Fodor's Touring Europe

Michael Spring

This book was previously published as
Great European Itineraries.

Fodor's Travel Publications, Inc.
New York and London

Fodor's Touring Europe

Editor: Nancy van Itallie
Contributors: Barbara Walsh Angelillo, Suzanne Brown, Thomas Cussans, Nigel Fisher, George Hamilton, Simon Hewitt, Alannah Hopkin, Helmut Koenig, Graham Lees, Bob Tilley
Art Director: Fabrizio La Rocca
Cartographer: David Lindroth
Illustrator: Karl Tanner
Cover Photograph: Comstock, Inc.

Design: Vignelli Associates

Contents

Maps

Foreword

While every care has been taken to ensure the accuracy of the information in this guide, the passage of time will always bring change, and consequently, the publisher cannot accept responsibility for errors that may occur.

All prices and opening times quoted here are based on information supplied to us at press time. Hours and admission fees may change, however, and the prudent traveler will avoid inconvenience by calling ahead.

Fodor's wants to hear about your travel experiences, both pleasant and unpleasant. When a hotel or restaurant fails to live up to its billing, let us know and we will investigate the complaint and revise our entries where the facts warrant it.

Send your letters to the editors of Fodor's Travel Publications, 201 E. 50th Street, New York, NY 10022.

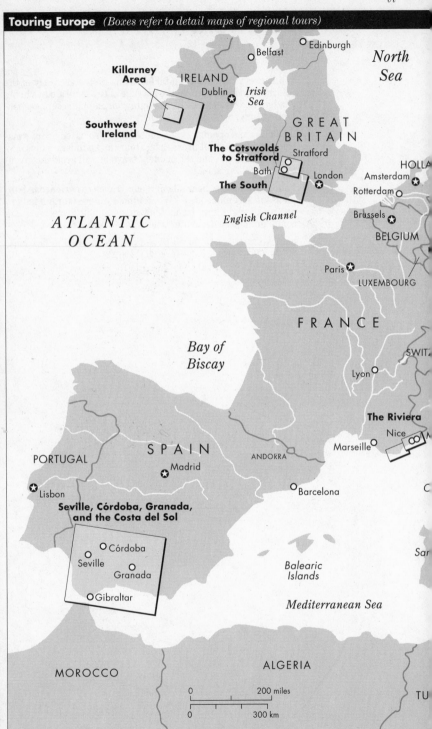

Touring Europe *(Boxes refer to detail maps of regional tours)*

North Sea

Edinburgh

Belfast

IRELAND

Dublin

Irish Sea

Killarney Area

Southwest Ireland

GREAT BRITAIN

Stratford

The Cotswolds to Stratford

Bath

The South

London

HOLLA

Amsterdam

Rotterdam

Brussels

BELGIUM

ATLANTIC OCEAN

English Channel

Paris

LUXEMBOURG

FRANCE

SWIT

Bay of Biscay

Lyon

The Riviera

Nice

Marseille

PORTUGAL

SPAIN

ANDORRA

Madrid

Lisbon

Barcelona

Seville, Córdoba, Granada, and the Costa del Sol

Córdoba

Seville

Granada

Gibraltar

Balearic Islands

Sar

Mediterranean Sea

MOROCCO

ALGERIA

TU

| 0 | 200 miles |
| 0 | 300 km |

Introduction

I wrote this guide for anyone who hates rubbing suit-cases with strangers on guided tours, but who needs help deciding where to go and how to organize his or her time.

I hope you'll see me as your travel agent and close friend, who sat down with you and helped you plan the vacation of your life. Because friends value honesty, I tried to sweep away the fluff and hyperbole of travel writing, and leave you with the truth. There are many places you won't hear about because I wouldn't send friends there or wouldn't choose to go back myself.

I've chosen the most popular trips in each of eight European countries, and shown you how to make do with a little money and how to spoil yourself with a lot. Each trip can be made by car or by public transportation. Major car rental companies include Avis (tel. 800/331–1212), Hertz (tel. 800/223–6472) and National/European (tel. 800/CAR–RENT). If you're looking for a bargain, try Kemwel (tel. 800/678–0678). If you're staying abroad more than three weeks, con-sider leasing a car from a company like Renault (tel. 800/221–1052). The itineraries are for three to five days, five to sev-en days, and seven to 14 days—but you can combine them into longer trips, or adjust them to meet your own schedule and needs. The countries can be visited individually or in the order I've presented them, starting in Ireland and mov-ing southeastward as far as Yugoslavia and then westward to complete the circuit in Spain.

To get you started, each itinerary includes (when appropri-ate) the following sections:

Introduction
Before You Go
Arriving and Departing
Getting Around
Essential Information
The Itinerary

I then take you on a day-by-day trip along the proposed route, suggesting things to do and places to stay and eat.

Here are some of the highlights:

Austria	Medieval towns along the Danube
England	Salisbury Cathedral and the Cotswold countryside
France	Saint-Tropez at dawn and the perched village of Peillon
Germany	The Royal Castles and Heidelberg
Ireland	Slea Head, on the wild west coast of Dingle Peninsula

Italy	The Temple of Neptune in Paestum and the hill town of Ravello
Spain	The Alhambra and the White Villages of Andalusia
Yugoslavia	The ancient stone city of Dubrovnik

Because I'm asking you to trust me, I had better say a word about my sensibilities. I have omitted many chain hotels because they could be anywhere in the world, and I'm partial to hotels that capture the spirit of a place; that are one of a kind; that could be nowhere other than where they are. On the other hand, I know that age is no guarantee of atmosphere or charm, and that many modern hotels have twice the character of so-called historic inns listed in the guides. I dislike yellow water glasses, all-weather carpeting, soft mattresses, and furnishings that are cute, overdecorated, or deliberately old-fashioned. I like to fall asleep in rooms softened with age. My favorite hotel organization is Relais & Châteaux (tel. 800/372-1323 or 212/696-1323), because the hotels it represents are historic buildings that are exquisitely furnished and maintained.

If you feel I've been too kind or too uncritical, or have overlooked interesting places, please let me know so that I can include the information in future editions. Write to Michael Spring, Fodor's Travel Publications, 201 East 50th Street, New York, N.Y. 10022.

Many people have helped make this book possible. I'd like to thank Hedy Wuerz of the German National Tourist Office, Pilar Vico of the National Tourist Office of Spain, Josephine Inzerillo of the Italian Tourist Board, Bedford Pace of the British Tourist Authority, Simon O'Hanlin of the Irish Tourist Board, Gerhard Markus of the Austrian National Tourist Office, and Vesna Loney of the Yugoslav National Tourist Office.

Material on Spain was prepared with the help of two very special guides, Angel López Macias and Julian Sarabia. Material on Austrian and German restaurants was prepared with the help of Konrad Sönnichsen.

I'd also like to thank Abe Pokrassa, Lucille Hosadjian, John Lampl, William Connors, Daphne Warner, and my editor, Nancy van Itallie.

Travel books that I found particularly helpful in formulating my own ideas are listed under Reading in the Before You Go section of each chapter.

1 Ireland

The South and the West

Introduction

Southwestern Ireland offers a wonderful range of scenery—wild mountain passes, rich green farm country, romantic seascapes; the view changes from one moment to the next. The weather changes, too, creating a sense of expectancy, as if you had stumbled on an unfinished bit of creation. If you're addicted to blue skies, stay away; Ireland is for those romantic fools who know that only on a misty day can you see forever.

Throughout the region you can piece together Ireland's history in ancient ruins, the Blarney Stone, restored mansions, and the daily life of the inhabitants. Every major town has craft stores selling everything from Waterford crystal to handknit Aran sweaters, and seafood restaurants serving fish as fresh as the day's catch. The west coast has a lively pub life where you can hear traditional Irish music—not made just for tourists. On the wild and unspoiled Dingle Peninsula the people still study and speak Gaelic.

You can also enjoy a summer's worth of outdoor activities: angling for shark or salmon, teeing off on championship golf courses, ambling along a riverside, or climbing some of the country's highest peaks. Killarney's romantic lakes invite rowing parties, and the Gap of Dunloe can be explored by pony cart.

Highlights

Seascapes and spectacular mountain passes on the Dingle Peninsula, where *Ryan's Daughter* was filmed.

A wealth of outdoor sports—golf, tennis, boating, fishing, and hiking—along the Ring of Kerry and among the beautiful mountains and lakes of Killarney.

The greatest collection of ancient monuments in Ireland, including the Rock of Cashel, where St. Patrick is said to have baptized Ireland's first Christian king.

The Blarney Stone.

Before You Go

Government Tourist Offices

The major source of information is the Irish Tourist Board. They produce numerous publications, many of them free and all useful.

Their addresses are:

In the U.S. 757 Third Ave., New York, NY 10017, tel. 212/418–0800.

In Canada 10 King Street E., Toronto, Ont. MC5 IC3, tel. 416/364–1301.

In the U.K. 150 New Bond St., London W1Y OAQ tel. 071/493–3201.

In Ireland local Tourist Information Offices will (for a nominal fee in certain cases) reserve accommodations and provide extensive information on all aspects of the surrounding areas. They are normally open weekdays 9–6, Sat. 9–1. The main office is in Dublin (14 Upper O'Connell St., tel. 01/747733). There are also offices at Dublin Airport (tel. 01/376387) and Shannon (tel. 061/61664).

When to Go

The main tourist season runs from June to mid-September. The attractions of Ireland are not as dependent on the weather as those in most other northern European countries, and the scenery is just as attractive in the off-peak times of fall and spring. Accommodations are more economical in winter, although some of the smaller attractions are closed from October to March. In all seasons the visitor can expect rain.

Currency

The unit of currency in Ireland is the pound, or punt (pronounced "poont"), written as IR£ to avoid confusion with the pound sterling. The currency is divided into the same denominations as in Britain (although Ireland doesn't have pound coins) with IR£1 divided into 100 pence (written *p*). There is likely to be some variance in the rates of exchange between Ireland and the United Kingdom (which includes Northern Ireland). This usually favors the visitor. Change U.K. pounds at a bank when you get to Ireland (pound coins not accepted); change Irish pounds before you leave.

Dollars and British currency are accepted only in large hotels and shops licensed as bureaux de change. In general, visitors are expected to use Irish currency. Banks give the best rate of exchange. The rate of exchange at press time (spring 1990) was about 58 pence to the U.S. dollar and IR£1.12 to the pound sterling.

Customs

Customs regulations for travelers entering Ireland are complex. There are three levels of duty-free allowance: one for residents of non-European countries; another for passengers arriving from other EC countries bringing in goods that have *not* been bought in a duty-free shop; and a third for residents of European countries not in the EC and for passengers arriving from other EC countries with goods that *have* been bought in a duty-free shop.

In the first category you may import duty-free: 400 cigarettes or 200 cigarillos or 100 cigars or 500 g (17.5 oz) of tobacco; plus one liter of alcoholic beverage of more than 22% volume or a total of two liters of alcoholic beverage of not more than 22% volume or sparkling or fortified wine, plus two liters of other wine; plus 50 g (1.75 oz) of perfume and a quarter of a liter of toilet water (½ pt); plus other goods to a value of IR£31 per person (IR£16 for children under 15).

In the second category you may import duty-free: 300 cigarettes or 400 g (14 oz) of tobacco or 150 cigarillos or 75 cigars; plus 1½ liters of alcoholic beverage of more than 22% volume or a total of three liters of alcoholic beverage of not more than 22% volume or sparkling or fortified wines plus four liters of other wine; plus 75 g (2.6 oz) of perfume and three-eighths of a liter of toilet water; plus, other goods to a value of IR£145 per person (IR£41 for children under 15).

Southwest Ireland

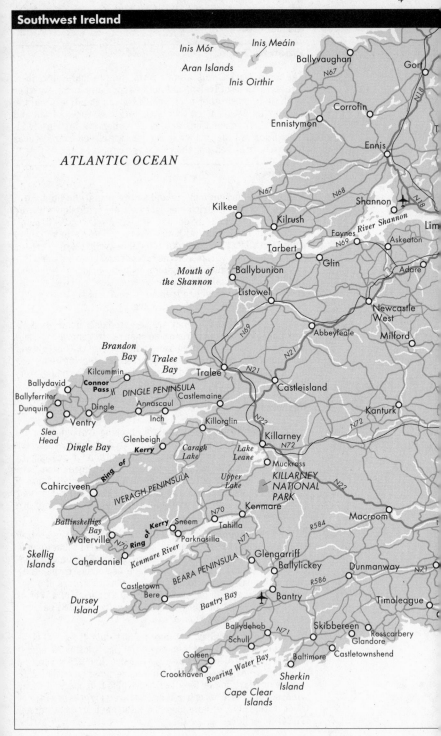

ATLANTIC OCEAN

Inis Mór
Inis Meáin
Aran Islands
Inis Oirthir
Ballyvaughan
Gort
N67
N18
Corrofin
Ennistymon
Ennis
N67
N68
Shannon
Kilkee
River Shannon
Lim
Kilrush
Foynes
N69
Askeaton
Tarbert
Glin
Adare
Mouth of
the Shannon
Ballybunion
Listowel
Newcastle
West
N69
Abbeyfeale
Milford
N21
N21
Brandon
Bay
Tralee
Bay
Tralee
N21
Castleisland
Kilcummin
Connor
Pass
DINGLE PENINSULA
Kanturk
Ballydavid
Castlemaine
Ballyferriter
Dingle
Annascaul
N22
N72
Dunquin
Ventry
Inch
Killorglin
Slea
Head
Killarney
Glenbeigh
N72
Dingle Bay
Kerry
Caragh
Lake
Lake
Leane
Cahirciveen
Muckross
IVERAGH PENINSULA
Upper
Lake
KILLARNEY
NATIONAL
PARK
N22
Ring of Kerry
Kenmare
Ballinskelligs
Bay
Sneem
Macroom
Waterville
N70
Ring of Kerry
Tahilla
R584
Caherdaniel
Parknasilla
N71
Skellig
Islands
Kenmare River
Glengarriff
BEARA PENINSULA
Ballylickey
Dunmanway
N71
Castletown
Bere
R586
Dursey
Island
Bantry
Timoleague
Bantry Bay
Ballydehob
Skibbereen
Rosscarbery
Schull
N71
Glandore
Goleen
Baltimore
Castletownshend
Crookhaven
Roaring Water Bay
Sherkin
Island
Cape Clear
Islands

In the third category you may import duty-free: 200 cigarettes or 100 cigarillos or 50 cigars or 250 g (8.75 oz) of tobacco; plus one liter of alcoholic beverage of more than 22% volume or a total of two liters of alcoholic beverage of not more than 22% volume or sparkling or fortified wine plus two liters of other wine; plus 50 g (1.75 oz) of perfume and a quarter of a liter of toilet water (½ pt); plus, other goods to a value of IR£31 per person (IR£16 for children under 15).

Note that in all three categories the tobacco and alcohol allowances apply only to those aged 17 and older. If you have nothing more than the duty-free allowance when you arrive, walk straight through the green "nothing to declare" channel. If you have more than your duty-free allowance, however, you must go into the red channel and declare the goods you are bringing in.

Visitors may import any quantity of currency, whether foreign or Irish, and nonresidents may export any amount of foreign currency, provided it was declared on arrival. Otherwise, you may export no more than IR£100, in denominations no larger than IR£20, and no more than the equivalent of IR£500 in foreign currency.

Language

Officially, the Irish language is the first language of the Republic, but the everyday language of the majority of Irish people is English. Except for the northwest, most signs are written in Irish with an English translation underneath. There is one important exception to this rule, with which all visitors should familiarize themselves: *Fir* and *mna* translate respectively into *men* and *women*. The *Gaeltacht*—areas in which Irish *is* the everyday language of most people—comprises only 6% of the land, and all its inhabitants are, in any case, bilingual.

Reading

A Motorist's Guide to the Dingle Peninsula (a small, useful guide sold in local shops).

Don Fullington, *An American's Ireland* (Panafast, New York).

Sean O'Suilleabhain's *Irish Walk Guides No. 1, Southwest*, which is available at local bookstores.

Arriving and Departing

By Plane

Flying to Dublin and returning from Shannon will save you about 3½ hours of driving time (224 km/140 mi) and about IR£20 in gas. The scenery grows more beautiful as you head west toward Shannon, so, on the principle that it's better to save the best for last, see Dublin first and fly home from Shannon. Three airlines operate between Ireland and the United States: **Aer Lingus** (tel. 800/223–6537, U.S.; 212/557–1110, NY); **Delta** (tel. 800/241–4141, U.S.; 800/722–9230, GA; 514/337–5520, Can.); **Pan Am** (tel. 800/212–1111, U.S. & Can.; 212/687–2600, NY; 416/368–2941, Toronto).

Aer Lingus flies direct to Dublin and Shannon from New York and Boston. Fares to Dublin are slightly higher. Delta flies to Shannon direct from Atlanta. Pan American flies to Shannon from New York.

Aer Lingus and **British Airways** (tel. 800/247–9297; U.K. 081/ 759–5511), **Ryan Air** (tel. 800/268–6755; U.K. 071/839–1192), and **Dan Air** (tel. 800/872–6677; U.K. 071/435–7107) have frequent services from the United Kingdom (London and most major regional airports) to both Dublin and Shannon.

By Car, Train, and Bus

All car ferry services from Britain are also served by motor coach and rail services to accommodate foot passengers. You can go direct from both Liverpool and Holyhead to Dun Laoghaire, a few miles south of Dublin. The crossing from Liverpool takes 7 hours; 3½ from Holyhead. If you are picking up the itinerary at Kilkenny or Cork, go via Fishguard or Pembroke to Rosslare, about 3½ hours. Crossings from Holyhead, Liverpool, and Fishguard are run by **Sealink British Ferries** (BritRail, 630 Third Ave., New York, NY 10017, tel. 212/599– 5400). In the United Kingdom contact Sealink Travel (tel. 0233/ 47074) for the nearest office. Pembroke to Rosslare is operated by **B & I Line** (c/o Lynott Tours, 350 Fifth Ave., New York, NY 10118, tel. 212/760–0101). In the United Kingdom call 071/734– 4681 for the nearest office.

Getting Around

By Car

Driving is on the left, as in Britain. Drivers and front-seat passengers must wear seat belts. While the country shifts from miles to kilometers, some signposts are in one, some in the other. Expect to be confused. There is a general speed limit of 88 kph (55 mph) on most roads; in towns, the speed limit is 48 kph (30 mph). In some areas, the limit is 64 kph (40 mph); this will always be clearly posted. At junctions, traffic from the right takes priority.

Rented cars will not have automatic transmission unless you request it in advance. If you are under age 21 or over age 70, you may be excluded from certain fly/drive packages; be sure to check. All the major car-rental companies have outlets in Ireland, as do a number of Irish firms.

One of the most reasonably priced Irish car rental companies is **Dan Dooley** (tel. 062/53103), which has desks at both Shannon and Dublin airports. Arrangements can be made in the United States by calling Dan Dooley (tel. 800/331–9301; NJ, 201/381– 8948). Mention this guide for a discount.

Aer Lingus has some attractive fly/drive packages. Some include prepaid vouchers for meals and/or accommodations.

By Public Transportation

This is the one trip that you would be advised to make by car. Trains and buses do exist, but they won't get you to many of the most beautiful, out-of-the-way spots. The best bet is simply to skip the south coast and take the train directly from Dublin to Killarney. From here you can take local buses or sign up for daily excursions to all local points of interest, including the Ring of Kerry and Dingle Peninsula. Rented bicycles will get you everywhere you want to go in the Killarney area.

Should you want to go from Dublin to Cork, the train takes 2 hours, 40 minutes. A bus goes from Cork to Kinsale in 50 minutes. The train from Cork to Killarney, via Mallow, takes 1 hour, 50 minutes. The train from Dublin to Killarney via Mallow takes 3 hours, 45 minutes. From Killarney there is regular bus service around the Ring of Kerry and to the town of Dingle. From Dingle, the bus to the Tralee train station takes 80 minutes. From Tralee the train back to Dublin takes 3 hours, 35 minutes.

If you plan to travel extensively, buy a Rail-only Ticket or a Rail-Road Rambler Ticket. The latter is valid on all trains and buses and is priced at $97 for 8 days' travel in a 2-week period, or $113 for 15 days within a month. They are available in the United States from CIE Tours (122 E. 42nd St., New York, NY 10168, tel. 212/972–5600), or from any bus or train station in Ireland. Both the Eurailpass and the Eurail Youthpass are valid in Ireland.

Essential Information

Important Addresses and Numbers

Tourist Information
Some of the smaller offices on the itinerary are only open high season as indicated.

Bantry Tourist Information Office: tel. 027/50229; open July and Aug.

Cashel Tourist Information Office: Town Hall, tel. 062/61333; open Mar.–Sept.

Cork Tourist House, Grand Parade, tel. 021/273251.

Dingle Tourist Information Office: tel. 066/51188; open June–Sept.

Kilkenny Tourist Information Office: Shee's Alms House, Rose Inn St., tel. 056/21755; open Mar.–Nov., weekdays 9–6, Sat. 9–1.

Killarney Tourist Information Office: Killarney Town Hall, opposite St. Mary's Church on Main Street, tel. 064/31633.

Kinsale's Tourist Information Office: Pier Rd., tel. 021/772234; open July and Aug. (Outside these months you might look up Peter Barry at the Scilly Store opposite the Spaniard Inn, or call him at 021/774026.)

Embassies
U.S. (42 Elgin Rd., Ballsbridge, Dublin, tel. 01/688777). **Canadian** (65 St. Stephen's Green, Dublin, tel. 01/781988). **U.K.** (33 Merrion Rd., Dublin, tel. 01/695211).

Emergencies
Police, tel. 999. **Ambulance,** tel. 999. **Doctor:** In Kilkenny, tel. 056/21702; in Cork City and county and in Kerry, tel. 021/545011. **Dentist,** tel. 01/978435. There are no late-night or all-night pharmacies in Ireland.

Opening and Closing Times

Banks Banks are open weekdays 10–12:30 and 1:30–3, and until 5 on selected days.

Museums Museums are usually open weekdays 10–5, Saturday 10–1, Sunday 2–5. Always make a point of checking, however, as hours can change unexpectedly.

Shops Shops are open Monday–Saturday 9–5:30, closing earlier on Wednesday, Thursday, or Saturday, depending on the locality.

Guided Tours

The following agents will organize day and half-day trips by private chauffeur-driven car or coach in the Killarney area:

Counihan's Travel Agency (High St., Killarney, tel. 064/31874).
Killarney and Kerry Tours (Innisfallen Mall, Main St., tel. 064/54041).
Cronin's Tours (College St., tel. 064/31521).
Deros Bus Tours (Main St., tel. 064/31251).
Destination Killarney (Scotts Gardens, Killarney, tel. 064/36238; in USA: 319 West 48th St., Suite 1419, New York, NY 10036, tel. 212/315–5034) will make all the arrangements for your stay, lining up accommodations, entertainment, special-interest tours, and sporting activities in one tailor-made package.

Shopping

VAT Refunds Visitors from outside Europe can take advantage of the "cash-back" system on value-added tax (VAT) if their purchases total more than IR£50. A cash-back voucher must be filled out by the retailer at the point of sale. The visitor pays the total gross price, including VAT, and receives green and yellow copies of the invoice; both must be retained. These are presented to—and stamped by—customs, as you leave the country. Take the stamped form along to the cashier and you will be refunded the VAT.

It's not necessary to go to Waterford to buy **Waterford glass**; the price is the same everywhere in Ireland, even at the factory store. The factory may have a wider selection, but there are no "seconds" available at reduced prices. Part of what you're paying for is the name; consider buying other Irish glass made in Kilkenny, Cork, Galway, and Dublin, at considerably lower prices.

Almost every town has a shop or two selling handwoven **tweeds**, undyed wool sweaters (the so-called **Aran knitwear**), and **linen**. Some of the knitted goods are made by hand, others—the less expensive ones—by machine. Some fabrics and knitwear are made locally, so goods vary from shop to shop. Prices vary, too; Aran-style sweaters, for instance, cost up to 40% more at the airport. The rule is to buy what you like when you see it, for you probably won't see one exactly like it again. The Design Workshop in Kilkenny has a large selection. Irish poplin is woven only in Cork.

Ireland is famous for its hand-thrown **pottery.** Some of the best shops are in Kinsale, Dingle Town, and Dunquin (on the west coast of the Dingle Peninsula).

The best bet for Irish crafts, fabrics, and knitwear is the Blarney Woolen Mills and Shop, at the entrance to Blarney Castle, 8.1 km (5 mi) north of Cork.

The tradition of Celtic ornamentation has inspired the jewelry and silverwork of present-day Irish craftsmen. Particularly popular are designs based on the Book of Kells.

In *Cork*, try the Savoy Centre or the Queen's Old Castle Shopping Centre on St. Patrick's Street. Egan's on St. Patrick's Street is famous for jewelry and silver. So is James Mangen. For antiques, try Macurtain Street across St. Patrick's Bridge or the Paul Street–Cornmarket area. Many shops and department stores sell locally made Glengarriff lace.

In *Kinsale*, you'll find several tasteful craft shops as you walk about town, notably Boland's Craft Shop on Pearse. Antiques, hand-knits and more crafts can be found in the narrow, twisty Main Street.

Sports

In **Bantry,** if you plan to spend more time, you can arrange to *angle* for trout and salmon (contact Justin McCarthy, tel. 027/50053); to go *sailing* or *windsurfing*, contact John Crowley (tel. 027/50030); to go *bike riding*, contact Kramers (tel. 027/50278); to play *golf*, contact the Bantry Golf Club (tel. 027/50579 or 027/50488); or to play *tennis*, contact the Bantry Community Tennis Club near Strand (tel. 027/50447 or 027/50113).

In **Killarney,** *ponies or jaunting cars* are available at the Muckross Road exit from town (near the Tourist Information Office), as well as at the entrance to the Gap of Dunloe and at the entrances to Muckross Abbey and Muckross House. *Horseback rides* through other areas of the National Park can be arranged through Donal O'Sullivan (Killarney Riding School, Ballydowney, tel. 064/31686). As elsewhere in Ireland, *inshore fishing* has been in dispute since 1988 when the government imposed a state license fee. At press time, a boycott is in operation and visitors are being asked to observe it. This effectively means no fishing except on privately owned rivers and lakes until the dispute is settled. Updated information can be obtained from Killarney Tourist Information Office (tel. 064/31633). For *golf*, the Killarney Golf and Fishing Club (tel. 064/31034) has two championship courses, at Mahoney's Point 4 km (2½ mi) from Killarney on the road to Killorglin, and at Killeen. For *boat hire and tours*, contact Henry Clifton at Ross Castle (tel. 064/32252) or Dermit O'Donoghue (High St., tel. 064/31068). For *windsurfing*, contact Killarney Windsurfing Centre (Lake Hotel, Killarney, tel. 064/31105).

For *bike rental*, contact O'Callaghan Bros. (tel. 064/31175), O'Sullivan's (tel. 064/31282), or O'neill's (tel. 064/31970).

In **Kinsale,** if you plan to spend some time in the area, there's river and deep-sea *fishing* (Trident Angling and Scuba Diving Center, tel. 021/774099); *golf* (tel. 021/772197); *tennis* at the Kinsale Community Tennis Club (no phone); and *windsurfing* at the Oysterhaven Boardsailing Centre (tel. 021/773738).

Walking tours of historic Kinsale can be arranged (tel. 021/772044).

Dining

Your safest bet, as you travel along the coast, is fresh fish, particularly salmon (either poached or grilled). Other favorites are sea and brown trout, sole grilled on the bone, oysters, and lobster. For meat dishes, try Irish mutton, spring lamb, or steaks.

Simplicity is the keynote of native Irish cooking, with such unpretentious dishes as Irish stew, bacon and cabbage, spring chicken with fresh vegetables, roast pork with applesauce, or eggs with homemade whole-meal bread. The leading restaurants lean toward French cuisine—either classic or nouvelle, with an emphasis on fresh local produce. The more imaginative establishments try to blend French and Irish influences: a sauce made with Irish whiskey, say, or Bailey's Irish Cream.

The word whiskey is derived from the Irish *uisce beatha*, meaning "water of life." You may want to try it in Irish coffee, topped with a thick layer of fresh cream.

For quick, inexpensive lunches, you can't go wrong with pub grub and a pint of cider, stout, or lager. Tipping is not expected at bars.

Some of the more expensive establishments add a 12% or 15% service charge; elsewhere a tip of 10% is adequate. At press time (spring 1990) there were 0.58 Irish pounds (IR£) to the dollar.

Category	Cost*
Expensive	over IR£25
Moderate	IR£15–IR£25
Inexpensive	under IR£15

Prices are per person and include a first course, main course, and dessert, but no wine or tip.

Lodging

The choice is yours between hotels—some modern high rises, others restored mansions—and private homes offering bed and breakfast. My vote would be to stay either in the best hotels or in private guest homes, or in a combination of the two. The exclusive hotels have the atmosphere and amenities that many travelers want. The second- and third-class hotels—many of them older hotels lacking the funds for renovations—are not in themselves objectionable, but the private homes are usually cleaner, friendlier, and more modern. The Irish Tourist Board publishes an indispensable guide to Irish bed-and-breakfast establishments, which shows you pictures of each home, and gives you information on prices and facilities, including availability of rooms with private bath. The Irish Tourist Board publishes a similar listing of hotels. Bed-and-breakfast reservations can be made through Tourist Information Offices in major Irish towns or by writing to the Central Reservations Service (14 Upper O'Connell St., Dublin 1). A fee of about $1.50

is added for each hotel booking and a 10% deposit taken; for accommodation in private homes there is no fee, but a deposit of 25% must be paid. Hotel reservations can, of course, also be made through your travel agent at home.

Published rates do not always include taxes and service charges; it pays to ask beforehand. The larger chain hotels that cater to the package-tour trade have gone the way of the world and begun charging extra for breakfast: tourists should boycott them on principle. It's not just a matter of dollars and cents: a breakfast "on the house" has always been part of the Irish (and British) experience, giving Americans the sense that they are guests in a foreign home.

At press time there were 0.58 Irish pounds to the dollar.

Category	Cost*
Very Expensive	over IR£100
Expensive	IR£70–IR£100
Moderate	IR£50–IR£70
Inexpensive	under IR£50

Prices are for 2 people in a double room based on high season (June–Sept.) rates.

The Itinerary

Orientation

Ireland is small enough that you can enjoy a wide range of scenery with a minimum amount of driving. This itinerary takes you around the south and southwest coasts of Ireland, primarily through Cork and Kerry. You can begin at either Shannon or Dublin and end at either airport. As you head south to Cork, you can stay in friendly guest houses or historic homes along the way. The road along the southern coast wanders through rich green farmland that borders the sea. As you head west, the scenery grows wilder. You pass through Killarney and the Ring of Kerry, with their ruins, historic sites, and opportunities for enjoying the outdoors, as well as the local life. Finally, you can take an unforgettable trip around the Dingle Peninsula. From here you'll return to either Shannon or Dublin.

The Main Route

3–5 Days *One night:* Cashel or Mallow
Day excursions to the Rock of Cashel and the Blarney Stone
One or two nights: the Killarney area
Day excursion through the Gap of Dunloe and around the Ring of Kerry
One night: Dingle
Day excursion around the Dingle Peninsula

It will take most of a day, leaving from Dublin, to tour the Rock of Cashel and the Blarney Stone. After reading the itinerary below, decide whether you want to see these sights or drive directly to the west coast.

If you plan to visit the Rock of Cashel and the Blarney Stone: From Dublin take Route N7 southwest to Port Laoise and continue on Route N8 to Cashel and Cork. Drive north 8 km (5 mi) to the Blarney Stone. Return to Cork and take Route N22 west to Killarney. Drive around the Ring of Kerry, seeing the south coast first: from Kenmare to Waterville, Cahirciveen and Killorglin. From Killorglin, drive around the Dingle Peninsula through the towns of Dingle, Dunquin, Ballyferriter, back to Dingle, and north across the Conor Pass to Tralee. Take Route N21 east to Castleisland, and north to Adare and Limerick. If you're returning to Shannon, drive northwest on Route N18 from Limerick to Shannon Airport. If you're returning to Dublin, take Route N7 from Limerick to Dublin.

If you don't plan to visit the Rock of Cashel or the Blarney Stone: From Dublin take Route N7 west to Limerick and Route N21 to Tralee. Following the itinerary in reverse, drive around the Dingle Peninsula, heading along the north coast, and crossing the Conor Pass to Dingle. From Dingle, follow a circular route west to Dunquin and Ballyferriter, and back to Dingle. From Dingle, head east to Castlemaine and south to Killorglin. Drive around the Ring of Kerry from north to south: from Cahirciveen to Waterville, Kenmare, and Killarney. From Killarney take Route N22 north and N21 northeast to Adare and Limerick. If you're returning to Shannon, drive northwest on Route N18 from Limerick to Shannon Airport. If you're returning to Dublin, take Route N7 from Limerick to Dublin.

5–7 Days Day excursion to Kilkenny, the Rock of Cashel, and the Blarney Stone
One night: Cashel, Mallow, or Kinsale
Three nights: the Killarney area
Day excursions through the Gap of Dunloe, across the lakes of Killarney, and around the Ring of Kerry
Two nights: Dingle
Day excursions around the Dingle Peninsula and to the Blasket Islands

From Dublin take Route N7 southwest to Port Laoise and continue on Route N8 to Cashel and Cork. The Blarney Stone is five miles north of Cork. From here you can take Route N22 direct to Killarney, which will give you more time to explore the beautiful west coast, or you can see more of the country by taking the slower but more scenic route along the south coast from Cork to Kinsale, Clonakilty, Skibbereen, Bantry, Ballylickey, Glengarriff, and Kenmare. Drive around the Ring of Kerry, through Waterville, Cahirciveen, and Killorglin to Killarney. Return to Killorglin and drive around the Dingle Peninsula through the towns of Dingle, Dunquin, Ballyferriter, back to Dingle, and north across the Conor Pass to Tralee. Take Route N21 east to Castleisland, and north to Adare and Limerick. If you're returning to Shannon, drive northwest on Route N18 from Limerick to Shannon Airport. If you're returning to Dublin, take Route N7 from Limerick to Dublin.

7–14 Days Day excursion to Kilkenny and the Rock of Cashel
One night: Mallow or Shanagarry
Day excursion to Cork and the Blarney Stone
One night: Kinsale
Day excursion: Beara Peninsula
One night: Ballylickey
One night: Kenmare

Five nights: The Killarney area
Day excursions through the Gap of Dunloe, across the lakes of Killarney, around the Ring of Kerry, and to the Skellig Islands
Three nights: Dingle
Day excursions around the Dingle Peninsula and to the Blasket Islands

From Dublin take Route N7 southwest to Naas and Routes N9 and N10 south to Kilkenny. From Kilkenny, drive west to Urlingford and south on Route N8 to Cashel and Cahir. Leave the main highway and follow signs south to Clogheen and Lismore, then west along the Blackwater River to Fermoy, and south on Route N8 to Cork. From Cork drive south to Kinsale, and west through Skibbereen, Bantry, Ballylickey, and Glengarriff. Drive around the Beara Peninsula to Castletown Bere and Kenmare. Drive around the Ring of Kerry, through Waterville, Cahirciveen, and Killorglin to Killarney. Return to Killorglin and drive around the Dingle Peninsula through the towns of Dingle, Dunquin, Ballyferriter, back to Dingle, and north across the Conor Pass to Tralee. Take Route N21 east to Castleisland, and north to Adare and Limerick. If you're returning to Shannon, drive northwest on Route N18 from Limerick to Shannon Airport. If you're returning to Dublin, take Route N7 from Limerick to Dublin.

Exploring

If your time is limited, take Routes N7 and N8 direct from Dublin to Cashel—a 2½-hour drive. With more time or a keen interest in Irish history, you can make a side trip to Kilkenny (2¼ hours), following Route N7 southwest from Dublin to Dorrow, and Route N77 south to Kilkenny.

Kilkenny

Kilkenny (*Cill Chainnigh*, Canice's Church) is billed as the best example of a medieval town in Ireland, but its historic roots are less than obvious to the casual visitor. Even with its narrow side streets with names like Collier's Lane, you'll have to use some imagination to envision its antiquity. What makes a side trip here worthwhile is St. Canice's Cathedral, with its ancient stone tower; the restored medieval Black Abbey; a restored 16th-century home, the Rothe House—a rare sight in a country whose past is so often glimpsed only in broken stone and rubble; and Kilkenny Castle.

Anyone who wants to understand Anglo-Irish relations has to go back at least to the infamous 1366 Statutes of Kilkenny, which were meant to strengthen English authority in Ireland, and to keep the Irish and the Anglo-Norman settlers apart. No Irish cattle could graze on English land. Marrying the Irish was punishable by death. Anglo-Norman settlers—many of whom went native—had their estates forfeited for speaking Gaelic, for giving their children Irish names, or for dressing in Irish clothes. Wearing Irish-made underwear was enough to get a person thrown in jail. The native Irish were not allowed within the town walls, but had to live in shanty Irishtowns—in their own country! The intermingling of Irish and Anglo-Norman elements was well under way when the Statutes of Kilkenny went into effect; if this fusion had been allowed to continue, who knows, there might be no civil war in Northern Ireland today.

By the early 17th century the Irish Catholics had had enough, and formed the Confederation of Kilkenny, which governed Ireland for six years and tried to bring about reforms. Pope Innocent X sent money and guns. Cromwell responded in 1650 by overrunning the town, sacking the cathedral, and using it to stable his horses.

Begin your tour at St. Canice's Cathedral, one of the finest in Ireland, despite Cromwell's defacements. The round tower is all that's left of the 6th-century monastic settlement around which the town developed. The cathedral, mostly Early English, is 13th century (restored in 1866), with a 12th-century marble font, a library you should ask to see, and a stone seat built into the north wall, said to be Saint Canice's. Within the massive walls is a Gothic structure with what one Irish writer calls, "all the exultant sensuality of the Provençal love poetry that the Normans brought to Ireland." The knights in full armor stare upward at eternity. Their faces are more Irish than French.

The tower is one of the few in Ireland you can climb.

From the cathedral, return to the road, turn right, and make your first left past the hairdresser's shop to reach the **Black Abbey,** a recently restored 13th-century friary, named after the black capes of the Dominican friars. Note how the transept is longer than the nave—a good example of how the Irish played tricks with Gothic forms, which never suited them, and a sad reminder of what the Irish could have accomplished architecturally if they had been permitted to develop styles that reflected their own Celtic sensibilities.

From the Black Abbey, turn left and follow narrow Abbey Lane—one of the town's more medieval-looking streets—to Parliament Street. Turn right. Two blocks down on your right and across the street is the late-16th-century **Rothe House,** the restored home of a Tudor merchant. Ask to see a small costume collection hidden away in an armoire. *Tel. 056/22893. Admission: 85p adults, 30p children. Open Apr.–Oct., weekdays 10:30–12:30 and 3–5, Sun. 3–5; Nov.–Mar., weekends 3–5.*

Continue down Parliament Street. Where the road splits, bear left on St. Kieran Street. On your left is **Dame Kyteler's Inn,** the 14th-century house of Dame Alice the witch. Perhaps because four husbands died on her, she was accused of holding witch's sabbaths, sacrificing black cocks, and mixing their innards with herbs, bugs, and the hair and nails of unbaptized children. She escaped without her maid, Petronilla, who was burned at the stake.

On your right at the junction of St. Kieran Street and Rose Inn Street is **Shee's Alms House,** founded as a hospital for the poor in 1582, now occupied by the Tourist Information Office.

Time Out   Turn left out of Shee's Alms House and left again at the edge of the River Nore to discover **Tynan's Bridge House,** one of the country's oldest pubs and a good bet for lunch.

From John's Bridge, left out of Shee's Alms House, you can look across the River Nore to **Kilkenny College,** the former St. John's College, where Jonathan Swift, William Congreve, and Bishop George Berkeley were educated.

Return to the bridge without crossing it, and continue along the path beneath **Kilkenny Castle.** A narrow break in the wall takes you up a flight of stairs to the castle. There's some lovely woodwork, an impressive Grand Hall, and a gallery of modern Irish art, but if you have only a passing interest in the arts, you may want to pass by. *Tel. 056/21450. Admission: IR£1 adults, 40p children and senior citizens. Open mid-Apr.–mid-Sept., daily 10–7; mid-Sept.–mid-Apr., daily 10–5.*

Two good alternatives are the extensive grounds and the **Kilkenny Design Workshop,** located in the castle's stables. One of the best in the country, it sells locally made woven textiles, silver and metal work, hand knits, and crystal. *Open Mon–Sat. 9–6, Sun. 10–5:30.*

Dunmore Cave, 11.3 km (7 mi) north of Kilkenny on N78 (follow signposts for Castlecomer and Athy), is modest in size yet has some beautiful formations that children in particular will enjoy. The bones found here belonged to 44 hapless individuals— 25 of them children—who were probably seeking refuge from a Viking attack. Scholars theorize that the coins found here fell from the armpit of a Viking: The Irish didn't use coins then, and the Vikings in those pocketless days wound them in a screw of cloth that they attached with beeswax to their armpit hair. A Viking probably dropped them in battle. "When you enter, a sudden Chilliness seizes all parts of the body," wrote an earlier visitor, "and a Dimness surrounded our lights, as if the Place were filled with a thick Fog. . . . Our Faces, through this Gloom, looked as if we were a Collection of Ghosts, and the Lights in our Hands seemed as if we were making a visit to the infernal Shades." *Tel. 056/27726. Admission: IR£1 adults, 30p children and senior citizens. Open mid-June–Sept. 30, daily 10–7:30; mid-Mar.–mid-June, Tues.–Sat. 10–5, Sun. 2–5; Oct. 1–mid-Mar., weekends 10–3.*

Dining   **Dame Kyteler's Inn.** The former home of Ireland's famous witch used to be a byword for touristic ballyhoo with its Friday night Witch's Banquet. New owner John Flynn has banished cabaret and fancy dress and restored some dignity to the stonework and exposed beams of the 14th-century interior. However, he can't resist serving witch's broth—a homemade vegetable soup—along with hybrid versions of French cuisine: pan-fried chicken cooked in whiskey, cream, and mushroom sauce; poached salmon served in a sauce of fresh herbs, white wine, and cream. *St. Kieran St., tel. 056/21064. Weekend reservations advised. Dress: casual. MC, V. Moderate.*
Langton's. This popular city center pub-cum-restaurant has been nominated "Pub of the Year" three times. The Edwardian interior, replete with mahogany paneling, polished brass, and potted plants, has been refurbished. The Edwardian theme is continued in the 90-seat restaurant, where a rear extension opens onto a walled garden. Fresh meat and fish are the menu's strength: try a peppered sirloin steak or roast spring lamb. *69 John St., tel. 056/65133. Weekend reservations advised. Dress: neat but casual. AE, DC, MC, V. Moderate.*

Lodging **Hotel Kilkenny.** The Kilkenny is a little closer to the city than the New Park and its public rooms have a little more character; otherwise, there's not much difference between the two. This property also has a charming Victorian house supplemented by cinderblock modern bedroom blocks that provide executive-style comfort in identical rooms. A pretty glass conservatory dominates the facade. *College Rd., tel. 056/62000. 60 rooms with bath. Facilities: restaurant, bar, indoor pool, saunas, sunbed, Jacuzzi, gymnasium, 2 lighted tennis courts, nightclub with disco Wed., Fri. and Sun. AE, MC, V. Expensive.*

New Park Hotel. This somewhat charmless hotel about 1.6 km (1 mi) from town has a Victorian house at the center of its modern extensions. The busy lobby is a popular meeting place for businessmen and also copes with tour bus trade in summer. The newer the rooms, the more modern the furnishings; go for one in the old block. *Castlecomer Rd., tel. 056/22122. 60 rooms with shower. Facilities: 2 restaurants, bar, indoor pool, saunas, sun beds, gymnasium. AE, DC, MC, V. Expensive.*

Club House. This is a 200-year-old inn in the center of town. The bedrooms have been refurbished in a comfortable but bland modern style, but the public rooms retain the elegance of old Ireland with fine plasterwork, gleaming wood paneling, polished brass fixtures, and hunting memorabilia. Light sleepers should ask for a room away from the main road. *Patrick St., tel. 056/21994. 27 rooms, most with bath or shower. Facilities: restaurant, bar. AE, DC, MC, V. Moderate.*

Lacken House. This compact Georgian guest house, a seven-minute walk from the center of Kilkenny, is set on an acre of grounds. It provides a welcoming atmosphere for those who value peace and quiet. Bedrooms are decked out in Laura Ashley prints. *Dublin Rd., tel. 056/61085. 8 rooms with shower. Facilities: restaurant (dinner only, closed Sun. and Mon.). AE, DC, MC, V. Inexpensive.*

On to Cashel Whether or not you visit Kilkenny, you'll be passing through Urlingford on the Dublin–Cork Road (N8) and then heading south to Cashel. It will add another 45 minutes to your trip to head west through Thurles and stop at the **Abbey of Holycross** en route to Cashel. You'll find it worth the time if you want to join the faithful who since the late 12th century have been making pilgrimages to this Cistercian Abbey to see a piece of the Cross.

Cashel

For anyone who cares about the past, a visit to the **Rock of Cashel** (*Causeal*, stone fort) is a high point of a trip to Ireland. The rock rises like a stone castle, 59.9 m (200 ft) above the town, and contains the best examples of medieval architecture in Ireland. It was here, it is believed, that St. Patrick baptized the Irish King Aengus, who thus became Ireland's first Christian ruler; here that St. Patrick plucked the shamrock that he used to explain the doctrine of the Trinity, which gave Ireland its national emblem; here that you can glimpse that Gaelic Ireland that has survived in spite of the Normans, the Danes, the British, and the tourists. *Tel. 062/61437. Admission: IR£1 adults, 40p children and senior citizens. Open June–Aug., daily 9–7:30; Sept.–May, Mon.–Sat. 10–4:30, Sun. 2–5. Optional 50-min guided tour.*

The most romantic route to the Rock is along the Bishop's Walk, a 10-minute hike from the Cashel Palace Hotel.

The rock dominates the surrounding landscape, which in the 5th century was covered with dense oak forests. Legend has it that the devil, flying back to England, took a bite from a nearby hillside and dropped it here in the Golden Vale. Ask a guide to point out the "bite" in the side of the Slieve Bloom Mountains.

As you enter this royal city, you'll see ahead of you a rough stone with an ancient cross, where Patrick is said to have baptized King Aengus. Patrick was old then and drove his staff into the earth to support himself. After the ceremony, it was discovered that the staff had passed through the king's foot, and that the grass was soaked with blood. Aengus never cried out because he thought that suffering was part of the Christian experience.

The stone is a replica; the actual one is on display in the museum across from the entrance. One piece is missing from the triple cross, which symbolizes the three crosses on Calvary. Carved on the back is the figure of a robed bishop. It is believed that the stone beneath the cross was once a coronation stone for pre-Christian Irish kings, and before that, a sacrificial altar. How emblematic of the blend of pagan/Celtic and Christian elements in the Irish character!

Behind the cross are **Cormac's Chapel,** which is the best preserved Romanesque ruin in the country, and the **cathedral.** When English writer and traveler H. V. Morton calls the chapel "whimsical"—an example of "gay Norman"—he is referring to its individuality, to the refusal of its builders to submit to foreign influences. Built by well-traveled Irish monks a half century before the Normans came, it has a uniquely Irish double roof, high-pitched to keep the rain away without pushing the walls out. The eastern end is not pointed directly east, as in other Romanesque churches, because the chapel was dedicated to Our Lady and built so that on her feast day, May 1, the sun streamed through two windows (now blocked up), and fell directly on the altar below. Similarly, the cathedral was built a few degrees off so that the sun could shine through three lancet windows and illuminate the altar on another feast day, March 17. Notice how the chancel arch (the rounded arch that separates the body of the chapel from the "front") is lopsided, symbolizing the drooping of Christ's head on the cross. Each column in both chapel and cathedral has a different shape, as if each had been carved by a different artist faithful to his own private vision. How contrary to European models, and how sad that these Celtic anomalies were eventually stuffed into an English form.

Compare the rough, simple chapel, built in the earliest days of Christianity, to the relatively grand, sophisticated Gothic cathedral, built in a later age when Christianity was more established, and faith more formalized. Ironically, it is the more modest chapel that has survived.

Dining **Chez Hans.** The heavily paneled nave of an old church gives this restaurant a unique ambience. The menu features an Irish variation on French cuisine: quenelles of turbot and brill in cream and red pepper sauce, rack of lamb *en croûte,* delicious homemade ice cream. The wine list is predominantly French. Be prepared for somewhat leisurely service. *Rockside, Cashel,*

tel. *062/61177. Reservations advised. Jacket and tie advised.
No credit cards. Closed Sun., Mon., first 3 wks Jan. Dinner
only. Expensive.*

Bishop's Buttery. This is the Cashel Palace Hotel's version of a
coffee shop. Elaborate Celtic-design hangings remind you that
you're in a palace, but the flagstone floor suggests you've ended
up in the servants' quarters. Try the substantial Irish stew:
mutton, onion, carrots, and potatoes; or Colcannon, a traditional mix of leeks, floury potatoes, butter, cream, and
nutmeg. *Cashel Palace Hotel, Main St., tel. 062/61411. No reservations. Dress: casual. AE, DC, MC, V. Moderate.*

Lodging   **Cashel Palace Hotel** is a conversation piece. The 18th-century
mansion was for 140 years the palace of the Archbishop of
Cashel. The Palladian architect Sir Edward Pearce also designed Parliament House in Dublin, now the Bank of Ireland.
One room has a 3.6- by 5.4-m (12- by 18-ft) bathroom, with
4.7-m (16-ft) ceilings. Running along the wall and across the
mirror is a family of Beatrix Potter rabbits—the work of the
Right Rev. Dr. Robert Wyse Jackson, Bishop of Limerick, who
resided here as dean of Cashel from 1946 to 1961. When I made
the mistake of lifting the heavy fabric from my night table, I
discovered that it was made from two pieces of interlocking
chipboard—which only added to the hotel's charm. The staff
here is friendly and accessible. The Four Seasons Restaurant is
outstanding. The Cellar Bar is a favorite with locals. Rooms are
unequal in quality; avoid 8; try for 25, which enjoys a view of the
Rock, or 21. *Main St. Cashel, Co. Tipperary, tel. 062/61411. 20
rooms with bath. Facilities: 2 restaurants, bar. AE, DC, MC,
V. Very Expensive.*

Cahir

Cahir (pronounce it "care"), 17.6 km (11 mi) south of Cashel,
has a fully restored 15th-century castle, with a massive keep,
high enclosing walls, and spacious courtyards. The entrance
fee includes a 12-minute audiovisual show. *Cahir center, tel.
052/41011. Admission: IR£1 adults, 40p children and senior
citizens. Open mid-June–mid-Sept., daily 10–7:30; mid-Apr.–
mid-June and mid-Sept.–Oct. 31, Tues.–Sat. 10–5, Sun. 2–5;
Nov. 1–Mar. 31, Tues.–Sat. 10–1 and 2–5.*

Lodging   **Kilcoran Lodge Hotel.** Located a few miles south of Cahir on
your right, this rural retreat makes an ideal overnight stop on
the Cork–Dublin road. The restaurant and lounge bar are
cheerful and homey with a spectacular view of the distant
mountains. A few rooms have antiques; ask for one that's quiet
and in the original hunting lodge. Rooms in the wings are not as
pleasant. *Cahir, Co. Tipperary, tel. 052/41288. 25 rooms, 22
with shower. Salmon and trout fishing on grounds. Facilities:
restaurant, bar, indoor pool, sauna, sunbeds, Jacuzzi. AE,
DC, MC, V. Expensive.*

On to Cork   The fastest route from Cahir to Cork is along the Dublin–Cork
Highway (N8) to Mitchelstown and Fermoy. If you appreciate
beautiful scenery, however, it's worth an extra half hour turning off N8 at Clogheen, driving over the mountains to Lismore,
and then heading west to Fermoy. About 48 km/30 mi northwest of Fermoy is the town of Buttevant. Cross-country horse
racing is said to have begun here in 1752 when Edward Blake
challenged a neighbor to race to the church at St. Leger 6.4

km/4 mi away. The steeple gave them a point to head toward; hence, the term steeplechase.

At Fermoy you have two choices: (1) To skip Cork and the south coast, and head directly west on Route N72 to Killarney. This makes sense if time is limited and you want to reach the west coast as soon as possible. The road takes you through Mallow, which has one of Ireland's better hotels. (2) To head south to Cork and the south coast. It's the latter route we'll be following.

Cork

Cork (*Corcaigh*, marsh) is so named because the area within the arms of the River Lee—the center and the oldest part of Cork —is filled-in marshland. If you're looking for a colorful old town with memorable walks, historic hotels, and first-class restaurants, Cork is *not* the place to visit, or at least not to stay. If you have a passing curiosity, plan to spend a morning or afternoon, and then overnight in Shanagarry (to the east), Mallow (to the north), or Kinsale (to the south). You may want to spend more time in Cork if you have a serious interest in its history as a center for the struggle for independence.

The Anglo-Normans invaded in 1172 and the native chieftain was forced to marry a Norman woman. The townspeople, led by merchants, won a good deal of independence over the years, but in 1492 they took up the cause of Perkin Warbeck, pretender to the throne, and the mayor and leading citizens were executed and Cork lost its charter. The city surrendered to Cromwell in 1649, and in 1690 had to surrender again to William III. The Fenian movement, the secret revolutionary society that sought independence from England by force, began here in 1858. These early terrorists played an important role in the War of Independence (1919–21), earning the city the name of Rebel Cork, which it kept until independence was won in 1922. The British burned down much of the city in 1920, so many of the buildings are relatively new.

It was here that William Thackeray composed *Vanity Fair* with the help of his mother-in-law, and here that the writers Frank O'Connor and Sean O'Faolain were born. It was nearby at Youghal that Edmund Spenser wrote the *Faerie Queene*, with financial help from the mayor, an Englishman named Sir Walter Raleigh. Raleigh may have been polite to women, but he recommended a ruthless policy against the Irish, helping to suppress rebellions and recommending assassination of their leaders.

You can tour the city's high points in about two hours. Begin near **St. Patrick's Bridge,** beneath the statue of Theobald Mathew (1790–1861), who championed at least one side of the Irish character by leading a nationwide temperance campaign. He looks young and dashing, but his right hand is raised, either to bless you or to say "no."

Follow St. Patrick's Street, the main street of town, toward the center of the island. Turn right on Academy Street to Emmet's Place and see the modern Irish landscapes on display in the **Crawford Municipal School of Art Gallery.** *Tel. 021/273377. Admission free. Open weekdays 10–4:30, Sat. 10–5.*

From the Gallery, follow Paul Street. On your right is the **City Park Shopping Centre,** where you can compare Waterford glass to less expensive Cork crystal. Turn right on Cornmarket Street, which contains the remnants of a once-thriving street market. Continue to the river. Turn left and walk to the bridge. Cross over and follow Shandon Street to Church Street. Turn right to **St. Ann's Shandon Church.** Sing "The Bells of Shandon" as you climb the 36-m (120-ft) bell tower for a gull's-eye view of the town: "With deep affection/ And recollection," wrote Father Francis Sylvester Mahoney, "I often think of/ Those Shandon bells,/ Whose sounds so wild would/ In the days of childhood/ Fling around my cradle/ Their magic spells." Is it any wonder many locals prefer Father Francis to O'Connor or O'Faolain?

Return down Shandon Street, recross the bridge, and continue along North Main Street. At the **Hilser Jewelry Store,** which is worth a visit, turn left on Washington Street, and then right on Grand Parade, past an enclosed vegetable and meat market, to the **Tourist Information Office.**

Time Out	Turn right out of the Tourist Information Office and follow Grand Parade around to the right into Patrick Street. In a narrow alleyway, Market Lane, on your right, **The Vine** has been in the same family since 1903, and its dark wood-paneled interior has recently been restored to the original Edwardian design. On weekday evenings at 6 PM it hums with lively locals enjoying a "quick one" after work.

Behind the Tourist Information Office is an **Entertainment Centre,** where you can take in a one-act Irish play at lunch. If you plan to spend the evening in the area, find out what's happening at the **Opera House,** which hosts both plays and recitals by visiting companies and popular artists.

Dining   **Arbutus Lodge.** The best reason to stay overnight in Cork is to dine at the Arbutus. This luxurious restaurant, in a late Victorian house on lovely grounds overlooking the River Lee high above the city, has won numerous awards. Monogrammed tableware and personalized napery enhance a dining room furnished with polished antiques and modern Irish paintings. Those on a budget can sample the cuisine at a lunchtime buffet in the bar, but splurging on dinner is recommended. Haute cuisine interpretations of Irish home cooking are a feature. Ninety percent of the produce is local. The wine list at the Arbutus is among the best in the country. *Middle Glanmire Rd., Montenotte, tel. 021/501237. Reservations required. Jacket and tie advised. AE, DC, MC, V. Closed Sun. Expensive.*
Clifford's. Michael Clifford, once the head chef at the Arbutus, now runs this small, fashionable city center restaurant with his wife Deirdre. A high standard is maintained in the fixed-price set menu that features dishes such as spinach soup with miniature chicken quenelles, veal garnished with apple and walnuts, or grilled chicken in Dubonnet and orange sauce. *23 Washington St., tel. 021/275333. Reservations advised. Jacket and tie required. AE, DC, MC, V. Wine license only. Closed Sun.; no lunch Mon. and Sat. Moderate.*

Lodging   **Arbutus Lodge.** Here is a place to satisfy anyone seeking a smaller hotel in town. It is a short (7-minute) drive from the city center. Rooms in this late Victorian house set in a garden overlooking the city are individually decorated, some with antiques. The restaurant is exceptional (*see* Dining). *Middle Glanmire Rd., Montenotte, Cork, tel. 021/51237. 20 rooms with bath. Facilities: restaurant, bar. AE, DC, MC, V. Expensive.*

Imperial Hotel. A sedate, old-fashioned institution, the Imperial is in the heart of Cork's legal and banking district. The spirit of an earlier age prevails in the carefully refurbished public rooms with high ceilings, marble floors, and crystal chandeliers. All bedrooms were fully renovated in 1989; room 115 is a good bet. *South Mall, Cork, tel. 021/274040. 101 rooms with bath. Facilities: 2 restaurants, 2 bars. AE, DC, MC, V. Expensive.*

Jury's Hotel. This modern two-story hotel with a striking smoked glass facade is situated on the banks of the River Lee, five minutes' walk from the downtown area. Cork's Pub is a lively bar, and the Fastnet Restaurant is better than hotel average. Despite the lime-colored cinderblock walls, rooms are spacious and comfortable, and the public rooms are big enough to absorb the package tour crowds attracted by the hotel's facilities. *Western Rd., Cork, tel. 021/266622. 185 rooms with bath. Facilities: 2 restaurants, 2 bars, indoor/outdoor heated pool, Jacuzzi, saunas, gymnasium, 2 tennis courts, squash courts. AE, DC, MC, V. Expensive.*

Gabriel House. This plain but friendly guest house is convenient for rail and bus stations. It once belonged to the Christian Brothers. *1 Summerhill St., St. Luke's, Cork, tel. 021/500333. 20 rooms with bath. Facilities: restaurant, bar. AE, MC, V. Inexpensive.*

Your choice of hotels outside Cork depends on your schedule. If you plan to tour Cork in the afternoon and take the slower but more scenic drive along the south coast, it makes sense to spend the night in Kinsale, which has several decent hotels and restaurants (*see* the town listings below). In a class by themselves, however, are Ballymaloe House in Shanagarry, and Longueville House in Mallow.

Longueville House, just west of Mallow on T30, toward Killarney, is 35.2 km (22 mi) north of Cork, so you wouldn't want to stay here unless (1) you plan to spend a few days in the area; (2) you arrive at the hotel in the evening, spend the night, and then, in the morning, continue south to Cork or west to Killarney; or (3) you're willing to go out of your way for a night in one of Ireland's best-loved country hotels. The Georgian mansion sits on 200 ha (500 acres) overlooking the Blackwater River, which supplies one of the country's top restaurants with its fresh fish. In spite of the owner's efforts to modernize the hotel, it has managed to keep its Old World charm, with an elegant drawing room, a library bound in silence, and lots of molded plaster, Waterford chandeliers, and beautiful, inlaid mahogany doors. The Presidents' Restaurant is outstanding. Ask for a bedroom with traditional furnishings overlooking the ruins of Dromineer Castle. *Mallow, Co. Cork, tel. 022/47156. 17 rooms with bath. Facilities: restaurant, bar. Fishing on grounds. AE, DC, MC, V. Very Expensive.*

Ballymaloe House is not directly on our proposed route. It would make sense staying here only if (1) you plan to spend a few days in the Cork area; (2) you arrive at the hotel in the evening, spend the night, and then continue to Cork the next morning on your way west; and/or (3) you're willing to go out of your way to stay in a family-run country hotel rich in charm (more than elegance) and character. The hotel, part of it dating back to the 17th century, sits on 160 ha (400 acres) of rolling farmland. William Penn, Oliver Cromwell, and Bishop Berkeley stayed here—in the days before it had swimming, tennis, and golf. The restaurant, lined with the paintings of Jack Yeats (William Butler's brother), is first-rate, particularly for Sunday dinner. To reach Shanagarry, pick up N25 at the traffic circle outside Cork City where N8 from Dublin terminates. Turn off N25 at Midleton and follow signs for Cloyne and Ballycotton. Ballymaloe is 3.2 km (2 mi) beyond Cloyne on the Ballycotton road. *Shanagarry, Midleton, Co. Cork, tel. 021/ 652531. 29 rooms with bath. Facilities: restaurant, bar. Outdoor heated pool, 8-hole golf course, tennis court. AE, DC, MC, V. Expensive.*

Blarney Castle

Kissing the Blarney Stone is like standing for the Hallelujah Chorus of Handel's *Messiah*—it's something you do. But the romantic ruins of Blarney Castle are also worth a visit, and so are the Woolen Mills—the largest emporium of Irish crafts in the country—located on the castle grounds. The castle is 8.1 km (5 mi) a 10-minute drive north of Cork off the main (N22) Killarney road; just follow the signs. If you're staying in Mallow, stop off at the castle en route south to Cork.

Why is there so much blarney about a simple stone? As the story goes, an emissary named George Carew was sent by Queen Elizabeth I to get the Lord of Blarney Castle, Cormac McDermot MacCarthy, to transfer his allegiance from his clan to her; in other words, to surrender his fortress. Again and again MacCarthy agreed, but at the last moment he always found another reason to delay. His excuses were so frequent and so reasonable that Carew became a joke at Elizabeth's court. Elizabeth is reported to have told Carew in exasperation, "This is all Blarney talk; what he says he never means." And so the word blarney has come to stand for smooth talk—charming, basically harmless, but meant to deceive.

High up on the battlements of the ancient castle, embedded in the outside wall, is the Blarney Stone. Kissing it is said to give one the gift of eloquence, which makes a person irresistible to the opposite sex. Of all visitors to the castle—Germans, Japanese, and so on—Americans, the manager tells me, are most likely to kiss the stone and be on their way, neglecting the romantic 15th-century castle itself, and the beautiful castle grounds.

Visitors, including the Irish, have been kissing the stone since the 18th century. No one knows exactly why. Some say MacCarthy rescued a drowning witch, who thanked him by telling him the secret of the magic stone. Others say the stone was brought from the Holy Land during the Crusades. The most palatable explanation is that the stone had some significance to the MacCarthy clan—perhaps as the stone on which the chieftain sat—and it was later incorporated into the battlements.

What will surprise you is the considerable effort you must make to kiss the stone. After climbing 127 very steep stone steps, you have to lie on your back and lean backward over the edge of the 42.75-m (150-ft) wall. Visitors were once dangled by their heels over the side of the castle, but in 1912 a hapless pilgrim fell ineloquently to the ground, and an iron guard rail was installed. Ninety-year-olds have kissed the stone, so there's no reason why you can't, too; and a photographer will take your picture to prove it. *Tel. 021/85252. Admission: IR£2 adults, IR£1.50 senior citizens, IR£1 children. Open May, Mon.–Sat. 9–7, Sun. 9–5:30; June and July, Mon.–Sat. 9–8:30, Sun. 9–5:30; Aug., Mon.–Sat. 9–7:30, Sun. 9–5:30; Sept., Mon.–Sat. 9–6:30, Sun. 9–5:30; Oct.–Apr., daily 9:30–sundown.*

The path leading to the castle veers left to the **Rock Close,** a grove of ancient yew trees—some of the oldest in the world— and weirdly shaped boulders. Don't miss it. The paths were probably laid out by an 18th-century owner of the castle, but when you see the witch's stone and wander through her kitchen, you'll agree with those who believe that this was once a center of Druidic worship.

If you want to do all your shopping at once, the best place to go is the **Blarney Woolen Mills** at the entrance to the castle. Prices are competitive, and the selection is impressive.

Lodging   **Blarney Park.** If you must overnight in Blarney (not a thing we recommend because of the package tour crowds unless dictated by time and logistics), this modern low rise is your best bet. It is pleasantly located a few minutes' walk from the hubbub of the castle green and is under enthusiastic new management. *Blarney, Co. Cork, tel. 021/385281. 70 rooms with bath. Facilities: restaurant, bar, indoor pool, saunas, gymnasium. AE, DC, MC, V. Moderate.*

Kinsale

Kinsale (*Ceann Saile*, head of the tide), 28.8 km (18 mi) southwest of Cork, is one of Europe's top deep-sea fishing and sailing centers. It also holds an important place in Irish history, for it was here, in 1601, in the Battle of Kinsale, that the Irish, aided by some 4,000 Spaniards, held the town for 10 weeks, before surrendering to English forces. This was the final effort by the medieval chiefs to fight the British; after the battle, the Irish were outlawed from the town (as in Kilkenny) and not permitted to live within its walls until the late 18th century. It was from Kinsale that the *Cinque Ports* set sail in 1703 with a sailor named Alexander Selkirk. Selkirk was marooned on the lonely Pacific island of Juan Fernandez and became the model for Defoe's *Robinson Crusoe.*

Kinsale today is one of Ireland's most attractive, sophisticated harborfront towns, with a reputation for good food. It is here that the annual Gourmet Food Festival is held in early October. Even if you don't plan to spend the night, it's worth stopping for lunch and a short walk around town.

Time Out   A five-minute climb in the Scilly/Summercove direction will take you to the **Spaniard Inn,** one of Ireland's most famous dives, situated on a hairpin bend overlooking the harbor. Inside a big log fire is always burning in the grate of the small front bar, which has a fishing net, wood beams, and sawdust on the floor. This is the place to meet the locals over a glass of Guinness.

The **museum** in the 17th-century Market House has models of local ships and examples of Kinsale lace. The 12th-century **St. Multose Church** has a Norman tower, and some stocks for unruly children.

Dining   **Blue Haven.** This old town house has earned international acclaim for its seafood. Inexpensive bar lunches are served in the lounge bar, patio, and conservatory. The rooms, which are decorated with pretty swagged curtains, hanging plants, and nautical brass, overlook a floodlit garden with a cherub-adorned fountain. Choose between the classical approach—lobster thermidor or turbot hollandaise—and chef Jean Michel's special seafood chow mein, which features the best of the day's catch. *3 Pearse St., tel. 021/772209. Reservations advised. Jacket and tie advised. AE, DC, MC, V. Closed mid-Jan.–mid-Feb. Expensive.*

The Vintage is a charming front-parlor restaurant, hidden away in a narrow back street and a minute from the center of town. It has a loyal clientele of discerning locals and celebrity visitors. The original front room, which has been discreetly extended, still gives patrons the impression of dining in a quietly chic, antique-filled private home. Hot oysters in a sauce of dry white wine, cream, and sorrel, and guinea fowl with red cabbage and apples are among the unusual specialties on the menu. *Main St., tel. 021/772502. Reservations advised. Jacket and tie advised. AE, DC, MC, V. Closed Sun. in winter, 2 wks in Nov., 3 wks late Jan.–Feb. Dinner only. Expensive.*

Man Friday. The log-cabin atmosphere of this restaurant's one large room—replete with stone walls and floor, rough-hewn beams, and coconut palms—is supposed to recall Robinson Crusoe's tropical paradise. It attracts a youngish crowd, and noise levels get high, especially on summer weekends. Seafood is given the "Irish nouvelle" treatment—a vast platter of monkfish, langoustine, salmon, brill, with a delicate sauce—or try chicken breasts stuffed with prawn mousseline and finished with a creamy chervil sauce. However, the place is best known for steaks. *Scilly, Kinsale (opposite the Spaniard Inn), tel. 021/772260. Weekend reservations advised. Dress: casual. MC, V. Closed Sun. and last 2 wks in Jan. Moderate.*

Lodging   **Acton's Hotel.** Kinsale's biggest hotel is constantly being refurbished without ever quite getting it right. It has a delightful seafront location on the town pier approach, but be sure to specify a room with a view; the other half overlooks a noisy back street. The bar and lobby, which are subject to invasions from the conference room, bus tours, and weddings, are taken over by jazz buffs on Sunday for a very popular brunch jazz session. *Pier Rd., Kinsale, tel. 021/772135, 55 rooms with bath. Facilities: restaurant, bar, gymnasium, sauna, indoor pool. AE, DC, MC, V. Expensive.*

Blue Haven. This carefully renovated town house is the first choice of individuals who value atmosphere and attention to detail above spaciousness, though some feel the decor verges on the precious. Rooms are small but individually decorated with antiques and paintings by local artists. The owner-managers have won numerous international awards. *Pearse St., Kinsale, tel. 021/772209. 10 rooms, 7 with bath. Facilities: restaurant, bar. AE, DC, MC, V. Closed 2–3 wks late Jan. Moderate.*

Trident Hotel. A modern low rise on the water's edge, this hotel is popular with visitors who come to Kinsale for deep-sea fishing—mainly all-male groups of Dutch or English. All rooms are identical cinderblock modern and all have a sea view. *Pier Head, Kinsale, tel. 021/772301. 40 rooms with bath. Facilities: restaurant, bar. AE, DC, MC, V. Moderate.*

The Old Presbytery. A tall, thin Victorian town house, this is among the most attractive of Kinsale's B&Bs. It is wittily furnished with a strange assortment of antiques and a bold primary color scheme. Host Ken Buggy bakes his own bread daily and serves an above-average breakfast. *Cork St., Kinsale, tel. 021/772027. 4 rooms, 2 with bath. No credit cards. Inexpensive.*

On to Skibbereen and Bantry The narrow road from Kinsale to Skibbereen and Bantry twists and turns through rich green farm country, cultivated to the very edge of the sea. The roller-coaster ride drops you down into hollows among fat sheep and peaceful cows, then up over the crests of hills where you can look out over a patchwork quilt of meadows extending in every direction, each patch a different shade of green, and see beyond them the colorful fishing boats and the sea. There's a domestic beauty here—a sense of fullness—you won't find elsewhere in Ireland. When you reach Ballydehob, the landscape becomes starker, leaner, and suddenly you realize you're in the west. Gone are the prosperous farms and the happy, gentle landscapes; suddenly you're in a world of wild seascapes and stone. You're sure to prefer one world to the other; but the joy of this trip is that you'll have an opportunity to experience both. There's a shortcut from Skibbereen inland to Bantry, but it's not worth saving a few minutes and missing some splendid views of the coast.

Dining **West Cork Hotel.** Tiny front-parlor restaurants come and go like wildflowers in this area. If you see one open, give it a try; otherwise, join the lawyers, doctors, priests, and merchants of Skibbereen at this reliable hotel restaurant. Ignore the mustard-colored modern decor and concentrate on the plainly cooked fresh Irish produce. There's always a choice of roast meat at lunchtime—generous portions of pork, lamb, beef, or chicken and ham—accompanied by a seemingly endless succession of potatoes and vegetables. At dinner hearty eaters should try the mixed grill. *Bridge St., Skibbereen, tel. 028/21277. Reservations advised for large parties (4 or more). Dress: casual but neat. AE, DC, MC, V. Inexpensive.*

Timoleague

Twenty-six kilometers (16 mi) west of Kinsale is **Timoleague.** Be sure to stop and walk through the 600-year-old ruins of the largest Franciscan friary in Ireland. People are still being buried among the rough grasses of the roofless church. A more romantic setting at the edge of the bay would be hard to find. Just inland from the abbey, signposted in the town, is Timoleague Castle Gardens. The castle is no more, but the pleasant Victorian manor has two large walled gardens—one for flowers, one for fruit and vegetables—and fine mature shrubbery. *Tel. 023/46116. Admission: IR£1 adults, 50p children. Open June–Aug., daily noon–6 PM.*

Castletownshend

If you have time to visit only one seaside village off the main road, stop in **Castletownshend.** Baltimore would be a good choice, too, but getting there involves a 25.6-km (16-mi) round-trip from the coastal road, while Castletownshend is only a few miles away and requires no backtracking. Leave the coastal road at Rosscarbery and follow signs to Glandore, Unionhall and Castletownshend. The town has only one main street that slides steeply down to the sea, passing around an ancient sycamore that keeps the tour buses away.

Time Out Stop for a drink at **Mary Ann's** (tel. 028/36146)—one of the noblest pubs in Ireland. Mary Ann, who never married, died in 1966, but the pub itself is some 300 years old. Play snooker (a type of billiards) or darts, enjoy your drink under the trees in the garden. Bar food is available in high season; by arrangement only off-season. One sighs at the bland and tasteless furnishings that destroy the atmosphere of so many venerable old Irish hotels and pubs; so drink a toast to Mary Ann, who understood the beauty that comes with age.

Lodging If you want to build memories on your trip, consider spending a night in one of Castletownshend's two hotels. Both can arrange for fishing, riding, golf, and tennis.

Bow Hall is as close as you'll come in Ireland to an American country inn—not surprising, as it's run by a family of bright, eager Midwesterners who fell in love with Ireland in the 1970s and decided to stay. The 17th-century house is bright and cheery, with American-made quilts and several summers' worth of books. Nowhere in Ireland will you be made to feel more of a welcome guest in a private home. *Mrs. Vickery, Bow Hall, Castletownshend, Co. Cork, tel. 028/36114. 3 rooms with bath. No credit cards. Inexpensive.*

The Castle. The water's-edge seat of the Townshend family that gave the town its name is the sort of place a pair of glassy-eyed teenagers might find themselves trapped in—in a late-night horror movie. Its torn carpets and peeling wallpaper evoke the ghostly presence of a bygone age. Anyone young at heart and/or in love should stay here—but probably only in the "Studio," with its fabulous antiques, or in a room called "Army." *Mrs. Rosemary Salter-Townshend, The Castle, Castletownshend, Co. Cork, tel. 028/36100. 5 rooms. Lunch and dinner by arrangement. No credit cards. Inexpensive.*

Bantry

Bantry (*Beann traighe*, the race of Beann) is delightfully situated at the head of Bantry Bay, one of the most beautiful bays along the Irish coast. If you're only passing through, try to find time to tour Bantry House, one of the great houses of Ireland—one of the very few whose furnishings do justice to their surroundings.

Bantry House has been the seat of the Earls of Bantry since 1765. The brick Georgian mansion was enlarged by the second Earl, who filled it with treasures from his travels around Europe—such as Flemish tapestries, fireplaces from Versailles, floor tiles from Pompeii. In one small dressing room is a dollhouse that is kept safe for examination by young visitors. If you can't spend the night here (*see* Lodging), consider staying for tea or homemade soups. *Tel. 027/50047. Admission: IR£2*

adults, IR£1 children and senior citizens. Open Mar.–Sept.,
daily 9–8; Oct.–Apr., daily 9–6.

Dining **The Admiral.** This small, quiet first-floor restaurant has a discreet art deco theme and serves French cuisine. Fresh local
produce is an additional bonus. *New St., tel. 027/51350. Reser-*
vations advised high season and weekends. Dress: casual but
neat. MC, V. Wine license only. Closed Jan. 1–Mar. 10 and
Nov. 1–Dec. 31. Dinner only. Moderate.

Lodging **Bantry House.** Imagine staying in a B&B among the treasures
and sumptuous gardens of this magnificent mansion. A selection of plainly decorated rooms in both wings can now be rented
overnight—the best one is the family room. *Bantry, Co. Cork,*
tel. 027/50047. 9 rooms, 6 with bath. No credit cards. Moderate.
Vickery's Hotel. A friendly, old-fashioned hotel in the town
center with a basic boardinghouse ambience, it has been in the
same family since 1822. *New St., tel. 027/50006. 15 rooms, 4*
with bath. Facilities: Restaurant, bar, no TV or direct dial
phones in rooms. AE, DC, MC, V. Inexpensive.

Ballylickey

From Bantry, head north 4.8 km (3 mi) around the head of the
bay to **Ballylickey.**

Lodging **Ballylickey Manor House** has a sophistication not easy to find
on the west coast of Ireland. The ambience is more country
French than Irish—which will be a plus or minus, depending
on why you're here. The four rustic pine chalets around the pool
seem out of place; best bet are the elegant rooms and suites in
the recently rebuilt, 300-year-old main house. Furnishings are
a blend of Cork and Provence—and, difficult as it is to believe,
it works! The hotel is surrounded by gardens on a hillside overlooking the bay. The grounds include a pool and private
streams for fishing. The candlelit French country restaurant is
in itself a good reason to stay. *Ballylickey, Co. Cork, tel. 027/*
⸱⸱⸱⸱. 11 rooms with bath. Facilities: restaurant, bar, fishing
on grounds. V. Closed Nov.–Mar. Moderate.
Sea View House Hotel is clean and well-run, with very friendly
owners who do their best to make you feel at home. Some rooms
and bathrooms are more basic than others. Best is Room 7.
Here, as elsewhere along the coast, owners can arrange for riding, boating, fishing, and golf. *Ballylickey, Co. Cork, tel. 027/*
50462. 13 rooms with bath. Facilities: restaurant, bar. AE, DC,
MC, V. Closed Nov.–Mar. Moderate.

Glengarriff

From Ballylickey, head west around the island-studded bay to
the tourist center of **Glengarriff** (*Gleann Garbh*, rugged glen),
which, because of its sheltered location, is famous for its semi-
tropical vegetation.

The top attraction is **Garinish Island,** a 10-minute boat ride
from town. Barren 50 years ago, it now has a lovely Italian garden with plants and shrubs from around the world. Shaded
paths lead to Roman statues, Grecian temples, a miniature Japanese garden, and an old Martello tower. It's also called Bryce
Island, after the family who gave it to the nation. Shaw was a

frequent visitor when he was living in the neighborhood, writing *Saint Joan*.

If time permits, or if you're partial to seascapes, follow a 107.2-km (67-mi) circular route around the Beara Peninsula from Glengarriff to Castletownbere, then north to Kenmare. The scenery is similar to but less spectacular than that of the Ring of Kerry and Dingle Peninsula, which you'll see later on, so you may prefer to head directly north from Glengarriff to Kenmare. This is a beautiful drive through wild mountain scenery, with cloud shadows racing across purple mountains, and pillars of golden gorse.

Kenmare

Kenmare (*Ceann mara*, head of the sea) is a delightful tourist center at the head of the Kenmare River, 32 km (20 mi) south of Killarney. If you want a single base from which to explore the entire west coast, you're better off closer to Killarney, which is central both to the Ring of Kerry and to the Dingle Peninsula. Kenmare, however, has the Park Hotel, which is the number one hotel on your itinerary. Kenmare is also much more sophisticated and uncommercial. If you want to enjoy some outdoor sports for a few days, or need a place to stop overnight before heading around the Ring of Kerry, Kenmare is ideal. At the very least, you should stop for lunch at one of its first-class restaurants, or have a deli make a picnic lunch for you. Sandwiches come on homemade brown bread—that's how sophisticated Kenmare is! If you're here on a Monday, the Town Fair on Main Street has some good buys on hand-knit sweaters.

Dining **Park Hotel.** The menu at this stately old hotel restaurant is nouvelle cuisine. Appetizers include salmon with champagne and basil sauce, and seafood chowder with pastry topping. For a main dish you might try turbot baked with crabmeat and apples in a saffron sauce or duck breast in pastry with port and orange sauce. Ask for a window table overlooking lawns that sweep down to the bay. *Kenmare, Co. Kerry, tel. 064/41200. Reservations advised. Jacket and tie required. DC, MC, V. Expensive.*

The Lime Tree. Located in a charming old stone house, it is a good bet for dinner if you'd rather not splurge in the Park Hotel next door. Entrées include mussels in garlic butter, smoked chicken with curried rice salad, and rack of lamb with red currant and almond sauce. *Kenmare, Co. Kerry, tel. 064/41225. Reservations advised high season. Dress: casual but neat. V. Closed Sun. and Nov. 1–Apr. 1. Dinner only. Moderate.*

The Star Restaurant. This light, bright modern restaurant is a half mile outside town and specializes in local seafood. Try pan-fried monkfish with Irish Mist and dill sauce. They also serve steaks, veal, and roast duckling. *Gortamullen, Kenmare, Co. Kerry, tel. 064/41099. Reservations advised high season. Dress: casual. MC, V. Open Oct.–Apr., Fri.–Sun. Moderate.*

Mickey & Ned's. For picnic sandwiches or a simple home-cooked lunch, this coffee shop and delicatessen is handy. *6 Henry St. Kenmare, tel. 064/41449. V. Open Mon.–Sat. 9:30–5:30; closed Sun. Inexpensive.*

Lodging **Park Hotel Kenmare** is a 90-year-old former bishop's palace on 11 beautifully kept acres overlooking Kenmare Bay. Here at last is a historic Irish hotel with bedrooms as distinguished as its public areas. Some rooms have four-poster beds, Liberty fabrics, and antique furniture from stately mansions of England and Holland. Others are smaller and more modern, but also decorated with flawless taste. The hotel grounds are a natural garden of dracaena palms, gladiolus, rhododendrons, fuchsia bushes, and other flora typical of southwestern Ireland. In its first incarnation the Park Hotel belonged to the chain of Great Southern Hotels built at the turn of the century for the English gentry who wanted their comforts away from home. *Kenmare, Co. Kerry, tel. 064/41200. 48 rooms with bath. Facilities: restaurant, bar, tennis, 9-hole golf course. DC, MC, V. Very Expensive.*

Lansdowne Arms. Kenmare's original coaching inn was established by the Marquis of Lansdowne when the town was first laid out in the 1790s. It has a friendly, homey atmosphere. Rooms are basic but adequate for an overnight stop, and there is live entertainment in the bar most nights. *Main St., Kenmare, tel. 064/41368. 22 rooms, 9 with bath. Facilities: restaurant, bar. DC, V. Inexpensive.*

Rockvilla. Mrs. Sheila Fahy's home is 6.4 km (4 mi) outside Kenmare on the Sneem/Ring of Kerry Road. She offers plain Irish hospitality in a comfortable modern house set in an acre of gardens. Unlike most B&Bs, this one has a chef in residence who prepares an à la carte evening meal of local seafood or steak. *Rockvilla, Templenoe, Kenmare, tel. 064/41331. 6 rooms, 5 with bath. Facilities: restaurant—dinner only, wine license only, tennis. V. Inexpensive.*

On to Killarney Kenmare is the starting point for drives around the Ring of Kerry to Killarney—a full day's trip. By taking this circular route, however, you'll miss the sensational drive north over the mountains from Kenmare to Killarney. Be sure to include this drive on an excursion from Killarney to Ladies' View.

Ring of Kerry

The famous **Ring of Kerry** is a road that skirts the coast of the Iveragh Peninsula, with dramatic seascapes, fine mountain scenery, and restaurants and hotels for every taste and budget. It's less wild than the Dingle Peninsula to the north, but it also has more amenities. If you have time for only one side trip from Killarney, tour the Dingle Peninsula instead; the Ring of Kerry is better suited for those who plan to stay in one of its resorts and take advantage of the outdoor activities—tennis, fishing, hiking, riding, and golf. The 176-km (110-mi) drive around the Ring is a full-day trip. Start in Kenmare, as most day-trippers will be heading in the opposite direction. The most dramatic views are west of Parknasilla on the south coast, and west of Glenbeigh on the north coast—particularly around Caherciveen.

Tahilla The village of **Tahilla** (17.6 km/11 mi west of Kenmare, 4.8 km/3 mi east of Parknasilla) consists of a Catholic church, a petrol pump, a post office, a school for 40 children, and lots of grazing cows and sheep.

Lodging **Tahilla Cove Country House** is a small, unpretentious guest house on 4.8 ha (12 acres) of undeveloped land along the bay. The physical layout is unmemorable, the furnishings are friendly in a sensible, boardinghouse sort of way, and there's almost nothing to do here but exist, but the secluded, out-of-the-way atmosphere and the friendliness of the hosts, Dolly, Deirdre, and James Waterhouse, make this a worthwhile stop. (The Prime Minister of Ireland reportedly came here before taking office to recover from his campaign.) Stay if you're passing through, or if you want to take a few days off to fish or simply to rest. Some rooms are plainer than others; of the four in the main house, Room 6 is best. The tiny bar is popular with local fishermen. The Sunday menu includes scallops, salmon, and lobster. *Tahilla, Co. Kerry, tel. 064/45104. 9 rooms, 8 with bath. Facilities: restaurant, bar. AE, DC, MC. Closed Sept. 30–Mar. 31. Inexpensive.*

Parknasilla   **Parknasilla** (24 km/15 mi west of Kenmare), located on the shores of the Kenmare River at the edge of the sea, is a center for sailing, fishing, tennis, pony trekking, and golf. Thanks to the Gulf Stream, the vegetation is tropical.

Lodging   **Parknasilla Great Southern Hotel** is one of those great, elegant turn-of-the-century hotels that were built for the English upper classes so they could brave the wilderness in comfort. The architect also designed the Park Hotel in Kenmare. (The Park seems to attract more Americans; the Parknasilla, more Europeans.) Among the most famous guests have been General de Gaulle, Princess Grace, the Dutch royal family, and George Bernard Shaw, who wrote much of *Saint Joan* while staying here in Suite 216. The atmosphere has an institutional edge to it, but also conjures up the glamor of a bygone age. Rooms are a bit plain, but very tasteful, with soft pinks and blues. Guests, most of whom prefer to stay in the old section, are greeted by a porter in frock coat and striped gray pants. *Parknasilla, Co. Kerry, tel. 064/45122. 60 rooms with bath. Facilities: restaurant, bar, indoor saltwater pool, sauna, horse trekking, sailing, windsurfing, waterskiing, angling, tennis, 9-hole golf course. AE, DC, MC, V. Closed Nov.–mid-Mar. Very Expensive.*

Sneem   In **Sneem** (27.2 km/17 mi west of Kenmare), buried in the Catholic church (1865) is Father O'Flynn of the famous song. The Protestant church, dating back to Elizabethan times, has a salmon as a weathervane. Along the main street are two stores selling hand-knit sweaters at attractive prices.

Staigue Fort   Beyond Sneem, the road winds inland for a few miles through wild scenery, meeting the coast again at Castlecove. Just past Castlecove, on the right, is a sign leading you 2.4 km (1½ mi) to **Staigue Fort,** one of the most remarkable prehistoric monuments in Kerry. You may wonder what the fuss is all about, as there's nothing to see but a circular wall of dry masonry 5.4 m (18 ft) high. But let your imagination lift you thousands of years back in time, to when the fort contained two thatched cottages and was used to shelter farmers and their animals from wolves. The walls, constructed without mortar, are 3.8 m (13 ft) thick at the base. Along the interior of the walls are several well-constructed flights of stairs. Staigue Fort is one of the finest of some 35,000 surviving ring forts scattered throughout Ireland, dating from the Iron Age to early Christian times. In spite of their name, they were not used as military forts but as homesteads and cattle enclosures.

Caherdaniel   Beyond Westcove is the village of **Caherdaniel.** In the vicinity, near the shores of Derrynane Bay, is the curious hermitage of St. Crohane, carved from solid rock. Slightly under 3.2 km (2 mi) southwest of Caherdaniel is Derrynane House, the former home of Daniel O'Connell (1775–1847), one of the most famous and revered fathers of Irish independence. If you know nothing of O'Connell, and care little for Irish history, you'll have no reason to visit—just as an Irishman might not go out of his way to visit the birthplace of Ethan Allen on a tour of the United States. O'Connell was committed to nonviolence. While living here he defended the poor in court, helped win emancipation for Catholics (he was the first Catholic Irishman to sit in the British Parliament), demonstrated to the Irish the power of numbers, and helped win back for them a sense of pride and self-respect. *Tel. 0667/5113. Admission: IR£1 adults, 40p children and senior citizens. Open mid-June–Sept. 30, daily 10–1 and 2–7, Sun. 2–5; Oct.–mid-June, Tues.–Sat. 10–1 and 2–5, Sun. 2–5.*

The Skellig Islands The views become more spectacular as you head north around the western rim of the peninsula. The road climbs above the sea, beneath smooth brown hills and sheep-colored rocks. Neat white cottages stand like sentinels among the green fields, running down to the very edge of the sea. There's something noble about this effort to claim every inch of available soil—a human drama you're not aware of in the richer country to the east.

The islands rising offshore are the **Skelligs.** The government's efforts to close the Skelligs to the public so that restorations can be made have been met with outrage from locals, whose livelihoods are at stake. Call Des Lavell on Valencia Island (tel. 0667/6124) for the latest word, and hope that he can take you. If you're young at heart and want a real adventure, this is the one trip you shouldn't miss; the memory will linger for a lifetime. The 14.4-km (9-mi) voyage from Valencia Island (north of Waterville) is made only in calm weather, and even then the sea can be rough; be sure to take motion-sickness pills before you sail.

The **Great Skellig** or **Skellig Michael** (Michael is the patron saint of high places) is the largest of the three—an enormous mass of rock rising more than 209.9 m (700 ft) above the sea. Steep and sometimes slippery steps lead up to the best-preserved early Christian monastic settlement in Europe. The ruins include a small, ancient church; a larger 10th-century church; two oratories (similar to the Gallarus Oratory you'll see on Dingle); six beehive cells rising up to 5 m (17 ft); several burial enclosures; crude crosses; and two wells. In former times Skellig Michael was a place of pilgrimage. Above "Christ's Saddle" is a projecting flake of rock inscribed with a cross that pilgrims kissed in an act of penance. En route to Skellig Michael you'll pass **Little Skellig,** home of 20,000 pairs of gannets—the second-largest gannetry in the North Atlantic.

Waterville The road from Derrynane House crosses the 209.9-m (700-ft) Pass of Coomakesta, and then winds down to **Waterville** (*An Coirean,* little waterfall). The popular angling center is on a strip of land between Ballinskelligs Bay and Lough Currane, one of the loveliest lakes in Ireland. Like Parknasilla, Waterville is a popular tourist destination with a few good restaurants and hotels. There's a summer's worth of outdoor activities, including sailing, tennis, hiking, and riding; but the main attractions are fishing and playing golf on an 18-hole championship course. You also have the exhilarating feeling of being on the ocean.

Dining **The Huntsman** features fresh, plainly cooked fish: lobsters from the tank (broiled, and served with roe), creamy seafood bisque, scampi Newburg, salmon with hollandaise, and delicious homemade bread. The color scheme, softened by candlelight, is bordello red: bright red carpets running up the side of the bar, red-colored chairs, and lampshades with red-tinted lights. *Waterville, Co. Kerry, tel. 0667/4124. Dress: neat but casual. AE, DC, MC, V. Closed Oct.–Apr., weekdays, except by prior arrangement for groups. Moderate.*

Lodging **Butler Arms.** Charlie Chaplin stayed here with his daughter. It is a large, established, residential-type hotel, neither sophisticated nor elegant, but friendly and old-fashioned in a distant-aunt sort of way. Best bet are rooms facing the sea. Ask for 215, or something comparable. *Waterville, Co. Kerry, tel. 0667/ 4144. 43 rooms, 27 with bath. Facilities: restaurant, bar, tennis, deep-sea and freshwater angling, pony trekking. AE, DC, MC, V. Closed Oct. 12–Apr. 15. Expensive.*

Waterville Lake Hotel. Waterville's deluxe hostelry is a smart, modern hotel particularly geared for fishermen and golfers. The 74-par course is one of the best in Europe. Fishing is in the ocean, on Lough Currane, or on mountain lakes with names like Derriana and Cloonaghlan, where the average size of spring salmon is 6.3 k (14 lbs). Rooms are very decorated with modern, serviceable furniture and fabrics. *Waterville, Co. Kerry, tel. 0667/4133. 50 rooms with bath. Facilities: restaurant, bar, indoor pool, sauna, tennis, 18-hole golf course, pony trekking, deep-sea and freshwater angling. AE, DC, MC, V. Closed Nov. 1–Mar. 31. Expensive.*

The Smuggler's Inn. Situated on Waterville's mile-long sandy beach, the small, family-run guest house has Old World charm. Rooms are basic, but pretty and clean with panoramic sea views. Chef/proprietor Harry Hunt runs a seafood restaurant. *Cliff Rd., Waterville, Co. Kerry, tel. 0667/4330. 6 rooms with bath. Facilities: restaurant (Moderate), bar. AE, DC, MC, V. Closed Nov. 3–Feb. 15. Inexpensive.*

Caherciveen **Caherciveen** (take it slowly: Ka-her-sigh-veen), located at the foot of 373.5-m (1,245-ft) Mount Bentee, and overlooking Valencia Harbor (where boats leave for the Skelligs), is the shopping center of the western end of the Ring of Kerry. Of all the towns on the Ring, Caherciveen has the most charm, in part because it enjoys a life independent of the tourists passing through. Stop for a pint at the Angel, one of the country's most famous pubs (but unknown to tourists), where writers and artists (Liam O'Flaherty was one of them) touch mugs with local farmers and fishermen. Down the street is the Iveragh Inn, a modest but friendly coffee shop for sandwiches or pies.

Lodging **Mount Rivers.** This bed-and-breakfast is one of the friendliest on the Ring. Books are everywhere in this late-19th-century home at the far end of town. *Mrs. N. McKenna, Mount Rivers, Carhan Rd., Caherciveen, Co. Kerry, tel. 0667/2509. 5 rooms with bath. Closed Oct. 1–Mar. 31. No credit cards. Inexpensive.*

Glenbeigh The road northeast from Caherciveen to **Glenbeigh** is scenically the highlight of the drive around the Ring of Kerry. Across the bay is Dingle Peninsula, which you'll be exploring in future days. Glenbeigh is the starting point for some of the best hikes in western Ireland, around the Glenbeigh Horseshoe, near Commasaharn Lake, and along the slopes of Drung Hill. Ask locally for details or consult the *Irish Walk Guides/1.*

A few minutes west of Glenbeigh is a 3.2-km (2-mi) long spit of land jutting into Dingle Bay, with soft yellow sand backed by high dunes, and breaking surf. Across the bay, on Dingle Peninsula, is a similar spit, perfect (at low tide) for walking or swimming. If the weather is right, don't wait for Dingle; in Ireland you never know when you'll see the sun again.

Caragh Lake A few miles northeast of Glenbeigh, on the Ring Road toward Killorglin, you'll see signs on your right pointing to **Caragh Lake.** This is a beautiful expanse of water, set among broom- and heather-covered hills with majestic mountains in the background. Much of the lakeside property is privately owned—as is much of the Killarney area—by Germans. If you're making a quick tour of western Ireland and want to see as much as possible, it makes little sense to base yourself on Caragh Lake. Stay here either (a) as a starting or ending point for a trip around the Ring of Kerry, or (b) as a place to stay put for a day or two that's near a lake and off the beaten track.

Lodging A hundred yards back from the lake are two lovely, secluded hotels surrounded by woods and gardens. Though both have access to the lake and their own boats for rowing and fishing, neither is close enough to enjoy lakeside views.

Ard na Sidhe. Its name pronounced *sheen*, and meaning "hill of the fairies," it is a secluded and peaceful Victorian mansion, with imposing gray walls covered with creeper. It is 4.8 km (3 mi) from the Ring Road, and the interior is tastefully furnished with antiques and open fireplaces. The hotel is now run by the same German group that manages Hotel Europe and Dunloe Castle (*see* Killarney, below). Rooms are a bit bare but have nice traditional furnishings. The main house is preferable to the annex. *Caragh Lake, near Killorglin, Co. Kerry, tel. 066/ 69105. 20 rooms with bath. Facilities: restaurant, bar, boating, fishing. AE, DC, MC, V. Closed Oct. 1–Apr. 30. Moderate.*
Caragh Lodge. Another secluded country house on the lake shore, 1.6 km (1 mi) from the Ring Road, the Lodge is smaller, friendlier, and more relaxed than its neighbor. Lounges and dining room are furnished with antiques and overlook the lake. It is situated in 3.6 ha (9 acres) of parkland with rare and subtropical trees and shrubs. *Caragh Lake, near Killorglin, Co. Kerry, tel. 066/69115. 10 rooms with bath. Facilities: restaurant (wine license only), sauna, fishing, tennis. AE, DC, MC, V. Closed Nov.–mid Apr. Moderate.*

Killorglin The best time to visit **Killorglin** is during the three-day Puck Fair in August, which is attended by people from all over Ireland. On the evening of the first day a procession assembles at the bridge and a large billy goat, his horns bedecked with ribbons, is borne in triumph through the streets to a platform on a square in the center of town. Here Puck is enthroned for two days, presiding over a great cattle, horse, and sheep fair, with nonstop dancing and entertainment. The tradition is a holdover either from pagan times, or from colonial days, when the stampeding of goats gave warning of the approach of English forces.

Killorglin is a pleasant 22.5-km (14-mi) drive from Killarney.

Killarney

There are two Killarneys—one, a spectacular region of mountains and island-studded lakes, wooded shores, and romantic glens; the other, a tourist-infested town, whose population more than triples in the summer months. The town—more a place of transit than a destination—is in the wrong place: on a flat plain more than a mile from the lakes. The only reason to come here is to satisfy a nostalgia for noise, traffic, and fast food; to mingle with the under-25 crowd; to shop; or to dine at one of the two quality restaurants. Fortunately, there are hundreds of guest houses and hotels in the surrounding countryside, so you don't need to visit the town too often.

What makes the scenery around Killarney so breathtaking is the rare combination of lushness and grandeur, of tropical vegetation and wild mountain scenery. A climate warmer than anywhere else in the British Isles encourages the growth of Mediterranean strawberry trees, cedars of Lebanon, and wild fuchsia sprouting from gray stone walls. Happiness, you'll find, has very little to do with the mind here. There are historic buildings to check off as you tour the country, but most of your time will be spent getting back in touch with yourself: biking along the shores of Muckross Lake, hiking to some windswept peak, angling for salmon, or simply watching the morning mist uncurl from a mountain lake.

A full-day pony or pony-cart ride through the Gap of Dunloe and boat trip through the three lakes of Killarney makes a memorable excursion. Hotels can make arrangements for you. For about IR£20 per person you can arrange for your own private ponies and boat. The trip was the standard Killarney adventure in the 19th century; today most visitors haven't time for a full day of anything, and make do with the pony trip alone, which is the least rewarding part of the tour.

If you're crossing the Gap on your own, drive west 7.2 km (4½ mi) on Route T67 to Beaufort, and follow the signs another 2.4 km (1½ mi) to the Gap of Dunloe. Men with pony carts—known locally as "jaunting cars"—will "assault" you along the way, but it's best to wait till you reach Kate Kearney's Cottage at the entrance, where the rates are regulated (but be sure to agree on a fee before you set off).

Have some ale or a cup of Irish coffee at Kate Kearney's Cottage, and toast the lady who was famous in her day for her moonshine and her beauty. Wrote Lady Morgan:

Oh, did you ne'er hear of Kate Kearney,
She lived on the banks of Killarney;
From the glance of her eye
Shun danger and fly
For Fate's in the glance of Kate Kearney.

For that eye is so modestly beaming,
You'd ne'er think of mischief she's dreaming.
Yet, oh, I can tell
How fatal's the spell
That lurks in the eye of Kate Kearney.

Though she looks so bewitchingly simple,
Yet there's mischief in every dimple,

And who dares inhale
Her sigh's spicy gale
Must die by the breath of Kate Kearney.

Kate never married. When the law came after her, she disappeared—some say to Australia or New Zealand. The Irish loved her because she flouted the law, and the law was British; and they continue to love wild, voluptuous women who flout the codes by which they're told to live.

On any given summer day the pony carts make some 300 90-minute trips about halfway through the Gap and back, so don't expect to feel like Lewis and Clark. It's a scenic and romantic trip, though, past a series of clear mountain lakes through a rift in the great MacGillycuddy's Reeks—surely an improvement over seeing the world framed through a car window. (Jaunting cars take 4 passengers at IR£4 per head). As the ponies leave their own trailmarkers along what is essentially an unimproved dirt road, you'll want to think twice about squishing forth on foot. If you're traveling off-season or want, because of health or children, to take a pony cart, a trip through the Gap is a great treat; otherwise, I'd suggest you take your feet or your rented ponies and explore other, equally spectacular areas of this beautiful country, such as the **Horse's Glen** described in Charles Kidney's *Visitor's Guide to Killarney*. A trip through the Gap makes sense, too, if you're leaving the crowds behind and taking a boat ride through the lakes.

The most romantic of the three lakes, **Upper Lake,** is also the least accessible. A road runs along a section of it, so, for the right price, you may be able to arrange through your hotel or through a tour agency to have a boat put in the water for you, or to get one at Lord Brandon's Cottage, at the western end of the lake. Speak to Henry Clifton at Ross Castle.

Ross Castle, a 16th-century stronghold of the O'Donoghue clan and the last castle to fall to Cromwell's army in 1652, is no longer open, but Henry Clifton runs a boat concession on the castle grounds, on the western shore of **Lower Lake.** You can row yourself around (rowboat hire is IR£1.50 per hour)—a memorable experience, particularly at dawn or dusk—or allow yourself to be taken to **Innisfallen Island.** (A waterbus tour of the Lower Lake from Ross Castle is IR£4 for adults, IR£2 for children. A rowboat trip to Innisfallen with guide costs IR£8.) If you have an interest in antiquity or a fondness for romantic ruins, you will want to visit the remains of a 7th-century abbey on Innisfallen, which, like the Rock of Cashel, goes back to the earliest days of Christianity. Brian Boru, the last High King of Ireland, and St. Brendan, who probably "discovered" America centuries before Columbus, are said to have been educated here. H. V. Morton writes that "there was once a Frenchman who said that Ireland was the jewel of the west, that Kerry was the jewel of Ireland, that Killarney was the jewel of Kerry, and that the little uninhabited isle of Innisfallen was the jewel of Killarney. I have nothing to add to this."

Another delightful half-day excursion from Killarney is south on Route N71 to Muckross Abbey, Muckross House, and Torc Waterfall, and around the southern shore of the three lakes to Ladies' View (32.2 km/20 mi round-trip). This trip will take you along a section of the spectacular road between Killarney and

Killarney Area

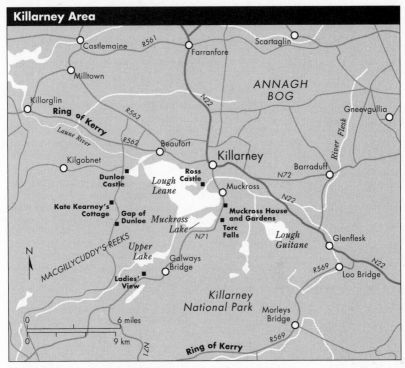

Castlemaine · R561 · Scartaglin · Farranfore · Milltown · ANNAGH BOG · Killorglin · Gneevgullia · Ring of Kerry · N22 · R563 · Laune River · R562 · Beaufort · Killarney · River Flesk · Kilgobnet · Ross Castle · Barraduff · N72 · Dunloe Castle · Lough Leane · Muckross · N22 · Kate Kearney's Cottage · Gap of Dunloe · Muckross Lake · Muckross House and Gardens · Glenflesk · MACGILLYCUDDY'S REEKS · Torc Falls · N71 · Lough Guitane · R569 · N22 · N · Upper Lake · Galways Bridge · Loo Bridge · Ladies' View · Killarney National Park · Morleys Bridge · 6 miles · 9 km · N71 · R569 · Ring of Kerry

Kenmare that you missed by driving from Kenmare around the Ring of Kerry. The abbey and house are located in wooded parklands along the tranquil shores of Muckross and Lower Lakes—an idyllic spot for walks, bicycle rides, or pony-cart rides (cars are not permitted on the grounds). There are several bicycle-rental shops in Killarney.

You'll reach Muckross Abbey first—a .4-km (¼-mi) walk from the parking lot, and 4 km (2½ mi) from Killarney. You can rent a pony cart here to take you on a delightful one- or two-hour ride to Muckross House and Torc Waterfall. (IR£10–IR£24 negotiable with guide/driver depending on time and route. Up to four people on one cart.) You can also arrange to ride to Muckross House and then walk back. What the drivers won't tell you is that you can return to your car after seeing the abbey and then drive directly to Muckross House without their services.

The 15th-century Franciscan **abbey,** partially restored in the past 20 years, was wrecked by Cromwell's forces in 1652, but is still amazingly complete, though roofless. An ancient yew tree rises up through the cloister and branches out over the broken abbey walls. The lakefront walk called Lovers' Lane, which runs halfway from the abbey to Muckross House, is one of the most beautiful in the park. Look at the islands in the lake—the abbey's treasures were buried on one of them in 1589 to avoid pillage and have not yet been found.

Muckross House is a 19th-century mock-Elizabethan manor house that no one knew what to do with for 32 years. It is now a craft center where blacksmiths, weavers, basket makers, and potters demonstrate their skills. Also on display are old tools and an assortment, more representative than exceptional, of 19th-century country furnishings. *Tel. 064/31440. Admission: IR£2 adults, IR£1 children. Open Mar. 17–June 30 and Sept. 1–Oct. 31, daily 10–7; July 1–Aug. 31, daily 9–9; Oct. 31–Mar. 17, Tues.–Sun. 11–5.*

Muckross House is clearly not for everyone; what shouldn't be missed, however, are the **Muckross Gardens,** with their many tender and exotic shrubs, and a stroll along Arthur Young Walk to Brickeen Bridge on a narrow strip of parkland between the two lakes. *Admission free. Opening hours are the same as those at Muckross House.*

Unless you go by pony cart, return to Route N71 and drive to **Torc Waterfall**—7.2 km (4½ mi) from Killarney. The falls are a 10-minute walk from the parking lot. Visitors whip out their cameras as the falls roar into view; if you want more privacy, continue up a long flight of stone steps for about 10 minutes to the second clearing. There's a marvelous view from here of the lakes of Killarney. If you need more exercise, bear right where the path splits and continue walking through the 8,000-ha (20,000-acre) national park.

Return to your car and continue west another 5 minutes or so to the **Ladies' View.** If I were Irish, I would feel a certain outrage at the fact that what is perhaps the region's most spectacular setting is named in honor of Queen Victoria's Ladies-in-Waiting—not even the queen herself—who once upon a time expressed their pleasure at the view. Stop at the café if you need some refueling; but the best view is at another parking area 90 m (100 yd) farther west. If you haven't had enough beautiful scenery, continue across the mountains to Kenmare; otherwise, return to Killarney.

A delightful way to end the day is to drive at dusk to the ruined tower on Aghadoe Heights, only 4 km (2½ mi) west of town, and watch the shadows creep over Lough Leane (Lower Lake).

Killarney Walks   The easiest walk, but one of the most delightful, is along the paved paths through the wooded parklands surrounding Muckross House.

Follow the steps past Torc Waterfall for a splendid view of the lakes of Killarney.

The most satisfying short walk—8.8 km (5½ mi) or three to four hours round-trip—is to the top of 529-m (1,764-ft) **Torc Mountain,** where you can enjoy breathtaking views of the entire region. Follow Route N71 past the entrance to Muckross House. Where the Kenmare road veers right, an unsurfaced road (the Old Kenmare Road) runs straight ahead into the forest. Drive uphill till you reach a locked gate beside the water supply station. Walk straight (disregarding forest roads to the left) to the bridge across the Owengarriff River above Torc Waterfall. The steep east face of Torc Mountain should be ahead of you. Continue uphill (left) along the road to the open moorland, where the river runs down from a mountain lake called the Devil's Punch Bowl. Continue till you come to a weather recording station within a wire enclosure. When a bridle path joins the road on the right, begin your ascent, making your own way up to the summit. Be sure to return the same way you came; descent by the steep east side of Torc would be foolhardy.

If you're partial to mountain lakes, take the 9.7-km (6-mi) walk (three to four and a half hours round-trip) to the **Devil's Punch Bowl,** the lake that feeds Torc Waterfall. The lake is 90 m (300 ft) below the summit of 689.9-m (2,300-ft) **Mangerton Mountain.** You should be able to arrange in advance to make most of the trip by pony, but because the ascent is gradual, the summit is accessible on foot to all age groups. Take Route N71 from Killarney toward Muckross House. Just past the Muckross Hotel (you might stop here for further details), take the road left to the Mangerton Viewing Park. At the upper end of the wood, swing right, past the car park, to the end of the surfaced road. Park by the concrete bridge. From here an old pony path leads up the mountain. The path swings right to an estate boundary fence, which runs left to the Punch Bowl. Just beside the outlet from the Punch Bowl is Bachelor's Well. Drink from its magic waters and you'll remain single all your life.

To enjoy what may be the wildest region in the country take a walk to the **Horse's Glen.** There are three lakes here suitable for swimming and fishing: Lough Garagarry, Lough Managh, and Lough Erhogh. The starting point, near Muckross Hotel, is only 9.7 km (6 mi) from Killarney, yet the lakes are seldom visited.

Dining   **Panorama Restaurant.** The best of the many hotel restaurants in town overlooks the lakes. There is live Irish entertainment most nights. The menu features such local specialties as oxtail soup, Irish stew, Dingle Bay lobster, and sea trout with toasted almonds. *Fossa, Killarney, tel. 064/31900. Reservations advised. Jacket and tie required. AE, DC, MC, V. Expensive.*

Foley's Seafood and Steak Restaurant. This smart pub-restaurant is either gay and lively or crowded and smoky, depending on your preferences. In either case, it has lots of atmosphere, thanks in part to the colorful characters playing turn-of-the-century ballads. The menu features local produce in classic French dishes: sole meunière, steak au poivre. *23 High St., Killarney, tel. 064/31217. Reservations advised high season. Dress: neat but casual. AE, DC, MC, V. Moderate.*

Gaby's. With crowded tables and wood-slat benches, this place gets low grades for atmosphere but high honors for the freshness of its fish. Try lobster bisque, black sole in cream sauce, seafood mosaic—an enormous shellfish platter—or fresh or smoked salmon. *17 High St., Killarney, tel. 064/32519. No reservations. Dress: neat but casual. AE, DC, MC, V. Closed Sun. Oct.–May. Moderate.*

O'Reilly's. Two restaurants give you a choice of atmosphere in this lively pub. Downstairs, diners are invited to play a piano. Go to the upstairs room if you want a quiet meal. Cooking is both Irish traditional and classic French: plain grilled steak or beef fillet with prawns. *46 New St., Killarney, tel. 064/33699. Reservations advised high season. Dress: casual. AE, DC, MC, V. Inexpensive.*

Lodging   **Aghadoe Heights Hotel** is a modern hilltop hotel 3.2 km (2 mi) northwest of Killarney, whose main attraction is its exquisite view over Lower Lake. Be sure to ask for a room with a lake view. Geared for the package-tour trade, it is part of a new breed of mass-market Irish hotels that charge extra for everything from ice to room service and have little time to deal with the problems of individual travelers. Still, it's a very clean, comfortable hotel that meets high international standards. *Aghadoe, Killarney, tel. 064/31766. 60 rooms with bath. Facilities: restaurant, bar, tennis. AE, DC, MC, V. Closed Nov.– Mar. Expensive.*

Cahernane is an 1877 Victorian mansion, the former home of the Earls of Pembroke. If you're looking for a small, peaceful hotel with a certain amount of character, this is the place to stay. Public areas have rich wood paneling and a sense of the past. Rooms in the main building vary considerably in furnishings and size. Best bet is 26, where the owner, a German lawyer, stays when he visits. Ask for a room with a lake view. Avoid rooms in the modern wing, which are very undistinguished. *Muckross Rd., Killarney, tel. 064/31895. 52 rooms with bath. Facilities: 2 restaurants, bar, tennis court, fishing, horseback riding, putting green. AE, DC, MC, V. Closed Nov. and Jan.–Mar. Expensive.*

Castlerosse is a Best Western hotel in a peaceful setting with lovely views, and lower prices than many other of Killarney's modern hotels. The ambience is Turnpike Modern—each room with its own parking place. Rooms are clean, charmless, functional, ample. *Killarney, tel. 064/31144. 40 rooms with bath. Facilities: restaurant, bar, tennis, sauna. AE, DC, MC, V. Closed Nov.–Mar. Expensive.*

Dunloe Castle, just south of Beaufort, on the road to the Gap of Dunloe, 7.2 km (4½ mi) west of Killarney, is not a castle, but a modern hotel built in the 1960s, under the same German management as the larger, more expensive and somewhat more elegant Hotel Europe. Public areas have classical statues and lovely terra-cotta floors, but rooms are Butcher-block Modern. Still, the castle is much classier than Killarney's mass-market hotels, such as Aghadoe Heights. *Beaufort, Killarney, tel. 064/ 44111. 140 rooms with bath. Facilities: 2 restaurants, 2 bars, indoor pool, sauna, gymnasium, tennis, horseback riding. AE, DC, MC, V. Closed Nov.–Mar. Expensive.*

Hotel Europe is a very spacious, modern, 170-room hotel under the same German management as Dunloe Castle Hotel. Though a bit impersonal (banquet facilities for 600), it attracts a well-heeled, educated clientele and has an old-fashioned elegance you won't find in hotels that cater exclusively to the package-tour trade. Ask for an upstairs room facing the lake. *Killorglin Rd., Fossa, Killarney, tel. 064/31900. 176 rooms with bath. Facilities: 2 restaurants, 2 bars, indoor pool, sauna, gymnasium, tennis, fishing, horseback riding. AE, DC, MC, V. Closed Nov.–Feb. Expensive.*

Killarney Great Southern Hotel is a good chain hotel that hasn't entirely lost that Old World feeling it had at the turn of the century when the British came by train and talked of Empire over their afternoon tea. The vast, rambling, creeper-clad town-center hotel dates from 1864 and is surrounded by pleasant gardens. Guests have included Caroline Kennedy and Pat Nixon. *Killarney, Co. Kerry, tel. 064/31262. 180 rooms with bath. Facilities: 2 restaurants, 2 bars, indoor pool, sauna, tennis. AE, DC, MC, V. Closed Jan. and Feb. Expensive.*

Arbutus Hotel, a former shelter for monks, is small and unpretentious—the best budget hotel for those who want to stay in town. Fully refurbished in 1989, it has turf fires and traditional music in its oak-paneled bar. The Buckley family has owned and managed it for more than 60 years. *College St., tel.*

064/31037. 35 rooms with bath. Facilities: restaurant, bar. AE, DC, MC, V. Inexpensive.

Carriglea is a clean, friendly, reasonably priced guest house on a farm set back from a main road. The rooms in the main house are generally preferable to those in the annex. More amusing than offensive is the extraordinary collection of clashing colors, as if one person were responsible for curtains, another for bedspreads, and so on. Rooms 1 and 8 are a bit more color-coordinated. The public areas are fussy in a delightfully proper Victorian way. *Mr. and Mrs. M. Beazley, Muckross Rd., tel. 064/31116. 9 rooms, 6 with bath. Breakfast only. No credit cards. Closed Nov.–Mar. Inexpensive.*

Tullig House, a B&B near Dunloe Castle, is a very basic but romantic and peaceful farmhouse where kids can help feed the chickens and milk the cows. The owner, Mrs. Joy, serves hearty, honest Irish fare. *Mrs. Debbie Joy, Tullig, Beaufort, Killarney, tel. 064/44183. 8 rooms, 5 with bath. Facilities: restaurant (wine license only). No credit cards. Closed Oct.–Feb. Inexpensive.*

East Avenue House. One of the newest hotels in Killarney, this centrally located mock-timbered building has meeting and banqueting facilities for up to 300 people and holds popular discos every weekend. The property is a good value, but not as quiet as its small number of bedrooms would lead you to expect. *Kenmare Place, tel. 064/32522. 16 rooms with bath. Facilities: restaurant, 2 bars. AE, MC, V. Inexpensive.*

Dingle Peninsula

Dingle Peninsula is the true wild west of Ireland—visually, because it has the grandest scenery; historically, because it has the most impressive number of Iron Age and early Christian monuments; and spiritually, because it was never tamed by the English (as the Ring of Kerry was), and has kept alive those Gaelic traditions that have all but disappeared from the rest of the country. The circular route around the peninsula from Killarney to Tralee is 166.4 km (104 mi), and should take the better part of a day. On a day's outing you'll drive through magnificent coastal scenery and cross the most spectacular mountain pass in Ireland. You'll walk or swim along soft, sandy beaches, visit quality craft shops, dine in first-rate restaurants and pubs. Should you want to spend more than a day here, you can base yourself in any number of charming guest houses and explore the Blasket Islands, play golf, go fishing, and hike some of the most dramatic trails in Ireland. The best places to stay are in the far west, around the towns of Dingle, Ventry, Dunquin, and Ballyferriter.

Inch Strand From Killorglin, head north to Castlemaine, and then west along the southern coast of Dingle about 16 km (10 mi) to the town of **Inch,** where John Millington Synge's *The Playboy of the Western World* was filmed. If the weather is behaving, and the tide is low (check the tides the night before), park your car, take off your shoes and socks, and let the wind blow through your hair as you wander out along **Inch Strand,** a wide, sandy beach stretching 3.2 km (2 mi) into the bay. (When you leave your hotel in the morning, bring a towel and wear a bathing suit under your clothes.)

From Inch continue west along the road to **Annascaul.** A right turn off the coastal road takes you to the South Pole Inn, named in honor of the local sailor who went to rescue Robert Scott and found him dead in his tent, having failed in his mission to reach the South Pole in 1912. Could anything be more wonderfully incongruous, and more appropriate, than a South Pole Inn in a tiny fishing village in western Ireland?

Dingle The road west from Annascaul is pleasant, but the real adventure begins in **Dingle** (*Daungean*, stronghold), the chief town and touring center of the district. Dingle was a Norman administrative center, a walled city in Elizabethan times, and chief port of Kerry in the old Spanish trading days. Today it's a center of Gaelic studies that attracts students from around the world—its existence does not depend solely on tourists. You'll want to walk around town, shopping for knitted goods, pottery, and yarn in several sophisticated craft shops such as **Commodum** (Green Street); and photographing many of the colorful old houses.

Time Out As you wander through town, refuel with a visit to **An Café Liteartha,** a café/bookstore with a marvelous collection of Irish books and records, many of them in Gaelic. *Dykegate St., tel. 066/51388. No reservations. Dress: casual. MC, V. Lunch only; closed Sun. Inexpensive.*

From Dingle you can arrange for a boat trip from Dunquin (16 km/10 mi west) to the Blasket Islands (*see* Dunquin, below). There's pony trekking in Ventry, 6.4 km (4 mi) to the west; golf at Sybil Head, near Ballyferriter; beaches at Ventry and Dunquin; deep-sea fishing off the coast of Dingle; trips to ancient monuments, spectacular drives around Slea Head and over the Conor Pass, and an endless variety of hikes to mountain ridges and lakes.

The high point of my visit to Dingle was an evening at **O'Flaherty's Pub,** drinking bitters with strangers and listening to some very local, traditional music played with guitars, flutes, accordions, and spoons. This is a place of great character where locals and tourists join together in the fun.

Dining **The Armada** is a less expensive, popular seafood restaurant near the pier, with homemade chowders, fresh Dingle cod, and seafood curries. *Strand St., tel. 066/51505. Reservations advised. Dress: casual. AE, DC, MC, V. Closed Mon. and mid-Dec.–mid-Mar. Moderate.*

Doyle's is the best, most sophisticated seafood restaurant in town. At the table across from mine was a Canadian couple who had come here on their 20th anniversary, and were back again for their 30th. The menu depends on the day's catch, but usually features cockle and mussel soup with garlic, grilled black sole, salmon cooked in parchment, and salmon poached with a sharp sorrel sauce. *John St., tel. 066/51174. Reservations advised. Dress: casual. AE, DC, MC, V. Closed Sun. and mid-Nov.–mid-Mar. Moderate.*

Half Door, next door to Doyle's, is considered the second-best seafood restaurant. Popular dishes include crab quiche, trout in oatmeal, mussels in garlic, seafood au gratin, and a variety of meat dishes. *John St., tel. 066/51174. Reservations advised. Dress: casual. AE, DC, MC, V. Closed Tues. and mid-Nov.–mid-Mar. Moderate.*

Whelan's hasn't a great deal of atmosphere, but no one faults its seafood pancakes, rainbow trout, crab salads, or Irish specialties, such as shepherd's pie or homemade soups and stews. *Main St., tel. 066/51121. Reservations advised. Dress: casual. AE, DC, MC, V. Closed Sun. and mid-Nov.–mid-Mar. Moderate.*

Lodging The Tourist Office has a complete list of hotels and guest houses.

Dingle Skellig Hotel. This extraordinary and rather bizarre modern building on the edge of the sea is supposed to remind you of the area's early Christian beehive-shaped hermit cells. It recently reopened after major renovations and offers the best sporting facilities in town. Its bar has traditional music. *Dingle, Co. Kerry, tel. 066/51144. 50 rooms with bath. Facilities: restaurant, bar, indoor pool, sauna, gymnasium, tennis. AE, DC, MC, V. Closed Nov.–mid-Mar. Expensive.*

Benner's Hotel. This famous 250-year-old hotel has recently been given a major face-lift. New carpets and lighting fail to enhance its slightly dingy Old World charm. The bedrooms, however, retain their antique furniture and some have four-poster beds. *Main St., Dingle, tel. 066/51638. 25 rooms with bath. Facilities: restaurant, bar. MC, V. Moderate.*

Ballymore House. A friendly B&B 2.4 km (1½ mi) beyond Cleevaun, this is another good choice. *Mrs. S. Birmingham, Ballymore, Ventry, Co. Kerry, tel. 066/59050. 7 rooms, 5 with bath. No credit cards. Inexpensive.*

Cleevaun is a B&B that's more comfortable and modern than many of Ireland's aging hotels. Rooms are spotlessly clean and cheery. The living room has a helpful collection of books on the Dingle area. *Mrs. U. Sheehy, Lady's Cross, Dingle, tel. 066/51108. 5 rooms with bath. No credit cards. Closed Nov.–Mar. Inexpensive.*

Mrs. Connor. A good bet if you're on a budget, this modern bed-and-breakfast is in the center of town. Rooms are plain, unfussy, clean, and pleasant. *Dykegate St., tel. 066/51598. 10 rooms, 9 with shower. Facilities: restaurant (dinner only; wine license only). AE, DC, MC, V. Inexpensive.*

Ventry There's a magnificent horseshoe of soft sand here; follow signs to the beach. Ventry Harbor was the scene of the ancient romantic tale, "The Battle of Ventry Strand," which, as told in a 15th-century manuscript now in the Bodleian Library at Oxford, describes how the King of the World, Daire Doon, landed at Ventry in an attempt to invade Ireland, and was defeated in a battle that lasted a year and a day. One of the loveliest walks in the region is to the lake on Eagle Mountain, to the west of Ventry. Inquire about the route in Ventry.

Dunbeg Past Ventry, about 3.2 km (2 mi) before Slea Head, look carefully for a small sign on the left pointing to a fort called **Dunbeg,** which is romantically situated on a promontory 27 m (90 ft) above the sea. This is the country's most notable example of an Iron Age promontory defense fort—a refuge of last resort. Note the underground tunnel, called a souterrain, leading from the center of the fort to an escape hatch in front of the entrance; when the enemy entered the fortification, the people inside could crawl out and trap the invaders within. Notice, too, the drainage system to stop the water coming down the mountain, and the guard rooms with spy holes on either side of the entrance. Because of sea erosion, the fort will probably disappear by the end of the century.

Slea Head   The road is cut from the slopes of Mount Eagle, and the views, if the weather is right, are as spectacular as any in Ireland. Where the land juts into the sea you'll see the rusted hulk of a Spanish freighter, sunk in a storm in 1982. Beneath the black cliffs is a magnificent beach, perhaps 90 m (100 yd) deep at low tide. Slea Head points to a group of islands and rocks known as the **Blaskets.** The largest, Inishmore or the Great Blasket, has an abandoned village that you can explore on a day trip from Dunquin (contact Michael O'Connor, tel. 066/56146). The island was the home of a remote and self-contained Irish-speaking community with a rich oral literature. In time, the younger islanders married into an easier life on the mainland, and in 1954, the remaining people were resettled near Dunquin. A walk along the high cliffs of the Great Blasket, above the crying gulls, is a memory to cherish for a lifetime.

The Blaskets acquired a new importance at the turn of the century when there was a revival of interest in Irish culture; the playwright J. M. Synge spent two weeks here in 1905, and it is believed that the character of Pegeen Mike in *The Playboy of the Western World* was inspired by his hostess. What is extraordinary is the literary outpouring from such a small, remote settlement: Maurice O'Sullivan's *Twenty Years A-Growing*, Thomas O'Criffan's *The Islander*, and Peig Sayers's *Peig*. Synge also wrote about the Blaskets, and so did the Englishman Robin Flower. What fun you can have reading their books (available in American libraries and in many Irish tourist shops), and then visiting the Blaskets and trying to identify the homes!

Dunquin   If it interests you, ask at the public house for directions to the *Ryan's Daughter* schoolhouse, which is on a nearby cliff. The film was shot nearby.

Of all the pottery stores on Dingle Peninsula, the finest is in **Clothar,** 2.4 km (1½ mi) past Dunquin. In addition to pottery, you can buy beautiful handwoven blankets, coveralls, wallhangings, and scarves.

Ballyferriter   From Ballyferriter you can look down on Smerwick Harbour where the old fortress of Dún an Óir (Fort of Gold) stands on a rock promontory. It was here in 1580 that some 600 Italian, Spanish, and Irish troops, supported by the Pope, held out against English Protestant forces, and were butchered by Lord Grey's troops. Grey's secretary was none other than the poet Edmund Spenser, who loved Ireland but not the Catholics, and who advocated starvation and genocide to bring the Irish under the sway of the Faerie Queene (Elizabeth I). Unsuccessful in its efforts to conquer England through the back door (Ireland), Spain made a frontal attack 8 years later, with a 130-ship Armada. The force was routed in the English Channel. The ships that were not destroyed fled around the top of Scotland and down the west coast of Ireland. Twenty-five Spanish ships were lost off the Irish coast, including two wrecked near the Blasket Islands. (Ironically, there's a modern Spanish ship aground there today.)

Lodging   **Dun an Oir Hotel.** Not to be confused with the Fort of Gold is this modern Best Western hostelry. Its name is its only Gaelic attribute. The hotel is essentially a complex of small white buildings squeezed together on a grassy field in the middle of the countryside, with virtually no trees or landscaping, sup posedly reminiscent of a typical Kerry village. In its favor, however, is the fact that it's the only modern resort on the western end of the peninsula; its motelish rooms are softened by tasteful fabrics, and the setting is as peaceful as anyone could wish. *Ballyferriter, Dingle Peninsula, tel. 066/56133. 22 rooms with bath. Facilities: restaurant, bar, outdoor pool, sauna, tennis, 9-hole golf course. Closed Oct.–mid-Apr. AE, DC, MC, V. Moderate.*

Gallarus Oratory Don't take the road south from Ballyferriter back to Ventry; follow signs toward the village of Ballydavid and **Gallarus Oratory.** The 7th- or 8th-century Oratory is one of the best-preserved early Christian churches in the country, and an unrivaled example of the use of corbeling—successive levels of stone projecting inward from both side walls until they meet at the top. Though made of unmortared stone, it is still watertight after more than 1,000 years. The two stones with holes in them on either side of the entrance were probably meant to hold the ends of wooden doorposts.

Kilmalkedar Church **Kilmalkedar Church,** 3.2 km (2 mi) north of Gallarus, is one of the finest examples of Romanesque (Early Irish) architecture in the country. Churches such as this replaced the more modest beehive huts in the 13th century, when a local and decentralized church developed into a formal system of dioceses and parishes. Kilmalkedar Church was founded in the 7th century, but the present structure, standing in a graveyard, dates from the 12th century. Note how—as at Cormac's Chapel at Cashel, by which it was inspired—the native craftsmen integrated foreign influences with their own local traditions: keeping the blank arcades and round-headed windows, for instance, but using stone roofs, sloping doorway jambs, and weirdly sculptured heads.

In the immediate vicinity you can "sample" a great variety of ancient Irish monuments. Just to the right of the entrance to the churchyard, beside a tomb, is a stone with mysterious decorations. It is usually regarded as a sundial, but could also be an early cross or even a pre-Christian monument. Nearby is an ogham stone with a hole in it. The writing on these stones, which date from the Late Stone Age and early Christian periods, consists of up to five strokes on either side of an imaginary vertical guideline. It begins on the bottom, continues upward and, if necessary, down the other side. The lines represent letters in the Roman alphabet, but the language itself is an early form of Irish. Most inscriptions commemorate the deceased and give details of their ancestry.

Near the church is **Caherdorgan Stone Fort,** which contains five almost complete beehive huts; **St. Brendan's House,** a two-story 15th-century building, now roofless but otherwise well preserved, where the local clergy probably lived; and the **Chancellor's House,** a two-room medieval building. The chancellor was a cathedral dignitary who occasionally resided there.

The Conor Pass From Gallarus Oratory return to the town of Dingle, and then head north across the **Conor Pass,** the most spectacular high-level crossing in Ireland. The parking area at the head of the pass is a good starting point for the ascent of **Ballysitteragh** (614.9 m/2,050 ft) to the west or **Slievanea** (605.9 m/2,020 ft) to the east. Neither walk should take more than an hour round-trip. You don't need a marked path on these treeless slopes; just head for the summit. The climb is gradual, so anyone with perseverance can make it to the top.

From the top of Conor Pass you can look down and see **Brandon Bay.** It was from here that St. Brendan the Navigator (484–577) is believed to have set sail at age 59 in a boat of skins and wood for "the Land of Promise." He got as far as Iceland, landing once on the back of a whale, which he thought was an island. On his second trip he may have reached either Newfoundland or Labrador, and "discovered" America more than 900 years before Columbus. In 1977 three men sailed 4,830 km (3,000 mi) to Newfoundland in a replica of Brendan's boat, proving that it could be done.

St. Brendan was a Kerryman from Tralee who founded an important monastery at Clonfert, in County Galway, and later became the patron saint of Dingle Peninsula. **Ballybrack,** 9.6 km (6 mi) north of Dingle, is the starting point for a grueling 3½-hour (one-way) hike to Brendan's hermitage (**St. Brendan's Oratory**) on the top of the peninsula's most famous landmark, **Brandon Mountain.** Don't go if the summit is shrouded in mist —which it usually is. The route follows an ancient pilgrim route, the Saint's Road, to the high point of an enormous 6.4-km (4-mi) ridge. Brandon was a sacred mountain in pagan times, when there was an annual pilgrimage to the summit to celebrate the festival of the Celtic god Lugh. After Christianity was introduced, the event was transformed into a pilgrimage in honor of Brendan.

Camp Head down the Conor Pass to Kilcummin, and right (east) to Tralee. If you want one final hike, visit a great prehistoric stone fort, one of the country's highest, on a 614.9-m (2,050-ft) spur of the 813.6-m (2,712-ft) **Cahercontree Mountain.** The fort can be reached from **Camp,** following signs to the Promontory Fort. Ask locally for details.

Adare From Tralee take Route N21 east to Limerick, and then head either north to Shannon Airport or east to Dublin. If you need to spend the night near Shannon, consider staying in **Adare,** 16 km (10 mi) southwest of **Limerick.** Voted the tidiest town in Ireland, it has some lovely thatched cottages on the banks of the Maigue River, three medieval abbeys, a 13th-century castle, and a popular inn with good food.

Lodging **Dunraven Arms Hotel.** Old World character envelops this country-house-style inn in the center of the village. For a special treat, try the Princess Grace and Prince Rainier Suite, named in honor of their visit. Good classic French cuisine will be found in the Maigue Restaurant, including eels in white wine sauce and stuffed pork steak. *Adare, Co. Limerick, tel. 061/86209. 44 rooms with bath. Facilities: restaurant, bar, horseback riding. AE, DC, MC, V. Expensive.*

What to See and Do with Children

Ireland is geared to family travel, which makes it an ideal country to visit with children of any age. Most hotels and private homes can make arrangements for babysitters.

Almost every town along the route offers swimming, hiking, biking, fishing, and pony rides. Families can rent ponies or pony carts for trips through the Gap of Dunloe. They can also take boat trips on the lakes of Killarney. The grounds of **Muckross House,** on the shores of two of Killarney's most beautiful lakes, are a safe and scenic place for kids to bike. Killarney has several bike-rental shops.

Kids will love **Blarney Castle** and a walk through its **Rock Close.** They should also enjoy exploring **Muckross Abbey** near Killarney, and climbing to the dizzying heights of the **Great Blasket Island,** off the coast of Dingle.

2 England

Bath, the Cotswolds, and Stratford-upon-Avon

Introduction

Within just two hours of London you can discover an extraordinary variety of scenery and architectural styles. Salisbury is the site of what many consider the most perfect cathedral in the country. Not far away are the mysterious pillars of Stonehenge. Wells, like Salisbury, is a famous cathedral town. Bath is the most sophisticated city in England after London, with theater, shops, and Georgian and Roman architecture. The National Trust town of Lacock, where the newest houses were built in the 18th century, is nearby. Northward are the stone villages and rich, rolling fields of the Cotswolds. Stratford-upon-Avon is the birthplace of the bard and home to the Royal Shakespeare Theatre. Blenheim Palace, where Winston Churchill was born, and the colleges and chapels of Oxford University are other highlights.

The region is rich in churches that were built and expanded over hundreds of years—each reconstruction reflecting the styles and values of a new age. Norman architecture (1066–c.1150) was named for the Normans, who brought their variant of the Romanesque style with them when they conquered Britain in 1066 and grafted it onto the existing English Saxon Romanesque style already begun by Edward the Confessor (1003?–1066). Early English (c.1150–c.1250) is, in effect, Early Gothic. Decorated (c.1250–c.1350) is mature Gothic. Perpendicular (c.1350–c.1520) is Late Gothic, an original and distinctively British style. In contrast to the Decorated style, the Perpendicular is marked by (1) a stress on straight verticals and horizontals, (2) window tracery with complex designs emphasizing the vertical, and (3) fan vaulting (ceiling ribs that fan outward).

Highlights

Three of England's greatest cathedrals—at Salisbury, Winchester, and Wells.

The Roman city of Bath—a fashionable 18th-century spa; today a sophisticated tourist center with elegant shops, music festivals, and first-class hotels and restaurants.

The mysterious standing stones of Stonehenge.

Stratford-upon-Avon—the Bard's birthplace and home of the Royal Shakespeare Theatre.

The picturesque stone villages of the Cotswolds.

Dining and lodging in restored manor houses and Elizabethan inns.

Before You Go

Vital Note In May 1990, all London telephone numbers were given new prefixes: 071 or 081. These digits must be dialed when calling from outside London.

The South of England

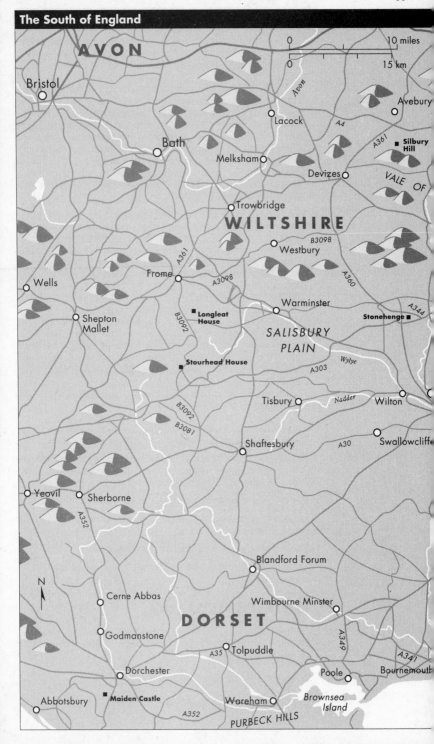

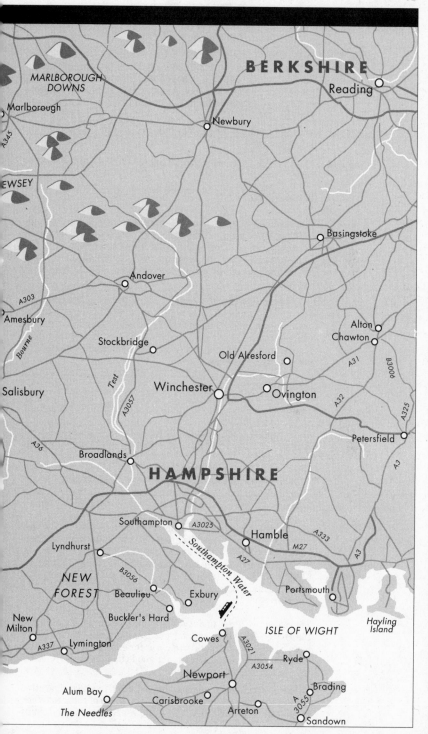

Government Tourist Offices

Contact the British Tourist Authority (BTA).

In the U.S. 40 W. 57th St., New York, NY 10019, tel. 212/581–4700; John Hancock Center, Suite 3320, 875 N. Michigan Ave., Chicago, IL 60611, tel. 312/787–0490; World Trade Center, 350 S. Figueroa St., Suite 450, Los Angeles, CA 90017, tel. 213/628–3525; 2305 Cedar Springs Rd., Suite 210, Dallas, TX 75201, tel. 214/720–4040.

In Canada 94 Cumberland St., Suite 600, Toronto, Ontario M5R 3N3, tel. 416/925–6326.

In the U.K. Thames Tower, Black's Rd., London W69EL, tel. 081/846–9000.

When to Go

The main tourist season in Britain runs from mid-April to mid-October. Spring is the time to see the countryside at its freshest and greenest. During July and August, when most of the British take their vacations, accommodations in the most popular resorts and areas are in high demand and at their most expensive.

In the main, the climate is mild, though the weather is changeable and unpredictable at any time of year. Summer temperatures can reach the 80s and the atmosphere can be humid, while in winter there can be heavy frost, snow, and thick fog. A good guide to what each day will be like is carried in the early morning radio forecast.

Special Events

March–December: Royal Shakespeare Theatre season at Stratford-upon-Avon
April: English Bach Festival, Oxford
May–June: Bath International Festival, music and the arts, Bath, Avon
May: Royal Windsor Horse Show
July: Cheltenham International Festival of Music

Currency

The unit of currency in Britain is the pound sterling, divided into 100 pence (p). The bills are 50, 20, 10, and 5 pounds (Scotland has £1 bills). Coins are £1, 50, 20, 10, 5, 2, and 1p. At presstime the exchange rate was about US$1.72 and Canadian $1.95 to the pound sterling.

Customs

There are two levels of duty-free allowance for people entering the United Kingdom; one, for goods bought outside the European Economic Community (EC), or for goods bought in a duty-free shop within the EC; two, for goods bought in an EC country but not in a duty-free shop.

In the first category, you may import duty-free 200 cigarettes or 100 cigarillos or 50 cigars or 250 g (8.75 oz) of tobacco (*Note:* If you live outside Europe, these allowances are doubled), plus one liter of alcoholic drinks over 22% volume or two liters of alcoholic drinks not over 22% volume or fortified or sparkling wine, plus two liters of still table wine, plus 50 g (1.75 oz) of perfume, plus nine fluid ounces of toilet water, plus other goods to the value of £32.

In the second category, you may import duty-free 300 cigarettes or 150 cigarillos or 75 cigars or 400 g (14 oz) of tobacco, plus 1.5 liters of alcoholic drinks over 22% volume or three liters of alcoholic drinks not over 22% volume or fortified or sparkling wine, plus four liters of still table wine, plus 75 g (2.6 oz) of perfume, plus 13 fluid ounces of toilet water, plus other goods to the value of £250. (*Note:* Though it is not classified as an alcoholic drink by EC countries for customs purposes and is thus considered part of the "other goods" allowance, you may not import more than 50 l [13 gal] of beer.)

No animals or pets of any kind may be brought into the United Kingdom. The penalties for doing so are severe and are strictly enforced.

Reading

Philip A. Crowl, *The Intelligent Traveller's Guide to Historic Britain* (Congdon & Weed).

Arriving and Departing

By Plane

Airlines serving London and other major cities in Britain include **American Airlines** (tel. 800/433–7300); **British Airways** (tel. 800/247–9297); **Delta** (tel. 800/241–4141); **Northwest Airlines** (tel. 800/447–4747); **Pan Am** (tel. 800/221–1111); and **TWA** (tel. 800/892–4141).

British Airways flies to London from more American cities than any other airline: from Boston, New York, Philadelphia, Baltimore, Washington, DC, Miami, Orlando, Tampa, Detroit, Chicago, Los Angeles, San Francisco, Seattle, and Anchorage. It's also the only airline that flies the Concorde there—from New York to London in three hours.

Getting Around

By Car

Driving on the left sounds frightening if you've never done it before; but when your life is on the line it's amazing how quickly it becomes second nature. The most important rule to remember is that the driver *inside* a traffic circle has the right of way. There's a 112 kph (70 mph) speed limit on highways (motorways to the British), but most drivers ignore it. Speeds of 128 kph (80 mph), even 144 kph (90 mph), are not at all unusual.

British Airways has a fly-and-drive package that saves about 20% on car rentals. **BritRail Travel** (tel. 212/599–5400) has a BritRail/Drive pass that lets you take the train and pick up a car at or near your destination. You can then leave the car at another station with no dropoff costs. (The BritRail/Drive pass won't make much sense if your trip is limited to our itinerary; because distances are short and you will probably want to travel the entire route either by car or by public transportation.)

You may want to visit London first and rent a car only when it's time to leave on this trip. If you're flying to and from London, arrange both to pick up and to return your car at Heathrow Airport *after* your stay in London.

Don't be satisfied with a general road map of England. The Ordnance Survey 1:50,000 maps indicate all back roads and footpaths, and allow you to discover the beauty of the countryside and avoid heavy traffic. These maps are sold in map stores in large American cities, and in gift shops throughout England.

By Public Transportation

You should follow this itinerary by car if you can; otherwise you will miss many of the small, out-of-the-way places. Still, it is possible to reach most of the major sites by train and bus.

There's good train service between London and Winchester (from Waterloo Station) and between London and Salisbury (also from Waterloo Station), but *not* between Winchester and Salisbury. To get from Winchester to Salisbury, you need either to backtrack to Basingstoke or to ride to Southampton. Unless Winchester Cathedral is high on your list of musts, consider skipping Winchester and taking the train directly to Salisbury. From here buses go regularly in season to Stonehenge, and direct trains go to Bath. From Bath there are regular bus service to Wells and frequent bus tours to Longleat House.

From Bath, take a train to Stratford-upon-Avon via Bristol and Birmingham. From Stratford-upon-Avon, ride to Moreton-in-Marsh, which is as close as you can get by train to the center of the Cotswolds. From Moreton-in-Marsh rent a car or a bicycle to tour the countryside. Trains go from Moreton-in-Marsh to Oxford, and back to Paddington Station in London.

Give a list of towns you want to visit to the **BritRail** office, and they will work out an itinerary for you and issue either a single-journey ticket or a BritRail Pass, depending on which is cheaper.

You *must* purchase the BritRail Pass before you leave home. They are available from most travel agents or from one of these BritRail Travel International offices: 630 Third Ave., New York, NY 10017, tel. 212/599–5400; Cedar Maple Plaza, 2305 Cedar Springs, Suite 210, Dallas, TX 75201, tel. 214/748–0860; 800 S. Hope St., Suite 603, Los Angeles, CA 90017, tel. 213/624–8787; 94 Cumberland St., Toronto, Ont. M5R 1A3, tel. 416/929–3333; 409 Granville St., Vancouver, B.C., V6C 1T2, tel. 604/683–6896.

The BritRail Pass allows unlimited rail travel through the entire British rail system for periods of 8, 14, 22, or 30 days and is available for both first- and economy-class travel. Even if you don't make full use of the pass, it saves time waiting on ticket lines. Passes are available through travel agencies or through offices of the BritRail Travel International in New York, Los Angeles, Chicago, and Dallas (addresses above). Children 5 to 15 receive a 50% reduction. There are also BritRail Youth

Passes for young people aged 16 through 25 and Senior Citizen Passes for travelers over 60.

The least expensive way to travel is by coach (as opposed to local buses). The Britexpress Card gives you a third off on all National Express services over a 6-month period. It can be purchased from travel agencies in the United States or from National Express at Victoria Coach Station (Buckingham Palace Rd., London SW1.). Unfortunately, there is no single pass good for both trains and buses.

BritRail also sells Open to View Tickets, good for one month, to hundreds of castles, historic homes, and sites.

By Bicycle

Flat or rolling countryside, short distances between towns, plenty of traffic-free back roads—all add up to a perfect landscape for bicycling. Bring bikes from home or rent them in London or in towns along the route, and, when you've had enough exercise, put them on the train with you at little or no cost. The British Tourist Authority (*see* Government Tourist Offices, above) has brochures, or you may want to join the **Cyclists' Touring Club,** the national body in Britain that promotes the interests of cycle tourists (69 Meadrow, Godalming, Surrey GU7 3HS, tel. 04868/7217).

Essential Information

Important Addresses and Numbers

Tourist Information

The Heart of England Tourist Board, 2–4 Trinity St., Worcester, Herefors & Worcs WR1 2PW, tel. 0905/613132. Information on Stratford and the Cotswolds. Open Mon.–Thurs. 9–5:30, Fri. 9–5.

The Southern Tourist Board, Town Hall Centre, Leigh Rd., Eastleigh, Hants S05 9JZ, tel. 0703/616027. Open Mon.–Thurs. 8:30–5, Fri. 8:30–4:30.

The West Country Tourist Board, Trinity Court, 37 Southernhay E., Exeter, Devon WX1 1QS, tel. 0392/76351. Information on Bath/Avon. Open weekdays 9:30–5.

Local tourist information centers are normally open Mon.–Sat. 9:30–5:30, but times vary according to season. Centers include:

Bath: Abbey Church Yard, tel. 0225/462831.
Chipping Campden: tel. 0386/840289.
Cirencester: tel. 0285/4180.
Salisbury: Fish Row (just off Market Sq.), tel. 0722/334956.
Stow-on-the-Wold: Talbot Court, tel. 0451/31082.
Stratford-upon-Avon: 1 High St., tel. 0789/293127.
Winchester: The Guildhall, The Broadway, tel. 0962/840222, ext. 2361.

Embassies and Consulates

U.S. Embassy (24 Grosvenor Sq., London W1A 1AE, tel. 071/499–9000).

Canadian High Commission (Canada House, Trafalgar Sq., London SW1Y 5BJ, tel. 071/629–9492).

Emergencies For police, fire brigade, or ambulance, dial 999.

Opening and Closing Times

Banks Banks are open weekdays 9:30–3:30. Some have extended hours on Thursday evenings, and a few are open on Saturday mornings.

Museums Museum hours vary considerably from one part of the country to another. In large cities, most open weekdays 10–5; many are also open on Sunday afternoons. The majority close one day a week. Holiday closings vary, so be sure to check individual listings.

Shops Usual business hours are Monday–Saturday 9–5:30. Outside the main centers, most shops observe an early closing day once a week, often Wednesday or Thursday. They close at 1 PM and do not reopen until the following morning. In small villages, many also close for lunch. Apart from some newsstands and small food stores, almost all shops are closed on Sunday.

Holidays **England and Wales:** January 1; March 29 (Good Friday); April 1 (Easter Monday); May 6 (May Day); May 27 (Spring Bank Holiday); August 26 (Summer Bank Holiday); December 25, 26 (Christmas).

Guided Tours

The Heart of England Tourist Board (tel. 0905/613132) and the **West Country Tourist Board** (tel. 0392/76351) have details of numerous guided tours within their regions, and the staff can book you with registered guides for outings ranging from short walks to luxury tours that include accommodations in stately homes.

National Holidays (tel. 0924/387387) runs five-day bus tours to the Cotswolds.

Wallace Arnold (tel. 0532/430691, head office; 081/202–5577, London reservations) offers five-day guided tours by bus from London to the Cotswolds and Shakespeare country.

Bath Free, 1¾-hour walking tours are conducted in season, weekdays at 10:30 AM and Sundays at 10:30 and 2:30. They begin outside the Pump Room, in the Abbey Church Yard.

Jane Austen Tours take you in the footsteps of the author and her characters. The 60-minute tour begins at the Beau Nash Gallery, York Street, 90 m (100 yards) from the Tourist Information Centre.

To tour Bath by bus, you can choose among several bus tour companies, some with open-top buses that leave both from near the Tourist Information Centre and from the bus terminal. Contact the Tourist Information Centre for schedules and prices.

For personal tours, contact **Beau Nash Guides** (tel. 0225/63030) or **The Red Guild of Tour Guides** (tel. 0225/312757).

Salisbury Guided walking tours begin outside the Tourist Information Centre, Fish Row, in August, daily at 10:30 and 2:30, late April–mid-October, daily at 2:30.

Ratings

Category	Cost*
Very Expensive	over £30
Expensive	£20–£30
Moderate	£10–£20
Inexpensive	under £10

Per person, for a three-course meal, including tip but not wine.

Lodging

If you haven't been to England for a while, you may be dismayed by the high price of a night's lodgings. You may be disappointed, too, by standards of service. The sorry truth is that many English hotels, especially middle-ranking ones, are both expensive and badly run, especially in comparison with those elsewhere in Europe. Of course, there are exceptions. You'll find that luxury hotels are in a class by themselves. Likewise, private homes offering bed-and-breakfast (B&B) accommodations are usually spotless and offer guests a great opportunity to make new friends. Large English breakfasts (though not private bathrooms) are standard. (You can take your chance with B&B signs along the road, or make reservations through regional tourist offices.) It may also be that for you staying in an old inn with creaky staircases and low-beamed ceilings is compensation for high rates, fading carpets, chipped paintwork, and uncertain plumbing. Adding insult to injury, the dead hand of hotel chains is evident everywhere, especially in cities and larger towns.

The best answer is to mix and match. You could, for instance, stay in a Georgian town house in Bath, a 350-year-old country inn in Lacock (near Bath), and both a B&B and a great manor house in the Cotswolds. But steer clear of fading second-class hotels.

Bath scores strongly on hotels in all price ranges. Hotels in Winchester and Salisbury offer little more than convenience. The best reason to stay overnight in Salisbury is to see the floodlit cathedral. If you're following the itinerary, there's little reason to stay in Winchester. Stratford has numerous hotels. Several are perfectly adequate for a night or two—you'll need to stay over if you're going to the Royal Shakespeare Theatre—but none is legendary. The best hotels are a few miles out of town. There are scores of hotels and ancient inns dotted around the Cotswolds, among them some of the best in the country. But if you blanch at the prices, stay at B&Bs.

Breakfast is usually, but not always, included in room rates. Most hotels quote prices per room, not per person.

Ratings

Category	Cost*
Very Expensive	over £100
Expensive	£80–£100

Moderate	£50–£80
Inexpensive	£30–£50

All prices are for a standard double room for two and include tax.

The Itinerary

Nothing is far away in England. Your trip will never take you more than two hours from London. You'll head southwest to Salisbury and Stonehenge. After a night in a Tudor inn or a Georgian manor house, it's on to Wells, and then to Bath, where you can dine in the home of Beau Nash's mistress, and end the day in a hotel where the elegance of 18th-century Bath has not been forgotten.

Next you can visit Lacock, and then you'll head north through the Cotswolds. Stow-on-the-Wold has some wonderful antiques shops, and makes a great base from which to explore the region —by car, on horse, or on foot. Farther north is Stratford-upon-Avon, where the play's the thing. On your way back to London you can visit Blenheim Palace and wander through Oxford University.

The Main Route

3–5 Days Day excursion to Salisbury and Stonehenge
One night: Bath
One night: Lacock
Two nights: Cotswolds, around Stow-on-the-Wold

5–7 Days Day excursion to Winchester, Stonehenge, Salisbury
One night: Lacock
Day in Bath, with side trip to Wells
Two nights: Bath
Two nights: Cotswolds, around Stow-on-the-Wold
One night: In or near Stratford-upon-Avon

7–14 Days Day excursion to Winchester, Stonehenge, Salisbury, Wilton, Longleat
One night: Near Salisbury/Wilton
One night: Lacock
Day in Bath, with excursion to Wells and Glastonbury
Two nights: Bath
Day excursion to Castle Combe, Cirencester, Fairford, Bibury, Burford, Northleach
Three nights: Cotswolds, around Stow-on-the-Wold
One night: Near Stratford-upon-Avon
Excursions to Warwick Castle
One night: Woodstock
Excursion to Blenheim Palace and Oxford

Exploring

Winchester

Winchester is a cathedral town 104 km (65 mi) from London by car on M3 and A33 (or 63 minutes from London's Waterloo Station by rail).

The Anglo-Saxons—Germanic-speaking peoples who settled in England after the Romans left—made Winchester the capital of their kingdom of Wessex. Threats from the Danes forced rulers from all over England to unite under the Wessex king, Egbert (reigned 802–39), and Winchester became, in effect, the capital of all England. The town flourished under Alfred the Great (reigned 871–99), and was later the seat of Canute (reigned 1016–35) and Edward the Confessor (reigned 1042–66). When the Normans conquered England in 1066, William the Conqueror (reigned 1066–87) made Winchester his capital, too, and power did not shift to London for another 100 years.

Winchester Cathedral—the largest church in Christendom when first built (1079)—is what draws most visitors to Winchester today. As you enter, you'll see long avenues of Norman columns encased in Gothic shells.

Walk down the left aisle. Set into the floor of the fourth bay is Jane Austen's gravestone. As the bronze plaque on the wall points out, it makes no mention of her talents as a writer because her fame followed her death. Farther down the aisle is a dark marble 12th-century **baptismal font,** where children were being baptized little more than 100 years after the Battle of Hastings.

Stand in the north transept (the transepts are the arms of a cross-shape church) and compare the sturdy grace of its rounded arches with the elegant pointed arches of the nave. These transepts are all that remain above ground of the original Norman church. To see more of the Norman building, go to the crypt. The entrance is in the north transept. It is the largest and oldest Norman crypt in the country and gives a strong sense of the simple style of the first cathedral. Access is limited in winter.

Then climb the rough-hewn stone steps to the choir—or Quire, as they call it here (English cathedrals guard their idiosyncracies jealously)—one of the glories of Winchester. The choir stalls are among the oldest in England.

Behind the quire is the retrochoir ("retro" means "behind"). Many of its battered red floor tiles date from around 1230.

Look along the north aisle for the tomb of Stephen Gardiner. When the Protestants under Cromwell ransacked the cathedral, they gave Gardiner's effigy the same rough treatment Gardiner gave the "heretics" during his lifetime. The Protestants were kinder to the blind and universally loved Bishop Richard Fox (1448–1528), whose effigy you'll find along the south aisle. Fox commissioned his own tortured effigy while he was still a young man—perhaps to remind himself that no one, not even a bishop, is free from corruption. How unlike the effigy of Cardinal Beaufort, all decked out in red, placidly awaiting his call to paradise.

As you walk through the chancel, look up at the painted mortuary chests that hold the bones of several Saxon kings: Egbert; Ethelwulf (reigned 839–58), who was father of Alfred the Great; and Canute, among others. The bones were scattered during the Civil War against Cromwell, so Egbert's head may be spending eternity with Ethelwulf's arms and Canute's legs.

A door on the south side of the south transept leads to the Cathedral Library and the Triforium Gallery. The library contains a 10th-century copy of the Venerable Bede's *Ecclesiastical History* and a 12th-century painted Bible.

Winchester Cathedral, tel. 0962/53137. Admission free, but suggested donation of £1.50. Open daily 7:30–6:30 (restricted access during services). Crypt, admission 20p; open Easter-Oct., daily 7:30–6:30 (water level permitting); tours 10:30 and 2:30. Library and Triforium Gallery, admission 40p; open mid-May–mid-Sept., Mon.–Sat. 7:30–6:30; Oct.–Apr., Sat. and Wed. only 7:30–6:30 (closed Jan.). Treasury, admission 20p; open mid-May–Oct., daily 11–5.

Make a sharp left as you leave the cathedral, and another left along a path beneath the buttresses. Notice how these buttresses, a Gothic invention, though in fact what you see are late-19th-century reconstructions of the Gothic originals, keep the walls from splaying out beneath the weight of the roof, and thus permit the building of churches with higher, thinner walls, using glass instead of solid masonry. Bear right. Ahead of you is a redbrick building; to your left, the flinty stone of the Deanery, the official residence of the Dean. Walk around it to the left, following a sign to the College/Water Meadows. Leave the cathedral close (where the clergy lived) and pass through the 14th-century town gate. To the right of the gate is the **Parish Church of St. Swithun upon Kingsgate,** founded in 1263. It seems odd that a tiny parish church would be built so close to a cathedral until you realize that cathedrals were used primarily by the clergy; that they had no seats or pulpits; that the naves were used primarily for processions; and that the laymen were encouraged by the clergy to build churches of their own.

Time Out Ahead of you as you pass through the gate is **The Wykeham Arms** (75 Kingsgate St., tel. 0962/53834), which dates from 1775. What was once one of the most run-down pubs in the city now houses an upscale restaurant (*see* Dining, below). It is also a good spot for an inexpensive plowman's lunch and a pint.

Turn left on College Street. A plaque indicates the house, now privately owned, where Jane Austen died from Addison's disease at age 42. She was born and spent most of her life elsewhere, but she was often in ill health and in 1817 put herself in the care of a Winchester doctor.

On the right side of College Street, at the end of a long, unbroken stone wall, is the arched entranceway to **Winchester College.** Founded in 1382, it is the oldest public school—an English "public" school is the equivalent of an American "private" school—in England. The college was established as a training ground for applicants to New College in Oxford.

Continue down College Street. On your left is the **Bishop's Palace,** a handsome 17th-century building reputedly designed by Sir Christopher Wren. It is not open to the public, but you can admire its facade from the footpath. Just beyond are the ruins of the **Old Bishop's Palace,** destroyed by Cromwell's forces in 1646. *College St., tel. 0962/54766. Admission: 80p adults, 40p children, 60p senior citizens. Open Easter–Oct., daily 10–6.*

Directly across from the palace is a sign to St. Cross via Water Meadows. If you have time, take this pleasant 1.6-km (1-mi) walk through the meadows and school playing fields. At the lock, cross the road, and continue along the river.

The Hospital of St. Cross, founded in 1133 by a grandson of William the Conqueror, may be the oldest functioning almshouse in the country. The gatekeeper maintains an ancient tradition of doling out beer and bread to all visitors, but you have to ask —and get there early: He has only two pints and two loaves. The 25 brothers wear gowns (black gowns if they are members of the original foundation, red gowns if members of the 15th-century order of the Brothers of Noble Poverty) and live in 15th-century quarters. Visitors can tour a 15th-century kitchen and a 12th-century Norman chapel with a bell tower you can get permission to climb. *St. Cross Rd., tel. 0962/51375. Admission: £1 adults, 50p students and senior citizens, 25p children. Open Mon.–Sat. 9:30–12:30 and 2–5.*

From the Hospital, take a mile walk or a bus ride back to town. St. Cross Road turns into Southgate Street. At High Street, turn left to the Great Hall, which is all that's left of a Norman castle. Hanging here is the legendary Round Table of King Arthur, now known to be from the 14th century, and looking very much like a giant dart board. Was there really a King Arthur? Of course. When the Romans left Britain in 410, towns decayed and the country was plunged into a Dark Age of lawlessness and civil unrest. Into this vacuum swept a number of military leaders and kings. One of them was Arthur. In the mid-6th century, the invasion of German-speaking Anglo-Saxons began. Arthur defended the Romanized Britons against the advancing Saxons in southwest England. Fighting like Roman cavalrymen against the Saxon foot soldiers—wearing helmets and chain mail against Saxon infantrymen with nothing but swords and spears—Arthur was able to keep them at bay for 50 years. He was probably Christian. Later English kings played up the Arthur legend to unite the country. Stories of Arthur and his Round Table were creations of the Age of Chivalry, and have no known basis in fact. *High St., tel. 0962/841841. Admission free (contributions welcome). Open Mar.–Oct., daily 10–5; Nov.–Feb., weekdays 10–5, weekends 10–4.*

Dining **Brann's.** Brann's is about the best restaurant in Winchester and the most conveniently located—right across the close facing the main (west) facade of the cathedral. The food, like the mood, is busy modern/chic and accordingly popular with Winchester's conspicuous movers and shakers. You can eat in the wine bar or in the more formal restaurant on the second floor. Breast of chicken with lemon, tarragon, and Pernod, and monkfish with shellfish sauce number among the specialties. Critics proclaim the wine list to be "thoughtful." *9 Great Minster St., The Square, tel. 0962/64004. Reservations advised for dinner. Dress: casual chic/jacket and tie. AE, MC, V. Closed Sun. Expensive.*

The Wykeham Arms. What was once a city-center dive is now an appealing pub/restaurant that combines sophisticated English food with the warm bustle of an old pub, just a step or two south of the cathedral close. The main dining room is at the rear of the building, divided from one of the two bars by an open fireplace. Have a drink first in the appealingly cluttered main bar, then move into the candlelit dining room. Salmon, veal, and rack of lamb are specialties. *75 Kingsgate St., tel. 0962/53834. Reservations advised for dinner. Dress: casual chic/jacket and tie. AE, DC, MC, V. Expensive.*

Old Chesil Rectory. The Old Chesil Rectory, with its gnarled, black-and-white exterior, is the oldest house in Winchester, built in 1450, and complete with the requisite low-beamed ceilings and creaky floors. Come for coffee in the morning, a snack or something more substantial at lunch, afternoon tea, or a full-blown Old English dinner, with roast beef, steak-and-kidney pie, sweetbreads, and boiled beef and carrots. The building is a 10- to 15-minute walk from the cathedral along the Stockbridge Road. *1 Chesil St., tel. 0962/53177. Reservations advised. Dress: casual chic/jacket and tie. AE, DC, MC, V. Moderate–Expensive.*

Lodging **Lainston House.** For luxury lodging the best in the area is Lainston House, about 3.2 km (2 mi) northwest of Winchester on A272 (and well signposted). A driveway lined with lime trees winds through parkland to an ivy-covered, 17th-century manor house built by staunch supporters of Cromwell. There's an ancient dovecote, the ruins of a 12th-century chapel, bird songs, and peace. Inside are beautifully turned moldings, a mahogany staircase, and a wonderful cedar-paneled bar. The furnishings, while tasteful, fall short of the tone of a 17th-century manor house. Rooms are large and comfortable, if rather simply decorated. Ask for one in the main building. The hotel caters principally to business types during the week and has an unmistakable expense-account atmosphere. *Sparsholt, Hants. S021 2LT, tel. 0962/63588. 32 rooms with private bath. Facilities: restaurant, bar, tennis, clay-pigeon shooting, croquet, fishing, horseback riding, golf, helicopter landing pad, numerous business amenities. AE, DC, MC, V. Very Expensive.*

The Royal Hotel. While offering nothing special, this is a comfortable enough place to spend a night. Public areas are soothingly decorated in quiet browns and reds. Bedrooms are standardized Motel Modern, but adequate; those in the modern annex are definitely more functional. There's a restful, glassed-in restaurant serving reasonable international-style food. Nonetheless, it's hard not to be reminded that this is now a Best Western hotel. *St. Peter St., Winchester, Hants. S022 8BS, tel. 0962/841582. 59 rooms with private bath. Facilities: restaurant, bar, garden, conference room. AE, DC, MC, V. Expensive.*

Wessex Hotel. Stay here if you value a central location only seconds from the cathedral and the reliable standards of Trusthouse Forte. There is little else to recommend this unsightly and slablike '60s building. The backlit "medieval" Plexiglas in the lobby says it all. *Paternoster Row, Winchester, Hants. S023 9LQ, tel. 0962/61611. 94 rooms with private bath. Facilities: restaurant, coffee shop, bar. AE, DC, MC, V. Expensive.*

Salisbury

From Winchester, drive 30 km (18.6 mi) west on A272/A30. (From London, bypassing Winchester, drive 149 km/93 mi on M3 and A30. By train: From Winchester, backtrack to Basingstoke, and catch another train to Salisbury. From London, it's a 90-minute ride from Waterloo Station.) Salisbury is the home of what many consider the most perfect English **cathedral** ever built. It owes its unity to the fact that it was constructed in 38 years (1220–58)—which was unheard of in those times—and therefore stands almost exactly as its designers conceived it more than 700 years ago. Winchester

Cathedral, which you just saw, is typical of most cathedrals in that it is an amalgam of styles, from Norman/Romanesque to Perpendicular/Late Gothic. Salisbury, in contrast, is in a single style, Early English—the purest expression of Early English in Britain.

Take your time walking around the cathedral grounds and looking up at the cathedral from different angles, appreciating its confidence, its restrained dignity, and its strength. Walk around on summer nights, too, when the cathedral is floodlit. The masons had trouble securing the weighty spire, which was added a century later, and it still leans slightly, despite the use of heavy arches to support it. At 121.1 m (404 ft), it's the tallest medieval spire ever built in England. Unfortunately, it is currently enclosed in scaffolding and likely to stay that way for some years during which time a major restoration project will be completed.

It has been said that the outside is all decoration, and the inside, all lines. You may find the uncluttered interior disappointing, in comparison: all ribs without flesh, appealing more to the mind than to the senses. This was due to an 18th-century housecleaning by some ill-advised ecclesiastical rationalists.

Near the west end of the north aisle—the aisle on your left as you face the altar—is the **oldest clock mechanism** (1326) in England, perhaps in the world. As you walk down the aisles, you'll see the tombs of knights who went on the Crusades or who died at Agincourt, where Henry V routed the French in 1415. In Salisbury, as in other English cathedrals, you'll notice that the aisles are lined with small chapels enclosing an altar and an effigy. These are called **chantries.** Wealthy laymen endowed these chapels, paying priests to say daily masses for their souls and for the souls of their families, in perpetuity or for a fixed number of years.

In the **Trinity Chapel** is a sheet of blue stained glass, the *Prisoner of Conscience,* glazed in 1980. Turn and compare it to the medieval shields and figures in the west window.

Leave by the **cloisters,** the earliest and longest in any English cathedral, and visit the adjoining **chapter house** (the room in a cathedral where business was conducted). You'll find here one of four extant copies of the **Magna Carta,** the foundation of English, and American, liberty. The Barons prepared it, and King John put his seal to it at Runnymede in 1215. In an effort to circumscribe the arbitrary powers of the king, Article 39 states that "no free man shall be seized or imprisoned, or stripped of his rights or possessions, or outlawed or exiled, or deprived of his standing in any other way, nor will we [the king] proceed with force against him, or send others to do so, except by the lawful judgment of his equals or by the law of the land." *Salisbury Cathedral, tel. 0722/28726. Admission free, but suggested donation of £1. Open daily 7:30–6 (restricted access during services). Chapter House, admission, 20p; open mid-Jan.–Mar., daily 1–3; Apr.–Oct., daily 10–4.*

Salisbury has the best **cathedral close** in the country, with houses from the 13th to the 18th century. It was in these stone and brick buildings surrounding the cathedral that the clergy lived. The clergy of monastic cathedrals consisted of monks who lived around a cloister. The clergy of Salisbury Cathedral were secular canons—clergymen who went out into the community and were not bound by monastic vows. These canons could live where they wanted, but usually chose to stay in houses near the cathedral, called a close. The secular cathedrals had cloisters, too, but they were often merely decorative.

Of particular note in the close are (1) **King's House,** home of the **Salisbury and South Wiltshire Museum,** which has some models of Stonehenge that will make your visit there more meaningful (63 The Close. Admission: £1.50 adults, 50p children. Open Apr.–Sept., Mon.–Sat. 10–5; July and Aug., Mon.–Sat. 10–5, Sun. 2–5; Oct.–Mar., Mon.–Sat. 10–4); (2) the **Museum of the Duke of Edinburgh's Royal Regiment** (The Wardrobe, 58 The Close; admission: £1.10 adults, 70p students and seniors, 50p children—free if accompanied by adult; open Apr.–June and Sept.–Oct., Sun.–Fri. 10–4:30; July and Aug., daily 10–4:30; Feb., Mar., and Nov., weekdays 10–4:30; closed Dec. and Jan.); and, above all, (3) the beautifully furnished **Mompesson House** (1701), with an exquisite Queen Anne interior (Choristers' Sq., The Close; admission: £1.50 adults, 70p children; open Apr.–Nov., Sat.–Wed. 12:30–dusk).

Exit through the north door of the cathedral and cross the lawn to where North Walk intersects with High Street. If you have only a few minutes, follow High Street past Mompesson House, and beneath North Gate. There's a National Trust Gift Shop here. Turn left on Crane Street. Just after the bridge cut left through the Queen Elizabeth Gardens to another bridge over the River Nadder. It was from here that John Constable painted his famous portrait of the cathedral. If time permits, follow a footpath from this bridge through open countryside, and enjoy changing views of the cathedral.

Time Out Any number of pubs offering reasonable food and atmosphere dot the city center. A good one to try is **The New Inn** (41–43 New St., tel. 0722–27679). It was built in the 15th century and has an impressively warped timbered facade. The gnarled mood is continued inside. To reach it, take the first right after leaving North Gate (the main entrance to the Close). It's about 90 m (100 yds) down the street on your right.

If you have an extra half hour, *don't* go up High Street; instead, turn right on North Walk to **St. Ann's Gate.** Handel is said to have given his first public concert in the room above. Turn left on St. John Street, which turns into Catherine Street and then into Queen Street. On your left is **Market Square,** where outdoor markets (Tues. and Sat.) have been held since 1361. Cross through the market to **St. Thomas's Church,** founded about 1220 in honor of Thomas Becket. It was rebuilt in the 15th century in the Perpendicular style, and has a notable fresco (1475) of the Last Judgment above the chancel arch (the arch separating the nave from the front of the church). From St. Thomas's, take High Street back toward the cathedral, turn right on Crane Street and take the abbreviated walking tour described above.

Dining **Rose and Crown.** The Club Restaurant of the Rose and Crown hotel offers what it likes to call Olde English Fayre. If not prize-winning, it's really much better than it sounds and features well-prepared, rather sturdy dishes. Deviled mushrooms and Butcher's Row pork fillet are specialties. The view over the River Avon is appealing, but the atmosphere is nothing special.

*Harnham Rd., tel. 0722/27908. Reservations advised. Jacket
and tie required. AE, DC, MC, V. Expensive.*

Harper's. Other than the city's hotel restaurants, this simple
spot on the second floor of a building overlooking the Market
Square is about the best Salisbury, not a town for gourmets,
can muster. The food is wholesome rather than sophisticated.
Try pan-fried haddock, chicken in tarragon cream sauce, or
grilled loin of pork. *7 Ox Row, The Market Square, tel. 0722/
333118. Reservations advised for dinner. Dress: casual. DC,
MC, V. Closed Sun. Moderate.*

Lodging   **Rose and Crown.** The two reasons for staying here are the location, just south of the cathedral but entirely removed from the
bustle of the city center, and the splendid half-timbered black-
and-white facade. Inside, it's something of a disappointment,
especially if you end up in the charmless annex out back (re-
deemed only by the views). But some of the older rooms have a
certain time-honored appeal, particularly those with four-poster beds. There's also an attractive garden on the banks of the
slow River Avon. *Harnham Rd., Salisbury, Wilts. SP2 8JQ,
tel. 0722/27908. 28 rooms with private bath. Facilities: restaurant, 2 bars, conference room, garden. AE, DC, MC, V.
Expensive.*

White Hart Hotel. A Georgian building not far from the cathedral, the White Hart is plushly comfortable, with spacious
public rooms and tasteful bedrooms. Rooms in the original
building are larger and more traditional than the faintly functional rooms in the newer building at back. Some rooms have
four-poster beds. *St. John St., Salisbury, Wilts. SP1 2SD, tel.
0722/412761. 68 rooms with private bath. Facilities: restaurant, bar, conference room. AE, DC, MC, V. Expensive.*

Red Lion Hotel. The Red Lion claims to be the oldest purpose-
built hotel in England, built in the 13th century (and almost entirely rebuilt in the 17th). Now, it's a Best Western property
with a Ye Olde atmosphere, complete with sagging floors and
low-beamed ceilings. The best rooms, some with floral four-
poster beds, are in the older part of the hotel. Those in the
newer wing are smaller. The hotel is conveniently located in the
city center. *Milford St., Salisbury, Wilts. SP1 2AN, tel. 0722/
23334. 57 rooms with private bath. Facilities: restaurant, bar,
conference room, golf, horseback riding, fishing, shooting.
AE, DC, MC, V. Moderate.*

On to Warminster   **Wilton House,** 6.4 km (4 mi) west of Salisbury on A30, is one of
England's greatest, most opulent mansions, designed by Inigo
Jones and his nephew by marriage, John Webb. The home of
the earls of Pembroke for more than 400 years, it contains a
world-famous collection of paintings, furniture, and sculpture;
an exhibit of 7,000 model soldiers; a palace dollhouse; a working
model railroad; even a lock of Queen Elizabeth I's hair. Jones's
state rooms are among the most palatial 17th-century rooms
left in England.

In about 1530, a Welshman named William Herbert married
the sister of Catherine Parr, who became Henry VIII's last
wife. When Henry confiscated the Church's lands, he abolished
Wilton Abbey and gave the property to his brother-in-law.
Herbert's eldest son later married Mary Sidney, sister of the
poet Philip Sidney, who wrote *Arcadia* while staying here.
Scenes from this famous poem are painted on the walls of the

Single Cube room. There's also a nude painting of the seventh earl's wife.

The famous double cube and single cube rooms, built to show off the paintings of Van Dyke, follow the rules of proportion that Jones learned from the Renaissance architect Palladio (1508–80); namely, that beauty consists of fixed, mathematical relationships between parts, none of which can be changed without destroying the harmony of the whole. The assumption is that God ordered the universe according to immutable mathematical laws, and that beauty comes from creating a similar order on Earth. *Tel. 0722/743115. Admission: £2 adults, £1 children. Open Easter–mid-Oct., Tues.–Sat. and Bank Holidays 11–6, Sun. 1–6.*

Stonehenge can be reached from Salisbury by taking A360 north 12.8 km (8 mi) and turning right about 3.2 km (2 mi) on A303. (From Wilton House, take A36 north to Stapleford, B3083 north, and then turn right on A303. Buses leave from the Salisbury Train Station frequently Monday–Saturday mid-April to mid-December. There's more frequent service from Salisbury Bus Station near Market Place, a few blocks from the cathedral.)

The best time to visit Stonehenge is early in the morning, or just before closing, when the shadows are longer than the lines. A fence keeps you from wandering among the stones, so you may want to avoid the entrance fee and look from the road. Even if the site is officially closed, you can see it quite well from the embankment, another reason to visit at sunrise or sunset, when the dim light creates an even greater sense of mystery.

What was this circular group of standing stones? An astronomical observatory? A Druidic temple? A navigational aid for flying saucers? Evidence seems to point to its being an open-air temple dedicated to sky gods. It was built from about 2200 to 1550 BC—later than the Great Pyramid, contemporary with the Minoan civilization on Crete, and 1,000 years earlier than the Great Wall of China. The Druids, a Celtic priesthood, did not get here until 250 BC.

The stones were shaped with hammers, and upended in holes dug with antler picks and spades made from the shoulder bones of cattle. The lintel stones ("henges") were set in place with the help of log platforms. The bluestones, which weigh up to four tons each, were brought some 384 km (240 mi) on logrollers and sledges, or lashed to the sides of rafts. The other stones weigh up to 50 tons each and were brought mostly uphill from 32 km (20 mi) away. At the time, only nomadic hunters lived on Salisbury Plain, so whoever built Stonehenge must have come from another, more sophisticated civilization.

The most important clues are the blue beads called *faience* that have been found in many parts of Britain and that could only have come from workshops in Egypt and Mycenae. The Egyptians and Greeks made these beads for trade with Europe. If you look where they have been discovered over the years, you find that they follow a trail along the southern coasts of France and Spain, up to Brittany, up the Dorset coast of England, to the greatest concentration—around Stonehenge. It was here that these beads were traded for Irish gold; here that Mycenaean civilization, through the medium of these traders, was introduced in Britain; and here that one of the traders or his associates must have been commissioned to build Stonehenge. It may seem farfetched, but how else do you explain the Mycenaean-type dagger carved into one of the Stonehenge stones, or the fact that the very same technique used to fasten the stone lintels to the uprights was used to construct the stone gateways at Mycenae?

Stonehenge—a temple dedicated to the sun—was needed by a people who were moving from a female-dominated society that worshiped earth goddesses, to a male-dominated society that worshiped gods of the sky. The same transition went on in Greece, when the old Achaean earth gods were replaced by Zeus and his cronies on Olympus. The transition took place in Greece about 1600 BC—the very same time that the Beaker Folk were engineering the final remodeling of Stonehenge.

If you stand at the center on the summer solstice, you can see the sun rising over the Heel Stone. So sophisticated were the techniques of these early astronomers that posts were placed to indicate where the moon rises over the horizon, as it shifts every two weeks in 18.61-year cycles. Yet Stonehenge was probably not an early version of Palomar Observatory, but a temple where the movement of the planets was observed for religious reasons. *Admission: £1.60 adults, 80p children 5–15. Open Mar.–Oct., daily 9:30–6:30; Oct.–Mar., daily 9:30–4.*

Warminster

From Stonehenge, drive 28.8 km (18 mi) west on A303 and A36 to Warminster, where there is an outstanding hotel.

Lodging **Bishopstrow House.** Standing in its own grounds about 3.2 km (2 mi) outside of Warminster on A36 is an elegant, late-Georgian mansion that is, if not the best hotel between London and Bath, then certainly a serious contender. There's no disputing the charm of the building, nor the substantial luxuries within. The formal lounge has Persian carpets, jade-green upholstery, antiques, and French windows overlooking the extensive grounds. Furnishings have a formal, decorated look, but are comfortable and in good taste. Whether you stay in the converted stables or the main house, furnishings are traditional, with soft, subdued pastels. The small rooms aren't quite worth the price; but the suites are wonderfully luxurious, some with Jacuzzis made for two. The tiled indoor pool, surrounded by classical pillars, is as elegant as the pool at the Palace Hotel in St. Moritz. The Conservatory dining room offers sumptuous nouvelle-inspired dishes in a light, sophisticated atmosphere. *Bishopstrow, Warminster, Wilts. BA12 9HH, tel. 0985/212312. 28 rooms with private bath. Facilities: restaurant, bar, indoor and outdoor tennis, indoor and outdoor pools, fishing, golf. AE, DC, MC, V. Very Expensive.*

On toward Wells A trip to **Stourhead House and Gardens** will add about 24 km (15 mi) to your drive, but anyone who loves gardens will find the trip worthwhile. From Stonehenge take A303 about 40 km (25 mi), then turn north on B3092 for about 4.8 km (3 mi). These are among the finest 18th-century gardens in England, laid out by the century's foremost landscape gardener, Lancelot "Capability" Brown. A river was dammed to create a three-part lake, whose shores are surrounded by various Italian temples and grottoes. The handsome Palladian house, furnished by Thomas Chippendale, can also be visited. *Tel. 0747/840348. Admission:*

gardens, Mar. and Apr. and July–Oct., £2 adults, £1 children 5–16; May and June, £2.50 adults, £1.30 children 5–16; Nov.– Feb., £1.50 adults, 70p children 5–16. House, £2.50 adults, £1.30 children 5–16. Gardens open daily 8–7 (or dusk if earlier). House open Easter–Oct., Sat.–Wed. 2–5:30.

From Stourhead House and Gardens, take B3092 north about 9.6 km (6 mi) and follow signs to **Longleat House.** (From Stonehenge, drive 28.8 km/18 mi west on A303 and A36 to Warminster, and follow signs.) What I remember most about Longleat House is the guide shaking the change in his pocket so we wouldn't forget to tip him at the end of the tour. The house itself is an exercise in wowmanship, with busloads of tourists tramping through the gilded halls among the priceless antiques, some more tasteful than others. Longleat is the only surviving 16th-century example of a Renaissance-style house in England. It was redecorated in the Italian Renaissance style during the 19th century, and stuffed with a dizzying collection of artifacts that the fourth marquess gathered on a grand tour of Europe. Chinese vases, Venetian ceilings lifted from the Doge's palace, Sicilian clocks, 19th-century saltshakers— Longleat has them all. Highlighting the tour are the erotic murals—apples hanging from phallic trees, and so on—painted in 1973 by the good Lord Weymouth, who is said to have had an unhappy childhood.

For children, the highlight of the trip to Longleat is a visit to the Dolls' Houses and a drive through Safari Park among the not-very-wild animals. There's also a maze, a 15-inch narrow-gauge railway, a 1:25 scale model of Longleat House, and safari-boat rides through a lake full of hippos and sea lions. This is a place that takes mass tourism seriously. *Tel. 09853/ 551. Admission: for all attractions, £8 adults, £6 children 4–14 and senior citizens; for house only, £3 adults, £1.50 children 4–14, £2.50 senior citizens; for gardens only, £1 adults, 50p children 4–14 and senior citizens (adults free if accompanied by children); for Safari Park only, £4 adults, £3 children 4–14 and senior citizens; charges for other attractions vary from 50p to £1. House open Easter–Sept., daily 10–6; Oct.–Easter, daily 10–4. Safari Park and Pets Corner open Mar.–Oct., daily 10–6 (or dusk if earlier). Other attractions open mid-Mar.– Oct., daily 11–6 (or dusk if earlier).*

Time Out A good bet for lunch near Longleat is the **Bath Arms** (Horningsham, tel. 09853/308), en route to Frome. Lord Christopher from Longleat likes to come here for a pint with the locals. In Frome itself, 5.6 km (3.5 mi) from Longleat on A362, try the **Settle** (Cheap St., tel. 0373/65975). The food and pastries are as memorable as the atmosphere. The lunch menu includes Somerset gammon (ham) with Damson sauce, pork in rough cider, and rabbit pie.

Wells

From Frome take A361 east 17.6 km (11 mi), or from Bath, take A39 south 33.6 km (21 mi) to Wells. (The 33.6-km/21-mi trip by bus from Bath takes 80 minutes. Buses leave hourly during the week, less frequently on Sunday, from the bus terminal one block from the train station.)

If you're spending several days in Bath, it makes sense to settle in and make a side trip to Wells. If time is limited, however, save time by visiting Wells en route to Bath.

Wells is the smallest cathedral city in England, but its cathedral, built by secular canons, is said to be the most graceful in the country. Because the complex of church buildings is so well preserved, it makes a great introduction to life in the Middle Ages. Try to visit on market days—Wednesday and Saturday.

The cathedral took three centuries to plan and build (1175–1508) and therefore offers a lesson in the history of architectural styles. As you enter, look up at the famous west facade and try to imagine the statues colored and gilded, as they were in the 13th century. The Puritans destroyed some of the 400 statues, but 297 remain—the greatest and richest display of 13th-century sculpture in England.

Ahead of you is a pair of strangely inverted scissor arches that were added to support the new tower, which was so heavy that it threatened to tumble into the nave. The arches look modern but were built 600 years ago. Some think them gross, others graceful, but all agree that they're unique, and that they worked.

Follow the left (north) aisle to the transept and look up at the clock. Knights rush out every quarter hour and fight with lances. One has been knocked down each time—since 1390. On the hour Jack Blandiver kicks the bells with his heels, and hammers one in front of him. No one knows how he got his name. Below the clock is a modern, life-size carving of Christ rising from the tomb (1955).

Continue toward the front (east) end of the church and look for the door to the **Chapter House**—the finest in the country. A flight of worn stone steps, themselves almost as memorable as anything else in the cathedral, leads up to it. In the octagonal room, 32 ribs fan out from the central pier like fronds on a giant palm tree. Don't miss it!

Look at the capitals (the heads of columns) in the south transept—on your right as you face the altar—and find the heads and animal masks hidden among the leaves. One has a toothache and seems to be waiting for a dentist to pass by.

The cathedral has some wonderful chantry chapels. Look especially for Bishop Thomas Bekynton's. The two views of him, in this life and the next, say more about mortality than a hundred sermons. Look, too, for chantries of Nicholas Bubworth, Bishop of Bath, and John Drokensford, who is waiting for Judgment Day with his feet on a lion and his head on a pillow. *Wells Cathedral. Admission free, but suggested donation of £1. Open daily 7:30–7 (may sometimes close earlier in winter; restricted access during services).*

From the cathedral walk through the 15th-century cloisters to the grounds of the **Bishop's Palace,** the only medieval bishop's palace still occupied. Because the bishop still lives here, the rooms we'd all like to see—bedrooms, bathrooms, and so on—are closed to the public. The 4.5-m (15-ft) thick walls and moat were added in the 14th century to protect the bishop from town riots. Guidebooks tell you that swans in the moat ring a bell for dinner; but the swans find it easier to be fed by tourists, and the bell hasn't tolled for years. *Tel. 0749/78691. Admission: £1.*

*Open Easter–Oct., Thurs. and Sun. 2–6; May–Sept., Wed.
11–6, Thurs. and Sun. 2–6; Aug. and Bank Holidays, open
daily 11–6.*

Wookey Hole is a cave and paper mill 3.2 km (2 mi) from Wells,
and very well signposted. If you dismiss it as a tourist trap run
by Madame Tussaud's, you're making a mistake. It *is* commercial, but it's great fun, too, and families in particular shouldn't
miss it. What makes a tour worthwhile is the fact that prehistoric folk once lived here, and it's fun imagining their lifestyle.
Watercolorists can buy handmade paper here, and children of
all ages can play prehistoric penny-arcade games and tour a
room filled with Madame Tussaud's retired wax figures. *Tel.
0749/72243. Admission: £4.10 adults, £2.85 children 4–17,
£3.65 senior citizens. Open mid-Mar.–Oct., daily 9:30–5:30;
Nov.–mid-Mar., daily 10:30–4:30.*

Bath

From Wells, take A39 33.6 km (21 mi) northeast, or from Salisbury, take A36 64 km (40 mi) northwest, to **Bath.** Bath is
England's most elegant city, famous for its history, its architecture, and its hot springs. It's also a clean, comfortable town
with sophisticated restaurants and first-class hotels. The shopping, along traffic-free pedestrian malls, is in some ways the
equal of London's. The major sights are the Roman Baths, the
Abbey, and the Georgian buildings where British society
stayed in the 18th century. None of this will mean much, however, unless you know something about Bath's history.

The Romans knew about the springs and their restorative powers when they began moving west in the 1st century AD to mine
lead. They built the baths around them—nothing as grand or elegant as the baths in Rome, but luxurious for such a distant
outpost. The baths are still well preserved and are today the best
Roman ruins in Britain.

The fame of Bath disappeared with the Romans in the 5th century. Medieval chroniclers knew about the health-giving properties
of the waters, but the spa was neglected until the 17th century.
The diarist Samuel Pepys wrote in 1668, "Methinks it cannot be
clean to go so many bodies together in the same water." Among
those who disagreed was Charles II, who brought his Queen
Catherine here to make her fertile and give the crown a legitimate
heir. It didn't work; but others followed, including Queen Anne,
who, suffering from dropsy and gout, came twice, in 1702 and
1703, bringing the rest of English society in her fashionable wake.

In 1704, a 31-year-old gambler, Richard "Beau" Nash, was chosen
to oversee the spa's restoration. In the next 40 years this obscure
Welshman virtually invented the resort business and became the
Arbiter of Elegance. His famous Code of Behavior, posted in the
Pump Room for all to see, included the following rules:

That ladies coming to the ball appoint a time for their footmen
coming to wait on them home, to prevent disturbance and
inconvenience to themselves and others.

That no gentleman give his ticket for the balls to any but
gentlewomen.—NB: Unless he has none of his acquaintance.

That the elder ladies and children be content with a second
bench at the ball, as being past or not come to perfection.

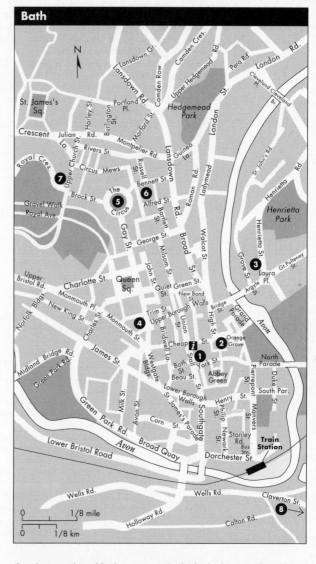

Bath

On three points Nash was particularly insistent: that there should be no dueling and wearing of swords; that women should never appear at assemblies in white aprons, and that men should never appear at fashionable gatherings in riding boots. The fight against white aprons was particularly severe. The climax came when the duchess of Queensberry arrived at the Assembly Room in an apron which Beau ruthlessly stripped from her and threw among the ladies-in-waiting. The duchess took the insult in stride, and meekly submitted to the uncrowned king of Bath.

Once Nash freed Bath from its rustic associations, the beau monde began to flock here, certain that dignity and decorum would prevail. By the middle of the century, Bath had become the center of Fashion and Polite Society during the long summer months. Richard Sheridan wrote *The Rivals* here in the 1770s while living on Terrace Walk. Jane Austen, who was often sick, came for the cures in the early 19th century. When you visit the Assembly Rooms you can imagine Catherine Morland, heroine of *Northanger Abbey,* and a projection of Jane herself as a young girl, being snubbed by fashionable visitors till she finds a suitable gentleman to show her around. A little later, Charles Dickens hung out in the card rooms (now the Assembly Rooms) and put the city in several chapters of *The Pickwick Papers.*

While Nash organized concerts and gambling, and lit the streets to make them safe, the architect John Wood (1700–54), with his son, also called John (1728–81), was busy transforming Bath into a city suitable for the People of Quality. Inspired by Bath's Roman past, Wood conceived a scheme to return the city to what he took to be its former architectural glory. Little of his original plan was executed, but what was built serves to underline just how much more magnificent Bath might have become. Not only can you still see these buildings today, you can stay in some of them, in hotels with appointments as splendid as the buildings themselves.

Begin your tour at the **Abbey,** a good example of late Perpendicular Style—one of the last great achievements of Catholic England. Do you see the angels climbing ladders on the west facade? The sculpture was inspired by a dream of Bishop Oliver King, in which he saw angels climbing to heaven and heard voices commanding a king (his own name) to restore the church. The designers were very anxious to have the church well lit, and so they built the large clerestory windows in the walls above the nave.

Time Out Combine your sightseeing with a bite to eat at **Sally Lunn's,** a Tudor building close to the Abbey that claims to be the oldest house in the city. Downstairs, there's a small museum (4 North Parade Passage, tel. 0225/461634). For more substantial meals, try the **Pump Room** itself, where you can eat surrounded by 18th-century elegance (Abbey Church Yard).

Cross the Abbey Church Yard, past the Tourist Information Centre, to the **Roman Baths and Pump Room.** The Pump Room —named for the reservoir below that provides 1,064,000 l (280,000 gal) a day of hot, sulfurous water at a constant temperature of 46.6°C (116° Fahrenheit)—is in fact a Georgian assembly hall. For a taste of 18th-century Bath, be sure to come from 9 AM to noon for coffee, a sip of the evil-tasting waters, and the sounds of violins. Be on your best behavior, for Nash—at least a painting and statue of him—is looking down on you. The Pump Room was actually built in 1789–99, after Nash's death, when the middle classes had begun to gate-crash, and the highborn and low-born were engaged in a frantic round of pleasure and diversion, both an easy prey to sharks and fortune-hunters. Close your eyes and think of the Pump Room as described by the novelist Tobias Smollett through the eyes of one of his heroines, Lydia Melford:

All is gaiety, good-humour, and diversion. The eye is continually entertained with the splendour of dress and equipage; and the ear with the sound of coaches, chaises, chairs, and other carriages. We have music in the Pump-room every morning, cotillions every fore-noon in the rooms, balls twice a week, and concerts every night, besides private assemblies and parties without number. The Squares and the Circus put you in mind of the sumptuous palaces represented in prints and pictures. At eight in the morning we go déshabillé to the Pump-room, which is crowded like a Welsh fair; and there you see the highest quality and the lowest tradesfolks, jostling each other, without ceremony. Hard by the Pump-room is a coffee-house for the ladies; but my aunt says young girls are not admitted, inasmuch as the conversation turns upon politics, scandal, philosophy, and other subjects above our capacity. . . .

Descend to the **Roman Baths.** Most of the excavations were made in the late 19th century, long after Nash's reign. The **Great Bath**—in essence, a warm swimming pool—is still unroofed, and has the original Roman lead plumbing; the columns and statues above are Victorian. There were no luxurious changing rooms in the 18th century; visitors arrived in carriages, wrapped in robes; after wallowing in the rather scuzzy waters, they wrapped themselves up, returned to their carriages, and niddlenoddled home. After you've seen the Great Bath, you can walk through the extensive excavations of Roman remains discovered on the site. *Roman Baths Museum, Abbey Church Yard, tel. 0225/462831. Admission: £2.70 adults, £1.40 children 5–16. Open Mar.–June, Sept., and Oct., Mon.–Sat. 9–6, Sun. 10–6; July and Aug., daily 9–7; Nov.–Feb., Mon.–Sat. 9–5, Sun. 10–5.*

Leave the Baths and turn right on Stall Street. You'll find many fashionable shops on this pedestrian mall and along the side streets. Follow Stall Street as it becomes first Union Street, then Milsom Street. After about 450 m (500 yd), you come to the **Octagon,** an 18th-century hall housing the National Centre for Photography, the oldest photographic society in the world. It offers a varied program of quality exhibits and contains a small permanent collection. *The Octagon, Milsom St. Admission: £1, children under 7 free. Open daily 9:30–5:30.*

Milsom Street runs into George Street. Turn right, then make the first left onto Bartlett Street, which has several **antiques shops,** and continue to Alfred Street. Turn left. On your right are the famous Assembly Rooms, built by John Wood's son in 1769–71 so that visitors didn't have to go all the way to the baths to socialize. The Assembly Rooms soon became the center of the town's social life, with balls, card playing, tea drinking, entertainments, and an endless stream of gossip and scandal.

A major restoration program was initiated in 1989 and the Assembly Rooms, along with the famous Museum of Costume beneath them, will be closed until sometime in 1991.

From The Assembly Rooms, turn left onto Bennett Street. This takes you to the Circus, a circle of identical Georgian houses that many consider John Wood's finest work. (A "circus" is a circle or ring.) Wood designed it, and it was completed by his son, who also designed the Royal Crescent (*see* below).

In order to appreciate the Georgian architecture of John Wood and his son, keep in mind that it was based largely on the concepts of the Italian Renaissance architect Palladio. If Wood's buildings seem cold to you, it's because they are meant not to overwhelm your senses, as, say, a Gothic or Baroque building would, but to appeal to your mind—to your sense of order and harmony and proportion. Every part has a fixed size and shape in relation to every other, and to the whole. This harmony, in the rationally conceived universe of the 18th century, was thought to be an echo of the harmony of the universe—a universe which, like a clock, was set in motion by a rational God. As you walk around the Circus, try to appreciate these harmonic ratios, and think fondly of an age when people could believe that Truth was known, and that the world was ruled by reason.

Leave the Circus and walk down Brock Street, which was built by John Wood the Younger in 1767. The street was conceived as an avenue connecting the town's two architectural masterpieces, the Circus and the Royal Crescent. You won't know what's in store for you until the moment you turn into the Crescent—which is exactly as Wood planned it more than 200 years ago.

The **Royal Crescent** is the severest expression of the Palladian style in England. Designed in 1767–74, it consists of 30 houses with a continuous facade of 114 Ionic columns. Ask yourself, Would you rather live here or in the Circus? I'd prefer the Circus; it seems more human. Yet Smollett seems unfair when he dismisses the Royal Crescent as "a pretty bauble, contrived for show, [that] looks like Vespasian's amphitheater [the Colosseum] turned inside out." Note that though the facade gives the buildings a uniform face, the interiors were all designed differently, by various contractors, and that the back sides, which no one was supposed to see, are, in comparison, rather shabby. How 18th-century, this distinction between a person's private life and the face he presents to the world!

The **Georgian House Museum** at 1 Royal Crescent is now a museum where you can capture a sense of life in 18th-century Bath. *Admission: £1.50 adults, £1 children 5–18, students, and senior citizens. Open Tues.–Sat. and Bank Holidays 11–5, Sun. 2–5.*

In the very center of this noble arc is the **Royal Crescent Hotel** (*see* Lodging, below). Note the fashionably understated hotel sign beside the door.

From the Royal Crescent, return to the Circus. Turn right (counterclockwise) in the Circus, past the hotel at number 6, and make your first right down Gay Street, across Queen Square and then into Barton Street. On your right is the most popular restaurant in town, Popjoy's (*see* Dining, below), where Nash once lived with his mistress, Juliana Popjoy. Beside the restaurant is the beautifully restored **Theatre Royal,** where you should get seats for an upcoming performance.

Cross the open square and turn left on Westgate Street, which will take you back to Stall Street, the Baths, and the Abbey. Between the Abbey and the River Avon are the lovely **Parade Gardens,** where you can rest your feet. To the right of the gardens (facing the river) is a bridge. Cross over, and turn immediately left on a path along the river bank. There's a place here to catch a boat for a peaceful 60-minute cruise on the Avon. Continue along the river to the next bridge, Pulteney Bridge, which has shops on it, inspired by the Ponte Vecchio in Florence. Cross the bridge, into Bridge Street. Turn left on High Street. On your left is the Guildhall, the banquet room of which is one of best interiors in Bath. Next door is the covered market. Continue down High Street and you're back at the Abbey.

Dining **Dower House Restaurant.** The restaurant of the Royal Crescent Hotel, the Dower House, is set in its own elegant building in the hotel garden and is the most formal restaurant in town. If you are not staying at the Royal Crescent, this is a great opportunity for you to tour John Wood's masterpiece and learn what 18th-century elegance was all about. The nouvellish menu includes lobster ravioli with a tarragon sauce and parcels of pigeon in a pastry case with red wine and mushroom sauce. *16 Royal Crescent, tel. 0225/319090. Reservations required. Jacket and tie required. AE, DC, MC, V. Very Expensive.*

Popjoy's. This is the place to dine if you have only one evening in Bath. It's conveniently located next door to the theater, and it comes closer than any restaurant in town to capturing the elegant atmosphere of 18th-century Bath. The limited, fixed menu features local fish and game, with such specialties as goat cheese profiterole, duck livers in pepper and sherry jelly, chargrilled duck with grapefruit and peppercorn sauce, and quail stuffed with pine nuts and raisins. Coffee is served upstairs. Nash lived here with his mistress; when he died she vowed never to sleep in a bed again, and ended her life in a hollow tree in Wiltshire. *Beau Nash's House, Sawclose, tel. 0225/ 460494. Reservations required. Jacket and tie required. AE, MC, V. Closed Sat. lunch, and Sun. and Mon. Expensive.*

Priory Hotel. The Priory Hotel, a late-Georgian villa a mile or so west of the city center, is considered Bath's best restaurant by many locals. The cuisine leans toward traditional French with nouvelle flourishes. Roast beef remains a consistent favorite, as do the asparagus (in season) and the watercress soup. Some critics maintain that, though excellent, the wines are overpriced. *Weston Rd., tel. 0225/331922. Reservations required. Jacket and tie required. AE, DC, MC, V. Expensive.*

Tarts. Located in a mazelike cellar of interconnecting rooms just south of the abbey, Tarts is a superior bistro-style restaurant offering excellent nouvelle food, fine wines at low prices, and a noisy, relaxed atmosphere. Chicken livers and lardons of bacon in puff pastry, escalope of salmon with rosemary butter, and terrine of salmon and sole are among the specialties. The desserts are rich and imaginative. *8 Pierrepoint Pl., tel. 0225/ 330280. Reservations advised. Dress: casual. MC, V. Closed Sun. Moderate.*

Lodging **Royal Crescent Hotel.** The Royal Crescent was the best address in Bath 200 years ago—and still is today. Staying in one of these lovingly restored town houses is as close as you'll come to recapturing the grandeur of Georgian Bath. Rooms in the renovated building behind the crescent are tastefully decorated in hushed pastels, but if you know the history of Bath, you may feel cheated unless you stay in the original building designed by John Wood. The atmosphere is formal and discreet, with most guests on the far side of 35. The larger rooms and suites are exquisite; the smaller, least expensive rooms are equally tasteful. The service is correspondingly polished. *16 Royal Crescent, Bath, Avon BA1 2LS, tel. 0225/319090. 13 suites and 32 rooms with private bath. Facilities: restaurant, bar, pool. AE, DC, MC, V. Very Expensive.*

Ston Easton Park. Located 19.2 km (12 mi) from Bath on A37, the Ston Easton is one of England's most elegant country hotels, with period antiques, a formal grand salon with ornate plaster ceilings, and other Palladian-style details. Forests of flowers protrude from huge vases. Some rooms have four-poster beds, and all are sumptuously decorated. The staff is discreet, attentive, and welcoming. The hotel stands in 11.2 ha (28 acres) of beautifully landscaped 18th-century gardens, with wonderful views in every direction. *Ston Easton, Nr. Bath, Avon BA3 4DF, tel. 076121/631. 5 suites and 15 rooms with private bath. Facilities: 2 restaurants, private dining room, croquet, archery, horseback riding, fishing, ballooning, helicopter landing pad. AE, DC, MC, V. Very Expensive.*

The Priory Hotel. If the Royal Crescent has the atmosphere of a city hotel, the rambling Priory, though little more than 1.6 km (1 mi) west of the city center, seems more like a country estate. The atmosphere is refined, but much more relaxed than at the Royal Crescent. There are rooms to curl up in here—one would never curl up in the Royal Crescent, at least not in public! Pay extra for the deluxe doubles; they're worth it. The best standard rooms are in the older wing. The restaurant is justly famous. *Weston Rd., Bath, Avon BA1 2XT, tel. 0225/331922. 21 rooms with private bath. Facilities: restaurant, croquet, heated outdoor pool. AE, DC, MC, V. Expensive.*

Apsley House Hotel. If you want to stay somewhere that seems more like a private home than a hotel, the Apsley House will appeal. It's small, immaculately clean, and run with warmth. The building itself is a stone mansion built in the reign of William IV. It's set back from busy A431, 1.6 km (1 mi) west of Bath. *Newbridge Hill, Bath, Avon BA1 3PT, tel. 0225/336966. 7 rooms with private bath. Facilities: restaurant, bar. MC, V. Moderate.*

Lacock

Take A4 about 19.2 km (12 mi) east of Bath, then turn right (south) on A350 if you want to see **Lacock,** an 18th-century village that hasn't been prettified or overwhelmed with tourist shops. It can be overwhelmed on summer days by tourists stalking the Real England, so stay overnight—before or after your trip to Bath—and explore the town when the day-trippers are gone. In the Middle Ages Lacock was a weaving community on an important Bath–London route. Prosperity continued through the 18th century, when—as with other towns you'll be visiting—the Industrial Revolution put the cottage weaving industry out of business. Unlike other towns, however, Lacock was owned largely by a single family, the Talbots, who preserved its heritage, and in 1944 put it safely in the hands of the National Trust. Thanks to the preservationists, the newest houses are 18th century, and the village remains one of the most homogeneous in England.

The main street, leading to the abbey, is High Street, lined with moss-covered stone houses spanning at least four centuries. Church Street, which parallels High Street, leads to **St. Cyriac Church.** This is a Perpendicular-style wool church—so-called because it was built by prosperous wool merchants during the 14th to 17th centuries. Note the memorial brass in the south transept to Robert Raynard and his 18 children. Note, too, the weird faces in the arches of the Lady Chapel (on the left, facing the altar).

Time Out For better-than-average pub food and a satisfyingly Old World atmosphere (only partly spoiled by the piped music), try **The Carpenter's Arms** (tel. 024973/203). It can get crowded in summer, so it's best to arrive early. The new Barn Restaurant in the back offers more substantial meals. The pub is located in the little square by the church.

Lacock Abbey was the last religious house in England to be suppressed at the Dissolution—when Henry VIII established the Church of England and appropriated church lands to fill his coffers. It is a good example of a medieval Augustinian priory that was converted into a private home, incorporating both the chapter house and the cloister. *Admission: £2.50 adults, £1.30 children (cloisters and grounds only, £1 adults, 50p children). House, cloisters, and grounds open Apr.–Oct., Wed.–Mon. 2–5:30 (Tues., cloisters and grounds only open).*

Visit the **Fox Talbot Museum,** which contains photos by Fox Talbot, who made the first photographic prints in 1833. *Admission: £1.50 adults, 70p children 5–16. Open Mar.–Oct., daily 11–5:30.*

Dining **At the Sign of the Angel.** You'll have to search long and hard to find a more perfect example of Merrie England than this beautifully maintained inn. Roasts predominate, with roast beef and Yorkshire pudding an enduring favorite (it's almost always rare, so be sure to tell the waiter if you prefer it well done). Braised kidneys in Madeira sauce, salmon mousse, and home-made pies, cheeses, and ice cream are other long-standing offerings. A few carping voices have been raised lately, complaining that the Sign of the Angel has succumbed to the pressures of tourism, and that it sometimes does little more than go through the motions. It may be wise to visit this extraordinary survival sooner rather than later. *Church St., tel. 024973/230. Reservations required. Dress: casual. AE, MC, V. Closed Sat. lunch, Sun. dinner, Christmas and New Year's. Expensive–Moderate.*

Lodging **Beechfield House.** If you want to experience an old Tudor inn, you can't do better than Sign of the Angel, but if you prefer the more polished atmosphere of an English country house, drive 3.2 km (2 mi) to Beechfield House. It's south of Lacock on A350 and well signposted. The hotel is in a sturdy late-Victorian building and stands on eight acres of grounds. It lacks the finesse of some of the country's grander country hotels, but the rooms are comfortable and large, with most decorated in a variety of floral prints and wallpapers. *Beanacre, Melksham, Wilts. SN12 7PU, tel. 0225/703700. 24 rooms with private bath. Facilities: restaurant, bar, outdoor pool, conference rooms. AE, DC, MC, V. Expensive.*

At the Sign of the Angel. If you're going to experience southwestern England, you should spend at least one night in a Georgian town house, another in a restored manor house, and a third in an old inn. The best of the inns is Sign of the Angel. This 15th-century wool merchant's house has low oak-beamed ceilings, even in the bathrooms, and whitewashed, stenciled bedroom walls. What makes the inn unique is that it hasn't been mucked up with tasteless modern furnishings, and has avoided the annex-expansion that has turned so many cozy English inns into tour-bus destinations. Each room is different. Number 3 is more spacious than some; if noise bothers you, avoid number 1. The breakfast omelets, with ham, mushrooms, and tomatoes, should see you through the day. *Church St., Lacock, Wilts. SN15 2LA, tel. 024973/230. 8 rooms with private bath. Facilities: restaurant, bar, garden. AE, MC, V. Expensive–Moderate.*

The Old Rectory. For a superior B&B, try the Old Rectory, a handsome Victorian house on the edge of town with 7 acres of land. It's run by a friendly, intelligent woman who turns guests into friends. The rooms are spacious and comfortable; two have four-poster beds. *Lacock, Wilts. SN1 2JZ, tel. 024973/335. 3 rooms with private bath. Facilities: tennis, croquet. Moderate.*

Castle Combe

From Bath: Take A46 north 9.6 km (6 mi) to A420. Turn right (east) to Ford, and follow signs north to Castle Combe. From Lacock: Take A350 north to Chippenham, A420 west, and follow signs on your right to Castle Combe.

The film *Dr. Doolittle* was a financial disaster, but it seems to have brought a lot of attention to **Castle Combe**, where it was filmed, and which subsequently won a national poll as the prettiest town in England. The old wool weavers' village hasn't changed much in the past 250 years, except for the sea of tourists in which, each summer, it threatens to drown. The problem with Castle Combe is that it's a one-street town jammed with traffic; there are no side streets to get lost in, no alleyways to discover. If you're collecting lovely villages, don't miss it; but don't expect to be overwhelmed by local color.

Lodging **Manor House Hotel.** The hordes of visitors that pour through Castle Combe during the day can make this seem more like a madhouse than a manor house. But if you spend your afternoons exploring, you will return at night to one of the most romantically situated country house hotels in England. The building stands on 10.4 ha (26 acres) with a trout-stocked lake, Italian gardens, and wooded trails. The public areas are filled with heirlooms and rich wood paneling. Furnishings are old-fashioned. If there's anything wrong with the Manor House it's that it's so Discovered—a place one does as part of the Olde Englande Experience. It's also expanding at an alarming rate. Be sure to get a room in the main house; the workmen's cottages look lovely from without but are in fact charmless, with worn carpets and small basic bathrooms. Two rooms have four-poster beds. *Castle Combe, Wilts. SN14 7HR, tel. 0249/782206. 34 rooms with private bath. Facilities: restaurant, bar, swimming pool, tennis. AE, DC, MC, V. Expensive.*

The Cotswolds

The Cotswolds are England's "green and pleasant land"—a region of soft stone villages and rich, rolling pastureland, where nothing seems to change, or matter, but the seasons. Americans love these picturesque villages because they have everything America lacks: tradition, homogeneity, local color, and a sense of place. The towns seem to spring organically from the soil, and no one needs an advanced degree to appreciate their timelessness, their beauty and their strength.

A "wold" is an upland common—in other words, a stretch of high land or plateau that's owned in common, usually as

The Cotswolds to Stratford

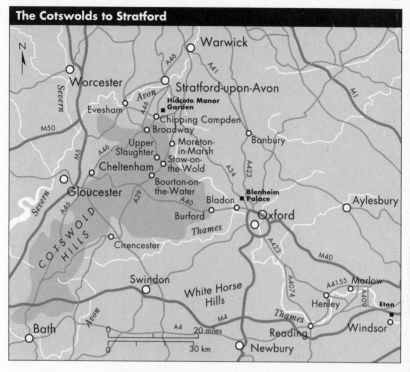

pastureland. The Cotswold Hills are about 160 km (100 mi) long and 64 km (40 mi) wide, and rise to about 300 m (1,000 ft); but the surrounding countryside, extending northeast roughly from north of the M4 expressway at Malmesbury to Stow-on-the-Wold, is often considered part of the Cotswolds, too.

From the 13th to the 15th century, the wool raised here was England's main export. The wool trade created great wealth and much of the money went into the construction of cottages, manor houses, and the so-called wool churches—buildings that give the Cotswold villages their unique architectural charm.

The cotton mills of Lancashire unraveled the wool trade. The commons were enclosed and turned into private farms by the Enclosure Acts (1795–1812). The drystone walls put an end to the small farmer and the great sheep runs; and when the bottom fell out of the wool trade in the 17th and 18th centuries, construction stopped and the towns remained suspended in time—until the tourists arrived and put the Cotswolds back on the map.

The challenge is to find some way to enter this world—not merely to pass through. It's not an easy task when you're one of hundreds of Americans sniffing around a tiny stone village, all searching for the Elusive Past.

Rule 1 is to avoid the main roads whenever possible. Get yourself a 1:50,000 map and drive down the backest of the back roads. Rule 2 is to pick your towns carefully. The itinerary below should give you some sense of which ones to visit or avoid. The area around Stow-on-the-Wold makes a great base, because it's centrally located, has restaurants, hotels, and shops for every taste and budget, and is large enough to absorb the crowds.

Rule 3 is to leave the pavement at least once and walk from one town to another, following a footpath through the meadows. One popular walk is from Stow-on-the-Wold to Lower Swell, Upper Slaughter, and Lower Slaughter; but wherever you are, ask a policeman or desk clerk to suggest a route, or pick up one of the hiking guides sold throughout the region. Among the best are *Along the Cotswolds Ways* by G. R. Crosher (Pan) and *A Visitor's Guide to the Cotswolds* by Richard Sale (Moorland).

There are some 2,560 km (1,600 mi) of pathways in the Cotswolds—along country lanes, footpaths, and ancient sheep tracks as old as Stonehenge. Most are marked with signposts and indicated on 1:50,000 maps. Villages are so close together that you rarely need more than an hour or two to hike between them. If a circular route is unfeasible, walk from A to B and arrange for a taxi to take you home.

Cirencester

From Castle Combe the fastest route is to Malmesbury and then north on A429 and A433. The more scenic route is via Tetbury.

Cirencester, known locally as "Ciren," is a busy district center, with markets and shops. It was once the second largest Roman town in Britain after London. During the Middle Ages it was the largest wool market town in the country.

The main reason to stop here, other than to admire the town's elegant and harmonious streets, is to visit **St. John the Baptist Church,** the finest of all the wool churches, and one of the largest parish churches in England. Because of its unusual length, 54 m (180 ft), it looks more like a small cathedral. The aisles are wide to accommodate the faithful, and give the church a sense of being of and for the people—an impression you don't always get in English cathedrals. The church was begun in the 12th century, but the **Tower,** the **Trinity Chapel,** and the **Lady Chapel** were built in the early 15th. The Norman nave was raised 4.5 m (15 ft) a century later in the new Perpendicular style. The 15th-century wineglass **pulpit** is one of a few left in the region from before the Reformation. To the right of the chancel arch is the **Boleyn Cup,** which Henry VIII gave to Anne two years before her execution. The Trinity Chapel has some great 15th-century brasses, which you can rub (contact Rev. Lewis, tel. 0285/3142).

From the church turn right and go down Castle Street. Bear right on Silver Street, which turns into Park Street. On your right is the **Corinium Museum,** the finest museum of Roman remains in the country, with reconstructions of a Roman kitchen, dining room, and workshop. (Corinium was the Roman name for Cirencester.) It also houses well-preserved mosaic pavements in replicas of rooms where they once stood. *Admission: £1 adults, 50p children, 70p students and senior citizens. Open Apr.–Sept., Mon.–Sat. 10–5:30, Sun. 2–5:30; Oct.–Mar., Tues.–Sat. 10–5, Sun. 2–5, closed Mon.*

Continue down Park Street. Bear right on Thomas Street and make your first right on Coxwell Street, which has many lovely old houses. At the end of Coxwell Street, turn right and return to the church.

A five-minute walk from the church takes you to the **Cirencester Workshops,** where you can buy hand-printed textiles and other crafts. To get there from the church, turn right to the light; turn left on Cricklade, then make your first right. *Admission free. Open Mar.–Oct., Mon.–Sat. 10–5:30; Nov.–Feb., Mon.– Sat. 10–5.*

Cirencester has the best of the **wool churches.** If you want to see some of the others, drive east on A417 to Fairford; north on A361 to Burford, and east on A40 to Northleach. From here take A429 north to Stow-on-the-Wold. If you've seen enough churches, take A429 direct from Cirencester to Stow-on-the-Wold.

Fairford

From Cirencester drive east 14.4 km (9 mi) on A417.

The main attraction of Fairford is **St. Mary's Church,** and the main attraction of St. Mary's is the stained glass windows. No other parish church in England has retained its complete set of medieval glass. The 28 windows serve as a picture book meant to teach the story of the Bible, beginning with Adam (the green glass that you'll see when you stand with your back to the organ), and ending with the Last Judgment. The "Short Guide," sold at the entrance, gives a brief description of each panel. Except for the base of the tower, itself very curious—it's at the head of the nave, in the crossing—the wool church was completely rebuilt in the Perpendicular style by John Tame (1470–1534), a rich wool merchant, and his son Edmund. Below the carpet in the Lady Chapel are commemorative brasses to Edmund and his two wives. His second wife commissioned it.

For examples of medieval humor, don't miss the misericords—the seat projections on the choir stalls. You'll see carvings of a woman giving grief to her husband, a couple draining a cider barrel, and so on.

As you leave, look for the little statue that commemorates Tiddles, the church cat, gravely dated 1963–1980. It's opposite the main door.

Lodging　**Bull Hotel.** Standing in Fairford's attractive Market Square, the long, low, gray-stone exterior of the Bull promises rather more than the interior delivers. It's very much a traditional Cotswold inn, with old beams, uneven floors, and exposed stone woodwork, but the rooms are plain and faded. One has a four-poster bed, another a sunken bath. Still, it's fine for overnighting. *Market Square, Fairford, Glos. GL7 4AA, tel. 0285/712535. 22 rooms, 18 with private bath. Facilities: restaurant, bar, conference room. AE, DC, MC, V. Moderate.*

Bibury

From Cirencester take A433 northeast for 11.2 km (7 mi). From Fairford, follow back-road signs.

Bibury is the town most often used on British Tourist Association posters—minus the crowds. In season, you'll find yourself among a gaggle of tourists on what is essentially a tiny, one-street village—much like Castle Combe. Yet Bibury is worth a stop because it's so pretty a town—William Morris thought it the most beautiful in England—and the Parish Church, Arlington Row, and Country Museum are all worth seeing. Here, as elsewhere in the Cotswolds, the ideal time to visit is in the early spring or fall.

About 90 m (300 yds) before the museum is a left turn leading to **St. Mary's Parish Church,** in an area of the town that many visitors miss. At Bibury the wool merchants did not completely rebuild the original Romanesque church, as they did at Cirencester, Fairford, and Northleach, so you'll be able to identify features that go back to Saxon times. There's a great Norman north door, and Saxon capitals. The north aisle is the earlier of the two—you can tell by the massive columns. The large windows of the north aisle are 14th-century work in the Decorated style. You won't see this in many Cotswold churches, because by the time the wool merchants had money for restorations, the Perpendicular style was in. The wall-cupboards (ambries) indicate that the church must once have had a great collection of plate or relics.

Arlington Row is a group of old Cotswold cottages that date back to the 14th century. Once the homes of shepherds, they were converted into houses in the 17th century to accommodate weavers from Arlington Mill. Don't peer into the windows; people are still living here. If you're ready for a walk, take the path uphill from Arlington Row to the gate, and follow the sign.

The **Cotswold Country Museum,** located in the former mill, has a fine collection of old carts and machines, and rooms showing how people lived and worked. *Admission: £1 adults, 50p children. Open mid-Mar.–mid-Nov., daily 10:30–7 (or dusk if earlier); mid-Nov.–mid-Mar., weekends only 10:30–dusk.*

Visit the **Bibury Trout Farm** next door to feed the fish (or to buy some—provided you have somewhere to cook them). It's a rather aggressively tourist-oriented place, with an Adventure Island, picnic areas, and the inevitable gift shop. But children appreciate it. *Admission: £1 adults, 40p children, 60p senior citizens. Open mid-Mar.–mid-Nov., Mon.–Sat. 9–6, Sun. 10–5; mid-Nov.–mid-Mar., Mon.–Sat. 9–5, Sun. 10–5.*

Lodging   **Bibury Court Hotel.** The stately stone Tudor mansion that is the Bibury Court, approached via a crunching gravel drive, stands on 2.4 ha (six acres) of land. Expansive lawns sweep away from the front of the building. Inside, dark wood paneling and antique furniture establish a convincingly old-fashioned mood. Nonetheless, and despite the best efforts of a scattering of four-poster beds, a number of the bedrooms exude a certain dowdiness. The best is the Sackville Suite. The restaurant offers substantial, if unexceptional, English food. *Bibury, Glos. GL7 5NT, tel. 028574/337. 18 rooms, most with private bath. Facilities: restaurant, fishing, gardens. MC, V. Moderate–Expensive.*

Swan Hotel. The Swan is another hotel that promises more than it delivers. The creeper-clad exterior, overlooking the River Coln, suggests something memorable inside, but, though the bedrooms are spacious, they remain faintly drab. Public rooms, too, bear witness to unsympathetic '60s modernization. Probably the best reason to stay here is to wake up to the view of the village outside your window—before the tour buses arrive. *Bibury, Glos. GL7 5NW, tel. 028574/204. 24 rooms with private bath. Facilities: restaurant, bar. MC, V. Moderate–Expensive.*

Burford

From Bibury, take A433 northeast 14.4 km (9 mi).

Burford is not directly on the route from Bibury to Stow-on-the-Wold; to get there you have to swing east. The extra miles are worthwhile, however, if you want to see one of the most beautiful wool churches and visit a half-dozen quality antiques shops strung along the main street of town.

The Church of St. John the Baptist is a late-12th-century Norman church that was transformed over the next 300 years into the Perpendicular building you see today. That's why the chapels and aisles are all at different levels.

Time Out There's a lovely 4-km (2½-mi) country walk east along the Windrush River to Asthall, where you can stop at the **Maytime Inn** for lunch. Ask locally for directions.

Northleach

From Burford take A40 west for 14.4 km (9 mi). From Bibury, follow the back-road signs from outside the Swan Hotel; it's a twisting 8.1 km (5 mi) to Northleach.

Northleach was a medieval wool-trading center on high ground between the valleys of the Coln and the Windrush. The wool church is one of the grandest—and a favorite among brass rubbers.

The Church of St. Peter and St. Paul was built by God-fearing wool merchants, and it looks as though it were made to last forever. Like most other wool churches, it is a Norman building that was rebuilt in the 15th century in the Perpendicular style. There's lots to see here: a 15th-century pulpit, a 14th-century carved baptismal font, and wonderful brasses of wool staplers, their feet resting on wool packs or sheep. For permission to rub brasses, contact the post office or the Tudor house on the Green.

Dining **Old Woolhouse.** Northleach is something of a gastronomic hot spot. The Old Woolhouse, an unpretentious building in the town square, is the kind of place where the chef/owner's personality tends to dominate from the moment you step over the threshold. Choice is limited: There are typically no more than two first courses and three main courses, followed by cheese and dessert. What's more, the cooking is idiosyncratically nouvelle: Most separate vegetable dishes, for example, are outlawed. Red mullet with fennel and a Pernod sauce, and hot foie gras mousse with mushrooms are two new stalwarts. The wines, though overpriced, are first class. *The Square, Northleach, Glos. GL54 3EE, tel. 0451/60366. Reservations (a week or two in advance) essential. Dress: casual. No credit* cards. *Dinner only (lunch sometimes by arrangement); closed Sun. and Mon. Expensive.*

Wickens. Come here for sturdy English cooking enlivened by sophisticated nouvelle touches. Seafood tartlet, beef casserole (more subtle than it sounds), and roast duckling with a plum and Armagnac sauce number among the specialties. Desserts and carefully chosen local cheeses complete your meal. The atmosphere is intimate; you dine in one of a series of small, tastefully decorated rooms. Those who visit the Cotswolds seeking no more than pretty towns and pub grub will be pleasantly surprised. If you're feeling adventurous, order one of the English wines. *Market Place, Northleach, Glos. GL54 3EJ, tel. 0451/60421. Reservations required. Dress: casual/jacket and tie. MC, V. Dinner only; closed Sun. and Mon. Expensive.*

Stow-on-the-Wold

From Northleach take A429 14.4 km (9 mi) north.

Stow-on-the-Wold is an ancient hilltop market town. At over 700 feet, it's the highest town in the Cotswolds. It sits at the junction of seven important roads, but—and this is what makes Stow unique—none runs through the town itself. The 17th-century stone buildings are clustered around a market square as a defense against the wind; if you squint you can imagine yourself back in the Middle Ages, when the town was famous for its fairs. Stow makes a great base for exploring the Cotswolds because it's so centrally located and has all the facilities you would want, including what, at first sight, looks like an antiques shop in every building (hotels and restaurants aside). In fact, Stow is now one of the most important centers of the antiques trade outside of London—and that includes Bath.

St. Edward's Church, in the town center, is Norman with many additions, including a Perpendicular tower dominating the square. The nave has a notable 17th-century Belgian painting of the Crucifixion.

Dining **Wyck Hill House.** The formal surroundings of the Wyck Hill House hotel's restaurant (*see* Lodging, below) provide a satisfying setting for French nouvelle food. If you're in the mood for a fancy night out you shouldn't be disappointed. A favorite appetizer is mousseline of chicken with Roquefort served on a bed of celeriac with a walnut-flavored cream sauce. Entrées include rolled fillets of Dover sole with smoked salmon served in a vermouth-and-wine sauce and garnished with caviar; and medallions of venison served with a pistachio-and-game mousse on a Port wine sauce. *Stow-on-the-Wold, Glos. GL54 1HY, tel. 04541/31936. Reservations required. Jacket and tie required. AE, DC, MC, V. Expensive.*

Mill House. Located 8.1 km (5 mi) east of Stow on B4450 in the village of Kingham, the restaurant of the Mill House hotel is light, somewhat formal, and, above all, upscale. Within its pink walls, accented by voluminous curtains and soft lighting, you'll dine on ambitious nouvelle-inspired dishes such as breast of duck with mango and lime sauce, breast of chicken stuffed with spinach, hot prune and Armagnac soufflé with kirsch-based cream, and hazelnut mousse. *Kingham, Glos. OX7 6UH, tel. 060871/8188). Reservations essential. Jacket and tie required. AE, DC, MC, V. BYOB. Expensive.*

Prince of India. For good-value Indian food, served swiftly and expertly, the centrally located Prince of India is hard to beat. The decor, with its lurid tapestries of bullfighters and assorted Indian scenes, may not be to all tastes, but the sheer value for money may well outweigh aesthetic considerations. *5 Park St., tel. 0451/31198. Dress: casual. Reservations not required. AE, DC, MC, V. Inexpensive.*

Lodging   **Wyck Hill House.** Set in expansive grounds about 3.2 km (2 mi) from town on A424, the Wyck Hill House is one of the most tastefully restored grand manor houses in the country. The cedar-paneled library, high French windows, oriental lamps, plants, and thick carpets show a fine attention to detail, which is matched by the attentive service. The hilltop view of the Windrush Valley is glorious. *Stow-on-the-Wold, Glos. GL54 1HY, tel. 0451/31936. 2 "Cottage Suites" in grounds and 18 rooms with private bath. Facilities: restaurant, bar, conference room, tennis, horseback riding, golf. AE, DC, MC, V. Very Expensive.*

Royalist Hotel. The Royalist is the oldest inn in England, in business since 947 and with an entry in the *Guinness Book of Records* to prove it. In fact, most of today's building is a positive youngster, having been put up only in 1615 (and much altered since). Stone walls and ancient beams still show its antiquity; many rooms have four-poster beds; all are individually decorated. *Digbeth St., Stow-on-the-Wold, Glos. GL54 1BN, tel. 0451/30670. 15 rooms with private bath. Facilities: restaurant, bar, conference room. MC, V. Moderate.*

Unicorn. The mellow stone of the Unicorn encloses a friendly, informal 17th-century hotel with an unpretentious, almost boardinghouse feel to it, despite now belonging to the Crest chain. Steep stairs lead to beamed rooms with bright furnishings. *Sheep St., Stow-on-the-Wold, Glos. GL54 1HQ, tel. 0451/30257. 20 rooms with private bath. Facilities: restaurant, bar, conference room. AE, DC, MC, V. Moderate.*

If you are in search of a good B&B in a bucolic setting, try **Mrs. Berry** (tel. 0451/30141). She has winning ways, a spotless house, and serves immense breakfasts. Her house is located on A424 on the right-hand side of the road as you drive to Burford, about 360 m (400 yds) before the Wyck Hill House.

Cotswolds Excursion

The following towns can all be reached on a one-day excursion from Stow-on-the-Wold. They are listed in the order in which you would reach them on a circular tour.

Bourton-on-the-Water   Kids and grownups who want Things to Do will love Bourton-on-the-Water.

Birdland is a world-famous 17th-century manor house with more than 600 species of birds from around the world, including, as it likes to boast, "the largest colony of penguins outside America." *Rissington Rd. Admission: £2 adults, £1.30 children, £1.50 senior citizens. Open Mar.–Nov., daily 10–6; Dec.–Feb., daily 10:30–4.*

The enterprising owner of Birdland also runs the **Cotswold Motor Museum;** a **Village Life Exhibition;** and the **Oscar Collection of Street Jewellery,** which contains the world's largest collection of vintage advertising signs. It's all under one roof, in an 18th-century water mill. *The Old Mill. Admission: 80p adults, 40p* *children 4–14. Open Feb.–Nov., daily 10–6; closed Dec. and Jan.*

On the opposite side of the High Street you'll find a **Model Railway,** housed in a superior toy shop. *Admission: 90p adults, 75p children 4–15. Open Apr.–Sept. and school holidays, daily 11–5:30; Oct.–Mar., weekends only 11–5:30.*

Finally, play Gulliver in Bourton's most famous attraction, the **Model Village.** It's an exact scale replica of the village, complete with miniature trees, made before World War II by the clearly obsessive landlord of The Old New Inn, behind which the model is located. *High St. Admission: 95p adults, 75p children. Open Easter–Nov., daily 9–7 (or dusk if earlier); Nov.–Mar., daily 10–4.*

Dining **Rose Tree.** Home-style meals, including rack of lamb, pot-roasted venison, and puddings are offered in this pretty cottage bordering the river. *Riverside, Bourton-on-the-Water, tel. 0451/20635. Dress: casual. MC, V. Moderate.*

Lower and Upper Slaughter These are two delightful back-road villages—completely unspoiled except for the tourists searching for an unspoiled village. If you're here in summer, visit in the early morning or evening, when the day-trippers are gone. The short distance (.8 km/½ mi) between the villages makes an ideal walk. Lower Slaughter is neater and prettier, with lovely stone bridges—which is why some people prefer Upper Slaughter.

Lodging **Lower Slaughter Manor.** An idyllic setting, a 17th-century manor house, and a multimillion-pound renovation by new owners have conspired to create one of the most elegant and gracious of the Cotswolds' many luxury hotels. Open fires, enormous sofas, hand-woven carpets, and pink and blue drapes strike sophisticated notes in the handsome public rooms. The bedrooms, many with four-poster beds, are large and tasteful; the restaurant, imposingly formal. The bells from the village church next door add a touch of Olde Englande to the designer chintz. *Lower Slaughter, Glos. GL54 2HP, tel. 0451/20456. 19 rooms with private bath. Facilities: restaurant, bar, conference room, indoor pool, sauna, solarium, croquet, tennis, fishing. AE, DC, MC, V. Very Expensive.*
Lords of the Manor Hotel. A mellow, honey-colored 17th-century one-time rectory, the Lords of the Manor stands in 7 acres of gardens. Ancient trees shield the house; lawns sweep down to the River Eye. Furnishings inside are old-fashioned in a quietly understated way. Floral drapes and hushed pastels predominate. That it is a family-run hotel is evident from the relaxed, friendly service. Two rooms have four-poster beds. *Upper Slaughter, Glos. GL54 2JD, tel. 0451/20243. 15 rooms with private bath. Facilities: restaurant, bar, croquet, fishing. MC, V. Expensive.*

Naunton For being less picturesque than other Cotswold villages, and for committing the unpardonable sin of permitting modern buildings, **Naunton** is blessed with an absence of tourists. The village won the 1981 Bledisloc Cup as Best Kept Village in England. "Most pleasant looking petrol station seen anywhere on the judge's rounds," says the award. "The telephone kiosk [behind the sign to the petrol station] adjoining the bus shelter cut into the face of the old building is ingenious." **Ye Olde Inn** is, despite its name, a good place for pub grub and a pint of anything.

Cotswold Farm Park Cotswold Farm Park is 4.8 km (3 mi) northeast of Guiting Power. Kids will love the rare breeds of farm animals, including the breed of sheep that brought prosperity to the region, and some Iron Age pigs. You're 270 m (900 ft) up—a great setting for walks among the enclosed animals. *Admission: £2 adults, £1 children, £1.50 senior citizens. Open Easter–Sept., daily 10:30–6.*

Sudeley Castle If your schedule is crowded, go directly from Naunton or the Cotswold Farm Park to Stanton (*see* below). But if time permits, spend an hour in **Winchcombe**, stopping at **Sudeley Castle** (.8 km/½ mi southeast of Winchcombe) on the way.

The fortified 14th-century manor house contains the tomb of Catherine Parr (1512–48), the sixth queen of Henry VIII. The king was Catherine's third husband—her second having died only months before the royal wedding. In the same year that Henry died, Catherine married a former lover, Thomas Seymour, who owned Sudeley Castle—and a year later she herself died in childbirth. Catherine of Aragon stayed here; so did Anne Boleyn. Elizabeth I lived here as a child. The modern **Queen's Garden** is laid out in authentic Tudor style. Inside, you'll find a wonderful collection of toys and dolls; the 18th-century Aubusson tapestries that belonged to Marie Antoinette; and paintings by Constable, Turner, Rubens, and Van Dyke. *Admission: £3.75 adults, £1.95 children 5–16, £3.25 senior citizens. Open Easter–Oct., daily 11–5.*

Winchcombe St. Peter's is a fine Perpendicular-style church, built in 1465, with a great gilded weathercock on top of the tower, and some 40 grotesque gargoyle waterspouts around the facade. The bullet marks are from the Civil War. The framed altar cloth behind blue curtains on the north wall is said to have been made by Catherine of Aragon. Look for the kneeling effigy of Thomas Williams of Corndean (d. 1636) in the chancel—he's staring at a space where his wife's image used to be: she remarried and is spending eternity with her second husband.

The church is on Queen Square. Opposite is the **Jacobean House** (1619), which is attributed to Inigo Jones and was restored in 1876. Exit the church, turn left, then right on Vineyard Street, which has some lovely old cottages running down to the river. It's also called Duck Street because of the witches who had their heads held under the water. If instead of turning right on Vineyard, you continue straight, you'll come to the Town Hall, where you can put your kids in the stocks. The Tourist Information Centre is here.

Kids will also enjoy the **Railway Museum** (admission: £1.25 adults, 25p children; open daily 1–6 or dusk if earlier). At **Toddington,** 6.4 km (4 mi) away, you can tour the disused train station (admission: 40p adults, 20p children). You can also ride on a steam train, a proud survivor from the once-mighty Great Western Railway, a precursor of the very much less-than-mighty British Rail (tel. 0242/69405; trains operate Sun., Easter–Oct.).

The Cotswold Way runs south from Winchcombe to Belas Knap and then circles back to Cleeve Hill on A46, 3.2 km (2 mi) south of Winchcombe. You'll need an extra day for this, but if you like walking, this is one of the most memorable hikes you can make. After passing a Stone Age burial mound—the finest in the Cotswolds—you'll continue to **Cleeve Common,** the highest point in the Cotswolds, which has breathtaking views. The bleak open wolds give you a wonderful sense of what the Cotswolds were like before the Enclosure Acts.

About 2 km (1 mi) north of Winchcombe, on A46, turn left to **Greet** and greet the potters who sell their wares at **Winchcombe Pottery.**

Stanton From Winchcombe, take A46 north about 8 km (5 mi), and look for signs on the right to **Stanton** (north of Stanway, and west of Snowshill).

With a terrain of steep pastures and much unclaimed marshland, there was nothing at Stanton to attract speculators and profiteers. Any move to commercialize the village was stopped in 1908, when Philip Sidney Stott, a builder of cotton mills, bought virtually the entire village. The restoration work that followed his arrival was tastefully done, and the village today seems unchanged from the 17th century. The result is a village that has kept its integrity, and that wins the Mike Spring award as the most perfect, unspoiled village in the Cotswolds. It's likely to stay that way, too.

Time Out Above the town is **Mount Inn,** a newish stone building with not much atmosphere, but some outdoor tables with a splendid view. A good bet for drinks or lunch.

Arrange with the owners of the **Vine** (*see* Lodging, below) to saddle up for a ride through the surrounding countryside.

The Church of Saint Michael and All Angels' is a 15th-century version of a Norman church, with a rare Decorated (1375) pulpit and a splendid font decorated with hares. The poppyheads on the medieval benches at the back of the nave are deeply ringed with marks of the chains of obedient sheepdogs, who sat through sermons with their masters.

Lodging **The Vine.** There is only one place to stay in Stanton, and this is it. It's a B&B, housed in a substantial vine-covered house at the junction of the village's only two streets. The owners, the Gabbs, have horses and can take you on rides through the glorious countryside. *Stanton, nr. Broadway, Glos. WR12 7NE, tel. 088673/250. 5 rooms, 2 with showers. No credit cards. Inexpensive.*

Buckland Just over 3 km (2 mi) south of the bustle of Broadway is the small, quiet village of Buckland. **St. Michael's Church** is Early English, with three panels of 15th-century glass releaded by William Morris, and some humorous gargoyles. **Buckland Rectory,** still in use, is the oldest, best-preserved parsonage in England. The main reason to visit Buckland, however, is to dine or lodge at the Manor.

Dining and Lodging **Buckland Manor.** Surely not *another* glorious old Cotswold manor house hotel? Yes, indeed. And this one, as everyone seems to agree, is the best of all, an old honey-colored house that sits among 4 ha (10 acres) of gardens and fields next to the village church. Inside, fine china, antiques, and crystal complement the exposed beams, dark paneling, and open fires to create a mood that is both formal and relaxed. The rooms are decorated with taste and great attention to detail. The restaurant offers sophisticated British nouvelle food that makes good use of fresh local produce. *Buckland, Glos. WR12 7LY, tel. 0836/852626. 10 rooms with private bath. Facilities: restaurant (reservations required), bar, heated outdoor pool, tennis, croquet, horseback riding, putting. Closed 3 wks from mid-Jan. MC, V. Very Expensive.*

Broadway   Just over 3 km (2 mi) north of Buckland is the popular resort town of **Broadway,** so named for its single main street. Most houses were built in the 17th and 18th centuries, when Broadway was an important staging post. The coming of the railway led to its decline. It was rediscovered in the late 19th century by William Morris and restored under his influence. It became an artists' colony before it was discovered by people like you and me.

What you will do in Broadway is walk down one side—at a faster pace, probably, than the traffic—and then back up the other, browsing in antiques stores and gift shops, and stopping for lunch or drinks in any of several restaurants and pubs. The quality of goods is geared more to the package-tour trade than it is, say, in Stow-on-the-Wold, but there's something to buy— Paddington dolls, lady mice, model Cotswold cottages, woolens, cashmeres—for every budget and taste.

If you've had enough sightseeing for a day, take A44 directly back to Stow-on-the-Wold. Just west of Broadway, A44 climbs to **Broadway Tower,** the second highest point in the Cotswolds. There's a park here for lovely walks and a 12-county view.

Dining   **Lygon Arms.** If you want a serious lunch, stop in the hotel's Great Hall Restaurant, and nibble on quail eggs in a royal hunting lodge atmosphere, complete with rich wood paneling and red barrel-vault ceiling—a real conversation piece. *Broadway, Worcs. WR12 7DU, tel. 0386/852255. Reservations required. Jacket and tie required. AE, DC, MC, V. Very Expensive.*
Hunter's Lodge. The Hunter's Lodge prides itself on providing a relaxed atmosphere in which to enjoy just a coffee—or to go the whole hog and have a full-blown feast. The cuisine is predominantly traditional English. Try baby guinea fowl, Dover sole, or noisettes of Highland venison. Fixed-price lunches help keep costs low. *High St., Broadway, Worcs. WR12 7DT, tel. 0386/853247. Dress: casual. AE, DC, MC, V. Closed Sun. for dinner and Mon. Expensive.*

Lodging   **Lygon Arms.** The Lygon Arms is a distinguished old hotel, as famous as the town. Both Charles I and Oliver Cromwell stayed here during the Civil War. Every year hundreds of groomed riders use the courtyard as the starting point for the North Cotswold Hunt. With so much expansion—there's a new wing and a newer wing—the Lygon Arms is less an inn than a luxury hotel on an inn-theme. Rooms in the modern wing are tasteful but conventional, some with unattractive views. Ask for Room 17 or something similar. Room 8 is nice, and so are rooms with four-poster beds. Best bet are the very expensive rooms in the old section; the smaller rooms are disappointing for the price. As for staying in Broadway: after a diet of stone cottages and sheep, an hour of window shopping can be fun—but not everyone will want to spend the night. *Broadway, Worcs. WR12 7DU, tel. 0386/852255. 5 suites and 58 rooms with private bath. Facilities: Goblet's wine bar, restaurant, tennis, snooker, conference room. AE, DC, MC, V. Very Expensive.*

Broadway Hotel. This is a 150-year-old half-timbered and stone house with cheerful modern furnishings and more character than a motel. Stick to rooms in the old inn. *The Green, Broadway, Worcs. WR12 7DU, tel. 0836/852401. 24 rooms, 20 with private bath. Facilities: restaurant, bar, conference room. AE, DC, MC, V. Moderate.*

Snowshill   The most scenic route back to Stow-on-the-Wold—indeed, one of the loveliest drives in the Cotswolds—is along a narrow country road from Broadway to Snowshill ("Snozzle" to the locals), Taddington, and Ford, then east on B4077.

The main attraction of this secluded village is **Snowshill Manor,** a 16th- and 17th-century manor house. Charles Wade bought it in 1919 and filled it with everything from toys to musical instruments, old clocks, farm carts, dead beetles, and butterflies. He gave it to the National Trust, which left it just as they found it. *Admission: £2.80 adults, £1.40 children. Open Apr. and Oct., weekends 11–1 and 2–5; May–Sept., weekends 11–1 and 2–6.*

Chipping Campden   Chipping Campden is not directly on our route, but it's too lovely to miss, should you have time to visit en route from Broadway or Stow-on-the-Wold to Stratford-upon-Avon.

"Chipping" means "market"—and by 1247, Chipping Campden had them every week. In the 14th century it was a major wool-market center, whose wealthy merchants built the Perpendicular church (**St. James**) and houses that make the town so special. The church has a handsome tower and some outstanding brasses.

High Street has several interesting craft and antiques shops, and a vitality that doesn't diminish at the end of the tourist season. Historian G. M. Trevelyan called it "the most beautiful village street in England."

If you care about gardens, stop at **Hidcote Manor Garden,** a National Trust Property north of town en route to Stratford-upon-Avon. These world-famous gardens were one of the first to group plants in "rooms," using hedges as walls—each room devoted to a particular color, species or combination of species. *Admission: £2.90 adults, £1.45 children. Open Easter–Oct., Mon., Wed., Thurs., and weekends 11–7.*

Lodging   **Noel Arms.** This is the oldest inn in town, built in the 14th century. In 1650, after the Battle of Worcester, Charles II, it is said, stayed here, when he was Prince of Wales. The mood is suitably timeworn, the furnishings friendly and old-fashioned, particularly in the older wing. There are four-poster beds in some rooms. *High St., Chipping Campden, Glos. GL55 6AT, tel. 0386/840317. 18 rooms with private bath. Facilities: restaurant, bar. MC, V. Moderate.*

Stratford-upon-Avon

From Stow-on-the-Wold take A429 north 20.8 km (13 mi), then take A34 12.8 km (8 mi) to **Stratford-upon-Avon,** the most popular destination in Britain after London. More than a half million tourists parade through its streets every year, visiting the Bard's birthplace and taking in a play at the Royal Shakespeare Theatre. Many Americans come prepared to sacrifice an evening in the name of Culture—as they would at home—and come away surprised at the wonderful fun a good Shakespeare pro-

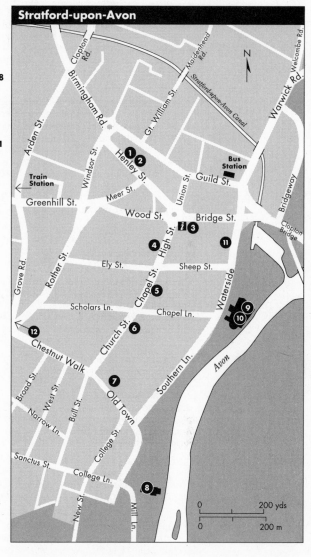

Stratford-upon-Avon

duction can be. It's only a half-hour drive from Stratford to Broadway, or 40 minutes to Stow-on-the-Wold, so you don't have to spend the night in Bardland; but should you decide to stay, you have a whole folio of hotels to choose from.

Mid-16th-century Stratford was a prosperous market town. People who wanted to rise in the world came here from the surrounding farms. One was John Shakespeare, who succeeded beyond his dreams, first as a maker of gloves, and then as a justice of peace and mayor. He had a son named William who did quite well for himself, too. John's wife, Mary, came from one of the oldest families in the region, so the image of Will as an untutored country lad is just not true.

Begin your tour where Shakespeare began his life (1564), in a half-timbered house on partly pedestrianized Henley Street, and called, naturally enough, **Shakespeare's Birthplace.** The houses on either side were destroyed to reduce the chances of fire. *Admission: £1.70 adults, 70p children. Open Easter–Oct., Mon.–Sat. 9–6, Sun. 10–6; Nov.–Easter, Mon.–Sat. 9–4:30, Sun. 1:30–4:30.*

The house is owned by the Shakespeare Birthplace Trust, whose headquarters, the **Shakespeare Centre,** are next door. The Trust owns five of the most important Shakespearean buildings in and around Stratford: the Birthplace, New Place (Nash's House), Hall's Croft, Anne Hathaway's Cottage, and Mary Arden's House and the Shakespeare Countryside Museum. If you have any serious interest in the man, it is worth seeing them all. You can buy a joint ticket (£5 adults, £2 children) to all five at any of the properties. Otherwise, just visit whichever interest you most, paying separately each time.

Turn left from the house and continue down Henley Street. The Tourist Information Centre is at the major crossing. Turn left on Bridge Street. You'll pass some lovely Shakespeare-period houses as you approach Clopton Bridge over the River Avon.

Turn right on Waterside (before the bridge). On your right is **Heritage Theatre,** the home of the **World of Shakespeare,** where you can submit to a continuous, 30-minute multimedia introduction to Elizabethan England. *Admission: £2.25 adults, £1.75 children and senior citizens. Open year-round, daily 9–5.*

Walk through the **Bancroft Gardens** (lit at night), watched over by a statue of the Bard surrounded by Hamlet, Lady Macbeth, Falstaff, and Prince Hal; and walk over to the **Royal Shakespeare Theatre.** No, this was not the Globe—that was in London, and burned down. The original Stratford theater was built in 1874. It was destroyed in a 1926 fire and rebuilt in 1932. You should have reserved seats, but it's sometimes possible to get them on the day of a performance (*see* The Arts, below).

Take the river path to the **Brass Rubbing Centre,** where you can make your own souvenirs. *Admission free. Rubbing charges (includes materials and instruction): 50p–£6. Open Apr.–Sept., daily 10–6; Oct., daily 10–4; closed winter.*

Continue to **Holy Trinity Church.** It was here that Shakespeare was baptized and buried. The 12 trees, as you approach from the north, are said to represent the 12 tribes of Israel; the 11 on the right, the 11 faithful apostles; and the one slightly back, Mathias, who took the place of Judas. The slab covering Shakespeare's grave was replaced a century ago, after the footsteps of tourists had almost obliterated the words on it. Look for the bust of Shakespeare in a monument in the north chancel wall (on your left as you face the altar)—it's believed to be the most authentic known portrait of the Bard. The charnel house—did it inspire the one in *Romeo and Juliet?*—is behind the north wall. Old bones were moved to make room for new ones—which is probably why Shakespeare wrote on his tomb, "And curst be he that moves my bones." Of course, he may also have wanted to prevent his wife, Anne—who lived seven years after his death—from spending eternity beside him.

Leave by the north door and bear left on Old Town Road to **Hall's Croft,** on the right. It's another of the Shakespeare Birthplace Trust buildings. It was here that Dr. John Hall lived with Shakespeare's daughter Suzanna. He had no medical degree, but that wasn't expected then. The timber-framed, late-16th-century house is carefully restored and gives you a good sense of life in a middle-class Tudor home. The enclosed gardens are authentic, too, though replanted during restorations in 1950. *Admission: £1.10 adults, 50p children. Open Easter–Oct., Mon.–Sat. 9–6, Sun. 10–6; Nov.–Easter, Mon.–Sat. 10–6, closed Sun.*

Continue down Old Town Road, and turn right on Church Street. On your right, behind a row of almshouses, is the **King's New Grammar School,** closed to the public, where Shakespeare learned "small Latin and less Greek." The sons of the most prominent men went to the same free grammar school as everyone else. The curriculum bore no relation to life after school; it was meant to turn out clerks for church positions, and little was taught but Latin. Every weekday, summer and winter, Shakespeare went here from 7 in the morning—6 in summer—to 5 at night, with a two-hour midday break to go home for dinner.

Continue down Church Street. On your right, on the corner of Chapel Lane, is the 15th-century Guild Chapel, which has a famous fresco of the *Last Judgment* above the chancel arch.

Church Street turns into Chapel Street. On your right is **New Place,** also a Shakespeare Birthplace Trust property. Shakespeare, now rich and famous, bought the house in 1597 and realized his father's dream of becoming a gentleman. If your name is Gastrell, don't tell anyone: in 1759, a neighboring clergyman named Francis Gastrell was so furious at the tourists trooping through that he had New Place torn down. The town fathers were so angry, they ordered that no one with that name could ever live there again. Only the cellar steps remain. The foundations are planted with an Elizabethan-style garden containing all the plants and shrubs mentioned in Shakespeare's plays. *Admission: £1.10 adults, 50p children. Open Easter–Oct., Mon.–Sat. 9–6, Sun. 10–6; Nov.–Easter, Mon.–Sat. 10–6, closed Sun.*

Time Out   The bar of the **Falcon Hotel** (Sheep St.), opposite New Place, is a fine place for some sustaining pub food and a pint of whatever takes your fancy.

Continue down Chapel Street, which turns into High Street. On the left is the **Harvard House.** It was built in 1576 by a butcher and alderman (local magistrate) named Thomas Rogers. His daughter Katherine was the mother of John Harvard, one of the founders of Harvard College.

You can drive to **Anne Hathaway's Cottage,** or take the lovely 1.6-km (1-mi) walk that the 18-year-old Shakespeare took to woo (or be wooed by) the 25-year-old Anne. From Harvard House, turn right on High Street, and a quick right again on Ely Street. Where the street ends, turn left on Rother Street. Where Rother intersects with Grove Road, there's a marked path leading to the cottage. Anne lived in this thatched cottage until Will married her in 1582. She was pregnant at the time, and some iconoclasts, like Anthony Burgess, delight in the notion that Anne did hath-her-way, and that Shakespeare was forced to act against his Will. Controversy still rages over the meaning of the rushed marriage. It was customary for couples to proclaim banns on three Sundays so that anyone who objected could be heard. The alternative was to get a special license and to post a bond to indemnify the court if objections were made later. Two farmer friends of Anne's father posted such a bond—were they also holding a shotgun to young Will? Anne may have been a Puritan, who viewed actors not just with contempt but as threats to salvation. If that's the case, it's no wonder that Will skipped town and lived alone in London for 20 years in hired lodgings. Perhaps, though, he simply left because Stratford was too small for him, as the village of Shottery had been too small for his ambitious father. *Admission: £1.60 adults, 60p children. Open Easter–Oct., Mon.–Sat. 9–6, Sun. 10–6; Nov.–Easter, Mon.–Sat. 9–4:30, Sun. 1:30–4:30.*

Excursions from Stratford-upon-Avon

Mary Arden's House (Wilmcote, north of Stratford off A34) is where Shakespeare's mother lived before her marriage. It, too, belongs to the Shakespeare Birthplace Trust. It was still used as a farmhouse until the 1930s, and so has seen little modernization. Mary was the youngest of eight. Before marrying John she would have slept on the kitchen or living-room floor with the servants. Getting married meant, among other things, having a bed. *Admission: £1.60 adults, 70p children. Open Easter–Oct., Mon.–Sat. 9–6, Sun. 10–6; Nov.–Easter, Mon.–Sat. 9–4:30.*

Warwick Castle (14.4 km/9 mi north on A46) is a great 14th-century castle, the most impressive in England after Windsor, with great towers and turrets on a steep rock over the Avon. You'll need two hours to tour some 30 state rooms (a number with tasteless waxworks, supposedly figures from an Edwardian country weekend), visit the grisly dungeons, and explore the gardens. *Admission: £4.50 adults, £3 children, £3.50 senior citizens (special family rates also available). Open Mar.–Oct., daily 10–5:30; Nov.–Feb., daily 10–4:30.*

Charlecote Park (6.4 km/4 mi east of Stratford off B4086) is an Elizabethan mansion in a 91.2-ha (228-acre) park. It was here, it is said, that Shakespeare poached deer, for which he was fined by the owner and local magistrate, Sir Thomas Lucy. Shakespeare got even by turning Lucy into Justice Shallow in *Henry IV, Part II*, and *The Merry Wives of Windsor*. The main buildings were greatly altered in the mid-19th century. The gardens were laid out by Lancelot Brown, nicknamed "Capability," in 1760. Brown (1716–83) designed some Palladian country houses but won lasting fame as a landscape gardener who broke away from the geometric formality that had hitherto been imposed on gardens, and created wide expanses of lawns, clumps of trees, and serpentine lakes. Kids will love the collection of carriages in the coach house. *Admission: £2.60 adults, £1.30 children (special family rates also available). Open Easter–Oct., Tues., Wed., and Fri.–Sun.*

Dining

Billesley Manor. Stylish French nouvellish dishes, such as beetroot consommé and crab, smoked salmon, and fresh salmon with dill mayonnaise, are served in the formal restaurant of the Billesley Manor hotel. Prices can be high, especially for the wines, but standards are reliable. The hotel is located 6.4 km (4 mi) west of Stratford on A422. *Billesley, tel. 0789/400888. Reservations required. Jacket and tie required. AE, DC, MC, V. Expensive.*

Chase Hotel. Modern British dishes are served with panache in the restaurant of the Victorian Gothic Chase Hotel. The mood is formal, but not intimidatingly so. The hotel stands some miles outside Stratford off A422. *Banbury Rd., Ettington, tel. 0789/740000. Reservations required. Jacket and tie required. AE, V. Closed Sat. lunch and Sun. dinner, and Christmas and New Year's. Expensive.*

Shepherd's. This is the restaurant of the Stratford House Hotel, located in the town center. The decor is light and airy, with an almost Middle Eastern touch to it. The food is unequivocally nouvelle: flaked chicken with mango and curried mayonnaise or rack of lamb with mint cream sauce, for example. *Sheep St., tel. 0789/68233. Reservations required. Jacket and tie required. AE, DC, MC, V. Closed Sun. dinner and Mon. Moderate–Expensive.*

Marlowe's Elizabethan Room. The oak-paneled walls of this second-floor restaurant in the town center establish a satisfactorily Tudorish atmosphere. Specialties are predominantly English. Try medallion of beef or any of the duck and lamb dishes. It's a good place for either pre- or posttheater dining. *18 High St., tel. 0789/204999. Reservations advised. Dress: casual. AE, DC, MC, V. Moderate.*

Lodging

Billesley Manor. A peaceful, gabled, 16th-century manor house in splendid grounds, the Billesley Manor, 6.4 km (4 mi) west of Stratford on A422, offers your best chance of a memorable night in Shakespeare country. Ask for one of the large rooms in the main house, some with four-poster beds. *Billesley, Warwks. B4G 6NF, tel. 0789/400888. 41 rooms with private bath. Facilities: restaurant, bar, indoor pool, tennis. AE, DC, MC, V. Expensive.*

Chase Hotel. A peacefully rural location outside the village of Ettington off A422 is the setting for this sturdy Victorian hotel. Magnificent views, substantial comforts, and a fine restaurant make it a reliable choice. *Banbury Rd., Ettington, Warwks. CV37 7NZ, tel. 0789/740000. 12 rooms with private bath. Facilities: restaurant, bar, garden. AE, MC, V. Expensive.*

Moat House International. If you value the convenience and comforts of a modern, centrally located chain hotel, the brick Moat House is more than adequate. Don't expect much in the way of atmosphere (the new, 650-space parking lot opposite is not an advantage). *Bridgefoot, Stratford-upon-Avon, Warwks. CV37 6YR, tel. 0789/414411. 249 rooms with private bath. Facilities: 2 restaurants, nightclub. AE, DC, MC, V. Expensive.*

Shakespeare. Of hotels actually in Stratford, this Trusthouse Forte property is about the best. The black-and-white exterior is newer than it looks, and a certain functional quality is evident inside the building, especially in some of the newer, smaller rooms. But for reliable standards and just a little authentic Stratford atmosphere, this hotel is not a bad bet. *Chapel St., Stratford-upon-Avon, Warwks. CV37 6ER, tel. 0789/294771. 70 rooms with private bath. Facilities: 2 restaurants, bar, conference room. AE, DC, MC, V. Expensive.*

White Swan. There's plenty of Ye Olde Trusthouse Forte atmosphere in this slightly less expensive spot facing the marketplace. Again, a functional quality is apparent in many rooms, which are still acceptable for overnighting. Those with four-poster beds are largest. The public rooms, which have ceiling beams, are extensive. *Rother St., Stratford-upon-Avon,*

Warwks. CV37 6NH, tel. 0789/297022. 42 rooms with private bath. Facilities: restaurant, bar, conference room. AE, DC, MC, V. Moderate.

On to Woodstock Your tour ends at Stratford-upon-Avon, a 2½-hour drive to London. If you want to extend your trip by another day, drive south on A34 (the main road back to London; follow the signs to Oxford) to the village of **Woodstock** to visit **Blenheim Palace,** one of England's greatest stately mansions, where Winston Churchill was born, and where you can visit his modest grave. Two of England's most famous inns are in Woodstock, the **Bear** (Woodstock, Oxfords. OX7 2SZ, tel. 0993/811511; Expensive); and **Feathers** (Market Street, Woodstock, Oxfords. OX7 2SZ, tel. 0993/812291; Expensive).

From Woodstock, it's only a short drive to **Oxford,** where you can tour the venerable colleges and chapels of one of the world's most famous universities. If time permits, stop at **Windsor Castle** en route back to London, and send our regards to the Queen.

What to See and Do with Children

Among the sights that will pique children's imaginations are the effigies of medieval knights in armor in various churches and cathedrals, particularly in Winchester, Wells, and Salisbury, King Arthur's Round Table in Winchester, and the costume and carriage museums at Bath. Most of the cathedrals and parish churches along the route have memorial brasses, which children (and adults) can rub for a small fee. The process is as simple as putting a coin beneath a piece of thin paper and rubbing with a pencil until the image comes through. Many churches sell equipment, but any art store will sell you masking tape, drafting paper, and a wax lumber crayon, and explain how to get started.

For action, try a back-road bike ride through the Cotswolds; the caverns, antique pinball machines, and wax figures at Wookey Hole, near Wells, and the wildlife park at Longleat.

The Arts

Bath Nothing could be more pleasant than an opera or a play at the historic **Theatre Royal** (tel. 0225/65065). Try to get seats while you're in London, or before you leave home. A good ticket agency is **Tickets** (Kingston House, Pierrepont St., tel. 0225/66541).

The internationally famous **Bath Festival** runs from late May through early June and features everything from choral music to opera and jazz. Get tickets when you reserve your hotel room.

Stratford-upon-Avon The **Royal Shakespeare Theatre** season runs from mid-April through December. Tickets are on sale from late March through **Keith Prowse & Co. Ltd.** (234 West 44th St., New York, NY 10036, tel. 212/398–1430 or 800/223–4446); and **Edwards and Edwards** (1 Times Sq., New York, NY 10036, tel. 212/944–0290 or 800/223–6108; for ticket information in Stratford, call 0789/69191; for reservations, tel. 0789/295623).

The Royal Shakespeare Company also performs at **The Other Place** (Southern La., tel. for information: 0789/69191; for reservations: 0789/295623). Plays include new musicals and dramas on their way to London's West End.

3 **Germany**

Heidelberg, the Romantic Road, Munich, and the Alps

Introduction

People who speak of romantic Germany are usually thinking of the south, with the ancient university town of Heidelberg, the winding Neckar Valley, the Romantic Road, and the fortified medieval town of Rothenburg ob der Tauber, filled with gabled houses and narrow, cobbled streets. It also includes Munich, a cosmopolitan city with the feel of a small town; Garmisch-Partenkirchen, Germany's most complete four-season resort and the most convenient and comfortable base for excursions into the Bavarian Alps; and the fairyland castles of Ludwig II.

Highlights

Heidelberg—the heart of German romanticism.

The Romantic Road, with two of Europe's most perfect medieval towns—Rothenburg and Dinkelsbühl.

Munich, capital of Bavaria.

The fantastic castles of mad King Ludwig II.

The breathtaking scenery of the German Alps, including the country's highest peak, the Zugspitze.

Before You Go

Government Tourist Offices

In the U.S. Contact the German National Tourist Office at 747 Third Avenue, New York, NY 10017, tel. 212/308–3300; or 444 South Flower Street, Suite 2230, Los Angeles, CA 90017, tel. 213/688–7332.

In Canada Box 417, 2 Fundy, Place Bonaventure, Montreal H5A 1B8, tel. 514/878–9885.

In the U.K. Nightingale House, 65 Curzon Street, London W1Y 7PE, England, tel. 071/495–3990.

When to Go

The tourist season in Germany runs from May to late October, when the weather is at its best. In addition to many tourist events, this period has hundreds of folk festivals. The winter sports season in the Bavarian Alps runs from Christmas to mid-March. Prices everywhere are generally higher during the summer, so you may find considerable advantages in visiting out of season. Most resorts offer out-of-season *(Zwischensaison)* and "edge-of-season" *(Nebensaison)* rates, and tourist offices can provide lists of hotels offering special low-price inclusive weekly packages *(Pauschalangebote)*. Similarly, many winter resorts offer lower rates for the periods immediately before and after the high season *(Weisse Wochen,* or "white weeks"). The other advantage of out-of-season travel is that crowds are very much less in evidence. The disadvantages of visiting out of season, especially in winter, are that the weather, which is generally good in summer, is often cold and gloomy, and many tourist attractions, especially in rural areas, are closed.

Special Events

January: International Winter Sports Week, Garmisch-Partenkirchen
March (early): International Fashion Fair, Munich
Mid-June–mid-September: Augsburg Opera and Operetta Festival
June: Munich Film Festival
June–July: "Der Meistertrunk" Festival, Rothenburg
July: Munich Opera Festival and "Kinderzeche" Festival, Dinkelsbühl
August: Heidelberg Open-air Theater
Late September–early October: Munich Oktoberfest (two weeks of beer drinking, dancing, and entertainment)

Currency

The units of currency in Germany are the Deutschmark (DM) and the pfennig (pf). The bills are DM 10, 20, 50, 500, and 1,000. Coins are DM1, 2, and 5; and 1, 2, 5, 10, and 50 pf. At press time (spring 1990) the exchange rate was about DM1.80 to the U.S. dollar, DM1.45 to the Canadian dollar, and DM2.80 to the pound sterling.

Customs

On Arrival There are three levels of duty-free allowance for visitors to West Germany.

Entering West Germany from a non-European country, you are allowed (1) 400 cigarettes or 100 cigars or 500 g (17.5 oz) of tobacco, plus (2) 1 liter of spirits more than 22% proof or 2 liters spirits less than 22% proof, plus (3) 2 liters of wine, plus (4) 50 g (1.75 oz) of perfume and ¼ liter of toilet water, plus (5) other goods to the value of DM 115.

Entering West Germany from a country belonging to the EC, you are allowed (1) 200 cigarettes (300 if not bought in a duty-free shop) or 75 cigars or 400 g (14 oz) of tobacco, plus (2) 1 liter of spirits more than 22% proof (1.5 liters if not bought in a duty-free shop) or 3 liters of spirits less than 22% proof, plus (3) 5 liters of wine, plus (4) 75 g (2.6 oz) of perfume and ⅓ liter of toilet water, plus (5) other goods to the value of DM 780.

Entering Germany from a European country not belonging to the EC (Austria or Switzerland, for example), you are allowed (1) 200 cigarettes or 50 cigars or 250 g (8.75 oz) of tobacco, plus (2) 1 liter of spirits more than 22% proof or 2 liters of spirits less than 22% proof, plus (3) 2 liters of wine, plus (4) 50 g (1.75 oz) of perfume and ¼ liter of toilet water, plus (5) other goods to the value of DM 115.

Tobacco and alcohol allowances are for visitors age 17 and over. Other items intended for personal use may be imported and exported freely. There are no restrictions on the import and export of West German currency.

Language

The Germans are great linguists, and English is spoken in virtually all hotels, restaurants, airports and stations, museums, and other places of interest. However, English is not always widely spoken in rural areas.

If you speak some German, you may find some regional dialects hard to follow, particularly in Bavaria. At the same time, however, all Germans can speak "high," or standard, German; even in the backwoods of Bavaria, the locals can alternate between dialect and standard German at will.

Arriving and Departing

By Plane

From North America
Because the air routes between North America and Germany are heavily traveled, the passenger has many airlines and fares to choose from. But fares change with stunning rapidity, so consult your travel agent on what bargains are currently available.

The Airlines
The U.S. airlines that serve Germany are **Northwest Airlines** (tel. 800/447–4747); **Delta** (tel. 800/241–4141); **TWA** (tel. 800/892–4141); **Pan Am** (tel. 800/221–1111); and **American Airlines** (tel. 800/433–7300). **Lufthansa** (tel. 800/645–3880) is the West German national airline.

From Britain
British Airways and **Lufthansa** are the main airlines flying from London to Germany.

For reservations and information: **British Airways** (tel. 081/897–4000); **Air Europe** (tel. 0345/444737); **Air UK** (tel. 0345/666777); **Lufthansa** (tel. 071/408–0442); **Pan Am** (tel. 071/409–0688); **Connectair** (tel. 0293/862971); **GTF** (tel. 071/229–2474).

By Train

British Rail operates up to 10 services a day to West Germany under its Rail Europe banner. Eight of the departures are from Victoria (via the Dover–Oostende ferry or jetfoil) with the other two from Liverpool Street (via Harwich–Hook of Holland).

By Bus

From Britain the fastest service is by **Europabus,** which has up to three departures a day from London's Victoria coach station. The buses cross the Channel on Sealink's Dover–Zeebrugge ferry service and then drive via the Netherlands and Belgium to Munich (22¾ hours).

Bookings can also be made through **Transline** (tel. 0708/864911), which runs a service to 35 smaller towns in West Germany.

By Car

British motorists are advised to acquire a green card from their insurance companies. This gives comprehensive insurance coverage for driving in Germany. The most comprehensive breakdown insurance and vehicle and personal security coverage is sold by the **Automobile Association** (AA) in its Five Star scheme.

Getting Around

By Car

Find a car-rental company that will let you pick up your car at Frankfurt Airport and return it to Munich Airport with no additional drop-off charges.

Darwin would have had a field day with the German Autobahns. The experience of cruising along at 112 kph (70 mph) and having a car going twice as fast screech on its brakes only inches from your rear bumper is something you won't quickly forget. Always stay to the right (except when passing), keep your cool, and remind yourself that the Germans drive by different rules. (At home we call it madness.)

By Public Transportation

If you plan to travel through Europe, get a **Eurail Pass,** valid for unlimited travel in 16 countries, either first- or second-class, for 7, 14, 21, or 30 days. Youths from 12 to 22, or students under 27, can get the less expensive **Eurail Youthpass.** All Eurail tickets must be purchased before you leave home. If your travel is limited to Germany, you have a choice: You can either buy a German Rail Pass, in dollars, before you leave, or you can buy a German Rail Tourist Card in West Germany. They are both valid for 4, 9, or 16 days, but the price can vary by a few dollars, depending on the exchange rate. A comparison is a good idea. You can also buy a Youth Pass, which, unlike the other two, restricts you to second-class travel. To qualify, you must be under age 26. The passes are valid on all trains and on Europa buses along the Romantic Road. The buses have reserved seats and attendants, and make one trip daily in each direction between Frankfurt, the Romantic Road, Munich, and Garmisch-Partenkirchen. In addition to bus and train privileges, the tourist card lets you borrow bicycles at one train station and return them to another.

German Federal Railroad (Germanrail or DB—Deutschebundesbahn) offices are located in: *New York* (747 Third Ave., New York, NY 10017, tel. 212/308–3100); *Boston* (625 Statler Office Bldg., Boston, MA 06116, tel. 617/542–0577); *Chicago* (9575 W. Higgins Rd., Rosemont, IL 60018, tel. 312/692–4209); *Houston* (13101 Northwest Fwy., Houston, TX 77040, tel. 713/462–6935); *Los Angeles* (11933 Wiltshire Blvd., Los Angeles, CA 90025, tel. 213/479–2772); *San Francisco* (442 Post St., San Francisco, CA 94102, tel. 415/981–5517); *Denver* (8000 Gerard St., Suite 518 South, Denver, CO 80231, tel. 303/695–7715).

All major towns on the itinerary can be reached by public transportation. Trains leave almost every hour from Frankfurt to Heidelberg. The trip takes about 60 minutes. A train goes from Heidelberg to Rothenburg (along the Romantic Road), but the Romantic Road Bus is more direct. By train, you need to change at Würzburg or Heilbronn and Steinach. The train trip takes about 3½ hours. The bus ride direct from Heidelberg to Rothenburg takes about an hour longer. Again, you could take the train or the Romantic Road Bus from Rothenburg to Munich, but the bus is preferable. Both train and bus take about 4½ hours. By train, however, you need to change at Ansbach.

From Munich to Garmisch-Partenkirchen there's train service almost every hour. The trip takes about 90 minutes. Tour buses leave daily in summer from Garmisch to the Royal Castles.

Essential Information

Important Addresses and Numbers

Tourist Information
The main regional tourist office for this itinerary is the Upper Bavarian Regional Tourist Office (Fremdenverkehrsverband Munchen/Oberbayern) at Sonnenstrasse 10, Munich, near the Karlsplatz (tel. 089/597–347). The local tourist-information offices (Verkehrsverein) in the cities and towns on this itinerary are located as follows:

Dinkelsbühl. On the main square (Marktplatz), tel. 09851/90-240. **Garmisch-Partenkirchen.** Verkehrsamt der Kurverwaltung, Bahnhofstrasse 34, tel. 08821–18–022. Open Mon.–Sat. 8–6, Sun. and holidays 10–noon. **Heidelberg.** Main office: in the train station (Hauptbahnhof), tel. 06221/21–341. Open Mon.–Sat. 9–7, Sun. 10–3. Branches: in the funicular station halfway to the castle (tel. 06221/29–641) and at Neckarmünzplatz, near the City Hall (tel. 06221/29–641). **Munich.** Main office: Sendlingerstrasse 1 (tel. 089/23–911). Open weekdays 8:30 AM–2 PM. Other offices are at the airport and at the Bayerstrasse exit of the main train station (tel. 089/2391–1256, open Mon.–Sat. 8:30 AM–9:30 PM, Sun. and holidays 1 PM–9:30 PM). **Nördlingen.** Städtisches Verkehrsamt, Marktplatz 2, tel. 09081/84–114. **Rothenburg ob der Tauber.** Marktplatz 2, tel. 09861/40–492. The office can help with accommodations.

Emergencies
In **Heidelberg:** *Police* (tel. 112); *Ambulance* (tel. 13013). In **Munich:** *Police* (tel. 110); *Urgent medical help* (tel. 558–661).

Consulates
U.S. Consulate General (Konigstrasse 5–7, Munich, tel. 089/23–011). **U.K. Consulate General** (Amalienstrasse 63, Munich, tel. 089/394–015). **Canadian Consulate** (Maximilianplatz 9, Munich, tel. 089/558–531).

Opening and Closing Times

Banks
Times vary from state to state and city to city, but banks are generally open weekdays from 8:30 or 9 to 3 or 4 (5 or 6 on Thursday). Branches at airports and main train stations open as early as 6:30 AM and close as late as 10:30 PM.

Museums
Most museums are open Tuesday–Sunday 9–6. Some close for an hour or more at lunch, and some are open on Monday.

Shops
Times vary, but are generally Monday to Saturday from 8:30 or 9 until 5:30 or 6; some close on Saturday at 2 or 2:30. On the first Saturday of each month, larger shops and department stores are open until 7:30 or 8.

National Holidays
January 1; March 29 (Good Friday); April 1 (Easter Monday); May 1 (May Day); May 9 (Ascension); May 20 (Pentecost Monday); June 14 (Corpus Christi, southern Germany only); June 17 (German Unity Day); August 15 (Assumption Day, Bavaria and Saarland only); November 1 (All Saints); November 20 (Day of Prayer and Repentance); December 25, 26 (Christmas).

Guided Tours

In **Dinkelsbühl,** escorted tours start from St. George's Church
(tel. 09851/90–240; Apr.–Oct., 2:30 and 8:30; cost: DM 2.50 adults, DM 1 children). In **Heidelberg,** contact the Tourist Office
at the main railway station or Heidelberg Service (Neckarmünzplatz, near the Town Hall, tel. 06221/29–641; mid-May–
Oct. only). Two-hour tours begin from Bismarckplatz and the
train station (Apr.–Oct., 10 and 2; off-season, Sat. only at 2). In
Munich, daily city sightseeing tours (minimum 1 hour) depart
at 10 and 2:30 from Bahnhofplatz, opposite the main entrance to
the Hauptbahnhof (tel. 089/591–504). Day trips to major attractions   outside   Munich   also   usually   depart   from
Bahnhofplatz (tel. 089/591–504 or 089/558–061); you can also inquire at the official Bavarian travel bureau, ABR, beside the
Hauptbahnhof (tel. 089/12–040).

Bike tours of Munich (the city is criss-crossed with bicycle
paths) are organized Tuesday–Sunday at 10 (tel. 089/272–
1131). In **Rothenburg,** guided tours leave from the Tourist Office on the Marktplatz (Easter–Oct., 11 and 2; DM 2). Also
beginning at the central square are horse-drawn carriage
rides.

Shopping

Popular items include **cameras, binoculars,** and **optical lenses;**
Rosenthal **crystal, china,** and **cutlery;** Nymphenburg **porce-
lains** (Munich); **leather goods; gourmet delicacies; handicrafts;**
and **antiques.**

In *Heidelberg,* Hauptstrasse is a pedestrian mall with many
gift shops. For **antiques** try Winnikes Antiquitäten, Hauptstrasse 138 (18th-century porcelain and furniture); B & B Antiques, Plöck 58 (old silver and glass), and several shops on
Haspelgasse.

In *Munich,* the most elegant shops are on Theatinerstrasse,
Maximilianstrasse, and Briennerstrasse. The pedestrian shopping mall runs from Karlsplatz to Marienplatz. Many of the
trendiest **boutiques** are in the suburb of Schwabing, a 10-min-
ute subway journey from Marienplatz.

For two floors of **mugs, folk costumes,** and **antiques,** try Wall-
ach, Residenzstrasse 3. Loden-Frey, Maffeistrasse 7–9, offers
an exclusive and expensive range of traditional Bavarian
clothes *(Trachten),* including dirndls. To see what contemporary **artisans** are up to, visit the Bavarian Association of
Artisans (Bayerischer Kunstgewerbeverein), Pacellistrasse 7.

The famous **porcelain** factory, Nymphenburger Porzellanman-
ufaktur, is on the grounds of the castle, 8 km (5 mi) northwest-
of the city (open weekdays 8–noon and 1–5). For **gourmet food**
specialties, don't miss Alois Dallmayr, Dienerstrasse 14–15.
For **clocks,** go to Andreas Huber, Weinstrasse 8, or Hauser,
Marienplatz 28. For **cameras** and **camera equipment,** the biggest selections can be found in Karstadt's department store
(ground floor) opposite Michaelskirche, or Pini at Karlsplatz
and Sendlinger-Tor Platz. For **optical goods** try Sohnges, at
both Briennerstrasse 7 and Kaufingerstrasse 34.

For **china, crystal,** and **cutlery,** try Rosenthal Porzellanhaus Zoellner, Theatinerstrasse 8, or Henckels, Weinstrasse 12. For **suitcases** and **leather goods,** Plaschke, Briennerstrasse 11, has a good selection.

The most expensive **antiques** are on Ottostrasse. Herbert M. Ritter, Prannerstrasse 5, is one of the best. The Antic Haus, Neuturmstrasse 1, near the Hofbräuhaus, has 50 dealers on three floors. The antiques market at Kirchenstrasse 15, Haidhausen (tram 18 to Wiener Platz), is a browser's paradise. Germany's largest secondhand market is also at Kirchenstrasse 15, Haidhausen. For fine **chocolates,** go to Elly Seidl shops at am Kosttor (off Maximilianstrasse) and Maffeistrasse 1.

Sports

Bicycling   In **Dinkelsbühl,** inquire at the tourist office. In **Heidelberg,** rentals are at the parcel counter in the main train station (Apr.–Sept.) In **Munich,** bikes can be rented at the English Gardens at the corner of Königinstrasse and Veterinärstrasse (tel. 089/397–016; May–Oct.). They can also be rented at Lothar Borucki (Hans Sachs Strasse 7, near Sendlinger Tor Platz, tel. 089/266–506); and at some stations of the electric suburban railway (S-Bahn). A current list is available at the main railway station (Hauptbahnhof).

Boating   In **Heidelberg** boat trips along the river valley leave from the Stadthalle (Congress House, tel. 06221/20–181) several times a day in summer (mid-May–Oct.). Boats can be rented at Theodor-Heuss Bridge and at the Stadthalle (tel. 06221/20–181).

Hiking   From Garmisch-Partenkirchen, serious hikers can take overnight trips, staying in mountain huts belonging to the German Alpine Association (Deutscher Alpenverein). Some huts are staffed and serve meals. At unsupervised huts, you'll need to get a key. For information, inquire at the local tourist office or write to the German Alpine Association (Praterinsel 5, 8000 Munich 22, tel. 089/235–0900)—preferably before you leave home.

Dining

Bavarian food is solid and not for people concerned about their daily caloric intake. The emphasis is on pork—from roast suckling pig to tender schnitzel—and the quality is exceptional. Traditional accompaniments include dumplings (*knödel*), which are made from either potato or bread and herbs, and salad with a variety of lettuces. Many menus are being internationalized, and beefsteak and the ubiquitous french fries are widely available. In the most expensive restaurants, French nouvelle cuisine with Bavarian touches is often featured.

The main meal is at midday. The fixed-price menu *(Tageskarte)* is the best bargain and sometimes includes soup, a main dish, and usually a dessert. Go to a café for coffee. All restaurants display menus outside. Though prices include taxes and service, it's customary in lower-priced restaurants to round out the bill to the nearest mark, and in expensive restaurants to add another 5%.

Department stores *(Kaufhäuser)* are a good bet for inexpensive lunches. Butcher shops, such as the Vinzenz-Murr chain in Munich, often serve hot snacks, such as *Warmer Leberkäs mit Kartoffelsalat* (baked meat loaf with mustard and potato salad).

Germany has some 1,200 breweries, more than the rest of Europe combined. The average German consumes 121.6l (32 gal) of beer each year—in Bavaria, he drinks 51, the highest per capita consumption in the world. Even the tiniest villages have breweries serving beer comparable to the best in the world, but drunk only locally: ask for the local brew as you're passing through. Bavarian beer gardens, hung with lanterns, are the center of Bavarian life in summer, particularly in Munich.

The most widely available draft beer styles are Export (known in Bavaria as *Helles*, which means pale) and the slightly stronger, more bitter pilseners. The cloudy amber brew served in tall glasses shaped like flower vases is wheat beer *(Weissbier)*. It's a slightly sour but very refreshing drink. Dark beer *(dunkles)* is usually available on request, but from the bottle.

Most German wines come from the midwest. The exception is around Lake Constance and along the Neckar River. Ask for Lake Constance wines when you're touring the Garmisch area, and for Neckar (Württemberg) wines when you're in Heidelberg or driving through the Neckar Valley between Heidelberg and Rothenburg. If you're uncertain what wine to order, remember that all German wines are grouped in one of three categories, *Tafelwein* (table wines), *Qualitätswein* (quality wines) and *Qualitätswein mit Prädikat* (award-winning wines).

Category	Cost*
Very Expensive	over DM 90
Expensive	DM 60–DM 90
Moderate	DM 40–DM 60
Inexpensive	DM 25–DM 40

Prices per person for a 3-course meal, excluding drinks.

Lodging

If you're looking for Laura Ashleyland, you're in trouble. Furnishings, even in many first-class hotels, tend to be functional. On the positive side, rooms tend to be cheerful, at least in an open-eyed, red-cheeked sort of way, and are always immaculately clean.

Taxes, service charges, and Continental breakfast are usually but not always included in quoted rates. Ask before you sign.

You can't go terribly wrong staying in one of some 70 Romantik Hotels, many of them old postal inns along medieval trade routes. To belong to this association a hotel has to be privately owned and at least 100 years old, and more than 85% of the rooms must have private baths or showers. Prices range from moderate to expensive. A brochure with photos and descriptions of each property is available for $6.50 from **Romantik Hotels** (Box 7038, Bellevue, WA 98007, tel. 206/885–5805; for reservations, tel. 800/826–0015). A free list of Romantik Hotels is available both from the association and from the German National Tourist Office. Check into the Romantik Hotel Open Voucher program, which entitles you to a car and six nights' accommodations, which don't have to be booked in advance.

Germanrail sells a Romantik Hotel package that includes lodging in Romantik Hotels, unlimited rail travel, sightseeing trips, and bicycle rentals.

Castle Hotels is an association of privately owned historic castles in attractive locations. Prices run from moderate to expensive. The German National Tourist Office has a free Castle Hotels brochure and information about Castle Hotels packages.

Lufthansa has several fly/drive packages, some of them including lodging in Romantik Hotels, Castle Hotels, and other properties.

Category	Cost*
Very Expensive	over DM 175
Expensive	DM 120–DM 175
Moderate	DM 75–DM 120
Inexpensive	under DM 75

Prices are for two people sharing a double room.

The Itinerary

Orientation

From Frankfurt, you head south to Heidelberg. A drive through the Neckar Valley takes you to the Romantic Road and Rothenburg. Next, you reach Munich, where you'll explore the past in palaces and museums, shop along convenient pedestrian malls, and then succumb to elegant restaurants, pastry shops, and beer halls. From Munich, it's only an hour's drive to Garmisch-Partenkirchen for skiing (December through May), mountain walks, dramatic cable car rides, and visits to the Passion Play town of Oberammergau and the castles of Ludwig II. After Garmisch you can head home or continue south to Austria or Switzerland.

The Main Route

3–5 Days *One night:* Heidelberg
Excursion along the Romantic Road
One night: Munich
One night: Garmisch-Partenkirchen
Tour of the Alps and the Royal Castles

5–7 Days *One night:* Heidelberg
Excursion through the Neckar Valley and along the Romantic Road
One night: Rothenburg
Two nights: Munich

Two nights: Garmisch-Partenkirchen
Tour of the Alps and the Royal Castles

7–14 Days *Two nights:* Heidelberg
Excursion through the Neckar Valley and the Romantic Road
One night: Rothenburg
Three nights: Munich
Four nights: Garmisch-Partenkirchen
Tour of the Alps and the Royal Castles

Exploring

Frankfurt to Heidelberg

Take the Autobahn (A5) south from Frankfurt to Darmstadt.
From here you can either continue south on A5 down the center
of the Rhine Valley, through flat agricultural country; or you
can turn off on the slower but more scenic Bergstrasse (Route
3). The drive along the Bergstrasse, the old main road on the
east side of the valley, is a pleasant rather than dramatic trip
through wine-producing villages at the foot of gently sloping
hills crowned with ruined medieval castles, some of them converted into restaurants and hotels.

About 19.2 km (12 mi) south of Darmstadt, between the towns
of Zwingenberg and Auerbach, look for signs to **Auerbach
Schloss** (Auerbach Castle). A 10-minute drive takes you
through a wooded *Naturpark*, with lovely hillside trails, to the
romantic ruins. Though the castle is losing its battle against nature, the ramparts are still intact, and children of all ages will
love scurrying in and out of its broken battlements. *Open May–
Oct., daily 10–6; Nov.–Apr., daily 10–5.*

Auerbach If you're partial to apple strudel and lovely parks, turn left at
the Hotel Krone in the center of **Auerbach,** and drive to
Fürstenlager Park. Leave your car at the Park Hotel Herrenhaus, spend an hour walking among the tropical trees and pa-
vilions, and then reward yourself with some strudel and a glass
of the hotel's own white Auerbach Fürstenlager wine.

Lodging The **Park Hotel Herrenhaus** is the former summer residence of
the Grand Dukes of Hessen-Darmstadt. The mansion, once a
bit run-down, has been beautifully modernized. There are just
seven guest rooms in the spacious interior, all with bath. The
owners are very friendly, and you couldn't ask for a more peaceful setting within a lovely 125-acre park. *6140 Bensheim 3.
Auerbach, tel. 06251/72–274. 7 rooms. Facilities: restaurant
(dinner for nonresidents only by reservation), gardens. MC.
Moderate.*

Heppenheim About 8 km (5 mi) south of Auerbach, still on Route 3, is the
town of Heppenheim. Stop at least long enough to appreciate
the 16th-century town hall and pharmacy.

Park where you see the brown marker with the words
HISTORISCHER MARKTPLATZ on your left, and spend a few minutes soaking up the atmosphere of the historic Market Place,
surrounded by 16th-century buildings and a Gothic church, the
so-called Bergstrasse Cathedral. Heppenheim offers only a taste
of what you'll see in Rothenburg, but it's virtually tourist-free,
with a sense of reality you won't find in the postcard towns along
the Romantic Road.

Heidelberg

Heidelberg has the mellow flavor of old Germany. The country's oldest university town, it nestles along the banks of the fast-flowing Neckar River, beneath an imposing red sandstone castle. In the early evening the sun turns the red to gold; a deep radiance lies upon the town and prints itself upon the inner eye.

The students transform what could be just another pretty tourist town into a place of youthful vitality. You'll mingle with them as you walk among the fashionable shops and cafés along the .8-km (½-mi) pedestrian mall, or wander down narrow alleyways in search of Heidelberg's past.

The city was the political center of a German state called the Rhineland Palatinate—the name deriving from the title "palatines," which was given to the highest officers in the Holy Roman Empire. After the Thirty Years' War (1618–48) the Protestant Elector (hereditary ruler) Karl Ludwig married his daughter to the brother of Louis XIV in the hope of bringing peace to the Rhineland. But when the Elector's son died without an heir, Louis XIV used the marriage alliance as an excuse to claim Heidelberg, and, in 1689, the town was sacked and laid waste. From the ashes of a devastating fire four years later arose what you see today: a Baroque town built on Gothic foundations, with narrow, twisting streets and alleyways. The new Heidelberg is changing under the influence of U.S. Army barracks and industrial development stretching into the suburbs; but the old heart of the city remains unchanged, and continues to exude the spirit of romantic Germany.

Longfellow wrote that, "Next to the Alhambra of Granada, the castle of Heidelberg is the most magnificent ruin of the Middle Ages." The imposing ruin is at its romantic best from a distance. You can drive up Neue Schlosstrasse, but parking can be a problem, so leave your car at your hotel and take the Königstuhl funicular (cost: DM 2 adults, DM 1.30 children).

The Castle should be seen early in the morning because it's the town's leading attraction, and you can spend 30 minutes in afternoon lines for the 60-minute guided tour.

The castle, dominating the town, should remind you of the time when Heidelberg was the capital of the Palatinate. There has been a fortress here since the 13th century, but it did not become the principal residence for the electors for another 300 years. Construction began about 1300 and continued for the next 400 years; the courtyard through which you enter is thus like the public square of a medieval town, surrounded by buildings representing four centuries of changing architectural styles. The best wings were built during the Renaissance and show a fine balance of strength and refinement, of might and grace. The late-Renaissance Heinrichs Wing, on the right side of the courtyard as you face the river, was built by Elector Otto-Heinrich in the mid-16th century. It is pure Italian Renaissance, made of warm red sandstone from the Neckar Valley, and has a dignity and a simplicity that stand in marked contrast to the riot of Baroque ornamentation that flourishes elsewhere. Otto's son Friedrich IV (1592–1610) added the Friedrichs Wing, also in late-Renaissance style. In 1693, less than 100 years later, the castle was badly damaged by the

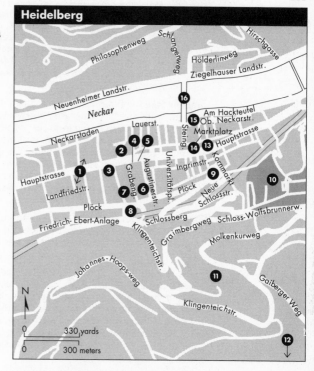

French and in 1764 it was struck by lightning and left in ruins until the end of the 19th century, when the shell and interior of the Friedrichs Wing were restored.

Do you see, over the entrance, the relief of two angels holding a wreath of five roses enclosing a pair of compasses? The story goes that the twins of the master builder fell from the scaffolding, and appeared as angels in the father's troubled dreams, holding the wreath of roses that covered their grave.

The castle's interiors are filled with a modest number of artifacts, arranged museum fashion, and do not breathe much living history; you may find the rooms much less impressive than the facades. What you're not supposed to miss is the mid-18th-century 186,200-l (49,000-gal) Great Vat. This is not a joke. It was built at a time when the Elector's subjects paid him one tenth of their wine in taxes. No one sent his best tenth, so it was customary to pour the whole amount into one cask and make a table wine for public celebrations or for payments to officials. The vat is made from 130 oak trees. The guardian was the jester dwarf Perkeo, known for his capacity to drink from its contents. Local lore says he died when he drank his first glass of water.

The one sight you truly shouldn't miss inside the castle is the Pharmaceutical Museum, the largest in the world. In a setting worthy of *The Sorcerer's Apprentice*, you'll see all the paraphernalia of medieval doctors. Kids in particular will love the dried beetles and toads, and the mummy with a full head of hair.

If you haven't time or patience to wait in line, don't leave without standing on one of the balconies and enjoying the magnificent view of the town below, with its spires and orange roof tiles spread along the river, and, stretching beyond them, the wooded mountains of the Palatinate. *Admission, including the tour: DM 4 adults, DM 2 children. Open daily 9–5; guided tours at 9, noon, 1:30 and 4.*

Walk or take the funicular back into town. From the funicular station, walk one block toward the river to the **Kornmarkt,** which has a fine 1718 Baroque statue of the Madonna. To your left is the oldest quarter of town, with narrow passageways leading to cozy wine taverns and pubs. You'll return here later. For now, make a short side trip to the right, to a square called Karlsplatz. On the far right corner (as you face the river) are two historic student pubs, the Seppl and the Roter Ochsen (Red Ox).

Return to the Kornmarkt. On the river side is the **Town Hall** (Rathaus). Next to it is another square, the **Marktplatz,** which has an outdoor flower market and good views of the castle.

Across from the Rathaus is the late Gothic **Church of the Holy Spirit** (Heilig-Geist-Kirche). Note how the aisles, though divided into galleries, are as high as the main body (the nave) of the church. This is the hallmark of the Hall Style. Slim pillars force your eyes upward toward God. In 1705 a wall was raised between choir and nave so that rival Christian sects could enjoy separate places of worship. The Roman Catholics fell heir to the choir and the Protestants were awarded the nave. Climb the tower for a view.

Leave by the west end of the church. On your left is the Ritter Hotel. When the armies of Louis XIV destroyed the town and castle in 1693, the only Renaissance building to survive was the Ritter. Its carefully preserved Renaissance facade is the finest and most fantastic you'll see in Germany.

Continue down Hauptstrasse, a pedestrian street and the commercial center of town, which has many stores and restaurants. Here and on side streets you'll find some first-rate antiques shops.

Continue to a large open square, the **Universitätsplatz.** This is the entrance to the **Old University.** It was founded in 1386 by Paris professors and students who were offered asylum when they refused to recognize the opposition Pope the French king had installed in Avignon. It was the first university in Germany, and, after the Reformation had swept Europe, the chief Protestant center of learning in the country.

In the back of the Old University is the **Students' Jail** (Studentenkarzer). Ancient tradition dictated that students couldn't be thrown in the town clink, so from 1712 to the early 20th century, the Studentenkarzer was filled with unruly undergraduates who spent their leisure time carving inscriptions commemorating their imprisonment—a distinction of which they were proud. Students could be confined for up to 14 days for such offenses as drunkenness, playing practical jokes, or disturbing the peace at night. After three days of bread and water they could accept food from outside, attend lectures, and receive visits from fellow prisoners. The walls are covered with cartoons, drawings, ribald verse—anyone who takes the time to examine signatures can probably find names of many who have achieved distinction in the arts, business, and politics. *Admission: DM 1 adults, 70 pf children. Open Mon.–Sat. 9–5.*

Nearby is the **University Library** (Universitätsbibliothek), in which you'll find some illustrated (illuminated) medieval books on display. *Admission free. Open daily 10–6.*

Return to Hauptstrasse, turn left, and continue to the **Electoral Palatinate Museum** (Kurpfälzisches Museum) and see the Altarpiece of the 12 Apostles (1509) by Tilman Riemenschneider. Riemenschneider is the greatest late-Gothic German wood carver, and this is his finest work. Compare the spiritual faces of the Apostles closest to Christ to the more worldly, worn faces of those farther away from Him. During the Peasants' War Riemenschneider sneaked the peasants of Würzburg into town by a secret path, and the Bishop of Würzburg punished him by mutilating his hands. *Admission: DM 1 adults, children free. Open Tues. and Wed. 10–5, Thurs. 10–9, Fri.–Sun. 10–5.*

Now cross Hauptstrasse and head toward the river on Grosse Mantelgasse (Big Coat Lane). When you can't go any farther, turn right. From here to the Old Bridge (Alt Brücke) there are several small side streets to explore. Cross the bridge and enjoy an unforgettable view of the town.

Go for a walk along the far side of the river, on Neuenheimer Landstrasse and Ziegelhäuser Landstrasse. You'll get your best views of the castle from here—preferably in the late afternoon, when the sun colors the town gold.

A more challenging and rewarding walk is along Philosopher's Walk (Philosophenweg), on the slopes above the riverside path. After you cross the Old Bridge, take the street called Schlangenweg that zigzags up the mountain.

Dining **Simplicissimus** provides an elegant setting for dinner and is considered by some to be Heidelberg's best kitchen. Chef Johann Lummer envelops regional style in French taste. Try his ravioli or duck in a delicious sauce. *Ingrimstr. 16, tel. 06221/ 13–336. Reservations required. Dress: dressy. AE, V. Dinner only. Closed Tues. and Aug. Very Expensive.*

Hirschgasse, the oldest inn in Heidelberg (built 20 years before Columbus discovered the West Indies), is across the river on the edge of town. Gaudeamus Igitur (Let's be happy . . .) is the name of the small, unpretentious hotel restaurant serving regional specialties. *Hirschgasse 3, tel. 06221/49–921/2. Dress: informal. AE, DC, MC, V. Dinner only. Closed Sun. and Dec. 23–Jan. 7. Expensive.*

Weinstube zum Kurfürsten in the Hotel Europa is Heidelberg dining at its best—either in a wood-paneled tavern or on a terrace. It serves regional specialties with a delicate nouvelle touch. *Friedrich-Ebert-Anlage 1, tel. 06221/5150. Reservations advised. Dress: informal. AE, DC, MC, V. Expensive.*

Kurpfälzisches Museum Restaurant is a garden restaurant back from the main street—a peaceful oasis for a pina colada, a milk shake, or lunch. *Hauptstr. 97, tel. 06221/24–050. Reservations not necessary. Dress: informal. DC, MC, V. Closed Jan. 1–5. Moderate.*

Inexpensive student restaurants include **Zum Roten Ochsen** (Hauptstrasse 217, tel. 06221/20–977); the 580-year-old

Schnookeloch (Haspelgasse 8, tel. 06221/22–733); and the more touristy **Zum Seppl** (Hauptstr. 213, tel. 06221/23–085).

Lodging Before you leave home, check with the German National Tourist Board for budget holiday packages that include three nights' accommodations, meals in student restaurants, entry fees, and guided tours.

Hirschgasse is across the river on the edge of town—a bit inconvenient if you want to go back and forth more than once a day. The original folksy look has been completely replaced by trendy Laura Ashley furnishings. The original house was here when Columbus was crossing the Atlantic. Downstairs is a friendly, rustic restaurant called Gaudeamus Igitur. *Hirschgasse 3, tel. 06221/49–921/2. 18 rooms. Facilities: restaurant. AE, DC, MC, V. Closed Dec. 23–Jan. 7. Very Expensive.*

Hotel Europa is a family-owned luxury hotel—the sort of place where an educated, well-heeled German would stay in Salzburg. The Red Baron would find himself outclassed in this classy hostelry, which has a marble entranceway flanked by carpeted lounges with wood newspaper racks, leather chairs, and crystal chandeliers. Celebrated guests have included Richard Strauss, King Edward VIII, and Maria Callas. Muhammed Ali signed the guest book, "Love is the net where hearts are caught like fish. Peace." Rooms vary significantly in size and decor, and many are decorated with money rather than taste; if you're unhappy, ask to see more. *Friedrich-Ebert-Anlage 1, tel. 06221/5150. 150 rooms, 4 apartments. Facilities: restaurant, bar, summer patio. AE, DC, MC, V. Very Expensive.*

Prinzhotel is a well-known, 75-year-old luxury hotel across the river from the old town. It reopened in 1985 after extensive renovations. The atmosphere is Trendy European, with some very smart, un-Teutonic colors—pink and gray. What the hotel lacks in warmth it makes up for in sophistication. Fight for a room with a river view. *Neuenheimer Landstr. 5, tel. 06221/40 –320. 50 rooms. Facilities: Italian restaurant, piano bar (closed Tues.) AE, DC, MC, V. Very Expensive.*

Romantik Hotel Zum Ritter St. Georg occupies the only surviving Renaissance house in town. The Red Baron would feel right at home in the dining room, complete with suit of armor, rough plaster walls, arched doorways, and ceiling beams. The hotel was fully modernized in 1987–88, and its 30 rooms (most with bath) have been refurnished in a mixture of "ancient and modern." Room 34 on the top floor is for romantics; it's under the roof and very cozy. *Hauptstr. 178, tel. 06221/24–272 or 20203. 32 rooms. Facilities: restaurant. AE, DC, MC, V. Very Expensive.*

Hotel Holländer is a renovated, centrally located, 17th-century house with lovely river views. Rooms are clean but fitted with undistinguished orange-and-brown Sears Modern furnishings; Headboards covered with an orangy velour. Room 452 has a skylight. *An der Alten Brücke, tel. 06221/42–12-091. 40 rooms. Facilities: restaurant. AE, MC, V. Expensive.*

Perkeo was recently renovated, so all rooms have the same decor. The ambience is a bit motelish, but with some homey, old-fashioned touches that you may find more agreeable than the deliberate Lederhosen Look of other hostelries. It's on a busy pedestrian street, so ask for a quiet room. Try for Room 25; it's extra quiet and very cozy. *Hauptstr. 75, tel. 06221/22–255. 25 rooms. Facilities: restaurant. MC. Moderate–Expensive.*

Anlage is a small but comfortable hotel nestling beneath the castle. *Friedrich-Ebert-Anlage 32, tel. 06221/26–425. 20 rooms, most with bath or shower. Facilities: restaurant. AE, DC, MC, V. Moderate.*

The Neckar Valley

Take Route 37 southwest through the Neckar Valley from Heidelberg toward Bad Wimpfen. The road is busy, particularly in summer, so don't expect to make rapid progress. Not that you'll be tempted to speed through the gentle, rural landscape of orchards and vineyards. Wooded hills crowned with castles rise above the soft-flowing river. When you reach Neckarelz, you have a choice of continuing to Bad Wimpfen or turning left on Route 27 to Mosbach.

Route 27 is the most direct route to the Romantic Road. Turn left on Route 27 through Mosbach to Route 292. Turn right to Bad Mergentheim. Drive east to Weikersheim and head south along the Romantic Road.

If you have time, are enjoying the scenery, and are partial to castles and medieval towns, continue south from Neckarelz to Bad Wimpfen. This is the route described below.

Neckargemünd During the busy tourist season you may want to leave Heidelberg and spend the night in the quiet surroundings of Neckargemünd (12.8 km/8 mi east of Heidelberg) in order to get an early start to the Romantic Road.

Lodging **Hotel zum Ritter** is comfortable and has a good restaurant that serves a multicourse Rittermahl (Knight's banquet). *Neckarstr. 40, tel. 06223/7035. 41 rooms. Facilities: restaurant. MC, V. Expensive.*

Hotel zum Rössl is a bed-and-breakfast-style hotel with a restaurant that enjoys a fine reputation. *Heidelberger Str. 15, tel. 06223/2665. 13 rooms, most with bath or shower. Facilities: restaurant (closed Mon., Tues.). No credit cards. Closed Jan., Feb., and 2 weeks during July/Aug. Inexpensive.*

Hirschhorn **Hirschhorn Castle Hotel** (12 km/7.5 mi east of Neckargemünd)
Dining and Lodging is not so much a castle hotel as a pleasant if undistinguished modern hotel inside an old castle. Hallways have that medieval rough-plaster look, lest you forget you're in a castle, and some rooms have double sinks, green velvet swag curtains, and canopied four-poster beds. The Grünes Zimmer and Hochzeitzimmer are the best rooms, but all have river views. Student Prince furnishings tend at times to confuse ornateness with class. Best bet may be to come for a meal (breakfast perhaps, after leaving Heidelberg), on a terrace overlooking the river. The view is splendid, and the restaurant enjoys a good reputation for lunch or dinner. *Schloss Hotel, Hirschhorn am Neckar, tel. 06272/1373. 34 rooms. Facilities: terrace/garden restaurant. MC. Moderate.*

Neckarzimmern Follow signs 1.6 km (1 mi) to the left to Hornberg Castle, part of which has been converted into a hotel.

Dining and Lodging **Berg Hornberg.** Best bet is lunch or dinner on the terrace overlooking the Neckar Valley. Specialties include fresh fish and venison at reasonable prices. Rooms are comfortable, but haven't much panache for an 11th-century castle. Ask for a room with a view and try for Room 26. The castle was the home of the picaresque knight Gotz von Berlichingen. He died here in

The Neckar Valley

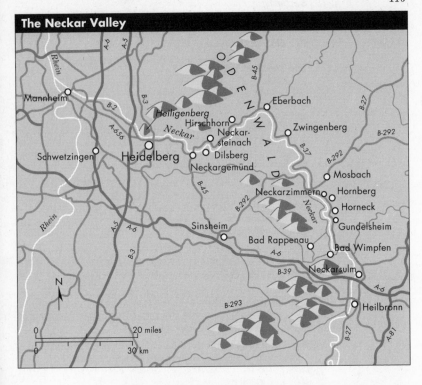

1562, and was immortalized in Goethe's drama of the same name. You can stroll around the rooms he once lived in, now a bit worse for wear and some of them roofless. His armor is on show in the castle museum. *Neckarzimmern, tel. 06261/406–465. 27 rooms. Facilities: restaurant (with occasional medieval-style banquets arranged). V. Closed Dec.–Feb. Expensive.*

Gundelsheim   A bridge beyond the town takes you 3.2 km (2 mi) out of your way to the romantic, fortified **Guttenberg Castle.** Sights worth stopping for include a library and an 18th-century herbarium, with plants grown in trick wood boxes. Return to the main road and drive about 7.2 km (4.5 mi) south to Bad Wimpfen.

Bad Wimpfen   The old fortified quarter of Bad Wimpfen was, in the 13th century, an imperial residence. The network of picturesque streets such as Klostergasse are lined with timber-framed houses, and are well worth an hour of your time. The 13th-century Gothic church, **St. Peter's** (Stiftskirche), has a lovely cloister. For an impressive view, climb the tower of the **Imperial Palace.** Wander down Schwibbogengasse, a street of broken cobbles, full of warmth and character. The four-story house beside the Hotel Sonne belongs in a fairy tale.

From Bad Wimpfen take country roads to Domeneck, Schöntal, and Krautheim, then turn north on Route 19 to Bad Mergentheim. The best restaurants in Bad Mergentheim are Zirbelstube in the Hotel Viktoria (tel. 07931/5930) and the less expensive Alte Jagdstube (tel. 07931/2526). Drive to Weikersheim and head south along the Romantic Road.

The Romantic Road

The road follows a medieval trade route through peaceful, rolling countryside, past vineyards and fields planted with sugar beets, potatoes, and wheat. This is not ooh-and-ah country, but a rural, daytime world of tractors and butterflies. The real romance is in the medieval towns along the route—the best preserved in Germany—particularly Rothenburg, Dinkelsbühl and Nördlingen.

Weikersheim The town developed around a castle (1580–1680), which has a first-rate collection of 16th- to 18th-century furniture and a marvelous Great Hall (Rittersaal), which is part Renaissance, part Baroque. Huntsmen track their prey on the ceiling, and carved deer and bear seem poised to spring from the walls. Visitors pass beneath the unblinking gaze of local royalty, each in his own regal frame, each one uglier than the next. *Admission: DM 2 adults, 50 pf children. Open Apr.–Oct., daily 8–6; Nov.– Mar., daily 10–noon.*

Dining **Hotel-Restaurant Deutschherren-Stuben,** which is known for its fresh regional cuisine and its reasonable prices, is a good bet for a quick lunch. *Marktpl. 9, tel. 07934/8376. Reservations not necessary. Dress: informal. No credit cards. Moderate.*

Creglingen A 1.6-km (1-mi) side trip takes you to the **Chapel of Our Lord** (Herrgottskirche), which has a famous carved wood altarpiece (1505–10) of the Virgin by Riemenschneider.

Dining and Lodging **Gasthof Krone** shares with the restaurant in Weikersheim a sound reputation for regional cuisine at reasonable prices. The Gasthof is also a comfortable hotel, run with a very friendly touch by the Ebert family. *Hauptstr. 12, tel. 07933/558. 25 rooms. Facilities: restaurant (closed Mon.). MC. Closed Dec. 10–Dec. 26. Inexpensive.*

Rothenburg ob der Tauber In spite of the museumlike atmosphere and the spate of tourists (2,000 tourist beds, 90 restaurants), Rothenburg is one of the most colorful medieval towns in Europe. Every street has its own arrangement of beautiful churches, gateways, fountains, and wrought-iron signs. No roof is like its neighbor. The gabled houses are half-timbered or plastered, and dripping with flowers and vines. In America a street is an open road that could, it seems, go on forever; but in medieval Rothenburg the streets turn in on themselves, and seem to shelter you from the world outside.

The town developed around two 12th-century castles that were destroyed in a mid-14th-century earthquake. From the ruins, the wealthy burghers built public monuments, such as St. James's Church (St-Jakobskirche), the Town Hall, and the gabled houses in the Herrngasse. The town turned Protestant and then never recovered from the depression brought on by the Thirty Years' War (1618–48). It languished through the 17th and 18th centuries—a sleepy, forgotten, regional market town, too poor to expand beyond its medieval walls. It was this neglect, ironically, that preserved the town—keeping it the perfect gem of a 16th-century village that tourists enjoy today.

Begin at the main square (Marktplatz). Notice how all main streets converge here, in the geographic and spiritual heart of town—and that wherever you go within the medieval walls, you're always moving in relation to this central space. It must

The Romantic Road

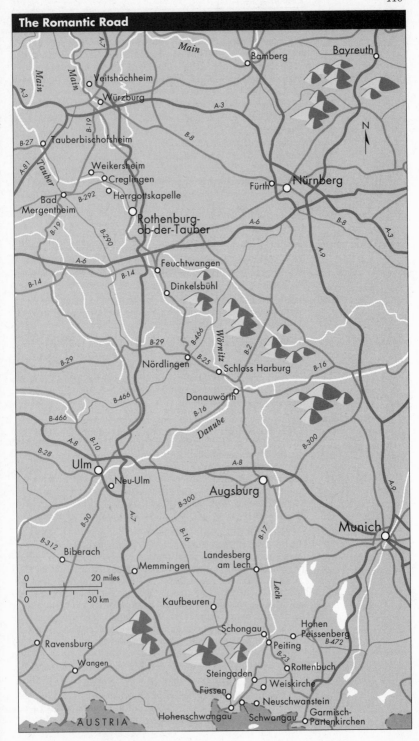

have been very satisfying, psychologically, always moving toward or away from a defined point; and it says something about our spiritual pilgrimage over the centuries that cities today no longer have this common center, these protective walls.

Look up at the **Town Hall,** off this main square, and see if you can distinguish between the 14th-century Gothic section, with a gable topped by a belfry; and the newer, Renaissance section facing the Marktplatz, which was built after a fire in 1501. Standing in the Marktplatz, you can appreciate the contrast between the horizontal lines of Renaissance architecture and the soaring, vertical lines of the earlier Gothic building. (The arcade in front was added in 1681.) Inside the town hall is a museum and a tower with striking views. *Admission: DM 2 adults, DM 1 children. Open Nov.–Apr., daily 10–5; May–Oct., daily 9–6.*

Also on the Marktplatz is the **City Councillor's Tavern** (Ratsherrntrinkstube), which you can recognize by the three clocks on its Baroque gable. If you're here at 11, noon, 1, 2, 9, or 10, you'll see the principal figures appear in what is referred to as the Drinking Feat of the Thirty Years' War. Rothenburg, a Protestant town, lay in the path of Catholic forces under General Cserklas Tilly, and was taken on October 30, 1631. The following day it was to be destroyed and its officers executed; but during the night the victorious general was offered a 3¼-l (.8-gal) tankard of heavy Franconian ale, which, to his embarrassment, he was unable to empty in a single draft. With his manhood at stake—so the story goes—he offered to pardon the town if one of its officials could down it in one go. A former mayor named Nusch succeeded in 10 minutes. It took him three days to recover, but the town was saved. The story is a bit hard to swallow, but who wants to question it? Skeptics can see the tankard in the museum and draw their own conclusions.

Cross the Marktplatz and walk down Obere Schmiedgasse (Upper Smithy's Lane). The second house (the **Master Builder's House**)—the one with the dragons on the gables—is the finest in town. The supporting figures at the upper windows represent alternately the seven vices and virtues; in the lower row Compassion, Gluttony, and Motherly Love stand side by side. The inner courtyard, unchanged for centuries, is today a café.

On the right, where Obere Schmiedgasse turns into Untere Schmiedgasse, is the Gothic **St. John's Church** (Johanniskirche). Adjoining it is the **Medieval Crime Museum,** where kids can unlock their imaginations among the instruments of torture. *Admission: DM 3.50 adults, DM 2 children. Open May–Oct., daily 9:30–5:30; Nov., Mar., and Apr., daily 2–4; Dec., daily 2–5; closed Jan. and Feb.*

Continue down Untere Schmiedgasse to Plönlein, a picturesque corner where two streets meet, both ending at gateways. If you have time, bear left and continue down Spitalgasse to the **Hospital** (Spital), a colorful group of 16th- and 17th-century buildings, including a notable Gothic **chapel** (Spitalkirche). Retrace your steps down Spitalgasse, back through the gate. Turn left and pass beneath the Koboldzell Gate.

If you skip the hospital, bear right to the Koboldzell Gate, make a sharp right turn, and follow the path along the outside of the wall, above the river. Pass through the arched entranceway into the **Burggarten.** Flowers bloom now where the two fortified castles used to be.

Follow the path through the public gardens. Pass through the fortified gateway (Burgtor), which was part of one of the original castles, and head back toward the center of town. Bear right on Herrngasse, a commercial street lined with mansions of the medieval burghers, and peer into some of the courtyards. Soon you'll be back to the Marktplatz. Behind the well—which supplied the town's water needs 550 years ago—is a half-timbered house where artists display and sell their wares. To the left is the picturesque Hofbronnengasse (Court Well Lane), leading to the **Dolls' Museum.**

Turn left on Kirchgasse and right on Klostergasse to **St. James's Church.** In the south aisle (on your right, facing front) is the famous 1504 Riemenschneider altarpiece, called the Holy Blood Altar because three drops of Christ's blood are said to be contained within a capsule of rock crystal in the gold-plated cross. Look closely at the facial expressions, particularly of Judas, in *The Last Supper.* Only John remains unperturbed.

Dining   **Eisenhut,** the number one hotel in town, has an attractive terrace restaurant overlooking the Tauber River. Popular dishes include "Franconian wedding" soup, saddle of venison with fresh mushrooms, and walnut ice cream with blackberries. Try the wines made from the hotel's own grapes. *Herrngasse 3, tel. 09861/7050. Reservations required. Dress: dressy. AE, DC, MC, V. Very Expensive.*

Baumeisterhaus, in a 16th-century building, displays irresistible pastries. Stop, too, for a lunch of regional specialties, such as dumplings in consommé, turkey schnitzel, and sauerbraten. *Obere Schmiedgasse 3, tel. 09861/3404. Reservations not necessary. Dress: informal. AE, DC, MC, V. Moderate.*

Zum Greifen, another inn with a long and colorful past, serves time-honored dishes. *Obere Schmiedgasse 5, tel. 09861/2281. Reservations not necessary. Dress: informal. AE, MC, V. Closed Sun., Mon., and Dec. 22–Jan. Inexpensive.*

Lodging   **Burg Hotel** is a bit flairless, but clean and comfortable. Ask for a room overlooking the Tauber River. *Klostergasse 1–3, tel. 09861/5037. 14 rooms. Facilities: indoor pool. AE, DC, MC, V. Very Expensive.*

Eisenhut is considered the top hotel in town, so be sure to reserve rooms in advance. Former guests include Winston Churchill, William Randolph Hearst, and the Shah of Iran. The century-old hotel was stitched together from four patrician houses. Old Bavarian furnishings are colorful in a busy, undisciplined sort of way; state your preference for modern or traditional decor. Smaller rooms are in back, facing the garden. Some of the marbleized bathrooms have twin sinks. Try for Room 102 or 108, or something comparable. The restaurant is excellent. What a lovely way to start the day, eating breakfast in the courtyard! *Herrngasse 3, tel. 09861/2041. 80 rooms. Facilities: restaurant, garden terrace. AE, DC, MC, V. Very Expensive.*

Romantik Hotel Markusturm is a family-type hotel just outside the walls, but only a few minutes' walk from town center. Some rooms have canopied four-poster beds. Most are small and unpretentious, and not without a certain character. Room 17 is as nice as any. In summer, you'll hear the night watchman going his rounds below your window. *Rödergasse 1, tel. 09861/2370.*

24 rooms. Facilities: restaurant serving local specialties. AE, DC, MC, V. Closed Jan. 10–Feb. 15. Very Expensive.

Goldener Hirsh. The better rooms here are comparable in price to those at the Eisenhut, but the standard rooms are considerably cheaper—and just as nice. The hotel has a delightful Louis XVI–style restaurant on a blue terrace overlooking the town. Not all units have baths. *Untere Schmiedgasse 16/25, tel. 09861/2051. 80 rooms, most with bath. Facilities: restaurant. AE, DC, MC, V. Closed Dec. 15–end of Jan. Expensive.*

Adam Hotel has the friendly, homey atmosphere of a wine house. It has a good kitchen, and its best rooms have carved wood beds with canopies—equal to those at the Eisenhut at half the price. Be careful, though, about your choice of rooms. Room 2 is nice but tiny; Room 1 has a small bathroom. Several other rooms have antique beds that are lovely to look at but not to sleep in—unless you're partial to the fetal position. Room 11 has a small but beautiful Bavarian farmer's bed. The Heart Room upstairs overlooking the garden has carved beds and stained-glass windows. There's no restaurant, but owner Hans-Karl Adam is a chef and will prepare something delicious for you if you look hungry. *Burggasse 29, tel. 09861/2364. 23 rooms. MC. Closed Nov.–Easter. Moderate.*

Hotel Roter Hahn. Painted reproduction furniture lends a certain stolid cheerfulness to the rooms. The newly renovated units are best. Rooms are clean and comfortable, but each is different, so tell the management what you have in mind. *Obere Schmiedgasse 21, tel. 09861/5088. 40 rooms. Facilities: restaurant. AE, DC, MC, V. Moderate.*

Dinkelsbühl Dinkelsbühl offers a smaller, less perfect portrait of the Middle Ages than Rothenburg—but it's also less precious. Rothenburg exists to be looked at, Dinkelsbühl to be lived in. There are fewer tourists here—more people getting on with the business of life. If you have time for only one town along the Romantic Road, it should be Rothenburg; but try to find time to see Dinkelsbühl, too. It's small enough that you can "do" it in less than an hour. On any street you can glance back through the centuries at 15th- and 16th-century houses—both gabled and frescoed—and at great half-timber structures up to six stories high. Don't miss the houses with rich Renaissance decoration on Martin-Luther Strasse. Particularly notable is the 15th-century **Deutsches Haus,** which now has a small 17th-century Virgin over the entrance. Two other streets not to miss are Segringer Strasse, its houses adorned with flowers and picturesque signs, and Nördlingen Strasse, where the houses are out of line.

St. George's is one of the finest Gothic churches of its type in southern Germany. The Romanesque tower rises nearly 200 feet and affords fine views. The interior is a Gothic hall with wonderful fan vaulting and a notable 15th-century Franciscan altar in the south aisle (on your right, facing the main altar).

Lodging **Deutsches Haus,** a 500-year-old half-timbered beauty, is the first choice of most visitors. The small, privately owned hotel has recently modernized its rooms to a high standard of comfort. *Weinmarkt 3, tel. 09851/2346. 11 rooms. Facilities: restaurant, serving local specialties. AE, DC, MC, V. Expensive.*

Gasthof Weisses Ross is an inexpensive guest house that has long been popular with artists. Rooms have old-fashioned family furniture. The kitchen has a sound reputation for fresh local food: asparagus with spicy ham; trout or carp from local ponds with melted butter and potatoes—and a glass of Frankenwein Bocksbeutel. *Steingasde 12, tel. 09851/2274. 26 rooms. MC. Closed Jan. 15–Feb. 15. Moderate.*

Goldene Rose is as venerable as the Deutsches Haus—Queen Victoria stayed here in 1891—but hasn't as much atmosphere. The restaurant, however, has a good reputation and is the scene of an annual "gourmet week." *Marktpl. 4, tel. 09851/831. 34 rooms. Facilities: restaurant. MC. Closed Jan. 8–Feb. 2. Moderate.*

Nördlingen Nördlingen is a less perfect medieval town than Rothenburg or Dinkelsbühl, and its buildings, made from a grayer stone, don't have the same ruddy glow. But the town does have some venerable buildings, and you may enjoy walking along the crumbling 14th- and 15th-century ramparts, which are punctuated by five huge gate towers.

Like every self-respecting German town, Nördlingen has a mighty church near the center, thrusting its stately tower hundreds of feet into the sky. The late 15th-century **St. George's Church** is near the Marktplatz. A late Gothic hall-style building, it has attractive fan vaulting, a Baroque organ gallery decorated with hanging keys, a late-15th-century pulpit, and a notable statue of Mary Magdalene that belonged to the original Baroque altarpiece. Climb the church steeple for a grand view.

The **Museum** has the original altarpiece from St. George's. *Admission: DM 1.50. Open Tues.–Sun. 9–4.*

Dining **Hotel Sonne,** in the center of town, is a good bet for a reasonably priced lunch. Try roast pork or grilled knuckle of veal with a salad. *8860 Nördlingen, Marktplatz 3, tel. 09081/51–749. AE, V. Moderate.*

Munich

If you arrive here from Hamburg or Berlin, you realize how much more easygoing the Bavarians are than their neighbors to the north. There, you have a sense that life is a serious business; here, that life is short and should be enjoyed.

Munich, West Germany's third largest city, is the capital of Bavaria. The city is the center of rapidly expanding technology and computer industries, yet it retains the status of being the German cultural capital. As well as housing important art galleries and museums, it is home to the greater part of the country's film industry. Munich is also renowned for its beer, breweries, and BMW cars. Its festive quality and proximity to the Alps make it the most popular city with Germans.

Why visit Munich? To shop and dine along its pedestrian malls, to wander among the dizzying smells and colors of the outdoor Viktualienmarkt food market, to clink mugs in a funky beer hall or dine in an elegant three-star restaurant. You'll also want to ride bikes or row boats through the beautiful English Gardens; visit two of Europe's most important museums—one for art, the other for science; and go to the opera. Above all you'll want to soak up the atmosphere of a city impressed with the stamp of royalty—and an "old" city center that was 70% destroyed by bombs during World War II but has been lovingly rebuilt.

The monk on the city's coat of arms recalls the city's origin as a monastic settlement (*München* comes from *Mönch*, which means "monk") around 1100. Eighty years later Bavaria was given to Otto of Wittelsbach—an underling of Holy Roman Emperor Friedrich Barbarossa—and for the next seven centuries, until 1918, the history of Bavaria and that of this family were intertwined. Munich became the ducal residence in 1255, and in 1503, the capital of Bavaria.

People say that the medieval **Church of Our Lady** (Frauenkirche) captures the essence of Munich today, but the city is basically modern and owes its beauty to the taste of Ludwig I of Bavaria (1825–48). Soon after he was crowned, Ludwig proclaimed, "I shall make Munich such an honor to Germany that no one who has not seen it can pretend to know the country"; and he proceeded to lay out avenues and found galleries, libraries, and churches. Through his love of Italy and Greece, he attracted architects and artists who built the **Pinakotheken** (art museums), enlarged the **Residenz** (Palace), and constructed Ludwigstrasse.

Ludwig was forced to abdicate as the result of an 18-month affair, at the age of 60, with a Spanish dancer named Lola Montez, the daughter of an Irish officer in India. She had burst into his quarters one day to protest her being banned from the stage.

Following the rule of Ludwig's son Maximilian II (1848–64), mad King Ludwig II (1864–86) assumed the throne. Ludwig II built the castles you'll see during your stay in Garmisch-Partenkirchen. It says much about the people of Munich that they still love Ludwig, and protect his memory as a person would protect his dreams.

When Ludwig II was declared insane and removed from the throne, his uncle, Prince Luitpold, son of Ludwig I, assumed the Regency. It was he who laid out the great thoroughfare that bears his name (Prinzregentenstrasse), built the **German Museum** (Deutsches Museum), and completed the **New City Hall** (Neues Rathaus).

Begin at **Karlstor,** one of the old city gates on **Karlsplatz,** also popularly known as Stachus. Beneath the square is an underground shopping arcade.

Pass through the Karlstor and enter the old part of the city, largely destroyed in the war, now the pedestrian street Neuhauserstrasse. On your left is **Bürgersaal Chapel,** which has a Rococo interior with some notable frescoes. Still on your left is the single-columned Richard Strauss fountain, which is decorated with scenes from the Munich-born composer's opera *Salome.* Next to the fountain is the **Church of St. Michael** (Michaelskirche), 1583–97, the first large Renaissance church in South Germany, and the inspiration for many others. Don't be surprised if you think you're in Rome, because this spacious, white stucco building was modeled on the Gesù. It was built for the Jesuits and restored after war. In the crypt is the tomb of Ludwig II of Bavaria (*see* the On to Ettal section, below, for notes on Ludwig).

Keep this church in mind as you visit (1) the Church of Our Lady (Frauenkirche), 1468–88; (2) the Church of the Theatines (Theatinerkirche), 1663–75; and (3) the Church of the Asam

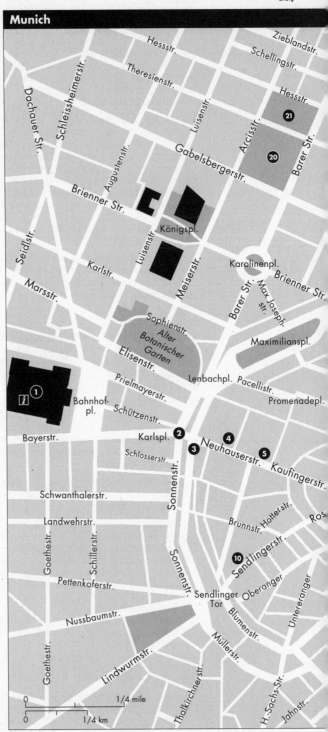

Munich

Alte Pinakothek, **20**
Altes Rathaus, **9**
Asamkirche, **10**
Bürgersaal, **4**
Englischer Garten, **18**
Feldherrnhalle, **16**
Frauenkirche, **6**
Hauptbahnhof, **1**
Haus der Kunst, **19**
Hofgarten, **14**
Karlsplatz, **2**
Karlstor, **3**
Marienplatz, **7**
Michaelskirche, **5**
Nationaltheater, **13**
Neue Pinakothek, **21**
Neues Rathaus, **8**
Residenz, **12**
Siegestor, **17**
Theatinerkirche, **15**
Viktualienmarkt, **11**

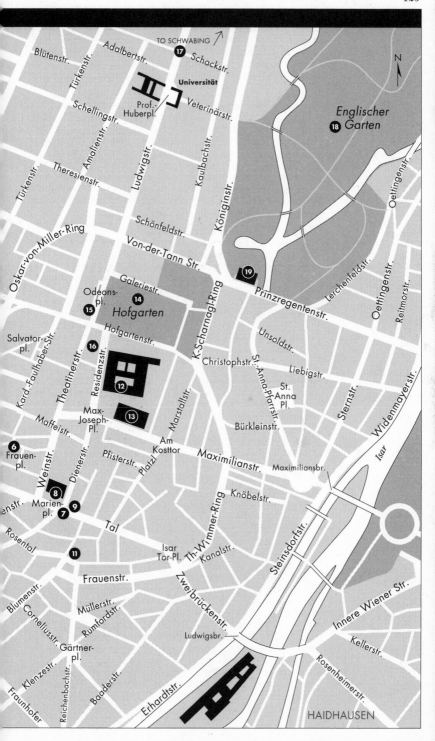

Brothers (Asamkirche), 1733. In these four churches you can trace the history of German architecture from Gothic to Baroque. The Frauenkirche is Bavarian Late Gothic; Michaelskirche is Renaissance; the Theatinerkirche is late Renaissance, but with the rich designs of the Italian Baroque; and the Asamkirche shows the full, riotous flowering of South German Baroque.

Neuhauserstrasse turns into Kaufingerstrasse. On your left, a block past St. Michael's, is a street leading to the **Church of Our Lady**. This late Gothic hall church has more character than originality, but its onion-shape domes have been symbols of Munich since they were added in 1525. One of them, purists will be glad to note, is three feet higher than the other. Notice, too, the absence of buttresses, and the walls running smoothly up to the roof. The redbrick exterior is strikingly plain but massive and has a strength and integrity missing from many of the more ostentatious, imitative churches around town.

The purity of line is unbroken inside, too. Largely restored since the war, the nave has 22 powerful pillars dividing it into three parts, and simple white walls that frame the light from the stained-glass windows. The interior is memorable for its stark whiteness, its height, and the way in which the pillars seem to hide the aisles. The ancient art and furnishings— hidden away during the war—stand out dramatically against the modern decor. In the south nave (on your right, facing the altar) is the black marble tomb (1622) of Ludwig the Bavarian. Not to be confused with his namesake, Ludwig II, Ludwig the Bavarian was one of the first Wittelsbachs, who went on to become king of Germany in 1314 and Emperor in 1328.

Continue along Kaufingerstrasse to the square known as Marienplatz—the heart of the city. You'll find luxury shops, cafés, and restaurants here. Marienplatz was the central market until 1853 and is still a lively meeting place for people from all walks of life. During the summer, street musicians, jugglers, and clowns perform here. At Christmas there is a big outdoor market, known as the Christkindlmarkt, with rows of gaily colored stalls selling tree decorations, small gifts, or **Gluhwein**, a hot punchlike alcoholic drink.

To the left of the square is the **New Town Hall** (Neues Rathaus), 1867–1908. One of Ludwig's more fanciful creations, it looks back on the golden age of the city during the Middle Ages, when the Wittelsbach realm included both North and South Germany and the Low Countries. Built in Flemish Gothic style, it was also meant to recall the rich autonomous towns of Flanders and thus the emancipation of Bavaria from the royal house. The Rathaus is nothing but a pastiche of styles, but it is fun and impressive, nonetheless. On clear days the view from the tower (open weekdays 9:30–4) extends as far south as the Alps. If you are in the square at 11 AM (also 5 PM in summer) or 9 PM, you can watch the figures in the *Glockenspiel* (the town hall clock) spring to life. Two knights joust in honor of a celebrated 16th-century marriage, ending in victory for the Bavarian nobleman. The coopers (makers of wood casks) dance in gratitude for the town's escape from a 16th-century plague. If you arrive too early, find a window table in a third-floor café across the square.

South of the Marienplatz is **St. Peter's** (Peterskirche), an old Gothic basilica in Rococo dress. The archways seem to squeeze the walls together, forcing the worshiper's eyes upward to God. At the same time, the 12 gilded apostles direct your gaze forward to the golden altar. The 90-m (300-ft) tower ("Old Peter") offers another view of the Alps.

From Marienplatz take a short side trip down Sendlingerstrasse (a quality shopping street) to the **Church of the Asam Brothers** on the right. This jewel box, this spiritual ballroom, was built by the brothers Asam from 1733 to 1746 and is the best example of late German Baroque architecture in town. The brothers built it at their own expense in a narrow space between two buildings—which is why the usual east–west axis (the entrance to the west, the altar to the east) has been reversed. Making a virtue of necessity, the brothers installed windows above the door. The light filtering through them forces your eyes from the altar to the suspended figure of Christ, and upward to the picture of the Ascension.

The Asam brothers would have understood what Descartes, that master of reason, meant when he said, "The nature of men is such that they value only those things which arouse their admiration, and which they cannot entirely grasp." Note how the walls are molded, as if made of wax or clay. Form, the essence of Renaissance art, dissolves. Everything moves, undulates, flows. Nothing *is;* everything *becomes.*

You may not like the Asamkirche because it is the art of the facade. In friends as in furnishings, you don't like to be fooled by surface charm, but want things to be what they seem. To the Asam brothers, however, as to all Baroque artists, the essence was revealed through appearances. The facade was not an escape from or a distortion of reality, but proof of God's kingdom here on Earth.

From the Asamkirche, walk to the busy, colorful outdoor **Food Market** (Viktualienmarkt), which moved here from Marienplatz in the last century. A wide selection of wines, cheeses, fruits, vegetables, and flowers is displayed daily here, together with game meat such as deer and boar. Some of the best and most intricate dried flower posies can be bought here, too.

Time Out If the scene brings on hunger pangs, stop for a Schweinswürstl or a bowl of hot soup at the **Münchner Suppenküche,** or an order of fish (*Fischsemmel*) at the **Nordseefischhalle.**

Return to St. Peter's Church, near Marienplatz. On the northeast side is a street called the Burgstrasse. At Number 5 is the **Weinstadl** (1552), the oldest house in town. At Number 10, take the passage right to the Lederstrasse. Turn left on the Orlandostrasse to the Platzl.

Here you'll find the **Hofbräuhaus,** the most famous of Munich's beer halls. The atmosphere is as heady as the ale, which is drunk from large glass mugs.

Take the Pfisterstrasse to the **Old Castle** (Alter Hof) on your left, and turn right on the Hofgraben to Maximilianstrasse. Cross over, to the Max Joseph Platz. On your right is the **National Theater,** which houses the Bavarian State Opera. Ahead of you, across the square, is the entrance to the **Residenz**

(Palace)—the home of the Dukes of Wittelsbach for more than 650 years.

Restored since the war, the Residenz contains a Treasury with beautiful crucifixes, diadems, and illuminated books; and a Palace Museum with both gilded State Rooms and Porcelain Rooms displaying masterpieces from Nymphenburg and Sèvres. *Admission: DM 3.50 adults, children under age 15 accompanied by an adult free. Open Tues.–Sat. 10–4:30, Sun. 10–1; closed Mon.*

The Residenz is bordered on the west by Residenzstrasse, which takes you to the Odeonsplatz (another square) overlooked by the lofty **Church of the Theatines,** 1663–75. The elaborate stucco work in the chancel and dome are indicative of Baroque at its best.

From Theatinerkirche, head back down Residenzstrasse to Maximilianstrasse. Many of Munich's most expensive shops are along this street.

If you find the following places too far to reach by foot, and you're taking public transportation, save money with either a multijourney blue *Streifenkarten* (strip tickets) or a 24 *Studenkarte* (24-hour ticket). Both are valid for use on the city's network of buses, subways (U-bahn), and trams.

Schwabing, a 10-minute subway ride from center city, is a fashionable suburb bordering the English Gardens (Englischer Garten). A onetime Greenwich Village–style student quarter, Schwabing is now a place for the chic pavement café set by day and the disco or jazz bar crowd by night. Schwabing's heart is Münchener Freiheit (take subway lines 3 or 6), home of the best ice-cream parlors. Try Cafe Münchener Freiheit, and be sure to notice the wonderful marzipan figures in the shop window.

While visiting Schwabing, stroll through the lovely **Englischer Garten**—Munich's most famous park, and the largest city park in Europe. You can jog, ride rented bikes, row boats on a lake, or quench your thirst beneath the chestnut trees at the Chinese Tower beer garden, which actually has a Chinese pagoda from which a Bavarian brass band entertains the crowd (weekends and Wednesdays). Here you can hire a horse-drawn carriage for a ride around the park (bus 54 stops at the beer garden).

Anyone with even a passing interest in art will want to visit the **Alte Pinakothek** (the old picture gallery), which houses the painting collections of several centuries of Wittelsbachs, beginning in the early 16th century. Under Ludwig I, the Alte Pinakothek became one of the top art museums in Europe. The collection includes notable works by Albrecht Dürer, Albrecht Altdorfer, Raphael, Titian, Leonardo da Vinci, Anthony Van Dyck, Peter Paul Rubens, Rembrandt, and El Greco.

Nearby is the **Neue Pinakothek,** featuring works by the French Impressionists (Claude Monet, Edgar Degas, and others), and modern German painting, beginning with the wonderfully tasteless, oversentimental works of the German Romantics.

Straddling an island in the Isar River is the **Deutsches Museum** (German Museum), one of the world's outstanding museums of science and technology. You can travel from prehistory into the space age in an hour, but the scale models and hands-on exhibits could keep you and your children happy for days.

Breweries can be visited by appointment. Contact Löwenbräu (tel. 089/52–001) or Paulaner-Salvator-Thomasbräu (tel. 089/41–151).

Nymphenburg—take tram 12 from Rotkreuzplatz (U-bahn 1)—is the former summer palace of the Bavarian rulers. The oldest part dates from 1664, with buildings and arcades added during the next century. The Rococo Hall of Mirrors is an exercise in wowmanship. In the Gallery of Beauty (Schönheits Galerie) Ludwig I collected portraits of beautiful women, both rich and poor, including his beloved Lola, for whom he forfeited his kingdom; see if you share his taste. It's not surprising that a back room upstairs was Ludwig II's favorite—it's so remote. In the peaceful park of woodland and lakes behind the palace you may spot wild deer. The park adjoins the colorful Botanic Gardens, which include tropical plant greenhouses. The high point is a visit to the Amalienburg hunting lodge, a Rococo masterpiece, where no one seems to have hunted for anything but pleasure. Animals, birds, leaves—all join in a Rococo dance that captures joy and movement of the chase. *Admission: DM 2.50 adults, children under 15 free when accompanied by an adult. Open Tues.–Sun. 10–12:30 and 1:30–4:00.*

Kids in particular will love the museum of Royal Carriages, where a mermaid holds the lamp on Ludwig II's carriage. Could anything be less appropriate? *Admission DM 2.50 adults, DM 1.50 children. Open Tues.–Sat. 10–4:30, Sun. 10–1PM.*

"Those who cannot remember the past are condemned to repeat it," says the brochure for the 4-hour morning tours to the Concentration Camp Memorial at **Dachau.** In this ultimate symbol of Nazi atrocities, 32 km (20 mi) northwest of Munich, you can see cell-block interiors and the Krematorium where more than 206,000 prisoners lost their lives (see Guided Tours, above). *Admission free. Open Tues.–Sun. 9–5 with a documentary film presentation in English at 11:30 and 3:30.*

Dining Müncheners, with their appetite for Bavarian specialties, keep scores of snack bar *(schnell imbiss)* stalls busy all day long. Try *Leberkäs,* a beef and pork meat loaf served with sharp mustard; *Fleischflanzerl,* spicy meatballs; and *Schweinswürstl,* small grilled pork sausages often served with sauerkraut. The best stalls are in the Viktualienmarkt.

A favorite late breakfast *(Brotzeit)* dish is *Weisswurst,* the succulent white sausage made with veal and parsley. Eat them either at **zum Spöckmeier** on Rosenstrasse, off Marienplatz, or the **Franziskaner** on Perusastrasse. Both places make Weisswurst on the premises.

Beer garden specialties include **Steckelfisch,** charcoal-grilled mackerel on a stick; **Radi,** a giant white radish sliced wafer thin; and **Obatz'n,** a spicy cocktail of Camembert cheese, butter, spring onions, paprika, and caraway seeds.

Aubergine, in the heart of the city, is run by chef Eckart Witzigmann, who believes in sharp modern decor to match his kitchen creations. Witzigmann also favors wild game meat, but fish dishes are a specialty, too. *Maximilianspl. 5, tel. 089/598–171. Reservations required. Jacket and tie required. MC. Closed Sun., Mon., first 3 wks of Aug. Very Expensive.*
Königshof serves some of the best hotel food in town. The Belle

Époque terrace restaurant has picture windows overlooking the busy Karlsplatz. The cuisine is a mix of nouvelle and classical, with such favorites as crab bisque, fillet of Angus beef, and grilled fresh trout. *Karlspl. 25, tel. 089/558–412. Reservations advised. Jacket and tie required. AE, MC. Very Expensive.*

Tantris is where Heinz Winkler presides over a kitchen that produces much that is delectable but little that resembles traditional Bavarian cooking. The award-winning Winkler likes to be innovative, so be ready for surprises. Try dishes with venison or pigeon breasts. *Johann-Fichtestr. 7, near Munchener Freiheit, tel. 089/362–061. Reservations required. Jacket and tie required. AE, DC, MC. Closed Sun., Mon., and most of Aug. Very Expensive.*

Alois Dallmayr's is Munich's answer to London's Fortnum and Mason: a black-tie gourmet food shop with a busy, sophisticated upstairs restaurant. An ideal trysting place for a hot lunch or salad, or a gooey dessert you'll be talking about for years. *Dienerstr. 14, tel. 089/213–5100. No reservations. Jacket and tie advised. MC, V. Expensive.*

Käfer Schänke, off Prinzregentstrasse, is another food delicacy store offering fresh fish, Caspian caviar and Hungarian goose liver. When you've had enough looking, dine in the charcuterie or in the upstairs Italian/French restaurant with a Bavarian flair. The ambience is gay and informal. *Schumannstr. 1, tel. 089/41–681. Reservations advised. Jacket and tie advised. AE, DC, MC. Closed Sun. and holidays. Expensive.*

Chesa Rüegg, close to the Hotel Vier Jahreszeiten, is an excellent Swiss restaurant with a yodelly, Engadine look, complete with copper pans and beamed ceilings. Popular dishes include fresh lobster, terrine of fish, and the best *Geschnetzeltes* (shredded veal) you've ever had. *Wurzerstr. 18, tel. 089/297–114. Reservations advised. Dress: casual. AE, V. Closed weekends and holidays. Moderate.*

Île de France, across the river Isar from the Deutsches Museum, is a nice French bistro with French specialties at reasonable prices. *Rosenheimerstr. 32, tel. 089/448–1366. Reservations advised. Jacket and tie advised. MC, V. Closed Sun., and Mon., Sat. lunch. Moderate.*

Augustiner Gastätte serves a broad selection of good-quality Bavarian dishes at reasonable prices. Wash down your meal with the favorite beer of the locals in a bustling Central European atmosphere. Best bets: *Schweinehaxen,* crispy knuckle of pork; or *spanferkel,* tender grilled chops. *Neuhauserst. 16 on the pedestrian mall, tel. 089/260–4106). No reservations. Dress: casual. No credit cards. Inexpensive.*

Ratskeller, where 1,000 people can dine at once, is another place to go for a *Knöedelsuppe* (clear soup with liver dumplings) or *Schlachtplatte* (roast pork or sausages on sauerkraut). *Marienpl. 8, tel. 089/220–313. Reservations not necessary. Dress: casual. No credit cards. Closed Sun. Inexpensive.*

Straubinger Hof, near the Outdoor Market (Viktualienmarkt), is the place to go for hard-to-find Bavarian specialties, such as baked udder and pudding, and pork with root vegetables. If you can pronounce it, try *kälberne Briesmilzwurst in aufgeschmelzter Brotsuppe*—a soup that will keep you strong for the rest of the day. Other popular dishes include roast suckling pig with potato dumplings, and *Kaiserschmarren,* a pancake with eggs and apples. One portion per family, please! *Blumenstr. 5, tel. 089/260–8444 near St. Peter's Church. Reser-*

vations not necessary. Dress: casual. No credit cards. Closed Sun., holidays, and Sat. lunch. Inexpensive.

A visit to Munich would be incomplete without sampling the atmosphere of a **beer hall** or **beer garden** in summer. The city has six big breweries plus a growing number of fashionable "house" breweries, where the beer is brewed in the pub and you can watch the process as you sit and sip! The most famous hall is the **Hofbräuhaus** (Am Platzl), but it's now so overrun with tourists it's worth a miss. For local earthiness try instead the **Mathäser** (Löwenbräu), arguably the biggest pub in the world, on Bayerstrasse, near Karlsplatz. The tiny **Isarbräu** brewery-pub is in a converted railway station on suburban S-bahn line 7 at Grosshesselohe. The train deposits you virtually in the pub! The most central beer garden is in the Viktualienmarkt.

Munich is also famous for its **wine taverns,** where the emphasis is on drinking rather than eating. Try the **Pfälzer Weinprobierstube** (Residenzstr. 1, tel. 089/225–628) for a wide selection of wines served in stone arched rooms with a thighslapping atmosphere; or the **Weinstadl** (Burgstr. 5, tel. 089/221–047).

Lodging Reservations are advisable, but if you arrive without a booking, the Münchner Hotel Verbund (Arnulfstr. 44, tel.089/554–614) can often help with decent and moderately priced rooms. You can also contact the city tourist office: Fremdenverkehrsamt (Postfach, 8000 Munich 1, tel.089/23–911) for a brochure.

Bayerischer Hof is a very large, traditional hotel with a clientele that's well heeled. The lobby has Italian marble floors, painted marble columns, and raw wood—an interesting blend of Caesar and Ludwig. The older bedrooms offer ornate comfort; the newer rooms offer functionalism. State your preference. For a taste of something different in central Europe, try the Polynesian food in Trader Vic's restaurant in the basement. *Promenade pl. 6, tel. 089/21–200. 440 rooms. Facilities: 3 restaurants, nightclub, rooftop pool, garage, sauna, masseur, hairdresser. AE, DC, MC, V. Very Expensive.*

Vier Jahreszeiten (Four Seasons) is on Munich's most exclusive shopping street and is one of the city's reknowned hotels. It is part of a chain but still retains its old charm and continues to attract the famous. A quiet dignity pervades the public rooms, with their rich mahogany paneling. Rooms have a friendly, residential hotel feeling to them—more Teutonic than Bavarian, with old-fashioned couches and framed botanicals. The less expensive rooms are smaller but thoughtfully furnished. *Maximilianstr. 17, tel. 089/230–390. 340 rooms with bath, plus 25 apartments. Facilities: restaurant, nightclub, pool, sauna, garage, car rental service. AE, DC, MC, V. Very Expensive.*

Eden Wolff Hotel, a large, ornate, and cozy place to base yourself, is next door to the main train station, information offices, and tour departure point. *Arnulfstr. 4, tel. 089/551–150. 210 rooms with bath. Facilities: restaurant, bar. AE, DC, MC, V. Expensive.*

Hotel Prinzregent is across the river. It may be newish, but some unobtrusive Bavarian touches, such as a breakfast room paneled with wood from an old farmhouse, make it an attractive place to stay. *Ismaninger Str. 42, tel. 089/470–2081. 70 rooms with shower. Facilities: bar, pool, sauna. AE, DC, MC, V. Expensive.*

Hotel Splendid, farther along Maximilianstrasse, offers excellent homey service in cozy surroundings. In warm weather, breakfast is served in a pretty inner courtyard. *Maximilianstr. 54, tel. 089/296–606. 37 rooms with bath. Facilities: bar serving light meals. AE, DC, MC, V. Expensive.*

Königshof is ideally located at the west end of the mall, and has a first-class restaurant overlooking Karlsplatz. The lobby is hushed and elegant. Rooms are decorated with soft, salmon-colored walls, swag curtains, and quality antique reproduction furniture. Corner rooms are best. *Karlspl. 25, tel. 089/558–412. 106 rooms with bath. Facilities: restaurant, piano bar. AE, DC, MC, V. Expensive.*

Domus, close to the heart of the city but also handy for the Englischer Garten and Haus der Kunst, an art gallery, and one of the few surviving examples of Nazi-commissioned architecture, is not cheap for a small hotel, but provides personal, friendly service. *St. Annastr., tel. 089/221–704. 45 rooms with bath. Facilities: bar serving snacks. AE, DC, MC, V. Closed Dec. 22–26. Moderate.*

Gästehaus am Englischer Garten is a converted, ivy-covered 19th-century mill only steps from Munich's largest and loveliest park. Rooms are plain, but the hotel is beautifully located and booking is necessary well in advance. Avoid the annex. Bed and breakfast only. *Liebergesellstr. 8, tel. 089/392–034. 34 rooms, not all with bath. No credit cards. Moderate.*

Kriemhild is an attractive place to stay if you are on a tight budget, have your family along, and don't mind being some way from center city. It's very close to the Nymphenburg Palace, botanic gardens, and Munich's biggest and most famous beer garden, the Hirschgarten. The family-run pension lays on the sort of breakfast that will keep you going through the day. *Guntherstr. 16, tel. 089/170–077. 40 rooms, 20 with bath. Facilities: bar. MC, V. Inexpensive.*

Pension Beck. This is very much a functional pension, but it is clean and well run. It is convenient to the old center, museums, and the Englischer Garten. Tram 20 stops outside. *Thierschstr. 36, tel. 089/220–708. 100 beds, including single, double, and multibed rooms, some with shower. No credit cards. Inexpensive.*

The Alps

The Autostrasse (A95) whirls you from Munich to Garmisch-Partenkirchen in only an hour. A slower, more scenic route is described below.

Andechs Take A96 west of Munich and follow exit signs to the Ammersee. If you are a beer drinker, you may want to take a somewhat roundabout route to Garmisch to taste what many Bavarians tell their overseas guests is one of the best beers in Germany—the dark, rich Andechser Bergbock—not a beer to be trifled with, especially if you're driving. It's brewed in a genuine monastery brewery (Klosterbrauerei), next door to the abbey in the village of Andechs, 6.4 km (4 mi) south of Herrsching—a terminus town on the Munich S-bahn railway system—and the 17.6-km (11-mi) long Ammersee (Ammer Lake). The Gothic **Abbey Church** (Klosterkirche), now in Rococo dress, is in itself well worth a visit.

Murnau The fast route is south from Munich on A95 for about 45 minutes to the Murnau exit. The more scenic route is via Andechs and Route 2.

Lodging **Alpenhof Murnau** is a tasteful, comfortable, modern hotel with traditional furnishings and the best nouvelle dining in the area. The hotel is in a peaceful, rural setting with a distant view of the Alps: a sensible place to stay if you leave Munich in the afternoon and don't want to deal with Garmisch till the following day. *Ramsachstr. 8, tel. 08841/1045. 48 rooms. Facilities: restaurant, outdoor heated pool, gardens. No credit cards. Expensive.*

Garmisch-Partenkirchen This is the largest winter sports complex in Germany, built almost entirely since World War I. The two towns—the hyphen is the stream that flows between them—sit in a valley ringed by the Bavarian Alps, including Germany's highest peak, the Zugspitze. Though originally a ski resort—the host for the 1936 winter Olympic Games—Garmisch-Partenkirchen has become a town for all seasons—the base for year-round sports and excursions into the countryside.

What Garmisch-Partenkirchen is not is a quaint Alpine village like Zermatt, huddled beneath towering peaks. It also lacks the panache of a St. Moritz, and seems to insinuate itself, rather than grow out of the Alpine setting. On the positive side, it can give you all the pampering you want after a day in the Great Outdoors, and has hotels and restaurants for all tastes and budgets. It makes a great base for hikes, scenic drives, cable car rides, and visits both to the Royal Castles of Ludwig II and to the Passion Play village of Oberammergau. If that's not enough to keep you busy, the town has six Olympic-size pools and three indoor skating rinks that seat 12,000! Furthermore, despite its success, Garmisch-Partenkirchen has remained small in scale, with nothing higher than an Alpine roof. Garmisch itself is the more fashionable and expensive part of town—more central to the cafés and nighttime activities; Partenkirchen is more low-key and family-oriented. But should both Garmisch and Partenkirchen be too commercial for your taste, you can stay in any of dozens of charming, family-run chalets on the roads up to the mountains, and, like the American troops stationed nearby, come into town for R & R.

The ski slopes are open from December through May, but the cog railway and cable car to the highest peak, the **Zugspitze** 2915.1m (9,717 ft), are open year-round, and a trip to the top is a must. For two different experiences, take the train one way and the cable car the other. It's a 2099.9-m (7,000-ft) climb from Garmisch to the summit, a trip that can be rough on the heart if made too quickly, so take the train up, and the faster cable car down. Trains leave almost hourly from 8 to 4 from Zugspitzbahn station in Garmisch and stop at **Lake Eibsee** on their way to the top. It's a 40-minute train ride just to the lake, so you may want to drive there—a 20-minute trip—and catch the train before it begins its ascent. The train bores through a 4-km (2½-mi) tunnel to the Hotel Schneefernerhaus at 2607.3 m (8,691 ft). From here you board a cable car to the summit—a trip as scenic (if there are no clouds) as flying over the Alps in a plane. The hotel, despite breathtaking views, is more for serious skiers than for lovers or tourists, since it has only single beds; and when the last train or cable car descends, there is nowhere to go. (The hotel does serve dinner, which is included in the rate.)

Another popular cable car ride if you have less time is a 20-minute trip direct from Partenkirchen to the 1,751.9-m (5,840-ft) summit of the **Wank.** The most dramatic high-altitude hike for the casual traveler in good condition is to take the cable car to the top of the Wank, and walk along the ridge.

Another dramatic walk—one anyone can make if the route is not blocked by snow—is through **Partnachklamm Gorge,** following a trail gouged from a ledge of rock above the frothing or frozen water. Park near the Partenkirchen Sports Stadium and walk or take a horse-drawn carriage to the Graseck cable car (the road is closed to cars). Take the cable car to the lower station. There's a modern hotel here, the **Forsthaus Graseck Inn** (tel. 08821/54–006), where you can stop for lunch or drinks and take in the view on the sun terrace at 899.75m (2,950 ft). From the inn, a path leads up one slope of the valley. Don't take the first right, which descends into the valley; continue past the Wetterstein-Alm Inn (a friendly place for a snack), and then turn right, to the bottom of the gorge, which you follow downstream. It's an easy walk, all downhill, back to your car.

Later, at the casino at the **Spielbank Garmisch-Partenkirchen** (Bahnhofpl. 74, tel. 08821/53–099) you can try your luck at roulette, baccarat, or blackjack from 3 PM daily.

Dining **Clausings Post Hotel** offers two dining venues to suit different tastes: romantic candlelit gourmet dinners are served in the Klause restaurant, or you can eat Bavarian style in the noisier Post Hörndl tavern, with dancing and folk music. *Marienpl. 12, tel. 08821/58–071. AE, DC, V. Expensive.*

Tonihof, 14.4 km (9 mi) from Garmisch, is one of the best restaurants south of Munich. A nouvelle menu features fresh fish, poultry, vegetables, and fruit. *Walchenseestr. 42, Eschenlohe; tel. 08824/1021. Reservations advised. Jacket and tie required. DC, MC, V. Closed Wed. Expensive.*

Restaurant Alpenhof im Casino has one adequate restaurant with local dishes at moderate prices, and a smaller "Casino Stube" for people who are willing to pay for a top French meal. *Bahnhofstr. 74, tel. 08821/59–055. Moderate–Expensive.*

Reindl-Grill in the Hotel Partenkirchner Hof focuses more on food than on decor. It's not just a grill, it's an above-average restaurant serving the very freshest fish, veal, venison, and seasonal vegetables. Popular favorites include Lady Curzon soup, and bouillabaisse. For dessert, try peach Melba. *Bahnhofstr. 15, tel. 08821/58–025. Moderate.*

Gasthof Fraundorfer offers a more down-to-earth evening. Try the *schnitzel* or the *schweinebraten. Ludwigstr. 24, tel. 08821/ 2176. Closed Tues. and Nov. 6–Dec. 6. AE, MC, V. Inexpensive.*

Haus Ingeborg. While driving to or from Lake Eibsee, stop for lunch or pastry at this terrace restaurant. For a more ambitious meal, try such local specialties—in season—as rainbow trout or roe deer with pears and cranberries. *Loisachstr. 38, Granau, tel. 08821/81–856. Inexpensive.*

Garmisch has many pleasant outdoor cafés where you can people-watch under a crowd of stars. Try the moderately priced **Café-Konditorei Kronner** on Achenfeldstrasse.

Many of the smaller restaurants and hotels in the town, and surrounding countryside, take a holiday break mid-November to mid-December before the hectic winter season.

Lodging Almost all hotels are low-roofed Alpine chalets with carved wood balconies. Ask for a room with a view.

Grand-Hotel Sonnenbichl, which welcomes you with an Italian-ate marble foyer, is an Old World hotel fed by new Arab money. The hotel's symbol is the peacock—could anything be more unBavarian? The only drawbacks are the hotel's lack of privacy (it's close to the road), and the necessity of looking out over the traffic to see the distant mountains. Be sure to get an upstairs room with a mountain view; at these prices, you don't want to stare out at the parking lot. *Burgstr. 97, tel. 08821/7020. 90 rooms, all with bath. Facilities: restaurant "Blauer Salon" (nouvelle cuisine), Bavarian-style bar, sauna, solarium, heated pool, tennis, golf. AE, DC, MC, V. Very Expensive.*

Dorint Sporthotel is a fairly recent addition to the choice of accommodation. It offers a wide range of facilities, particularly for the athletically inclined, but you can also retire to your rustic-style apartment after an unenergetic evening at the in-house wine tavern. If your children are along, they can keep themselves busy in the playroom while you try your hand at tennis or bowling or take a skiing lesson in the hotel school run by German champions Rosi Mittermaier and Christian Neureuther. *Mittenwalderstr. 59, tel. 08821/7060. 156 apartments. Facilities: 2 restaurants, 2 bars, nightclub, indoor pool, solarium, sauna. AE, DC, MC, V. Expensive.*

Obermühle. An old waterwheel turns outside to remind you of the hotel's antiquity—it dates from 1634, although there's not much of the original left to see. It has all the modern facilities of a Best Western hotel, plus some Bavarian-style rustic decor. *Mühlstr. 22, tel. 088821/7040. 102 rooms with bath, plus several suites. Facilities: restaurant, wine bar, indoor pool, sauna, solarium. AE, DC, MC, V. Expensive.*

Posthotel Partenkirchen. This, one of the oldest buildings in the locality, dates from 1542 and claims to have entertained Bavarian kings on their journeys through the district. It's a classic of the "post house" style—that of the staging places where horse-drawn coaches carrying travelers and mail stopped to rest. There's lovely paneling and stuccowork, and some colorful antiques, including old painted chests and carved armoires. *Ludwigstr. 49, tel. 08821/51–067. 60 rooms, most with bath. Facilities: restaurant (offering a mix of French style and Bavarian cooking). AE, DC, MC, V. Expensive.*

Garmischer Hof, centrally located close to the train station, offers country Bavarian-style comfort, rooms with mountain views, and pleasant gardens. The room price includes a generous Bavarian buffet breakfast—just the thing to set you up for a day in the fresh mountain air. *Bahnhofstr. 53, tel. 08821/51–091, 38 rooms with bath. AE, DC, MC. Moderate.*

Hotel Roter Hahn is only three minutes from the station and the Zugspitzbahn, the special railway to the mountain peak. It's a fairly functional place for people who are not going to spend a lot of time at home although, surprisingly for a hotel of its class, it boasts an indoor pool. *Bahnhofstr. 44, tel. 08821/54–065. 32 rooms, most with bath. Facilities: pool. No credit cards. Moderate.*

Gasthof Fraundorfer is a colorful family-run Bavarian inn located in old Partenkirchen. Josef and Bärbel Fraundorfer provide traditional Bavarian hospitality—from the kitchen to the musical evenings featuring accordion music and folk dancing. *Ludwigstr. 24, tel. 08821/2176. 24 rooms, most with bath. Closed Tues. and Nov. 6–Dec. 6. AE, MC, V. Inexpensive.*

Haus Kornmüller is an ornate, wood-balconied guest house set in colorful gardens with mountain views. It offers excellent value if you are on a tight budget. In addition to the main house, there is an adjoining apartment house. *Höllentalstr. 36, tel. 08821/3557. 18 rooms, 9 with bath, 8 apartments. AE, MC, V. Inexpensive.*

On to Ettal A must trip from **Garmisch** is to the three Royal Castles identified with Ludwig II: Neuschwanstein, Hohenschwangau, and Linderhof. You have a choice of two routes: a northern route through Oberammergau, and a southern route past Linderhof. The mountainous southern route is considerably more dramatic and has the added perk of a trip to another country (Austria). Best bet is to take one route going, and the other back. If you plan to visit Linderhof, begin with the southern route so you reach the castle early in the day; otherwise, you won't get there until after it's closed. The following itinerary takes you to the castles by this southern route, and returns you by the northern route. It's going to be a long day, so leave early in the morning, and don't expect to return to Garmisch till dark.

Ettal Take Route 23 north from Garmisch-Partenkirchen to Oberau, and continue about 4.8 km (3 mi) to **Ettal.** The size of the abbey —now a boarding school—is extraordinary. It was founded by Ludwig the Bavarian in 1330, but wears 18th-century Baroque dress.

The road splits past Ettal. The right fork (Route 23) continues north to Oberammergau. Take the left fork to Linderhof.

Dining **Ludwig der Bayer** is a hotel-restaurant in the center of town, opposite the abbey. Stop for some yellow or green Kloster Liqueur produced by the monks or for one of the five varieties of beer they brew. *Kaiser Ludwig Pl. 10, Ettal, tel. 08822/6601. Reservations advisable. Dress: casual. No credit cards. Moderate.*

The Royal Castles (Königsschlösser)

Of the three castles, Neuschwanstein is the most impressive, Linderhof the least. But whether you have time to see one castle or three, it helps to know about the man whose life was intimately entwined with all of them—Ludwig II. It's important, too, to understand the symbolism of the swan, which you'll see so often as you tour the castles.

Ludwig II, the son of Maximilian II, was born in 1845 in Nymphenburg Castle (which you saw in Munich) but spent almost all his youth at his father's castle, Hohenschwangau, in the Bavarian Alps. This was a fairy fortress, capturing the spirit of the Middle Ages, where Maximilian could escape the pressures of official life in Munich. The walls of Hohenschwangau were covered with paintings of the swan knight Lohengrin, and the young, impressionable Ludwig fell under their spell. Maximilian gave his son a Spartan education, seldom allowing him to see the real world of Munich. The boy turned his back on his stern father, and played not with soldiers but with puppets and dolls. His mother—one of the few women he ever saw—read him the Greek myths, including the story of how Zeus created swans from the waves.

When news came that his father was dying, Ludwig was absorbed in the text of Wagner's *Lohengrin.* The opera is based on a medieval German story of the knight Lohengrin, son of Parsifal, who sets off from the Castle of the Grail on the back of a swan to rescue the Princess Elsa. In the German legend, he saves her and is given her hand in marriage; but when she asks his name, in violation of a pledge, he must return to his castle, and the swan turns into Elsa's brother.

In 1864, at the age of 18, Ludwig became the king of Bavaria. One of his first royal wishes was to meet with the German composer Richard Wagner, who was at the time living at the Bayerischer Hof in Munich, in flight from his creditors. Ludwig had seen *Lohengrin* four years earlier and lived for the moment when he could meet its creator and help produce his plays. The 51-year-old composer met the 19-year-old king at Hohenschwangau and thereafter became his soul mate, his confidant, his adviser.

Three years after assuming the throne, Ludwig became engaged to his cousin, Princess Sophie of Bavaria, a sister of the Austrian empress, Elizabeth. He is said never to have kissed her on the lips, only on the forehead, but he was wildly in love with her—why else would he spend his days rowing with her in a swan-shape boat? And why else would he call her Elsa?

As the wedding day approached, Ludwig ordered his trousseau brocaded with scenes from *Lohengrin*. But then, at a ball for the royal couple, he rushed off to catch the last act of an opera without saying good-bye to anyone, including Sophie, and everyone knew the engagement was in trouble. Sophie, he had discovered, was only human. "When I marry, I want a Queen, a Mother for my country, not an imperious mistress," he explained later. But he never married. Instead, he flew back to Wagner. And on the ruins of an ancient castle near his father's, he decided to build an even grander castle of his own.

Neuschwanstein is a child's idea of a medieval knight's castle. It took 17 years to build, but was never finished. As Ludwig became embroiled in hopeless wars, he withdrew more into himself and emptied his country's treasury to satisfy his fantasies. He began Linderhof, a Rococo pleasure palace with an artificial Blue Grotto in imitation of the one at Capri. He built Herrenchiemsee, modeled on Versailles, on an island in the Chiemsee, a large lake in southeast Bavaria.

In June 1886, Ludwig was declared insane by a state commission, which visited Neuschwanstein and diagnosed him to be suffering from advanced paranoia. He was taken to Berg, overlooking Starnberg Lake, near Munich. On June 13—three days after his uncle Luitpold had been named his successor as prince regent—both Ludwig and Dr. Bernhard von Gudden, the psychiatrist into whose care he had been entrusted, were found dead in the lake. The official version of the deaths is that Ludwig committed suicide and von Gudden died trying to save him. But there has been considerable speculation over the years that Ludwig was murdered because he had become an embarrassment to the authorities. In the stables of a nearby friend there were 10 horses instead of two—was he trying to escape? Most important of all, was he truly insane, or merely the victim of a plot? After all, he was judged by physicians who never examined him. What was taken for madness may have been merely hypersensitivity. "If I were a poet I might be able to reap praise by putting [my thoughts] into verse," Ludwig told an interviewer. "But the talent of expression was not given me, and so I must bear being laughed at, scorned at, and slandered. I am called a fool. Will God call me a fool when I am summoned before Him?"

The Bavarian people have always loved Ludwig, and if they could play God, even today, they would redeem him, or at least forgive him. An affront to him is an affront to their fierce sense of regional pride. In a workaday world, here was a man who played. In a land of beer and sausages, here was a man who dreamed. The Bavarians know that the final laugh is on those who condemned Ludwig, for the castles that almost bankrupted the royal treasury now bring fortunes in tourist revenues; and the money taken from the public coffers to support Wagner gave the world some of its most treasured music.

Linderhof   The royal villa of **Linderhof** (1869–79) was once an annex of Ludwig's father's hunting lodge. It is said to have been inspired by the Petit Trianon—though, as one critic points out, it looks more like a small casino in southern France. Ludwig reportedly spent hours in the Moorish Pavilion—bought at the Paris Exhibition of 1867—playing the oriental potentate dressed in a bearskin. The grotto is a modern version of Aladdin's cave, where a rock moves back at the touch of a button. On an illuminated pond is a conch-shape boat recalling the Venusberg episode in Wagner's opera *Tannhäuser*. More attractive than the house is the surrounding parkland—once the royal hunting grounds—with pools, Italian-villa-style waterfalls, and formal gardens with pyramid-shape hedges.

The influence of the Bourbons is seen in the royal sun—symbol of Louis XIV—on the ceiling. In the ornate Gobelin or Music Room, notice how the Rococo wall paintings are meant to simulate tapestries. The Hall of Mirrors is a stage set for Ludwig's fantasies, in which nothing is what it seems. The bedchamber is a child's dream of luxury and opulence. Royal insignias, gilt-edged angels, and tapestries fill every inch of space, as if Ludwig were afraid of what lay beyond. *Open Apr.–Sept., daily 9–12:15 and 12:45–5; Oct.–Mar., daily 9–12:15 and 12:45–4.*

Hohenschwangau   From Linderhof drive 27.2 km (17 mi) through Austria to Reutte and 12.8 km (8 mi) north to Füssen. Follow signs east 3.2 km (2 mi) to the castle.

Ludwig's father purchased the ruins of a 12th-century castle and restored it in 1832–36. Ludwig spent most of his youth here; you can imagine him, a young child, staring up at the murals depicting scenes from medieval legends. What he saw must have encouraged his own romantic inclinations without satisfying them, for the young visionary built an even more fanciful castle of his own. Maximilian's castle, unlike his son's, looks almost livable—which is why visitors prefer Neuschwanstein.

Today, 14 rooms are furnished for public view. The Authari Room is where Wagner stayed; he never set foot in Neuschwanstein. The Music Room or Room of the Hohenstaufen contains the square maplewood piano on which Wagner played his works for Ludwig—who was an accomplished pianist himself. The bedchamber ceiling is painted to look like a night sky, with stars that could be made to light up. From a window the king could watch through a telescope the work progressing at Neuschwanstein. In the Hall of Heroes is a bust of Ludwig by an American sculptor; the king posed for it in 1869. *Open Apr.–Sept., daily 8:30–5:30; Oct.–Mar., daily 10–4.*

Neuschwanstein Bavarian kitsch—that's how you'd describe Ludwig's castle. Yet in its own tacky, overstated way it has the purity of, say, Versailles, because it remains faithful to a single vision. As a 19th-century fortress, its bulwarks and its position on a mountain spur are wonderfully useless—which somehow makes the king's vision even grander.

Maximilian II had thought of building a castle here, too, on the ruins of an ancient family fortress, so in a sense Ludwig was merely carrying out his father's designs. In 1869, influenced by Wagner's operas, Ludwig asked the court stage designer, Christian Jank, to draw up plans. Only later did he consult an architect. What he got, therefore, was a stage set where he could play the role of Lohengrin.

The castle tour takes you through an artificial stalactite cavern that recalls Wagner's *Tannhäuser*. The bedroom is decorated with a young boy's dreams—14 sculptors worked 4½ years to build it. The curtains and coverings are light Bavarian blue— Ludwig's favorite color. Throughout, the upper walls are covered with paintings from a world of fantasy—windows into a world of the mind. There's something sadly appropriate about the Oriental Throne Room without a throne. Ludwig lived in his castle only 102 days, and died before the gold-and-ivory chair could be completed. *Open Apr.–Sept., daily 8:30–5:30; Oct.–Mar., daily 10–4.*

After the tour, take an hour's walk (round-trip) to the **Pöllat Gorge** and stand on the same bridge (Marienbrücke) across the ravine where Ludwig II came at night to look up at his empty castle.

Wies Church Returning to Garmisch-Partenkirchen by the northern route, drive north 24 km (15 mi) on Route 17, about 3.2 km (2 mi) past Steingaden, and look for signs on the right to **Wies.** A 2.4-km (1½ mi) side trip (one-way) takes you to this Baroque masterpiece. The pilgrimage church (1746–52) is the work of the celebrated Baroque architect, Dominikus Zimmerman. The simple exterior is in marked contrast to the intensely rich interior. There's a similar contrast between the plain lower walls— symbolizing the Earth—and the rich stucco work of the "heavens." The pulpit and organ loft are high points of Rococo art in southern Germany.

Oberammergau Return to Route 17 and turn right (east) toward Echelsbach Bridge, above the River Ammer. Head south on Route 23, through Saulgrub to **Oberammergau** (17.6 km/11 mi), a town famous for its Passion Play. When a devastating plague stopped short of the town in 1634, the villagers vowed to perform the play every ten years. The first took place in that same year, and since 1680 it has been performed every decade, with an additional 350th anniversary performance in 1984. When villagers are not acting out the Passion of Christ they are turning out wood carvings in their colorful painted homes. The Heimat Museum has a large collection of handmade Christmas crèches (nativity scenes).

It's 16 km (10 mi) on Route 23 from Ettal back to Garmisch-Partenkirchen—where your trip ends. From here, you can take one of four main routes:

1. Return to Munich and fly back home.
2. Drive to Salzburg, Austria, and follow the Austrian itine-

rary described below. (The most scenic route is south from Garmisch-Partenkirchen through the lovely village of Mittenwald to Innsbruck.)

3. Drive to Zurich for a tour of Switzerland. (If you're going to Switzerland, don't return to Garmisch-Partenkirchen, but continue from the Royal Castles to Konstanz.)

4. Return to Frankfurt through the Black Forest and fly home.

What to See and Do with Children

Heidelberg: boat trips, bike rides, a visit to the castle.

Rothenburg: the whole medieval town is a child's dream come true.

Munich: the largest science and technology museum in the world; the famous glockenspiel at the New Town Hall; bike riding, boating, and buggy rides in the English Gardens; ice skating at the Olympia Tower; Hellabrunn Zoo, which has a children's section where animals can be hand fed.

Garmisch-Partenkirchen: four seasons' worth of outdoor sports, including skiing (Dec.–May) and hiking, cable car and cog railway rides, and a stagecoach ride from Garmisch to Grainau. The former site of the Winter Olympics has seven indoor pools, including one with waves and man-made surf; indoor tennis; and three indoor skating rinks.

The Arts

In **Heidelberg,** there are summer performances in the Castle (the Schlosspiele), including *The Student Prince*. Check for frequent organ recitals in the Church of the Holy Ghost (Heiliggeistkirche).

In **Munich,** the tourist office publishes a monthly events brochure, available in bookshops and newspaper kiosks. Munich has a fairy-tale Opera House (Bayerisches Nationaltheater) on Max Joseph Platz. The renowned company, which goes back 450 years, performed two premieres by Mozart and no fewer than five by Wagner. Richard Strauss conducted the opera orchestra for seven years. Tickets are sold at agencies and at the Opera Ticket Office at Maximilianstrasse 11 (open weekdays 10–1 and 4–6, weekends 10–1). Tickets are in great demand, so arrange to buy them when you make your hotel reservations.

Agencies specializing in concert tickets for the Bavarian State Orchestra and the famous Bach Choir include Otto Bauer Musikalienhandlung (in the Rathaus, tel. 089–221–757), Residenz Bücherstube (Residenzstrasse 1, tel. 089–220–868), and Buchhandlung Lehmkuhl (Leopoldstrasse 45, tel. 089/398–045). An increasing number of concerts are now being held at the new entertainment center, **Gasteig** (Rosenheimerstr. 13, tel. 089/418–1614) near the City Hilton Hotel and at the **Deutsches Museum** (tel. 089/480–980). Check with the Tourist Office for upcoming church concerts in St. Michael's, St. Matthew's, and the Frauenkirche. There's a summer concert series from mid-June to mid-July in Nymphenburg Castle.

4 Austria

Salzburg to Vienna

Introduction

The region between Salzburg, where Mozart was born, and Vienna, former capital of the Habsburg empire, is a trove of natural and cultural riches. The lakes and wooded hills of the Lake Country are a paradise for sailors and hikers, and the Wachau river valley enchants with crumbling castles, terraced vineyards, and walled medieval towns. Throughout the year, outstanding music is performed not just in modern concert halls, but in Baroque palaces under stucco skies filled with saints and angels. The history and art of seven centuries of Habsburg rule are embodied in the churches and palaces of Vienna.

Highlights

The imperial city of Vienna, home of the Spanish Riding School, the world-famous Boys' Choir, and a Baroque confection of music and art.

The Wachau Valley, the most romantic stretch of the Danube, with magnificent abbeys and castles overlooking terraced vineyards and medieval towns.

Salzburg, a city of historic beauty and natural charm—an ideal stage set for the world-famous music festival.

The Lake Country, a natural setting of sparkling blue lakes and wooded hills.

Before You Go

Government Tourist Offices

In the U.S. 500 Fifth Ave., 20th Floor, New York, NY 10110, tel. 212/944–6880; 500 N. Michigan Ave., Suite 544, Chicago, IL 60611, tel. 312/644–5556; 11601 Wilshire Blvd., Suite 2480, Los Angeles, CA 90025, tel. 213/477–3332; 4800 San Felipe, Suite 500, Houston, TX 77056, tel. 713/850–9999.

In Canada 1010 Sherbrooke St. W., Suite 1410, Montreal, Quebec H3A 2R7, tel. 514/849–3709; 736 Granville St., Suite 1220–1223, Vancouver Block, Vancouver, British Columbia V6Z 1J2, tel. 604/683–5808; 2 Bloor St. E., Suite 3330, Toronto, Ontario M4W 1A8, tel. 416/967–3381.

In the U.K. 30 George St., London W1R OAL, tel. 071/629–0461.

When to Go

Austria has two main tourist seasons. The summer season starts at Easter and runs to about mid-October. The most pleasant months weather-wise are May, June, September, and October. June through August are the peak tourist months, and aside from a few overly humid days when you could wish for wider use of air-conditioning, even Vienna is pleasant; the city literally moves outdoors in summer. The winter cultural season starts in October and runs into June. Some events—the Salzburg Festival is a prime example—make a substantial difference in hotel and other costs. Nevertheless, bargains are available in the (almost nonexistent) off-season.

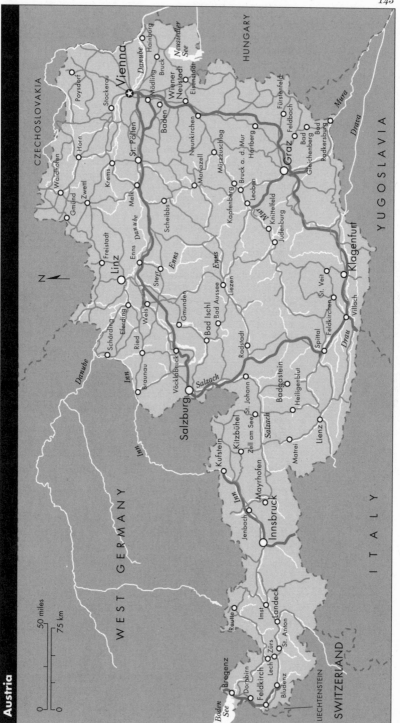

Austria

Special Events

Late July–late August: Salzburg Summer Festival, an international festival of concerts, opera and ballet.

Late May–late June: Vienna Music Festival, with concerts in Baroque palaces and gardens.

Currency

The unit of currency is the Austrian schilling (AS), divided into 100 groschen. There are AS 20, 50, 100, 500, and 1,000 bills; AS 1, 5, 10, and 20 coins; and groschen 1, 2, 10, and 50 coins. The 1- and 2-groschen coins are scarce, and the AS 20 coins are unpopular—though useful for some cigarette machines. The 500- and 100-schilling notes look perilously similar; confusing them can be an expensive mistake.

At press time (spring 1990); there were about AS 12.6 to the dollar, and about AS 20 to the pound sterling.

Customs

Austria's duty-free allowances are as follows: 200 cigarettes or 100 cigars or 250 g (8.70 oz) of tobacco, two liters of wine and one liter of spirits, one bottle of toilet water (about 300-ml/9 oz size); 50 ml (1½-oz) of perfume for those age 18 and over arriving from other European countries. Visitors arriving from the United States, Canada, or other non-European points may bring in twice the above amounts.

Language

German is the official national language. In larger cities and most resort areas, you will have no problems finding people who speak English; hotel and restaurant staff, in particular, speak English reasonably well. Most younger Austrians speak at least passable English, even if fluency is relatively rare.

Reading

Diane Buregwyn, *Salzburg: A Portrait* (sold in local gift shops).

Richard Rickett, *A Brief Survey of Austrian History* (Heinemann) and *Music and Musicians in Vienna* (Heinemann. Out of print; check your library.)

Edward Crankshaw, *Vienna: The Image of a Culture in Decline* (MacMillan).

Vienna from A to Z (Vienna Tourist Bureau).

Henriette Mandl, *Vienna Downtown Walking Tours* (Uebereuter).

Arriving and Departing

By Plane

For the 3 to 5-day trip, fly to and from Vienna. **ALIA Royal Jordanian Airlines** (535 Fifth Ave., New York, NY 10017, tel. 212/949–0077) flies nonstop to Vienna from New York and Chicago, and direct from Los Angeles. **Pan Am** flies direct to Vienna from New York.

For stays of 5–7 or 7–14 days, fly to Munich and return home from Vienna. (If you need to arrive and depart from the same European airport, end your trip with a train ride from Vienna back to Munich.) Germany's reliable airline, **Lufthansa,** flies nonstop from New York and Chicago to Munich. Lufthansa also flies to Munich via Frankfurt from San Francisco, Los Angeles, Dallas, Houston, Philadelphia, Boston, Miami, and Atlanta. Pan Am and **TWA** fly nonstop to Munich from New York. **Delta** flies direct to Munich from Chicago.

Getting Around

By Car

If you're taking the 3-to-5-day trip, you'll be flying direct to Vienna. It makes no sense to rent a car here. Parking is difficult and public transportation is good. Rent a car only for the visit to Melk and the Wachau Valley—preferably at the end of the trip, when you can return the car to the airport.

If you're taking the 5- to 7- or 7- to 14-day trip, fly direct to Munich and then either rent a car or take the train to Salzburg, where your trip begins. The train from Munich to Salzburg takes 90 minutes. The drive takes two to three hours. After seeing Salzburg, drive to Vienna and return your car at the Vienna airport on your way home.

Is it better to rent your car in Munich or in Salzburg? If money is no issue and you can pick up the car at the Munich airport and return it at the Vienna airport, do so. Otherwise, catch a train directly from Munich to Salzburg and pick up your car in Salzburg when you're ready to leave. The bus ride from Munich's airport to the city train station takes 30–45 minutes.

If you have to pick up and return your car from the same location, fly to Vienna, drive directly to Salzburg on A1 (a three-hour trip), and then follow the itinerary below back to Vienna. You can also fly to Munich, follow the itinerary to Vienna, and then drive directly back to Munich.

By Public Transportation

You can follow essentially the same itinerary by car or by a combination of bus, train, and boat. What you'll miss traveling by public transportation are a few towns in the Lake District and the side trip to Mühlviertel.

Austrian Rail Passes, sold at train stations, are good for reduced rates on trains and Danube cruises.

If you're taking the 3- to 5-day trip, which begins in Vienna, you have three ways to reach Melk and the Wachau Valley:

1. Join an escorted tour, which can be arranged through any hotel or travel agency in Vienna. Make sure the tour includes a boat ride between Melk and Dürnstein.

2. Take a Danube cruise from Vienna to Melk; tour the abbey; take the train back to Dürnstein; spend the night in Dürnstein, and then take a train or boat back to Vienna. You can't take the steamship round-trip because it arrives in Melk at 3:50 PM and doesn't return until 3:20 the next afternoon. Your nights away from Vienna should be spent not in Melk but in Dürnstein.

3. The third and best alternative is to take the train from Vienna to Melk; visit Melk Abbey; take the steamship back to Dürnstein; spend the night in Dürnstein, and then take either the train or boat back to Vienna.

The evening sail from Dürnstein back to Vienna takes four hours. It's not nearly as scenic as the trip along the Wachau, so if you're pressed for time, take the train instead.

Make sure you arrive in Melk in time to tour the abbey, which closes at 4 or 5 PM, depending on the season. Melk has two docks, one for the local Wachau ferry, and one for the ship to Vienna. If you want to sail directly back to Vienna, ask a cab driver to take you to the Schiffahrt-Wien. Both ferries stop at Dürnstein, where you'll be spending the night.

The local ferries leave Melk in season at 9, 12:30, 2:30 and 6. The trip from Melk to Dürnstein, along the most beautiful stretch of the Danube, takes less than two hours. (Check current schedules.)

Combination train/ship tickets can be purchased through travel agencies or directly from the First Danube Steamship Company (DDSG Travel Dept., A-1021 Vienna, Handelskai 265, tel. 266536/443 or 444).

If you're taking the 5- to 7-day trip, you'll be flying to Munich. Take the 30- to 45-minute bus ride from the airport to the train station. The ride to Salzburg takes 90 minutes. After touring Salzburg, take the four-hour train ride to Melk. (One train leaves Salzburg at 9:57 AM and arrives at Melk at 1:41 PM.) For the boat and train ride along the Danube, see the 3- to 5-day trip above.

If you're taking the 7- to 14-day trip, you'll also be flying to Munich. It's a 30- to 45-minute bus ride from the airport to the train station, and a 90-minute train trip to Salzburg. After touring Salzburg, take the train or bus to Hallstatt in the Lake Country. Both take about 90 minutes, plus connecting time. A boat meets the train at the northern end of Hallstatt Lake (Hallstätter See) and brings you to the village of Hallstatt. If bus or train connections are poor, join an excursion bus direct from Salzburg to Hallstatt. Tickets can be purchased through hotels and tourist offices in Salzburg. From Hallstatt, return by bus or train to Salzburg.

St. Florian is difficult to reach from Salzburg by train, so save the abbey for another trip, and take the train direct from Salzburg to Melk. If you're determined to visit St. Florian, take the train from Salzburg to Linz, then change to a local train to Asten-St. Florian. After visiting St. Florian, return to Linz and continue by train to Melk. For the boat and train ride from Melk to Vienna, see the 3- to 5-day trip, above.

Essential Information

Important Addresses and Numbers

Tourist Information
Dürnstein: Im Rathaus, tel. 02711/219. **Krems:** Wichnerstr. 8, tel. 02732/2676. **Melk:** Im Rathaus, tel. 02752/2307. **Salzburg:** Auerspergstr. 7, tel. 0662/80–7–20. There's also an information center at Mozartplatz 5, tel. 0662/84–75–68, and at the main train station, tel. 0662/71–7–12. **Vienna:** City Tourist Office, Kärntnerstr. 38, behind the opera, tel. 0222/513–88–92. Open daily 9–7.

If you're driving from Salzburg or Dürnstein, there's an Auto Information Center (tel. 0222/97–12–71) off the Autobahn (A1) as you approach Vienna. Hotel reservations can be made here. There's another information office at the airport (tel. 0222/777–02–617).

For a taped list of events, tel. 1515. For general train information, tel. 1717; for train information at the West Train Station (Westbahnhof), tel. 0222–1552 or 0222/1700. For airport information, tel. 7770. For information on travel in Austria, contact Osterreich Information, Margaretenstrasse 1, tel. 0222/587–20–00.

Emergencies
Salzburg
Police, tel. 0662/133; **U.S. Consulate,** Giselakai 51, tel. 0662/28–6–01.

Vienna
Police, tel. 122; **ambulance,** tel. 144; **doctor,** American Medical Society of Vienna, Lazaretteg. 13, tel. 0222/42–45–68; **pharmacies,** open weekdays 8–6, Sat. 8–noon; **embassies:** *U.S.,* Gartenbaupromenade (Marriott Bldg.), tel. 0222/51–4–51; *Canadian,* Dr. Karl Leuger-Ring, tel. 0222/63–36–91; *U.K.,* Jauresg. 10, tel. 0222/75–61–17.

Opening and Closing Times

Banks
Doors open weekdays 8–12:30 and 1:30–3. Principal offices in cities stay open during lunch.

Museums
Opening days and times vary considerably from city to city and depend on season, the size of the museum, budgetary constraints, and assorted other factors. Your hotel or the local tourist office will have current details.

Shops
These open weekdays from 8 or 9 until 6, Saturday until noon or 1 only, except the first Saturday of every month when they stay open until 5. Many smaller shops close for one or two hours at midday.

Guided Tours

Vienna
Escorted walking tours leave from various points in the city and cover various subjects, such as Freud, the "Third Man," and musicians. Ask hotels or travel agencies for details, or call 0222/93–90–88, 0222/220–66–20, or 0222/676–41–64.

Bus tours are convenient to the Belvedere, Schönbrunn Palace, and the Vienna Woods. Two companies offer escorted bus tours: **Cityrama Sightseeing Tours** and **Vienna Sightseeing Tours.** Make reservations through hotels or travel agencies. Some leave from the Opera, others from in front of the Stadtpark subway station across from the Intercontinental Hotel. Most tours will pick you up at your hotel.

Shopping

For purchases over 1,000 schillings (about $75), request a refund on the Value Added Tax (VAT) when you leave the country. Ask for special forms to be filled out at shops where purchases are made.

Salzburg Best buys here are folk costumes (Lederhosen and dirndls), leather goods, sporting equipment, pottery, and candles.

Vienna In the capital you can shop for porcelain, crystal, petit point, leather goods, folk costumes, local handicrafts and antiques. The **Dorotheum** (1, Dorotheergasse 17. Tel. 0222/51–5–60) is the state-run auction house, which has sales almost every day. There's also a flea market (Sat. 8–6) at the end of the Naschmarkt, between Districts V and VI.

The shops listed below are along the streets and squares you'll be visiting in District I. Almost all are on three connecting streets, Kärntnerstrasse, Graben, and Kohlmarkt. Serious shoppers should begin at the Opera, stroll down Kärntnerstrasse to St. Stephen's, turn left on Graben, and left again on Kohlmarkt.

Porcelain and Glass: *Lobmeyr* (Kärntnerstre 26). **Dirndls and Lederhosen:** *Lanz* (Kärntnerstr. 10); *Loden-Plankl,* (Michaelerplatz 6); *Trachten Schlössl* (Kohlmarkt 2). **Local handicrafts:** *Österreichische Werkstätten* (Kärntnerstr. 6). **Leather:** *Nigst* (Neuer Markt 4). **Watches:** *Wagner* (Kärntnerstr. 32). **Silverware:** *Rozet & Fischmeister,* (Kohlmarkt 11). **Linen:** *Zur Schwäbischen Jungfrau* (Graben 26). **Jewelry:** *A. E. Koechert,* (Neuer Markt 15).

Dining

Take your choice of sidewalk *wurstl* (frankfurter) stands, quick-lunch stops *(imbisstube),* cafés, Heuriger wine restaurants, self-service restaurants, modest *gasthäuser* neighborhood establishments with local specialties, and full-fledged restaurants in every price category. Most establishments post their menus outside. Shops selling coffee beans (such as Eduscho) also offer coffee by the cup at considerably lower prices than those in a café.

Austrians often eat up to five meals a day—a very early Continental breakfast of rolls and coffee; a slightly more substantial breakfast *(Gabelfrühstück)* with egg or cold meat, possibly even a small goulash, at mid-morning (understood to be 9, sharp); a main meal at noon; afternoon coffee *(Jause)* with cake at teatime; and, unless dining out, a light supper to end the day. Cafés offer breakfast; most restaurants open somewhat later. Lunches usually cost more in cafés than in restaurants.

A jacket and tie is generally advised for restaurants in the top price categories. Otherwise, casual dress is acceptable, although in Vienna formal dress is preferred in some moderate restaurants at dinner. When in doubt, it's best to dress up.

Prices include taxes and service (you may wish to leave small change, in addition). At press time (spring 1990), there were 12.6 schillings (AS) to the dollar.

Category	Major City	Other Areas*
Very Expensive	over AS 800	over AS 600
Expensive	AS 500–AS 800	AS 400–AS 600
Moderate	AS 200–AS 500	AS 170–AS 400
Inexpensive	under AS 200	under AS 170

Prices are per person and include soup and a main course, usually with salad, and a small beer or glass of wine. Meals in the top-price categories will include a dessert or cheese and coffee.

Lodging Austrian hotels and pensions are officially classified from one to five stars. These gradings broadly coincide with our own four-way rating system. No matter what the category, standards for service and cleanliness are high. All hotels in the upper three categories will have bath or shower in the room; even the most inexpensive accommodations will have hot and cold water. Accommodations include castles and palaces, conventional hotels, country inns *(Gasthof)*, motels (considerably less frequent), and the more modest pensions.

Though exact figures will vary, a single room will generally cost more than 50% of the price of a comparable double room. Breakfast—which can be anything from a simple roll and coffee to a full and sumptuous buffet—is always included in the room rate. At press time (spring 1990), there were 12.6 schillings (AS) to the dollar.

Category	Major City	Other Areas*
Very Expensive	over AS 2,300	over AS 1,800
Expensive	AS 1,250–AS 2,300	AS 1,000–AS 1,800
Moderate	AS 850–AS 1,250	AS 700–AS 1,000
Inexpensive	under AS 850	under AS 700

Prices are for 2 people in a double room.

Austrian Baroque Architecture

In this region are the greatest examples of Austrian Baroque: Salzburg Cathedral (very early Baroque); the abbeys of St. Florian and Melk, and the Karlskirche in Vienna. The Baroque style was imported from France and Italy, but for the Austrians it expressed architecturally the joy they felt after their triumph over the Turks in 1683. It was also the art of the Counter-Reformation—a form of visual propaganda to win Catholic Austrians back to the Mother Church by a direct appeal to the senses. It's hard to believe today that a person could get very close to God in such a worldly setting, but each age approaches God in its own way.

In Austrian Baroque churches, the original Gothic columns direct your eye both upward to God and forward to the altar; but the flowing lines and ornate decorations force your eye to stop along the way, almost as if you were being diverted by this world on your way to the next.

Renaissance architects worked on the Platonic assumption that there was an order in the universe that a building could capture by following certain rules—a certain ideal relationship, say, between the width of a column and its height. What the Baroque artist tried to do was not to satisfy some ideal form of beauty, but to satisfy the direct, emotional needs of the worshiper. Perhaps that's why Renaissance art has always belonged to the cultivated minority, while Baroque belongs to the masses.

One might be tempted to dismiss these Baroque churches as spiritual ballrooms—as ill suited for repentance as for salvation. But this would miss the essence of Baroque, which is to bring heaven down to earth, and to hold out an image of joy unsullied by guilt or sin. The Baroque church was meant to be God's castle. Created in the spirit of the age, heaven became a dwelling place for God's appointed, the Habsburg kings and queens. Overwhelmed by such splendid surroundings, worshipers became royal, too.

The three great Baroque architects whose major works you'll be seeing along the route are **Johann Bernhard Fischer von Erlach** (1656–1723): Karlskirche (Vienna), University Church (Salzburg); **Johann Lukas von Hildebrandt** (1668–1745): Upper and Lower Belvedere (Vienna); and **Jakob Prandtauer** (1660–1726): Abbeys of St. Florian and Melk.

The Itinerary

Orientation

This itinerary takes you on a scenic and historic route eastward from Salzburg to Vienna, with stops in the Lake Country and along the most romantic stretch of the Danube. You'll begin in Salzburg and then relax in the Lake Country. After exploring the magnificent Baroque abbeys of St. Florian and Melk, you'll wander through the gentle, rolling farmland of the Muhlviertel. From here you'll drive or sail through the romantic Wachau Valley. Rested by the slow, dreamy pace of the Danube, you'll be ready for Vienna.

The Main Route

3–5 Days *One night:* Salzburg
Two nights: Vienna
One night: Dürnstein

5–7 Days *Two nights:* Salzburg
Two nights: Dürnstein
Two nights: Vienna

7–14 Days *Two nights:* Salzburg
Two nights: Lake Country
Two nights: Dürnstein
Four Nights: Vienna

Exploring

Salzburg

Vienna absorbs its tourists; Salzburg exists for them. Vienna spreads out; Salzburg nestles. Vienna acknowledges the seasons; Salzburg opens its arms to them. Vienna is ethnically diverse; Salzburg is so homogeneous that Hitler chose nearby Berchtesgaden as the headquarters for his Thousand-Year Reich.

Like Vienna, Salzburg was redone in Baroque dress. Both cities are monumental, but Salzburg, with its clusters of ancient homes and narrow, cobbled streets, has a much more intimate, medieval feeling to it.

When visitors speak of Salzburg they're referring not to the modern town but to Old Salzburg, nestled between the Salzach River and the cliffs of Mönchsberg and the Hohensalzburg fortress. It's difficult not to love Old Salzburg—its setting is idyllic, its streets safe and clean, its people friendly and polite. It is a show town, a pretty stage set with no apparent purpose but to entertain its paying guests. During the day everything is yours to peek into, buy, listen to and explore—but by 11 at night all the shutters are closed and you can hear your footsteps echoing on the empty squares. There is something unreal about all this, but who needs reality on a vacation?

You'll find yourself drawn down picturesque alleys, exploring monuments to this world and the next. Nearly everything is within walking distance: the Baroque churches, the humble house where Mozart was born, the shopping streets with wrought-iron signs as intricate as lacework. Ideally, you should come during the summer music festival, but there are concerts all year long, performed in a Baroque setting as sumptuous as any in the world.

The **cathedral** (Dom) is the physical and spiritual center of the town, so let's begin here. A Romanesque cathedral once stood on this spot, but Archbishop Wolf Dietrich either set fire to it or did nothing to stop it from burning down. He wanted the cathedral to be another St. Peter's, but he died before its completion. Though its interior is influenced by St. Peter's, particularly in its geometric use of space, it's more closely modeled on Rome's Il Gesù.

Wolf Dietrich was the most notorious of the prince-archbishops who ruled Salzburg and the surrounding territory for over 1,000 years, controlling everything from breweries to the salvation of souls. When he became archbishop in 1587, he wasn't yet ordained. Educated in Rome, he shared with Alberti and Palladio the notion that a house of worship should stand isolated on a beautiful square; and so he tore down much of the medieval city and built Italian-style piazzas with lovely fountains, both around the cathedral and around the Residenz, where he planned to live.

Living with Wolf Dietrich, probably out of wedlock, was a Jewish woman named Salome Alt, who bore him 15 children. She tolerated his extravagances more than the townspeople, who rose up and imprisoned him in the Hohensalzburg—a fortress

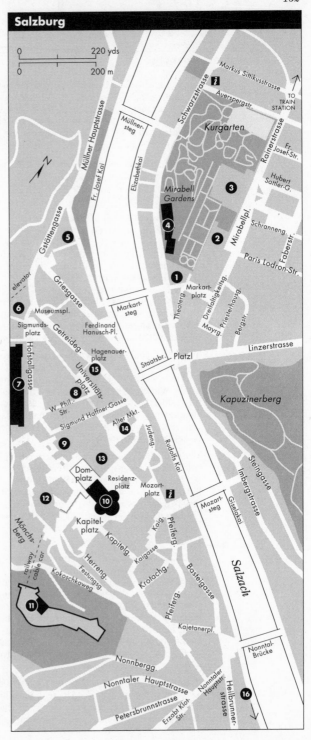

built, ironically, to protect archbishops from the people. When Wolf Dietrich died five years later, his only finished project was his mausoleum, which you can see in St. Sebastian's Cemetery, not far from the tombs of Mozart's wife and father.

After Wolf Dietrich came Archbishop Markus Sittikus, a man who apparently played as hard as he prayed, building a fun palace called Hellbrunn and renaming Salome's castle Mirabell after one of his own mistresses.

The last of the three great archbishops who gave Salzburg the face it wears today was Paris Lodron (1619–53), who completed the Residenz and a more modest version of the cathedral in Italian Mannerist style. Though he was a more gentle, peace-loving fellow than his predecessors, he was accompanied wherever he went by 30 personal guards, 14 lords chamberlain carrying enormous gold keys, and a dozen children of the nobility dressed in red velvet.

It was Napoleon who put an end to the line of prince-archbishops; should we be grateful to him? The rulers of Salzburg were often selfish autocrats who led extravagant lives at the expense of their people, yet they loved art and created beauty; can they be forgiven? (Salzburg still has an archbishop, but his domain is limited to matters of the spirit.)

The cathedral's bronze **doors** and **altar** are postwar. To the left of the entrance is the baptismal **font** in which Mozart was christened in 1756. In the **crypt** is the grave of an early Irish bishop named Virgil, who created waves 12 centuries ago by insisting that the world was round. In the treasury are Baroque chalices, Romanesque miters, and a traveling flask belonging to the late-7th-century priest, Rupert of Worms. Rupert founded St. Peter's Church, which you'll be visiting soon.

Head south, away from the river, and cross Kapitelplatz. The square has an 18th-century drinking trough for horses in the shape of a monumental fountain—a reminder that some prince-archbishops may have treated their animals better than their subjects. Walk to the funicular that goes to the **Hohensalzburg.** Buy a one-way ticket. This fortress—one of the best-preserved medieval structures in the world—gets top billing in Salzburg, so go in the morning to beat the lines. (Tours begin at 9 AM.) The Hohensalzburg was built to protect the prince-archbishops, and was virtually impregnable. The fourth-floor apartments offer fine examples of Late Gothic secular architecture, but there's little else that's memorable on the tour, so if lines are long, pass it up, and admire the breathtaking view of Salzburg.

Near the fortress is **Nonnberg Convent,** which has a late-14th-century church. It was while staying here that Maria heard the sound of music, or at least the voice of Baron George von Trapp. The real Maria, according to a delightful account in *Salzburg: A Portrait,* lost both parents at age nine and was turned over to an uncle who beat her and put her in an asylum. She escaped to Salzburg and asked to be placed in the strictest convent. While at Nonnberg, she was sent to care for the Baron's children, fell in love with him, and in 1938 escaped with him to the United States. After *The Sound of Music* was released, the Von Trapps bought 600 acres in Vermont and turned a farmhouse into a Salzburg-type chalet with a Trapp family gift shop selling Trapp family postcards. The real Von Trapps lived not in

Leopoldskron Castle, as the film suggests, but in a Salzburg
suburb. A baroness much sturdier than Julie Andrews married
George von Trapp, not in the church in Mondsee but in the convent; and if they had followed the mountain route they took in
the movie they would have ended up in Germany. The people of
Salzburg don't appreciate songs like "Do Re Mi," which insult
their religiously inspired folk melodies; but this doesn't stop
them from cheerfully exploiting the film for every tourist dollar
they can get—much as they exploit Mozart, who was born here
but fled to Vienna.

Time Out   Stay on the ridge above the city and enjoy a delightful 30-min-
ute walk through parklands to the **Winkler Café.** (If you make
this walk in reverse, starting at the Winkler Café, you'll have a
very steep climb to the fortress.) The Winkler terrace is overrun with tourists, but is still a scenic spot for coffee or lunch.
*Am Mönchsberg 32, tel. 0662/841215. Reservations advised.
Dress: informal, but no shorts. AE, DC, MC, V. Closed Mon.
Expensive.*

A more peaceful and elegant alternative is the terrace at the
Mönchstein Hotel, a 10-minute walk farther along the bluff.
*Am Mönchsberg 26, tel. 0662/848555. Reservations required.
Dress: elegant casual or jacket and tie. AE, DC, MC, V. Ex-
pensive.*

From the Winkler, take the elevator back down to the town and
wander along Getreidegasse, the main shopping street. Here
and on Judengasse, the continuation of Getreidegasse, you can
buy dirndls, needlework, leather goods, candles, and ski equipment.

At **Getreidegasse 9** is the humble apartment, now a museum,
where Johannes Chrysostomus Wolfgangus Theophilus (Ama-
deus) Mozart was born in 1756. Mozart's clavichord is here; you
can imagine his father Leopold standing over him while he
played. When Mozart was four, a court musician named
Andreas Schatner came here with a friend to play trios with
Leopold. Wolfgang begged to play the violin, but Leopold said
no: The boy had never taken a lesson in his life. Schatner convinced Leopold to let Wolfgang try. The four-year-old took up
the same violin you see on display here and played the piece so
perfectly that Schatner could not compete with him, and Leopold was reduced to tears.

At age six, when most children were reading nursery rhymes,
Wolfgang was brought to Vienna, where he performed for Maria Theresa at Schönbrunn Palace. Six years later the Emperor
commissioned him to write an opera. Mozart's problems with
Salzburg began in 1771 when a new archbishop tried to limit
what he called Mozart's "begging expeditions" across Europe.
What the archbishop really wanted was a less brilliant, less ambitious court musician—someone content to fulfill his obliga-
tions at court. Mozart, in turn, felt unappreciated in provincial Salzburg, where "the audience is all tables and chairs."
Eventually he left Salzburg for good.

In 1890 Mozart's fame was sweetened by the arrival of
Mozartkugeln (Mozart balls)—pistachio-flavored marzipan
rolled in nougat cream and dipped in dark chocolate; you can
buy them anywhere along Getreidegasse. The factory at

Mirabell turns out 150,000 of these tin-wrapped morsels every day; look for the word *echte*, which distinguishes them from the competition.

Next stop are the catacombs of **St. Peter's Church.** If you want to trace Salzburg's history through its monuments, you should begin not at the cathedral or fortress, but here. A landslide in 1669 killed 200 people and revealed these crude stone chambers where the early Christians came to pray as far back as AD 200. On the 20-minute tour you can try to imagine the faith of these early believers, who prayed in secret and died for their beliefs. Some two centuries later a Christian church was built nearby. In the 7th century, Rupert of Worms poured the church's profits from salt mining into the monastery and Church of St. Peter. Salzburg (which means "castle of salt") thus began life as a monastic settlement long before the era of the prince-archbishops. The secular town, where employees of the monastery lived, grew up along the river. You'll get a sense of these early days when you look at the massive Romanesque walls of the church and compare them to the 18th-century Baroque interior. It was here in St. Peter's that Mozart first performed his C Minor Mass, with his wife singing solo soprano. Nearby is a peaceful 17th-century cemetery where anyone would be happy to spend eternity. The seven old iron crosses belonged to the family of a stonemason named Stumpfegger who died at age 79 after burying six wives.

You can trace the history of Western architecture in the nearby **Church of the Franciscans** (Franziskanerkirche). Stand near the back and let the massive Romanesque columns pull your eyes forward to the Baroque altar. The effect is that of standing in the 14th century and looking toward the 18th; of standing in a shaded forest and staring out at a distant sunlit clearing in the woods. The Gothic choir was begun by the Tyrolean wood sculptor Michael Pacher, whose work you'll see again in St. Wolfgang. He worked on the High Altar, too; but then Fischer von Erlach, the greatest of all Austrian Baroque architects, was called in, and put Pacher's gentle madonna in a Baroque heaven. Von Erlach's other masterpiece in Salzburg is the **University Church** (Kollegienkirche).

To understand the worldly power of the prince-archbishops, tour the 180-room, Renaissance-style **Residenz.** The staircase, commissioned by Wolf Dietrich, was built to be ascended on horseback. The cathedral, St. Peter's, and the Church of the Franciscans were all so close to the archbishop's home that he could commute from palace to pulpit without stepping outdoors.

Across the Residenzplatz is the **New Building** (Neugebäude), which Wolf Dietrich began in 1590 for visiting royalty. Climb up to see the **Glockenspiel** (carillon) in action. It came broken from Antwerp in 1695 and is still slightly off-key.

If you've had enough walking for a day, rent a *Fiaker*—a horse-drawn carriage—and clip-clop around town.

In the early evening, cross over the Salzach River, turn left, and enjoy a delightful walk or bike ride along the water.

The same walk will take you at another time to (1) the Mozarteum, (2) Mirabell, and (3) the Marionettentheater.

The **Mozarteum** has two concert halls and a one-room summer house imported from Vienna where Mozart supposedly wrote *The Magic Flute.*

Mirabell was the palace Wolf Dietrich built for Salome. Because of an early 19th-century fire, little remains of the Baroque alterations except for the Marble Room upstairs and the playful white marble staircase, where stubby-legged cherubs ride the waves. The gardens, left as Wolf Dietrich designed them, are a delightful place to doze or sunbathe. Archbishop Franz Anton von Harrach was partial to dwarfs and commissioned the squat, hunchbacked marble figures in the Dwarf Garden.

The elegant dining hall of the 90-year-old Hotel Mirabell is the home of the famous **Salzburger Marionettentheater.** Holography—the art of the laser—creates the illusion of three-dimensional sets for abbreviated, taped performances of *The Magic Flute, Die Fledermaus,* and other famous operas. *The Nutcracker* uses more than 100 lifelike puppets. Performances are in a sense more realistic than live opera, because there are no actors behind the masks, no real people standing between the characters and our vision of who they should be.

A few miles south of town is **Hellbrunn,** the pleasure palace of Archbishop Markus Sittikus. It was apparently built in 1612 for Madame de Mabon, the wife of the captain of the guard; look for her likeness in the Orpheus Grotto, wearing a portrait of Sittikus around her neck. The archbishop had a child's fascination with water and a child's sense of play. The stone dining table, for instance, has a trough down the center to cool wine, and holes in the benches where jets of icy water drenched unsuspecting guests. The warbling in the Birdsong Grotto is created by water pressure. In the Neptune Grotto is a Groucho Marx–type figure who, when his mouth fills with water, sticks out his tongue and rolls his eyes.

Dining **Alt Salzburg.** This restaurant has several small, relatively elegant dining rooms. It has one of the best reputations in town, particularly for its *Tafelspitz* (boiled beef), lamb, and salads, but quality can be uneven. *Sigmundspl. 2, tel. 0662/84–14–76. Reservations useful. Jacket and tie required. AE, DC, MC, V. Closed Sun. except during Festival weeks. Expensive.*
Mirabell. Although it's housed in a chain hotel (the Sheraton), some will argue that the Mirabell is the city's top restaurant. The menu mixes international dishes with adventurous versions of local specialties such as Wiener Schnitzel and *wildschwein* (wild boar). *Auerspergst. 4, tel. 0662/79–32–15. Reservations advised. Jacket and tie required. AE, DC, MC, V. Expensive.*
Zum Eulenspiegel. The intimate rooms of an old city house contribute to the charm of this city restaurant. *Hagenauerplatz 2, tel. 0662/84–31–80. Reservations advised. Jacket and tie required. AE, DC, MC, V. Closed Sun. and holidays in winter. Expensive.*
Moserstuben, in the very heart of the old town, serves regional dishes. *Rainerstr. 4, tel. 0662/74–0–80. Reservations useful. Dress: informal. AE, DC, MC, V. Closed weekends. Moderate.*
Stiffskeller St. Peter. Tucked under the mountain, this vast restaurant offers good food and service in its winding set of rooms. Both fish and game are excellent, or ask the waiter about Salzburg specialties. *By St. Peter's Church, tel. 0662/84–12–68.*

Dress: informal. No credit cards. Closed Mon. in winter. Moderate.

Coffeehouses For a morning or afternoon coffee break along one of the narrow, winding streets near Getreidegasse, stop at a coffeehouse.

Mozartkugel is a great place for afternoon coffee and pastries. Ask for a Dobos torte—the best you'll ever have. *In Hotel Österreichischer Hof. Schwarzstr. 5–7, tel. 0662/72–5–41. Reservations useful. Dress: elegant casual. AE, DC, MC, V. Expensive.*

Kaffee-Häferl is cozy. *In passageway between Universitätspl. 6/Getreidegasse 25, tel. 0662/84–32–49. No reservations. Dress: informal. No credit cards. Closed evenings. Moderate.*

Ratzka has the best pastries, including *Marillenknödel*, petit fours, and tarts with fresh fruits. *Inpergstr. 45, tel. 0662/70–9–19. Reservations essential but often impossible. Dress: elegant casual. No credit cards. Closed Mon., Tues., except during festival weeks, closed Mon. only. Moderate.*

Schatz Konditorei is a dollhouse of a pastry shop, serving Mozartkugeln, cakes with candied fruit, and Krapferln. *Getreidegasse 3, tel. 0662/84–27–92. No reservations. Dress: informal. No credit cards. Closed evenings, Sun. Moderate.*

Tomaselli. At this coffeehouse the coffee could be better, the cake fresher, and the waiters more polite, but you haven't been to Salzburg (some say) until you've been here. *Alter Markt 9, tel. 0662/84–44–88. Reservations essential at festival time. Dress: elegant casual. No credit cards. Moderate.*

Lodging The **Goldener Hirsch,** an 800-year-old house with rag rugs and old painted chests, is a young American's idea of what a small, charming Austrian inn should be. It's just off the main street, which is a plus or minus, depending on how close to center city you want to be. *Getreidegasse 35–37, tel. 0662/84–85–11. 75 rooms with bath. Facilities: restaurant. AE, DC, MC, V. Very Expensive.*

Österreichischer Hof. Salzburg's grande dame occupies a lovely riverside location, and some of the rooms give views of the fortress and the old city. All four restaurants are excellent, but reservations are essential. *Schwarzstr. 5–7, tel. 0662/72–5–41. 120 rooms, 118 with bath or shower. Facilities: 4 restaurants. AE, DC, MC, V. Very Expensive.*

Schloss Mönchstein is a castle in a peaceful garden overlooking the city. Filled with serious antiques and softened with dark wood paneling, it has more the atmosphere of a private residence than of a hotel. Some of the rooms are exquisite, others small and tasteless. Room 20 is a good bet; so is 23, if you like pink. Avoid 34. *Mönchsberg 26, tel. 0662/84–85–55. 17 rooms with bath. Facilities: restaurant, garage, tennis. AE, DC, MC, V. Very Expensive.*

Kaserer Bräu. Keep your head up so you can ignore the carpets and appreciate the lovely old painted furniture and ornate armoires. Request a room with antiques. *Kaigasse 33, tel. 0662/84–24–45. 37 rooms with bath. Facilities: restaurant. AE, DC, MC, V. Expensive.*

Other friendly hotels include **Weisse Taube** (Kaigasse 9, tel. 0662/84–24–04; 30 rooms with bath or shower; nearby parking garage; AE, DC, MC, V; moderate) and **Vier Jahreszeiten** (Hubert-Sattlergasse 12, tel. 0662/72–4–08; 28 rooms with bath; restaurant; AE, DC, MC, V; moderate).

The Lake Country

East of Salzburg is the **Salzkammergut,** a land of blue lakes and green mountains, where you can swim, boat, fish, or simply slow down to the pace of the season. This is a popular tourist area, but a short stroll or sail will take you away from the crowds and leave you in the company of birds and pines.

Salt *(salz)* was mined here for at least 1,500 years before the Romans came and was the principal source of wealth for the prince-archbishops of Salzburg. Because the managers permitted no visitors, it remained a sealed domain. The situation changed when Emperor Franz Josef (1867–1916) moved his summer court to Bad Ischl. Great families soon moved in and built their estates overlooking the lakes. Painters drew postcards of the Lake Country, and soon the region became one of the most popular resort areas in the country.

Lake Fuschl From Salzburg, continue your tour on Route 158 24 km (15 mi)
(Fuschlsee) to **Lake Fuschl.**

Dining **Schloss Fuschl.** This elegant 16th-century hotel-castle over-
and Lodging looks the delightful lake. It's only 24 km (15 mi) from Salzburg, so consider staying here while you tour the city or stopping for lunch. No luncheon setting could be lovelier than the terrace above the lake. *A–5322 Hof bei Salzburg, am Fuschlsee, tel. 06229/2253. 55 rooms with bath. Facilities: outstanding restaurant, swimming, sauna, tennis, 9-hole golf course, AE, DC, MC, V. Very Expensive.*

St. Gilgen Continue on Route 158 8 km (5 mi) to **St. Gilgen,** where Mozart's mother was born.

Dining **Nannerl** is a good café and patisserie for snacks or lunch. *St. Gilgen, tel. 06227/368. No reservations. Dress: informal. No credit cards. Moderate.*

St. Wolfgang Continue south on Route 158 along the southern shore of **Lake Wolfgang** (Wolfgangsee). Either leave your car at Gschwandt near the eastern end of the lake, and take the ferry; or drive to Strobl, turn left, and head back up the western side of the lake about 5.6 km (3.5 mi). The boat trip is the best part of a visit to St. Wolfgang, so if time permits, take the ferry, checking the schedule the night before.

From the ferry landing at St. Wolfgang, walk to the **Parish Church,** wander down narrow lanes, lunch on a terrace overlooking the lake, rent a rowboat, and then enjoy a peaceful boat ride back to your car. The drawing cards of St. Wolfgang are the lake view and Michael Pacher's altarpiece in the 16th-century Parish Church, one of the most famous Gothic wood carvings in the world. The work is done with such detail that you can see the stitches in the Virgin's robes. Perspective had just been mastered in 1481, and Pacher delights in it like a child who has just learned to walk. Give thanks to the artist who sculpted the Baroque side altar; he was commissioned to update Pacher's work in Baroque style and deliberately made it the wrong size so that the original would not be replaced.

Dining **Lachsen** is the best restaurant in town. *St. Wolfgang, tel.*
and Lodging *06138/2432. Reservations advised. Jacket and tie required. AE, DC, MC, V. Expensive.*
White Horse Inn. The pilgrims who visited St. Wolfgang seven

centuries ago have been replaced by busloads of tourists who during the day saunter in and out of the famous hotel. Rooms are clean and comfortable, but renovations have eclipsed much of the hotel's natural charm. Request a room with traditional furnishings and a balcony overlooking the lake. *Hotel Weisses Rössl, St. Wolfgang, tel. 06138–2306. 120 rooms with bath or shower. Facilities: restaurant, lake swimming, indoor pool. AE, DC, MC, V. Closed Nov.–Dec. 20. Expensive.*

Bad Ischl Continue east about 19.2 km (12 mi) on Route 158 to **Bad Ischl.** From May through September take the 60-minute tour of **Kaiservilla,** where Emperor Franz Josef held his summer court. His bedroom, with an iron bedstead, plain pine wardrobe, and uncomfortable armchair, is simplicity itself and reflects the emperor's austere tastes. He was a great hunter who shot selectively, protecting the breeds of deer. His nephew, Franz Ferdinand—the one shot at Sarajevo, precipitating World War I—was not permitted to hunt here because of his passion for indiscriminate slaughter. As you stand in the emperor's bedroom, think of him as a man so set in his Imperial ways that he refused to carry money or speak on the phone—a man who drove in a car only once, as a gesture to Edward VII of England, who came here to offer the emperor an alliance with Britain if Austria-Hungary would agree to break with Germany. If only Edward VII had been more persuasive or Franz Josef less obstinate—"You must not forget that I am a German prince," he said—World War I might have been averted.

Dining **Cafe Zauner** is world renowned for its pastries, particularly *Zaunerstollen. Pfarrgasse 7, tel. 06132/3522. Reservations advised. Dress: casual. AE, DC, MC, V. Closed Tues. in winter. Expensive.*
Weinhaus Attwenger is a good bet for a complete meal. *Leharkai 12, tel. 06132/3327. Reservations advised. Jacket and tie required. AE, DC, MC, V. Closed Mon. Expensive.*

Hallstatt From Bad Ischl take Route 145 south about 16 km (10 mi) and make a right turn on Route 166. **Hallstatt** is about 11.2 km (7 mi) farther south along Lake Hallstatt.

The charming village of Hallstatt clings to the side of Dachstein Mountain above the deep blue Hallstatt Lake. Consider spending the night; there are no first-class hotels, but when the day-trippers have left, you'll enjoy one of the loveliest natural settings in the Lake Country. You can rent boats and use the town as a base for excursions. The **Parish Church** is reached by steps from the center of the village.

Hallstatt is the oldest known settlement in Austria, and many prehistoric graves have been discovered nearby. The cemetery is overcrowded, and skeletons have been periodically dug up and displayed in the **charnel house**—some inscribed with dates and causes of death. Kids will love it!

Dining and Lodging **Grüner Baum** is a terrace restaurant overlooking the lake. *Hallstatt, tel. 06134/263. Reservations useful. Dress: casual. No credit cards. Closed Nov.–Mar. Expensive.*
Gasthof Zauner is simple but friendly. Ask for a room with antiques. *Hallstatt, tel. 06134/246. 12 rooms with shower. MC. Closed Nov.–mid-Dec. Moderate.*

Excursions **Lake of Gosau:** From Hallstatt, turn left on Route 166 to Gosau, and then turn left again to the Lake of Gosau. The surface of this small lake reflects the rock walls and majestic peaks of the nearby mountains. This is the most dramatic setting in the Lake Country, particularly if you arrive in the morning or evening, when the lake is still and the busloads of tourists are absent. The hour-long walk around the lake is a delightful experience.

Salt Mines: From Hallstatt, drive to Lahn, take the funicular to the restaurant, and then a 10-minute walk to the salt mines. You can descend by a staircase or down the same smooth woodslide used by the miners. A guided walk takes you past an underground lake. The trip ends with a mile-long underground train ride.

The Ice Caves and **Mount Krippenstein:** From Hallstatt, drive around the southern end of the lake. Just before Obertraun turn right on the road to the Ice Caves (Dachsteineishöhle). Take the cable car to the station Schönbergalpe, and follow signs to the Eishöhle. There are 60-minute guided tours daily from May to mid-October. After the tour, continue up the cable car to Mount Krippenstein (2,075.6 m/6,919 ft) for lunch. The view is breathtaking, particularly from Pioneer's Cross (Pionierkreuz), a short walk from the cable car.

On to Linz Return to Bad Ischl and take Route 145 about 17.6 km (11 mi) north to **Ebensee.** If you're partial to panoramic views, take the cable car to the winter sports area of **Feuerkogel.**

From Ebensee, continue for about 4 km (2½ mi) along the lovely west shore of the Traunsee to **Traunkirchen.** The Parish Church has ornate Baroque furnishings and a famous Fisherman's Pulpit in the form of a boat, representing the Apostle's craft with dripping nets. Overhead is the scene of a lobster returning to St. Francis Xavier a crucifix he lost when shipwrecked near Japan.

Continue north about 8 km (5 mi). **Gmunden** is famous for its ceramics. Stretch your legs on a 1.6-km (1-mi) walk under chestnut trees along the shores of the Traunsee. **Ort Chateau** is on an island linked to the mainland. A nephew of the emperor acquired it in 1878. He gave up his title after the death of Franz Josef's son Rudolf, and lived here under the assumed name of Johann Ort.

Linz Take Route 144 north to A1, and drive east to **Linz.**

Dining **Allegro** is the best and most expensive restaurant in the old town. The nouvelle menu features lamb, *Tafelspitz* (boiled beef), and *Geschnetzeltes* (sliced veal with mushrooms in a cream sauce). The desserts are worth saving room for. *Schillerstr. 68, tel. 0732/66–98–00. Reservations essential. Jacket and tie required. AE, DC, MC, V. Closed weekends and Aug. Expensive.*
Traxlmayr is a typical Austrian café where you can read the *International Herald Tribune* for the price of a cup of coffee. *Promenade 16, tel. 0732/27–33–53. Reservations useful. Dress: casual. AE, DC, MC, V. Closed Sun. Expensive.*

The Mühlviertel

If you're in a hurry, go directly to the Abbey of St. Florian. But if time permits, and the weather cooperates, consider a loop north through the district of **Mühlviertel.** This will take you down back roads, through rolling farmland seldom seen by foreign tourists. There's a Grandma Moses quality to this landscape, with stone barns, milk cans, laundry lines flapping their shadows on lengths of lawn, and everywhere the smells of the good earth.

It's about 80 km (50 mi) round-trip from Linz to Freistadt. Leave A1 and follow A7 north toward Linz. Continue past Linz, following signs to Route 125 and Freistadt. About 11.2 km (7 mi) before Freistadt, turn right on a small country road to **Kefermarkt.** In the chancel of the Gothic **Church of St. Wolfgang** is a great carved wood altarpiece about 11.9 m (40 ft) high. (If the church is locked, ask in the building behind, n. 2, for the key.) Continue north to **Freistadt.** The town has a lovely main square with a **Parish Church** and old, arcaded houses.

Dining and Lodging **Zum Goldenen Adler** is an informal, reasonably priced hotel-restaurant that's been in the same family for 200 years. Regional dishes popular with tourists include roast pork with *Speckkrautsalat;* and *Zwiebelrostbraten* (roast beef) with *Bratkartoffeln.* Don't miss the *Apfelstrudel* or a sweet called *Esterhazyschnitte. Salzgasse 1, tel. 07942/2112. 30 rooms with bath. Facilities: restaurant, pub, pool, solarium, sauna, fitness room. AE, DC, MC, V. Moderate.*

On to St. Florian You can continue your back-road tour from Freistadt to **Bad Leonfelden** on Route 128, then south to **Glasau** on Route 126 and back to Linz. Part of this trip takes you through a forest and along a broodingly romantic gorge; but if you've had enough of back roads or need to reach St. Florian before the last tour (4 PM), take Route 125 direct from Freistadt to Linz, and continue to St. Florian.

St. Florian

The abbey at Melk, crowning a bluff above the Danube, is more imposing; but **St. Florian** has a greater variety of things to see, so it would be a mistake to pass it up for Melk. The **abbey** has been occupied for more than 900 years by the Canons of St. Augustine (canons, unlike monks, are not confined to an abbey, but do ministerial work in their district). It was entirely rebuilt under Carlo Antonio Carlone and Jacob Prandtauer (1686–1751) and is today one of the purest examples of Baroque architecture in Europe.

St. Florian was a Roman administrator who was martyred in AD 304 and thrown into the nearby river Enns with a millstone around his neck; it was on the site of his grave that the monastery was built. The saint is traditionally invoked against fire with the prayer, "Good St. Florian, spare my house and rather burn my neighbor's." His figure can still be seen in many Austrian houses, dressed as a Roman legionary holding a pail of water to douse the flames.

A great stairway leads to the **Marble Hall,** which has a ceiling depicting Austrian victories over the Turks. Science and Virtue join hands with Religion in allegorical paintings on the **Library** ceiling—a reminder that the Augustines have always regarded the intellect as an ally in their search for spiritual truth.

There were no hotels fit for royalty in those days; hence, the **Imperial Apartments,** lavishly furnished as they were when

Empress Maria Theresa and other members of the royal family stayed here. On display, too, is the bed of Anton Bruckner, who died here in 1896. Bruckner, the country's greatest 19th-century composer of organ music, was accepted into the abbey's choir school at age 13, when his father died. Most of his symphonies and masses were composed here after 1845, when he was appointed church organist. He became famous when he went to Linz and Vienna as an organist and teacher, but his roots were here, and he was buried, as he requested, in the crypt beneath the church organ.

Don't miss the exuberant Baroque **Abbey Church** (Stiftskirche). You'll wonder why the architect tried so hard to keep you in this world when you should be thinking of the next—until you realize that he has tried to bring God's kingdom down to you, and overwhelm you with its glory. The organ's 7,343 pipes make music during summer concerts, daily at 4:30. In the crypt below lie Bruckner's coffin and the very un-Baroque bones of some 6,000 early Christians, dug up when the original Gothic church was built, and arranged like so many oranges in a market.

The abbey's most valuable paintings, which you'll see on the tour, are 14 works by Albrecht Altdorfer (1480–1538), the master of the early-16th-century Danube school of painting. The works are noted for their warm, rich colors, their expressiveness, and their use of landscapes not just to provide background, but to influence the total mood of the painting—a technique that foreshadows the Romantics several centuries ahead of its time.

On to Melk If you're anxious to reach Dürnstein or to make the last tour at Melk (summers at 5; off-season at 4), take A1 direct from Linz to Melk Abbey. The alternative is to follow A1 only as far as Enns, cross the Danube on Route 123, take Route 3 east along the Danube, and then recross the river at Melk. This route takes you to **Mauthausen** (25.6 km/ 16 mi from Linz), the granite quarry used as a concentration camp where nearly 200,000 prisoners were killed. A 90-minute tour takes you to the remaining huts where prisoners waited to be summoned to their deaths.

Melk

There's nothing modest about **Melk;** straddling a rocky bluff 45 m (150 ft) above the Danube, it is the embodiment of the Church Militant and the Church Triumphant. The Babenbergs—the family that ruled Austria for 270 years, before the Habsburgs took over—established their rule here in the late 10th century. The second Babenberg, Heinrich I (994–1018), founded the monastery and turned it over to the Benedictines. The Turks gutted it in 1683, and 19 years later Jacob Prandtauer turned it into what many consider the greatest monument to the Baroque imagination in Austria.

The high points of the tour are the **Library,** one of the richest in Europe, where the light of learning continued to burn during the Middle Ages; and the **Abbey Church.** Leaving the church is like stepping from daylight into a shaded room.

The Wachau Valley

From Melk take Route 3 east along the north shore of the Danube to Krems.

The region along the Danube from Melk to Krems, scarcely 56 km (35 mi) long, is known as the **Wachau:** one of the dreamiest, most romantic river valleys in the world. Imposing castle ruins loom above as you drive along the wide, silent river past the terraced orchards and vineyards. In spring, apple, plum, and apricot trees burst into bloom. Medieval vintners' towns with narrow cobbled streets and fortified churches spread along the banks. You're only 90 minutes from Vienna, yet there's little commercial development to mar the beauty of the landscape.

The economy rests on the vineyards, the source of Austria's finest white wines. In 1301 a man named Ritzling, whose vineyards lay along a brook that meets the Danube just west of Dürnstein, developed his own grapes, which were cultivated in Germany's Rhineland and then brought back to Austria under the name Riesling. Today more than 1,000 winegrowers belong to the Wachau cooperative, with headquarters in the 1719 castle outside Dürnstein. Wherever you stay, you'll be able to enjoy these local wines from family-owned vineyards. Route 3, the most popular route, takes you through the most historic towns, including Dürnstein, where you should spend the night. The other town not to miss is Weissenkirchen.

From Melk, cross the Danube and turn right on Route 3. About 5 km (3 mi) along, on the opposite shore, you'll see an early 19th-century castle (closed to the public) called Schönbühel. The orchards begin after Grimsing. Looming up from the highest point across the river, past the village of **Aggsbach Markt** (11.2 km/7 mi east of Melk), is Aggstein Fortress. You'll return here later.

Spitz After Aggsbach Markt comes **Spitz,** an ancient market town hidden behind apricot and pear trees. Schlossgasse is one of its most picturesque streets. The Gothic Parish Church has an elegant chancel that is out of line with the nave (the central aisle). If you need to stretch, hike through the vineyards to the Red Door, a wall built to keep out the Turks, and enjoy a sweeping view of the valley.

Dining **Christines Weinlöchl** is a historic house with modern paintings, some charcoal-grill specialties, and a great choice of regional wines. *Ottenschlägerstr. 4, tel. 02713/2230. No reservations. Dress: informal. No credit cards. Moderate.*
The Strand Restaurant is a delightful spot for lunch or dinner overlooking the river at the far end of town. Try the venison or some fresh Danube fish with a glass of homemade apricot brandy. *Donaulände 7, tel. 02713/2320. Reservations useful. Dress: informal. No credit cards. Closed in winter. Moderate.*
Mühlenkeller is in the cellar of an ancient mill. The dishes are better on quantity than quality, but the wines are excellent. The restaurant has some rooms to rent, so you won't have to drink and drive. *Auf der Wehr 1, tel: 02713/2352. No reservations. Dress: informal. No credit cards. Closed mid-Dec.–mid-Jan. Inexpensive.*

Lodging **Frühstückspensionen Hans Burkhardt** is a friendly guest house. *Krenserstr. 19, tel. 02713/2356. 5 rooms with bath. No credit cards. Closed Nov.–Mar. Inexpensive.*

Frühstückspensionen Zur alten Mühle is another guest house with a friendly atmosphere. *AUF der Wehr 1, tel. 02713/2352. 20 rooms with bath. Facilities: bakery on premises. No credit cards. Inexpensive.*

Weissenkirchen This charming medieval village, dominated by a fortified Gothic church, is 14.4 km (9 mi) past Aggsbach. It's less perfect than Dürnstein, but also less precious and less well known to tourists.

Dining **Jamek** is more expensive than Florianihof, but enjoys a somewhat better reputation for its local wines and daily specials, particularly the cream soups, fillet of beef, and pork cutlets with caraway. *Joching 45, tel. 02715/2235. Reservations essential. Jacket and tie required. AE, DC, MC, V. Closed Sun., Mon., and mid-Dec.–mid-Feb. Expensive.*

Florianihof is one of the best restaurants along the Danube. The family Mandl takes credit for the friendly service and top cuisine. Popular dishes include fish from the Danube and *Vanillerostbraten.* For an apéritif, try a dry Dürnsteiner Auslese; and with your meal, a Riesling or Veltiner. *Weissenkirchen/Wösendorf 74; tel. 02715/2212. Reservations advised. Jacket and tie required. AE, DC, MC, V. Closed Wed. and Thurs. Moderate.*

Prandtauerhof is a perfect choice for an outdoor lunch or dinner of lamb, venison, and excellent wines from the owner's own vineyards. *Joching 36, tel. 02715/2310. Reservations useful. Dress: casual. AE, MC, closed mid-Dec.–mid-Jan. Moderate.*

Lodging **Raffelsbergerhof** is the former home of the controller of river traffic. Not even the modern furnishings can destroy the charm of this 16th-century manor house. *Weissenkirchen, tel. 02715/ 2201. 12 rooms with bath. AE, DC, MC, V. Closed Nov.–Apr. Moderate.*

Dürnstein **Dürnstein,** 4 km (2½ mi) past Weissenkirchen, is the most picturesque village along the Danube. It sits below terraced vineyards, at the most dramatic turn of the river. The main road passes through a tunnel beneath the town, so the modern world—except for the tourists—hardly intrudes. Richard the Lion-hearted would probably recognize Dürnstein, though he might wonder what has happened to the castle where he was imprisoned, as it lies today in ruins.

During the Third Crusade, Richard the Lion-hearted, King of England, offended Leopold V, the Duke of Austria, by removing his banner from a tower during the assault on Acre in Palestine. On his way home Richard was shipwrecked off the Yugoslavian coast and had to pass through his rival's lands dressed as a peasant. His royal ring gave him away near Vienna, however, and he was shuttled off to prison in Dürnstein. In the spring of 1193, so the story goes, Richard's faithful servant Blondel was wandering from town to town in search of his master, when Richard, standing in a fortress window, overheard Blondel singing his favorite song, and finished the verse himself. The king was later set free, after paying a king's ransom.

It's only a 10-minute walk from one end of Dürnstein to the other. Wander along the main street (Hauptstrasse), which is lined with turreted 16th-century houses dripping with flowers.

The 15th-century **Parish Church** was redone in Baroque dress
—compare the simple Gothic nave to the ornate 18th-century
pulpit and high altar.

Don't miss the view of Dürnstein from the ruins of the castle
above the town. The 20-minute walk should be made in the early morning or at dusk. Also enjoy a mile-long walk along a
riverfront promenade, and a 4-km (2½-mi) walk through the
vineyards to Weissenkirchen. Time your trip so you can return
by ferry.

If you're partial to boat rides on romantic rivers, take the local
ferry round-trip from Dürnstein to Melk. You can get off the
ferry at Melk if you missed seeing the abbey en route from Salzburg, and then catch another ferry back to Dürnstein later in
the day.

The road along the southern bank of the Danube is just as scenic as the one you took (Route 3) along the north shore. The
southern route misses the major towns but lets you see them
from a distance, framed by vineyards and orchards. To get to
the southern route, drive east from Dürnstein toward Krems,
cross the bridge at Mautern, and head west along the Danube,
back to **Aggstein Fortress**—one of Austria's most romantic castle ruins. The present owner runs a modest restaurant in the
old retainer's hall. From the ramparts, 288 m (960 ft) above the
Danube, there's a breathtaking view of the Wachau Valley.
Standing at this dizzying height you can decide whether you
would rather jump or starve to death—a choice given to prisoners of Schreckenwald ("Terror of the Forest"), the robber
baron who stretched a chain across the Danube here and imprisoned those who didn't pay a toll. (Justice was served when
an escaped prisoner set the castle on fire, and the Terror was
reduced to a wandering beggar.)

Bicycles can be rented at train stations in Krems and Melk and
returned at other stations along the route. The ferries take bicycles (for a fee), so you can bike, say, from Dürnstein to
Aggsbach, and then return by ferry. Most tourists take the
north route, so the relatively flat south route is ideal for biking.
A ferry recrosses the Danube at Spitz.

Dining **Bacher.** The Bacher is one of Austria's best restaurants, elegant but entirely lacking in pretension. Dining in the garden in
summer adds to the experience. *Südtirolerpl. 208, Mautern,
tel. 02732/2937. Reservations advised. Jacket and tie required.
Closed Mon. May–Oct., Mon. and Tues. Nov.–Apr. Expensive.*
Schloss Dürnstein is the top restaurant in town. It's also the
most expensive, but how often do you get to dine in a 17th-
century castle? *Dürnstein 2, tel. 02711/212. Reservations essential weekends; otherwise advisable. Jacket and tie required.
AE, DC, MC, V. Closed Dec.–Feb. Expensive.*
Sänger Blondel is more a family restaurant popular with tourists. Meals are less elegantly prepared than at the Schloss, but
almost as satisfying, and at half the price. Try the clear soup
with liver dumplings; the roasted pork or stuffed brisket of
veal; and the house specialty, the *Sänger-Blondel Torte.
Dürnstein 64, tel. 02711/253. Reservations advisable. Jacket
and tie required. AE, DC, MC, V. Moderate.*

Lodging **Schloss Dürnstein** spares no pains to capture the elegance of the original 17th-century castle, high on a cliff overlooking the Danube. There's a swimming pool, a famous gourmet restaurant, and a shaded terrace where you can sip local wines and watch the boats gliding along the river. The vaulted salons are decorated with antique furniture from the family of Count Starhemberg, who kept the Turks from Vienna in 1683. Introduce yourself to the owner/manager, Johann Thiery; he takes a personal interest in the happiness of his guests. *Dürnstein 2, tel. 02711/212. 37 rooms with bath or shower. Facilities: restaurant (reservations required), sauna, pool. Closed Dec.–Feb. AE, DC, MC, V. Very Expensive.*

Hotel Richard Lowenherz is run by Johann Thiery's brother Raimund. This is more a hotel you check into than a castle where you become a privileged guest, and antiques are in the hallways, not in the rooms; yet the hotel does have some character, and rooms are less expensive than at the Schloss. *Dürnstein 8, tel. 02711/222. 50 rooms with bath. Facilities: restaurant, terrace café, pool. AE, DC, MC, V. Expensive.*

Pension Altes Rathaus, Beate Fürtler is a private home that provides budget lodging for travelers. *Dürnstein 26, tel. 02711/252. 8 rooms, 3 with shower. No credit cards. Closed Dec.–Apr. Inexpensive.*

Vienna

It's about 96 km (60 mi) from Dürnstein to Vienna. As you head east from Dürnstein to Krems, the mountains recede, and the scenery loses much of its drama. Cross the bridge at Krems, and drive south past Herzogenburg to A1. There's a Tourist Information Office on A1 before you reach Vienna.

Vienna says Empire—that's why Americans love it so much. Only a people raised under Jefferson could embrace an imperial city so uncritically and with such longing. We may have left the Old World behind, but not our need for splendor. And splendor, imaginary or not, is what Vienna has to offer.

The people, the palaces—everything about Vienna seems suspended in the 18th century, frozen in time. It is a city under glass. The people, born to another age, still hold to courtly forms: addressing each other by titles long abolished; kissing hands; loving food and beauty; ignoring time. It is, literally, a city of dreams—dreams that become your own as you wander through palaces, sip champagne at the opera, or indulge yourself at pastry shops once frequented by Haydn and Mozart, Adler and Freud.

There's a reverse side to this dream, of course. "The Blue Danube," which isn't blue, was written partly to make Austrians forget their humiliating defeat by Prussia, which reduced them to a second-rate power. Coffeehouses thrive in part because of a housing shortage and cramped living conditions. Few cities have been so unkind to their musicians—while they were alive. The Viennese loved Schubert's pretty songs, but the poignancy of his greatest works escaped them.

Between the Franco-Prussian War and World War I Vienna changed from the center of an empire of 50 million to the capital of a small Alpine nation. It remains today an imperial city without an empire. It is fitting that it is a Baroque city, for Baroque is the art of the facade, the perfect stage set for fantasy. To say that its splendor exists only in the mind's eye, however, makes it no less splendid. If Vienna is a dream, let's dream on.

The oldest part of Vienna, bounded by the Ringstrasse and the Danube (Donau) Canal, is called District I. The major sights of District I are described below on the walking tour of "Old Vienna and the Ring." Other sights—Schönbrunn, the Belvedere, and the Prater—are described in a subsequent section called **"Outside the Ring."**

The Hofburg (the Habsburg Palace) is the number one attraction in Vienna, so visit in the morning, particularly because the Spanish Riding School and the National Library, both part of the Hofburg, are only open then. In the afternoon either (1) visit museums near the Hofburg (the Fine Arts Museum for paintings; the Neue Burg for porcelain and silver, arms and armor); or (2) wander the streets of Vienna, shopping and visiting churches and pastry shops. Whichever you choose not to do should be saved for the following day and combined with tours of Schönbrunn Palace, the Belvedere, and the Prater. If any time is left, take a streetcar ride around the Ring. The "1" line does the full circuit clockwise, the "2" line counterclockwise. Plan to spend at least one evening dining in Old Vienna and going to a concert or opera. Save another evening for a drive through the Vienna Woods and dinner at a Heuriger (new wine tavern) at Grinzing or Nussdorf.

Old Vienna and the Ring Let's begin at the **Vienna Booking Service tourist office** in the subway station and shopping mall beneath Opera Square. Pick up maps and brochures, and listings of weekly events. Be sure to get the latest schedule of opening and closing times, which can vary from building to building; ignoring these times could ruin your trip. Buy a valuable city publication called *Vienna from A to Z*, which describes the major sights by numbers that match numbered plaques on the buildings. Also purchase a money-saving Three-Day Transportation Ticket valid on all subways, streetcars and buses.

From the tourist office, cross back inside the Ring and head down Kärntnerstrasse, past the **State Opera House** (Staatsoper). If you don't plan on going to the opera, take a tour (daily, June–Sept., depending on rehearsal schedules).

Continue down Kärntnerstrasse toward **St. Stephen's Cathedral.** Just past the Opera House is Philharmonikerstrasse. Turn left. At Number 4 is one of Vienna's most illustrious hotels, the **Sacher,** where the nobility conducted its affairs, both political and social, during the days of the Empire. Franz Josef's guests used to come here after dining at the Imperial Palace (the Hofburg); etiquette demanded that no one eat after the Emperor finished a course, and Franz Josef, who had Spartan tastes, was a light eater. If the hotel lobby is quiet, a porter may be willing to show you the paneled lounge, private dining rooms, and collection of autographed menus. The Sachertorte, a chocolate-frosted cake with an aside of whipped cream, was first made here for one of Metternich's banquets.

It's said that Franz Josef's son and heir, the Crown Prince Rudolf, began his affair here with 17-year-old Mary Vetsera. Probably because Franz Josef refused to delegate authority to his son, the 31-year-old boy found his own way of growing up by drinking, partying, and associating with liberals and other

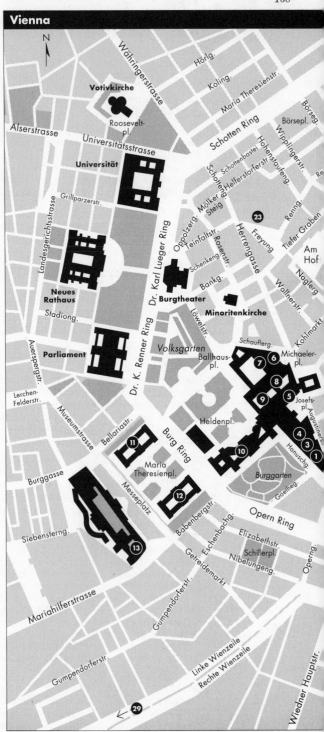

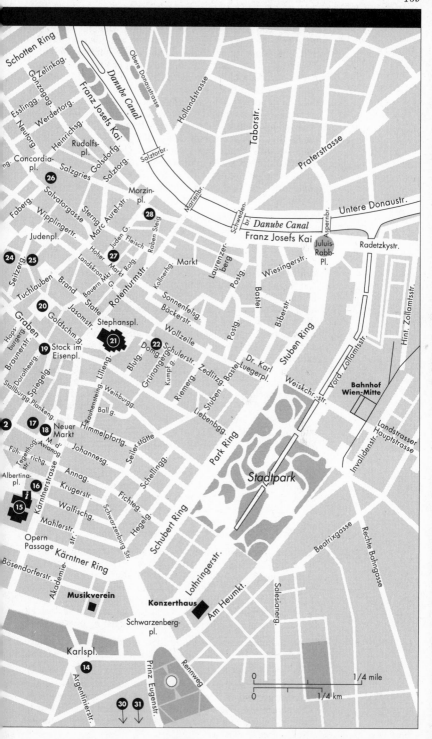

freethinkers. In late 1888, Rudolf wrote a letter to the Pope. What he said nobody will ever know, but when his father got wind of it, he severely chastised the boy, and the next day Rudolf and Mary were found dead at his hunting lodge at **Mayerling,** about 32 km (20 mi) southwest of Vienna. Mary had been shot first and covered with flowers. To cover up the scandal, she was spirited away in a rainstorm, sitting up fully dressed in a carriage between two uncles, and buried in a nearby monastery under police supervision. Rudolf left notes for his wife and his mother, but not for his father. That the young couple had a suicide pact seems clear, but that the lovers took their lives because Franz Josef demanded that they part seems doubtful. Rudolf was a man of many affairs—he had, in fact, spent the night before with an actress he had been seeing for some time—so more than likely he was in trouble for his liberal views.

At the end of Philharmonikerstrasse is a large plaza (Albertina), now site of a disputed war memorial.

Cross over to the **Capuchin's Crypt.** Three centuries of Habsburgs are buried here—or at least their bodies: their hearts are gathering dust in the crypt of the **Augustinerkirche,** and their entrails are resting in the catacombs of **St. Stephen's.** Maria Theresa used to pay respects to her husband, Franz, here, and an elevator was installed when she got too stout for the trip. Stuck one day, she cried out, "Look, the dead don't want to let me go"; and a week later she too was dead. Maria and Franz now stare into each other's eyes on the lid of their sarcophagus—an angel waits at their heads with a trumpet to awaken them on Judgment Day. The only non-Habsburg here is Caroline Fuchs, governess to Maria Theresa's 10 surviving children, including Marie Antoinette. History should note that it was Caroline Fuchs who made it possible for Maria Theresa to have both a family and a career. The most recent—and presumably last—burial in the crypt took place in 1989, when Zita, widow of Austria's last Kaiser, was interred with all state honors, those of Hungary included.

Bear right on Augustinerstrasse. On your left is the **Albertina Gallery.** Stop here now, or return another day on your visit to the museums. The Albertina houses one of the largest and best collections of graphic art in the world, including many drawings by Albrecht Dürer. Unfortunately, many works are shown only in facsimile, except during special exhibits.

Continue down Augustinerstrasse to the 14th-century **Augustinerkirche.** Though remodeled, it gives off an aura of great age and captures the spirit of the early Habsburgs, who came here to pray. They all left their hearts here—buried in urns. Franz Josef gave *his* heart away here to 17-year-old Elisabeth. It was here that Napoleon married Marie-Louise, though he decided not to show up and sent someone to marry her by proxy.

Continue a few steps down Augustinerstrasse to a large square (Josefsplatz). On your left is the **National Library.** The **Great Hall** is a masterpiece of Baroque decoration.

You are now in the **Hofburg,** the winter residence of the Habsburgs, and still today the seat of Austrian government. The palace was begun in the 13th century and continued to grow and change for the next 700 years. Styles change from one building to the next—the public halls are usually lavish, the private rooms relatively plain and comfortable.

Your tour of the Hofburg is a voyage into Austria's past. In 976 the Holy Roman Emperor Otto I gave land to a German nobleman named Leopold of Babenberg for his help in crushing a Bavarian revolt. The Babenbergs ruled Austria for the next 270 years. When the last Babenberg died without an heir, Count Rudolf of Habsburg fought his way to power. From this family of minor Swiss nobility came the Habsburg dynasty, the strongest in European history, which ruled continuously from 1278 until 1918. The emperors were brilliant and mad; they wrote music; they built palaces. Their goal was not to win slavish allegiance to Austria but to acquire wealth and land, and they accomplished this less by aggression than by diplomacy, marrying their daughters off to foreign kings. From the Hofburg they ruled most of Central Europe, as well as Spain and Spanish colonies in South America.

Vienna has always been a frontier town on the border between East and West. The Turks attacked in 1529 and were repelled. More than 150 years later, the Turks tried again. While the Emperor and his court fled the city, 24,000 men under Count Starhemberg held out for two months against a force of 200,000. With the aid of Polish King John Sobieski, the Turks were finally routed, ending forever the Ottoman threat to Europe. If Vienna had fallen, so might have Christendom. For decades the Viennese had faced outward, bracing themselves for the attack. Victory released a flood of pent-up energy, and with joy, pride and relief the Viennese created the Baroque city you see today.

Before Maria Theresa came the three so-called Baroque emperors: Leopold I (reigned 1658–1705); Josef I (reigned 1705–11) and Karl VI (reigned 1711–40). Maria Theresa had much in common with Queen Victoria: the long reign (1740–80); the large family (16 children); the insistence on duty and morality; the goodness and sincerity; the enlightened despotism. With her death the age of monuments, and, some would say, the glory of the Habsburgs, came to an end.

Her son Josef II (reigned 1780–90) tried to continue his mother's reforms, but he pushed too hard and too fast. He reacted against excesses of luxury, but the people loved pomp and splendor. He tried to protect nightingales in the public gardens, but the people preferred keeping songbirds caged.

When Napoleon's empire fell apart, the crowned heads of Europe gathered in Vienna to pick up the pieces. Vienna was now the center of Europe. The main figure at the Congress of Vienna (September 1814–July 1815) was the Austrian statesman, Prince Metternich. For centuries, European powers had struggled to dominate by force; what Metternich sought was a balance of power, with Austria as the vital buffer between Russia and France. While Metternich schemed, the Congress danced and dined its way from one wild entertainment to the next. This was the gay, licentious Vienna that lives on in our dreams: Czar Alexander of Russia dancing for 40 nights; the fat King of Würtemberg cutting a hole in the dinner table so he could reach his plate; Castlereagh's wife wearing a garter ribbon in her hair. *"Le Congrès danse, mais il ne marche pas"* is the quote to remember; "The Congress dances, but it gets nowhere."

The period from 1815 to 1848 is known as the Biedermeier Age, the age of the middle class. Tired of war, the country turned to Schubert songs, pastry, and new wine. Gone was the stately minuet—the dance of the aristocracy; in its place came the rhythms of a Jewish innkeeper's son named Johann Strauss. While twilight fell over Imperial Vienna, his son Johann Strauss the younger had some 230 musicians working for him in the huge, resplendent ballrooms of Vienna. "Vienna, be gay!" they sang to the strains of the "Blue Danube." "Well, why court sorrow?/There's still tomorrow,/So laugh and be merry."

Metternich ruled under a weak emperor. Discontent grew as liberties were repressed, and Metternich was finally forced to flee to London in the Vienna uprising of 1848.

Franz Josef reigned for 68 years, from 1848 to 1916. When he was crowned, James Polk was in the White House; when he died, Woodrow Wilson had been elected to serve a second term.

Until the mid-19th century "Old Vienna" was encircled by the walls that kept the Turks from overrunning Europe. In order for the city to expand, Franz Josef had the walls torn down and replaced by the Ringstrasse—a ring of wide boulevards lined with the monumental, late-19th-century public buildings you see today.

Tearing down the walls was one of Franz Josef's few gestures toward the future. He was a man of simple, austere tastes who hated reform. He was an anachronism—an 18th-century figure in a 19th-century world; a man who worked long hours, fumbling with documents while the world collapsed around him. His son Rudolf committed suicide at Mayerling; his wife, Elisabeth, was struck down by an assassin's dagger; his nephew Franz Ferdinand was assassinated at Sarajevo. Helplessly he watched the growing might of Prussia. It was perhaps a blessing that he died in 1916 and did not live to see his successor, the Emperor Karl, renounce the throne in 1918, bringing to an end more than six centuries of Habsburg rule.

Across the Josefsplatz, on the far right, is the Stallburg, the stable for the **Spanish Riding School.** A passage in front of the Stallburg leads to the Spanish Riding School itself.

The idea of noble purebred horses smacks of Empire, which helps explain the lasting appeal of the milk-white Lippizan stallions who perform to capacity crowds in the City of Dreams. Hitler, who, as the world knows, had a fondness for selective breeding, sent the horses to Czechoslovakia to protect them during the war; General Patton, another horse lover, eventually brought them back.

It seems fitting that during the Congress of Vienna, kings and queens danced in the same sumptuous hall where the horses performed. As Edward Crankshaw wrote in 1938,

The cabrioling of the pure Lippizaners is, by all our standards, the absolute of uselessness. The horses, fine, beautiful and strong, are utterly divorced from all natural movement, living their lives in an atmosphere of unreality with every step laid down for them and no chance whatsoever of a moment's deviation. And so it was with the 19th-century Habsburgs. The

Court, intent on cabrioles and ballotades, was lost to all reality.

True as this may be, what visitors seek and discover at performances today are qualities often missing from our modern world: grace, beauty, and dignity—all born of discipline and self-control. *Performances March–June, Sept. Nov.; Sun., 10:45 AM, Wed., 7 PM, Sat. 9 AM. Training sessions, Tues.–Fri., 10 AM. Check schedules for Sun. performance; write at least 3 months in advance to the Spanische Reitschule, Hofburg, A 1010 Vienna. Line up by 9:30 for training sessions.*

Return to Josefsplatz. To your right, beside the National Library, is a passageway that leads to the Swiss Court, named for the soldiers who once stood here on guard. On the right is the **Imperial Treasury,** where you'll see the crown of the Holy Roman Emperor, Charlemagne's lance, and fabulous 15th-century embroidered vestments. Even when the imperial crown was padded it failed to fit most heads, and Maria Theresa had a good silent laugh when it slipped down over the ears of her husband, Franz, at his coronation.

From the Treasury, return to the Swiss Court. To your left are steps leading to the beautiful Gothic **Castle Chapel** (Hofburgkapelle), where the Vienna Boys' Choir sings. The choir, founded in 1498 by Emperor Maximilian, is chosen from some 7,000 applicants every year. *(See* The Arts, below, for ticket information).

Return to the Swiss Court, turn left, and pass into the central palace courtyard called In Der Burg (Inside the Castle). Turn immediately right and pass beneath a rotunda. On the left is the **Collection of Court Porcelain and Silver.** On the right are the Imperial Apartments.

The **Imperial Apartments** are impressed with the personalities of Franz Josef and his wife, Elisabeth. The emperor's iron bed is as austere as the one he slept in in Bad Ischl. Elisabeth had exercise equipment in the room next to her bedroom because she loved sports and was afraid of getting fat. In the Empire-style Conference Room is a portrait of Elisabeth with the face of both an empress and a playful little girl. What must it have been like for a 17-year-old to become an empress with 50 million subjects? According to British writer Rebecca West, it was Elisabeth who convinced her husband to create the Dual Monarchy with Hungary, which permitted the empire to survive into the 20th century. By 1860 Elisabeth had become a withdrawn, sensitive lady, who hardly ever visited her husband and was seldom at Court. She may have gone a bit mad. If her tyrannical mother-in-law, Sophie, had let her raise her son Rudolf, who knows, the boy might have lived, and Elisabeth with him; and together they might have restrained Austria's imperialist ambitions and avoided World War I. Without them, Franz Josef stood fast against reform. A conscientious but unimaginative man (though liked by his people), he ruled a dying empire. Three years after his son Rudolf took his life at Mayerling, Franz Josef wrote to Elisabeth, "I should like to put into words how very, very deeply I love you, though I am not very good at showing it and I would only bore you if I could." The most satisfying and disturbing room on your tour is the **Banquet Hall,** set for a royal feast to which the guests will never come.

Return to the rotunda and, leaving the Hofburg, turn right to **St. Michael's Church** (Michaelerkirche) on a square called Michaelerplatz. The high altar, with angels and saints in a golden heaven, is the essence of Baroque.

At No. 3 Michaelerplatz is the 1910 **Loos House,** considered the first example of modern architecture. Adolf Loos was a New Functionalist who believed that style should be the servant of use. By eliminating meaningless detail and decoration—the essence of Baroque—Loos paved the way for the familiar glass-and-concrete slabs that define our cities today. Now beautifully restored, the building houses bank offices instead of the tailors for which the lower floors were designed. Go inside to view the splendid staircase and exhibits of some of the original furnishings.

From St. Michael's, turn right and take your first right along the pedestrian shopping street called Kohlmarkt. Turn right on another shopping street called Graben. If you want to see one of the most sumptuous Baroque churches in Vienna, make your first left off Graben to **Peterskirche.**

Halfway up the Graben is the **Plague Monument** designed by Fischer von Erlach to celebrate the end of a plague in 1679. Though it's not particularly satisfying—it looks like a mound of dirty whipped cream—it does capture the essence of Baroque in the way that the artist completely transforms his material to satisfy his artistic needs.

The Graben ends at **St. Stephen's** (Stephansdom), the spiritual heart and soul of Vienna. This is one of the few Austrian churches whose Gothic austerity has not been retouched with the lightness and color of Baroque. The slender south tower has been hit by lightning and artillery; look for the window where the watchkeeper kept a lookout for Turks. The builder, Hans Puchsbaum, was told not to look down, but did anyway, and fell to his death. For a great view, climb 344 steps up the tower, past the bench where Count von Starhemberg watched the Turkish assault. An elevator takes you to the bell in the northern tower.

The Romanesque (13th-century) main doorway, decorated with stiff apostles, animals, and demons, is the oldest part of the church. In medieval times men and women sat on opposite sides, which is why there are only male saints over the southwest door, where the men entered; and only the Virgin and female saints over the northwest door used by women. Behind the cathedral is a suffering Christ called the "Toothache God."

Immediately on your left as you enter is the Cross Chapel (Tirnkapelle). The iron grillwork on the doors is copied from the gates at Belvedere Palace. Look for reliefs depicting scenes from the Turkish wars.

Near the middle of the church, on the left, is the early-16th-century pulpit carved from solid blocks of stone. The artist peers through a window near the bottom, looking quite fatigued after so much work. The animals climbing up the railing represent sins.

More beautiful than the black marble main altar is the Wiener Neustadt altarpiece (1447) in the chapel to the left. This is one of the most richly carved altarpieces in the world. In the right chapel is the remarkable late-15th-century tomb of Emperor

Friedrich III, made from red Salzburg marble. Evil animals try to disturb Friedrich's sleep, while good spirits, in the form of local personages, keep them away.

A 30-minute guided tour of the catacombs takes you past the entrails of the Habsburgs preserved in copper jars.

A block behind the cathedral, at Domgasse 5, is the **Mozart Memorial** (Figarohaus) where Wolfgang lived from 1784 to 1787 and wrote *The Marriage of Figaro*. Haydn came here as a guest and heard the first performance of Mozart's *Haydn Quartets*. Mozart died in 1791 in dire poverty. His body was taken to the cemetery on a cold, snowy day, and no one marked where it was placed. (Freemasons, at that time, advocated extremely simple burials, without markers or tombstones.)

The choice now is yours: to cross the square (Stephansplatz) and walk up the main shopping street, Kärntnerstrasse, back to the Opera; or to take a short side trip through the Old University district, the oldest part of the city. Let's begin with the Old University District; if your legs refuse to cooperate, skip down to the section below called Kärntnerstrasse, and save the old town for another day.

The Old University District   As you exit through the main door of St. Stephen's, turn right and head down Rotenturmstrasse. Turn right at Lugeck, and bear right on Bäckerstrasse. You're in the Old University district now (the university has since moved), with lots of narrow lanes and beautiful courtyards. The courtyard at No. 7 has Renaissance arcades; the French writer Madame de Staël lived in No. 8 after Napoleon banished her from France. Continue to Old University Square (Dr. Ignaz Seipel-Platz). To your left, at the far end of the square, is the dignified **Church of the Jesuits** (Jesuitenkirche). The domed ceiling isn't curved at all—a good example of Baroque trompe l'oeil (optical illusion).

From the church entrance, walk straight on Sonnenfelsgasse (behind the Academy) and turn right on Schönlaterngasse, which is lined with houses that have not changed much since the days of the Turkish siege. In a niche at No. 7 is an image of a beast, perhaps 750 years old. Legend has it that a dragon poisoned the water in the well within the courtyard. A hero climbed down with a mirror. When the beast saw himself, he died of fright.

Just before the street turns right, you'll pass **St. Bernard's Chapel,** which has a peaceful courtyard where you can rest your feet. The monastery was the winter home of monks from the Vienna Woods.

Leave the courtyard by the far entrance, make your first right, and then a left on Fleischmarkt (Meat Market). Turn left again on Rotenturmstrasse and right at Lugeck to the **Hoher Markt,** the old Roman forum, where Vienna began. In the Middle Ages the square was used as both a market and a pillory, where pickpockets and adultresses got their due. The great personages of Viennese history march from the **Anker Clock** as the hour strikes.

From the center of the square turn right up Judengasse to the Romanesque **Church of St. Rupert** (Ruprechtskirche), the town's oldest church. Though altered, its simplicity provides relief from the bright extravagances of the Baroque, and reminds you that the Viennese must have believed once in guilt and sin. Rupert was the patron saint of the Danube salt merchants, and you can see his salt bucket with his statue outside the church.

Retrace your steps a short way down Judengasse and turn right on a narrow lane called Sterngasse. At the *T*, turn left, and then at the **Old Town Hall** (Altes Rathaus), next to St. Salvador Church, turn right down a narrow street to **Maria Am Gestade.** Many consider this the loveliest church in Vienna. Before the Danube was diverted, an arm flowed by the church steps and fishermen moored there to pray. The late 8th-century church was rebuilt in Gothic style in the early 15th century and has been restored since World War II.

From Maria Am Gestade, turn down the narrow Schwertgasse. The first wide street you come to is Wipplingerstrasse. Turn left and pass between the Altes Rathaus and the old **Chancellery of Bohemia,** which has a Baroque facade by Fischer von Erlach. Turn right around the chancellery, and right again, to a square called **Judenplatz,** the heart of the old ghetto. There was a synagogue here around 1200, but in the 15th century the Jews were burned or imprisoned and the synagogue razed. The Jews gradually returned but were again expelled during the Counter-Reformation.

Cross the square and turn left down another narrow street, Parisergasse, which empties into a small square. On your left is the **Vienna Clock Museum** (Uhrenmuseum der Stadt Wien), which has a wonderful collection of timepieces, from medieval sundials to electronic clocks, which perform on the hour. To your right, on the main square (Am Hof), is the **Church of the Nine Choirs of Angels** (Kirche am Hof), a 14th-century Gothic church with a simple, early Baroque facade. The church faces onto Am Hof square, surrounded by buildings with Baroque facades. It was here that Franz II announced the end of the Holy Roman Empire in 1804. Turn left as you enter the square and at the corner turn left again on Bognergasse or walk across into the Naglergasse, with its small shops and sidewalk restaurants. A quick right at the end of the street takes you back to Kohlmarkt. Turn left on Graben and return to St. Stephen's Cathedral.

From St. Stephen's walk along Kärntnerstrasse, the main shopping street, back to the Opera House (Staatsoper), where your walk began.

Kärntnerstrasse If your feet are holding up, continue south along Kärntnerstrasse past the Ring to a large park. To your left, at the far end of the park, standing beneath a magnificent dome, is the **Karlskirche,** one of the most important Baroque churches in Vienna. There's a story that Fischer von Erlach got the idea for it while standing on Pincio, Rome's famous hill, seeing Trajan's column and St. Peter's in a single vision in the setting sun. The Karlskirche is a fascinating synthesis of pagan Rome and Christianity, of East and West, of clerical and secular. There's no long nave (central aisle) leading to the altar, so you feel as though you're standing at the center of a cross, or a giant egg, overwhelmed by color and light. It's not surprising that this was the first church built after the victory over the Turks.

Return to the Ring and turn left. The first park you come to on the right is the delightful **Burggarten.** There's a café on the back terrace. The park is bordered by the Neue Burg, which has museums of old musical instruments, and of arms and armor.

Across the Ring is the **Museum of Fine Arts,** which no one who cares about art will want to miss. There are entire galleries devoted to the paintings of Pieter Bruegel the Elder, Sir Anthony Van Dyck, Peter Paul Rubens, and Albrecht Dürer. The paintings come from the collection of the Habsburgs, who must have had a particular fondness for Venetian colors.

If you're partial to wide, busy boulevards and monumental mid-19th-century public buildings, continue right around the Ring to the canal. The Ring that encircles the original, medieval city is a rather ponderous monument to a dying empire that barely survived its completion. The original ramparts, which stood along the Ring until Franz Josef tore them down, were so wide that carriages could ride on top, four horses abreast. Outside the walls was a moat, and then a level area with no buildings, so that enemies could be spotted. The Ring today consists of 8 interlocking boulevards, about 4 km (2.5 mi) around and 18 m (60 yd) wide. Though its buildings are not Baroque, they are, in their monumental way, as much a part of Vienna as the Baroque. A village lad, seeing them for the first time, wrote, "The entire Ringstrasse affected me like fairy out of the Arabian Nights." The boy's name was Adolf Hitler.

Outside the Ring The three most popular trips outside the Ring are to the Belvedere Palace, Schönbrunn Palace, and the Prater amusement park.

Belvedere Palace, the summer residence of Prince Eugene of Savoy (1663–1736), is marked by lightness and grace. You may prefer visiting Schönbrunn because of its historical importance as summer residence of the Court, but you would probably prefer living here. The Prince lived, between campaigns, in the Lower Belvedere; today it houses a museum of Baroque and medieval art. Modern paintings are in the Upper Belvedere. Be sure to enjoy a peaceful stroll through the gardens.

The grounds of **Schönbrunn Palace,** Austria's answer to Versailles, are rigidly formal. In the gardens of the Belvedere man has tried to cooperate with nature; here he has tried to conquer her. The Belvedere is a graceful tribute to the Baroque in the years of peace following the Turkish defeat; Schönbrunn, in contrast, depends for effect on size and is decorated with all the frivolity of Rococo. Aristocratic, gay, voluptuous in a pale, fleshy sort of way; pleasant rather than strong or spiritual—these are the impressions associated with the Rococo, the last flowering of the Baroque. What is extraordinary is the fact that this world of leaping tendrils and gilded peacocks, this riot of curved and twisted lines, was the choice of Maria Theresa—that model of sobriety, that pillar of church and state. Can you imagine Queen Victoria, whom Maria Theresa is often compared to, decorating Schöbrunn? Yet what a pleasant relief it must have been for the empress, with all her awesome responsibilities, to have this opportunity to set her imagination free! And what a pleasure it must have been to stay in Schönbrunn after a winter in the dark and gloomy Hofburg!

It was here in Schönbrunn that Marie-Antoinette, ninth child of Maria Theresa, spent her youth, and here that the six-year-old Mozart amazed Maria Theresa with his skill. (In the white-and-gold music room little Mozart slipped on the polished floor, and when Marie-Antoinette, who was about the same age, helped him up, he vowed to marry her.) Here, too, Napoleon established his headquarters from 1805–9; here Franz Josef was born and died; and here the empire came to an end, in 1918, when Franz Josef's successor, Karl I, signed the renunciation papers in the Chinese salon.

After touring the apartments, stroll through the formal gardens. Don't miss the grand carriages in the old palace coach house (Wagenburg).

The **Prater** was once the Court game preserve, but Maria Theresa's son Josef II turned it over to the people, and now it's a lovely public park with biking and jogging trails, lakes with rowboats to rent, a golf course, tennis courts, and an amusement park highlighted by a toy train and a giant 19th-century Ferris wheel. Bikes can be rented from the **Fahrradverleih Prater** (Praterstern Bahnhof, Wien Nord Lok 28, tel. 0222/26–85–57).

The Vienna Woods (Wienerwald) City planners could take a lesson from the Habsburgs who—from a wish to protect their hunting grounds as much as a sense of civic duty—declared that the woods and mountains surrounding Vienna should forever remain inviolate, free from development. Hence, the pastoral charm of the Vienna Woods, which encircle the city today. When people speak of the Vienna Woods they're referring to one of two distinct areas—one to the southwest that includes Baden and Mayerling, where Rudolf took his life; and the other, the Kahlenberg Heights, to the west and northwest. If you must choose between the two, go to the Heights: they're closer and offer splendid views of Vienna. A scenic highway takes you from one vantage point to another. It makes sense to combine tours of Schönbrunn and the Heights, and to stop on your way back to Vienna at a new wine tavern in Grinzing.

The best approach is from the south. Take the scenic mountain road called the Höhenstrasse for 8.8 km (5½ mi) and then drive another 24 km (15 mi) to Klosterneuburg Abbey. There are scenic lookouts, restaurants, and hiking trails along the route.

Turn right and follow a winding road to the summit of **Gallitzinberg,** where there's a restaurant.

Walk to **Hermannskogel,** one of the less touristy areas.

Turn left on Sieveringerstrasse toward **Weidlingbach** and drive to the **Jägerwiese Restaurant.** Park and walk to the summit. (If you're using public transportation, take bus 39A to the end, and follow Sieveringerstrasse.)

Continue to **Kahlenberg.** There's a church, hotel, and restaurant near the summit, and the view is impressive. By public transportation, take the streetcar to Grinzing and then a bus. It was on this summit that the Polish King John Sobieski gathered his forces for the attack that routed the Turks.

Take a few minutes' drive or a 30-minute walk to **Leopoldsberg,** the mountain with the best view and the biggest crowds.

Continue north to **Klosterneuburg.** The 11th-century monastery wears Baroque dress. High point of the visit is the famous Verdun Altar, which has 51 enameled scenes by a late-12th-century goldsmith. *Open Mon.–Sat. 9:30–11, 1:30–4; Sun. 1:30–4.*

From the monastery, either drive 11.2 km (7 mi) east along the Danube back to Vienna, or return south on the Höhenstrasse, past Leopoldsberg and Kahlenberg, and turn left on Cobenzlgasse to the wine town of Grinzing.

If you want to Do Vienna, you need to visit a Heurigen tavern, many of them in the suburb of **Grinzing**. Streetcar 38 goes directly there. When the new wine is ready, vintners hang an evergreen branch over their doors. The wine tastes as innocent as soda water—until you stand up. When the weather cooperates, tables are set in outdoor gardens. The Viennese used to bring their own picnic dinners, but most Heurigen now serve meals for the tourist trade. When you're not drinking, you can sing along with the musicians playing old Viennese folk songs on violins, accordions, and zithers. Among the best Heurigen are **Das Alte Haus Rolde** (Himmelstrasse 35, tel. 0222/32-23-21) and **Figlmüller** (Grinzingerstrasse 55, tel. 0222/32-42-57). Another good bet is **Berger** (Himmelstrasse 29, tel. 0222/3220703), or try **Martin Sepp** (Cobenzlgasse 30, tel. 0222/3244875) with its newish but intimate rooms. For additional names, pick up a booklet called *Heuriger in Wien* at any tourist information office.

Dining   Viennese food makes up in heartiness what it lacks in subtlety. A legacy of the Austro-Hungarian Empire is **Hungarian goulash** and **stuffed cabbage and peppers** (*gefüllte Paprike* and *gefülltes Kraut*). **Soup with dumplings** is another specialty, particularly *Leberknödelsuppe* (liver dumpling soup). **Veal** is featured on most menus, particularly *Wiener Schnitzel*—veal dipped in egg batter and fried. Other specialties include *Backhuhn* (fried chicken), *Rehfilet* (venison), and *gebackene Champignons* (fried mushrooms). For dessert, try the small wild strawberries from the Vienna Woods, topped, of course, with fresh whipped cream.

Steirereck, located near the Rotunden Bridge across the Danube Canal, is strong on elegant ambience. The menu features fresh, lightly prepared international and regional dishes, including excellent cream soups, ravioli stuffed with Saibling (a fresh-water fish), and wild duck in a juniper cream sauce. *Rasumovskygasse 2, tel. 0222/713-31-68. Reservations essential. Jacket and tie required. AE, DC, MC, V. Closed weekends. Expensive.*

Zu Den 3 (Drei) Husaren ("The Three Hussars"), located just off Kärntnerstrasse, near St. Stephen's, is an elegant restaurant with an Old World atmosphere. Some 45 hors d'oeuvres are wheeled around on four trollies. The excellent French cuisine features goose-liver pâté, fresh lobster, and, best of all, a saddle of venison for two. Luncheon prices are slightly lower than dinners. *Weihburggasse 4, tel. 0222/512-10-92. Reservations essential. Jacket and tie required. AE, DC, MC, V. Closed Sun. Expensive.*

Zum Kuckuck, located on a side street between the Opera and the cathedral, is a modern restaurant with a growing reputation for its creative French cuisine. *Himmelpfortgasse 15, tel. 0222/512-84-70. Reservations advisable. Jacket and tie required. AE, DC, MC, V. Closed weekends. Expensive.*

Bei Max, located on a side street off the Herrengasse, not far from the Opera, is known for its large servings and plain, wholesome meals at reasonable prices. *Landhausgasse 2, tel.*

63–73–59. Reservations useful. Jacket required. AE, MC, DC, V. Closed weekends. Moderate.

Chez Rainer is a unpretentious restaurant in the south part of town catering more to middle-class Austrians than to tourists. The menu features simply prepared, hearty Austrian dishes at reasonable prices. *Wiedner Hauptstrasse 27, tel. 0222/50–11–10. Reservations useful. Jacket and tie required. AE, DC, MC. Moderate.*

Figlmüller is a folksy restaurant in a historic courtyard. Popular regional dishes include its own huge *Figlmüller Schnitzel* (veal cutlet), *Tafelspitz, Powidltascherl,* and *Palatschinken* (small crepes with jam), and excellent fruity wines. *Wollzeile 5 passage, tel. 0222/512–61–77. Reservations essential. Dress: casual. No credit cards. Closed Sat. eve and Sun. Moderate.*

Oswald & Kalb, very near the cathedral, is an Old World restaurant with a young crowd. Dinner only. *Bäckerstrasse 14, tel. 0222/512–69–92. Reservations essential. Dress: elegant casual. No credit cards. Evenings only 6 pm. Moderate.*

Wine Cellars Below the streets are a number of wine cellars with a cavernous, medieval feel to them that students or newcomers to Europe will love. Some serve modest meals. Among the best are **Melkerstiftskeller** (Schottengasse 3, tel. 0222/533–55–30) and **Urbanikeller** (Am Hof 12, tel. 0222/63–91–02).

Coffeehouses Sitting at a café is not a pastime but a way of life. Each Viennese has his own favorite, where he comes to talk, read, or dream. Here he becomes a man of leisure, a nobleman from the Court. Once your order has been taken, feel free to stay all day; for a waiter to pressure you to move is un-Viennese. When the Turks fled in 1683, they left behind bags of a dark, bitter-tasting bean called coffee. The first coffee shop was opened by a Pole named George Kolschitsky, who was rewarded with some of these beans for having sneaked through Turkish lines with messages to relieving troops. The *Kipfel* or crescent-shape pastry was conceived at the same time by a baker tasting victory over the Turks (whose symbol is the crescent). Among your choices: **Einspänner** (black coffee with whipped cream); **Kapuziner** (coffee with a little milk: brown in color like the habit of a Capuchin monk); **Mit Schlag** (with whipped cream and milk); **Doppelschlag** (with more whipped cream than coffee); **Schale licht** (with more milk than coffee).

Pastry Shops Among the best are **Demel's** (Kohlmarkt 14, tel. 0222/635–51–60), which also serves a fine lunch; **Sluka** (Rathausplatz 8, tel. 0222/42–71–72); **Gerstner** (Kärntnerstrasse 15, tel. 0222/512–49–63); **Heiner** (Kärntnerstrasse 21, tel. 0222/512–68–63); and **Lehmann** (Graben 12, tel. 0222/512–18–15).

Cafés Don't miss the historic **Café Central** (Herrengasse 14, tel. 0222/5333763) where Trotsky and Stalin used to play chess, and where Trotsky still owes for an unpaid black coffee; **Café Europa** (Kärntnerstr. 18, tel. 0222/51–59–40), and **Café Hawelka** (Dorotheergasse 6, tel. 0222/512–82–30). At **Café Sacher** (Philharmonikerstr. 4, tel. 0222/51–45–60) you can decide whether the Sachertorte is worth its reputation. Eduard Sacher, the rebellious son of the owner of the Sacher Hotel, apparently slipped the recipe to the owner of **Demel's** (Kohlmarkt 14, tel. 0222/533–55–16) and claimed that his recipe was the original. After 10 years of litigation—only a city of dreams could have a 10-year court battle over pastries!—the judge decided that

Sacher could claim the original and that Demel's should call its own "Eduard Sacher Torte." Why not try both?

Lodging **Hotel Bristol** rivals the Sacher in prestige and tradition. Its location opposite the Opera House, at the head of the main shopping street, is equally convenient. The bedrooms are larger than those at the Sacher, and the black marble bathrooms are more opulent. *Kärntner Ring 1, tel. 0222/51–51–60. 152 rooms with bath. Facilities: restaurants, bar. AE, DC, MC, V. Very Expensive.*

Hotel Imperial was completely restored after 10 years as the Russian headquarters during the Four Power occupation of Vienna (1945–55). Though it is a palatial indulgence (Wagner liked to stay here), it lacks the nostalgic feeling of the Sacher and Bristol. The service is faultless, however, and many consider the Imperial their favorite hotel. *Kärntner Ring 16, tel. 0222/50–11–00. 151 rooms with bath or shower. Facilities: beauty parlor, conference rooms. Very Expensive.*

Hotel im Palais Schwarzenberg occupies part of a palace within 7.6 ha (19 acres) of gardens. The rooms are decorated with modern French elegance, with great attention to detail. If you want to be in walking distance of the shops and sights, stay at the Sacher or Bristol; if you want a quiet retreat, and the sense of staying in a private palace, stay at the Schwarzenberg, a 10-minute cab ride to center city. *Schwarzenbergplatz 9, tel. 0222/ 78–45–15. 38 rooms with bath. Facilities: restaurant, bar. AE, DC, MC, V. Very Expensive.*

Hotel Sacher, next to the Opera, is still the place to stay for character and tradition. Bathrooms can be small, but the hotel is truly 19th century, with hallowed, paneled lounges regal in crystal and Habsburg maroon. The Sacher attracts a crowd of intellectuals and artists, which makes its appeal perhaps a bit narrower and deeper than that of the equally opulent Bristol. *Philarmonik, erstr. 4, tel. 0222/51–45–60. 117 rooms with bath or shower. Facilities: restaurant, café. AE, DC, MC, V. Very Expensive.*

Ambassador has rooms grouped around a central courtyard. The red plush drapes and upholstery are, well, typically Viennese. If the top four hotels are booked or too expensive, stay here for comfort and Old World charm. *Neuer Markt 5, tel. 0222/51–4–66. 107 rooms with bath or shower. Facilities: restaurant, bar. AE, DC, MC, V. Expensive.*

Astoria. Though the Astoria is one of Vienna's traditional old hotels, the rooms are modernized. The paneled lobby has been preserved, however, and retains an unmistakable Old World patina. The location is central, but because of the street musicians and the late-night crowds in the pedestrian zone, rooms overlooking the Kärntnerstrasse tend to be noisy in summer. *Kärntnerstr. 32–34, tel. 0222/51–57–70, 108 rooms with bath or shower. Facilities: outstanding restaurant (Fürichgasse 1). AE, DC, MC, V. Expensive.*

Hotel Kaiserin Elisabeth is in a building that dates back to the 14th century. Home to Wagner, Liszt, and Grieg, it offers all the creature comforts of the 5-star hotels, without the trappings of luxury, or the expense. *Weihburggasse 3, tel. 0222/51– 5–26. 70 rooms with bath or shower. AE, DC, MC, V. Expensive.*

König von Ungarn. This utterly charming, centrally located hotel is tucked away in the shadow of the cathedral. The historic facade belies the modern efficiency of the interior, from the atrium lobby to the guest rooms themselves. The restaurant (just next door in a house that Mozart once lived in) is excellent, though not inexpensive, and is always packed at noon. *Schulerstr. 10, tel. 0222/51–58–40. 32 rooms with bath or shower. Facilities: restaurant (tel. 0222/5125319), bar. AE, DC, MC, V. Expensive.*

Geissler is one of the few reasonably priced pensions in District I (near the Danube Canal). *Postgasse 14, tel. 0222/533–28–03. 22 rooms, 16 with bath or shower. Facilities: garage. No credit cards. Moderate.*

Pension Zipser. This has become a favorite with regular visitors to Vienna. It is slightly less central than some others on our list, but very comfortable. *Lange Gasse 49, tel. 0222/42–02–28. 46 rooms with bath or shower. Facilities: bar. AE, DC, MC, V. Moderate.*

Wandl faces St. Peter's Church (Peterskirche), off Graben. Rooms are comfortable and reasonably priced. *Petersplatz 9, tel. 0222/53–45–50. 134 rooms with bath or shower. No credit cards. Moderate.*

Music and the Arts in Vienna
Why did Vienna spawn so many musicians, but so few writers? Perhaps because ideas were censored under the Habsburgs, and one can say most anything in music. Perhaps, too, music is the voice of nostalgia.

Musicians came here in the 18th and early 19th centuries because the aristocracy maintained small orchestras and groups of performers. A musician who joined a household was treated as a footman and lived and ate with the servants. The intimacy among the Viennese composers is legendary: Mozart and Haydn were friends; Beethoven took lessons from Haydn; Schubert was a pallbearer at Beethoven's funeral; Arnold Schönberg (1874–1951) taught his 12-tone system here to Alban Berg and Anton von Webern.

The Haydn Museum is where Haydn (1732–1809) gave lessons to Beethoven and composed *The Creation*. When Franz Joseph Haydn arrived in Vienna at age 17 he was alone and friendless; at the time of his death, here at this house, he was considered the greatest composer in Europe. He came of peasant stock from a nearby village and was brought to sing in the choir of St. Stephen's. To make ends meet he sang at weddings and funerals. Eventually he was offered the position of Kapellmeister to a prince, at whose estate he composed most of his works. *Haydngasse 19. Open Tues.–Fri. 10–4; Sat. 2–6; Sundays, 9–1.)*

The **Mozart Monument** (Figarohaus). *See* above.

The **Beethoven House** is where the composer lived from 1805 to 1815. Ludwig van Beethoven came to Vienna from Bonn at age 22 and stayed for life. He was a terrible neighbor, playing piano at odd hours, and was forced to move some 25 times. It was at this charming house that he composed *Fidelio* and the Fourth, Fifth, and Seventh symphonies. Here too he wrote the Moonlight Sonata, dedicated to an early love of his. It was a walk in the Vienna Woods that may have inspired the Pastoral Symphony. In his house in Heiligenstadt, which can be visited on a trip to the Vienna Woods, Beethoven wrote his bitter Heiligenstadt Testament: "What humiliation when someone is standing near me and hears a far-off flute and I cannot hear it, or when someone hears the shepherd singing and I can hear nothing. Such experiences nearly drove me to despair, and it would have taken little to make me end my own life. One thing alone, the art of music, restrained me." When Beethoven conducted the Ninth Symphony in Vienna in 1824, the orchestra watched not him but the concert master. After the second movement there was thunderous applause, but Beethoven didn't hear it; the singer had to turn him around so that he could see the clapping hands and acknowledge the ovation. Beethoven died in Vienna. According to one source, he died saying to his friend Hümmel: "I had a certain talent, hadn't I?" *Mölker Bastei. Open Tues.–Fri. 10–4; Sat. 2–6; Sun. 9–1.*

The **Schubert Museum** is the birthplace of the only one of the major composers who was actually born in Vienna. Franz Peter Schubert was the son of a poor schoolmaster—a small boy with glasses and an angelic voice. When his voice broke, he had to leave the Vienna Boys' Choir and find some other way to earn a living. He started teaching in his father's school, but hated it and spent most of his time writing music instead. He was never able to afford his own room (except for a short time), or even his own piano. Many of his songs were written on the backs of menus in neighborhood cafés, where he went with devoted friends. At Beethoven's deathbed he toasted, "To the one of us who is next"; and 19 months later, at age thirty-one, he himself was dead. *Nussdorferstr. 54. Open Tues.–Fri., 10–4; Sat. 2–6; Sun. 9–1.*

In the **Central Cemetery** (Zentralfriedhof) is "Musician's Square," where you'll find the graves of Schubert, Hugo Wolf, Christoph Willibald Gluck, Johannes Brahms, Beethoven, and Johann Strauss (father and son).

On from Vienna You will probably fly home from Vienna or Munich. If you're continuing south to Yugoslavia, drive to **Graz,** and take the highway to **Ljubljana** and **Rijeka** (*see* Chapter 5, Yugoslavia).

What to See and Do with Children

In Salzburg: the Glockenspiel (carillon); the catacombs at St. Peter's; the torture chamber in the fortress; the mummified Ice Age rhinoceros in the Natural History Museum; Hellbrunn, especially the mechanical theater; and above all, the Marionettentheater.

In the Lake District: windsurfing, swimming, fishing, and boating on the lakes.

In the Abbey of St. Florian: the 6,000 skeletons in the crypt.

Along the Wachau: the ramparts of Aggstein Castle; bike riding along the less-traveled southern route (bikes can be rented at train stations in Melk and Krems and returned to these or other stations).

In Vienna: the children's armor collection in the Neue Burg; the Prater amusement park, particularly the Ferris wheel; the zoo; the royal coaches in the Wagenburg coach house outside Schönbrunn Palace; the walk to the top of St. Stephen's; a Sunday morning concert by the Vienna Boys' Choir; a training session or performance of the Lippizzaner horses at the Spanish Riding School. For babysitters, contact the Austrian Student Service Society, Mühlgasse 20, tel. 0222/5873525 or Babysitter Zentrale, Herbststrasse 6–10, tel. 0222/95–11–35.

The Arts

The **Vienna Festival** features four weeks of operas and concerts in late May and June. For details, contact any Austrian Tourist Office or contact the Wiener Festwochen (Bestellbüro, Lehargasse 11, A-1060 Vienna, tel. 0222/586–16–76).

The **Summer of Music** (late June–Aug.) is a summer-long festival of daily concerts. Complete programs are available at Tourist Offices or by mail from Wiener Musiksommer (Friedrich Schmidt-Platz 5, A-1082 Vienna).

The season at the **State Opera** (Staatsoper) runs Sept.–June. Strauss-type operettas or light operas are performed at the **Volksoper** in summer. It's worth a trip to the Staatsoper just to see the "show" at intermission when the formally dressed Viennese, with their stiff collars and pearly bosoms, sip champagne and nibble on chocolate-dipped strawberries as they promenade up and down the hall. No monument gives you such a sense of living in a City of Dreams. Tickets are sold at box offices and travel agencies. Credit card telephone orders from anywhere in the world can be made six days in advance of performance by calling 0222/513–15–13.

The tourist office has monthly listings of concerts. The **Vienna Philharmonic** performs in the **Musikverein** (Dumbastrasse 3, tel. 0222/505–81–90). The **Vienna Symphony** and other groups perform in the **Wiener Konzerthaus** (Lothringerstrasse 20, tel. 0222/712–12–11). Concerts are also held in the **Schubert Museum** (Nussdorferstrasse 54). Church music can be heard Sunday mornings at St. Stephen's, Karlskirche, and Augustinerkirche. Special summer concerts are held in the Belvedere Garden and at Schönbrunn. Candlelit Baroque concerts, with performers in 18th-century dress, are given in the Palais Pallavicini at Josefsplatz. To see the **Vienna Boys' Choir** write at least two months in advance to Hofmusikkapelle, Hofburg, A-1010 Vienna. You'll be sent a reservation card to present at the box office when you pick up your tickets. Additional tickets are sold at travel agencies and at the Burgkappelle (in the Hofburg) every Friday at 5 PM. Line up by 4:30.

The two English-speaking theaters are **The English Theater** (Josefgasse 12, tel. 0222/42–12–60) and **The International Theatre** (Porzellangasse 8, tel. 0222/31–62–72).

5 Yugoslavia

The Adriatic Coast

Introduction

The Adriatic Coast, a wildly beautiful stretch of land between the mountains and the sea, alternates between dramatic moonscapes of shattered stone and fertile coastal plains in a balmy Mediterranean world of cypresses, olive groves, and vineyards. Strung along the coast are medieval towns within whose walls little has changed, visually, since the Renaissance. As they were under Venetian control, they are filled today with loggias, clock towers, white stone piazzas, and princely palaces that might as easily have graced the streets of Venice.

In the late 6th century the Roman towns along this coast were invaded by the Avars and the Slavs. The Slavs are still there today in the Slavic nation of Yugoslavia, created after World War II in the form of a federation of six autonomous republics. The coast lies within three of the republics: most of it is in Croatia, a short strip south of Dubrovnik is in Bosnia-Herzegovina, and the southernmost part is in Montenegro. The other three republics are Macedonia, Serbia, and Slovenia. In addition to its six republics, Yugoslavia today has two alphabets (Cyrillic inland and Latin along the coast), three main religions (Roman Catholic, Eastern Orthodox, and Muslim), four main languages (Slovene, Croatian, Serbian, and Macedonian), and five Slavic nationalities (Slovenes, Croats, Serbs, Macedonians, and Montenegrins). In the wake of the political upheavals in Eastern Europe, long-standing frictions among the nationalities have led to recent outbursts of violence in some parts of the country, but the Adriatic Coast appears not to be involved as we go to press. Check with your travel agent and the Yugoslav tourist office before you finalize your plans.

Highlights

Walled medieval towns, such as Rab, Trogir, and Split, strung along a wild, romantic coast.

Two thousand years of art and architectural treasures, from the Roman palace of Diocletian in Split to the contemporary sculpture of Ivan Mestrovic.

Dubrovnik, a 14th-century city of ancient white stone—one of the most graceful and dignified cities in the world.

Before You Go

Government Tourist Offices

In the U.S. **Yugoslav National Tourist Office,** 630 Fifth Avenue, Suite 280, New York, NY 10111, tel. 212/757–2801.

In the U.K. **Yugoslav National Tourist Office,** 143 Regent Street, London W1R 8AE, tel. 071/734–5243.

When to Go

The tourist season runs from April or May through October. Outside this period, many resort hotels close, but you will find good bargains in those that don't. July and August are the hottest and most crowded months, to be avoided unless you've planned to attend one of the major festivals. Spring and fall have all the advantages of good weather and reduced rates for accommodations.

Along the coast, winters are relatively mild, although rain can be heavy through April. Summers are hot. There can be strong winds: *bura* (dry, northerly, mainly in winter), *Yugo* (humid, southerly, mainly in winter), and *maestral* (steady, generally westerly, and the most frequent). Summer storms are fierce but brief.

Special Events

Mid-June–mid-Aug.: Split Summer Festival, with music and drama performed within the walls of Diocletian's Palace, and in the Venetian-style Republic Square beyond the walls.
July 10–Aug. 25: Dubrovnik Summer Festival, with music and dance performed against a backdrop of ancient palaces and churches.
July–Aug.: Musical evenings in Zadar, inside the 1,000-year-old Church of St. Donat.
July–Aug.: Korčula Sword Dance, symbolizing Yugoslavia's struggle against oppression. Thursdays and July 27.

Currency

The unit of currency is the dinar. Bills are in denominations of 50, 100, 500, 1,000, 5,000, 10,000, 20,000, and 50,000 dinars. Coins are 1, 2, 5, 10, 20, 50, and 100 dinars.

In January 1990, Yugoslavia revalued its inflated dinar and tied it to the West German mark in an effort to stabilize skyrocketing prices and wildly fluctuating exchange rates while restructuring the economy. Nevertheless, at press time (spring 1990), the dinar was fluctuating so radically that it was impossible to fix an average exchange rate. Traveler's checks can be exchanged at banks, exchange bureaus, travel agencies, and many hotels. Major credit cards—American Express, Diners Club, MasterCard, and Visa—are widely accepted.

Visas

U.S. and Canadian citizens are required to have both a valid passport and a visa to enter Yugoslavia. A visa can be obtained free at Yugoslav embassies or, for a small fee, at Yugoslav entry points.

All British citizens need a passport to enter Yugoslavia; visas are not required. The British Visitor's Passport is accepted, but if it has less than three months' validity, you must obtain a Tourist Pass, valid for 30 days, at entry points; these are issued free.

Customs

On Arrival Visitors are permitted to bring in personal effects and normal amounts of photographic, recording, and sports equipment. All travelers age 16 and older may also bring in 200 cigarettes or their equivalent in tobacco, one liter of wine, one liter of liquor, a quarter liter of eau de cologne, and small quantities of perfume.

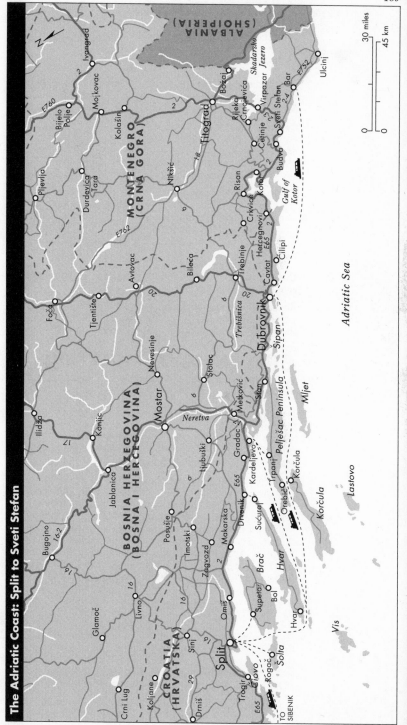

The Adriatic Coast: Split to Sveti Stefan

ALBANIA (SHQIPERIA)

MONTENEGRO (CRNA GORA)

BOSNA I HERCEGOVINA)

BOSNA HERZEGOVINA

CROATIA (HRVATSKA)

Adriatic Sea

Ivangrad
Mojkovac
Bijelo Polje
E760
Kolašin
Pljevlja
Durdevica Tara
Titograd
Nikšić
Rijeka Crnojevića
Božaj
Virpazar
Sveti Stefan
Skadarsko Jezero
Cetinje
Budva
Bar
E752
Ulcinj
Foča
Tjentište
Avtovac
Bileća
Trebinje
Risan
Crkvice
Herceg Novi
Kotor
Gulf of Kotor
Cavtat
Cilipi
Trebišnica
Dubrovnik
Šipan
Nevesinje
Mostar
Stolac
Neretva
Ston
Metković
Mljet
Konjic
Ilidža
Jablanica
Ljubuški
Gradac
Kardeljevo
Pelješac Peninsula
Trpanj
Orebić
Korčula
Posušje
Drvenik
Sućuraj
Korčula
Lastovo
Bugojno
Imotski
Zagvozd
Makarska
Hvar
Brač
Supetar
Bol
Livno
Glamoč
Omiš
Sinj
Hvar
Vis
Crni Lug
Koljane
Trogir
Split
Čiovo
Rogač
Šolta
Drniš
E65
TO ŠIBENIK

30 miles
45 km

On Departure A special permit is needed only if you have purchased goods of historical or cultural value. If you have any questions on this point, be sure to ask the seller when you make your purchase.

Language

Where you're going, along the Dalmatian coast, people use the same Latin alphabet you use at home. There are a few different sounds, though, which you should learn:

ć = t as in picture
č = ch as in chuckle
dž = dg as in jungle
j (at the end of a word) = ye as in yeshiva
š = sh as in shenanigan

English is widely spoken among the young and those in the travel industry. Away from tourist areas, you're likely to have some communication problems, although German is understood by many of the older generation.

Reading

Dusko Doder, *The Yugoslavs* (Vintage), gives a pre-1989 recent view of Yugoslav politics and society.

Rebecca West, *Black Lamb and Grey Falcon: A Journey Through Yugoslavia* (Penguin) is somewhat dated, but remains the most literate and intelligent book on Yugoslavia.

Arriving and Departing

By Plane

If you're taking the three- to five-day or five- to seven-day trip, fly to and from Dubrovnik. Yugoslav Airlines (JAT) has direct service from New York; Pan American has connecting service from New York. (On direct flights you don't change planes, on connecting flights you do.)

If you're taking the seven- to 14-day trip, fly to Zagreb or Ljubljana, and return from (1) Zagreb or Ljubljana, (2) Dubrovnik, or (3) Belgrade. These alternatives are discussed below. When you arrive in Zagreb or Ljubljana, take a bus, train, or rented car to Rijeka (near Opatija) on the coast, where the itinerary begins. The trip from Ljubljana is shorter. Only Yugoslav Airlines has direct service between New York and Zagreb, Ljubljana, Dubrovnik, and Belgrade. Pan Am has connecting service between New York and Zagreb, Belgrade, and Dubrovnik.

By Car

If you're driving to Yugoslavia from Vienna, take the road from Graz (Austria) to Rijeka, via Ljubljana. The border crossing on the main highway between Graz and Maribor can be slow in tourist season; if lines are very long, take Route 69 east about 16 km (10 mi) to Mureck, and cross the border there.

If you're driving from Western Europe, there are car trains from major cities to Rijeka. If you're continuing from Yugoslavia to Italy, there are overnight car ferries from Dubrovnik and Bar to Bari, Italy.

Getting Around

By Car

Driving is on the right; at intersections, traffic from the right has priority, except on main highways or where otherwise indicated. The speed limit in cities and towns is 60 kph (37 mph); otherwise it's 80 kph (50 mph), 100 kph (62 mph), or 120 kph (75 mph) as indicated. Seat belts are compulsory. Penalties for drunk driving are severe.

If you're taking the three- to five- or five- to seven-day trip, pick up and deliver your rented car at Dubrovnik's airport.

If you're taking the seven- to 14-day trip, you have three main alternatives:

1) Rent a car at Ljubljana or Zagreb; drive south along the coast, exploring the islands along the way; leave your car at Dubrovnik's airport, and fly home.
2) Rent a car at Ljubljana or Zagreb; drive south along the coast, exploring the islands along the way; continue south, past Dubrovnik, to Bar; either leave your car at Bar and take the train to Belgrade, or drive to Belgrade, and fly home.
3) Rent a car at Ljubljana or Zagreb; drive south along the coast to Dubrovnik; take a car ferry back to Rijeka, stopping at islands along the way; drive back to Ljubljana or Zagreb; leave your car at the airport, and fly home.

The car ferries run both from the mainland to the islands and from one island to another the entire length of the coast. For reservations and schedules, contact the **International Cruise Center** (250 Old Country Rd., Mineola, NY, 11501, tel. 516/747–8880 or 800/221–3254). In Yugoslavia, contact any travel agency or **Jadrolinija** (the Yugoslav Adriatic Shipping Co.). They have offices in each port you'll be visiting: Rijeka, Zadar, Šibenik, Split, Dubrovnik, Korčula, Hvar, and Rab.

Gas coupons purchased in foreign currency at the border will save you about 5%.

By Train, Bus, or Boat

If you're taking the three- to five-day or five- to seven-day trip, you'll arrive in Dubrovnik, where you can take bus excursions to the Gulf of Kotor and ferries to all the major towns and islands along the coast.

If you're taking the seven- to 14-day trip, fly to Zagreb or Ljubljana and take a train or bus to Rijeka. From here you can take buses or boats anywhere along the coast. Buses are crowded in summer, so coastal ferries are preferable. There's at least one coastal ferry daily in season, and any number of local ferries between islands. The trip from Rijeka to Dubrovnik takes about 24 hours, but you'll want to disembark at Rab, Zadar, Šibenik, Split, Hvar, and Korčula. The International Cruise Center can make arrangements, including private staterooms, overnight stays at island hotels, and transportation across the Adriatic to Italy.

Essential Information

Important Addresses and Numbers

Tourist Information
Dubrovnik: The Tourist Information Center (Turistički Informativi Centar, Poljana P. Milicecica 1, tel. 26302) is on the corner of the Placa next to the Onofrio Fountain near the Pile Gate. Outside the Gate, the Atlas travel agency (tel. 27333) represents American Express.

Hvar: The Tourist Office (Turistički Savez Općine Hvar, tel. 74058) is on the main square.

Korcula: The Tourist Bureau (Turist Biro Marko Polo, tel. 711067) is near the main square.

Opatija: Contact Kvarner Express (tel. 711111) or the Tourist Office Opatija (M. Tita 183, tel. 711310).

Rab: The Tourist Bureau (Turist Biro Rab, Maršala Tita 1, YU51280 Rab, tel. 051/871123).

Senj: Kvarner Express (Titovo Obala, tel. 881068).

Sibenik: The Tourist Bureau (Turističko Društo, tel. 22075) borders the Municipal Park, near the Church of St. Francis; the Tourist Association Office (tel. 059/22–346) is at XIX Divizije bb next to the square named Palih Sibenskih Boraca, but referred to locally as Medulic.

Split: The Tourist Bureau (Turist Biro, Titova obala 12, tel. 42142) is on the waterfront at the southwest corner of the palace.

Trogir: The Tourist Office (Turisticko Drvstvo, tel. 73554) is in the Cipiko Palace directly across from the Cathedral.

Zadar: The Tourist Information Center (tel. 22146) is on Omladinska Ulica just off Narodni Trg, the main square of the old town.

Emergencies
Police: tel. 92. **Ambulance:** tel. 94. **Breakdown service,** Yugoslav Automobile Association: tel. 987. **Doctors:** IAMAT (International Association for Medical Assistance to Travelers, 417 Center St., Lewiston, NY 14092, tel. 716/754–4883) has a list of approved English-speaking doctors in major Yugoslavian cities.

Embassies
U.S.: Kneza Milosa 50, Belgrade, tel. 011/645–655; **Canadian:** Kneza Milosa 75, Belgrade, tel. 011/644–666; **U.K.:** Generala Zdanova 46, Belgrade, tel. 011/645–055.

Opening and Closing Times

Banks
Banks in major cities are open weekdays 7–7, Saturday 7–1.

Museums
Museums are normally open 9–1, sometimes 10–noon; also 2–6 or 4–7; normally closed one day a week, usually Sunday or Monday. Always check before going.

Shops
Most stores are open weekdays, 8–8, Saturday 8–3. Some close for three or four hours in the middle of the day, and some are open Sunday morning. In tourist resorts small shops stay open until late in the evening. Markets usually operate in the morning, 5:30–12:30.

Shopping

Art books are top quality and, pricewise, a real steal. For old books with beautiful line drawings, check out the shops on side streets in Dubrovnik. Liqueurs in decorative bottles, such as maraschino and plum brandy (*šljivovica*), are distilled in Zadar and sold along the coast. The best filigree jewelry is in Montenegro, south of Dubrovnik. The quality of fine lacework varies from shop to shop; the best I saw was sold by peasant women along the benches of the seaside park in Opatija. The best place for antique ceramics is Zadar. For modern art, visit the galleries in Split. Old icons are not for sale, but you can find quality reproductions in Split and Dubrovnik. Inexpensive peasant handicrafts—costumed dolls, embroidered blouses, and so forth—are sold everywhere; the best quality is usually in the gift shops in the more expensive hotels. Prices are fixed, except in outdoor markets.

Peasant women sell hand-embroidered tablecloths, napkins, and shawls in parks along the waterfront in Opatija.

In Hvar, treat yourself to some essence of lavender, which is extensively cultivated on the island for soaps and perfumes and sold by island women along the rim of Hvar's harbor near the Palace Hotel.

Sports

Boating and Fishing An indented coast with offshore islands is ideal both for saltwater fish—swordfish, mullet, tuna, and sea bass—and fishermen. Deep-sea fishing is popular, so you won't have trouble arranging trips through hotels and travel agencies. Another popular sport is underwater spear fishing, best around the Kvarner Islands and off the seaward coasts of Rab, Cres, and Pag. You can reach these islands from Opatija, Rijeka, and Zadar. From Sibenik, fishermen angle on the River Krka and on Lake Visovačko for trout, chub, and barbel. From Split, they play the River Jadro for trout.

Nautical tourism has evolved on a big scale in recent years, with a string of ambitious super-modern marinas inlaid into the coast and islands, offering sailboat rentals, charter boat arrangements, and sailing schools, as well as, in certain cases, deluxe accommodations and some of the most satisfactory restaurants in Yugoslavia.

Swimming Most beaches along the Dalmatian coast are pebbly; in many areas you have to clamber over rocks to get wet. Fortunately, most postwar higher quality hotels have pools.

Opatija, built as a winter resort, has concrete platforms along its shore. Zadar has a good beach at the Borik Hotel complex. Rab has some great rocky coves; rent a boat to take you there. Beaches on Hvar and Korčula are mostly rocks and pebbles. Dubrovnik's pebbly beach is often crowded; take a boat to the sandy beaches on the nearby islands of Lopud and Lokrum. Near Budva, you'll find good beaches at the Hotel Avala and at Jaz and Beči. There are good sand and pebble beaches along the causeway to Sveti Stefan.

Dining

East meets West in Yugoslavia, not only in architectural styles but in food as well. Along the coast, from Opatija to Dubrovnik, cooking is to some extent influenced by the region's long association with Italy and Austria; farther south the culinary accent is Greek and Turkish. Over the years, however, the distinctions have blurred, and, with occasional notable exceptions, menus of restaurants along the coast and islands tend to be virtually identical. The reason for this is that with the current economic crisis, few native Yugoslavs (with the exception of expense account business and professional types) can afford to eat out except in the most modest restaurants. As a result, restaurants are geared strictly to the tourist trade, catering to the tastes of Austrians, Germans, Swiss, Dutch, and British, at prices that remain far out of reach for those living here. Some of the best eating along the coast is in the restaurants of the new marinas.

If possible, avoid eating in hotels on a package plan at all costs. The food is terrible, atmosphere nonexistent, service impossible. On the other hand, most hotels maintain à la carte restaurants, either colorfully decorated tavernas or pleasant restaurants serving authentic regional specialties in romantic settings.

The floor of the Adriatic dips toward the Yugoslav coast—is that why the fish and crustacea are so delicious? As expected in coastal cities, your best bet is almost always fresh seafood: *škampi* (prawns), *mušule* (mussels in wine), *jastog* (lobster), *lignje* (baby squid), *barbbuni* (red mullet), *skuše* (mackerel), *brodet* (a bouillabaisse-type fish soup), and *oštrige* (oysters). The shrimps, remember, come in their shells with little beady eyes that stare at you as you tear them apart. Fish is often sold in restaurants by weight. In the smaller, family restaurants, you'll be shown a platter with the day's catch, from which you choose your meal.

Meat dishes, as a rule, are not exceptional. Best are lamb, veal, and mutton. Also tasty are *ražnjiči* (skewered, barbecued lamb, pork, and veal) and pršut (smoked Dalmatian ham).

Of late there's been a trend to serving steak, as though it were a national dish. Some can be surprisingly good, but it's nothing you can count on. A better choice for meat-and-potato types might be a *Schnitzel*, Austrian-style veal cutlets. For no-nonsense eating (with no surprises) ask for a *Naturschnitzel*, with boiled rice on the side, a mixed salad, and a carafe of local wine. You can't go wrong.

Yugoslavia produces many good, inexpensive, full-bodied wines. Until you find what you like, ask for a *dva deci* (two-tenths liter) of a local wine—either *crno* (red) or *belo* (white). Zilavka is a relatively dry white wine. Lighter white wines include Posip and Vugava. Dingač is a heavy, sweet red wine. Lighter reds are Postup and Plavac. Šljivovica, a fiery plum brandy, used to be the national drink; now it is Loza. Locally made liqueurs include cherry (Maraschino) and walnut (Orahovac).

Fruit juices (*vočni sokovi*) are special, particularly *marelica* (peach juice). Shops that sell juice also sell wonderful ices and sorbets, and delicious pastries such as warm *štrudla* filled with fruit.

Limited top-of-the-line establishments at Sveti Stefan, Dubrovnik, Opatija, and yacht club marina restaurants at Split and Zadar offer outstanding meals, ambience, and service; otherwise it's all likely to be somewhat ordinary.

Expect to pay about $25–$35 per person for a complete meal with wine in the best restaurants. Meals in smaller atmospheric seafood restaurants run considerably less, although fish, scampi, and lobster (invariably sold by weight) are among the priciest items on the menu. The same is true for Dalmatian smoked ham. Even here a meal with wine can easily add up to $50 for two.

Category	Cost*
Very Expensive	$25 and over
Expensive	$15–$25
Moderate	$10–$15
Inexpensive	$10 and under

Per person for a three-course meal, including half of wine cost.

There are no taxes on meals in Yugoslavia, and in theory the service charge is included in the price of the meal. No tipping is necessary beyond the bottom-line figure, although most visitors feel more comfortable leaving some token of their appreciation if the service is acceptable. You can tip if you want, but under no circumstances tip more than 5% of the bill.

Casual dress can be considered appropriate for just about all restaurants in all price categories along the coast. If you are dining at either of the two Sveti Stefan hotels (Sveti Stefan and Milocer), in the more elegant restaurants of such luxury hotels as Dubrovnik's Belevedere or Cavtat's Croatia, or in the Villa Dalmacija, you might feel more comfortable if you are dressed up for evening meals.

Lodging

In 1948 Yugoslavia had 60,000 foreign visitors; in 1980 it had 6.5 million. Since then that figure has been climbing steadily. Starting in late May and early June tourists come by the tens of thousands in their Audis, Mercedeses, and BMWs, beneath canopies of surfboards and bicycles. They drag campers, powerboats and miniyachts behind them, clogging the narrow roads and causing massive gridlock in coastal communities as they head for campgrounds, trailer park cities by the seaside, "naturist" colonies that function as towns in their own right where no one wears clothes, and vast resort complexes. Others arrive by charter flights from Britain and Scandinavia.

To deal with this annual invasion, state-controlled companies have constructed huge, 600-room, ferroconcrete hotels in complexes several miles outside the main towns. The principle seems to be that one 600-room hotel is more economical than six 100-room hotels. These compounds, complete with pools, shopping arcades, discos, and beauty parlors, were built not to isolate foreigners from the Real Yugoslavia, but to provide them, at minimum cost, with the motellike comforts of home.

Functional, cavernous, cold—these are words that come to mind to describe these late-20th-century Diocletian palaces, built not to awe emissaries from Nicomedia but to accommodate the package-tour trade from Manchester and Liège. Furnishings, too, are Socialist Modern. On the bright side, there's a certain comfort knowing your room will be relatively new and clean, with the amenities you expect at home. It's nice, too, to have tennis courts, swimming pools, and tour desks with clerks who speak English.

In Yugoslavia, older hotels are usually not more charming but more run-down, so if you want spaciousness and comfort, check into the newest hotel you can find. The country-inn set should do this, too, unless you stay in a private home or in one of the few prewar hotels that has kept its Old World charm.

The Yugoslavs rate their hotels L (luxury), A, B, C, and D. Most Americans will be content with A and B. Bear in mind that a B-class hotel may be as comfortable as an A-class hotel, but gets a lower rating because it lacks, say, a pool.

The following hotel rates for two people in a double room, including Continental breakfasts, are approximate and can vary from resort to resort and hotel to hotel. The more popular the resort, the higher the prices. All coastal and island hotels levy a "resort" tax of about $1 a day per person.

Category	Cost*
Very Expensive	$150 and over
Expensive	$85–$150
Moderate	$60–$85
Inexpensive	$60 and under

For two people in a double room, including breakfast, tax, and service.

These rates are for the July–August season; rates drop by about 20% for June and September, 35% or more for May and October, and 50% or more the rest of the year.

Conditions in July and August can be all but impossible. June and September turn out to be somewhat better; best of all, if you can schedule an off-season visit, are May and October.

If you're adventurous, traveling with kids, or on a tight budget, spend at least one night in a private home. Rooms, which are as safe and comfortable as bed-and-breakfast houses in Britain, are somewhat more personal than facilities at the big resort complexes. Chances are you will no longer be moving in with a family but staying in a separate building outfitted as minihotel, with perhaps five or six rooms or apartments. Arrangements can be made through travel agencies at home or through tourist offices and tour operators in every major town along the coast.

If you are considering a longer coastal or island holiday, bungalows, villas, and apartments with cooking facilities are available by the week. Contact the Yugoslav National Tourist Office (*see* Government Tourist Offices, above).

Architecture of the Adriatic Coast

The coast has been built up in many important architectural styles in the centuries since it was first settled.

Roman. The best example is Diocletian's Palace in Split. Its monumental scale was a form of architectural propaganda, meant to advertise the greatness of the emperor. The Romans were the first city planners, and you can see their ancient street plans—appropriate for a military camp with main thoroughfares crossing at right angles—both in Split and Zadar.

Early Croatian. These Pre-Romanesque churches, strongly influenced by Byzantium (the Eastern Roman Empire), are usually small and circular, and surmounted by a dome. The interiors, like the interiors of Romanesque churches, are based on Roman basilicas: oblong halls with a central corridor (nave), flanked by aisles. The best examples are St. Donat's in Zadar, the Church of the Holy Cross in Nin, and the basilica of St. Barbara in Trogir.

Romanesque. The dominant features are the rounded arch and the stone barrel ceilings (vaults). The best examples are the Cathedral of St. Tryphon in Kotor, the churches of St. Mary and St. Andrew in Rab, and the Cathedral of St. Lawrence in Trogir.

Gothic. The Gothic influence came from Venice and showed a strong continuity with Romanesque forms. In Northern Gothic churches, the high ceilings and delicate columns force you to look upward to God, but in Italian Gothic churches the thrust is still forward to the altar. The best examples of Venetian Gothic are the cathedrals in Šibenik, Korčula, and Split. The master of Late Venetian Gothic was the Croatian sculptor and architect, George of Dalmatia.

Renaissance. Renaissance architecture was almost always mixed with Gothic and Romanesque, as in Trogir, Zadar, Šibenik, and Dubrovnik. Only in the work of Nikola of Florence does the early Florentine Renaissance find expression, notably in the chapel of Ivan Ursini in the Trogir Cathedral and in the dome of the Šibenik Cathedral.

Baroque. The Baroque came via Italy and Austria and can be seen in Dubrovnik, both in the cathedral and in the façades of buildings along the main street (Placa). The Baroque arrived at a time when cities were losing their independence and the great age of building was over.

The Dalmatian painters whose work you should follow are Blaž of Trogir (early 15th century), Lovro Dobričenic (late 15th century), Nikola Božidarević (the most important Croatian Renaissance painter, early 16th century), and Mihajlo Hamzić (early 16th century).

The Itinerary

Orientation

The Yugoslav itinerary takes you down a 824-km (515-mi) stretch of the Adriatic, through stark, rocky wastes and sunny coastal plain, to medieval towns where visitors stop to swim, dine, shop, and explore.

You can enter Yugoslavia with nothing but a toothbrush and a sense of possibilities, and no one will ever ask where you're headed, or when, or why. Without reservations you may have trouble finding rooms in high season. Almost all medium-range hotels have been built in the past 30 years to meet international standards—many with tennis courts, pools, saunas, discos, and boutiques. These so-called American-style hotels have all the charm of turnpike motels, but they *are* clean, with freshly laundered sheets, private baths, bedside phones, and at least one desk clerk who speaks English. The best of the family guest houses have all the amenities of country inns at home. The ships that ply the coast have private staterooms for those who want them, and keep to schedules that commuters would be proud of. The coastal road is no turnpike, but it's well marked and generally well paved.

The Main Route

3–5 Days   *Two nights:* Dubrovnik
One night: Split
One night: Hvar

5–7 Days   *Two nights:* Dubrovnik
Two nights: Split
Excursions to Šibenik and Trogir
Two nights: Sveti Stefan

7–14 Days   **Land route:**
One night: Opatija
One night: Rab
One night: Zadar
Three nights: Split
One night: Hvar
Three nights: Dubrovnik
Excursion to Korčula
Two nights: Sveti Stefan

7–14 Days   **Land and sea route:**
One night: Opatija
One night: Zadar
Three nights: Split
Three nights: Dubrovnik
Two nights: Sveti Stefan
One night: Hvar
One night: Rab

Exploring

Opatija

If you're partial to middle-class German resort towns with concrete beaches, you'll love Opatija. If you aren't—well, there are still reasons to visit.

Opatija was a fishing village until the 1880s, when a Viennese doctor began shipping his patients here to recuperate. The high concentration of ozone in the air was said to work wonders. In the late 19th century the resort flourished as a fashionable watering hole for the nobility of Austria and Hungary. Hotels and villas were built in the classical (Roman) style—a form of visual propaganda for the declining Habsburgs. The architecture plays for effect rather than supporting high intellectual ideals, but it does have a certain opulence that suggests a bygone age.

Today elderly couples come in buses and stroll among the lush, subtropical flowers. They nod at the camellias and promenade along the sea, breathing in the sweet, lime-scented air. Have you stumbled into an octogenarian convention, you may wonder. And yet the experience will put you in a frame of mind to slow down and enjoy life, too.

You may need a little luck with climatic conditions on your stay in Opatija. If the wind is wrong, the place can get socked in by nasty smog and pollution from the refineries and heavy industry south of Rijeka, something the Austrian nobility didn't have to contend with a century ago.

Mass tourism in a 19th-century setting—that's what makes Opatija so compelling, and so off-putting. My favorite image is of a middle-aged Italian couple entering the regal ballroom of the Imperial Hotel, where kings once danced, sitting among the crumbs of an uncleared table, and biting into the uneaten rolls.

Opatija is worth visiting if only to compare a town under Austro-Hungarian influence to all the Venetian-style cities you'll see along the coast. It's also a convenient place to rest up after a transatlantic flight; it's certainly more attractive than the industrial city of Rijeka. The climate is balmy, and you can offer your face to the sun for a few days before heading down the coast. Built as a winter resort, it has limited beach facilities, so find yourself a hotel with a pool. Hotels can arrange for waterskiing, windsurfing, boat rentals, tennis, and other activities.

Excursions Opatija makes a good base for day trips to Trieste, the Plitvičke lakes, and the island of **Rab** (*see* below). Try to overnight on Rab so you can see it when the day-trippers are gone. If you have only an afternoon to spare, leave your car in Opatija and (in season) take the hydrofoil. It's only an hour's trip. Tours can be arranged through hotels or Kvarner Express (tel. 711070 or 711111).

The **Postojna Caves** are 72 km (45 mi) north—if you drove from Austria, you passed them en route. These are the second-largest underground caverns in the world. A narrow-gauge railroad takes you in, and a guide leads you on a mile-long walk to a chamber that can seat 10,000. En route you'll pass a pool that contains the eyeless, pencil-thin *Proteus anguineus*. It must have been such creatures, half-fish, half-mammal, that Thomas Wolfe had in mind when he wrote about the first forms of life crawling out of the primeval mud and then, finding the change unpleasant, crawling back in again. Half-day tours can be arranged through Kvarner Express (tel. 711070 or 711111).

Dining **Restaurant Ariston.** On the outskirts of town, in a meticulously restored turn-of-the-century villa in a private seaside park, this fine restaurant offers impeccable service in a romantic setting. Menus feature French specialties (a trout soufflé with white wine), the freshest of seafood, roast duckling, and flaming desserts. Opt for a table on the terrace overlooking Kvarner Bay. (There are also nine high-ceilinged rooms and a royal suite available at Vila Arison.) *M. Tita 243, tel. 711379, 711919. Reservations suggested. Jacket and tie recommended. AE, DC, MC, V. Expensive.*

Zelengaj. This is probably Opatija's most popular restaurant. In the center of town, down a short flight of steps from the main street, the large, plain terrace restaurant is set in the greenery behind the ancient Kvarner Hotel. The food, without frills, includes tasty seafood risotto, scampi, grilled fish, *Schnitzel*, and fine wines at modest cost. *M. Tita 179, tel. 051/711–870. Reservations unnecessary. Dress: casual. AE, DC, MC, V. Moderate.*

In the neighboring port of Volosko (a 10-minute walk along the scenic waterfront promenade known as Lungo Mare), three notable seafood restaurants are set virtually side by side along the rim of this Cote d'Azur–style harbor: **Bevandica, Mili,** and **Plavi Podrum.** Each offers fish soups and stews, risottos, scampi, and grilled and fried fish. The quality is high, but the service tends to be erratic. In season you may be hustled through your meal to make way for the next wave of customers; out of season you may have a lengthy wait before anyone takes your order. But the setting could hardly be faulted. Forget about reservations. See which one appeals to you, or has a table. *AE, DC, MC, V. Moderate–Expensive.*

Lodging **Admiral.** Opatija's newest big-time hotel is pyramid-shaped, built around a small marina at the seaside away from the resort center. *M. Tiba bb, tel. 051/711–533. 180 rooms. Facilities: restaurants, bars, indoor and outdoor pools, sauna, fitness center, shopping mall. AE, DC, MC, V. Expensive.*

Ambassador. This conveniently located luxury-class high-rise hotel features a wide range of facilities. *F. Persica 1, tel. 051/ 712–211. 300 rooms. Facilities: restaurants, bar, indoor and outdoor pools, hairdresser, duty-free shop. AE, DC, MC, V. Expensive.*

Krystal. This centrally located, recently renovated hotel on the waterfront is typical of Opatija's older hotels that have been upgraded. Furnishings may be Early Sears, but rooms have high ceilings and balconies that suggest the elegance of another era. *M. Tita 207, tel. 051/711–333. 135 rooms. Facilities: restaurant, bar with live music, indoor pool, sauna. AE, DC, MC, V. Moderate.*

Other similar (centrally located) hotels, all on the main street, M. Tita, are **Astoria** (tel. 051/711–411), **Avala** (tel. 051/712–411), **Bellevue** (tel. 051/711–011), **Belvedere** (tel. 051/711–433), **Imperial** (tel. 051/712–533), **Istra** (tel. 051/711–826). The last has been entirely renovated: 130 rooms, indoor swimming pool; right on the water, with its own (stone) beach.

Rijeka

Rijeka (9.6 km/6 mi from Opatija) is a modern port city with some old buildings—more a point of transit than a place to stay. Rebuilt after heavy damage during the war, it has emerged as Yugoslavia's largest port, the busiest on the Adriatic after Trieste. Only those with more than a passing interest in architecture will want to explore its sights.

Park near the tourist office (on the main square of Trg Republike, just off the waterfront, identified by a large *i*) and walk inland three blocks to the **Old Town** (Stari Grad). One of the few historic buildings that survived the war is the **Cathedral of the Assumption** (Uznesenje Marijini). Here's your first chance to appreciate the sometimes awkward juxtaposition of styles in Yugoslavian churches. The 13th-century cathedral preserves both Romanesque and Gothic features but was given a 17th-century Baroque face-lift and a 19th-century neoclassical facade. Alongside the cathedral is a slightly askew Romanesque bell tower, the upper portion redone in High Gothic.

Senj

Look out to sea: The channel between the mainland and the island of Krk widens to 16 km (10 mi) here, making a fairway for the north wind. Another channel runs past the south end of Krk, and where the two channels meet, the seas become as violent as they do anywhere in the world.

In the early 16th century, refugees from Turkish-held lands fled to Senj, and, mastering the currents, became the scourge of the Adriatic for almost 200 years. There were only 1,000 of these Uskok buccaneers, but they built a navy with light, quick boats that could leap the waves and lure Turkish and Venetian ships to destruction. Folk songs are still sung of the ferocity of these pirates, who nailed Turkish turbans to Turkish heads, and tore out Turkish hearts and ate them.

There are few signs today of the town's stormy past. If your time is limited, continue on to Jablanac and take the ferry to Rab. If you have a serious interest in architecture, however, you may want to explore some of Senj's notable buildings.

While the Turks were mounting their fiercest attack, a fortress called the **Dreadnaught** (Nehaj) was built above the town. It survives in its original form—ask at the tourist office for a key.

Rab

At Jablanac (36.8 km/23 mi from Senj), a road twists down to the landing for the car ferry to the island of Rab, and the town of the same name. This is the shortest crossing, but lines in season can be long. You may have better luck taking ferries from Opatija, Rijeka, or Senj. Ask local hotels and tourist offices for advice.

If you have time for only one afternoon visit to an island, visit **Rab,** if only because the town, with its graceful towers and white stone facades, is so distinctive. Try to spend the night so you can experience Rab when the day-trippers are gone and the late afternoon sun turns the stone to gold. (The island of Hvar has a wonderful hotel and more to see than Rab, so if you have time for only one night on an island, stay on Hvar and visit Rab in an afternoon.)

Rab is a Venetian jewel rising above a blue-green sea. The oldest section (the Kaldanac) sits on a peninsula surrounded by 12th- and 13th-century walls. It was abandoned during a 15th-century plague; you can still see houses with windows and doors that were walled up to check the spreading contagion.

Start at the tourist office by the harbor. The Sea Gate (Morska Vrara) leads to the main square, which has been the center of town since the 14th century, when the population was four times what it is today. There are only three main streets—Lower (Donja Ulica), Middle (Ivo Lola Ribar), and Upper (Gornja Ulica)—all parallel to the harbor and connected to each other by steep narrow steps and passageways. It's only a five-minute walk to the top, where you'll see the four graceful bell towers (campaniles) that give the town its famous skyline.

It's almost impossible to get lost in Rab, but I suggest you try. Wander through this stone citadel as you would stroll through a church, absorbing its atmosphere, stopping to appreciate its elegant Gothic and Renaissance facades. The town has such balance and grace, it really is very much like a single, open-air, white stone church, its four Romanesque bell towers confidently reaching up toward the sky.

Follow Lower Street to the **Dominis-Nimira Palace,** a distinctive secular Gothic building. From the palace climb to Upper Street. In front of you is Trg Slobode (*trg* means "square") and the small 12th-century **Cathedral of St. Mary Major** (Sveta Marija Velika), also known as **Rab Cathedral.** Though rebuilt in the 13th and 15th centuries, it's one of the most distinctive Romanesque buildings along the coast. The clumsy but powerful early 16th-century pietà over the doorway expresses the tragedy of a subject people. Notice the lightness of the stone canopy; British writer Rebecca West calls it "as weightless as candleflame."

Continue along Upper Street to the Franciscan **Church of St. Anthony the Abbot** (Sveti Antum opat). The convent was founded in 1497 by a princess who sought refuge from the advancing Turks; today it's closed to the public by nuns seeking shelter from advancing tourists.

Retrace your steps past the cathedral, and continue along Upper Street to the **Church of St. Andrew,** which has a resplendent Baroque altar and a 12th-century bell tower.

Next, you'll come to the almost pure Renaissance **Church of St. Justina** (1573–78), which has an onion-shaped cupola on its bell tower. Farther along is **Komrčar Park,** which contains the Gothic **Church of St. Francis,** redone in Renaissance style, and the ruins of a late-15th-century monastery. Walk down from the park to the **Franciscan Friary of St. Euphemia,** and tour its lovely cloister and garden.

Dining   **Santa Maria.** Located on the ground floor of a one-time palace at the far end of the old town, this is surely the most atmospheric (and expensive) restaurant on the island. Choice of seating is beneath graceful arches of an ancient courtyard or in the wood-paneled interior, which is decked out in a nautical motif—old-time ship models, nets, glass floats, and so on. It is strictly for the tourist trade, but what can you expect on this tourist-oriented island? Nor are there any surprises on the menu: the usual fish soup, Dalmatian ham, risotto, grilled meat platter, and *Riblja Fritura*, a grilled (or fried) fish platter. Still, if you're going to have only one meal on Rab, this is the place to have it. With a chilled bottle of the famous Mostar Zilavka white wine, you may just experience a moment of levitation. *Loza 6, tel. 051/771–196. Reservations suggested only for prime-time seating at top of season. Dress: casual. AE, DC, MC, V. Expensive.*

Lodging **Padova.** Located directly across the harbor from the old town, Hotel Padova makes for an ideal choice to spend the night. *Obala Banjol, tel. 051/771–444. 175 rooms. Facilities: restaurants, night club with cabaret, dancing, indoor and outdoor swimming pools, sauna. AE, DC, MC, V. Moderate.*

In-town choices include **International** (on the waterfront, Obala XIII Proleterske Udarne Brigade, tel. 051/771–266; 130 rooms; AE, DC, MC; moderate) and **Imperial,** above the old town in Komrčar Park (Šetalište VI, Ličke Divizije, tel. 051/771–522; AE, DC, MC; moderate). The International has an indoor pool, Imperial does not.

Novigrad

If you have a car, it's important at least once to leave the coast and discover a town that hasn't been transformed by tourism. Novigrad is only 9.6 km (6 mi) off the coast road, but a trip here is a voyage back in time. The turnoff to Novigrad is just past the town of Ravanjska. The village preserves a layout typical of medieval Dalmatia, with steep, narrow streets flanked by close-packed rows of stone houses. Park at the harbor. When you're tired of staring at people staring at you, climb to the medieval **Church of St. Catherine**—all that remains of a former abbey.

Zadar

If you like to put your nose up against the past, you may be disappointed in **Zadar** (116.8 km/73 mi from Jablanac). Heavily bombed during the war, it's less precious, less museumlike than other cities you'll be visiting farther south. The past is less well defined here: The present insinuates itself through broken walls. But how delightful to find a medieval quarter where local people come to shop, a town that exists not just to be admired.

Gothic styles came to Yugoslavia through Venice; what is uniquely Croatian belongs to the earlier Romanesque and Pre-Romanesque periods. It's in Zadar that you'll discover this early Croatian world, including Dalmatia's outstanding early Christian monument, St. Donat's—a wonderful setting for summer concerts. The hotel complex in Zadar is Motel Modern but includes a pool and private beach where you can relax after a busy day on the road.

Park at the harbor (Radnička Obala), near the kiosk with the SUNTURIST sign. Through the Sea Gate (Morska vrata) on your left is the almost pure Romanesque **Church of St. Christopher.** One wonders what the saint, executed under Diocletian's orders, would think of the Baroque marble altar covering his bones.

The street that began at the Sea Gate passes the **Tourist Office,** which has street maps of Zadar and information on obtaining keys to locked churches. The third street beyond the gate, Ulica Ive Lole Ribara, is the main street of the medieval town. On your left is a delightful 16th-century building containing the **Archeological Museum.** Turn right on the main street to the strong but graceful **Cathedral of St. Anastasia** (Sveta Stošija), which contains some of the country's most beautiful, delicately carved choir stalls. The Romans laid out their towns like military camps, with a series of rectangular blocks and two main streets intersecting at right angles; you'll get a sense of this plan from the top of the cathedral's 55-m (184-ft) bell tower.

Turn left from the cathedral and walk one block to the remains of the old **Roman Forum.** The forum was discovered after houses were razed during air raids in World War II. The 13.7-m (46-ft) column, once part of the forum, was used as a pillory as late as 1840. Cross the forum and stroll along Obala Maršala Tita, at the water's edge, where young people come for their nightly stroll.

Retrace your steps one block northeast (inland) to Ulica Borisa, turn left, and walk to the eastern end of the peninsula. Across a square is the **Franciscan Monastery** and the **Church of St. Francis** (Sveti Frane). This aisleless 13th-century church has a treasury with one of the country's few remaining painted, 12th-century crucifixes. These crucifixes used to be the dominant religious symbol in coastal churches, standing in the center of the chancel screen, on the altar, or in the center of the nave. The image of Christ Triumphant, more a God than a man, must have been painted by an artist under Byzantine influence, for Eastern emperors did not allow Christ to be shown dying or in pain.

Return to the forum and turn right on Stomorica to the Early Croatian **St. Donat's Church** (Sveti Donat), a high stone fortress, one of the oldest surviving buildings in Dalmatia. Its 9th-century foundations are built entirely of Roman masonry, including fragments of pillars and altar stones dedicated to Jupiter and Juno. Its strength is overwhelming: It's no wonder that of all the buildings in the area it alone survived the air raids in World War II.

From Sveti Donat, continue down Stomorica to the Romanesque **St. Mary's Basilica** (Sveta Marija), once part of a Benedictine convent. Follow Ulica Ive Lole Ribara to the city's main square (Narodni Trg), where suddenly you're transported from Croatia to 16th-century Venice. The **Café Central** is an ideal stop for a glass of local cherry brandy, called *Vishnievacha.*

Nearby is **St. Simeon's Church** (Sveti Šimun). On the high altar is the saint's sarcophagus borne by two 249-kg (550-lb) Baroque angels. Ask a nun to lift the lid so you can see the saint under glass.

Dining **Restoran Maestral.** This is by far Zadar's finest restaurant, part of the marina operation—bright, modern, with nautical decor and gleaming brass. It has a bar and café downstairs. The restaurant upstairs features picture windows overlooking boats and the old town across the water. The menu includes bouillabaisse, French onion soup, risotto, steaks, mixed grill, fish, and Yugoslavia's best wines. *In marina, Obala Oktobarska Revolution, tel. 057/430–549. Reservations suggested in season. Dress: casual. AE, DC, MC, V. Expensive.*

Konoba, Gostionica Dva Ribara, Dalmatija, Zadar, Balkan Grill, and Riblja are all run by the Jadera Company. In the heart of the old town, these six simple restaurants offer fish, mixed grills, and crisp salads, with beer or wine, at modest cost. One, identified only by the Jadera sign, is set up in a courtyard directly behind the church of Sveti Krsevan. They are very popular in summer. *No phone. No reservations. Dress: casual. No credit cards. Inexpensive.*

Lodging **Borik Hotel Complex.** Located 3.2 km (2 mi) from the old town on the Borik peninsula, this "hotel city" consists of six hotels and campgrounds.

Hotel Barbara, a modern high-rise, is your best bet if you are coming by car. Follow the signs to Borik. *Entrance on Put Matije Gupca, tel. 057/24–299. 180 rooms. Facilities: 3 restaurants, indoor and outdoor pools, sauna, shopping arcade, gambling casino. AE, DC, MC, V. Expensive.*

Zagreb. A somewhat run-down "grand hotel" of long ago, but conveniently situated in the old town, facing the bay, this is the best choice if you don't have a car, or if you want to be close to historic Zadar. Some spacious corner suites rent at very reasonable rates. *Obala Marsala Tita, tel. 057/22–071. 100 rooms. Facilities: terrace café. AE, DC, MC, V. Moderate.*

Šibenik

Šibenik (72 km/45 mi past Zadar) has been developing into an industrial town, but you should stop at least to see the cathedral, one of the most important along the coast. The road passes through a modern world of high rises and factories, down to the harbor. Leave your car here. Everything you want to see is within a few blocks' radius.

The **Cathedral of St. James** (Sveti Jakov) took 124 years to build (1431–1555), during which time styles changed from Gothic to Renaissance. The stone roof seems to defy gravity, covering the nave and aisles with no visible support. The satirical portraits around the outer wall of the apse were carved by George of Dalmatia. Some say they were George's way of getting even with those who refused to contribute to the building's cost. Turks and Venetians, cooks and warriors—what a colorful and disparate lot! If you want to meet George, there's a statue of him on the square by Ivan Meštrović.

It's worth visiting the Gothic **Church of St. Barbara** (Sveta Barbara) to see the polyptychs by the Venetian-style painter Nikola Vladanov. Notice the individuality of the faces of those kneeling below the cloak of the Madonna: each unique yet all joined together by a common faith.

If you're into scenic waterfalls, make a short side trip from Šibenik to **Skradin Falls** on the Krka River. There's a restaurant on a stone patio under some pines, and steps leading down to a grassy picnic area. It's a lovely spot, but don't expect to be alone. You can sign up here for a boat ride to a Franciscan convent on an island in the Krka.

Trogir

Trogir, surrounded by water, is a beautiful museum town—a place to look at rather than enter into. Yet because it is so well preserved, you get a sense of the past unequaled along the coast. When you cross the bridge, you enter a world of glowing stone that has remained essentially unchanged since the Renaissance.

Above the entrance gate is the lion of St. Mark, the symbol of Venice: a reminder that Trogir was under Venetian rule for more than 350 years. Make your first left and continue around the island to the **Cathedral of St. Lawrence** (Sveti Lovro). Most memorable of all Trogir's glories is the portal of this 13th-century cathedral, a treasury of Romanesque sculpture by the Croatian master Radovan. A griffin plucking out the eye of a pig, a centaur, a sea horse, a mermaid, the apostles accompanied by their zodiacal signs—all remind you that, to the early Croatian mind, there were mysteries unanswered by the rituals and dogma of the church—mysteries that were part of their spiritual baggage as they migrated to the Balkans from the east. Pass through Radovan's doorway, flanked by statues of Adam and Eve on their way east of Eden (among the first nudes in medieval art), and you'll find yourself in the dimly lit interior of a Romanesque church. Notable features include the 13th-century stone pulpit, the 14th-century ciborium (canopy) over the high altar, the Gothic choir stalls, and the great barrel roof of the Chapel of John Orsini. The treasury contains works by one of Dalmatia's greatest painters, Blaž of Trogir. The play of light and shadow on flesh and fabric is a trademark of the Dalmatian School of painting.

Stand outside the cathedral and notice how the walls exude the raw, massive power of the Romanesque, while the bell tower—the first two stories Gothic, the third, Renaissance—expresses the grace and elegance of a more refined age.

The cathedral rises above **National Square** (Narodni Trg), which could be in Venice. Beside the City Tower is the oldest of Trogir's churches, the small, tunnellike **Basilica of St. Barbara** (Sveta Barbara). The 9th-century church (rebuilt in the 11th) is a rare example of early Croatian architecture.

In the 14th-century **Church of St. Nicholas** (Sveti Nikola) is a crucifix painted against a modest red background—a reminder that gold was not always affordable in this outpost of Christianity. There's no more Byzantine influence here: Both the Virgin's face and the face of St. John (in the right trefoil) are rich with feeling.

In the 14th-century **Church of St. Dominic** (Sveti Domjan), near the quay, is a tomb with an enraged lion, erected by a widow to her husband who was murdered by the Venetians: a reminder that the Venetian occupation was not always a civilizing influence.

Dining and Lodging There are a number of cafés and private restaurants set on the narrow passageways off the cathedral square, serving more or less fast food and typical coastal specialties. None is really geared for serious dining.

Plavi Jadran, in a courtyard, is a pleasant setting for a light lunch. *27 Gradski, no phone. No reservations. No credit cards.*

While the itinerary doesn't include Trogir as an overnight stop, should you want to spend the night, then two hotel complexes are located several miles west on the coastal highway: the 150-room **Jadran** (tel. 058/73–688), and the 680-room **Medena** (tel. 058/73–788).

Salona

The road passes through the rich, green Riviera of the Seven Castles (Kaštel Riviera), the most fertile region of Dalmatia. About 6.4 km (4 mi) before Split are the ruins of **Salona.** Stop here only if you have more than a passing interest in antiquity or want to feed your sense of mortality. Lizards dart among the broken stones of this 1st-century Roman town, which is scattered across a hillside. Some 70,000 people, including the Roman Emperor Diocletian, once lived here—more than the present-day population of Dubrovnik. The town was destroyed by the Avars 14 centuries ago, but you can still see the ruins of the arena, the public baths, the Roman theater, and several early Christian churches. When the town was destroyed, the survivors fled to Split.

Split

You'll wonder what the fuss is about as you drive through the sprawling suburbs of Dalmatia's largest town, with its shipyards, cement factories, and ferroconcrete flats. The fuss, you'll discover when you reach the harbor, is the 1,685-year-old palace of Emperor Diocletian—one of the most imposing Roman monuments in the world. Here is an odd twist in the history of urban planning: not a palace built within a town, but a town built within a palace.

The Roman Emperor Diocletian was ruler of all lands from Brittany to Persia, but when he retired in AD 305, he chose this spot near his birthplace to build his palace. Some 310 years after his death, survivors from Salona found shelter within its abandoned walls. They waited for peace so they could return home, but peace never came, and so they settled in, partitioning the Emperor's quarters into apartments, building homes in courtyards, up against the palace walls, and within the ancient arcades—turning broad Roman streets into alleyways so narrow that two people had to turn sideways to pass. Centuries later the Venetians came and built grand palaces beside the medieval homes. The medieval and Renaissance town spread beyond the western walls; and beyond that stretches the modern town you see today.

Recent plans to restore the palace to its ancient glory were dropped when it was discovered that the palace would crumble without the medieval and Renaissance homes to support it. What a fine example of architectural symbiosis! The palace was never a great example of Roman architecture, but what a jumble, what a patchwork of styles you'll see in Split today; and what a sense of continuity, as past and present merge in this living testimony to almost 17 centuries of human history. Laundry lines hang today where imperial banners once unfurled. What was once an emperor's mausoleum is now a cathedral. A Renaissance palace has become a disco, a medieval home, a café. Miraculously, it all holds together, an amalgam of shapes and styles from Roman to Romanesque, Gothic, Renaissance, and Baroque.

Split

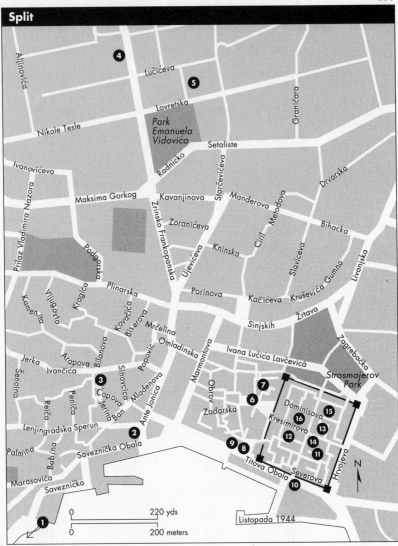

Aljinovića
Lučićeva
Lovretska
Nikole Tesle
Park Emanuela Vidovića
Setaliste
Ivanovićeva
Radnicko
Maksima Gorkog
Kavanjinova
Starčevićeva
Manderova
Drvarska
Prilaz Vladimira Nazora
Zrinsko Frankopanska
Zoranićeva
Ciril Metodova
Bihacka
Podgorska
Ujevićeva
Kninska
Slavićeva
Kruševića Gumno
Livanjska
Granićara
Kamen Ila
Viligasta
Kragica
Plinarska
Kovočića
Bis erova
Mrčelina
Porinova
Kačićeva
Sinjskih
Žttava
Zagrebačka
Jerka
Senoina
Aropova
Bilanova
Sinovica
Popović
Omladinska
Ivana Lučića Lavčevića
Strosmajerov Park
Ivančića
Copova
Jertna Ban
Mladenova
Ante Jonica
Marmontova
Obrov
Zadarska
Dominisova
Kresimirova
Reiča
Peniča
Lenjingradska Sperun
Saveznička Obala
Titova Obala
Severova
Hrvojeva
Palmina
Babina
Marasovića
Saveznička
Listopada 1944

0 220 yds
0 200 meters

N

Archeological Museum, **4**

Gallery of Fine Arts, **5**

Kaštelet Mestrović (Museum of Croatian Archeological Monuments), **1**

Narodni Trg, **6**

Sveti Frane, **2**

Sveti Mikula, **3**

Tourist Office, **9**

Town Hall, **7**

Trg Preporoda, **8**

Palace of Diocletian

Baptistery, **12**

Church of St. Philip Neri, **13**

Church of St. Roch, **14**

Cindro Mansion, **16**

Papalic Mansion, **15**

Porta Aenea (Bronze Gate), **10**

Sveti Duje, **11**

The palace has a striking monumentality that visitors tend to overpraise. It is, in fact, one of the most pretentious private residences ever built—the monument of a man not born to wealth; the boast of a local boy made good. It was also the creation of a theocracy in which architecture existed to trumpet the divinity of the emperor to the people. Diocletian, who reigned from 284 to 305, was a true autocrat, an emperor-god, whose concepts of magnificence came not from Rome but from Persia. Jovius was what he called himself—son of Jupiter; subjects had to fall on their knees before they dared to speak.

And yet Diocletian was a sad, lonely man with few friends. His wife converted to Christianity; his daughter was beheaded and thrown into the sea. He spent 11 years building his palace, and when it was complete he abdicated, at age 61. For eight years or so he lived here, cultivating cabbages, watching the decay of the empire that his reforms had merely held in check. His palace must have been—as Monticello was for Jefferson—a brave attempt to give himself a form of immortality.

The palace was built like a Roman fort, with two main streets intersecting at the central courtyard (peristyle), dividing the palace into four parts. The southern half, facing the sea, was reserved for the imperial apartments and religious buildings; the northern half was for warehouses and for the emperor's bodyguards and staff.

Begin your tour with a walk along the seafront promenade, beneath the southern wall. In Diocletian's day the sea slapped against this wall, which was fronted by a great portico, and a central hall leading to the emperor's apartments. Houses today cling like barnacles to the facade, but near the southeastern tower you can see how this loggia once appeared to visitors arriving by sea.

Enter through the **Bronze Gate** (Porta Aenea) and descend on the left into the dark, vaulted chambers. This basement floor corresponds roughly to the imperial apartments, which were directly above, but which sadly no longer exist; in fact, there's really very little to see here but the massive walls and some broken columns.

Return to the gate. As you climb the steps to the central courtyard, imagine yourself delivering a message to Diocletian some 1,700 years ago, perhaps informing him of another barbarian invasion. Pause to admire the columns along the courtyard, which, like the 15th-century black granite sphinx, were brought here from an Egyptian temple. Walk south (toward the sea) to the vestibule (antechamber) of the imperial apartments, where you would have had to prostrate yourself before the emperor and kiss the hem of his robe.

To the east of this courtyard is **Diocletian's mausoleum.** You have to imagine statues in the niches and mosaics in the dome; otherwise, the octagonal building has kept its original Eastern appearance. As for Diocletian's remains, they disappeared one day; perhaps they'll show up again beneath the basement of some medieval home. In the 7th century the pagan statues were removed and the mausoleum consecrated as the **Cathedral of St. Mary,** commonly known as the **Cathedral of St. Dominius** (Sveti Duje). The conversion included construction of a solid but graceful Romanesque-Gothic bell tower. What a contrast between the refined lines of this bell tower and the rough Roman exterior of the mausoleum. Walk between the two 13th-century lions by Radovan (you met him in Trogir) and climb the bell tower for a great view of the palace. Of special note in the cathedral are the doors by Andrija Buvina of Split (1214) portraying the life and agony of Christ; the 13th-century pulpit to the left of the entrance; the Altar of Anastasius (1428) by George the Dalmatian; and the Romanesque choir stalls, which are similar to those you saw in Rab and Zadar.

When you leave the cathedral, recross the peristyle and follow a narrow street called Kraj Sveti Ivana to the Imperial Temple. Though converted during the Middle Ages into St. John's **baptistery**, it remains one of the world's best examples of a small classical temple. Look closely at the 11th-century altar screen on the baptismal font: Is that an Adoration of Christ or a portrait of a Croatian king with his subjects?

Crowded within the palace walls is a maze of medieval streets lined with Romanesque and Gothic buildings. Worth visiting are the 18th-century Baroque **Church of St. Philip Neri,** the small Renaissance **Church of St. Roch** (a miniature Šibenik Cathedral), the **Papalić Mansion** (designed by George the Dalmatian, it is the best Late Gothic building in the city), and the 17th-century **Cindro Mansion** (a typical Venetian-style patrician palace, the most beautiful Baroque building in Split).

Medieval Split spreads beyond the western walls of the palace. Among buildings worth visiting here are the 9th-century, Pre-Romanesque **Church of St. Michael** (Sveti Mikula), and, near the harbor, the 13th-century **Church of St. Francis** (Sveti Frane), which has a lovely cloister.

National Square (Narodni Trg), once reserved for the upper classes, is directly across from the West Gate. You'll find here the Venetian Gothic **Town Hall** (1433) and the Renaissance **Karepić Mansion.** Follow the western wall south toward the harbor and you'll come to another lovely Venetian square, **Trg Preporoda.**

The findings at Salona are displayed in the **Archeological Museum** (13 Zrinsko-Frankopanska St.). The most important remains of early Croatian culture are exhibited in the **Museum of Croatian Archeological Monuments** (Kaštelet Mestrović) on Šetalište Moše Pijade. The **Art Gallery** (11 Lovretska St.) has paintings from the 14th century to the present, and a fine collection of icons.

From the bus station it's a 7.2 km (4½-mi) ride to the high, wooded **Marjan Hill,** the Emperor's former hunting grounds. The road passes the gallery and castle that house some 200 of Ivan Meštrović's sculptures and reliefs. **Holy Cross Chapel,** 495 m (550 yd) from the Meštrović Museum, contains his New Testament cycle of bas-relief wood carvings, said to be his best work.

Dining **Adriatic.** This restaurant, located in the ACY marina complex, high on a promontory overlooking the harbor, is surely the finest restaurant in Split, and among the best in Yugoslavia. The dining room is handsomely appointed with pale blue Tiffany lamps, blue tablecloths, modern paintings, and picture windows looking out to sea. An ambitious menu concentrates on the freshest seafood, along with steaks, chops, salads, and a range of Yugoslav wines. Adjoining is the Skipper Bar and a popular pizzeria. *Uvala Baluni, tel. 058/587–090. Reservations suggested in summer. Dress: casual. AE, DC, MC, V. Expensive.*

Bellevue. This hotel-restaurant is perhaps the best-kept secret in Split. In summer you can dine under the arcades, looking out on the square. The chef prepares daily specials—hearty stews, boiled beef with tomato sauce, "black" risotto. *Ante Jonica 2 (entrance on Trg Republike), tel. 058/47–175. Reservations unnecessary. Dress: casual. AE, DC, MC, V. Moderate.*

Other restaurants worth considering: **Adriana** for fresh fish. *(Titova obala 8, tel. 058/44–072; dress: casual; AE, DC, MC, V; moderate).* **Sarajevo** for Bosnian specialties. *(Ilegalaca 6, tel. 058/47–454; dress: casual; AE, DC, MC, V; moderate).*

Lodging **Villa Dalmacija,** once a part-time residence of Tito's, was opened as a super-luxury hotel in 1989. Three handsomely furnished villas are situated in a vast seaside park along the city's western edge. The elegant gourmet restaurant is exclusively for those staying here. *Setaliste M. Pijade 41, tel. 058/511–333. 11 apartments and suites. Facilities: restaurant, beach, pool, tennis. AE, DC, MC, V. Very Expensive.*

Lav is a pleasant complex 9.7 km (6 mi) west of town on the coastal highway. It is difficult to reach because of traffic jams. *Milijevac, tel. 058/551–444. 360 rooms. Facilities: swimming pool, beach, bars, several restaurants. AE, DC, MC, V. Expensive.*

Marjan. The lobby of this boxlike structure has recently been treated to a face-lift, with a jazzy art nouveau piano bar, a disco, a nightclub, and an atmospheric national restaurant. Still, the rooms are ordinary at best. *Obala J.N.A. 15, tel. 058/ 42–930. 330 rooms. AE, DC, MC, V. Expensive.*

Bellevue. This small, old-fashioned hotel has a certain rundown charm and has benefited from some recent renovations. Be choosy about rooms, because some are infinitely superior to others. Ask for a *quiet* room, which usually means on the Trg Republike side, except during summer music festival time when you can forget about sleep until very late. *Ante Jonica 2, tel. 058/47–175. 46 rooms. AE, DC, MC, V. Moderate.*

Ston

If you want to make time between Split and **Ston** (166.4 km/104 mi from Split), there's no overwhelming need to stop en route. Desolate 1,500-m (5,000-ft) peaks slope down to the sandy beaches of the Makarska Riviera. The island on your right is Brač, whose quarries provided the marble for Diocletian's Palace, the White House, and the UN. Beyond Gradac the mountains recede and the road winds inland through rocky rolling countryside. The reed beds in the delta near Ploče look like Chinese rice paddies. A right turn about 64 km (40 mi) north of Dubrovnik takes you 8 km (5 mi) to the fortified Roman and medieval settlement of Ston—a side trip worth making if you're interested in early Slavic architecture.

Ston, once the second most important city in the republic of Ragusa, sits on a narrow strip of land connecting the peninsula of Pelješac with the mainland. On Sveti Mihajlo Hill is the well-preserved Pre-Romanesque **St. Michael's Church** (11th or 12th century). The earliest Croatian kings and bishops worshiped here, as they did in Nin. On the plain below was an ancient settlement with eight churches, two of which still stand: the Romanesque **Church of Our Lady of Lužina** and the small Pre-Romanesque **Church of St. Martin.**

In **Greater Ston,** see the late Romanesque **Church of St. Nicholas** (1347), which preserves a large painted crucifix by Blaž of Trogir. Other buildings to see are the Gothic **Chancery of the Republic;** the Gothic **Sorkočević-Djurdjević Mansion,** and the Renaissance **Bishop's Palace.**

Hvar

The 3,000-year-old town of Hvar, on the island of the same name, is reached by car ferry or hydrofoil from Split or Dubrovnik. The passage can be rough, so bring motion-sickness pills. You can depart at 8 AM and return at 4:30 PM, but why not spend the night and experience this most Venetian of Venetian towns when the day-trippers have departed?

You can also visit Hvar on a guided tour from Split or Dubrovnik—any mainland hotel or tourist office can arrange it —or join a group tour once you reach the island. Arrange for private guides in Dubrovnik or Split.

Hvar was destroyed by the Turks in 1571, so what you'll see is a late-16th-century town. Within the ancient walls are palaces weathered to the color of gold. Pass through the **Sea Gate** to the main square—the largest in Dalmatia. The town rises on either side: the medieval quarter, with its steep, narrow streets, to the north; the Venetian section to the west. The square is surrounded by notable buildings: the Renaissance **Cathedral of St. Stephen** (Sveti Stefan), which has a bell tower you can climb; the Gothic-Renaissance **Paladini Palace;** the beautiful **Vukašinović Palace;** and the **Arsenal** (1579–1611), which houses the oldest surviving theater (1612) in Yugoslavia.

The dining hall in the mid-15th-century **Franciscan Monastery** (a five-minute walk along the sea wall) contains one of the best collections of paintings along the coast, and a library that includes a 1524 Ptolemaic atlas and some exquisite 16th-century music books. The small garden behind the refectory has a 300-year-old cypress.

For exercise and a great view, follow the cactus-lined walk that zigzags up to the **Spanish Fort.** Fortify yourself with a glass of wine at Konoba Lepurini or at one of the other ancient taverns en route.

If you're spending the night, rent a motorboat or rowboat at the harbor and explore the coast. The tiny island of **St. Clement** (Sveti Kliment) has better beaches than Hvar, and a colorful display of tropical plants.

If you bring your car to Hvar, you can drive the length of the island to Sućuraj and take the short ferry ride back to the mainland at Drvenik. The road climbs hundreds of feet above the sea, offering breathtaking views of the mountainous coast. Farmers have imposed a semblance of order on this rocky terrain by building stone walls and planting the enclosures with grapevines and lavender. The geometric stone patterns look like hieroglyphics from the dawn of time. From Drvenik, return to Split or head south to Dubrovnik.

Dining **Palace.** Enjoy a fine meal in an idyllic setting overlooking the main square and harbor, or in the elegant indoor dining room. *Titor Trg, tel. 058/74–906. Reservations in summer. Dress: casual. AE, DC, MC, V. Expensive.*

A series of small restaurants (featuring Dalmatian specialties and seafood) is strung along the waterfront, across from the palace, where ships dock, including **Konoba. Kop Kapetna** is on the opposite shore, near the Adriatic hotel. *No phones. No reservations. No credit cards. Moderate.*

Lodging **Adriatic.** Situated along the harbor on the palace side, this satisfactory small hotel has its own beach. *Titov Trg, tel. 058/74–024. 58 rooms. Facilities: indoor pool. AE, DC, MC, V. Expensive.*

Amfora. Somewhat inconveniently located, this mammoth hotel complex overlooks the sea. *Obala Pakleni, tel. 058/74–202. 375 rooms. Facilities: indoor pool, fitness club, casino. AE, DC, MC, V. Expensive.*

Palace. One of the coast's most elegant hotels, the Palace was built into a Venetian palace with a loggia and clock tower and modernized without losing a sense of continuity with the past. *Titor Trg, tel. 058/74–966. 76 rooms. Facilities: indoor pool. AE, DC, MC, V. Expensive.*

Korčula

There's regular car-ferry service to Korčula from Split and Dubrovnik. You can also take a ferry from Orebić on the Pelješac Peninsula and stop at Ston en route either to or from the coastal highway.

Korčula, like the town of Hvar, sits on an island of the same name. It's similar in size to Hvar but more compact. It's also marked with the same Venetian imprint: the same narrow winding streets opening out on squares surrounded by 16th-century palaces and loggias; the same wheat-colored stone that the late afternoon sun turns to gold.

The historical nucleus lies within the 14th- to 16th-century walls that protected the town from attacks by Turks and pirates. The main street changes directions three times to reduce the impact of the winter wind; the side streets join it at an angle, like veins on a leaf, to reduce the heat of the midday sun. It may have been Greek settlers who thought up this plan in the 4th century BC.

A building not to miss is the **Cathedral of St. Mark.** The first masons worked in the Gothic spirit; then came the florid southern Italian influence, and, finally, features of the early Renaissance. Churches were built to teach as well as to provide a sanctuary for prayer; hence, the biblical allegories carved by an itinerant French artist on the cathedral doors. Projecting from a gable above the door is a carving of an old woman with the same questioning, morbid features that you saw in Radovan's work in Trogir. If you're looking for a sensibility that's distinctly Croatian, you'll find it in this face, which, as British writer Rebecca West points out, assumes that all is not known, and that order and proportion may not be the only principles that govern the world. If you want to see what modern Croatian artists have done with these notions, study the 20th-century works of art on the ground floor of the bell tower. In the cathedral treasury is a polyptych (1421) by Blaž of Trogir.

From the square you can see the courtyard side of a mansion with a tower. This is reputedly the birthplace of the famous medieval explorer Marco Polo (1254–1324). Venice also claims Marco as its own; but what is not contestable is the fact that Polos still live on Korčula and that back in 1298 Marco Polo commanded a Venetian fleet of 10 ships within sight of the island and was captured by the Genoese. It was in jail that he dictated to a fellow prisoner the story of his journey to China.

In the southeast part of the walled town is the renovated early-15th-century **Church of All Saints** (Svi Sveti), which has another polyptych by Blaž and an impressive collection of Greek icons.

Come Thursdays in season for the Moreška, when armed dancers in magnificent costumes act out a great battle between the Moors and the Turks for possession of a beautiful princess. The dance symbolizes more than 1,000 years of Yugoslav history—one dancer representing attack, the other defense.

Dining **Adio Mare.** Here regional specialties are served on the vine-covered terrace of a fine late Gothic-Renaissance building in the heart of the old town. Try the local fish soup, which is really a thick seafood stew. *Glavni Graski Trg, tel. 050/711–253. Reservations advised for dinner only at top of season. AE, V. Closed Oct. 15–April. Moderate.*

Planjak. This is a long-time favorite with the locals who come here to enjoy their meals on the restaurant's covered terrace by the sea. Accompany a meal of seafood with the locally produced Grk white wine. *Korcula Obala, tel. 051/711–015. No reservations. AE, DC, MC, V. Moderate.*

Lodging **Liburna.** Located on a wooded promontory, with its own rocky beach, Liburna is a short walk from the old town. It opened in 1985 and has the best facilities of any hotel in Korcula, with many choices for water-sports fans. *Naselje, tel. 050/711–026. 84 rooms, 25 apartments with bath or shower. Facilities: pool, tennis, miniature golf, windsurfing, boat and bicycle rental, ping-pong, billiards. AE, DC, MC, V. Expensive.*

Korčula. Renovated in 1982, this seaside hotel is in the heart of the old town. About 186 m (200 yd) from a beach, the Korcula is ideal if you want to feel part of the local scene or if you prefer accommodations on a smaller scale. Ask for a room *not* facing the street if you want to be spared late-night noise. *Korcula Obala, tel. 051/711–078. 24 rooms with bath. AE, DC, MC, V. Closed Nov.–Apr. Moderate.*

Dubrovnik

If you're driving or sailing south, you'll arrive in the suburb of Gruž. The travel agencies are here, along the harbor, and so are most of the large, modern hotels. Don't worry, this is not Dubrovnik. The old walled city is 3.8 km (2.4 mi) farther south, sitting on a huge rock formation jutting out into the sea.

The tourist department has billed Dubrovnik (62.4 km/39 mi from Ston) as the country's number one attraction, so you may be surprised by how small it is: only 40,000 people, compared to 300,000 in Split. Americans who like to discover new continents may not appreciate the 55,000 fellow tourists, all searching for the Real Yugoslavia; yet the magic of the city somehow survives.

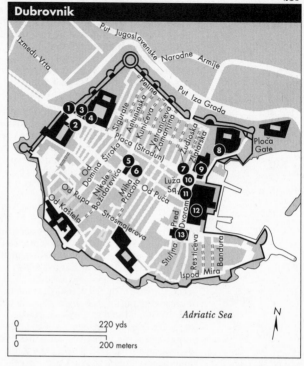

Dubrovnik

Adriatic Sea

0 — 220 yds

0 — 200 meters

N

It survives because the city is visually one of the most pleasing in the world. It envelops you. It shelters you within its huge, protective walls. The polished white stone makes everything seem both new and everlasting. Each building has its own decoration, but all were built to conform to strict medieval building codes—the same slant of the roof, the same kind of cornice—and the result is an expression in stone of both the unity and uniqueness people seek in their own lives.

Houses, churches, monasteries, fountains—all are built with the same aristocratic poise and dignity you'll find in the people themselves. Unlike Vienna, where every monument says money, monarchy, and power, Dubrovnik is built to human scale. There is no ostentation here; no building stands out at the expense of another. Despite its Baroque facades, added after a 17th-century earthquake, Dubrovnik is still essentially a Gothic-Renaissance city, and when you enter its walls you are whirled back into the 16th and 17th centuries.

In the 12th century, Dubrovnik (called Ragusa until World War I) became an independent city-state. It had only 40,000 citizens but was a greater sea power than Britain at that time, and for many decades was Venice's chief rival in the Adriatic. Caravans started from here to Constantinople. Pilgrims visited Ragusa's brothels on their way to Jerusalem—the madam was called "the abbess of the sinners." Goods from the eastern Mediterranean sailed to England in Ragusan ships called *raguisies;* hence, the word *argosy.* In the 16th century Ragusa had 50 consulates and more than 180 ships sailing the Mediterranean.

Ragusa grew rich on the principle that it's better to negotiate and buy off the enemy than fight him. The people were shrewd businessmen, not fighters, and bought with money what their neighbors, the Montenegrins, bought with their lives. When Constantinople fell to the Turks, the Ragusans sent an annual tribute to the Sultan in return for retaining their trading and maritime rights; they also paid tribute to the Hungarian king and agreed to pray for him in church.

The shipowners were the aristocracy of Ragusa. Under their rule, 500 years ago, doctors were salaried and forbidden to charge fees except to foreigners—and then only if their remedies did some good. Street sweepers were contracted in 1415 not only to sweep up garbage, but to report those who threw it in the streets. Every shopkeeper and homeowner was required by law to sweep up in front of his own property on Saturday mornings. Europe's first orphanage was established in Ragusa in 1432; unmarried women were allowed to give birth there and then leave their children—in complete secrecy. A person who traded in slaves in 1417 would have been fined and put in jail; 50 years later he would have been sentenced to death. Four hundred forty-six years before the Emancipation Proclamation (1863), it was written in Ragusa's lawbooks that "It must be held to be base, wicked and abominable, and to redound to the great disgrace of our city, that the human form, made after the image and similitude of our Creator, should be turned to mercenary profit, and sold as if it were a beast." This did not stop the Ragusans from holding slaves of their own; but they were not permitted to trade in slaves, an attitude considerably ahead of its time; and in the 17th century the Ragusans refused to profit from the slave trade to the American colonies.

In 1667, Ragusa was destroyed by an earthquake and rebuilt under strong Venetian influence. Napoleon occupied the city in 1806 and dissolved the Republic. While the town was under Austrian occupation from 1814 to 1918, the nobility vowed not to have children until they regained their freedom, and many old families disappeared or lived in drafty houses full of cats.

Enter through the **Pile Gate** (Vrata od Pila) on the west, surmounted by statues of St. Blaise, the city's patron saint. If you're feeling sick, say a prayer to him—he was known for curing diseases, particularly sore throats.

Opening before you is the Placa, a street of glistening white paving stones polished by the feet of merchants and sailors, priests and patricians for more than 300 years.

Everything in Dubrovnik seems to flow down and meet in the Placa. Whatever is social, whatever is public in human nature seems to find expression here. In it you'll feel part of a noble procession that began hundreds of years before you were born and will continue long after you are gone.

The young people gather along the Placa in the early evening. Up one side of the street they strut, and down the other—a pride of boys and girls, in groups, in pairs, offering themselves to each other's gazes. It's something not to be missed.

Join this pavane, this polonaise, then return to the West Gate (preferably at sunset) and climb the fortifications—among the most remarkable in Europe. From here, 23.9 m (80 ft) up, you'll get a fine overview of the town. It's a 45-minute walk around the walls.

In front of you as you enter the Placa through the West Gate is a **fountain** (Velika Onofrijeva česma) by the Neapolitan architect Onofrio della Cava, looking much like the dome of a mosque. Onofrio got the contract to build an aqueduct to bring water here, then indulged his Renaissance fancy to build the fountain. It's said that buildings that survived the 1667 earthquake had been constructed with fresh water from the aqueduct; those built with mortar diluted with seawater were destroyed.

To the left of the fountain is the small but beautiful **Church of the Holy Savior** (Sveti Spas). The **Franciscan Church** next door is mostly Baroque (though completed in 1343), and has a noble 15th-century pietà over the doorway.

Don't miss the Romanesque cloister in the **Franciscan Friary.** The Roman arcades are supported by graceful double columns crowned with grotesque figures that must have amused or horrified the monks. In the treasury is a painting of Dubrovnik before the earthquake. In the lower cloister is a 14th-century pharmacy that is still in use.

The **Museum of Icons** (Muzej Starih Ikona) near the **Serbian Church** has a great collection of old icons.

On Zudioska Ulica (Jew Street), near the Eastern (Ploče) Gate, is a 14th-century **synagogue,** the third-oldest in Europe. Jews came here to escape persecution in Spain and Italy. They were allowed to draw water only from their own fountain, yet some worked as doctors or secretaries to patrician families. Dubrovnik had 5,000 Jews before the war; now it hasn't enough to form a congregation.

The nearby **Dominican Church** has a graceful cloister and paintings by some of Dalmatia's most venerated artists (including a famous model of Dubrovnik by Nikola Božidarević in the Bundić Chapel).

Walk to Luža Square, at the far, eastern end of the Placa. The **Column of Orlando** (Roland) was the medieval symbol of a free merchant city. It was here that festivities were announced and laws proclaimed. To your left is the original 14th-century Customs House, known as the **Sponza Palace** (Palača Sponza). Dubrovnik in its heyday served as a storage depot between East and West, and packages were stored here on the ground floor. A second floor was added in Venetian Gothic style for literary gatherings; later, a third floor was completed in Renaissance style and the house was faced with a loggia. Inside is a beautiful courtyard.

To the right of the square is the **Church of St. Blaise** (Sveti Vlaho), a Baroque mass built by a second-rate Venetian architect. The famous sculpture of the saint holding a model of the town now stands on the high altar.

Across the street, to the right (as you face the harbor), is the two-storied, flowery Gothic **Rector's Palace** (Knežev dvor), the glory of Dubrovnik, the most beautiful civic building in the city.

Turn right from the palace and cross to the **Cathedral of Our Lady** (Stolna crkva), which was given a flashy Baroque dress after the earthquake. The treasury has some notable relics, including a hand of St. Blaise, and his skull adorned by an 11th-century Byzantine crown.

When you've seen enough sights, make an excursion to the island of **Mljet**. It has three lovely lakes surrounded by pines. In the largest is an islet with a 12th-century Benedictine convent, now a modest hotel called **Melita** (tel. 050/89–010).

Unless you have time to spare, don't bother visiting **Trebinje**. It's a popular excursion spot, but there's little to see except two mosques, which will probably be locked.

A cable car leaves every 30 minutes to the top of **Mount Srdj**, where you'll enjoy a breathtaking view of Dubrovnik.

Dining In addition to some 30 eating places in the old town, most hotels have à la carte restaurants. Numerous pizzerias, cafés, bars, and snack bars serve fast food or light meals. The following is a list of personal favorites. Casual wear is fine in all of them. Reservations are suggested in summer unless otherwise indicated.

Domino Steak House. This is the city's most ambitious restaurant, with the most complete menu. The interior is a two-story affair with stone walls in a historic structure; tables are set up in the courtyard out front. Start with caviar, steak tartare, oysters, or a shrimp cocktail before sampling the fresh seafood or excellent steaks. *Domino 3, tel. 050/32–832. AE, DC, MC, V. Expensive.*

Konavoski Dvori. Thirty-two kilometers (20 mi) south of Dubrovnik (turn off the coastal highway below Cavtat at Gruda, and follow the restaurant signs to the mouth of the River Ljuta), this showplace alongside a working water mill serves up authentic regional specialties. It's a little hokey—waitresses dressed in national costumes, atmosphere laid on with a trowel—but the lamb, cooked on a spit or in iron pots in a charcoal fire, cannot be faulted. *Gruda, tel. 050/79–039. Reservations recommended. AE, DC, MC, V. Moderate–Expensive.*

Ombla. Six kilometers (4 mi) west of town in a former sea captain's house, you can dine on fresh fish. *Rijeka Dubrovacka, Komolac, tel. 050/78–713. AE, DC, MC, V. Moderate–Expensive.*

Ragusa 2. Run by the same family for over 60 years, this popular restaurant features a limited menu of Dalmatian specialties. Two small rooms sport nautical fittings; tables are set along the narrow streets outside. *Zamanjina 12, tel. 050/22–435. AE, DC, MC, V. Moderate–Expensive.*

Riblji. In the center of Dubrovnik, just off the Placa, this is the city's top fish restaurant. The setting is no-nonsense, with a few fishnets as decor. Fresh fish, prepared to your specification, is what matters here. *Siroka Ulica 1, tel. 050/27–589. AE, DC, MC, V. Moderate–Expensive.*

Jadran. This popular restaurant next to the Onofrio fountain near the Pile Gate occupies the courtyard of a former monastery. It serves typical Dalmatian specialties. *Paska Milicevica 1, tel. 050/23–547. AE, DC, MC, V. Moderate.*

Nada. This is a typical restaurant on a side street off the Placa. *Zudioska 8, tel. 050/28–752. AE, DC, MC, V. Moderate.*

Cavtat. This minuscule establishment on a narrow passageway parallel to the Placa serves the closest approximation to home cooking in the city. It is very popular and always crowded. *Od

Puca bb, tel. 050/27–499. No reservations. No credit cards. Inexpensive.

Lodging **Belvedere.** Dubrovnik's number one international luxury hotel —for a time a Holiday Inn—is about a mile south of the city, in other words a fairly long walk for sightseeing, although there is frequent bus service. The hotel offers all the amenities anyone could ask for, in a dramatic setting, and is a good choice if you don't mind spending top dollar. Opened in 1985, it is near a rocky beach with dining terraces overlooking the sea. The property is a favorite among Americans. *Frana Supila 28, tel. 050/28–655. 230 rooms with bath or shower, some suites. Facilities: 3 restaurants, 3 bars, nightclub, saunas, 2 pools, gym, solarium. AE, DC, MC, V. Very Expensive.*

Dubrovnik President. Built in 1976, the frequently renovated President is on the Lapad Peninsula across the harbor from Gruz and 4 km (2½ mi) from the old town. Its five streamlined stories rise above a pebble beach. Every room has its own balcony with a sea view. *Dubrava- Babin Kuk, tel. 050/22–666. 163 rooms with bath, plus suites. Facilities: drugstore, pizzeria, saunas, pool, tennis; sports facilities at nearby Dubrava Center. AE, DC, MC, V. Closed Jan.–Mar. Very Expensive.*

Argentina. One of the original old-time luxury hotels, located east of the city, the Argentina is currently undergoing a major renovation. The old wing offers fairly spartan rooms with fine views out to sea or over the old city. *F. Supila 24, tel. 050/23–855. 150 rooms. Facilities: restaurant, café, bar, indoor pool, children's outdoor pool, tennis, sauna, massage, hairdresser. AE, DC, MC, V. Expensive.*

Dubrovnik Palace. In a quiet location on a wooded headland, 4 km (2½ mi) from the old town in the Lapad district, the Palace has long been popular with Americans. This modern hotel, renovated in 1985, has its own rocky beach. *Masarykov put 18, tel. 050/28–556. 320 rooms with bath or shower. Facilities: saunas, pool, tennis. AE, DC, MC, V. Expensive.*

Villa Dubrovnik. A gem of a small luxury hotel, tucked away on a hideaway cove between the Belvedere and the Argentina, with a rocky beach out front, this is an insider's pick as best of the best. *V Bukovaca 8, tel. 050/22–933. 54 rooms. Facilities: Restaurant, terrace, bar. AE, DC, MC, V. Expensive.*

Grand Hotel Imperial. Though no longer quite a "grand hotel," the Imperial, a short walk west of the Pile Gate, is a good choice for anyone arriving in Dubrovnik by ship or bus. *M. Simoni 2, tel. 050/23–688. 132 rooms. Facilities: restaurant. AE, DC, MC, V. Moderate.*

Rooms to Rent In and around Dubrovnik are many private apartments and homes that accept overnight guests. Arrangements can be made through the Tourist Information Center (Poljana P. Milicecica 1, tel. 050/26–302) or on one's own wherever rooms for rent are indicated. If you request a room in the old city through the Tourist Center, you might be sent to **Cetinic** (Prijeko 17). Ring the bell, and a waiter of the restaurant in front will give you the keys to the apartment. Upstairs, there's one room and bath on the second floor, similar accommodations on the third floor. The facilities are clean and functional and rent for about $20 a night (without breakfast). Turning private apartments into rooms for rent is part of the "new look" of Yugoslav tourism.

Outside the City **Croatia.** This, one of the coast's most luxurious hotels, is dramatically situated on high ground overlooking the sea, the two islands of Mrkan and Borbara, and Cavtat. *Sustjepan Peninsula, tel. 050/78–022. 450 rooms, several suites. Facilities: 2 restaurants, bars, nightclub, saunas, fitness center, 2 pools, tennis courts, bowling alley, shopping arcade, gambling casino. AE, DC, MC, V. Very Expensive.*

Grand Hotel Albatross, right on the beach, is the star of the Hotel Cavtat complex. *Tiha Obala, tel. 050/78–044. 288 rooms. Facilities: 2 outdoor pools, 1 indoor pool, waterskiing, boat and canoe rental, windsurfing, sports center with tennis courts. AE, DC, MC, V. Expensive.*

Montenegro

When you reach Hercegnovi, at the entrance to the Gulf of Kotor, you'll have left Croatia and entered **Montenegro.** No American loves his country more than the Montenegrin loves his poor, rocky land. Yet no part of Yugoslavia has suffered more from oppression, mostly from the Turks. Wrote Tennyson:

> O smallest among peoples! rough rock-throne
> Of Freedom! Warriors beating back the swarm
> Of Turkish Islam for five hundred years . . .

The identity of these people comes not from their monuments, but from their struggle. Living in continuous fear, being subjected to massacres and decapitations, has created its own set of moral values: a love of excess, a talent for revenge, a fondness for self-glorification. Fierce and uncompromising in times of war, the Montenegrins also have a reputation for laziness in peacetime. They joke about it themselves. (Why does the Montenegrin sleep with a chair next to his bed? To take a rest after sleeping. Why is the Montenegrin a bad lover? Because he's too proud to get underneath, and too lazy to climb on top.)

The Montenegrins are the only people on the Balkan Peninsula never wholly conquered. Throughout their history they have held to the idea of national independence, rising above the temptation of an easier life under the wing of a stronger power. If this is praiseworthy, how should we react to the citizens of Dubrovnik, who said prayers for their enemies and bartered their way to freedom?

As you drive through Hercegnovi, you'll sense a greater Turkish, Byzantine presence. This is the meeting place of East and West—of Roman and Byzantine, Catholic and Orthodox, Christian and Muslim. At the narrows at Kamenari you can save time by taking the ferry to Lepetane, but don't—not unless the weather is terrible or you plan to explore the Gulf of Kotor on your drive back to Dubrovnik.

Risan Continue instead around the Gulf to **Risan** (72 km/45 mi from Dubrovnik). Illyrian tribes lived here around 230 BC, when Rome was crossing the Adriatic and colonizing Dalmatia. The story of how the Illyrian widow Teuta took up the standard of her fallen warrior husband against the Roman invaders would wear well on late-night TV, preferably dubbed in English; it would end in the town of Risan, where Teuta plunged into the gulf rather than acknowledge defeat.

Crkvice The road that climbs over a 1,037-m (3,400-ft) pass to **Crkvice** offers breathtaking views of the gulf below. The two small islands are **St. George** (Sveti Juraj) and **Our Lady of the Rocks** (Gospa od Škrpjela). The cypress trees on St. George mark a sailors' burial ground and the ruins of a 12th-century Benedictine monastery. It was this island that inspired Böcklin's painting *The Island of the Dead*, which in turn inspired Rachmaninoff's music of the same name. **Our Lady of the Rocks** was once a reef to which sailors contributed stones for the foundations of a church.

Perast The Gulf of Kotor gave the Adriatic many of its most accomplished seamen, and some of its best came from Perast. Peter the Great sent young Russian noblemen to the naval school founded here in 1698, and they became the nucleus of the Russian navy in the Baltic. There was probably a shipyard here in the early 14th century. In the 18th century, Perast had more than 50 cargo vessels sailing the Adriatic and the coast of Greece.

The town today is overgrown and neglected. Lizards dart through the portals of an unfinished church. Wisteria vines hang over balustrades of Venetian Gothic palaces, and Judas trees grow among the broken stones. It's all deliciously melancholy—and worth a visit.

Kotor This walled medieval city was badly damaged by an earthquake in 1979, but most monuments are once again open to the public. A hidden, inland port that had some 600 ships in the 18th century, it was of great strategic importance to the Venetians, who gave it semi-independence that lasted until it was occupied by Napoleon's forces in 1807. Later it became the base for Austria's Adriatic fleet.

The town has kept its medieval appearance, with churches and patrician mansions from the 12th through the 18th centuries. Most impressive is the 12th-century Romanesque **Cathedral of St. Tryphon** (Sveti Tripun), flanked by two Renaissance towers added after the earthquake of 1667. Two unusual features are the single wide arch that spans the porch between the towers, and the 9th-century doorway taken from a church that stood on the same site. Legend has it that in 890 a ship carrying sacred relics for sale in Europe found shelter here. Having no patron saint, the people of Kotor bought the head of a Byzantine saint named Tryphon, the patron saint of gardeners. His story is told in reliefs carved in the stone canopy (ciborium) over the high altar. The treasury has several bodies' worth of votive legs and arms, and crosses carried in wars against Turks.

Behind the town is a steep flight of steps leading to the **Gospa od Zdravlja Church** (1500), and, farther up, **Fort St. John** (Sveti Ivan). Walk at least partway for a fascinating view of this devastated town.

The Lovćen Pass The mountains above the gulf seem to rise forever: How, you wonder, could a road ever be built there? Yet a road there is— one of the most dramatic in Europe. There's a legend, which I hope is true, that an Austrian engineer built the road in the shape of an *M* in honor of a princess named Marija. The stolid Austrians fired him, of course, for squandering good money.

On top of the plateau are the fertile fields of Njeguši, birthplace of Montenegro's poet/ruler, Petar II. There's a restaurant here famous for its smoked ham and cheese, served with a mixture of wine and beer that you may not want to try more than once.

Cetinje The former capital of Montenegro sits in a fertile valley at the foot of Mount Lovćen. It's a peaceful, unassuming town today, more interesting for its historical associations than for its monuments. The graves of freedom fighters are reminders that Cetinje was the center from which Montenegro organized and waged its battle for independence. When freedom came in 1878, Montenegro was officially recognized as a sovereign state, and Cetinje became its capital—the smallest in Europe. The palace, museum, and banks were all built at the turn of the century.

The railings around the 15th-century **Vlah Church** (Vlaška crkva) were made in 1897 from barrels of 1,550 captured Turkish rifles.

The present monastery, dating from 1785, has a treasury rich in ancient manuscripts, icons, and paintings. Adjoining the monastery is the **Biljarda Palace** (1837–38), where Njegoš lived. Though he died at 38 (he reigned from 1830 to 1850), he was considered the greatest of the Orthodox bishop-princes to rule Montenegro since the 16th century. He was six feet eight, a great poet, and a great billiard player. (The palace is named after the table brought up from the coast by mules.) He knew five foreign languages, and read Shakespeare, French philosophers, and German classical writers in the original. He was a marksman, too, and liked to throw lemons in the air and shoot them, an impressive feat for a bishop.

Colorful Montenegrin costumes are displayed in the palace's **Ethnographic Collection.** A fascinating relief map of the mountainous terrain will show you why no one ever conquered Montenegro.

A good road climbs 25.6 km (16 mi) from Cetinje to the 1,735.4-m (5,785-ft) summit of Mount Lovćen, topped by the **Njegoš Mausoleum.** The bishop-prince built himself a small chapel here, but the Austrians destroyed it during World War I and brought his remains back to Cetinje. After the war he was reinterred in a mausoleum built by the country's most famous sculptor, Ivan Meštrović. Mount Lovćen is the symbol of Montenegrin independence, the beacon of the homeland, and has inspired many heroic poems, including Njegoš's own famous epic, *The Mountain Wreath.* Here's a verse to recite as you're climbing the 461 steps to Njegoš's tomb.

Some Montenegrin chieftains are talking. Drashko, who has just returned from Venice, says,

> Brother, many a handsome man I saw,
> But 10 times more of ugly folk;
> Too ugly much to look upon. . . .
> They like better egg or chicken
> Than sheep's flesh or ball of cheese;
> Untold the quantity of chickens
> That they eat up within a year!
> From this lordly life they die,
> With bellies big and no moustaches,
> Their craniums dusted o'er with powder
> And, like ladies, dangling rings at ear!

When they reach their 30th year,
They get a face like some old hag,
Too ugly are they to be seen;
And even should they climb a stair,
All pale they grow and linen-white,
And something rattles in their throat,
As if had come their dying night!

Budva From Cetinje you'll zigzag down to the coast again, and enjoy breathtaking views along the way. Budva was one of the most attractive walled cities along the coast until it was devastated by an earthquake in 1969. It has been meticulously restored, and it looks as good as old, if not better.

Lodging **Avala.** This hotel was built in 1983 on the site of the Hotel Avala that was destroyed in the 1979 earthquake. Its aggressively modern boxlike design may strike a jarring note, because it is built right up against the restored walls of the lovely old town. *Mogren Obala, tel. 086/41–022. 223 rooms. Facilities: 2 restaurants, several bars, sand beach, indoor and outdoor pools, nightclub, disco, casino, shopping center. AE, DC, MC, V. Expensive.*

Sveti Stefan There's really no reason to come here except to stay in the Sveti Stefan Hotel—but what a splendid way to end your trip!

Lodging **Sveti Stefan.** After World War II, a fortified 15th-century island fishing village was converted into the coast's most luxurious hotel complex and connected to the mainland by a causeway. Eighty stone fishermen's cottages have been turned into beautifully appointed rooms, suites, and apartments to create a fantasy hideaway. If you want to be pampered at least once on your trip, here's the place to do it. Rooms 90 and 93 are particularly lovely—and expensive. With a pool hewn out of solid rock, a terrace bar affording views of sunsets you'll never forget, and true gourmet dining (entrées on the dinner menu include grouper, lobster, venison with médoc sauce, wild boar, and braised hare) in a setting worthy of the great ocean liners of the past, this surely ranks among Europe's most prestigious hotels. *Sveti Stefan, tel. 086/41–411. 118 rooms. Facilities: restaurant, bar, pool. AE, DC, MC, V. Very Expensive.*
Milocer, the former summer residence of the royal family, in a nearby parklike setting with its own beach, is part of the Sveti Stefan operation. It offers elegance (and fine dining) at somewhat lower rates. *Sveti Stefan, tel. 086/41–411. 27 rooms. AE, DC, MC, V. Closed Nov.–Apr. Very Expensive.*

On from Yugoslavia From Sveti Stefan, you have several choices. (1) Return to Dubrovnik and fly home. (2) Return to Dubrovnik and take the car ferry back to Rijeka. (3) Drive to Belgrade and fly home. (4) Drive to Bar, and take the train to Belgrade. Train buffs will love the dramatic 9-hour, 473.6-km (296-mi) train ride, through 154 tunnels and over 234 bridges, including the longest bridge (503 m/550 yd) in Europe.

What to See And Do with Children

Yugoslav teenagers strut every night along the main street of every town. This daily ritual begins in the early evening and can continue to midnight—the later the hour, the younger the crowd. Medieval buildings along the streets are now ice cream parlors, cafés, and discos, where young people do what young people do.

If your kids have a limited tolerance for the past, spend mornings with them, exploring the ancient cities, and then send them back to the beaches and pools. The resort complexes have tennis courts and can arrange for waterskiing, underwater spear fishing, and windsurfing.

Stay in private homes with English-speaking children the same age as yours. If you have young children, find families willing to baby-sit.

Near **Opatija,** visit the Postojna Caves. In **Split,** visit the zoo and aquarium. In **Korčula,** see the sword dance Moreško on Thursdays in summer.

6 Italy

*Pompeii, Capri,
and the Amalfi Coast*

Introduction

The region south and west of Naples offers the traveler an extraordinary variety of landscapes and experiences.

Volcanic ash and mud preserved the Roman towns of Pompeii and Herculaneum almost exactly as they were on the day Vesuvius erupted in AD 79. What you'll see are not just archeological ruins, but living testimony of daily life in the ancient world. You'll walk through the baths and brothels, the bars and bakeries, the sumptuous villas of wealthy patricians and the cramped quarters of the servants. You'll even see the food they ate, the wooden beds they slept in, and the graffiti they wrote on the walls. "Many a calamity has happened in the world," wrote Goethe, "but never one that has caused so much entertainment to posterity as this one."

When the ancients imagined the entrance to hell they had a specific place in mind—Lake Avernus—a silent, lonely spot in the Phlegrean Fields just west of Naples. Here also is the dark vaulted chamber where the Cumaean Sybil rendered her oracles. This was one of the most venerated sites in antiquity; the English writer H. V. Morton calls it the most romantic classical site in Italy today.

The magnificent Amalfi Drive snakes above deep gorges and fantastically shaped rocks. Sparkling white towns cling to the precipitous walls among lemon trees and vineyards. Visitors dine on fresh fish and sleep in rooms overlooking the sea.

Off shore are the islands of Ischia and Capri. The volcanic isle of Ischia offers mineral springs surrounded by tropical gardens and white wine-growing villages. The pleasure island of Capri is famed for its hotels and restaurants, its grottoes, its rich tropical vegetation, and its scenic walks.

On the mainland, south along the coast, lies Paestum. Though unknown to many tourists, Paestum has three magnificent Greek temples—one of them as wonderful in its own way as the Parthenon in Athens.

Highlights

The most spectacular drive in Italy, along the wild, romantic Amalfi coast.

Positano—the most popular town on the Amalfi Drive.

The excavated Roman town of Pompeii—brought back to life as it was almost 2,000 years ago.

The magical island of Capri, with fairy-tale grottoes, comfortable hotels, dozens of first-class seafood restaurants, and dramatic walks high above the sea.

Paestum—site of the Greek Temple of Neptune, a building as memorable as the Parthenon.

The National Museum of Naples, housing the most important collection of classical art in the world.

Before You Go

Government Tourist Offices

In the U.S. Contact the Italian National Tourist Offices at 630 Fifth Ave., Suite 1565, New York, NY 10111, tel. 212/245–4822; 500 N. Michigan Ave., Chicago, IL 60611, tel. 312/644–0990; 360 Post St., Suite 801, San Francisco, CA 94108, tel. 415/392–6206.

In Canada 1 Place Ville Marie, Montreal, Quebec H3B 2E3, tel. 514/866–7667.

In the U.K. 1 Princes St., London W1R 8AY England, tel. 071/408–1254.

When to Go

The main tourist season runs from mid-April to the end of September. The best months for sightseeing are April, May, June, September, and October, when the weather is generally pleasant and not too hot.

If you can avoid it, don't travel at all in Italy in August, when much of the population is on the move. The heat can be oppressive, and vacationing Italians cram roads, trains, and planes.

Currency

The unit of currency in Italy is the lira. There are bills of 100,000, 10,000, 5,000, and 1,000 lire. Coins are 500, 100, and 50 lire. At press time (spring 1990) the exchange rate was about 1,240 lire to the U.S. dollar, 1,040 to the Canadian dollar, and 2,010 to the pound sterling.

Customs

On Arrival Non-European visitors can bring into Italy duty-free: 400 cigarettes or 200 cigarillos or 100 cigars or 500 g (17.5 oz) of tobacco; 1 liter of alcohol or 2 l of wine; 50 g (1.75 oz) of perfume; ¼ l (17.5 oz) of toilet water. European visitors can bring in duty-free: 300 cigarettes or 150 cigarillos or 75 cigars or 400 g (14 oz) of tobacco; 1.5 l (1.75 oz) of alcohol or 3 l (.5 pt) of sparkling wine and 3 l (14 oz) of table wine, and 90 cc of perfume. Officially, 10 rolls of still camera film and 10 reels of movie film may be brought in duty-free. Other items intended for personal use are generally admitted, as long as the quantities are reasonable.

Language

In the main tourist cities, language is no problem. You can always find someone who speaks at least a little English, albeit with a heavy accent; remember that the Italian language is pronounced exactly as it is written (many Italians try to speak English as it is written, with disconcerting results). You may run into a language barrier in the countryside, but a phrase book and close attention to the Italians' astonishing use of pantomime and expressive gestures will go a long way.

Try to master a few phrases for daily use, and familiarize yourself with the terms you'll need to decipher signs and museum labels.

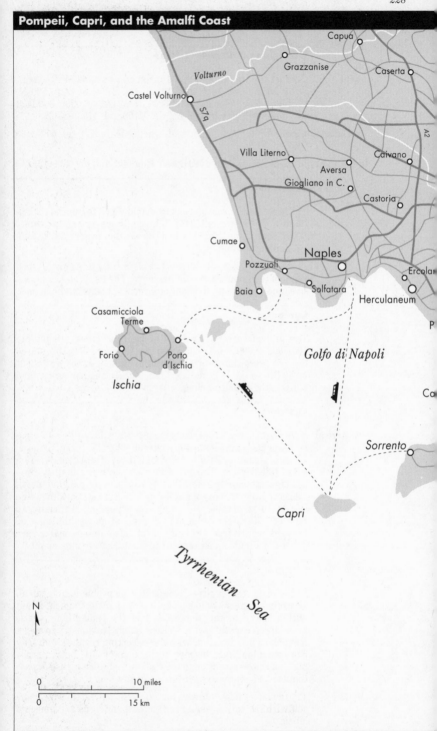

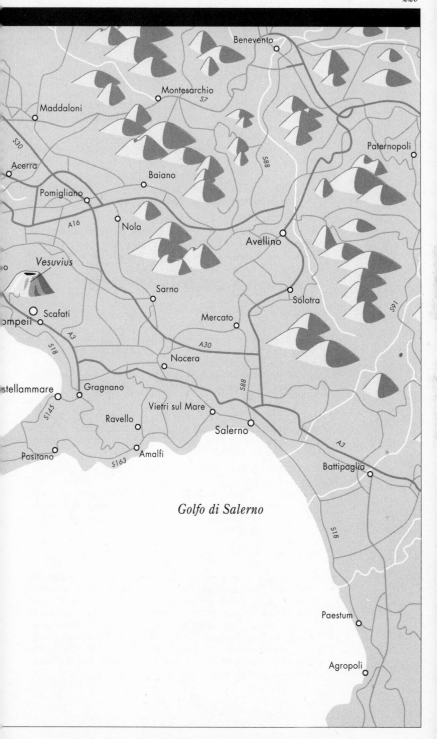

Golfo di Salerno

The exhortation "Va via!" (Go away!) is useful in warding off begging gypsies and the advances of wolfish men.

Reading

H. V. Morton. *A Traveller in Italy* (Dodd, Mead). Witty and intelligent.

Edward Bulwer-Lytton. *The Last Days of Pompeii* (Buccaneer Books). The classic 1834 novel that brings Pompeii to life during its final days.

Michael Grant. *Cities of Vesuvius: Pompeii and Herculaneum* (MacMillan). The best unscholarly introduction to the two cities.

Virgil. *The Aeneid*. Book VI in particular is essential reading for a trip to the Sibyl's Cave and Lake Avernus in the Phlegrean Fields.

Pompeii-Herculaneum: A Guide with Reconstructions. A guide to both sites with plastic overlays that let you see buildings as they are today and as they were before the eruption.

Arriving and Departing

By Plane

There are no direct flights from the States to Naples, where the trip begins. Your best bet is to fly to Rome, which is a three-hour drive or a two-hour train ride from Naples. Three airlines fly nonstop from the United States to Rome: TWA (from New York and Los Angeles), Pan Am (from New York), and Alitalia (from New York).

Alitalia (tel. 01/602–7111) and **British Airways** (tel. 01/897–4000) operate direct flights from London (Heathrow) to Rome and Naples. Flying time is 2½ to 3 hours. There's also one direct flight a day from Manchester to Rome.

Capodichino Airport (tel. 081/780–5763), 8 km (5 mi) east of Naples, serves the Campania region. It handles domestic and international flights, including several flights daily between Naples and Rome (flight time: 45 min). During the summer, **Eliambassador** (tel. 081/789–0644) provides direct helicopter service between Capodichino Airport and Capri.

By Train

If you're traveling by public transportation, take the new express train from the airport to the Ostiense terminal (about 30 minutes), then taxi or subway (Metropolitana) to the Termini train station. There are trains every hour between Rome and Naples. Intercity and Rapido trains make the trip in less than two hours. Trains take either the inland route (through Cassino) or go along the coast (via Formia). Express trains to Naples stop at **Stazione Centrale** (Central Station) on Piazza Garibaldi (tel. 081/264–644).

By Bus

Cital, a Rome-based bus line (tel. 06/327–1347) runs direct, air-conditioned service from Rome to Campania, stopping at Pompeii and Sorrento year-round, and Positano-Amalfi June–mid-September only.

By Car

If you're renting a car, arrange to pick it up at the Rome airport. If you're driving from northern Europe, and the distances seem too great to drive, there's always the Motorail from the channel ports. However, no car/sleeper expresses run beyond Milan.

Italy's main north–south route, heading out of Rome (A2, also known as the Autostrada del Sole), connects the capital with Naples and Campania. In good traffic the ride takes less than three hours.

Getting Around

By Car

If you're driving your own car, save money on gas and tolls by purchasing special coupons from the Italian Auto Club (ACI) at ports and border crossings. The ACI package includes free breakdown service.

To drive in Italy you need both a valid U.S. driver's license with Italian translation, available through your local AAA, and a Green Insurance Card. If you're driving your own car, get the Green Card from your insurance company. If you're renting a car in Europe, make sure the Green Card is in the glove compartment. You're required to have a red warning triangle in your car for use in emergency halts.

Driving is on the right. The speed limit is 130 kph (81 mph) on the autostrada and 90 kph (56 mph) on other roads. Other regulations are largely as in the United States except that police can levy on-the-spot fines—as high as $500.

Driving through Naples is a nightmare. Keep it to an absolute minimum and adopt tight security. Don't keep cameras or purses in sight even when you're in the car, and never leave luggage, even in a locked trunk.

Autostrada A3, a southern continuation of A2 from Rome, runs through Campania and into Calabria, to the south. Take S18 south for Ercolano (Herculaneum), Pompeii, and the Sorrento peninsula; for the Sorrento peninsula and the Amalfi coast, exit at Castellamare di Stabia. To get to Paestum, take A3 to the Battipaglia exit and take the road to Capaccio Scalo/Paestum. All roads on the Sorrento peninsula and Amalfi coast are narrow and tortuous, although they have outstanding views.

By Train

Save money on train tickets by purchasing a **Family Pass** before you leave home. Contact the Italian State Railways. Avoid lines at stations by buying tickets at authorized travel agencies. A network of suburban trains connects Naples with several points of interest. The **Circumflegrea** (tel. 081/55–13–328) runs from the Piazza Montesanto station in Naples to the archaeological zone of Cumae, with three departures in the morning. The **Ferrovia Cumana** (tel. 081/55–13–328) runs from the Piazza Montesanto station to Pozzuoli and Baia. The line used most by visitors is the **Circumvesuviana** (tel. 081/77–92–444), which runs from Corso Garibaldi station and stops at Stazione Centrale before continuing to Ercolano (Herculaneum), Pompeii, and Sorrento. Travel time between Naples and Sorrento on the express train is one hour.

By Bus

There is an extensive network of local buses in Naples and throughout Campania. Buses connect Naples with Caserta in one hour, leaving every 20 minutes from Piazza Porta Capuana (tel. 081/70–05–091).

SITA buses (tel. 081/55–22–2176) for Salerno leave every 30 minutes on weekdays and every two hours on weekends from the SITA terminal on Via Pisanelli, near Piazza Municipio. SITA buses also serve the Amalfi Coast, connecting Sorrento with Salerno.

By Boat

Hydrofoil and passenger- and car-ferries connect the islands of Capri and Ischia with Naples and Pozzuoli. Check ahead, as schedules and connections vary according to season. Boats and hydrofoils for these islands, and also for Sorrento, leave Naples from the **Molo Beverello,** Piazza Municipio, near the Castle Nuovo.

Caremare (tel. 081/55–13–882) has frequent passenger- and car-ferry services, as well as some hydrofoil services. **Alilauro** (tel. 081/684–288) and **SNAV** (tel. 081/660–444) also provide hydrofoil services. In the summer, these lines have a residents-only policy for cars.

Essential Information

Important Addresses and Numbers

Tourist Information The main EPT (regional tourist board) offices for Campania are in **Naples** (Via Partenope 10, tel. 081/406–289; Stazione Centrale, tel. 081/268–779; Stazione Mergellina, tel. 081/76–12–102; and Capodichino Airport, tel. 081/78–05–761). These offices provide information on transportation, accommodations, and cultural events throughout the region. Local tourist offices in Campania are useful for information on festivals, changing opening hours, and maps of towns and villages:

Amalfi (Corso Roma 19, tel. 089/872–619). **Anacapri** (Via G. Orlandi 19/A, tel. 081/83–71–524). **Capri** (Marina Grande pier, tel. 081/83–70–634; Piazza Umberto, tel. 081/83–70–686). **Ischia Porto** (Piazzale Trieste, tel. 081/991–146). **Naples** (Piazza del Gesù, tel. 081/55–23–328; Piazza Garibaldi, mobile unit, no phone; Hydrofoil pier at Mergellina, tel. 081/660–816; Castel dell'Ovo, tel. 081/411–461, summers only). **Paestum** (Temple zone, tel. 0828/811–016). **Pompeii** (Piazza Esedra, near Porta Marina gate, tel. 081/86–10–913). **Positano** (Via Saraceno, tel. 089/875–067). **Ravello** (Piazza Duomo, tel. 089/857–096). **Salerno** (Piazza Amendola 8, tel. 089/224–744). **Sorrento** (Circolo Forestieri, Via de Maio 35, tel. 081/87–82–104).

Emergencies   **Police,** tel. 112. **Motoring,** tel. 116 (Automobile Club of Italy). **Ambulance,** tel. 081/75–20–696. **Doctors and Dentists,** tel. 113.

Consulates   **U.S.:** Piazza della Repubblica, 80122 Naples, tel. 081/76–14–303.**U.K.:** via Francesco Crispi 122, 1-80122 Naples, tel. 081/663–511.

Opening and Closing Times

Banks   Banks are open weekdays 8:30–1:30 and from 3 or 3:30 to 4 or 4:30.

Churches   Churches are usually open from early morning to noon or 12:30, when they close for about two hours or more, opening again in the afternoon until about 7 PM.

Museums   National museums are usually open until 2 and closed on Monday, but there are many exceptions. Other museums have entirely different hours, which may vary according to season. Archaeological sites are usually closed Monday. At all museums and sites, ticket offices close an hour or so before official closing time. Check with the local tourist office for current hours.

Shops   Shops are open, with individual variations, from 9 to 1 and from 3:30 or 4 to 7 or 7:30. They are open from Monday through Saturday, but close a half day during the week; for example, in Rome most shops (except food shops) close Monday morning, or, in July and August, on Saturday afternoon.

Shopping

Leather goods, coral, jewelry, and cameos are some of the best items to buy in Campania. In Naples, where many of the top leather and fashion houses have their factories, you'll find good buys in bags, shoes, and clothing, but it's often wise to make purchases in shops rather than from street vendors. The coastal resorts have maintained some of their traditional crafts, although some shops try to pass off poor-quality machine-made goods as handmade items.

Capri   Prices tend to be high. For trendsetting designer clothes, try **La Parisienne,** on the main square. **Yves Dupris** (Via Canfora) sells men's and women's fashions on opposite sides of the street. For jewelry, go to **La Campanina** (Discesa Quisana 18) or **Angela Puttini** (Via Botteghe 12). For good buys in pottery, try **Sea Gull** (Via Roma 25).

Naples   The **Galleria** is a good introduction to shopping in Naples; a wide variety of retail outlets trade in the four glass-roofed arcades. Other areas and streets are more specialized: The area immediately around **Piazza dei Martiri** is the heart of luxury shopping, with perfume shops, fashion outlets, and quality antiques on display. **Via Roma** and **Via Chiaia** are better bets for bargains.

Positano   The picturesque streets of this coastal resort are lined with boutiques selling trendy casual fashions and beachwear in splashy colors and extravagant fabrics.

Sorrento This is the place to buy embroidered table linen and crocheted lace. Also, the wood-inlay art of intarsia is a centuries-old tradition here. Shops today offer everything from jewelry boxes to trays and coffee tables with intarsia decorations. **Ferdinando Corciano,** in his shop on Via San Francesco, gives demonstrations of his intarsia work, producing decorative plaques with classic or contemporary motifs.

Sports

Sun, sand, and sea combine in this region to offer the visitor a number of sporting options, but be prepared to encounter pollution in some of the beaches nearest Naples (*see* Beaches, below). The top hotels often offer sports facilities such as private beaches, swimming pools, and tennis courts, and many will allow nonresidents to use these facilities: Contact the hotels themselves or the local tourist office.

Fishing For information on licenses and water quality, contact **Federazione Italiana Pesca Sportiva** (Piazza Santa Maria degli Angeli, Naples, tel. 081/41–75–79).

Golf **Afsouth Golf Club** (tel. 082/42–99–20) is a nine-hole course in Pozzuoli, just west of Naples.

Horseback Riding For information on riding contact the **Federazione Italiana Sport Equestri** (Via Ruggieri 12/B, Naples, tel. 081/76–09–379).

Sailing **Nantic Coop** (Piazza Amedeo 15, Naples, tel. 081/41–53–71).

Tennis Most top hotels have courts: Contact them or local tourist boards about use of these courts. The following are public courts.

Naples (Via Giochi del Mediterraneo, tel. 081/76–03–912).

Porto d'Ischia (Lungomare Colombo, tel. 081/99–34–86).

Waterskiing **Sci Nautico Partenopeo** (Lake Averno, Pozzuoli, tel. 081/86–63–526).

Beaches The waters of the Bay of Naples are notoriously polluted. Beaches tend to be pebbly and crowded. Capri and some, but not all, of Ischia's beaches offer clean swimming. Pollution is intermittent along the Amalfi coast, where the deep waters are generally clean. Beaches in the Salerno area are best avoided; the water is cleaner the farther south you go.

Dining

The region is famous for its seafood, particularly shellfish soups and grilled bass. Ask for the fresh fish of the day: *triglie* (red mullet), *spigola* (sea bass), or *tonno* (tuna). Order *vóngda*, (clam), *cózze* (mussel), or other seafood sauces on pasta, which is the other specialty of the region. Pasta comes in all shapes—not just spaghetti, but also ziti, cannelloni, vermicelli. Most everything is served with local tomatoes; meat dishes are often served *alla pizzaiola* (with tomato sauce and garlic). Naples is said to be the birthplace of the pizza, so go ahead and try it. Neapolitan pizza tends to be served lukewarm, with a bit of runny tomato sauce floating on a sea of oil; once I had to pour the oil into a cup and soak up the rest with a napkin.

This is mozzarella (buffalo cheese) country, which puts our own to shame. If it's made of cow's milk, it's called *fior di latte*. Other locally produced cheeses are scamorza and various types of smoked, fresh, or aged provolone.

For wines try Falerno, immortalized by Horace; the red and white Ischia and Capri wines; the wines from the volcanic slopes of Vesuvius—white Lacrima Christi (tears of Christ) with fish; red Gragnano with meat. Ravello (where you'll be staying) also has its own local wines.

For desserts try the famous *sfogliatelle*, a multilayered pastry filled with custard or ricotta. Happiness is a profiterole—a pastry puff filled with custard or whipped cream and topped with hot bittersweet chocolate sauce.

Prices are almost always listed in restaurant windows or just inside the door. Be prepared for a cover charge (*pane e coperto*) for the privilege of sitting down. The additional 15% service charge goes only partially to the waiter, so in finer restaurants be prepared to add another 5% to the tip.

Category	Cost*
Very Expensive	over 85,000 lire
Expensive	60,000–85,000 lire
Moderate	25,000–60,000 lire
Inexpensive	under 25,000 lire

Per person, including house wine, service, and tax.

Lodging

The most attractive rooms overlook the water—some of them (usually upstairs) with full views, and others (downstairs) with partial views. The better the view, as a rule, the higher the price. Ask for rates and then specify what you want.

Rooms even in better hotels tend to be decorated with a confusion of different brightly colored tiles—the more clashing the better. This busy Moorish-Italian look tends to compete with the naturally lush colors of the landscape.

Service charges and taxes are usually included in the rates, but it pays to ask in advance. It's a good idea, too, to check the quoted rates against those listed on the back of your hotel door.

Rooms with showers prevail. If you want a tub, specify when booking.

Category	Cost*
Very Expensive	over 300,000 lire
Expensive	140,000–300,000 lire
Moderate	80,000–140,000 lire
Inexpensive	under 80,000 lire

All prices are for a standard double room for two, including service and 10% VAT (18% for luxury establishments).

The Itinerary

Orientation

The Italian itinerary takes you through a wide range of countryside and atmospheres in a minimum amount of traveling time. At no point are you more than two hours from Naples, yet you'll be exploring Pompeii and climbing to the heights of Vesuvius, dining on terraces above the spectacular Amalfi coast, and visiting fantastic grottoes on the magical Isle of Capri.

The Main Route

3–5 Days   *One to two nights:* Sorrento
Arrive Naples in morning, visit museum, then Pompeii or Herculaneum, and on to Sorrento; visit Vesuvius and Pompeii or Herculaneum.
One to two nights: Capri or Positano
Boat to Capri for tour and overnight; or day tour, return boat to Sorrento or Positano (in summer).
One night: Positano or Ravello
Day trip along the Amalfi Drive; Salerno, Paestum

5–7 Days   *One night:* Naples
Arrive Naples in morning, visit museum, then Vesuvius and Pompeii *or* Herculaneum
One night: Sorrento
Visit Pompeii or Herculaneum, then boat to Capri
One to two nights: Capri
Tour island, then return by boat to Sorrento, and on to Positano
Two nights: Positano or Ravello
Trip along the Amalfi Drive; Salerno, Paestum

7–14 Days   *Two nights:* Naples
Arrive Naples in morning, visit museum, then Vesuvius and Pompeii *or* Herculaneum; visit Pompeii or Herculaneum; day trip to Phlegrean Fields and (in season) on to Pozzuoli for ferry to Ischia (off season, ferry from Naples)
One to two nights: Ischia
Explore, then (in season) boat to Capri (no tourists' cars allowed on Capri in season), or to Naples or Sorrento, then boat to Capri
Three to five nights: Capri
Explore, then boat to Sorrento
Three to four nights: Positano or Ravello
Amalfi Drive; Salerno, Paestum or
Two to three nights: Positano or Ravello
One night: Salerno or Paestum

The 3- to 5- Day Trip

By Car   On the 3- to 5-day trip, you have to decide whether or not to visit Naples. On one hand, it would be easier on the nerves to miss the city altogether. Security is a serious problem here—thieves commonly snatch purses or cameras from pedestrians or even out of cars stopped in traffic. On the other hand, Naples is home of the San Carlo Opera House, and of the National Archaeological Museum, which contains many of the most important discoveries from Pompeii and Herculaneum. A visit to the museum will make your trip to these sites a much more rewarding experience.

If you decide to visit the Archaeological Museum (which I recommend): Take Route A2 from Rome to Naples, check into your hotel, and go directly to the museum.

You still have the afternoon open to visit **Vesuvius** or **Herculaneum** or **Pompeii.** If you can't get to the Herculaneum-Pompeii-Vesuvius area until after 2 PM, save Pompeii for another day, as the excavations take at least a full half day to explore. See Herculaneum instead, which can be toured in about two hours. Spend the night in Sorrento.

If you decide not to visit the Archaeological Museum, take A2 and A3 from Rome directly to Herculaneum, Vesuvius, and Pompeii. It's impossible to do justice to all three in one day, so you'll have to make a choice. I'd vote for Herculaneum for two hours in the morning and Pompeii in the afternoon. If you want more time for Pompeii, follow Route 145 to the resort town of **Sorrento,** where you can spend the night with a room overlooking the Bay of Naples.

On your second day drive or take the bus (which does not run after 2 PM) to the top of Vesuvius (the road to the crater begins near Herculaneum), and then return to complete your tour of Pompeii. Return to Sorrento (off-season) or the Amalfi Drive down to Positano (at Easter or in summer only).

After a night in Sorrento or Positano, leave your car and take the hydrofoil to Capri. After either a day trip or an overnight on Capri, return to Sorrento or Positano and continue east along the Amalfi Drive to Amalfi. Spend a night at Ravello. Continue along the coast to Salerno and Paestum. From Paestum, take A3 back to Naples and Highway A2 back to Rome.

By Public Transportation You'll be arriving at the Stazione Centrale in Naples. To get from Naples to Herculaneum and Vesuvius, take the Circumvesuviana Suburban Railway (tel. 081/77–92–444) from the Corso Garibaldi stop on the lower level of the Stazione Centrale to the Ercolano Station; it's a 40-minute bus ride to the top of Vesuvius. To get to Pompeii from Naples, Herculaneum, or Sorrento, take the same Circumvesuviana Railway. The trip takes less than 30 minutes. To get to the Amalfi Drive (Positano, Amalfi) from Pompeii, take the train to Sorrento, and then a bus along the drive. Buses leave almost every hour. To get to Ravello, which is in the mountains above the drive, you may need to change buses in Amalfi. From Salerno, take the train to Paestum. From Paestum, take the train back to Naples (you may have to change trains in Salerno). From Naples, take the train back to Rome.

The 5- to 7- Day Trip

By Car or Public Transportation This is essentially the same as the 3- to 5-day trip, except that it gives you more time at each destination and includes an optional side trip either to the Phlegrean Fields or to the island of Ischia. For the route through the Phlegrean Fields, see the 7- to 14-day trip below. For the day trip to Ischia, take a hydrofoil or ferry from Naples or Pozzuoli.

The 7- to 14- Day Trip

By Car   As with the 3- to 5-day trip, take A2 south from Rome. You may want to stop en route at Caserta, north of Naples. Check into a Naples hotel, and visit the National Archaeological Museum.

Take A2, then A3 East to Ercolano (Herculaneum), Vesuvius, and Pompeii. Follow directions under the 3- to 5-day trip above for visits to these sights. Then spend a half day visiting the Phlegrean Fields, leaving Naples by the Quattro Giornate Tunnel, then taking Route S7 Quater west toward Pozzuoli. In the Phlegrean Fields, stop at the Solfatara, where sulfurous gases steam from the ground; then continue west to the Sibyl's Cave at Cumae. Visit Lake Avernus, which the ancients considered the gateway to the Underworld, and the baths at Baia, where Julius Caesar, Nero, and other famous Romans had their villas. The excursion should take three to four hours. After touring the Phlegrean Fields, take the ferry to Ischia (in season) from Pozzuoli or the Tangenziale back toward Naples.

Alternatively, visit the Phlegrean Fields first and on succeeding days visit Vesuvius, Herculaneum, and Pompeii. From Pompeii drive south to Castellammare di Stabia and continue on Route 145 south to Sorrento. Take your car with you on the ferry from Sorrento to Ischia. (Direct service, summer only; via Naples, Nov.–Mar.)

Save Capri for later. You can reach Capri from Ischia or from Sorrento or Positano. You won't need a car on Capri off-season; and in-season you're not allowed to have one. If you want to go from Ischia to Capri—doing both islands at once—leave your car on Ischia and pick it up on your way back to Naples or Sorrento.

As on the 3- to 5-day trip, drive from Positano to Ravello. From here, continue along the coast to Salerno and on to Paestum. For a more leisurely pace, spend your last night in either Salerno or Paestum before returning on A3 to Naples and then heading north on Route A2 back to Rome.

By Public Transportation   Hotels and travel agencies in Naples can arrange for you to join scheduled tours to Caserta, the Phlegrean Fields, Herculaneum, Vesuvius, Pompeii, the Amalfi Drive, and Paestum. Here's some help if you want to do it on your own.

To Caserta from Naples: Buses leave from Piazza Porta Capuana in the old city. Look for the bus with a yellow placard; it goes to Caserta via A1 and takes only 30 minutes. Trains are less frequent, leaving from the Stazione Centrale.

To the Phlegrean Fields from Naples: There are two trains, the Ferrovia Dello Stato (Metropolitana), which stops at Pozzuoli and the Solfatara, and the Ferrovia Cumana, which leaves from Piazza Montesanto and stops in Pozzuoli and Baia. The Circumflegrea local railway leaves from Piazza Montesanto and has six departures for Cumae daily, three of them in the morning.

To Herculaneum, Vesuvius, and Pompeii from Naples: See the 3- to 5-day trip above.

To Ischia: Ferries leave from Capri or Sorrento, in season, or Pozzuoli and Naples.

To Capri: Ferries leave in season from Ischia, Naples, Sorrento, Positano, and Amalfi. You go from Positano in season, or from Sorrento year-round.

To the Amalfi Drive (Positano, Amalfi, Ravello, and Salerno) from Naples, Pompeii, or Sorrento: Take the train from Naples or Pompeii to Salerno. From Salerno there are hourly buses along the Amalfi Drive. To reach Ravello, which is up in the mountains, change buses in Amalfi.

From Salerno to Paestum: Infrequent express trains take about 35 minutes; local trains take about 50 minutes. The station at Paestum is in walking distance of the ruins.

From Paestum back to Naples: The train from Paestum to Salerno takes 35 to 50 minutes. Express trains from Salerno to Naples take about 50 minutes; locals take up to 1¾ hours. Naples has several stations; if you're heading back to Rome, take the train to the Central Station (Napoli Centrale), where you can catch the express train back to Rome.

Exploring

Caserta

Visit **Caserta** (29 km/18 mi from Naples), Italy's answer to Versailles, only if you have a special interest in architecture and history or have time to spare. It's off Highway A2, 28.8 km (18 mi) north of Naples, so you may want to stop here on the drive from Rome.

The Baroque furnishings and decorations show you how Bourbon royalty lived in the mid-18th century. The Royal Palace was built by Charles III, the first Bourbon king of Naples, later to wear the crown of Spain. Charles was in his late 30s when he built this Hollywood-style extravaganza, this monument to megalomania, at Caserta. It was here, in what Eisenhower called "a castle near Naples," that the Allied High Command had its headquarters in World War II; and here that German forces in Italy surrendered in April 1945. Most enjoyable are the gardens and parks, particularly the Cascades, where a life-size Diana and her maidens stand waiting to be photographed. *Piazza Carlo III. Admission: royal apartments, 3,000 lire; park, 2,000 lire; minibus, 1,000 lire. Open daily (except national holidays); royal apartments, 9–1:30; park, 9–1 hr before sunset.*

Dining **La Castellana.** Located in Casertavecchia, Caserta's medieval nucleus on the hillside overlooking the modern town, this tavern has atmosphere and hearty local specialties, such as *stringozzi alla castellana* (homemade pasta with a piquant tomato sauce served in individual casseroles) and *agnello alla castellana* (lamb sautéed in red wine). *Via Torre 4, tel. 082/33-71-230. Reservations required on weekends. Dress: casual. AE, DC. Closed Thurs. Moderate.*

Antica Locanda Massa 1848. Near the Reggia, this large, informal restaurant is decorated in browns and white in 19th-century rustic style. In fair weather you eat alfresco under an arbor. The specialties are *linguine al cartoccio* (pasta steamed with fresh tomato and shellfish) and *pazzielli alla borbone* (*gnocchi* with cheese and truffle sauce). *Via Mazzini 55, tel.*

082/33–21–268. Reservations advised. Dress: casual. AE, DC, V. Closed Mon. and Aug. 5–20. Inexpensive.

Naples

Is it the sense of doom, living in the shadow of Vesuvius, that makes the people of **Naples** so volatile, so seemingly blind to everything but the pain and pleasure of the moment? Poverty and overcrowding are the more likely causes; but whatever the reason, Naples is a difficult place for the casual tourist to like. The Committee of Ninety-nine (Napoli 99), formed to counter the city's negative image, has its work cut out. If you have the time, and if you're willing to work at it, you'll come to love Naples as a mother loves her reprobate son; but if you're only passing through and hoping to enjoy a hassle-free vacation, spend as little time here as you can.

John Steinbeck must have had Naples in mind when he called Italian traffic "a deafening, screaming, milling, tire-screeching mess." I came to Naples determined to dismiss its noise, dirt, and confusion as so much local color; but after an hour, standing motionless in a traffic jam while a pride of policemen looked indifferently on, I was ready to search for color elsewhere.

Why visit Naples at all? First, Naples is the most sensible base —particularly if you're traveling by public transportation— from which to explore Pompeii, Herculaneum, Vesuvius, and the Phlegrean Fields. Second, it's home of the National Archaeological Museum. The most important findings at Pompeii and Herculaneum are on display here—everything from sculpture to carbonized fruit—and seeing them will add to the pleasure of your trip to Pompeii and Herculaneum. The museum closes at 2 PM (1 PM Sunday) except in summer, so spend the morning here, and the afternoon visiting either the Phlegrean Fields or Herculaneum and Vesuvius (remembering that the last bus to the volcano is at 2 PM). Spend the night back in Naples— perhaps at an opera or concert at the world-famous San Carlo Opera House—and the following morning set off on your tour of Pompeii.

The **National Archaeological Museum** was designed as a cavalry barracks in the 16th century. The ground floor is devoted to marble sculpture, notably the Farnese Hercules and Farnese Bull. On the mezzanine is a collection of ancient frescoes and mosaics, including *Alexander's Battle*, taken from the floor of the House of the Faun, which you'll see in Pompeii. On the first floor are works from Herculaneum. Don't miss the room with musical and surgical instruments. *Piazza Museo, tel. 081/440–166. Admission: 4,000 lire. Open May–Sept., Mon.–Sat. 9–7:30, Sun. 9–1; Oct.–Apr., Mon.–Sat. 9–2, Sun. 9–1.*

The **San Carlo Opera House** is famous for its near-perfect acoustics and its sumptuous decoration. *Via San Carlo, tel. 081/79–72–370. Box office open weekdays 10–1, 4:30–6:30.*

Dining   **Casanova Grill.** Soft lights and a trendy art deco look set the tone in the Casanova Grill, the Hotel Excelsior's restaurant. The seasonal specialties and antipasti arranged on the buffet will whet your appetite for such traditional Neapolitan dishes as the simple *spaghetti al pomodoro* (with fresh tomato sauce) and the classic *carne alla pizzaiola* (meat with tomato and oregano). *Hotel Excelsior, Via Partenope 48, tel. 081/417–111.*

Reservations advised. Jacket and tie advised in the evening. AE, DC, MC, V. Expensive.

La Fazenda. Overlooking the sea at Marechiaro, in one of the city's most picturesque spots, this restaurant is a favorite for leisurely dining and an invitingly informal atmosphere. The pastas, many with vegetable sauces, are particularly good. The specialty is seafood, but chicken and rabbit *alla cacciatora* (in a tangy sauce) also are good. Desserts are homemade. Note that you must take a taxi to get to La Fazenda. *Calata Marechiaro 58, tel. 081/76–97–420. Reservations advised. Dress: casual. V. Closed Sun. and Aug. 13–29. Expensive.*

La Sacrestia. Popular with Neapolitans because of its location and the quality of its food, La Sacrestia is set on the slopes of the Vomero hill, with marvelous views of the city and bay. The specialties range from appetizing antipasti to *linguine con salsetta segreta* (pasta with a sauce of minutely chopped garden vegetables). Seafood has a place of honor on the menu, and there are interesting meat dishes as well. If you swim clear of fish, the check can stay in the moderate category. *Via Orazio 116, tel. 081/664–186. Reservations advised. Dress: casual. AE, V. Closed Wed., Sun. in July, and all Aug. Expensive.*

Bergantino. This bustling trattoria, located near the central station, is a favorite with business people and is open only for lunch. Courteous and efficient waiters serve a variety of classic Neapolitan dishes, including hearty *maccheroni con ragù* (pasta with meat sauce) or *sartù di riso* (rice casserole with bits of meat and cheese). Anything made with mozzarella is sure to be good here, or order plain mozzarella—it's light and fresh. *Via San Felice 16, tel. 081/310–369. No reservations. Dress: casual. No credit cards. Open lunch only. Closed Sat. and all Aug. Moderate.*

Bersagliera. Most first-time visitors to Naples want to dine once on the Santa Lucia waterfront in the shadow of the medieval Castel dell'Ovo, and this is one of the best places to do so. It's touristy but fun, with an irresistible combination of spaghetti and mandolins. The menu offers uncomplicated classics, such as *spaghetti alla pescatora* (with seafood sauce) and *melanzane alla parmigiana* (eggplant with mozzarella and tomato sauce). *Borgo Marinaro 10, tel. 081/415–692. Reservations advised. Dress: casual. No credit cards. Closed Tues. Moderate.*

Ciro a Santa Brigida. Centrally located off Via Toledo near the Castel Nuovo, Ciro is a straightforward restaurant popular with business travelers, artists, and journalists who are more interested in food than frills. In dining rooms on two levels, customers enjoy classic Neapolitan cuisine. Among the specialties: *sartù di riso* (rice casserole with meat and peas), and *scaloppe all Ciro* (veal with prosciutto and mozzarella). There's pizza, too. *Via Santa Brigida 71, tel. 081/55–24–072. Reservations advised. Dress: casual. No credit cards. Closed Sun. and all Aug. Moderate.*

Dante e Beatrice. A simple trattoria on central Piazza Dante, this popular spot features typical Neapolitan dishes in an unassuming setting. The menu may offer *pasta e fagioli* (very thick bean soup with pasta) and *maccheroni al ragù* (pasta with meat sauce). *Piazza Dante 44, tel. 081/349–905. Reservations advised in the evening. Dress: casual. No credit cards. Closed Wed. and Aug. 24–31. Moderate.*

Don Salvatore. Head just west to the little port of Mergellina to find an unpretentious-looking place known for good local dishes and seafood. *Linguine cosa nostra* (with shellfish) and other pastas with seafood sauces are specialties, and the *fritto misto* (mixed fried fish) is as light as a feather. *Via Mergellina 5, tel. 081/681–817. Dress: casual. Reservations advised. AE, DC, MC, V. Closed Wed. Moderate.*

Lodging

Excelsior. This CIGA hotel is located on the shore drive, with views of the bay from front rooms. The lobby and lounges are lavish, with Oriental carpets and gilt or glass chandeliers. Off the large semicircular lounge are a chic little bar and the Casanova restaurant. Rooms are decorated either in CIGA's standard Empire style (with ormolu trim and soft pastels) or in more typically Neapolitan floral prints. *Via Partenope 48, tel. 081/417–111. 138 rooms with bath or shower. Facilities: restaurant, bar. AE, DC, MC, V. Very Expensive.*

Jolly Ambassador. This hotel occupies the top 12 floors of the only skyscraper on the downtown skyline (if you don't count the new business center beyond the station), and the bedrooms and roof garden-restaurant command sweeping views of Naples and the bay. Decorated in the uninspired but functional style of the Jolly chain, with dark brown and white predominating, it promises comfort and efficiency in a city where these are scarce commodities. *Via Medina 70, tel. 081/416–000. 251 rooms with bath or shower. Facilities: restaurant, bar, garage. AE, DC, MC, V. Expensive.*

Paradiso. Stay here if you want something special a step or two off the beaten track. A modern air-conditioned building perched on the slopes of the hill above the port of Mergellina, the Paradiso is just a few minutes by taxi or funicular from downtown, and it has fabulous views from huge window walls in the lobby and all front rooms. The decor, in tones of blue and beige, is restful and attractive. Be sure to ask for a room with a view; there's no extra charge. There are terraces for sitting, dining, and contemplating the entire bay as far as Vesuvius and beyond. Rates are in the lower level of this category. *Via Catullo 11, tel. 081/660–233. 74 rooms with bath or shower. Facilities: restaurant, bar. AE, DC, MC, V. Expensive.*

Cavour. Located in the rundown Stazione Centrale area, on the square in front of the station and handy to all transportation, including the Circumvesuviana, the Cavour is gradually being renovated and can now offer clean and comfortable rooms. It's especially convenient for those using Naples as a touring base. The hotel's contribution to urban renewal in the area is its elegant street-level restaurant and piano bar. *Piazza Garibaldi 32, tel. 081/283–122. 92 rooms, 70 with bath or shower. Facilities: restaurant. AE, DC, MC, V. Moderate.*

Rex. One of the few inexpensive hotels in Naples that can be recommended, the Rex has a fairly quiet location near the Santa Lucia waterfront. Situated on the first two floors of an Art Nouveau building, it has no elevator; decor ranges from '50s modern to fake period pieces and even some folk art, haphazardly combined. Though it has no restaurant, there are many in the vicinity. *Via Palepoli 12, tel. 081/416–388. 40 rooms, 34 with bath or shower. AE, DC, MC, V. Inexpensive.*

On to Vesuvius, Herculaneum, and Pompeii

If you're going directly from Naples to Ercolano (Herculaneum), take A3 to the Ercolano exit. The ruins of Herculaneum are here, and also the 12.8-km (8-mi) road up the western face of Vesuvius. (There's another road from Pompeii up the south face of Vesuvius, but it's more difficult and requires more walking.)

The road up Vesuvius splits twice. At the first split, a right turn takes you to the observatory. Stay left. At the second split, bear left to a parking area, where you set off on a 30-minute climb up a soft, slippery cinder track.

To drive direct from downtown Naples to Pompeii on A3 takes about an hour. To go by train, take the Circumvesuviana, which leaves from the Corso Garibaldi–Stazione Centrale stop. It's a 30-minute ride to the Pompeii-Villa dei Misteri Station. From here it's only a short walk to the Porta Marina (Sea Gate), the main entrance to Pompeii.

To drive to Pompeii from Herculaneum or Vesuvius, return to A3 and continue east about 11.2 km (7 mi). To go by train, take the Circumvesuviana from the Ercolano Station to the Pompeii-Villa dei Misteri Station.

After touring Pompeii, you can get a train almost every 20 minutes to Sorrento. It's a 30-minute trip. If you're going to return to Pompeii, you can spend the night in Sorrento as an alternative to returning to Naples. From Sorrento, you can catch a boat to Capri or (in season) to Ischia, or begin your trip along the Amalfi Drive.

An Introduction to Vesuvius, Herculaneum, and Pompeii

Lava is extremely fertile. In less than 20 years it sprouts greenery that in time becomes luxuriant vegetation. Memories of former eruptions are forgotten. The rich land attracts farmers, and villages are built. Two such towns, Herculaneum and Pompeii, grew up in the shadow of Vesuvius. On the slopes above the town, oaks and chestnuts grew; below were fig and lemon trees, chestnut forests, vineyards, and the yellow blossoms of the mimosa.

In 80 BC, the Roman General Sulla turned Herculaneum and Pompeii into Roman colonies, where wealthy patricians came to escape the turmoil of city life and relax in the sun. The sea lapped against Herculaneum's walls then, and the citizens were mostly fishermen. Pompeii was a thriving commercial center in a rich agricultural region. Herculaneum and Pompeii were ideal resort towns for overworked Romans seeking a delightful climate and a respite from the frantic pace of everyday Rome.

The towns were laid out on grid patterns, with two main intersecting streets. The wealthiest took a whole block for themselves; those less fortunate built a house and rented out the front rooms, facing the street, as shops. The facades of these houses were relatively plain and seldom hinted at the care and attention lavished on the private rooms within.

When a visitor entered, he passed the shops and entered an open area (atrium). In the back was a receiving room. Behind was another open area called the peristyle, with rows of columns and perhaps a garden with a fountain. Only good friends ever saw this private part of the house, which was surrounded by the bedrooms and the dining area.

How different these homes are from houses today—and how much they say about changing attitudes toward family and society! Today we build homes that face the streets, that look out over the world; in Pompeii and Herculaneum, houses were designed around an inner garden so that families could turn their backs on the world outside. Today we install picture windows that break down visual barriers between ourselves and our neighbors; the people in these Roman towns had few windows, preferring to get their light from the central courtyard—the light within. How pleasant it must have been to come home from the forum or the baths to one's own secluded kingdom with no visual reminders of a life outside one's own.

Not that public life was so intolerable. There were wine shops on almost every corner, and frequent shows at the amphitheater. The public fountains and toilets were fed by huge cisterns connected by lead pipes beneath the sidewalks. Because garbage and rainwater collected in the streets of Pompeii, the sidewalks were raised and huge stepping stones were placed at crossings so pedestrians could keep their feet dry. Herculaneum had better drainage, with an underground sewer that led to the sea.

The ratio of freemen to slaves was about three to two. A small, prosperous family had two or three slaves. As all manual labor was considered degrading, the slaves did housework and cooking, including the cutting of meat, which the family ate with spoons or with their fingers. Everyone loved grapes, but figs were popular, too. Venison, chicken, and pork were the main dishes. Oranges weren't known, but people used quinces (a good source of vitamin C) against scurvy. Bread was made from wheat and barley (rye and oats were unknown) and washed down with wine made from grapes from the slopes of Vesuvius.

The government was considered a democracy, but women, children, gladiators, and Jews couldn't vote. They did, however, express their opinions on election day, as you'll see in campaign graffiti left on public walls.

Some 15,000 graffiti were found in Pompeii and Herculaneum. Many were political announcements—one person recommending another for office, for example, and spelling out his qualifications. Some were bills announcing upcoming events —a play at the theater, a fight among gladiators at the amphitheater. Others were public notices—that wine was on sale, that an apartment would be vacant on the Ides of March. A good many were personal, and give a human dimension to the disaster that not even the sights can equal. Here are a few:

At the Baths: "What is the use of having a Venus if she's made of marble?"

At a hotel: "I've wet my bed. My sin I bare. But why? you ask. No pot was anywhere."

At the entrance to the front lavatory at a private house: "May I always and everywhere be as potent with women as I was here."

"Everyone writes on this wall but me."

"We are as full as wineskins."

"You sell us this watery liquid and drink pure wine yourself."

"Oh, I would rather die than be a god without you."

"Victoria, I greet you, and wherever you are, may your sneeze bring you good luck."

"Lucilla makes money from her lover."

"Virgula to her friend Tertius: Thou art too ugly!"

"Methea loves Chrestus with all her heart. May Venus favor them, and may they ever live in amity."

"Vivius Restitus slept here alone and thought with longing of his Urbana."

In the year AD 63 Vesuvius was considered an extinct volcano. The crater had become a dense forest filled with wild boars. Spartacus and his slaves had lived here during their rebellion against Rome.

An earthquake in that year caused so much destruction that the citizens of Pompeii and Herculaneum considered abandoning their towns and settling elsewhere. Nero was in the 10th year of his reign, and the people had to turn to him for help. What was rebuilt was therefore done in Roman style, which was splendid but not always in the best taste—a definite departure from the noble and simple lines of Greek art. Not that everyone minded or even noticed the difference. With so many wealthy visitors, it was only natural that the people in these provincial towns would imitate the manners of the Roman nobility and look to Rome for the latest styles. The Pompeiian artists mostly reproduced famous Greek paintings, not from inspiration but from memory. There were no allegories—just pleasant, agreeable images, mostly mythological love stories—Jupiter carrying off Europa, Apollo pursuing Daphne, Venus in the arms of Mars. False pilasters were painted in fresco, imitating the example of the rich. Artists worked fast and art became an industry.

August 24, AD 79, was a hot summer day. On the previous day the annual Festival of Vulcan, the Roman fire god, had been celebrated. At both Herculaneum and Pompeii tremors had been felt for four days. Then came the explosion.

The younger Pliny, age 17, was at the house of his uncle, the elder Pliny, at Misenum (which you passed if you drove from Baia to Cumae), when the family's attention was drawn to a cloud of unusual size and appearance. As Pliny reported later in a famous letter to Tacitus*:

It was not clear at that distance from which mountain the cloud was rising (it was afterwards known to be Vesuvius). Its general appearance can best be expressed as being like an umbrella pine, for it rose to a great height on a sort of trunk and then split off into branches. . . . In places it looked white, elsewhere blotched and dirty, according to the amount of soil and ashes carried with it. My uncle's scholarly acumen saw at once that it was important enough for a closer inspection, and he ordered a boat to be made ready, telling me I could come with him if I wished. I replied that I preferred to go on with my studies. . . .

Pliny the elder, both a historian and commander of the naval base at Misenum, was diverted by a note from the wife of a friend, begging him to rescue her husband, whose house was at the foot of Vesuvius. And so he ordered the warships launched with the intention of bringing help to those who were trapped. The letter continues:

---

*The younger Pliny, Letters, VI, 20, 6, 8–9, 16. Trans. B. Radice.

He [steered] his course straight for the danger zone. He was entirely fearless. . . . Ashes were already falling, hotter and thicker as the ships drew near, followed by bits of pumice and blackened stones, charred and cracked by the flames: Then suddenly they were in shallow water, and the shore was blocked by the debris from the mountain. For a moment my uncle wondered whether to turn back, but when the helmsman advised this he refused, telling him that Fortune stood by the courageous. . . .

The wind was in my uncle's favor, and he was able to bring his ship in. He embraced his terrified friend, cheered and encouraged him. . . . Meanwhile, on Mount Vesuvius broad sheets of fire and leaping flames blazed at several points, their bright glare emphasized by the darkness of night. My uncle tried to allay the fears of his companions by repeatedly declaring that these were nothing but bonfires left by peasants in their terror, or else empty houses on fire in districts they had abandoned.

Then he went to rest. . . . By this time the courtyard giving access to his room was full of ashes mixed with pumice stones, so that its level had risen, and if he had stayed in the room any longer he would never have got out. He was awakened, came out and joined [his friend] Pomponianus and the rest of the household. They debated whether to stay indoors or take their chances in the open, for the buildings were now shaking with violent shocks, and seemed to be swaying to and fro as if they were torn from their foundations. Outside, on the other hand, there was the danger of falling pumice stones; however, after comparing the risks, they took the latter. As a protection against falling objects they put pillows on their heads tied down with cloths.

Elsewhere there was daylight by this time, but they were still in darkness, blacker and denser than any ordinary night, which they relieved by lighting torches and various kinds of lamps. My uncle decided to go down to the shore and investigate the possibility of escape by sea, but he found the waves still wild and dangerous. A sheet was spread on the ground for him to lie down on. . . . Then the flames and smell of sulphur which gave warning of the approaching fire drove the others to take flight and roused him to stand up. He stood leaning on two slaves and then suddenly collapsed, I imagine because the dense fumes choked his breathing by blocking his windpipe. . . .

When daylight returned on the sixteenth—two days after the last day he had been seen—his body was found intact and uninjured, still fully clothed and looking more like sleep than death.

This is the oldest-surviving realistic description of a major natural disaster.

The eruption actually began at 1 PM, with flames and a cloud of ashes that whirled with the wind and covered the region in a shroud of darkness. Red-hot boulders were hurled thousands of feet into the air, and rained down on the surrounding countryside. By the following day, Pompeii was covered to a depth of 3.7 m (12 ft) by a sudden fall of ashes, pumice, and stones. Later eruptions buried the town another 1.8 m (6 ft). When excavators uncovered the town, they found 600 bodies in the streets and the bodies of many others who had tried to flee. An estimated 2,000 people—one tenth of the total population—had perished.

What covered Herculaneum was not pumice and ash, but mud. Vesuvius belched forth steam at 1,093°C (2,000°F), which mingled with seawater. Torrents of liquid mud swept down upon the city, leapt the walls, and penetrated into every crevice. Until a few years ago it was believed that most of the estimated 5,000 inhabitants had managed to escape by sea, as few skeletons were found in the city. Excavations at Porta Marina, the gate in the seawall leading to the beach, revealed instead that many perished there. As the mud solidified, it acted as a prop to buildings that otherwise would have collapsed. The pressure from this and subsequent eruptions converted the mud into a compact mass of rock *(tufa)* 18.3–30.5 m (60–100 ft) deep.

So effective was the covering that eggs and fish were found on a dining room table, and in a bakery 81 carbonized loaves were discovered in the half-opened oven. At Herculaneum, the mud scorched papyrus and cloth but did not destroy them. Wood beds, stairs, cupboards—all were saved and are on view today. In one house excavators found the bread, salad, fruit, and cake that were being served for lunch when the catastrophe struck.

In 1864 Giuseppe Fiorelli, in charge of the excavations at Pompeii, had the idea of forcing liquid plaster into the lava molds that had solidified around the fallen bodies. The plaster forms (which you will see) are so true to life, you can see the pubic hair shaved in semicircles to duplicate the look on certain statues, and the tormented expressions on the faces.

The first deaths at Pompeii must have been caused by the huge stones falling from the sky. Some people hid in their homes; others fled. Many who stayed must have suffocated beneath the falling ash, or, like Pliny the elder, been asphyxiated by fumes. Many who fled must have been struck down by falling pillars and masonry.

At the House of Meander at Pompeii the doorkeeper fled to his room with his little girl, and covered their heads with pillows. That's how they were found 1,800 years later. In another house, a mother and daughter escaped through a skylight into a garden. That's where they were found. A woman and her three maids were found with the jewelry and the silver mirror they had squandered time gathering. A man with teeth marks in his flesh was found beside his dog. The Roman sentry at the gate at Herculaneum was found trying to cover his dog with his cloak. Two gladiators with manacled wrists were discovered in the prison cell. More than 60 gladiators were found dead in their barracks; with them was a richly dressed woman: No one will ever know why.

In 1748, when excavators turned over the ashes that for 1,700 years had covered Pompeii, they had one objective: to find masterpieces for the king's museums. Excavations were by chance; if nothing was found, the site was abandoned. Litter was thrown back; frescoes not worthy of the museum were left exposed to the influence of the sun and rain; walls cracked and fell. It was only later, in 1863, that the collection of works of art became secondary to the goal of restoring an ancient Roman city. That is why so much of the priceless art is found today in the National Museum in Naples and not where it belongs, in Pompeii. The situation in Herculaneum was somewhat different. Because the town was buried in solidified mud rather than ash, citizens could not return after the disaster, as many did in Pompeii, to recover possessions. Excavations began much later, so much of the art was left where it was found. Though Herculaneum had only one fourth the population of Pompeii and has only been partially excavated, the things that have been found there are generally better preserved than those discovered at Pompeii.

Herculaneum

The best guide is a small red book called *Pompeii-Herculaneum: A Guide with Reconstructions.* Photos are covered with plastic overlays, so you can see how various sites look both today and 2,000 years ago. I found a copy at the entrance to Pompeii but not at Herculaneum; pick one up in Naples if you can.

If you want a personal guide, make sure he has certification papers (a booklet with his photo and a stamp). Agree beforehand on the length of the tour and the price. Write the figures down.

Whether you're with a guide or not, be sure to have some 500-lire pieces handy to tip the guards who open the locked houses for you.

You could easily get lost in the streets of Pompeii, but not here. Most important buildings can be seen in about two hours. If you feel closer to the past at Herculaneum than at Pompeii, it's in part because there are fewer hawkers here, and visitors tend to show a certain quiet respect for antiquity that's not always evident in such a famous Tourist Spot as Pompeii. Though there's much less to see here, houses are better preserved, with bright frescoes and mosaics. In some cases, you can even see the original wood beams, staircases, and furniture. *Corso Ercolano. Admission: 4,000 lire; children under 12 free. Open daily 9–1 hr before sunset; ticket office closes 2 hrs before sunset.*

The following route will help you locate the most important sights:

The sole entrance is at the east corner. You'll walk halfway around the perimeter of the site and enter on Cardo III. Only three main streets have been excavated: Cardo III, Cardo IV, and Cardo V. The two cross streets are Decumanus Inferior and Decumanus Maximus. As you walk around the excavated site, you can see how it was unearthed like hidden treasure from a pit below the surface of the existing town. Excavations are still going on; the best perhaps is yet to come.

On Cardo III, make the first right, in front of the badly damaged **Casa dell'Albergo,** and turn left on Cardo IV. The first building on the right is the **House of the Mosaic Atrium** (Casa dell'Atrio a mosaico). The atrium (entranceway) is still paved with mosaics. The floors rippled under the weight of the lava. You can still see the wood window frames in the courtyard (peristyle). Don't miss the bedrooms and the large dining room.

Continue up Cardo IV (to the right). On your left is the **Wooden Trellis House** (Casa a Graticcio). This is the only surviving example of the use of trellises to make walls—a money-saving technique used by the Romans for shops and secondary rooms.

Next door is the **House of the Wooden Partition** (Casa del Tramezzo di legno), which has the charred remains of a bed and a well-preserved facade.

Cross Decumanus Inferior. The first house on the right is **Casa Sannitica,** which has a beautiful atrium surrounded by Ionic columns. The house retains the simple plan of the Samnites, the people that lived here before the Romans came.

A few steps farther along, across the street, is the entrance to the **Baths** (Terme), which have separate rooms for men and women. The dressing room has cubicles for clothing. There's a series of chambers that grow progressively hotter, and a sweating room for people with bad livers. Hot air from furnaces circulated in cavities under the floor and through ducts in the walls and ceilings. Soap was reserved for medical treatment or hair dye, but bathers brought their own oils, scrapers, and towels. The baths usually opened at noon, when the furnaces were lit. Many bathers came to these early health and fitness clubs in the evening, after dinner. They sang, bathed, splashed, brawled, got massaged, drank wine, ate pastries and sausages, and sweated off the pressures of the day.

Continue (left) up Cardo IV. Across the street is the **House with Charred Furniture** (Casa del Mobilio carbonizzato), a small, elegant house with an attractive courtyard and the remains of furniture.

Next to it is the **House with the Neptune and Amphitrite Mosaic** (Casa del Mosaico di Nettuno e Anfitrite). The annexed shop is the best-preserved example we have of a Roman shop.

At the end of Cardo IV, turn right on Decumanus Maximus. The first entrance on the right is **Casa del Bicentenario,** so called because it was unearthed in 1938, 200 years after excavations began. The living room has a marble floor and frescoes. In a small upper room (many houses in Herculaneum had two floors) is a small cross in a panel above a wood altar—the oldest evidence of Christianity in the Roman Empire.

Make your first right down Cardo V. Halfway down the street, on the left, is the **Bakery** (Pistrinum), which has two original flour mills, an oven, and bread molds.

Continue down Cardo V and turn left at the first cross street, Decumanus Inferior, for a look at the **Palestra,** the sports center, which has a swimming pool in the shape of a cross.

Return to Cardo V and continue left. On your right is the **House of the Stags** or **Deer** (Casa dei Cervi), one of the most beautiful patrician houses, which has two marble statue groups of stags being assailed by dogs. At the end of Cardo V, outside Porta Marina, the **Suburban Baths** (Terme Suburbane) are elegantly decorated and illuminated by skylights.

Return to Cardo III and make your way back to the entrance.

Vesuvius

You can visit Vesuvius either before or after Herculaneum. The mountain tends to be clearer in the afternoon, though then you must have your own car, as the last bus up the volcano is at 2 PM. If possible, save the mountain till after you've toured the buried city and learned to appreciate the volcano's awesome power. The most important factor is whether the summit is lost in mist—when it is, you'll be lucky to see your hand in front of your face. The volcano is visible from Naples and everywhere else along the Bay of Naples; the best advice is, when you see the summit clearing, head for it. The view then is magnificent, with the curve of the coast and the tiny white houses among the orange and lemon blossoms.

If you decide to take the 30-minute walk, wear your hardiest shoes: It's a steep, relentless climb over pulverized ash and lapilli—definitely not for everyone. If the weather's bad and you've never seen a volcano, it's still worth driving to the parking area, past fields of black twisted lava from the 1944 eruption.

When you think of earlier generations being tougher than we are, imagine Goethe in 1787 making his way to the top hanging on to the belt of a guide.

Pompeii

If your time is limited and you have to choose between Herculaneum and Pompeii, choose Pompeii: The buildings are not as well preserved as at Herculaneum, but the size of the town and the extent of excavations are considerably more impressive. It would be a shame to miss either, however; and as the two towns are so close, there's no reason not to see both. This is one of the few times when it would be preferable to know two things superficially than to know one in somewhat greater depth.

If you want a personal guide, make sure he's registered and that he's standing *inside* the gate. Agree beforehand on the length of the tour and the price.

Many houses will be locked. Ask one of the many guards to open them for you. Be persistent! And have some small change ready if persistence is not enough.

For a self-guided tour, you'll need a map. Most, unfortunately, list only the major streets. The best comes with a useful English guide, *How to Visit Pompeii*, sold at the entrance. Also helpful, particularly for families with children, is the small red guide *Pompeii-Herculaneum: A Guide with Reconstructions*, which includes transparent overlays so you can see the various sites as they looked in AD 79.

You'll be spending many hours negotiating rough paving stones; be sure to wear your most comfortable walking shoes.

The following route will help you locate the most interesting sights:

Enter through **Porta Marina,** so called because it faces the sea. It is near the Pompeii-Villa dei Misteri Circumvesuviana Station.

On your right is the **Antiquarium,** which contains casts of human bodies and a dog.

Past the **Temple of Venus** is the **Basilica,** the law court and the economic center of the city. These oblong buildings ending in a semicircular projection (apse) were the model for early Christian churches, which had a nave (central aisle) and two side aisles separated by rows of columns. Standing in the Basilica

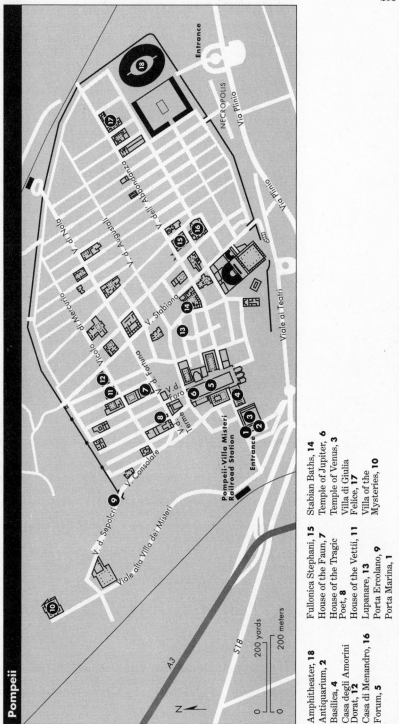

Pompeii

you can recognize the continuity between Roman and Christian architecture.

The Basilica opens onto the **Forum** (Foro), the public meeting place surrounded by temples and public buildings. It was here that elections were held and speeches and official announcements made. America's answer to the forum was the village green. The closest we come to it today is the mall.

Turn left. At the far (northern) end of the forum is the **Temple of Jupiter** (Tempio di Giove). Walk around the right side of the temple, cross the street, and continue north on Via del Foro. On your left a low building houses a cafeteria, coffee bar, souvenir shop, and rest rooms.

The next cross street becomes Via della Fortuna to your right, and Via della Terme to your left. Turn right on Via della Fortuna. On your left is **The House of the Faun** (Casa del Fauno), one of the most impressive examples of a luxurious private house, with wonderful mosaics (originals in the National Museum in Naples).

Retrace your steps along Via della Fortuna to Via del Foro. Cross the street. You're now on Via della Terme. The first entrance on the right is the **House of the Tragic Poet** (Casa del Poeta Tragico). This is a typical middle-class house from the last days of Pompeii. Over the door is a mosaic of a chained dog and the inscription *Cave canem*, "Beware of the dog."

Continue west on Via della Terme to the end. Turn right and bear left along Via Consolate. Pass through the beautiful **Porta Ercolano** (Gate of Herculaneum)—the main gate that led to Herculaneum and Naples.

Now outside of Pompeii, walk down Via dei Sepolcri, lined with tombs and cypresses. The road makes a sharp left. At the four-way crossing, turn right to the **Villa of the Mysteries** (Villa dei Misteri). This patrician's villa contains what some consider the greatest surviving group of paintings from the ancient world, telling the story of a young bride (Ariadne) being initiated into the mysteries of the cult of Dionysus. Bacchus (Dionysus), the god of wine, was popular in a town so devoted to the pleasures of the flesh. But he also represented the triumph of the irrational—of all those mysterious, chthonic forces that no official state religion could fully suppress. The cult of Dionysus, like the cult of the Cumaean Sybil, gave people a sense of control over Fate, and, in its focus on the Other World, helped pave the way for Christianity.

Return along Via dei Sepolcri back into Pompeii. Retrace your steps down Via Consolare, which joins with Vicolo di Narcisco. Make your first left on Vicolo di Mercurio. Six blocks down is Vicolo dei Vettii. Around the corner, to the left, is the **House of the Vettii** (Casa dei Vetti). This is the best example of a rich middle-class merchant's house, with beautifully frescoed walls and a garden.

Return back around the corner to Vicolo di Mercurio. Turn left, the direction you took before you turned the corner to visit the House of the Vettii. Continue east one more block. You've now reached Via Stabiana, one of the two major intersecting streets of the town. Around the corner to the left is **Casa degli Amorini**

Dorati (House of the Gilded Cupids), an elegant, well-preserved home with original marble decorations in the garden.

From the door of Casa degli Amorini Dorati, turn right down Via Stabiana. Your fourth left should put you on Via Augustali. Your first left will take you to the **Lupanare** (the brothel) on Vicolo del Lupanare. An uneaten plate of pasta and beans was found here. On the walls are scenes of erotic games that clients could request. The beds have shoe marks left by visitors.

Continue south on Vicolo del Lupanare. Your first left will put you on Via dell'Abbondanza, the other main street of the old town. The first door on your left is the **Stabian Baths.** It was here that people came in the evening to drown the burdens of the day. The baths were heated by underground furnaces. The heat circulated among the stone pillars supporting the floor, rose through flues in the walls, and escaped through chimneys. Water temperature could be set for cold, lukewarm, and hot. Bathers took a lukewarm bath to prepare themselves for the hot room. A tepid bath came next, and then a plunge into cold water to tone up the skin. A vigorous massage with oil was followed by rest, reading, horseplay, and conversation.

Continue in the same direction, east on Via dell'Abbondanza (a left turn as you leave the baths). Two blocks down on your right is the **Fullonica di Stefanó,** a house converted into workshops for the cleaning of fabrics. All Roman citizens were required to wear togas in public, which weren't exactly easy to keep clean. It's not hard to imagine why there were more toga-cleaners (fullers) in Pompeii than anything else, except perhaps bakers. The cloth was dunked in a tub full of water and chalk, and stamped upon like grapes. Washed, the material was stretched across a wicker cage and exposed to sulfur fumes. The fuller carded it with a long brush, then placed it under a press. The harder the pressing, the whiter and brighter it became.

Go south, completely around the block. Behind the Fullonica di Stefano is the entrance to the **Casa di Menandro,** a patrician's villa with many paintings and mosaics.

Return to Via dell'Abbondanza and turn right. If you've had enough walking, head back to Porta Marina, where your tour began, making a short detour to the left on Via di Stabia to the **Grand Theater** (Teatro Grande) and **Triangular Forum** (Foro Triangolare).

The recommended alternative is to continue east on Via dell'Abbondanza seven blocks to the **Casa di Loreius Tiburtinus,** a large and richly decorated patrician house.

Two blocks farther is the **Villa di Giulia Felice** (House of Julia Felix), which has a large garden with a lovely portico. The wealthy lady living here ran a public bathhouse annex and rented out ground floor rooms as shops—no one knows why.

Turn right past the villa and continue to the **Amphitheater** (Anfiteatro). The games here were between animals, between gladiators, and between animals and gladiators. There were also Olympic Games and chariot races. The crowds rushed in as soon as the gates opened—women and slaves to the bleachers. When the emperor or some other important person was in attendance, exotic animals—lions and tigers, panthers, elephants, and rhinos—were released. At "halftime," birds of prey were set against hares, or dogs against porcupines—the animals tied to either end of a rope so neither could escape. Most gladiators were slaves or prisoners, but a few were Germans or Syrians who enjoyed fighting. Teams of gladiators worked for impresarios, who hired them out to wealthy citizens, many of whom were running for office and hoping that some gory entertainment would buy them some votes. When a gladiator found himself at another's mercy, he extended a pleading hand to the president of the games. If the president turned his thumb up, the gladiator lived; if he turned his thumb down, the gladiator's throat was cut. The arena grew pretty bloody after a night's entertainment and was sprinkled with red powder to camouflage the carnage. The victorious gladiator received money or a ribbon exempting him from further fights. If he was a slave he was often set free. If the people of Pompeii had had trading cards, they would have collected portraits of gladiators; everyone had his favorite. Says one graffito: "Petronius Octavus fought 34 fights and then died, but Severus, a freedman, was victor in 55 fights and still lived; Nasica celebrates 60 victories." Pompeii had a gladiator school (Caserma dei Gladiatori), which you can see behind the Grand Theater on your way back to Porta Marina.

Return to Porta Marina, where your walk began, or exit through the **Ingresso Anfiteatro** and find a cab for the 1.6-km (1-mi) trip back to Porta Marina. You could, of course, begin your trip at Ingresso Anfiteatro, and make the tour in the opposite direction.

From Pompeii return to Naples or head south through Castellammare di Stabia. Continue on Route S145 until it intersects with Route S163. From here continue on to Sorrento on route S145 unless you plan to skip it and go on to Capri from Positano.

The Phlegrean Fields

The **Phlegrean Fields**—the fields of fire—was the name once given to the entire region west of Naples, including the island of Ischia. The whole area floats freely on a mass of molten lava very close to the surface. The fires are still smoldering. Greek and Roman notions of the underworld were not the blind imaginings of a primitive people; they were the creations of poets and writers who stood on this very ground—here in the Phlegrean Fields—and wrote down what they saw. The main sights today are (1) the **Solfatara,** the sunken crater of a volcano, where visitors walk among the sulfurous steam jets and pools of bubbling mud; (2) Italy's third-largest and best-preserved **Amphitheater** at **Pozzuoli;** (3) **Lake Avernus,** which the ancients believed was the entrance to the Underworld; (4) **Baia,** the resort town of ancient Rome, where you can see the remains of a spa frequented by Pompey, Julius Caesar, Nero, and Cicero; and (5) the **Cave of the Cumaean Sibyl,** described by Homer and Virgil.

Whether it's worth the half day it takes to tour these sites really depends on your interests. If you've never seen volcanic activity, don't miss the Solfatara (it's quite safe, so long as you stick to the path). The Amphitheater at Pozzuoli is fascinating because of its well-preserved underground passages and chambers, which give you a good sense of how the wild animals were hoisted up into the arena. At Lake Avernus you'll be standing at the very spot that the ancients considered the entrance to Hades. The ruins at Baia won't mean too much unless you have more than a passing interest in antiquity. The Oracle at Cumae was as famous as the one at Delphi; if you've read *The Aeneid*, you'll want to enter the very cave described in Book VI, where Aeneas sought the Sibyl's aid for his journey to the Underworld.

The **Solfatara.** From Naples, take Route S7 Quater, "Via Domiziana," west toward Pozzuoli. You'll see a sign to the Solfatara on your right, about 2 km (1.3 mi) before Pozzuoli. The only eruption of this semiextinct volcano was in 1198. *Open 9–1 hr before sunset.*

Legends about this smoldering landscape are based on conflicts between the neolithic gods of the soil and the newer Olympian gods brought to Greece by the Achaeans about 1600 BC. One legend tells of how Zeus hurled a 100-headed dragon named Typhon—the pre-Olympian god of volcanoes—down the crater of Epomeo on the island of Ischia; and of how every crater in the Phlegrean Fields is one of Typhon's mouths, flashing steam and fire. In a similar legend pitting old values against new, the sulfurous springs of the Solfatara are said to be the poisonous discharges from the wounds the Titans received in their war with Zeus before he hurled them down to hell. Both legends, of course, are efforts to dramatize man's struggle to overcome the mysterious and dangerous forces of nature.

The **Amphitheater** at **Pozzuoli** is about 2 km (1.3 mi) farther west on S7. It's the third-largest arena in Italy, after the Colosseum and that of Santa Maria Capua Vetere, and could accommodate 40,000 spectators, who were sometimes treated to mock naval battles when the arena was filled with water. *Open 9–1 hr before sunset.*

You may want to make a short side trip to Pozzuoli's harbor and imagine St. Paul landing here in AD 61 en route to Rome. His own ship had been wrecked off Malta, and he was brought here on the *Castor and Pollux*, a grain ship from Alexandria that was carrying corn from Egypt to Italy 18 years before the eruption at Vesuvius.

If time is limited, visit Lake Avernus and Cumae (the Sibyl's Cave) and then return toward Naples on a highway called the Tangenziale. A longer route takes you on a 17.7-km (11-mi) loop from Pozzuoli south to Baia, around Lake Miseno (a volcanic crater believed by the ancients to be the Styx, across which Charon ferried the souls of the dead), and around Lake Fusaro. This 30-minute side trip lets you see the baths at Baia and enjoy some fine views of Pozzuoli Bay and the Phlegrean Fields.

To reach **Lake Avernus** (Lago d'Averno) continue west on S7 toward Cumae and then turn left (south) on the road to Baia. About 1.6 km (1 mi) along this road, turn right and follow signs to Lake Avernus. The best time to visit is at sunset or when the moon is rising. There's a restaurant on the west side, near the tunnel (closed to the public) to Cumae, where you can dine on the terrace. Forested hills rise on three sides; the menacing cone of Monte Nouvo rises on the fourth. The smell of sulfur hangs over this sad, lonely landscape at the very gates of hell. No place evokes Homer, Virgil, and the cult of the Other World better than this silent, mysterious setting.

The ancient city of **Baia** (5.7 km/3.6 mi from Pozzuoli) is now largely under the sea, but it was once the most opulent and fashionable resort area of the Roman Empire. Sulla, Pompey, Julius Caesar, Tiberius, Nero, Cicero—these are some of the men who built their holiday villas here. Petronius's *Satyricon* is a satire on the corruption and intrigue, the wonderful licentiousness of Roman life at Baia. (Petronius was hired to arrange parties and entertainments for Nero, so he was in a position to know.) It was here at Baia that Emperor Claudius built a great villa for his wife Messalina, who spent her nights indulging herself at public brothels; here that Agrippina poisoned her husband and was in turn murdered by her son Nero; here that Cleopatra was staying when Julius Caesar was murdered on the Ides of March. *Open 9–1 hr before sunset; closed Mon.*

Cumae is perhaps the oldest Greek colony in Italy. In the 6th and 7th centuries BC it was the most important settlement in the Phlegrean Fields and in the entire Naples area.

The **Sybil's Cave** (Antro della Sibilla) is here—one of the most venerated sites in antiquity. In the 5th or 6th century BC, the Greeks hollowed the cave from the rock beneath the present ruins of Cumae's acropolis. Visitors walk through a dark, massive stone tunnel that opens into a vaulted chamber where the Sibyl rendered her oracles. Standing here, imagine yourself having an audience with her, her voice echoing off the dark, damp walls. The sense of mystery, of communication with the Invisible, is overwhelming. "This is the most romantic classical site in Italy," writes H. V. Morton. "I would rather come here than to Pompeii." *Open Tues.–Sun. 9–1 hr before sunset. Closed Mon.*

Virgil wrote the epic *The Aeneid*, the story of the Trojan prince Aeneas's wanderings, partly to give Rome the historical legitimacy that Homer had given the Greeks. On his journey, Aeneas had to descend to the Underworld to speak to his father, and, to find his way in, he needed the guidance of the Cumaean Sybil. She told him about the Golden Bough, his ticket through the Stygian swamp to the Underworld.

Virgil did not dream up the Sybil's cave or the entrance to Hades—he must have stood both in her chamber and along the rim of Lake Avernus—as you yourself will stand there. When he wrote, "The way to hell is easy"—*Decensus Averno est facile*—it was because he knew the way. In Book VI of *The Aeneid*, Virgil describes how Aeneas, arriving at Cumae, seeks Apollo's throne (remains of the Temple of Apollo can still be seen) and "the deep hidden abode of the dread Sibyl,/An enormous cave. . . ."

The Sibyl was not necessarily a charlatan; she was a medium, a prophetess, a woman who the ancients believed could communicate with the Other World. The three most famous Sibyls were at Erythrae, Delphi, and Cumae. Foreign governments consulted the Sibyls before mounting campaigns. Wealthy aristocrats came to consult with their dead relatives. Businessmen came to get their dreams interpreted or to seek favorable omens before entering into financial agreements or setting off on journeys. Farmers came to remove curses on their cows. Love potions were a profitable source of revenue; women from Baia lined up for potions to slip into the wine of handsome charioteers who drove up and down the street in their gold-plated, four-horsepower chariots.

With the coming of the Olympian gods, the earlier gods of the soil were discredited or given new roles and names that reflected the change from a matrilineal to a patrilineal society. Ancient rites, such as those surrounding the Cumaean Sybil, were carried out in secret and known as the Mysteries. The Romans tried in vain to replace these Mysteries by deifying the state in the person of its rulers. Yet even the Caesars appealed to forces of the Other World. And until the fourth century AD the Sibyl was consulted by the Christian Bishop of Rome.

From the Phlegrean Fields, take S7 back from Cumae to Pozzuoli, where you can take the boat to Ischia, or toward Naples. If you are going to Naples, less than 3.2 km (2 mi) east of Cumae turn off on the Tangenziale, an expressway that goes along the northern edge of Naples.

Sorrento

Sorrento (27.2 km/17 mi from Pompeii) is a large, attractive tourist town on the Gulf of Sorrento. You can stay here if you need an extra day to tour Pompeii. You may also need to stay here if you're headed for the islands of Ischia or Capri and miss the ferry.

The most interesting historical site is the Gothic-cum-Baroque **Church of St. Francis** (San Francesco), which has an attractive 13th-century cloister. The **Belvedere,** with orange and lemon trees and a terrace with a beautiful view, is behind the **Correale Museum.** The museum features a collection of decorative antiques. *Via Capasso. Admission: 3,000 lire. Open Mar.–Sept., Mon. and Wed.–Sat. 9:30–12:30 and 4–7, Sun. 9:30–12:30; Oct.–Jan., Mon. and Wed.–Sat. 9:30–12:30 and 3–5, Sun. 9:30–12:30; closed Tues. and Feb.*

Dining **Parrucchiano.** Centrally located and popular, this is one of Sorrento's oldest and best restaurants. You walk up a few steps to glassed-in veranda dining rooms filled, like greenhouses, with vines and plants. The menu offers classic local specialties, among them *panzerotti* (pastry shells filled with tomato and mozzarella) and *scaloppe alla sorrentina* (veal with tomato and mozzarella). *Corso Italia 71, tel. 081/878–216. Reservations advised. Dress: casual. AE, V. Closed Wed. (Nov.–May). Moderate.*
Zi'Ntonio. Prices are reasonable at this bright, cheerful restaurant that has the look of a country inn. It's located just off the main square, Piazza Tasso. The specialties are classic *spaghetti al pomodoro* (with fresh tomato sauce and basil) and *melanzane alla parmigiana* (eggplant). *Via De Maio 11, tel. 081/87–81–623. Reservations advised. Dress: casual. AE, DC, MC, V. Closed Thurs. and all Feb. Moderate.*

Lodging **Cocumella.** This hotel is set in a cliff-top garden in a quiet residential area on the edge of Sorrento. Occupying a historic old villa that was a monastery in the 17th century, it has been totally renovated and features a tasteful blend of antique and contemporary decor, with vaulted ceilings and archways, a dining veranda, and stunning tiled floors. It's exclusive and elegant without being stuffy. *Via Cocumella 7, tel. 081/87–82–933. 60 rooms and suites with bath or shower. Facilities: res-*

taurant, bar, garden, pool, tennis court. AE, DC, MC. Expensive.

Excelsior Vittoria. In the heart of Sorrento, but removed from the bustle of the main square, this historic hotel perches on the cliff. It has Art Nouveau decor and some quite grand, though faded, furnishings. Tenor Enrico Caruso's bedroom is preserved as a relic; guest bedrooms are slightly less elegant but spacious and comfortable. The views are wonderful. *Piazza Tasso 34, tel. 081/87–81–900. 125 rooms and suites with bath. Facilities: restaurant, bar, pool, garden. AE, DC, MC, V. Expensive.*

Bellevue Syrene. A palatial villa in a garden overlooking the sea, the Bellevue has solid, old-fashioned comforts and plenty of charm, with Victorian nooks and alcoves, antique paintings, and worn oriental rugs. Rooms are pleasant, with good views. *Piazza della Vittoria 5, tel. 081/87–81–024. 50 rooms, most with bath. Facilities: restaurant, bar, garden, pool. AE, DC, MC, V. Moderate.*

Eden. In a quiet but central location, the Eden has a garden and bright but undistinguished bedrooms. The lounge and lobby have more character. Some smaller rooms are in the inexpensive category. *Via Correale 25, tel. 081/87–81–909. 60 rooms with bath. Facilities: restaurant, garden, pool. AE, V. Closed Nov.–Feb. Moderate.*

Ischia

Ischia takes time to cast its spell. Give Ischia a week and you'll probably grow attached to its special character, its hidden corners and familiar views. An overnight stay is probably not long enough for the island to get into your blood. It does have its share of white, wine-growing villages beneath the lush volcanic slopes of Monte Epomeo; and it does enjoy a life of its own that survives when tourists head back home. But there are few signs of antiquity here; the architecture is unremarkable; the beaches are small and pebbly; there's little shopping.

Ischia is volcanic in origin. From its hidden reservoir of seething molten matter come the thermal springs said to cure whatever ails you. As early as 1580 a doctor named Iosolini published a book about the mineral wells on Ischia. "If your eyebrows fall off," he wrote, "go and try the baths at Piaggia Romano. Are you unhappy about your complexion? You will find the cure in the waters of Santa Maria del Popolo. Are you deaf? Then go to Bagno d'Ulmitello. If you know anyone who is getting bald, anyone who suffers from elephantiasis, or another whose wife yearns for a child, take the three of them immediately to the Bagno di Vitara; they will bless you."

Today the island is covered with thermal baths surrounded by tropical gardens—if you've never been to one before, don't miss the opportunity. The most picturesque part of Ischia today is the port (**Ischia Porto**), with its small shops and charming seafront restaurants. If you're coming for the day, your best bet is to recapture your youth at one of the mineral baths such as Poseidon Gardens and then lose it at a harborfront restaurant in Forio or Ischia Porto.

Ischia also has some lovely hotel-resorts high in the hills, offering therapeutic programs and rooms with breathtaking views of the sea. If you want to plunk down in the sun for a few days

and tune out the world, this is an ideal place to go—
remembering that you're unlikely to find many Americans to
talk with.

It's a 33.6-km (21-mi), two-hour drive around the island from
Ischia Porto. Poseidon Gardens and the port of **Forio** are on the
opposite side. Take the southern route and you'll come to
Fontana, the start of an invigorating one-hour climb to the top
of **Mount Epomeo,** a huge volcano that last erupted in 1302.

Poseidon Gardens (south of Forio on the west coast) is a complex
of thermal pools, waterfalls, limestone cliffs, and tropical vegetation. There's also a cafeteria and changing rooms. You can sit
like a Roman senator on a stone chair recessed in the rock and
let the hot water cascade over you. All very campy—and fun.
Baths, such as those on the north coast, at **Lacco Ameno** and
Casamicciola, are more formal and reputed to be highly therapeutic.

Near the port is the **Castello,** which looks the way a fort is supposed to look. It was built by Alphonso V of Aragon in 1450. A
sunset stroll in front of the castle, overlooking the Bay of Naples, is a treat.

Dining **Padrone del Mare.** On the seafront, it has a pizzeria on the
street level, a restaurant upstairs, and a terrace for outdoor
dining overlooking the sea. Its specialty is *zuppa di pesce* (thick
fish soup/stew served not in a soup bowl but on a plate). *Via
Circumvallazione 4, tel. 081/986-159. Reservations advised.
No credit cards. Closed Tues. and Nov. 15–Feb. 15. Expensive.*
Purticiullo. This rustic restaurant is on the port at Ischia. *Via
Porto 42, tel. 081/992-917. Reservations advised. AE, DC,
MC, V. Open Mar.–Nov., July–mid-Sept. evenings only. Ex-
pensive.*
San Montano Hotel. The terrace is a peaceful setting for lunch.
*Lacco Ameno, tel. 081/994-033. Reservations advised. AE,
DC, MC, V. Expensive.*
La Bussola. On the harbor at Forio, La Bussola has a large, rus-
tic indoor dining room with a fireplace, as well as outdoor
dining on a terrace. Its specialties include fettuccine alla
bussola (with zucchini, prosciutto, onions, and cream), linguine
all' aragosta (with lobster), and charcoal-grilled meat and fish.
*Via Marina 36, Forio, tel. 081/998-464. Reservations not nec-
essary. AE, DC, MC, V. Closed mid-Nov.–late Mar.
Moderate.*
Gennaro. This small family restaurant on the seafront at the
port where the boats from the mainland dock serves excellent
fish. *Via Porto 66, tel. 081/992-917. Reservations advised
weekends and July–Aug. AE, DC, MC, V. Closed Nov.–mid-
Mar. and Tues., Mar., Apr., and Oct. Moderate.*
La Romantica has a terrace for outdoor dining. Seafood specialties include spaghetti *con vongole* (with clam sauce) and
alla marinara (with seafood and tomato sauce). *Via Marina
46, Forio, tel. 081/997-345. Reservations not necessary. AE,
DC, MC, V. Closed Wed. Oct.–Apr. Moderate.*

Lodging **Grand Hotel Punta Molino.** Right in the town of Ischia, but set
in a quiet zone near the sea and framed with pine trees and gardens, is one of the best hotels on the island. Decor is bright and
contemporary, with some luxury touches, and many rooms
have sea views. There's a heated pool on one of the terraces.
Half-board is required. *Lungomare Telese, tel. 081/991-544. 88*

rooms with bath or shower. Facilities: spa treatments, garden, outdoor pool. AE, DC. Closed Nov.–Apr. 24. Expensive.

Regina Palace. Located near the beach of Ischia Porto is the Regina Palace. Entirely renovated in 1987–88, it has an elegant art deco look, with pink-toned wood the keynote. Almost all bedrooms have terraces or balconies overlooking the grounds, on which there's a large pool. *Via E. Cortese 18, tel. 081/991–344. 60 rooms with bath or shower. Facilities: restaurant, garden, outdoor pool, tennis courts, spa treatments, parking. AE, V. Closed Nov. 16–Dec. 19, Jan. 11–Mar. 15. Moderate.*

Villarosa. You'll find this welcoming hotel in the heart of Ischia Porto and only a short walk from the beach. It is a gracious family-run villa with bright and airy rooms. There's a heated pool in the villa garden. Half-board is required, and you must reserve well in advance. *Via Giacinto Gigante 3, tel. 081/991–316. 37 rooms with bath or shower. Facilities: restaurant for hotel guests only, garden, outdoor pool. No credit cards. Closed Nov.–Mar. 19. Moderate.*

Capri

The summer scene on Capri calls to mind the stampeding of bulls through the narrow street of Pamplona: If you can visit in the spring or fall, do. Yet even the crowds are not enough to destroy Capri's very special charm. The town is a Moorish opera set of shiny white houses, tiny squares, and narrow, medieval alleyways hung with flowers. You need to take a funicular to reach the town, which rests on top of rugged limestone cliffs, hundreds of feet above the sea.

The mood is modish but somehow unspoiled. The summer set is made up of smart, wealthy types and college kids. The upper crust bakes in the sun in private villas. The secret is for you, too, to disappear while the day-trippers take over—offering yourself to the sun at your hotel pool, or exploring the hidden corners of the island. Even in the height of summer you can enjoy a degree of privacy on one of the many paved paths that wind around the island hundreds of feet above the sea—if you're willing to walk, you can be as alone here as you've ever wanted to be.

The Blue Grotto (La Grotta Azzurra) is renowned, but there are other, lesser-known grottoes to explore at leisure on boat trips around the island. You can also make a day trip to the nearby island of Ischia. When you've seen enough and tanned enough, it's time to go shopping in some trendsetting boutiques or succumb to Capri's cafés, where you'll be watching everything but your waist. As for dinner—there are enough fine restaurants that you can try a different one each night.

In his book *Italian Holiday*, Ludwig Bemelmans offers an entertaining way to picture Capri. Turn a coffee cup upside down, he says, and next to it invert an oversized cup with a chipped lip. Put a matchbox between them and drape a green handkerchief on top. This is the island of Capri, about 6.4 km (4 mi) by 3.2 km (2 mi). The small cup is Mount Tiberio at 328.7 m (1,096 ft); the large cup, Mount Solaro at 576 m (1,920 ft). The matchbox is the saddle between them. On the saddle is the town of Capri. Lean a match against the matchbox—that's the funicular from the harbor (Marina Grande) to town. Put two pieces of limp spaghetti on the other side of the matchbox: These are the roads leading down to the smaller port and beach at Marina Piccola. A strand of spaghetti from the matchbox to the larger cup is the road to the town of Anacapri. Another strand from the matchbox to the top of the smaller cup is the path to Villa Jove, where the Roman Emperor Tiberius spent his declining years. The chip in the cup is, of course, the Blue Grotto.

The boat will disgorge you in a north coast settlement called **Marina Grande.** Here you'll find a few medium-priced restaurants, the tourist information office, boats to the Blue Grotto, and the funicular to the town of Capri. If you're staying at one of the larger hotels, a representative will be at the harbor to take your bags. To reach the upper town, take the funicular, minibus, or cab (expensive!). The funicular lines can be long; if you're coming for the day, it helps to be the first off the boat.

The funicular lets you off at the Piazzetta (Piazza Umberto I), which was probably here when Emperor Tiberius was living on the island in the first century. This open-air drawing room is surrounded by the medieval quarter of the town.

Time Out	Just down Via Roma from the piazzetta is **Verginiello** (tel. 081/83–70–994), one of the island's best-value restaurants for lunch. Try the calamari (squid).

There are three spectacular walks.

From the main square of Capri, follow either Via Longano or Via Le Botteghe to the crossroads. Take Via Matromania to the **Natural Arch,** a remarkable phenomenon of geological erosion. Then descend the nearby steps to the **Grotto of Matromania,** a natural cave that was transformed by the ancient Romans into a nymphaeum (a shrine and resting place adorned with a fountain, plants and statues). From here, continue down the steps leading to the **Terrace of Tragara.** Here you'll enjoy views of the famous Faraglioni, rocky islets carved into fantastic shapes by the sea. (The best time to see the Faraglioni is in the early evening light.) Follow the picturesque Via Tragara amidst sumptuous villas and flowering gardens back to the town center. The walk takes about 90 minutes round-trip.

From Capri's central plaza, follow either Via Longano or Via Le Botteghe until you reach a crossroad. Take the road to the left that passes by the little **Church of San Michele.** In 45 minutes you'll reach the summit of **Mount Tiberio** and the ruins of the **Villa Jovis.** This was the largest and most sumptuous of Emperor Tiberius's many villas on Capri. You can imagine him sitting here with Caligula on his 92-m (300-ft) front porch, planning an orgy in one of the grottoes or watching for imaginary enemies approaching by sea. *Via Tiberio. Admission: 2,000 lire. Open daily 9–1 hr before sunset.*

Via Krupp takes you below the beautiful **Augustus Gardens** (Parco Augusto) to the port and beach of **Marina Piccola.** Stop for a drink or pastry here, and then take the 10-minute bus ride back to Capri.

An excursion to the **Blue Grotto** (a 45-minute trip from Marina Grande) is something you have to submit to, if only to have an opinion about one of the most celebrated tourist attractions in the world. The boat ride can be rough; if you have a weak stomach, sit in the back looking forward, rather than on one of the side seats. You can also reach the grotto by cab from Anacapri, but it would be a shame to miss the 10-minute boat ride beneath the towering cliffs. At the entrance to the grotto you'll step from your 14-passenger motorboat (expect to get a bit wet) into a tiny rowboat and duck low as you pass through the narrow entrance of the cave on a surge of the sea. The cliff wall doesn't extend to the bottom of the sea, so the sun's rays are refracted about a yard below the surface and indirectly illuminate the cavern from underneath. It's difficult to feel much wonder when it's paid for with a ticket and called for on demand—when in under three minutes you're spewed back out into the world again, among the fleets of boats bobbing at the entrance, waiting for their turn—but it's worth seeing what all the fuss is about and imagining how wonderful the experience might have been if only you had had this beauty to yourself. *Cost, including 2,000-lire admission to the grotto: 12,800 lire. Daily 9:30–2 hr before sunset; departures less frequent in winter months.*

To make this wish (almost) come true, rent a boat that follows *your* schedule and visit the less frequented green, yellow, pink, and white grottoes around the island. The trip around the island takes 90 to 120 minutes by motorboat. *Round-island boat: at Marina Grande, cost, 13,750 lire.*

Dining **La Pigna.** Ensconced in a glassed-in veranda and offering outdoor dining in a garden shaded by lemon trees, the Pigna is among Capri's favorite restaurants. The specialties are a house-produced wine, *linguine alla Mediterranea* (pasta with herbs), and *aragósta alla luna caprese* (lobster). The cordial host organizes party evenings with feasts of seasonal specialties and seafood. *Via Roma 30, tel. 081/83–70–280. Reservations required in the evening. Dress: casual. AE, DC, MC, V. Closed Tues. Expensive.*

La Capannina. La Capannina is only a few steps from the busy social hub of the Piazzetta. It has a vine-draped veranda for dining outdoors by candlelight in a garden setting. The specialties, aside from an authentic Capri wine with the house label, are homemade *ravioli alla caprese* (with a cheese filling, tomato sauce, and basil) and regional dishes. *Via delle Botteghe 14, tel. 081/83–70–732. Reservations required in the evening. Dress: casual. AE, V. Closed Wed. (except Aug.) and Nov. 10–Mar. 15. Moderate–Expensive.*

Al Grottino. This small and friendly family-run restaurant, which is handy to the Piazzetta, has arched ceilings and lots of atmosphere; autographed photos of celebrity customers cover the walls. House specialties are *gnocchi* (dumplings) with tomato sauce and mozzarella, and *linguine ai gamberetti* (pasta with shrimp and tomato sauce). *Via Longano 27, tel. 081/83–70–584. Reservations required in the evening. Dress: casual. AE, DC, MC, V. Closed Tues. and Nov. 3–Mar. 20. Moderate.*

Lodging **Quisisana.** Catering largely to Americans, this is the most luxurious and traditional hotel in the center of town. Spacious rooms are done in traditional or contemporary decor with some antique accents; many have arcaded balconies with views of the sea or the charming enclosed garden, in which there's a pool. The bar and restaurant are casually elegant. *Via Camerelle 2, tel. 081/83–70–788. 143 rooms with bath or shower. Facilities: restaurant, bar, garden, pool. AE, DC, MC, V. Closed Nov.–Mar. Very Expensive.*

Scalinatella. The name means "little stairway," and that's how this charming but modern small hotel is built, on terraces following the slope of the hill, overlooking the gardens, pool, and sea. Bedrooms are intimate, with alcoves and fresh, bright colors. The hotel has a small bar, but no restaurant. Ask for a room high up. *Via Tragara 8, tel. 081/83–70–633. 28 rooms with bath or shower. Facilities: pool. No credit cards. Closed Nov.–Mar. 14. Expensive.*

Villa Brunella. This quiet family-run gem nestles in a garden setting just below the lane leading to the Faraglioni. Comfortable and tastefully furnished, the hotel also has spectacular views and a terrace restaurant known for good food. *Via Tragara 24, tel. 081/83–70–279. 19 rooms with bath. Facilities: restaurant (tel. 081/83–70–122; reservations required for nonguests; moderate), pool. AE, DC, V. Closed Nov. 6–Mar. 18. Moderate–Expensive.*

Villa Sarah. This quiet, family-run hotel, located about 10 minutes from the center of town, is on the path leading to Tiberius's Villa Jovis. The facility is a Capri-style villa with a pretty garden and nice views. Rooms are bright, though simply furnished. *Via Tiberio 3/a, tel. 081/83–77–817. 20 rooms with bath or shower. Facilities: bar. AE. Closed Nov.–Mar. Moderate.*

Florida. In the heart of downtown Capri off Via Fuorlovado, this modern building overlooks its own small garden and those of nearby hotels. Rooms are cheery and functional; those on upper floors have views and many have balconies. It's booked way ahead by regulars in season, so reservations are essential. *Via Fuorlovado 34, tel. 081/83–70–710. 19 rooms, most with bath or shower. AE, DC, MC, V. Closed Nov.–Mar. Inexpensive.*

Villa Krupp. Among the hotels that are open all year, this historic hostelry is a good choice. In a quiet location above the Gardens of Augustus, it has marvelous views. Bedrooms are ample; some have a balcony. *Via Matteotti 12, tel. 081/83–70–362. 12 rooms with bath. Facilities: garden. No credit cards. Inexpensive.*

Anacapri **Anacapri** (about 4 km/2 ½ mi from Capri) has little to offer the casual visitor, so it's difficult to understand why one would choose to stay there; but the ride along the corniche road, gouged from the edge of the cliff, is spectacular. From Anacapri, take the chairlift to the top of **Mount Solaro** for panoramic views. Small buses run on schedule from Capri to Anacapri. If you have to catch an afternoon boat back to the mainland, leave plenty of time; lines both in Anacapri for the bus back to Capri and in Capri for the funicular back down to the harbor can be a good 30 minutes long in season. Most people wait for the return bus at the main square in Anacapri; to make sure you get on the bus, walk away from the square to an earlier stop. From the bus terminal in Anacapri follow Via San Michele to the **Villa San Michele,** which was built for a Swedish doctor who lived here until 1910. No cars are allowed from April 1 to October 31.

Lodging **Europa Palace Hotel.** A modern resort atmosphere prevails at this large Mediterranean-style hotel set in lovely gardens. Each of four junior suites has a private pool and terrace. Bedrooms are tastefully decorated in contemporary style, with white predominating; marble is featured in the bathrooms, and many rooms have balconies. *Via Capodimonte 2/b, tel. 081/83–70–955. 103 rooms with bath. Facilities: pool, garden, restaurant (moderate), AE, DC, MC, V. Closed Nov.–Mar. Expensive.*

San Michele. Surrounded by luxuriant gardens, the San Michele offers solid comfort and good value along with spectacular views. The decor is contemporary, with some Neapolitan period pieces adding atmosphere. Most rooms have terraces or balconies overlooking either the sea or island landscapes. *Via G. Orlandi 5, tel. 081/83–71–427. 60 rooms with bath or shower. Facilities: 2 restaurants, garden, tennis courts, outdoor pool. AE, DC, MC, V. Closed Nov.–Mar. 24. Inexpensive–Moderate.*

The Amalfi Drive

This is the most romantic drive in Italy. The road is gouged from the side of rocky cliffs plunging down into the sea. Small boats lie in quiet coves like so many brightly colored fish. Erosion has contorted the rocks into mythological shapes and hollowed out fairy grottoes where the air is turquoise, and the water, an icy blue. White villages, dripping with flowers, nestle in coves or climb like vines up the steep, terraced hills. The road must have 1,000 turns, each with a different view, on its dizzying, 69-km (43-mi) journey from Sorrento to Salerno.

Positano   The most popular town along the drive, particularly among Americans, is **Positano** (27.2 km/17 mi from Sorrento), a village of white Moorish-type houses clinging dramatically to slopes around a small sheltered bay. When John Steinbeck lived here in 1953, he wrote that it was difficult to consider tourism an industry because "there are not enough [tourists]." Alas, Positano has since been discovered. The artists came first, and, as happens wherever artists go, the wealthy followed and the artists fled. What Steinbeck wrote, however, still applies:

Positano bites deep. It is a dream place that isn't quite real when you are there and becomes beckoningly real after you have gone. Its houses climb a hill so steep it would be a cliff except that stairs are cut in it. I believe that whereas most house foundations are vertical, in Positano they are horizontal. The small curving bay of unbelievably blue and green water laps gently on a beach of small pebbles. There is only one narrow street and it does not come down to the water. Everything else is stairs, some of them as steep as ladders. You do not walk to visit a friend, you either climb or slide.

In the 10th century Positano was part of the Amalfi maritime republic, which rivaled Venice as an important mercantile power. Another heyday was in the 16th and 17th centuries, when its ships traded in the Near and Middle East, carrying spices, silks, and precious woods. The coming of the steamship in the mid-19th century led to the town's decline, and some three-fourths of the town's 8,000 citizens emigrated to America, mostly to New York. One major job of Positano's mayor has been to find space in the overcrowded cemetery for New York Positanesi who want to spend eternity here.

What had been reduced to a forgotten fishing village is now the number one attraction on the coast, with hotels for every budget, charming restaurants, and dozens of boutiques. From here you can take hydrofoils to Capri in season, escorted bus rides to Ravello, and tours of the Emerald Grotto near the town of Amalfi.

If you're staying in Positano, your hotel may have a parking area; if not you will have to pay for space in an open-air garage. If you're here only for the day, a parking place in summer is almost impossible to find. If you are day-tripping, get to Positano early enough to find space in a garage. No matter how much time you spend in Positano, make sure you have some comfortable walking shoes—no heels, please!—and be aware that you will have to negotiate steps.

Do you see the three islands offshore? They're called **Li Galli** (The Cocks). The local king wanted a castle quick, legend says, and a sorcerer agreed to build one in three days if the king would give him all the roosters in Positano. (The sorcerer had a passion for fowl.) The king ordered them all slaughtered and sent to the sorcerer, but the young daughter of a fisherman hid her rooster under her bed. At dawn the rooster did what a rooster does. The workmen, flying by with rocks for the castle, realized that the king had broken his contract and dropped their loads into the sea.

Positano may not have a castle, but it does have another attraction that brings the town considerable wealth: extravagantly styled summer clothes. From January to March buyers from all over the world come to Positano to buy the trendsetting resort clothes that are sold in more than 50 boutiques. One size, loose-fitting cotton dresses; full skirts, plain or covered with lace—some in light pastel colors with handprinted designs, others in bold block colors: bright oranges, pinks, and yellows—the choice is endless, and the prices—well, you're on vacation, and the same dresses would cost twice as much in New York or Rome.

Because the streets are narrow and winding, and many hotels are accessible only on foot, make sure you get explicit directions on how to reach your hotel. The tourist office is little help because it's down near the beach and inaccessible by car.

The town rises up on either side of a cove. Most shops and restaurants are near the beach on the east side (the side away from Sorrento), where you'll find both the domed Parish Church and Le Sirenuse Hotel. Le Sirenuse is in an ideal location: high enough for breezes and dramatic views, yet close enough to restaurants and shops. There are other, less expensive hotels in the same vicinity.

Dining **Buca di Bacco.** After an apertif at the town's most famous and fashionable café downstairs, you dine on a veranda overlooking the beach. The specialties include *spaghetti alle vongole* (with clam sauce) and *grigliata mista* (mixed grilled seafood). *Via Rampa Teglia 8, tel. 089/875–699. Reservations advised in the evening. Dress: casual. AE, DC, MC, V. Closed Nov. 6–Mar. 31. Moderate.*

Capurale. Among the popular restaurants on the beach promenade, this one has the best food and lowest prices. Tables are set under vines on a breezy sidewalk in the summer, upstairs and indoors in winter. *Spaghetti con melanzane* (with eggplant) and *crepes al formaggio* (cheese-filled crepes) are among the specialties. *Via Marina, tel. 089/875–374. Reservations advised for outdoor tables and weekends off-season. Dress: casual. No credit cards. Closed Dec. 16–Mar. Moderate.*

Lodging **Il San Pietro.** Spreading across a rocky ledge outside of town, the spacious Il San Pietro is an elevator ride down from the road (there's a shuttle service to town and back. Decor is tasteful, with fabrics that complement, rather than fight against, the bright colors of the landscape. Nature intrudes everywhere: in the pitchers of wild purple orchids; in the bougainvillea spilling over the terraces and balconies; in the roses and hibiscus growing through the windows and spreading over the lounge and dining-room ceilings. *Amalfi Coast Rd., 84017, tel. 089/875–455. 55 rooms with bath or shower. Facilities: restaurant, 2 bars, pool, private beach and dock, hotel boat, tennis court, garden, parking. AE, DC, MC, V. Closed Nov. 3–Mar. Very Expensive.*

Le Sireneuse. Older and somewhat smaller than Il San Pietro, Le Sireneuse is a converted 18th-century villa with seven floors both above and below the road. Located in town, it appeals to a younger, snappier clientele. Rooms have panoramic views from balconies and terraces, and top-floor suites have Jacuzzis. *Via Cristoforo Colombo 30, tel. 089/875–066. 58 rooms with bath or shower. Facilities: restaurant, bar, heated pool, parking. AE, DC, MC, V. Very Expensive.*

Casa Albertina. One of the few hotels here that is open all year, Casa Albertina is a pleasant place with a friendly owner-manager. Rooms are bright with color, some have views, and you can enjoy the panorama from the terrace, where you can have breakfast or drinks in fair weather. It's a few steps up from one of the town's social hubs, the Bar De Martino. There's no restaurant, and rates are low in its category. *Via Tavolozza 4, tel. 089/875–143. 21 rooms with bath or shower. AE, DC, MC, V. Moderate.*

Palazzo Murat. The location is perfect—in the heart of town, near the beachside promenade, but set in a quiet walled garden. The old wing is a historic palazzo with tall windows and wrought-iron balconies; the new wing is a whitewashed Mediterranean building with arches and terraces. You can relax in antique-accented lounges or in the charming vine-draped patio, and because there's no restaurant you will avoid the half-board requirement applied in most hotels here in high season. *Via dei Mulini, tel. 089/875–177. 28 rooms with bath or shower. Facilities: bar, garden. No credit cards. Closed Oct. 16–Mar. Moderate.*

On to Amalfi Because you're heading directly east from Positano to Amalfi, it's best to drive in the afternoon, when the sun is behind you.

Drive past the towns of **Véttica Maggiore** and **Praiano.** The 4.8-km (3-mi) stretch of the Amalfi Drive between Praiano and the Emerald Grotto is the most dramatic. The road passes the gorge of Furore, where abandoned fishermen's houses cling to the cliff above a tiny beach. Wild vegetation sprouts in the crevices and clambers up the sides. A path goes up one side of the gorge, which you'll see after you pass through two tunnels after Praiano. (Trails along the Amalfi Drive are indicated on a tourist map—carta turistical—called "Penisola Sorrentina, Costiera Amalfitana," which is sold in tourist shops in Positano and Amalfi.)

The Emerald Grotto About 4.8 km (3 mi) farther along is the **Emerald Grotto** (Grotta dello Smeraldo). An elevator takes you down to a rocky terrace. A small rowboat takes you around a cave with stalactites and an underwater Nativity scene. With tourists lined up to Do The Grotto, it's not easy to experience the awe the first visitors must have felt; but the luminescent, emerald-colored water is still magical, and a trip is worthwhile just to be able to enter into the argument over whether the Emerald Grotto is more beautiful than the Blue Grotto on Capri. You can also reach the Emerald Grotto by boat from Amalfi or from Positano in season.

Amalfi
Amalfi (12.8 km/8 mi) from Positano) is your third choice after Positano and Ravello as a town to stay at along the drive. It would have to be a distant third, however, because of the congestion caused by tour buses, which make Amalfi the main stopping point on their excursions. The town is romantically situated at the mouth of a deep gorge and has some quality hotels and restaurants. It's also a convenient base for excursions to the Emerald Grotto and to Ravello.

During the Middle Ages Amalfi was an independent maritime state—a little Republic of Venice—with a population of 50,000. The ship compass—trivia fans will be pleased to know—was invented here in 1302.

The main historical attraction is the **Duomo** (Cathedral of St. Andrew), which shows an interesting mix of Moorish and early Gothic influences. The interior is a 10th-century Romanesque skeleton in an 18th-century Baroque dress. The transept (the transverse arms) and the choir are 13th century. The handsome 12th-century campanile (bell tower) has identical Gothic cupolas (domes) at each corner. Don't miss the beautiful late-13th-century Moorish cloister, with its slender double columns. At least one critic has called the cathedral's facade the ugliest piece of serious architecture in Italy—decide for yourself. The same critic snickers at the tourists who fail to note the cathedral's greatest treasure, the 11th-century bronze doors from Constantinople.

The parking problem here is almost as bad as in Positano. The small lot on the waterfront fills quickly.

Time Out
On the main piazza, facing the fountain, **Panza** is Amalfi's best bakery, offering pastries, candies, and jumbo *sfogliatelle* (cream- or preserves-filled pastry dusted with confectioners' sugar) fresh from the oven.

If the sea is calm, you can take a boat back along the coast to the Emerald Grotto.

The main street leads back through town from the cathedral to the mountains and passes a ceramic workshop and some water-driven paper mills where handcrafted paper is made and sold.

Dining
La Caravella. You'll find this welcoming establishment tucked away under some arches lining the coast road, next to the medieval Arsenal, where Amalfi's mighty fleet once was provisioned. La Caravella has a nondescript entrance but pleasant interior decorated in a medley of colors and paintings of Old Amalfi. It's small and intimate; specialties include *scialatelli* (homemade pasta with shellfish sauce) and *pesce al limone* (fresh fish with lemon sauce). *Via M. Camera 12, tel. 089/871–029. Reservations advised. Dress: casual. AE, MC, V. Closed Tues. and last 2 wks in Feb. Moderate.*

Lodging
Santa Caterina. A large mansion perched above terraced and flowered hillsides on the coast road just outside Amalfi proper, the Santa Caterina is one of the best hotels on the entire coast,

offering gracious living in a wonderfully scenic setting. Rooms are tastefully decorated; most have small terraces or balconies with great views. There are lovely lounges and terraces for relaxing, and an elevator whisks guests to the seaside saltwater pool, bar, and swimming area. On grounds lush with lemon and orange groves, there are two romantic villa annexes. Some rooms and suites are in the luxury category. *Strada Amalfitana, tel. 089/871–012. 54 rooms with bath. Facilities: restaurant, bar, pool, swimming area, beach bar, parking. AE, DC, MC, V. Expensive.*

Hotel Dei Cavalieri. This terraced white Mediterranean-style hotel on the main road outside Amalfi has three villa annexes in grounds just across the road that extend all the way to a beach below. Bedrooms are air-conditioned and functionally furnished, with splashy majolica tile floors contributing a bright note throughout. An ample buffet breakfast is served, and, though half-board is mandatory during high season, you can dine either at the hotel or at several restaurants in Amalfi by special arrangement. *Via M. Comite 26, tel. 089/831–333. 70 rooms with bath. Facilities: restaurant, bar, beach (via stairs), parking, garage, minibus service into town. AE, DC, MC, V. Moderate.*

Miramalfi. A modern building perched above the sea, the Miramalfi has wonderful views, simple but attractive decor, terraces, pool, and sunning/swimming area on the sea, as well as a quiet location just below the coast road, only a half mile from the center of town. Many rooms boast balconies with sea views. *Via Quasimodo 3, tel. 089/871–588. 48 rooms, most with bath or shower. Facilities: restaurant, garden, parking. AE, DC, MC, V. Inexpensive–Moderate.*

Atrani A few minutes past Amalfi is the less-known but impressively situated town of **Atrani,** which is just waiting to be discovered. The valley here is narrower than at Amalfi, and its flanks steeper.

The **parish church** is worth a visit.

Porcelain and ceramics are sold in Atrani and in nearby towns along the Amalfi Drive. Among the mass-produced turnpikeware are some lovely, simple, hand-painted plates, vases, pillboxes, and the like.

Just past Atrani is the road winding up the mountain to Ravello. The road heads east, paralleling the coast, then switches back. As it turns again and climbs up the valley, there's a turnoff that ends in a trail climbing 305 m (1,000 ft) up to Ravello. It's a walk you might want to make going down. Both walk and drive take you up the spectacular Dragon Valley (Valle del Dragone), which is planted with vines, fruit trees, and olives, and offers a breathtaking view of Atrani and the Amalfi coast.

Ravello Envy Gore Vidal for living here in what André Gide calls "a town closer to the sky than to the shore." Because **Ravello** (4.8 km/3 mi from Amalfi) is a long, steep drive above the sea, tour buses are discouraged and crowds are less overwhelming than at Positano and Amalfi. By early afternoon the day-trippers have departed and Ravello becomes one of the most reposeful settings in the world.

Not that Ravello is everyone's glass of chianti: There's very little to do here except walk through peaceful gardens, admire the view, and exist. Those who need a more active life, with shops and restaurants, should avoid the rarefied air and stick to Positano. But after so much traveling, you may welcome this excuse to come to a complete stop.

There are two estates to visit, Villa Cimbrone and Villa Rufolo. Don't miss either, but particularly don't miss Villa Cimbrone.

Villa Cimbrone is a scenic 15-minute walk from the main square. The cloister to the left of the entrance looks medieval but was built in 1917. The unusual crypt was finished in 1913. What make the villa so memorable are its peaceful gardens, with small secluded grottoes and temples hundreds of feet above the sea. The Viale dell'Immensita, a long, straight avenue flanked by oleanders, leads to a belvedere with an unforgettable view of the coast. Few places lend themselves so thoroughly to contemplation. Most construction was carried out in the early 20th century by the former valet of a British lord. Was the mood of melancholy merely a pose that suited a classical garden? In the Belvedere of Mercury, the god faces away from the view as though tired of running; and on the bench is a quote from D. H. Lawrence:

Lost to a world in which I crave no part,
I sit alone and commune with my heart,
Pleased with my little corner of the earth,
Glad that I came, not sorry to depart.

Under the cupola of the little temple of Bacchus are verses by Catullus, which say, in translation, "What is sweeter than to return home free of care, and, tired of toiling for others, to repose in one's own bed?" *Off Piazza Vescovado, by way of Via San Francisco, Via San Chiara, and Via Cimbrione. Admission: 3,500 lire. Open daily 9–1, 3–1 hr before sunset.*

Villa Rufolo is a crumbling 11th-century palace that has a famous Moorish cloister, ancient trees, and a belvedere with a fantastic view. In 1880, while working on *Parsifal*, Richard Wagner stayed at the Villa Palumbo in Ravello, and on a morning walk he visited Villa Rufolo. In the hotel register he wrote, "The magic garden of Klingsor has been found: May 26, 1880." It's fitting that this beautiful garden-terrace has become the site of summer concerts dedicated to Wagner. *Off Piazza Vescovad. Admission: 2,000 lire. Open daily 9–1, 3–1 hr before sunset.*

The 13th-century **cathedral** (Duomo di San Pantaleone) was redone five centuries later in Baroque dress and has a notable late-13th-century Byzantine pulpit decorated with fantastic beasts and resting on a pride of marble lions.

Dining **Cumpa Cosimo.** This family-run restaurant a few steps from the cathedral square offers a cordial welcome in three simple but attractive dining rooms. There's no view, but the food is excellent. Among the specialties are cheese crepes and roast lamb or kid. *Via Roma 44, tel. 089/957–156. Reservations advised on weekends and summer evenings. Dress: casual. AE, DC, MC, V. Closed Mon. (Nov.–Mar). Inexpensive.*

Lodging **Palumbo.** Occupying a 12th-century patrician palace furnished with antiques and endowed with modern comforts, this hotel has a warm atmosphere that gives you the feeling of being a guest in a private home, under the personal care of Swiss host Signore Vuilleumier. Rooms are conversation pieces—a bit cramped for the price but marked by character and good taste. *Palazzo Confalone, tel. 089/857–244. 20 rooms with bath or shower. Facilities: restaurant, bar, garden. No credit cards. Very Expensive.*

Belvedere Caruso. Charmingly old-fashioned, spacious, and comfortable, this rambling villa hotel has plenty of character and a full share of Ravello's spectacular views from its terraces and balconied rooms. The restaurant is known for fine food and locally produced house wine. Rates are low in the category. *Via Toro 52, tel. 089/857–111. 26 rooms with bath or shower. Facilities: restaurant, garden. AE, DC, MC, V. Closed Feb. Moderate.*

Villa Maria. This family-run pension is set in a pretty garden, where you can enjoy a drink or dine under the trees. Rooms are simple but homey, and the atmosphere is restful. *Via Santa Chiara, tel. 089/857–170. 7 rooms, some with bath or shower. Facilities: restaurant, bar, garden. AE, DC, MC, V. Inexpensive.*

Salerno

The Amalfi Drive ends at Salerno (32 km/20 mi from Ravello). There's no overwhelming reason to stay here except to get an early start to Paestum the next morning or to catch a morning train back to Naples. Worth seeing before you leave are the **cathedral** and the Via dei Mercanti, a picturesque old street with shops selling jewelry and other gift items at less-than-tourist-area prices. Drive along the harborfront, past the port. When you see a wide, grassy seafront promenade on your right, park. Via dei Mercanti is a few blocks in from the promenade, depending on where you park. The cathedral won't be more than 15 minutes away. Built in 1085 and remodeled in the 18th century, it has an unusual Moorish atrium, beautiful Byzantine doors (1099) from Constantinople, outstanding 12th- and 13th-century pulpits, and a crypt bright with multicolored marble inlays and frescoes.

Lodging **Plaza.** A dignified old building conveniently located opposite the train station, the Plaza has been entirely renovated for comfort and efficiency without losing its character. Rooms are quiet, with functional modular furnishings and bright new white-tiled baths; bedrooms and the small lounges and bar are well maintained, with a fresh, clean look. The management is friendly and helpful. *Piazza Ferrovia, tel. 089/224–477. 42 rooms with bath or shower. Facilities: air-conditioning on request. AE, DC, MC, V. Inexpensive–Moderate.*

On to Paestum Trains run several times daily from Salerno to Paestum. Buses leave about every hour. To drive, take the road along the Salerno harbor and continue south to Paestum.

Paestum

For most visitors, a trip to **Paestum** (40 km/25 mi from Salerno) is justified by three classical temples: the Basilica, the Temple of Ceres (Tempio di Cerere) and, above all, the Temple of Neptune (Tempio di Netuno). If a building like the Parthenon does nothing for you, don't waste your time here. But if you can be moved by the harmony and proportion of Greek architecture, Paestum may be the highlight of your trip.

You probably won't need more than an hour or two. On one side of the main street are the souvenir shops and a museum. On the other are three of the largest and best-preserved Greek temples in the world—surely the greatest Greek buildings in Italy—two of them older than the Parthenon.

The temples were originally part of a sacred area within a Greek colony founded about 600 BC by the people of Sybaris, which is located on the opposite (eastern) coast of Italy. The Sybarites didn't like the loss of revenues from ships sailing from Greece and Asia Minor through the Straits of Messina (between Sicily and the toe of Italy), so they convinced merchants to unload goods at Sybaris and send them overland to the new town of Paestum, rather than make the dangerous trip through the straits. Eventually Sybaris was razed in a war among competing political parties. Paestum became a Roman colony in 273 BC. The opening of the Via Appia from Rome to Brindisi in about 22 BC spelled the end of Paestum as an important port. Its harbor gradually silted up and inhabitants succumbed to malaria from the marshes. An 11th-century visitor found the town deserted. Malarial marshes and thick forests hid the temples until road builders came upon them in the 18th century. In the 19th century, only a few foreigners bothered traveling south of Pompeii; one of them was the poet Shelley. When a train station was built, the station-master was given gloves and veils against the mosquitoes (no problem today).

The English writer H. V. Morton points out that the **Temple of Neptune** has "a primitive grandeur that recalls the Great Hall of Karnak rather than the lighter constructions of classical Greece." It may be ruder, less perfect than the Parthenon, but it has a raw, almost animal power that the Parthenon lacks. What makes the Temple of Neptune so extraordinary is its blend of brutal strength and constraint; of defiance and grace. And there it sits, this 2,400-year-old temple, among the grasses in a forgotten field. It was called the Temple of Neptune (the Roman name for Poseidon) by some 17th-century visitors because the town was named Poseidonia before it became a Roman colony; but the temple was in fact dedicated to Hera (Juno).

The Temple of Ceres, which was originally dedicated to Athena (Minerva), dates from the end of the 6th century BC. The **Basilica** (so called by some 18th-century archaeologists who thought it was a secular building) is the oldest of the three temples, dating back to the mid-6th century BC. Like the Temple of Neptune, it was dedicated to Hera. Like all Greek temples, it faces east because it is from the east that the sun (the first god of all ancient peoples) rises daily. The **museum** (museo) contains bronze vases, unique 5th-century BC paintings, and decorated stone slabs from a nearby cemetery depicting details of daily life in the 4th century BC. *Admission: 3,000 lire (ticket also valid for museum). Open Tues.–Sun. 9–1 hr before sunset.*

Dining and Lodging **Martini.** Directly across the road from the Porta della Giustizia and only a few steps from the temples, the Martini has 30 cottage-type rooms, each with minibar, in a garden setting and a pleasant restaurant serving local specialties and seafood. *Zona Archeologica, tel. 081/811–020. 30 rooms with bath or shower. Facilities: restaurant (reservations advised; dress: casual), beach 1 km (½ mi) away. AE, DC, V. Inexpensive.*

On to Naples   If you're driving from **Paestum** to **Naples,** take Route SS18 north to Battipaglia and pick up Highway A3 toward Naples. Turn off on Highway A2 back to Rome. If you're taking the train, there's daily service from Paestum to Naples, with a change in Salerno.

What to See and Do with Children

Capri: the Blue Grotto, the hotel pools, the walk to the Natural Arch, the cable car from Anacapri, the 960 steps from Anacapri back down to the harbor.

Pompeii: the casts of bodies and animals exhibited in the Antiquarium. (The more children read beforehand about Pompeii, the more interested they will be.)

The Amalfi Drive: the Emerald Grotto, the hotel tennis courts and pools, the crowded, pebbly beaches, the Italian ices and pizza.

7 France

The Riviera

Introduction

In the popular imagination, the Riviera is a golden stretch of beach along the southern coast of France. Life here is a dialogue of sun and flesh, where nothing is meant to be built, just to be burned up. That's one Riviera—but there's another, a few miles inland, where fortified medieval towns are perched on mountaintops, high above the sea.

It's impossible to be bored along the Riviera. You can try a different beach or restaurant every day. When you've had enough sun, you can visit pottery towns like Vallauris, where Picasso worked; or perfumeries at Grasse, where three-quarters of the world's essences are produced. You can drive along dizzying gorges, one almost as deep as the Grand Canyon. You can disco or gamble the night away in Monte Carlo, and shop for the best Paris has to offer, right in Cannes or Nice. Only minutes from the beaches are some of the world's most famous museums of modern art, featuring the work of Fernand Léger, Henri Matisse, Pablo Picasso, Pierre Auguste Renoir, Marc Chagall—all the artists who were captivated by the light and color of the Côte d'Azur.

The myths have changed, but not the beauty or the sybaritic pleasures. You can go in search of them, or stand still and let them find you. The Riviera will always know where you are.

Highlights

The fabulous casino at Monte Carlo. The colorful old town of Nice. Lavish festivals at Cannes. The beach scene at Saint-Tropez. And everywhere, the luminescent light and brilliant sunshine of the Côte d'Azur.

Historic churches and castles, modern art museums, fortified medieval hill towns where dedicated artists work and sell their wares.

A bouillabaise of first-class restaurants, offering the best in classic, nouvelle, and Provençal cuisine.

Hotels for every taste and budget—from friendly, family-run pensions to some of the most palatial resorts in the world.

Before You Go

Government Tourist Offices

Contact the French Government Tourist Offices for information on all aspects of travel to and in France.

In the U.S. 610 Fifth Ave., New York, NY 10020, tel. 212/315–0888; 645 N. Michigan Ave., Chicago, IL 60611, tel. 312/337–6301; 2305 Cedar Springs Rd., Dallas, TX 75201, tel. 214/720–4010; 9401 Wilshire Blvd., Beverly Hills, CA 90212, tel. 213/271–6665; 1 Hallidie Plaza, Suite 250, San Francisco, CA 94102, tel. 415/986–4174.

Contact the Monaco Tourist and Convention Bureau (845 Third Ave., New York, NY 10022, tel. 212/759–5227) for information on Monte Carlo.

In Canada 1981 McGill College, Suite 490, Montreal, Quebec H3A 2W9, tel. 514/288–4264; 1 Dundas St. W, Suite 2405, Box 8, Toronto, Ontario M5G 1Z3, tel. 416/593–4723.

In the U.K. 178 Piccadilly, London W1V OAL England, tel. 071/491–7622.

When to Go

On the whole June and September are the best months to be in France, because both are free of the mid-summer crowds. June offers the advantage of long daylight hours, while slightly cheaper prices and frequent Indian summers (often lasting well into October) make September an attractive proposition. Anytime between March and November will offer you a good chance to soak up the sun on the Riviera, though, of course, you'll tan quicker between June and September.

Special Events

January: Monte Carlo Auto Rally.
February: Nice Carnival, for two weeks before Shrove Tuesday.
May: Cannes Film Festival, Monaco Grand Prix motor race.
June: Nice Festival of Sacred Music.
July: Monaco: classical concerts in the palace courtyard.
August: Menton Music Festival.

Currency

The units of currency in France are the franc (fr.) and the centime. The bills are 500, 200, 100, 50, and 20 francs. Coins are 10, 5, 2, and 1 francs, and 50, 20, 10, and 5 centimes. At press time (spring 1990), the exchange rate was about 5 francs to the U.S. dollar, 4.90 to the Canadian dollar, and 9.40 to the pound sterling.

Customs

Travelers from the United States and Canada may bring into France 400 cigarettes or 100 cigars or 100 g (3.5 oz) of tobacco, 1 l (1 q) of liquor of 22% volume and 2 l (2 q) of wine, 0.50 l (1 pt) of perfume and 0.25 l (½ pt) of toilet water, and other goods to the value of 300 frs.

Adults traveling from the United Kingdom may bring into France 300 cigarettes or 150 cigarillos or 75 cigars or 400 g (14 oz) of tobacco; 1.5 l (1 q) of liquor over 22% volume or 3 l (3 q) of liquor under 22% volume or 3 l (3 q) of still wine; 0.9 l (1.8 pt) of perfume and 0.375 l (.7 pt) of toilet water; plus other goods to the value of 2,400 frs.

Language

The French study English for a minimum of four years at school (often longer) but to little general effect. English is widely understood in major tourist areas, however, and, no matter what the area, there should be at least one person in most hotels who can explain things to you, if necessary. Be courteous and patient and speak slowly: The French, after all, have plenty of other tourists and are not dependent for income on English-

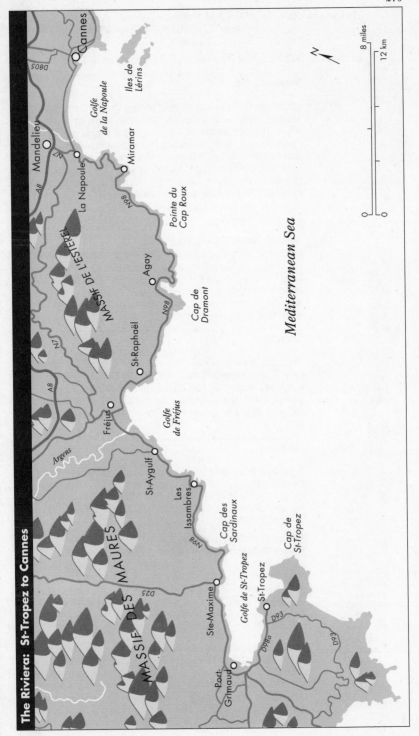

The Riviera: St-Tropez to Cannes

Cannes

D805

Golfe
de la Napoule

Iles de
Lérins

Mandelieu

A8

N7

La Napoule

Miramar

N98

MASSIF DE L'ESTEREL

Pointe du
Cap Roux

Agay

N98

St-Raphaël

Cap de
Dramont

A8

N7

Fréjus

St-Aygulf

Golfe de Fréjus

Argens

Les
Issambres

N98

Cap des
Sardinaux

Mediterranean Sea

MASSIF

DES

MAURES

D25

Ste-Maxime

Golfe de St-Tropez

Cap de
St-Tropez

St-Tropez

Port-
Grimaud

D98a

D93

D93

N

8 miles

12 km

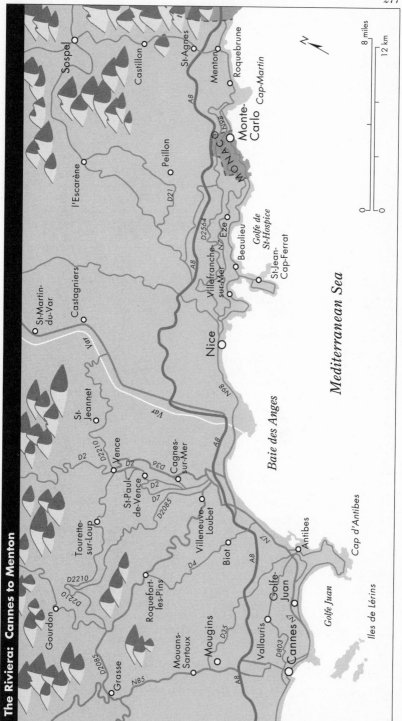

The Riviera: Cannes to Menton

speaking visitors. And while it may sound cynical, remember the French respond quicker to charm than to anything else.

Even if your own French is terrible, try to master a few words: The French are more cooperative when they think you're making at least an effort to speak their language. Basic vocabulary: *s'il vous plaît* (please), *merci* (thanks), *bonjour* (hello—until 6 PM), *bonsoir* (good evening—after 6 PM), *au revoir* (goodbye), *comment ça va* (how do you do), *oui* (yes), *non* (no), *peut-être* (maybe), *les toilettes* (toilets), *l'addition* (bill/check), *où* (where), *anglais* (English), *je ne comprends pas* (I don't understand).

Reading

What's Hot, What's Not: French Riviera Guide (available in shops along the coast). ·

Arriving and Departing

By Plane

Pam Am and **Air France** fly nonstop from New York to Nice.

If you're renting a car, arrange either to pick it up at the Nice Airport or to have it delivered to your hotel.

By Train

If you're arriving in Paris and traveling by train, go by cab, or by bus and subway, from **Charles de Gaulle Airport** to the **Gare de Lyon** train station. The airport bus goes to the RER, which is, in effect, a rural extension of the Paris metro. Change at Châtelet-les-Halles for Gare de Lyon. There are about six trains daily from Gare de Lyon to the Riviera. The trip takes slightly under five hours to Marseilles (via Lyons), another two hours to Cannes, and an additional half hour to Nice. The Paris–Lyons train is one of the fastest in the world—up to 272 kph (170 mph). You can also take an overnight sleeper from Paris to Nice (about 11 hours) and save the cost of a hotel. One train, for instance, leaves Paris at 10:36 PM and arrives at Marseilles at 7:20 the next morning.

The reduced-rate **Billet Touristique** (Tourist Ticket) and the **Billet de Famille** or Carte kiwi (family tickets) can be purchased at major train stations in France.

By Car

If you're driving from Paris, it's 880 km (550 mi) to Cannes and 912 km (570 mi) to Nice. The Autoroute goes from Paris to Lyons and then swings north of Marseilles to Cannes and Nice. You can arrange to have your car transported on the train, but arrangements must be made in France.

Getting Around

By Train

The **Metrazur** is the local train linking all major towns on the Riviera from Monte Carlo to Saint-Raphaël and Marseilles. The ride from Nice to Monte Carlo takes 23 minutes; from Nice to Cannes, 39 minutes; from Nice to Saint-Raphaël, 60 minutes; from Nice to Antibes, 24 minutes. For information, contact Gare SNCF (av. Thiers, Nice, tel. 93/87–50–50; for reservations, tel. 93/88–89–93).

If you want to reach Saint-Tropez by public transportation, take the train to Saint-Raphaël and then the bus or (preferably) the hydrofoil to Saint-Tropez. There's also helicopter service by Heli Air Monaco at Nice Airport (tel. 93/21–34–95).

By Bus

Motorcoaches run between Nice Airport and most major towns along the Riviera. There are 11 buses daily, for instance, between the airport and Cannes, and seven between the airport and Monte Carlo. Coaches from Nice Airport to downtown Nice leave every 12 minutes. For information, contact Gare Routière (Blvd Jean-Jaurès, Nice, tel. 93/85–61–81).

If you're traveling by public transportation, the perched towns of **Èze** and **St-Paul-de-Vence** are the most accessible by bus from Nice. To visit other medieval towns in season, sign up for bus excursions at any hotel or travel agency in Cannes or Nice.

By Hydrofoil

There's daily hydrofoil service in season along the coast. It's slower than the train, but can be faster than driving in high season. Check with hotels and travel agencies.

By Car

You may use your own driver's license in France but you must be able to prove you have third-party insurance. Drive on the right. Be aware of the French tradition of yielding to drivers coming from the right. Seat belts are obligatory, and children under 12 may not travel in the front seat. Speed limits are 130 kph (80 mph) on expressways, 110 kph (70 mph) on divided highways, 90 kph (55 mph) on other roads, 60 kph (40 mph) in towns. French drivers break these limits and police dish out hefty on-the-spot fines with equal abandon.

The best regional maps are published by Michelin. If unavailable in local bookstores, order them directly from Michelin Tire Co. (Guides and Maps Dept., Box 1007, Hyde Park, NY 11042, tel. 516/488–4477 or 212/895–2342). A road map of France isn't detailed enough to help you negotiate the back roads of Provence. Best bet is yellow regional map 245, "Provence/Côte d'Azur."

If you're planning to spend at least three weeks in Europe, look into the option of leasing a car from Renault Inc. (650

First Ave., New York, NY 10016, tel. 212/532–1221 or 800/221–1052).

By Motorbike or Bicycle

Mopeds and motorbikes are ideal for negotiating traffic on crowded beachfront roads, particularly for short distances, such as from Cannes to Cap d'Antibes or from Nice to Cap Ferrat. Contact, in **Nice:** *Nicea Location* (Gare SNCF, av. Thiers, tel. 93/82–42–71); in **Cannes:** *Cycles Remy* (22 av. des Hesperides, tel. 93/43–44–66), *Cannes Location Rent* (5 rue Allieis, tel. 93/39–46–15), or *Cycles Corot* (tel. 93/39–22–82); in **Antibes:** *French Riviera Location* (43 blvd. Wilson, tel. 93/67–65–67); in **Beaulieu:** *Au Tour de France* (36 blvd. Maréchal Leclerc, tel. 93/01–04–51). Bikes, mopeds, or motorbikes are particularly useful in Saint-Tropez, because the main beaches are several miles from town.

Essential Information

Important Addresses and Numbers

Tourist Information
Beaulieu: The tourist office is at Place Gare, tel. 93/01–02–21.
Cannes: Office de Tourisme, 1 La Croissette, 06400 Cannes, tel. 93/39–24–53.
Cap Ferrat: 59 avenue Denis Demis-Semeria, tel. 93/01–36–86.
Monaco: 2a boulevard des Moulins, tel. 93/30–87–01.
Nice: Office de Tourisme, avenue Thiers, 06000 Nice, tel. 93/87–07–07.
Saint-Tropez: Quai Jean-Jaurès, tel. 94/97–45–21.
Saint-Paul-de-Vence: The tourist office is at rue Grande, tel. 93/32–86–95.

Emergencies
Police: Dial 17 anywhere in France.

Consulates
United States: 36 rue Maréchal Joffre, 06000 Nice, tel. 93/88–89–55.
United Kingdom: 12 rue de France, 06000 Nice, tel. 93/82–32–04.

Opening and Closing Times

Banks
In general, banks are open weekdays 9:30–4:30, but times vary. Most close for an hour to an hour and a half for lunch.

Museums
Most museums are closed one day a week (usually Tuesday) and on national holidays. Usual times are from 9:30 to 5 or 6. Many museums close for lunch (noon–2); many are open afternoons only on Sunday.

Shops
Large shops in big towns are open from 9 or 9:30 to 6 or 7 without a lunch break. Smaller shops often open earlier (8 AM) and close later (8 PM), but take a lengthy lunch break (1–4). Corner grocery stores, often run by immigrants, frequently stay open until around 10 PM.

Shopping

Jewelry, designer clothing, perfume—whatever you would buy in Paris is sold along the Riviera, particularly in Cannes, Monte Carlo, and Nice. The price and quality are about the same, too. Look for good buys in silk scarves, perfumes, scented soaps, sportswear, and bathing suits (particularly bikinis).

Handmade **pottery** is sold in Vallauris, some based on original Picasso designs, and in Moustiers-Ste.-Marie (near the Grand Canyon of the Verdon). The town of Biot specializes in hand-blown glass. Paintings and local crafts—pewter, batik, jewelry, olive-wood carvings, handprinted cotton shoulder bags, etc.—are made and sold in the hilltop villages, particularly in Saint-Paul-de-Vence and Tourrette-sur-Loup. The more commercial villages, such as Èze and Gourdon, also sell scented soaps, candles, herbs, and essences. The town of Grasse is famous for its (not particularly subtle) **perfumes.** *Poivre d'âne* is a wild savory found only in this region.

There are some first-rate **antiques** shops in Nice and Antibes, and along the road from Cagnes-sur-Mer to Vence. Monaco is the place for stamps.

For refunds of up to 20% on purchases exceeding 1,200 francs, fill out a Value Added Tax (TVA) form in larger stores and give a copy to customs when leaving the country. A refund will be sent to you. Shops with duty-free signs in windows give this discount on the spot.

Cannes   Rue d'Antibes, a few blocks behind the Croisette, is one of the coast's most glamorous shopping streets. At **Saint Laurent** (No. 21) you can pay $1,000 for an evening dress. **Claire-fontaine-Maiffret** (No. 31) sells chocolates and candied everything. **Rimay** (No. 46) is known for perfumes. **Miss Apollinaire** (No. 62) is a popular boutique for Saint Laurent's second line, at affordable prices. Other boutiques are on nearby streets such as Notre Dame and rue des États-Unis. Many, such as **Brutus** (13 Rue Notre Dame), are for men.

The most exclusive shops are along the Croisette. Some of Paris's most fashionable boutiques have branches in the **Gray d'Albion** (17 La Croisette). **Cartier** is at No. 57; **Van Cleef et Arpels** is at No. 61. If the prices make you dizzy, buzz over to the flea market on Saturday.

Monte Carlo   The shop windows are for many visitors as interesting as the historic sites. Certainly, some of the couturier clothing is as dazzling and, for many, as inaccessible as the furnishings in the palace.

Most of the boutiques—Cartier, Dior, Yves Saint Laurent, and the like—are on streets surrounding the casino: place du Casino, avenue des Beaux-Arts, boulevard de Moulins, and avenue Princesse Grace. The somewhat younger, trendier boutiques are in the Park Palace complex (Les Allées Lumières) at the head of the casino gardens.

To help support local artisans, Princess Grace set up two shops called **Boutique du Rocher,** selling handicrafts and goods made from Provençal fabrics. One is at 1 Avenue de Madone in Monte Carlo; the other is on the Rock at 11 Rue Emile de Loth.

Nice Best bet for designer bathing suits is **La Boutique du Méridien,** one flight up in the Hotel Méridien. There are several pricey boutiques in the Royal Salon of the Hotel Negresco, some selling designer clothes made exclusively for these shops.

In the old town, the most elegant and trendy boutiques are along rue Masséna, place Magenta, and rue Paradis (Saint-Laurent at No. 8, Gladys Falk at No. 2, Façonnable at No. 7–9). On rue de la Liberté is Dorothée Bis at No. 20, Gigi at No. 10, Caroll for women and children, at No. 9, and Trabaud, for men, at No. 10.

Boulevard Risso has a flea market daily except Sunday.

Saint-Tropez Saint-Tropez has many boutiques at the port, in the old town around the Hôtel de Ville, and along the narrow streets between quai Suffren and place des Lices. Place des Lices has a market for clothing and antiques on Tuesday and Saturday morning.

Sports

Beaches Beaches between Monte Carlo and Cannes are mostly small and pebbly. Cannes has a sandy beach (with imported sand). The best beach is at Saint-Tropez. Most resorts tend to have a single stretch of sand divided into a public area and a series of private beaches, each with its own distinctive character and clientele. The private beaches charge admission that includes use of a changing room and rental of a sun umbrella and mattress. They also usually serve light lunches. You're free to wander, so find a beach that suits your taste and budget and then go exploring.

Cannes Of the public beaches, **Plage du Midi,** to the west of the old harbor, is best in the afternoon; **Plage Gazagnaire,** to the east of the new port, is best in the morning. Between the two are private beaches where anyone can swim for around 100 francs—a fee that includes a mattress, a sun umbrella, and waiters who will take your orders for lunch. As elsewhere along the Riviera, each section of the beach has its own character. An older, Middle Eastern crowd, for instance, gathers at the **Plage Gray d'Albion.**

Monte Carlo **Plage du Larvotto** is a man-made public beach squeezed between two pieces of man-made land. Next door is the private Monte Carlo Sea Club, which has a heated seawater pool free to guests at the Beach Plaza Hotel. If you want to come close to experiencing some of the dazzle that Monte Carlo once knew, the only place to swim is at the exclusive **Monte Carlo Beach** (tel. 93/78–21–40). A fee of around 100 francs will admit you to a heated Olympic-size saltwater pool, restaurants, a pebbly beach with cabanas, and a bevy of pretty boys and aspiring Bardots.

Saint-Tropez Beaches close to town—**Plage des Greniers** and the **Bouillabaisse**—are great for families; but holiday people snub them, preferring a 9.7-km (6-mi) sandy crescent at **Les Salins** and **Pampellone.** These beaches are about 3.2 km (2 mi) from town, so it helps to have a car, motorbike, or bicycle (*see* Bicycling, below, for rentals).

The most magnificent stretch of beach is divided into a number of private beaches, each with its own atmosphere and clientele.

Tahiti, for instance, tends to get a 30- to 35-year-old singles crowd. For around 100 francs you'll get a mattress and sun umbrella—then you're free to wander up and down the beach at will. Each beach has its own lunch area open to the public. The one at **Club 55** began as the canteen for the film crew of *And God Created Women.*

Bicycling In high season bicycles can be faster than cars. Two lovely trips on fairly level terrain are around Cap d'Antibes from Nice and around Cap Ferrat from Cannes. Bicycles are ideal at Saint-Tropez, since the beach is a few miles from town. Bicycles can be rented at train stations in Antibes, Cannes, Juan les Pins, and Nice. They can be taken with you on trains.

Saint-Tropez To prepare yourself for Muscle Beach, rent a bike at **Peretti** (2 av. du Général-Le-Clerc, tel. 94/97–00–11) and bike to the beach every day.

Boating Windsurfers and sailboats are for rent at all major resorts. Waterskiing is also available.

Cannes Sailboats and motorboats are rented at **Sun Way** (Port de la Napoule, tel. 93/93–03–04). For Windsurfers, try the **Centre Nautique Municipal** (9 rue Esprit-Violet, tel. 93/43–83–48).

For deep-sea fishing, call **Hotel Sofitel-Méditerranée** (tel. 93/39–00–84).

Saint-Tropez Rentals for windsurfing at Tahiti and Pampelonne beaches are available from the **Surfing Shop** (av. du Général-Le-Clerc, tel. 94/97–40–52) or **Windsurf** (rue Paul-Roussel, tel. 94/97–44–02).

Golf **Golf Bastide du Roy** (Biot, tel. 93/65–08–48), **Golf Club de**
Cannes **Cannes Mandelieu** (tel. 93/49–55–39), **Country Club de Cannes Mougins** (tel. 93/75–79–13), and **Golf de Valbonne** (tel. 93/42–00–08 or 93/42–11–88).

Monte Carlo **Monte Carlo Golf Club** (Mont Agel, tel. 93/41–09–11).

Tennis Resorts that offer tennis (white outfits only, please!) include:

Antibes **Hotel du Cap** and **Résidence du Cap.**

Cannes **Hotel Montfleury.** Ask hotels to reserve a court at **Complexe Sportif Montfleury** or the **Gallia Tennis Club.** Lessons are served up at the **Cannes Tennis Club** (11 rue Lacour, tel. 93/43–58–85).

Cap Ferrat **Grand Hotel du Cap.**

Saint-Paul-de-Vence **Mas d'Artigny.**

Vence **Chateau St. Martin.**

Saint-Tropez There are clay courts at **Tennis de Saint-Tropez** (tel. 94/97–36–39), **Hotel dei Marres** (tel. 94/97–26–68), and **Tennis-Club des Salins** (tel. 94/97–44–84).

Dining

A set or fixed menu is usually cheaper than à la carte.

The cuisine takes its inspiration from Paris, Provence, and Italy. The closer to the Italian border you are—from Nice eastward—the more pronounced the Italian influence. You'll find essentially three types of meal: classic French, nouvelle cuisine, and regional or Provençale. Classic and nouvelle cui-

sine are served in the more formal restaurants; regional cuisine, in the small, family-run establishments. The telltale sign
of a classic meal is the use of rich, heavy sauces. Nouvelle em-
phasizes small portions of fresh local produce, cooked simply to
enhance natural flavors and attractively arranged. Many
meals, of course, are a blend of classic and nouvelle. A dinner
served à la Provençale is usually cooked with garlic, tomatoes,
and fresh herbs, particularly rosemary or thyme. The emphasis is on simple, robust flavors. A popular local taste is *aïoli:*
mayonnaise with garlic, olive oil, and saffron. The most popular
dish is fish—broiled, grilled, cooked in a stew, or in a sauce
with pasta.

Bouillabaisse is a fish stew with eel, shrimp, crabs, and other
fish and shellfish, cooked with olive oil, tomato, garlic, saffron,
fennel, and a touch of anise liqueur—all served with garlic
toast and a garlic-and-pepper-flavored mayonnaise.

Pistou is a thick vegetable soup with beans, onions, or leeks,
fresh herbs (especially basil), garlic, and grated cheese.

Soupe de poisson is fish soup made with tomatoes, saffron, garlic, and onions.

Salade niçoise begins with tomatoes, anchovies, radishes,
green peppers, olives, and a vinaigrette dressing. Added to
these basics are green beans, tuna, and/or hard-boiled eggs.

Crudités are raw vegetables.

Loup de mer (sea bass) is a specialty of the Riviera, particularly
flambéed with fennel. Less expensive is *daurade* (sea bream),
often grilled or baked with onion, tomato, and lemon juice.
Rouget is red mullet grilled or baked in foil with lemon. Grilled
scampi is often imported, frozen. *Moules* (mussels) are served
in white wine *à la marinière* or in soup.

Leg of lamb *(gigot d'agneau)* or brochettes of skewered lamb
are best in the spring. *Daube de boeuf* is a beef stew with a
wine-flavored mushroom sauce, popular in Nice.

Chicken is served roasted with herbs *(poulet rôti)* or with white
wine, herbs, tomatoes, and black olives *(niçoise)*. Also popular
is *lapin* (rabbit) in a mustard sauce.

As you head east toward Italy, try various kinds of pasta, particularly with fresh fish sauce.

Of the various fresh vegetable dishes, the best of all is
ratatouille—a vegetable stew with tomatoes, onions, eggplant, zucchini, and green peppers. Other local favorites are
asparagus and artichokes with herb stuffing.

You can try a different cheese every night for a year without
having the same one twice. Be sure to try local goat and sheep
cheeses.

For dessert, you can't go wrong with fresh local fruits: particularly melons and strawberries dipped in *crème fraîche*. Fruit
sorbets are special, too.

For quick snacks on the beach, try a simple ham and cheese
sandwich on a long thin loaf of french bread, or *pain bagnat* (a
sandwich with tomatoes, hard-boiled eggs, olives, anchovies,
onions, olive oil, and sometimes tuna).

Anise-flavored *Pastis* is the number one drink.

Category	Cost*
Very Expensive	over 350 francs
Expensive	200–350 francs
Moderate	100–200 francs
Inexpensive	under 100 francs

*per person for a three-course meal, including tax and service but not wine

Lodging

Most but not all hotels include a European breakfast (coffee and croissant) in the price.

A *salle de bain* is a bathroom that may have a shower or a bathtub *(baignoire)*. Specify which you want. A bathtub is more expensive. In less expensive hotels with shared bathrooms, you may have to pay extra each time you take a bath or shower.

Many of the most splendid properties—most of them castles and other historic buildings that have been converted into hotels—belong to an organization called Relais & Châteaux, represented by David Mitchell Co. in New York.

The best of the simpler and less expensive hotels are grouped together in an organization called **Logis et Auberges de France** (Country Hotels and Inns of France). These clean and inexpensive family hotels are located in quiet neighborhoods or on back roads. (It helps to have a car to reach them.) About 30% of the rooms in the inexpensive range hotels have private baths. Rooms average 170 francs a night for two, or 250 francs a night with three meals. That's the cost of a good bottle of wine in a luxury-class hotel. Most have restaurants that serve fresh, well-prepared family meals. You can recognize these hotels by the distinctive yellow and green signs in front. Members are listed in the *Logis et Auberges de France* guide, which can be obtained by writing to: Federation Nationale des Gites de France (35 rue Godot de Mauroy, 75009 Paris, France).

A traditional itinerary—moving from place to place—makes no sense on the Riviera. What you should be doing is learning how to relax, not how to pack and unpack every day. Your best bet, therefore, is choosing a limited number of hotels and using them as bases from which to make daily excursions both inland and along the coast.

Begin by answering two important questions: (1) Do you want to spend all your time in one or more seaside resorts, or to split your time between these resorts and one of the walled medieval towns in the interior? (2) Of the time you spend on the coast, do you want to stay in towns where there's lots of activity, or in relatively isolated resorts, or in a combination of the two?

You want to spend all your time in seaside resorts. Stay (1) in or around Cannes and/or (2) in or around Nice. You can also stay in Saint-Tropez and/or Monte Carlo, but Cannes and Nice are more centrally located for excursions. (Picture the Riviera as a straight line along the southern coast of France. Saint-Tropez is at the southwest end, and Monte Carlo is at the northeast end. Cannes is in the middle. Nice is midway between Cannes and Monte Carlo.)

You want to split your time between seaside resorts and perched villages. Stay in one or more of the seaside resorts listed above and also in the hill towns of Saint-Paul-de-Vence or Peillon.

You want to stay along the coast, but only in towns with lots of activity. Stay in (1) the city of Nice, (2) the city of Cannes, (3) the village of Saint-Tropez, and/or (4) Monte Carlo.

You want to stay on the coast, but only in quiet, isolated resorts. Stay (1) on Cap d'Antibes near Cannes and/or (2) in Beaulieu or Cap Ferrat, near Nice. The two capes, though different in character, are both off the main coastal road and therefore more tranquil. Village and beach life in Saint-Tropez are pretty frenetic, but there are some peaceful resorts (*see* the Itineraries, below) outside of town.

You want to stay on the coast and experience both quiet resorts and active towns. For a quiet resort, stay in either (1) Beaulieu or Cap Ferrat or (2) Cap d'Antibes. For city life, stay in (1) Cannes, (2) Nice, (3) the village of Saint-Tropez, or (4) Monte Carlo.

Return to these questions after you've read the Itineraries.

Category	Cost*
Very Expensive	over 750 francs
Expensive	450–750 francs
Moderate	200–450 francs
Inexpensive	under 200 francs

*All prices are for a standard double room for two, including the tax (18.6%) and service charge.

The Itinerary

Orientation

On your trip you'll be traveling both along the coast, from Monte Carlo to Saint-Tropez, and to the so-called perched villages. This makes sense, because until recently the beaches were nothing but extensions of the hill towns.

The Riviera trip, unlike others in this book, won't be taking you from Points A to B, checking off important sights along the way. Happiness, as all travelers know, is staying put whenever possible. Even if you're in southern France for several weeks, there's no need to stay in more than two hotels—three at most. From any of these bases you can make daily excursions to all the places recommended below, and then come back to the same room, the same drawer of underwear and socks.

This itinerary, then, is divided into two main parts:

The First is a description of the four areas where most visitors prefer to stay: (1) Monte Carlo, (2) the Nice area, including

Beaulieu and Cap Ferrat, (3) the Cannes area, including Cap d'Antibes, and (4) Saint-Tropez.

Then follows a description of the various excursions you can take from any of these four areas. Two of the excursions are to the perched villages of Saint-Paul-de-Vence and Peillon, where you may want to stay, too.

It's important to begin with a realistic sense of Riviera life so you won't spend your holiday nursing wounded expectations. The Riviera conjures up images of fabulous yachts and villas, movie stars and palaces, and budding Bardots sunning themselves on ribbons of golden sand. The truth is that most beaches, at least east of Cannes, are small and pebbly. In summer, hordes of visitors are stuffed into concrete high rises or roadside campsites—on weekends it can take two hours to drive the last 9.7 km (6 mi) into Saint-Tropez. Yes, the film stars are here—but in their private villas. When the merely wealthy come, they come off-season, in the spring and fall—the best time for you to visit, too.

That said, I can still recommend the Riviera, even in summer, so long as you're selective about the places you choose to visit. Back from the coast, the light that Renoir and Matisse came to capture is as magical as ever. Fields of roses and lavender still send their heady perfume up to the fortified towns, where craftspeople make and sell their wares, as their predecessors did in the Middle Ages. Some resorts are as exclusive as ever, and no one will argue that French chefs have lost their touch.

The Main Route

3–5 Days *Two nights:* Nice, Beaulieu, or Cap Ferrat
Visits to Nice, Monte Carlo, Saint-Paul-de-Vence, Tourrette-sur-Loup
Two nights: Cannes or Cap d'Antibes
Visits to Cannes, Antibes, L'Esterel, Vallauris, Cagnes.

5–7 Days *Two or three nights:* Nice, Beaulieu, or Cap Ferrat
Visits to Nice, Monte Carlo, Peillon, Saint-Paul-de-Vence, Tourrette-sur-Loup, Villefranche
Two or three nights: Cannes or Cap d'Antibes
Visits to Cannes, Vallauris, Antibes, Biot (Léger Museum), Cagnes, L'Esterel, Saint-Tropez
One night: Saint-Paul-de-Vence or Peillon

7–14 Days *Three nights:* Nice, Beaulieu, or Cap Ferrat
Visits to Nice, Cap Ferrat, Monte Carlo, Èze, Peillon, Saint-Paul-de-Vence, Vence, Tourrette-sur-Loup, Gorges du Loup, Grasse
Three nights: Cannes or Cap d'Antibes
Visits to Cannes, Vallauris, Antibes, Biot, L'Esterel, Saint-Tropez, Cagnes, Grand Canyon of the Verdon, Moustiers-Ste-Marie
One night: Peillon, or *two nights:* Saint-Paul-de-Vence
Two nights: Saint-Tropez
Trips to Ramatuelle, Gassin.

Exploring

The first step is to find a place to stay. Let's begin with the most popular areas along the coast—Monte Carlo; the Nice area, including Beaulieu and Cap Ferrat; the Cannes area, including Cap d'Antibes; and Saint-Tropez. Then we'll discuss the various excursions, including visits to Saint-Paul-de-Vence and Peillon—two medieval hill towns where you might want to stay, too.

Monte Carlo

Trains run direct from both Cannes and Nice to Monte Carlo. If you're driving, there are three scenic roads at varying heights above the coast between Nice and Monte Carlo, a distance of about 19.3 km (12 mi). All are called "corniches"—literally, a projecting molding along the top of a building or wall. The Lower Corniche *(Corniche Inférieure)* is the busiest and slowest route because it passes through all the coastal towns. The Middle Corniche *(Moyenne Corniche)* is high enough for views and close enough for details. It passes the perched village of Èze, which is discussed below. The Upper Corniche *(Grande Corniche)* winds some 389.9 to 479.9 m (1,300 to 1,600 ft) above the sea, offering sweeping views of the coast. The Upper Corniche follows the Via Aurelia, the great Roman military road that brought Roman legions from Italy to Gaul (France). In 1806, Napoleon rebuilt the road and sent Gallic troops into Italy. Best advice is to take the Middle Corniche one way and the Upper Corniche the other. The view from the upper route is best in the early morning or evening.

The Principality of Monaco is 189.2 ha (473 acres) small and would fit comfortably inside New York's Central Park or a family farm in Iowa. Its 5,000 citizens would take up only a small percentage of seats in the Astrodome. The country is so tiny that residents have to go to another country to play golf.

The present ruler, Rainier III, traces his ancestry back to Otto Canella, who was born in 1070. The Grimaldi dynasty began with Otto's great-great-great-grandson, Francesco Grimaldi, also known as Frank the Rogue. Expelled from Genoa, Frank and his cronies disguised themselves as monks and seized the fortified medieval town known today as the Rock. That was in 1297, almost 700 years ago. Except for a short break under Napoleon, the Grimaldis have been there ever since, which makes them the oldest reigning family in Europe. On the Grimaldi coat of arms are two monks holding swords: Look up and you'll see them above the main door as you enter the palace.

Back in the 1850s a Grimaldi named Charles III made a decision that turned the Rock into a giant blue chip. Needing revenues, but not wanting to impose additional taxes on his subjects, he contracted with a company to open a gambling facility. The first spin of the roulette wheel was on December 14, 1856. There was no easy way to reach Monaco then—no carriage roads or railroads—so no one came. Between March 15 and March 20, 1857, one person entered the casino—and won two francs. In 1868, however, the railroad reached Monaco, filled with wheezing Englishmen who came to escape the London

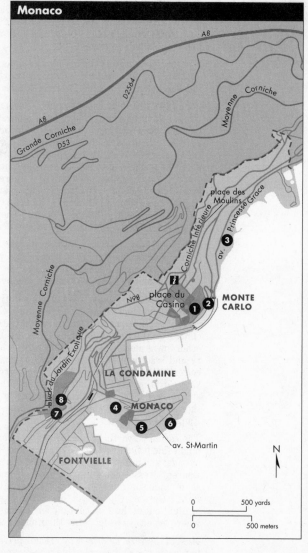

fog. The effects were immediate. Profits were so great that Charles eventually abolished all direct taxes.

Almost overnight a threadbare principality became an elegant watering hole for European society. Dukes and their mistresses, duchesses and their gigolos danced and dined their way through a world of spinning roulette wheels and bubbling champagne—preening themselves for nights at the opera, where artists such as Vaslav Nijinsky, Sarah Bernhardt, and Enrico Caruso came to perform.

Monte Carlo—the modern gambling town with elegant shops, man-made beaches, high-rise hotels, and a few Belle Epoque hotels—is actually only one of four parts of Monaco. The second is the medieval town on the Rock ("Old Monaco"), 59.9 m (200 ft) above the sea. It's here that Prince Rainier lives. From July through September the prince goes a-traveling and the palace is open to the public.

The third area is La Condamine, the commercial harbor area, with apartments and businesses. The fourth is Fontveille, the industrial district on 8 ha (20 acres) of reclaimed land.

Today only about 3% of the country's revenues come from gambling; other chips are invested in chemicals, glass, ceramics, plastics, food products, and beer. Monaco may be a handkerchief-size state, a golden ghetto, but it's also a serious country with some 95 consulates around the world. Rainier has been adept financially, and citizens still don't have to pay taxes. (If you're thinking of becoming a citizen, there are long residency requirements before you can even apply, and even then it isn't easy: There are no huddled masses here.) Of some 33,000 residents, only about 5,000 are citizens. They are called Monégasque, and they are not allowed to gamble.

The principality has the lowest crime rate in Europe, perhaps because it has one security officer for every 122 residents. The navy, such as it is, has the fastest boat on the coast—so don't think of robbing the casino and escaping by sea.

When the Monégasques want to expand, they build upward or reclaim land from the sea. The result is a clean, sparkling concrete jewel set in a ring of mountains at the edge of the sea. The climate is the next best after Southern California's. Unlike other towns along the coast, Monaco has a highly defined history and tradition. It is also a town dedicated to conspicuous consumption. The borders with France are open; one moment you're driving through France, the next, through Monaco. The spoken language is French. French money is freely circulated, though there are Monégasque coins stamped with the image of Rainier III.

The casino is worth a visit, even if you don't bet a cent. You might find it fun to count the Jaguars and Rolls-Royces parked outside, and breathe on windows of shops selling $1,200 Saint-Laurent dresses and fabulous jewels. The Oceanographic Museum under Jacques-Yves Cousteau is a treat, and so is the Exotic Garden. Should you decide to stay, there's one hotel straight out of the 19th century and a comfortable beach hotel where expensive people offer their oiled bodies to the sun.

Most of the very wealthy stay in their private villas, of course, barricaded behind a wall of old money, and the people you will meet are people like yourself—holidaymakers, sunseekers, coming to Monte Carlo to cloak themselves in the opulence of a world that no longer exists. But no matter. The contrast between yesterday and today is sad and wonderful, funny and obscene—but it's still worth seeing. And while you're mourning what has been lost, a bit of the old glamour, miraculously, rubs off, too.

As you approach Monte Carlo from Nice, you'll see signs on the right to the Jardin Exotique (Tropical Gardens), the Musée d'Anthropologie Préhistorique (Museum of Prehistoric Anthropology), and the Observatory Caves. All three are worth a visit. The garden has some 9,000 species of cacti and succulents clinging to a rocky cliff 92 m (300 ft) above the sea. The view of the palace and the coast is spectacular. Steps take you down to the museum (which has a great collection of skeletons and stone-age tools of interest to the nonspecialist) and to the caves. The caves are not enormous; but you'll still enjoy wandering through an Arthur Rackhamish world of fantastic shapes and shadows. Keep in mind that it's a long, steep walk down to the caves and back again. *Blvd. du Jardin Exotique. Admission: 27.50 frs. adults, 18 frs. senior citizens, 14 frs. children. Open daily 9–7 (dusk in winter).*

Next stop is Old Monaco—the Rock—to tour the palace.

Leave your car in the Fontveille Car Park on your way into town. From Easter to the end of October there is bus service between the car park and the Rock. The walk takes about 30 minutes.

There's little room on the Rock for anything but official buildings, tourist shops, and restaurants. The marble staircase in the **palace** was inspired by the one at Fontainebleau. The tour takes you through ornate state rooms filled with priceless antiques and paintings, where you can imagine Princess Grace greeting visiting royalty. Families with kids should come early to see the Changing of the Guards in front of the palace, daily at 11:55 AM. *Admission: 20 frs. adults, 10 frs. children. Joint ticket with Musée Napoléon: 30 frs. adults, 15 frs. children. Open June–Oct., daily 9:30–6:30.*

One wing of the palace, open throughout the year, is taken up by a **museum** full of Napoleonic souvenirs and documents related to Monaco's history. *Admission: 15 frs. adults, 7 frs. children. Joint ticket with palace apartments: 30 frs. adults, 15 frs. children. Open Tues.–Sun. 9:30–6:30.*

The **Oceanographic Museum** has an aquarium asplash with playful sea lions and turtles. *Av. St-Martin, tel. 93/30–15–14. Admission: 45 frs. adults, 23 frs. children. Open July–Aug. daily 9–9; Sept.–June daily 9:30–7.*

Time Out Take the museum's elevator to the roof terrace for a fine view and restorative drink.

Also on the Rock is the **cathedral,** a neo-Romanesque monstrosity (1875–84) with several important early paintings of the Nice School. This school, led by Louis Bréa—you'll see his work in churches along the coast—flourished from the mid-15th to the mid-16th century under strong Gothic and Italian Renaissance influence. The simplicity and humanity of Bréa's work have led some critics to call him a Provençal Fra Angelico.

The **casino** is a must. Nowhere in the world will you see a more striking contrast between yesterday and today. Wandering through a world of gold-leaf splendor are gamblers looking as though they had just stumbled off the bus to Reno or Atlantic City. Beneath the gilt-edged Rococo ceiling, busloads of women from Dubuque and Jersey City jerk the arms of one-armed bandits. Don't miss it! The main gambling hall, once called the European Room, has been renamed the American Room and fitted with 150 one-armed bandits from Chicago. Adjoining it is the Pink Salon, now a bar where unclad nymphs float about on the ceiling smoking cigarillos. The private rooms (Salles Privées) are for high rollers. Even if you don't bet, it's worth the price just to see them. The stakes are higher here, so the mood is more sober, and well-wishers are herded farther back from the tables. On July 17, 1924, black came up 17 times in a row on Table 5. This was the longest run ever. A dollar left on black would have grown to $131,072. On August 7, 1913, the number 36 came up three times in a row. In those days, if a gambler went broke the casino bought him a ticket home. *Open 10 AM–the last die is thrown. Back rooms open 4 PM; ties and jackets required. Bring your passport.*

It seems in the true spirit of Monte Carlo that the **Opera House,** with its 18-ton gilt bronze chandelier, is part of the casino complex. The designer, Charles Garnier, also built the Paris Opera.

The serious gamblers, some say, play at **Loew's Casino,** nearby. You may want to try parking here, because parking near the old casino is next to impossible in season. *Open weekdays 4 PM, weekends, 1 PM.*

The **Museum of Dolls** is in the **National Museum,** a short walk to the left as you exit the casino. Your children will thank you for taking them! *17 av. Princesse Grace, tel. 93/30–91–26. Admission: 22 frs. adults, 12 frs. children. Open daily 10–12:15 and 2:30–6:30; closed holidays.*

Time Out Head for the **Place d'Armes** in the port below the Rock and munch on hot *socca* (a thin pancake made with chickpea flour) or a slice of *pissaladière* (thick pizza with onions) in the open-air market.

Dining **Le Bec Rouge** has the best classic French cuisine in town. Specialties include cold mussels with a mayonnaise of hot pepper and garlic, fresh house *foie gras*, lobster or prawn gratin, bouillabaisse, Alpine lamb, and fresh bass. *11 av. Grande-Bretagne, tel. 93/30–74–91. Reservations essential. Dress: smart. AE, DC, MC, V. Expensive.*

Café de Paris is a *brasserie*-type lunch spot for jet-setters who want to see and be seen, and for ladies with poodles and heavy Arpels bracelets. *Pl. du Casino, tel. 93/50–57–75. Reservations advised. Dress: elegantly casual. AE, DC, MC, V. Expensive.*

Rampoldi draws a fashionable and exuberant yachting crowd for Italian food in a 1930s-ish setting. Try Risotto primavera or grilled lamb. *3 av. Spélugues, tel. 93/30–70–65. Reservations essential. Dress: smart. AE, DC, MC, V. Expensive.*

Restaurant du Port is a popular Italian restaurant with outside tables and efficient service. A large, varied menu includes prawns, pastas, lasagna, Bolognese, fettuccine, fish risotto, and veal with ham and cheese. *Quai Albert I, tel. 93/50–77–21. Reservations advised. Dress: elegantly casual. AE, DC, MC, V. Closed Mon. and Nov.–early Dec. Expensive.*

Pizzeria Monégasque is a chic pizza house. *4 rue Terrazzani, tel. 93/30–16–38. Reservations advised. Dress: elegantly casual. MC, V. Closed lunchtime. Moderate.*

Pinocchio, featuring French-Italian specialties, is the most popular eaterie on the Rock. Bronzed women and men fighting their age relax in a cozy atmosphere beneath a vaulted ceiling. *30 rue Comte Félix-Gastaldi, tel. 93/30–96–20. Reservations essential. Dress: elegantly casual. MC, V. Closed Dec.–Jan. and Wed. out of season. Moderate.*

Lodging Monte Carlo is only a half-hour drive from Nice, so there's no need to stay here unless you're an inveterate gambler or like the idea of waking up in the land of Princess Grace. If you're looking for a luxurious hotel, the Negresco in Nice is as luxurious as the Hotel de Paris in Monte Carlo, and the food is better; if you need a moderately priced or inexpensive hotel, you'll have a better choice in Nice. Don't come to Monte Carlo in season without a reservation.

The Beach Plaza is part of the respected Trusthouse Forte chain. It is large and modern. *22 av. Princesse-Grace, tel. 93/30–98–80. 313 rooms with bath. Facilities: restaurant, 3 pools, private beach. AE, DC, MC, V. Very Expensive.*

The Hermitage is another grand Belle Epoque palace. The dining room is a tribute to a bygone age, with pink marble columns holding up a gilded, frescoed ceiling. The recently reappointed rooms are comfortable but disappointing after you've seen the lavish public areas. *Square Beaumarchais, tel. 93/50–67–31, 230 rooms with bath. Facilities: restaurant, pool. AE, DC, MC, V. Very Expensive.*

Hotel de Paris, located a bone's throw from the casino, is one of the most famous hotels in Europe. Just as the new Loew's Hotel is the offspring of the modern travel world of conventions and gambling junkets, so the ornate Hotel de Paris is the child of a vanishing age of privilege and luxury. It was here in this heavy, Second Empire splendor—this Belle Epoque tour de force—that Escoffier worked his magic for empresses, dowagers, and queens. *Pl. du Casino, 98000, tel. 93/50–80–80. 255 rooms with bath. Facilities: restaurant (closed Tues., Wed.—except dinner July–Aug.—and Nov.–Dec.). AE, DC, MC, V. Very Expensive.*

Monte Carlo Beach Hotel has small, modern, elegant rooms with balconies overlooking the sea. It also has the best hotel food in town. It is exactly what its name says—a beach hotel, where guests are given privileges at the exclusive Monte Carlo Beach Club, which occupies the same site. A minibus takes guests to the casino and shops, which are too far to reach by foot. *06190 Roquebrune, tel. 93/78–21–40, 46 rooms with bath. Facilities: restaurant, pool, private beach. AE, DC, MC, V. Closed mid-Oct.–Easter. Very Expensive.*

The Balmoral. Although some rooms have recently been renovated, it remains a sad reminder of a lost age. The nicest thing a travel writer can say about it is that it's an old-fashioned family hotel. *12 av. Costa, tel. 93/50–62–37. 75 rooms with bath. Facilities: snack-restaurant. AE, DC, MC, V. Expensive.*

The Terminus, near the train station, is the closest thing to a budget hotel. *9 av. Prince-Pierre, tel. 93/30–20–70. 54 rooms, some with bath or shower. DC, MC, V. Moderate.*

Excursion to Èze Almost every tour to Monte Carlo includes a visit to the medieval hill town of Èze, which is perched on a rocky spur near the Middle Corniche, some 389.9 m (1,300 ft) above the sea. (Don't confuse Èze with the beach town of Èze-sur-Mer, which is down by the water.)

Èze is one of several beautifully preserved medieval towns on mountaintops behind the coast. It would be a shame to tour the Riviera without seeing at least one of these towns, and Èze, directly on the road between Nice and Monte Carlo, is the most accessible. But because of its accessibility it's also the most crowded and commercial. Èze has its share of serious craftspeople, but most of its vendors make their living selling perfumed soaps and postcards to the package-tour trade.

If Èze is your first perched village, you'll be delighted with it, but if you've been to Saint-Paul-de-Vence (also commercial but visually more beautiful), Tourrette-sur-Loup, Peillon, or others, you may be disappointed with Èze. If time is limited, certainly, visit Èze, particularly in the early evening when the buses have returned to Nice.

Enter through a fortified 14th-century gate and wander down narrow, cobbled streets with vaulted passageways and stairs. The church is 18th century, but the small **Chapel of the White Penitents** dates to 1306 and contains a 13th-century gilded wood Spanish Christ and some notable 16th-century paintings. Tourist and craft shops line the streets leading to the ruins of a **castle**, which has a scenic belvedere. Some of the most tasteful craft shops are in the hotel/restaurant Chèvre d'Or.

Near the top of the village is a garden with exotic flowers and cacti. It's worth the admission price, but if you've time for only one exotic garden, visit the one in Monte Carlo.

If you're not going to Grasse, the perfume capital of the world, consider visiting a branch of a Grasse perfumerie called **La Parfumerie Fragonard,** located in front of the public gardens.

Dining and Lodging
Château Eza is trying hard to match the well-established Chèvre d'Or in comfort and class. Rooms here are more spacious, though the atmosphere is a bit "Ye Olde." The hotel occupies the former home of the King of Sweden. The view from the terrace is, as they say, breathtaking. *Rue Pise, tel. 93/41–12–24. 6 rooms and 3 suites with bath. AE, DC, MC, V. Very Expensive.*
Chèvre d'Or is a restored medieval manor house with six well-appointed but smallish rooms and three apartments (no. 9 is a good bet). The small pool is surrounded by a terrace: a lovely, peaceful place to take the sun or end the day. The hotel belongs to the prestigious Relais & Châteaux group. Classic French cuisine is served in the restaurant. Specialties include *Saumon mariné, filet de loup* (local bass), and pigeon with fresh truffle pâté. The dining area is formal, without much warmth; the terrace may be more appealing if you are here only for the day. *Rue du Barry, 06360, tel. 93/41–12–12. 15 rooms with bath. Facilities: restaurant, café, bar, terrace, pool. AE, DC, MC, V. Closed Dec.–Feb. Very Expensive.*

Nice (including Beaulieu and Cap Ferrat)

Near the busy city of Nice is a cape called Cap Ferrat, jutting out into the sea. On the far side of the cape is the coastal village of Beaulieu. A village, a cape, a city—which of these three is right for you? Let's look at the alternatives.

Nice is less glamorous, less sophisticated, and less expensive than Cannes. It's also older—weathered-old and faded-old, like a wealthy dowager who has seen better days but who still maintains a demeanor of dignity and poise. Nice is a big, sprawling city of 350,000 people—five times as many as in Cannes—and has a life and vitality that survive when tourists pack their bags and go home. Cannes, on the contrary, exists for its visitors; it was dreamed up by them and blinked into existence almost overnight.

Nice

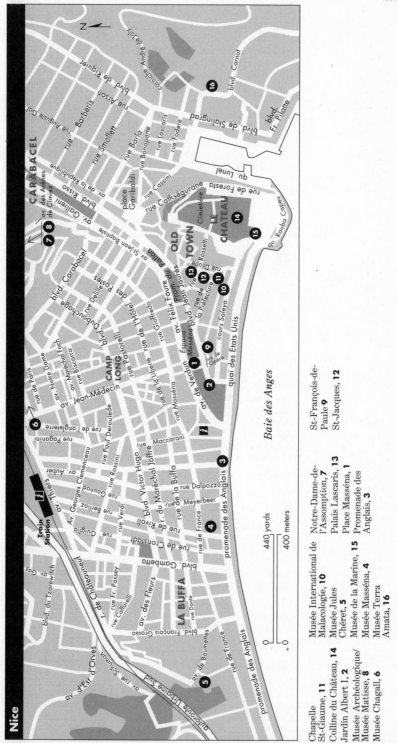

Baie des Anges

Chapelle
St-Giaume, **11**
Colline du Château, **14**
Jardin Albert I, **2**
Musée Archéologique/
Musée Matisse, **8**
Musée Chagall, **6**

Musée International de
Malacologie, **10**
Musée Jules
Chéret, **5**
Musée de la Marine, **15**
Musée Masséna, **4**
Musée Terra
Amata, **16**

Notre-Dame-de-
l'Assomption, **7**
Palais Lascaris, **13**
Place Masséna, **1**
Promenade des
Anglais, **3**

St-François-de-
Paule **9**
St-Jacques, **12**

The glitter has moved to Cannes, but Nice has kept some of the local Marseilles flavor that Marseilles has lost and Cannes never had. Cannes is smart, stylish, and international, like nouvelle cuisine; Nice has the simple robust flavor of a meal cooked à la Provençale, with lots of garlic, tomatoes, and herbs.

It's easy to picture Nice, stretching behind the beautiful blue Baie des Anges: Along a narrow strip of pebbly beach is the Promenade des Anglais, lined with hotels and cafés. If you follow the promenade to the west, you'll come to the fabulous Hotel Negresco. If you follow the promenade to the east, you'll reach a hill called the Château, crowned with the ruins of an old fortress. Below the fortress are both the old town—*la vieille ville*—and the harbor. That's it, essentially, as far as visitors are concerned: After the promenade, the old town, and the museums and ruins in an area called Cimiez, you're left with a busy, modern city where nothing goes on but life.

The old town of Nice is one of the delights of the Riviera. Cars are forbidden on streets narrow enough for their buildings to crowd out the sky. The winding alleyways are lined with faded 17th- and 18th- century buildings where families sell their wares. Flowers cascade from window boxes on soft, pastel-colored walls. You wander down cobbled streets, proceeding with the logic of dreams, or sit in an outdoor café on a Venetian-like square bathed in a pool of the purest, most transparent light. At the edge of the old town is the **flower market,** a swirl of colors and smells as intoxicating as wine.

Nice is worth a visit, but should you stay here? On the negative side, its beaches are cramped and pebbly. Except for the luxurious Negresco, most of its hotels are either rundown or being refurbished for the convention crowd. On the positive side, Nice is likely to have hotel space when all other towns are full, and at prices you can afford. It's also a convenient base from which to explore Monte Carlo and the medieval towns in the interior. It does have its share of first-class restaurants and boutiques, and an evening stroll through the old town or along the Promenade des Anglais is not easily forgotten.

Nice was "colonized" in the mid-18th century by Englishmen fleeing the harshness of northern winters. The Promenade des Anglais got its name because, in the 1820s, the Reverend Lewis Way got the English colony to pay for widening a 4-km (2.5-mi) footpath along the Baie des Anges, thus creating jobs for fruit pickers thrown out of work by a terrible frost. The eastern end of the boulevard, bordering the old town, is now called the Quai des États-Unis in deference to changing commercial realities. You can lunch in your bathing suit at any of the private beaches along the promenade.

A few blocks inland, to the west of the Negresco Hotel, is a first-rate fine arts museum, **Musée Jules Chéret.** It contains paintings by masters of the Belle Epoque and Picasso ceramics created in the pottery village of Vallauris in the 1950s. *33 av. des Baumettes, tel. 93/44–50–72. Admission free. Open May–Sept., Tues.–Sun. 10–noon and 3–6; Oct. and Dec.–Apr., Tues.–Sun. 10–noon and 2–5.*

The **Masséna Museum,** a few blocks west of the Negresco, has a fine collection of Provençal ceramics, and paintings by the early Nice School, including works by Bréa. *67 rue de France, tel. 93/*

62–18–12. Admission free. Open Tues.–Sun. 10–noon and 2–5; closed 2 weeks in Nov. or Dec.

At the end of the Quai des États-Unis are steps and an elevator leading to a viewing platform at the top of the **Château.** From here, continue inland, down to the old town. At **Place Garibaldi** there's a morning fish market. Walk down **Rue St.-François** and bear left on **Rue Droite.**

On your right is the **Palais Lascaris.** This mid-17th-century palace has an 18th-century pharmacy and a Rococo interior with a grandiose staircase and an interesting trompe l'oeil ceiling. *15 rue Droite, tel. 93/62–05–54. Admission free. Open Dec.–Oct., Tues.–Sun. 9:30–noon and 2–6.*

Continue down **Rue Droite.** On your left is the 17th- century **St. Jacques Church,** known as the Gesú, because it was modeled on that church in Rome. Three short blocks in from the bay, and paralleling it, is the tastefully restored **Cours Saleya,** once the elegant promenade of Old Nice, now a street lined with shops and restaurants and home to a daily flower market.

Time Out Shop for the best crystallized fruits in Nice at **Henri Auer** *(7 rue St-François-de-Paul)*, and have an ice-cream and pastry in his cozy tea room.

Cimiez, site of ancient Nice, is now a residential neighborhood on a hill back from the bay. The **Marc Chagall Museum** houses the most important permanent collection of the painter's work, including the 17 canvases of the *Biblical Message. Av. du Dr-Ménard, tel. 93/81–75–75. Admission: 16 frs. adults, 8 frs. children and senior citizens; free Wed. Open July–Sept., Wed.–Mon. 10–7; Oct.–July, Wed.–Mon. 10–12:30 and 2–5:30.*

The ruins of a Roman bath and amphitheater will not be high on your list of musts unless you have a special interest in antiquity. Nearby is the 17th-century Villa des Arènes, which houses the **Matisse Museum,** with some 30 examples of the painter's work, drawn from different stages of his life. *164 av. des Arènes-de-Cimiez, tel. 93/81–59–57 or 93/53–17–70. Admission free. Open May–Sept., 10–noon and 2:30–6:30; Oct.–Apr., 10–noon and 2–5.*

Also near the ruins is a **Franciscan Monastery** with several masterpieces of the Nice School, including a 1475 *Pietà* by Louis Bréa. *Admission free. Open weekdays 10–noon and 3–6.*

Nice is a good base for half-day or full-day excursions to Monte Carlo and Èze; to the perched villages of Peillon and Saint-Paul-de-Vence; to the Léger Museum at Biot; and to Cap Ferrat, Villefranche, Antibes, and Cannes.

Dining Dining in Nice is a mixture of Italian, Provençal, and Parisian. Lunchtime specialties include *pissaladière* (pizza with black olives, onions, and anchovies) and *pan bagnat* (French bread soaked in olive oil and filled with tomatoes, radishes, hard-boiled eggs, black olives, and parsley).

Le Chantecler is the top restaurant for nouvelle cuisine. The *menu de gustation* includes tiny, elegant portions of a dozen dishes. Other specialties include *Charlotte de St-Pierre* (a fish dish), lobster salad with asparagus tips, melon and grapefruit soup with sauterne wine, and lobster ravioli in a shellfish bouillon. Chef Dominique le Stanc forged a name for himself in Monte Carlo. *37 promenade des Anglais, 06000, tel. 93/88–39–51. AE, DC, MC, V. Very Expensive.*

L'Ane Rouge is the best of the many harborfront restaurants. Its specialties include *bourride* (a fish stew), lobster, sweetbreads, and chocolate cake. *7 quai des Deux-Emmanuel, tel. 93/89–49–63. Reservations advised. Dress: elegant casual. AE, DC, MC, V. Closed Sat., Sun., and mid-July–Sept. Expensive.*

Los Caracolès, located near the flower market and the opera, is an alternative for fresh fish. *7 rue Terrasse, tel. 93/80–98–23. Reservations essential. Jacket and tie required. AE, DC, MC, V. Closed July, part of Feb., Sat. lunch and Mon. Expensive.*

Chez Don Camillo, a tiny, quiet, comfortable restaurant with attentive service and a good but limited menu, serves Italian specialties. Try the fettuceine or fillet of sole. *5 rue Ponchettes, tel. 93/85–67–95. Reservations essential. Dress: smart. AE, MC, V. Closed Sun. Expensive.*

La Mérenda is a popular old town bistro near the flower market. Specialties cooked to order include *tripes niçoises, pâte au pistou* (pasta with garlic and basil sauce), pizza, and stew Provençale. This is your best bet for a first-rate meal at a low price. *4 rue de la Terrasse. Reservations not accepted. Dress: casual. No credit cards. Closed Sat. dinner, Sun., Mon., Feb., and Aug. Inexpensive.*

Most tourists are directed to restaurants on the eastern side of the harbor, where glass-enclosed terraces muffle the sound of traffic. None has a very strong reputation among locals.

Le Scampi, serving good simple meals of pastas, fresh fish, and, of course, scampi, is the best bet here. *59 quai des Etats-Unis, tel. 93/85–72–90. Reservations advised. Dress: casual. MC, V. Moderate.*

Lodging Except for the Negresco, which has succeeded in maintaining the elegant standards of a bygone age, Nice's major hotels are either fading or undergoing restoration to satisfy the demands of the package-tour trade. The older hotels in all categories have beautifully ornate facades. Dining rooms, hallways, and stairways also have a certain fading charm. But the rooms are almost always a disappointment. It's not that they're uncomfortable or unclean, but that they lack character and fail to live up to the promise of the public areas.

Elysée Palace. This glass-fronted addition to the Nice hotel scene lies close to the sea; all guest rooms feature views of the Mediterranean. The interior is spacious and ultramodern, with plenty of marble in evidence. The large restaurant is a sound bet for nouvelle cuisine, served amid contemporary works of art. *59 promenade des Anglais, 06000, tel. 93/86–06–06. 150 rooms with bath. Facilities: restaurant, bar, pool, sauna, health club. AE, DC, MC, V. Very Expensive.*

Méridien is a modern, impersonal hotel with a rooftop pool. *1 promenade des Anglais, tel. 93/82–25–25. 305 rooms with bath. Facilities: restaurant, pool. AE, DC, MC, V. Very Expensive.*

The Negresco, a turn-of-the-century turreted white castle, is the only hotel in France that the government has declared a national monument. Doormen greet you in red-lined capes, knee-high boots, and blue hats with cockades. The massive suites are designed around different periods of French history— Romantic, Louis XIV, Empire, and others. The marble bathrooms are big enough to throw parties in. The lobby is a huge oval rotunda encircled with columns reaching up to a stained-glass dome. Hanging above its center is a gigantic Baccarat crystal chandelier. The hallway carpet, when woven, represented one tenth of the cost of the hotel. *37 promenade des Anglais, 06000, tel. 93/88–39–51. 130 rooms with bath. Facilities: 2 restaurants, bar, private beach. AE, DC, MC, V. Very Expensive.*

La Pérouse is at the eastern end of the Baie des Anges, near the Château. The reception area is tacky, but rooms are clean and the rooftop pool is a quiet oasis with a spectacular view. *11 quai Rauba-Capéu, tel. 93/62–34–63, 63 rooms with bath. Facilities: restaurant, pool. AE, DC, MC, V. Very Expensive.*

Grand Hotel Aston has a lovely roof garden overlooking the old city. *12 av. Félix-Faure, tel. 93/80–62–52, 160 rooms with bath. Facilities: restaurant. AE, DC, MC, V. Expensive.*

Sofitel-Splendid is a family-run, in-town hotel with rooftop pool and sun terrace. *50 blvd. Victor-Hugo, tel. 93/88–69–54. 116 rooms with bath. Facilities: restaurant, pool. AE, DC, MC, V. Expensive.*

Hotel Busby is one of a group of hotels back from the bay that cater heavily to the package-tour trade. If you're stuck for a room, they're likely to come up with something. *38 rue du Mal-Joffre, tel. 93/88–19–41. 80 rooms with bath or shower. Facilities: restaurant. AE, DC, MC, V. Moderate.*

Hotel Harvey is just off the ocean behind the Méridien. There's no lobby, the wallpaper in rooms I saw was peeling, the closets were unpainted, and carpets needed vacuuming. But the location is great, and the rooms are cheap. *18 av. Suède, tel. 93/88–73–73. 62 rooms, most with bath or shower. DC, MC, V. Closed Nov.–mid-Feb. Moderate.*

On to Beaulieu and Cap Ferrat The **Beaulieu–Cap Ferrat** area, just east of Nice, is the quietest, most understated, most refined area along the Riviera. People come here not to see and be seen, but to be left alone. Because of the limited nightlife, the absence of sandy beaches, and the distance from Cannes, guests tend to be families or couples on the far side of 30—particularly off-season. If a hotel is nothing more to you than a place to put your head after a full day of sightseeing, stay in Nice; but if you want to escape the frenetic pace of summer life along the Riviera and merely exist in the sun for a few days, stay in Beaulieu or on Cap Ferrat. You will want to have a car here and perhaps a rented bicycle for rides around the cape.

Beaulieu The one Thing to Do in Beaulieu is visit the **Villa Kérylos.** In the early part of the century a rich amateur archaeologist named Theodore Reinach asked an Italian architect to build him an authentic Greek house. The villa, now open to the public, is a faithful reproduction made from cool Carrara marble, alabaster, and rare fruitwoods. The furniture, made of wood inlaid with ivory, bronze, and leather, is copied from drawings of Greek interiors found on ancient vases and mosaics. *Tel. 93/01–01–44. Admission: 14 francs. Open July–Aug., daily 3–7; Sept.–June, Tues.–Sun. 2–6.*

Dining **Les Agaves** is a local restaurant that serves regional, home-style meals. *4 rue du Mal-Foch, tel. 93/01–12–09. Reservations essential. Dress: casual. DC, MC, V. Closed Nov., Sun. evening and Mon. out of season. Moderate.*

La Pignatelle offers regional food in a home-style atmosphere.

10 rue Quincenet, tel. 93/01–03–37. Reservations advised. Dress: casual. MC, V. Closed Mon. Inexpensive.

Lodging The **Métropole,** at the edge of the sea, is visually relaxed, with comfortable couches in the public areas and 1 ha (2.5 acres) of gardens leading past rocky ledges to the sea. *15 blvd. Gal-Leclerc, tel. 93/01–00–08. 50 rooms with bath. Facilities: restaurant, pool, private beach. DC, MC, V. Closed Nov.–late Dec. Very Expensive.*

La Réserve, nearby, is a bit more reserved, in an elegant sort of way, with a lounge that resembles the reception room in Rome's Farnese Palace. *5 blvd. Gal-Leclerc, tel. 93/01–00–01. 50 rooms with bath. Facilities: restaurant, pool. AE, MC, V. Closed mid-Nov.–end of Dec. Very Expensive.*

Cap Ferrat Cape Ferrat (Saint-Jean-Cap-Ferrat), originally the southern tip of the cape, now gives its name to the entire peninsula. It resembles Cap d'Antibes, near Nice, in that it's a rocky finger extending into the sea, covered with sumptuous mansions hidden behind walls of lush vegetation. Because of its proximity to Cannes, Cap d'Antibes tends to attract a noisier, more aggressively star-studded clientele; guests on the more inaccessible Cap Ferrat want nothing but privacy, understated elegance, and seclusion. Land values on Cap Ferrat are second only to those in Monaco.

The cape is a fine, peaceful place to visit, even if you're not staying here. There's a lovely one-hour **walk** along the coast from Paloma Beach around Pointe St. Hospice—ask for directions to the Tourist Path (Sentier Touristique). There's also a **zoo** (open mid-June–mid-September, 9–7; off-season, 9:30–6) with a tropical garden and some 350 species of animals and exotic birds, including a condor and a school of chimps who put on a daily show.

Best of all is the **Ephrussi de Rothschild Foundation,** a 6.8-ha (17-acre) estate with magnificent gardens and a villa-museum called the Musée Ile-de-France. The museum reflects the sensibilities of its former owner, Madame Ephrussi de Rothschild, sister of Baron Edouard de Rothschild. An insatiable collector, she lived surrounded by an eclectic but tasteful collection of Impressionist paintings, Louis XIII furniture, rare Sèvres porcelain, and objets d'art from the Far East. *Villa Ile-de-France, tel. 93/01–33–09. Admission: 25 frs. adults, 15 frs. students, children free. Open Dec.–Oct., Tues.–Sat. 10–noon and 2–6, Sun. 2–6. Guided tours only.*

Dining **Les Hirondelles** is a good bet for fresh fish, bouillabaisse, and grilled lobster, all served on a vine-covered terrace overlooking the harbor. *52 av. Jean-Mermoz, tel. 93/76–04–04. Reservations essential. Dress: smart. MC, V. Closed Nov.–Easter. Expensive.*

Petit Trianon serves meals on a flowery terrace. *1 blvd. Gal-de-Gaulle, tel. 93/76–05–06. Reservations essential. Dress: jacket and tie. AE, DC, MC, V. Closed mid-Oct.–Jan., Wed. evening, and Thurs. Expensive.*

Provençal, overlooking the harbor of Saint-Paul-du-Cap, is a first-class choice on the cape. *2 av. Denis-Séméria, tel. 93/76–03–97. Reservations essential. Dress: smart. MC, V. Closed mid-Nov.–New Year, Tues. Moderate.*

Lodging As in Beaulieu, you have a choice of two first-class hotels. The mood difference between these two, however, is marked.

Grand Hotel du Cap Ferrat is a grand but modernized resort standing back from the cliffs in isolated splendor at the very southern tip of the cape. A walk across sweeping lawns takes you to the funicular, which leads down to the seaside pool. Anyone can use the pool for a fee (a plus for visitors, a minus for guests), so if you're only passing through, bring your bathing suit and stay for lunch. The restaurant serves good classical French cuisine. *71 blvd. Gal-de-Gaulle, tel. 93/76-00-21. 57 rooms with bath. Facilities: restaurant, pool, private beach, tennis. AE, DC, MC, V. Closed Nov.-Mar. Very Expensive.*

Voile d'Or is a smaller, smarter, younger hotel overlooking the pleasure boats in the colorful harbor of Saint-Jean-du-Cap. It has a private pool and is near the boutiques, restaurants, and antiques shops of an active but generally unspoiled seaside village. The sophistication of the clientele is reflected in the tasteful furnishings: white marble floors, chenille spreads, soft pastel-colored walls covered with hand-loomed tapestries. *Av. Jean-Mermoz, tel. 93/01-13-13. 41 rooms with bath. Facilities: restaurant, pool. AE, DC, MC, V. Closed Nov.-mid-Mar. Very Expensive.*

Brise Marine is a clean, friendly, unpretentious villa with lovely views (try Room 3) and reasonable prices—reasonable, that is, for Cap Ferrat. *5 av. Jean-Mermoz, tel. 93/76-04-36. 15 rooms with bath or shower. Facilities: restaurant. MC, V. Closed Nov.-Jan. Moderate-Expensive.*

Cannes

Cosmopolitan, sophisticated, smart—these are words that describe the liveliest and most flourishing city on the Riviera. It's a resort town—unlike Nice, which is a city—that exists only for the pleasure of its guests. It's a tasteful and expensive breeding ground for yuppies, a sybaritic heaven for those who believe that life is short and that sin has something to do with the absence of a tan.

Whatever you would want to buy in Paris you can find in Cannes, and at about the same price. There are hair-raising salons where trendies get their New Wave cuts, and boutiques for the model man and fashion-page woman. There are frozen kiwi parlors and late-night clubs for Arab princes, playgirls, and pretty boys. Everywhere—along the coast, high up in the hills —are restaurants where chefs make an art of arranging asparagus and peas. The day's catch is swaddled in ice outside bistros where film stars sit at red-checkered tables, trying not to get oyster juice on their black ties. Couples sip wine at open-air cafés behind the beach, where coeds display their pampered bodies. There are few historic monuments, but people come here for the present, not the past.

Picture a long, narrow beach. Stretching along it is a broad, elegant promenade called La Croisette bordered by palm trees and flowers. At one end of the promenade is the modern Festival Hall, a summer casino, and an old harbor where pleasure boats are moored. At the other end is a winter casino and a modern harbor for some of the most luxurious yachts in the world. All along the promenade are cafés, boutiques, and luxury hotels like the Carlton and the Majestic. Speedboats and water-skiers glide by; little waves lick the beach, lined with prostrate bodies. Behind the promenade lies the town, filled with shops, restaurants, and hotels; and behind the town are the hills with the villas of the very rich.

The first thing to do is stroll along the Croisette, stopping at cafés and boutiques along the way. Near the eastern end (turning left as you face the water), before you reach the new port, is the **Parc de la Roserie,** where some 14,000 roses nod their heads. Walking west takes you past **Palais des Festivals** (Festival Hall), where the famous film festival is held each May. Just past the hall is a square called Place du Général-de-Gaulle. On your left is the old port, where boats leave for the Iles de Lérins. If you continue straight beyond the port on Allés de la Liberté, you'll reach a tree-shaded area where flowers are sold in the morning, *boules* is played in the afternoon, and a flea market is held on Saturday. If instead of continuing straight from the square you turn inland, you'll quickly come to Rue Meynadier. Turn left. This is the old main street, which has many 18th-century houses—now boutiques and specialty food shops, where you can buy exotic foods and ship them home.

Time Out Be sure to stop at Number 53 for ice cream; best bet is La Marmite du Diable—a "devil's dish" laced with cocoa and nougat.

Rue Meynadier leads to a covered market, **Marché Forville.** Ahead of you is **Le Suquet,** the fortress in the center of medieval Cannes, and narrow, steep streets leading to a tower with a lovely view.

You, like St. Honorat almost 1,500 years ago, may want to visit the peaceful Iles de Lérins (Lerins Islands) to escape the crowds. The ferry takes 15 minutes to Ste-Marguerite, 30 to Saint-Honorat (tel. 93/39–11–82 for information).

Sainte-Marguerite, the larger of the two, is an island of wooded hills, with a tiny main street lined with fishermen's houses. Visitors enjoy peaceful walks through a forest of enormous eucalyptus trees and parasol pines. Paths wind through a dense undergrowth of tree heathers, rosemary, and thyme. The main attraction is the dank cell in **Fort Royal** where the Man in the Iron Mask was imprisoned (1687–98) before going to the Bastille, where he died in 1703. The mask that he always wore was in fact made of velvet. Was he the illegitimate brother of Louis XIV or Louis XIII's son-in-law? No one knows.

Saint-Honorat is wilder but more tranquil than its sister island. It was named for a hermit who came to escape his followers; but when he founded a monastery here in 410, his disciples followed and the monastery became one of the most powerful in all Christendom. A pope was among the pilgrims who came to walk barefoot around the island. It's still worth taking this two-hour walk to the **old fortified monastery,** where noble Gothic arcades are arranged around a central courtyard. Next door to the "new" 19th-century monastery (open on request) is a shop where the monks sell handicrafts, lavender scent, and a home-brewed liqueur called Lerina. *Monastère de Lérins. Admission free. Open May–Oct., daily 9:45–4:30; Nov.–Apr., daily 10:45–3:30. High Mass at the abbey Sun. 10:45.*

Dining You may have great success with a classical or nouvelle meal, but your best bet, as a rule, is to stick with simply prepared seafood.

Chez Félix is popular with film folk and with those who don't mind paying for the ambience of the Croisette. *63 La Croisette, tel. 93/94–00–61. Reservations advised. Dress: casually smart. V. Expensive.*

La Mirabelle is a popular bistro in the old quarter. The limited menu includes pastas with Saint Pierre fish, salad with foie gras and honey, and homemade sorbets. *24 rue St-Antoine, tel. 93/38–72–75. Reservations advised. Jacket and tie required. MC, V. Closed Dec., first half of Mar. and Tues. Expensive.*

La Poêle d'Or is very plain, perhaps a bit somber, but it has a solid reputation for dishes such as mousseline of trout and chicken in a creamed morelle sauce. *23 rue des Etats-Unis, tel. 93/39–77–65. Reservations essential. Dress: smart. AE, DC, MC, V. Closed mid-Nov.–mid-Dec., Mon. and Tues. lunch. Expensive.*

Le Festival is busy and gay—exactly what you'd expect from a restaurant across from the Palais des Festivals. Lunchtime is best. Specialties include salmon à la menthe and pastries. *52 La Croisette, tel. 93/38–04–81. Reservations essential. Dress: smart. AE, DC, MC, V. Closed Dec. and part of Feb. Moderate.*

Mère Besson is a crowded, fashionable Provençal restaurant with regional specialties. *13 rue des Frères-Pradignac, tel. 93/39–59–24. Reservations advised. Dress: casual. AE, MC, V. Closed Sun.; July–Aug., dinner only. Moderate.*

Au Bec Fin. Here the owner and his son turn out simple, homemade dishes—thick steaks, grilled fish with fennel, salad niçoise, homemade tarts—in a cheerful crowded restaurant near the train station. *12 rue du 24-Août, tel. 93/38–35–86. Reservations advised. Dress: casual. AE, DC, MC, V. Closed Sat. dinner, Sun., and Christmas–late Jan. Inexpensive.*

Part of the Cannes Experience is to drive out of town for dinner, to the hills or to other resorts along the coast. Here are some possibilities:

In **Golfe Juan** (about 15 minutes east of Cannes on the coastal road to Antibes):

Chez Tetou is a friendly, informal restaurant with wood tables on a lovely terrace. Sole meunière and bouillabaisse are outstanding. *Av. des Frères-Roustan, Golfe Juan, tel. 93/63–71–16. Reservations advised. Dress: smart. AE, DC, MC, V. Closed mid-Oct.–Christmas, most of Mar., Wed. Very Expensive.*

In **Mougins** (a hill town about 15 minutes north of Cannes on the road to Grasse):

Le Moulin de Mougins is one of the best-known restaurants in the country, where you can expect patrician treatment—and prices. An inventive nouvelle cuisine is served in a converted olive mill, with such specialties as lobster fricassee, escallop of fresh salmon, and cold wild-strawberry soufflé. *Notre-Dame-de-Vie, 06250, tel. 93/75–78–24. Reservations required. Jacket and tie required. AE, DC, MC, V. Closed Feb.–Mar., Mon. (except summer), and Thurs. lunch (times are variable). Very Expensive.*

L'Amandier. The chef and the old-olive-mill ambience are the same as at Le Moulin de Mougins, but the prices are lower. The nouvelle menu includes a creamy mussel and oyster soup with saffron, crayfish bisque, sea bass, young rabbit pâté, farm cheeses, and homemade tarts. *Pl. Cdt-Lamy, Mougins, tel. 93/ 90–00–91. Reservations advised. Dress: jacket and tie. AE, DC, MC, V. Closed Sat. lunch and Wed. Expensive.*

Le Relais à Mougins is another favorite (though some say it rests too heavily on its reputation) that has been under the supervision of André Surmain, formerly of New York's Lutèce. Mougins is a lovely old town; consider coming here for lunch, when prices are less dear. *32 Pl. Cdt-Lamy, Mougins, tel. 93/ 90–03–47. Reservations essential. Dress: smart. MC, V. Closed mid-Feb.–mid-Mar., mid-Nov.–mid-Dec., Tues. lunch, and Mon. out of season. Expensive.*

Bistro de Mougins features such regional dishes as beet pie, sardines with mint, stuffed rabbit, guinea hen with cabbage, and a good selection of local cheeses. The low prices keep the restaurant crowded. *Pl. Cdt-Lamy, Mougins, tel. 93/75–78– 34. Reservations advised in midsummer. Dress: casual. MC, V. Closed Dec.–mid-Jan., Tues. and Wed. (except evenings in midsummer). Moderate.*

Lodging Because Cannes exists for its tourists, hotels in season aren't cheap; expect to pay 450–1,250 francs a night for a room for two on or near the Croisette. If you're on a budget, best bets are the smaller hotels closer to the train station.

The Carlton has been modernized but still retains the feeling of a luxurious Belle Epoque hotel. The west wing is quieter, with the best views. *58 La Croisette, 06400, tel. 93/68–91–68. 325 rooms with bath. Facilities: Restaurants, bar, terrace, private beach. AE, DC, MC, V. Main restaurant closed Nov.– Christmas. Very Expensive.*

Gray d'Albion provides free video, bathroom phones, and other state-of-the-art amenities. The restaurant, **Le Royal Gray,** is one of the best in town, with an imaginative nouvelle menu that includes rack of lamb with fresh herbs, fresh salmon salad marinated in ginger on a bed of vegetables, prawn salad with orange dressing, and duck aiguillette with apple sauce. For dessert, succumb to the hot walnut cake. *38 rue des Serbes, 06400, tel. 93/68–54–54. 174 rooms with bath. Facilities: 3 restaurants, disco, private beach. AE, DC, MC, V. Restaurant closed Feb., Sun., and Mon. (open Mon. dinner July–Aug.). Very Expensive.*

The Majestic is another of the grand old hotels, perhaps just a notch below the Carlton. There's a great heated seawater pool in a palm grove. The renovated rooms are preferable. *14 La Croisette, tel. 93/68–91–00. 249 rooms with bath. Facilities: restaurant, pool, private beach. AE, DC, MC, V. Closed mid-Nov.–mid-Dec. Very Expensive.*

Beau Séjour has its own pool and garden not far from the beach. *5 rue Fauvettes, tel. 93/39–63–00. 46 rooms with bath. Facilities: restaurant, pool. AE, DC, MC, V. Closed Nov.–mid-Dec. Expensive.*

Novotel-Montfleury has 10 tennis courts, two heated pools, an ice-skating rink, and three restaurants on a nine-acre hillside estate with great views. Its remoteness will be a plus or minus, depending on your priorities. *25 av. Beauséjour, tel. 93/68–91– 50, 183 rooms with bath or shower. Facilities: restaurants, 2 pools, tennis, ice-skating. AE, DC, MC, V. Expensive.*

Victoria nestles among the fancy boutiques on the main shopping street. There's a garden with a small pool and stylish rooms with electrically controlled shutters and other amenities. *122 rue d'Antibes, tel. 93/99–36–36. 25 rooms with bath or shower. Facilities: pool. AE, DC, MC, V. Expensive.*

Cheval Blanc is back from the beach but relatively lower-priced. *3 rue Guy-de-Maupassant, tel. 93/39–88–60. 16 rooms, some with shower. V. Moderate.*

Palma is a small, less expensive hotel near the east end of the promenade. Rooms are small and bright. *77 La Croisette, tel. 93/94–22–16. 52 rooms with bath or shower. AE, DC, MC, V. Moderate.*

Roches Fleuries is back from the beach and even less expensive. *92 rue Georges-Clemenceau, 06400, tel. 93/39–28–78. 24 rooms, 15 with bath. No credit cards. Closed mid-Nov.–Dec. Inexpensive.*

On to Cap d'Antibes Strictly speaking, Cap d'Antibes refers to the southern tip of the cape, but it has come to mean the entire peninsula, including even the resort towns of Antibes and Juan-les-Pins. Though we'll discuss the three together, be sure to distinguish among them, for each has its own character and clientele. On the eastern side of the cape is the village of Antibes, which boasts a Picasso Museum and, like Nice, a charming old section with restaurants, antiques shops, and boutiques. You'll want to visit Antibes but probably not stay, because it has no memorable hotels. On the western side of the cape, closer to Cannes, is the village of Juan-les-Pins, which has a shoreline backed by ferro-concrete high rises where French families spend their two-week vacations. Visitors under 25 enjoy the crowded public beaches and the neon nightlife, but others may have less reason to stay. The place to stay is on the cape itself—a lush and peaceful garden with sumptuous villas, guest houses, and hotels. Cannes is perhaps 20 minutes away, so you can take advantage of everything the city has to offer and then return here at night. If you're single or into crowds, stay in Cannes. But if you want to be alone with someone you want to be alone with, look no farther than Cap d'Antibes.

Cap d'Antibes

The main reason to visit the cape, even if you're not staying here, is to enjoy the view at Pointe Bacon; to walk through the Thuret Gardens (open weekdays 8–12:30 and 2–5:30; closed weekends); to have lunch or a swim at the exclusive Hotel du Cap; and to imagine yourself living in the palatial estates discreetly hidden behind hedges and trees.

Follow D2559 along the eastern shore to **Pointe Bacon,** where you should be able to see as far east as Nice and Cap Ferrat. Continue south along the eastern shore of the cape on Boulevard de Bacon, which merges with Boulevard de la Garoupe. At the end of the boulevard turn left to visit the Hotel du Cap (*see* Lodging, below), or turn right on Boulevard F. Meilland and right again on Chemin des Nielles to the top of the hill, where the road ends. There's a great view here, and a church, La Garoupe, which has two aisles, each built at a different time and dedicated to a different saint.

Return down Chemin des Nielles and make the first right on Boulevard du Cap to the **Thuret Gardens.** Created by a botanist in 1856, they contain exotic cacti, palms, mimosas, and some 141 species of eucalyptus.

Continue straight on Boulevard du Cap and make a left on Chemin des Sables. Bear right and return to Cannes, about 11.2 km (7 mi) west on N7.

Dining Many day-trippers have their limousines take them to lunch at the **Pavilion Eden Roc,** the restaurant of the exclusive Hotel du Cap (*see* below). The menu is nouvelle.

Auberge du Bacon is near Pointe Bacon, which you'll pass as you drive down the east shore of the cape. The bouillabaisse is, some say, the best on the coast. Seafood dishes are served on a terrace with a lovely view. Specialties include steamed bass, prawn salad, and grilled mullet. *Blvd. de Bacon, Cap d'Antibes, tel. 93/61–50–02. Reservations essential. Jacket and tie required. AE, DC, MC, V. Closed Sun. dinner, Mon., and mid-Nov.–Jan. Expensive.*

Lodging **Hotel du Cap d'Antibes** is the best-known and most expensive resort on the Riviera. The elite of the world stay in this baronial, Second Empire–style resort, which is said to have a staff-guest ratio of one-to-one. The room I saw was about to be occupied by Jimmy Stewart; the *Who's Who* list of recent guests includes Henry Kissinger, Dustin Hoffman, and the members of Duran Duran. Charles Graves tells in his book *The Azure Coast* how George Raft walked down from the hotel to the pool with Norma Shearer, passing hairy-legged Charles Boyer. While Marlene Dietrich was checking out, Edward G. Robinson and Erich Maria Remarque were sitting at the bar—Robinson looking at himself, Remarque just looking glum. F. Scott Fitzgerald of course stayed here with Zelda and is said to have used the hotel as his model in *Tender Is the Night*. That said, it should be added that the atmosphere today is a shade self-conscious. Day-trippers can pay to use the pool—which is great for them, but not for guests. A child would be an anomaly here—unless he were dressed in white, with knee-high socks. There is no library, no sequestered bar, no place to relax except at the pool and in the privacy of your room. *Blvd. Kennedy, 06600 Antibes, tel. 93/61–39–01. 130 rooms with bath. Facilities: restaurant, tennis, pool. No credit cards. Closed Nov.–Apr. Very Expensive.*

Hotel Levant is a rectangular, motellike building by the sea. It has no special charm, but is clean and new and very friendly. *Plage Garoupe, blvd. de la Garoupe, tel. 93/61–41–33. 27 rooms with bath. Facilities: private beach. V. Closed Oct.–Easter. Expensive.*

La Gardiole has 20 simple, quiet rooms among the pines, away from the sea. *Chemin de la Garoupe, tel. 93/61–35–03. 21 rooms with bath or shower. Facilities: restaurant. AE, DC, MC, V. Closed Nov.–Feb. Moderate.*

Antibes What makes a visit to **Antibes** worthwhile are the picturesque old streets, lined with shops and cafés, and the Picasso Museum.

The **Musée Picasso** is housed in a Grimaldi castle overlooking the sea. Picasso had part of the castle at his disposal when he arrived on the Riviera in 1946. His output was extraordinary—some 145 works in six months; and most of what you'll see was produced during his first season here. Particularly noteworthy are his ceramics from Vallauris and his joyful Antibes paintings, inspired by the marine and mythological life of the Mediterranean. Don't miss them! *Pl. du Château. Admission:*

*15 frs. adults, 8 frs. children and seniors. Open Dec.–Oct., 10–
noon and 2–6; closed Tues.*

Just north of the museum is the **Church of the Immaculate Con-
ception,** which has a wood crucifix from 1447 in the choir and an
early 16th-century altarpiece by Louis Bréa in the south transept.

From either the church or the museum walk inland one block
and turn left to the colorful marketplace at **Cours Masséna.**
Ahead of you is Rue de la Touraque. Spend an hour in this area,
strolling through the streets of the old town, among the antiques and pastry shops.

Antibes is the rose capital of Europe. Some 250 ha (625 acres) of
carnations, tulips, and gladioli grow here, too. Anyone who
loves color will want to visit the flower market near the Pont
Vauban (Vauban Bridge).

Dining **La Bonne Auberge** (north of Antibes on N7—near La Brague)
is expensive but is one of the most famous restaurants on the
coast. Dinner, a blend of classic and nouvelle, is served either in
a Provençal dining room or on a flowery terrace. Specialties include lobster soup, artichoke salad with lobster, and grilled
bass (*loup*). *Quartier de la Brague, Antibes, tel. 93/33–36–65.
Reservations strongly advised. Jacket and tie required. AE,
MC, V. Closed Mon. (except for dinner mid-Apr.–Sept.), and
mid-Nov.–mid-Dec. Expensive.*

La Marguerite has white-lacquered paneling and lots of flowers. Prices are reasonable, particularly for the fixed menu. Try
the veal and rice salad, stuffed chicken, fresh fish, and regional
cheeses. *11 rue Sadi-Carnot, tel. 93/34–08–27. Reservations
advised. Dress: casually elegant. MC, V. Closed Mon., Tues.
lunch, and Sun. evening out of season. Expensive.*

Les Vieux Murs sits on the ramparts close to the sea. The decor—
stucco walls, arched ceilings—is regional. The classical menu
includes fish soup and lobster thermidor. *130 prom, Amiral-de-
Grasse, tel. 93/34–06–73. Reservations advised. Dress: smart.
AE, DC, MC, V. Closed mid-Nov.–Christmas and Wed. Expensive.*

L'Oursin, on the edge of the old town, is a crowded family restaurant with little atmosphere, but it has a solid reputation for
fresh seafood and reasonable prices. *16 rue de la République,
tel. 93/34–13–46. Reservations advised. Dress: casual. V. Closed
Aug., Sun. eve, and Mon. Moderate.*

Auberge Provençale is located on a lovely old square behind the
Picasso Museum. Specialties include smoked trout, coq au vin,
and beef fillet. *61 pl. Nationale, tel. 93/34–13–24. Reservations
advised. Dress: smart. AE, DC, MC, V. Closed mid-Apr.–
mid-May, mid-Nov.–mid-Dec., and Mon. Moderate.*

Juan-les-Pins **Juan-les-Pins** splashed into life in the 1920s, thanks to its mile-
long beach (an improvement on the man-made beach at Cannes)
and its amenities. The ambience is—with two notable
exceptions—strictly fast-food. If you're alone and don't want
to be, hang out on the beach and wait for night, when the bar
and disco lights outshine the stars.

Dining and The two luxury-class hotels in Juan-les-Pins have no trouble
Lodging filling their rooms in-season, but it's not easy to understand
why. What use is elegance in discoland?

Belles Rives. Here rooms are rather small and basic, but the location is lovely, with a stone terrace overlooking the harbor. *33 blvd. Edouard-Baudoin, tel. 93/61–02–79. 40 rooms with bath. Facilities: restaurant, private beach. AE, DC, MC, V. Closed Nov.–Mar. Very Expensive.*

Juana is the more tasteful of the two. Though hidden behind hedges, the pool sits at the very edge of a busy road near the center of town. Juan-les-Pins is only 10 minutes from Cannes by train—20 by car—so you may want to come for dinner at the Terrasse Restaurant, which enjoys a first-class reputation. *Av. Gallice, 06160 Juan-les-Pins, tel. 93/61–08–70. 45 rooms with bath. Facilities: restaurant, bar, pool. No credit cards. Closed late Oct.–mid-Apr. Very Expensive.*

Eden is located between the train station and the beach and is lower priced. *16 av. Louis-Gallet, tel. 93/61–05–20. 17 rooms, some with bath or shower. No credit cards. Closed Nov.–Jan. Moderate.*

Saint-Tropez

There's only one main road from Sainte-Maxime to Saint-Tropez, and in season the 13.6-km (8.5-mi) trip can take two hours. If you're planning to drive down from Cannes for the day, be sure to leave in the early morning and to return in the early afternoon or late at night. Stick to Autoroute A8 and avoid the coast as long as possible. The worst time to come is on summer weekends, when you're competing with the rest of France. Best bet is to take a hydrofoil from Cannes or Saint-Raphaël and avoid the road altogether. If you want to combine trips to the Esterel and Saint-Tropez, drive southwest along the coast from Cannes to Saint-Raphaël and take the hydrofoil from there. Make arrangements through any travel agency or hotel. Cabs in Saint-Tropez are available at 94/97–05–27. For bus information, call 94/97–01–88.

Old money never came to Saint-Tropez, but Brigitte Bardot did. She came with her director Roger Vadim in 1956 to film *And God Created Woman*, and the resort has never been the same. Actually, the village was "discovered" by Guy de Maupassant and by the French painter Paul Signac (1863–1935), who came in 1892 and brought his friends—Matisse, Bonnard, and others. What attracted them was the pure, radiant light, and the serenity and colors of the landscape. Colette moved into a villa here between the wars and contributed to its notoriety. When the cinema people staked their claim in the 1950s, Saint-Tropez became Saint-Trop (*trop* in French means "too much").

Anything associated with the past seems either detestable or absurd in Saint-Tropez, so you may not want to hear the story of how it got its name. In AD 68, a Roman soldier named Torpes from Pisa was beheaded for professing his Christian faith in the presence of the Emperor Nero. The headless body was put in a boat between a dog and a cock and drifted out to sea. The body eventually floated ashore, perfectly preserved, still watched over by the two animals. The buried remains became a place of pilgrimage, which by the 4th century was called Saint-Tropez. In the late 15th century, under the Genovese, it became a small independent republic.

Nowadays, the beaches are filled with every imaginable type of human animal: aggressively cheerful volleyball players searching for meaningful one-night relationships, supergirls with Cartier bracelets, golden boys with big dogs, aspiring Bardots, college girls with organic faces, middle-aged men with mirrored shades, bare-breasted mothers with children and dogs. The atmosphere is part Benetton, part Tarzan-and-Jane. In summer the population swells from 7,000 to 64,000.

Off-season is the time to come, but even in summer you can find reasons to stay. The soft, sandy beaches are the best on the coast. Beauty is beauty—even if it wears gold chains. Take an early morning stroll along the harbor or down the narrow medieval streets—the rest of the world will still be comatose from the Night Before—and you'll see just how pretty Saint-Tropez is, with its tiny squares and its rich, pastel-colored houses bathed in light. There's a weekend's worth of trendy boutiques to explore—to be delighted by or shocked at—and many cute cafés where you can sit under colored awnings sipping wine and feeling very French. The restored harbor front has a reputable art museum. Five minutes from town and you're in a green world of vineyards and fields, where you'll see nothing more lascivious than a butterfly fluttering around some chestnut leaves or a grapevine clinging to a farmhouse wall. Above the fertile fields are mountains crowned with medieval villages, where you can come at dusk for wild strawberry tarts and fabulous views. Perhaps it's the soft light, perhaps the rich fields and faded pastels, but nowhere else along the coast will you experience so completely the magic of Provence.

Time Out | Food at the **Café des Arts** may be ordinary, but the café is a popular place to sit and feel part of the in-crowd. *Pl. Carnot. Closed Oct.–Mar.*

Near the waterfront is the **Chapelle de l'Annonciade**, a well-known museum of works by Impressionist and Postimpressionist painters who loved Saint-Tropez: Maurice de Vlaminck, Georges Braque, Georges Seurat, Pierre Bonnard, Raoul Dufy, Georges Rouault, and others. *Quai de l'Epi, Admission: 16 frs. adults, 8 frs. children. Open Wed.–Mon. 10–noon and 3–6; closed Tues.*

You may enjoy a trip through **Port-Grimaud**, a modern architect's idea of a Provençal fishing village-cum-Venice, built out into the gulf for the yachting crowd—each house with its own mooring. Particularly appealing are the harmonious pastel colors, which have weathered nicely, and the graceful bridges over the canals.

From Saint-Tropez take D93 south about 11.2 km (7 mi) to the old Provençal market town of **Ramatuelle.** The ancient houses are huddled together on the slope of a rocky spur 13 m (440 ft) above the sea. The central square has a 17th-century church and a huge 300-year-old elm. Surrounding the square are narrow, twisting streets with medieval archways and vaulted passages.

From Ramatuelle, follow signs to the old village of **Gassin**, which is less than 3.2 km (2 mi) away. The ride is lovely, through vineyards and woods, and takes you over the highest point of the peninsula (320.9 m/1,070 ft), where you can stop and enjoy a splendid view. The perched village of Gassin, with its venerable old houses and its 12th-century Romanesque church, has somehow managed to maintain its medieval appearance. The best time to visit is in the late afternoon, when the shadows deepen and the tourists have gone home. Find yourself a table at an outdoor café, order a fruit tart, and watch the sunlight turn the fields to gold. From Gassin, return to Saint-Tropez or continue back along the coast to Sainte-Maxime and Cannes.

Dining Saint-Tropez has many charming restaurants, but no great ones. If film stars like Catherine Deneuve leave the privacy of their villas, it's to dine in Le Mas de Chastelas or Le Byblos (*see* Lodging, below). Best bets are restaurants big on atmosphere that specialize in fresh fish. The busy waterfront is lined with small restaurants where you can sit in tiny back rooms or people-watch in front, beneath colored awnings.

Les Mouscardins is a busy Provençal-type restaurant in the old city, serving such local favorites as bouillabaisse and grilled sea bass. *Rue Portalet, tel. 94/97–01–53. Reservations essential. Dress: casually smart. DC, MC, V. Closed Nov.–Jan. Expensive.*

Le Café des Arts in the quieter, old part of town is where you can join the locals. The one-price menu includes zucchini, stuffed eggplant, veal in wine sauce, grilled fish, and all the wine you can drink. *Place Carnot, tel. 94/97–02–25. Reservations advised. Dress: casually elegant. MC, V. Closed mid-Oct.–Feb. Moderate.*

L'Escale is the best (try the bouillabaisse) and busiest of the waterfront restaurants. Families come at 8, singles at 10. *9 quai Jean-Jaurès, tel. 94/97–00–63. Reservations advised. Dress: casual. V. Moderate.*

Le Girelier, also near the port, offers fishy fare at reasonable prices. *Quai Jean-Jaurès, tel. 94/97–03–87. Reservations not required. Dress: casual. AE, DC, MC, V. Closed mid-Jan.–early Mar. Moderate.*

Pizzeria Romana is a popular eaterie with a more ambitious menu and higher prices than its name implies. The fresh pasta is tops. *Chemin des Conquetes, tel. 94/97–13–16. Reservations advised in midsummer. Dress: casual. MC, V. Moderate.*

Lodging **Le Byblos** is a smart, flashy hotel-village where the gold-chain set should feel right at home. The look is New York Casbah, with Persian carpets on the dining room ceiling, a genuine leopard-skin bar, raw stone and brick walls, and lots of heavy damask and hammered brass. It's a real conversation piece, with an imaginative use of space. *Av. Paul Signac, 83990, tel. 94/97–00–04. 97 rooms with bath. Facilities: restaurant, pool, sauna, exercise room, disco, nightclub. AE, DC, MC, V. Closed Nov.–Feb.; restaurant closed early Oct.–early May. Very Expensive.*

Le Mas de Chastelas is a renovated 17th-century manor house in a rural setting just outside of town, with a heated pool, tennis courts, and sophisticated dining. *Rte. de Gassin, 83990, tel. 94/56–09–11. 31 rooms with bath. Facilities: restaurant, pool. AE, DC, MC, V. Closed Oct.–Mar. Very Expensive.*

Levant, located just out of town, has 28 modern rooms, a heated pool, and a beautiful garden. *Rte. de Salins, tel. 94/97–33–33. 28 rooms with bath. Facilities: restaurant, pool. AE, DC, MC, V. Closed mid-Oct.–Easter. Expensive.*

Ponche is an old inn with a chic but peaceful terrace restaurant serving such specialties as saffron mussel soup, giant shrimp in tarragon sauce, lamb stew, and a homemade lemon pie. *Pl. Revelin, tel. 94/97–02–53. 19 rooms with bath. Facilities: restaurant. AE, MC, V. Closed mid-Oct.–Easter. Expensive.*

L'Ermitage is next door to Le Byblos, but the ambience is more subdued. It's one of the few hotels with a view of the town. *Av. Paul-Signac, 83990, tel. 94/97–52–33. 27 rooms with bath. AE, DC. Moderate.*

Lou Troupelen is a modernized farmhouse with gardens, not far from the beach or town. *Chemin des Vendanges, tel. 94/97–44–88. 44 rooms with bath or shower. AE, DC, MC, V. Closed mid-Oct.–Easter. Moderate.*

There are several small, family-run hotels among the farms and vineyards along the road to Tahiti Beach—one of the most tranquil settings on the Riviera.

La Figuière is the only one with dining facilities. *Rte. de Tahiti, Ramatuelle, tel. 94/97–18–21. 45 rooms with bath or shower. Facilities: restaurant, pool, tennis. MC, V. Closed Oct.–Easter. Moderate–Expensive.*

Saint-Vincent is pleasant and friendly, with a pool, and vineyards outside the door. *Rte. de Tahiti, Ramatuelle, tel. 94/97–42–48. 16 rooms with bath. Facilities: pool. MC, V. Closed Nov.–Easter. Expensive.*

Excursions from Nice and Cannes

Here are some of the most worthwhile excursions from the Nice area (including Beaulieu and Cap Ferrat), and from the Cannes area (including Cap d'Antibes).

Peillon Peillon and Monte Carlo are both about 19.2 km (12 mi) east of Nice and can be combined in a single excursion from Cannes or Nice. Monte Carlo is along the coast; Peillon is about 9.6 km (6 mi) inland. From Nice take D2204. Turn right on D21. Turn right, up the mountain to Peillon. If you're returning to Nice, return the way you came. If you're continuing to Monte Carlo, return to D21. Turn right. Turn right again on D53 to the medieval town of Peille. Continue south on D53 to Monaco.

To picture Peillon, just close your eyes and imagine a fortified medieval town perched on a craggy mountaintop more than 305 m (1,000 ft) above the sea. Of all the perched villages along the Riviera, Peillon is the most spectacular and the least spoiled. Unchanged since the Middle Ages, the village has only a few narrow streets and many steps and covered alleys. There's really nothing to do here but look—which is why the tour buses stay away. Some 50 families live in Peillon—including professionals from Paris who think it's chic summering in a genuine medieval village and artists who sincerely want to escape the craziness of the world below. Visit the studio of a very talented and well-known French sculptor; visit the **White Penitents' Chapel** (key available at the Auberge); spend a half hour exploring the ancient streets, and be on your way.

Time Out Stay for lunch or dinner at the charming **Auberge de la Madone** (Peillon 06440, L'Escarene, Alpes-Maritimes, tel. 93/91–91–17). The ideal arrangement is to arrive in the late afternoon and spend the night at this lovely, family-run *auberge* (inn), far away from the traffic and heat along the coast.

Roquebrune If you haven't seen enough medieval towns, continue south on D53 (en route from Peillon to Monte Carlo) and then take the Upper Corniche road to **Roquebrune.** From here, head south to Monaco.

The ancient town of Roquebrune is spread out along the slopes. Shops are filled with the wares of painters and artisans. The Carolingian castle was restored in the early 16th century by the Grimaldis. The keep is the oldest in Provence, with walls from 1.8 to 3.8 m (6 to 13 ft) thick.

Dining **Vistaero** is 3.2 km (2 mi) from Roquebrune. A good deal of what you pay for is the fabulous view. *Grande Corniche, tel. 93/35-01-50. Reservations essential. Dress: smart. AE, DC, MC, V. Closed lunch in summer. Expensive.*

Villefranche Villefranche is on the coastal road (N98, the Lower Corniche), only 3.8 km (2.4 mi) east of Nice on the way to Cap Ferrat and Beaulieu.

The harbor town of **Villefranche,** only about 10 minutes from Nice or Cap Ferrat, is a miniature version of old Marseilles, with steep narrow streets—one, Rue Obscure, an actual tunnel—winding down to the sea. The town is a stage set of brightly colored houses—orange buildings with lime-green shutters, yellow buildings with ice-blue shutters—the sort of place where *Fanny* could have been filmed. If you're staying in Nice, include Villefranche on a tour of Cap Ferrat. To see the Cocteau Chapel (*see* below), you'll need to arrive by 4 PM. If you can skip the chapel, best bet is to come at sundown (for dinner, perhaps) and enjoy an hour's walk around the harbor, when the sun turns the soft pastels to gold.

The 17th-century **St. Michael Church** has a strikingly realistic Christ, carved of boxwood by an unknown convict. The **Chapel of Saint-Pierre-des-Pêcheurs,** known as the **Cocteau Chapel,** is a small Romanesque chapel once used for storing fishing nets, which the French writer and painter Jean Cocteau decorated in 1957. Visitors walk through the flames of the Apocalypse (represented by staring eyes on either side of the door) and enter a room filled with frescoes of St. Peter, gypsies, and the women of Villefranche. *Open May–Oct., daily 9–noon and 2–4:30; Nov.–Apr. 9–noon and 2:30–7.*

Dining **Mère Germaine** overlooks the port. *7 quai Amiral-Courbet, tel. 93/01-71-39. Reservations advised. Dress: casual. AE, MC, V. Closed mid-Nov.–Christmas and Wed. out of season. Moderate.*

La Campanette, near St. Michael Church, is an inexpensive bistro with turn-of-the-century decor, serving meals such as fish ravioli in shellfish sauce, mussels in pastry with chicory, and chicken with clementines. *2 rue du Baron-de-Brès, tel. 93/01-79-98. Reservations unnecessary. Dress: casual. V. Inexpensive.*

Cagnes From either Cannes or Nice take Autoroute AB to the Cagnes exit.

There are actually three "Cagnes"—**Le-Gros-de-Cagnes,** the seaside resort on the coast; **Cagnes Ville,** the modern commercial section; and **Haut-de-Cagnes,** the old town leading up to the castle. From Cagnes Ville follow signs to the Renoir Museum.

The **Renoir Museum** is at Lès Collettes, the house that Pierre Auguste Renoir built for himself in 1908 and where he spent the last 12 years of his life. One of his well-known canvases, *Les Collettes Landscape*, is on view on the ground floor, and his bronze statue of *Venus* stands in the garden surrounded by fruit trees. But what you'll remember most are Renoir's studios, preserved just as he left them, and the gardens where he walked and painted. The sense of his presence is overwhelming as you stroll among the olive trees, gazing out across the fields through the most magical, luminescent light at the ancient town of Cagnes, rising in the distance like a fortress in a dream. *Av. des Collettes, tel. 93/20–85–57. Admission: 6 frs. adults, 3 frs. children. Open Apr.–Oct. daily 2:30–6:30; Nov.–Mar., Wed.–Mon. 2–5.*

If time is limited and you're planning to visit Saint-Paul-de-Vence and Tourrette-sur-Loup, consider seeing Haut-de-Cagnes only from Renoir's house and continuing to the Escoffier Museum in Villeneuve-Loubet (*see* below). Haut-de-Cagnes is a lovely old medieval village, but it doesn't have the craft shops you'll see in the other villages; and the streets are very steep and look down on a modern town. If you do decide to visit Haut-de-Cagnes—it's only a few minutes' drive from Renoir's house—park near the top of the town, at the Castle Museum.

The **Castle Museum** is a feudal castle restored by the Grimaldis when they lived here from the 14th century to the French Revolution, at which time it was looted and sold. The marble stairway, inspired by the one at Fontainebleau, leads to state rooms with ornately painted ceilings and notable collections of objets d'art and paintings. The throne room is most sumptuous. In the cellar the olive gets its due in the **Museum of the Olive Tree.** On the second floor is a **Museum of Modern Mediterranean Art.** *Pl. du Château, tel. 93/20–61–07. Admission: 6 frs. adults, 3 frs. students. Open Easter–mid-Oct., daily 10–noon and 2:30–7; mid-Nov.–Easter, Wed.–Mon. 10–noon and 2–5; closed Tues.*

Dining **Le Cagnard** offers a nouvelle cuisine menu that includes duck liver pâté, crayfish in sauternes au gratin, and veal with mushrooms. The fixed-price lunch is reasonably priced. *Haut de Cagnes, tel. 93/20–73–22. Reservations essential. Dress: smart. AE, DC, MC, V. Closed Nov.–mid-Dec. and Thurs. lunch. Very Expensive.*

Josy-Jo is well known for its regional cuisine, including duck pâté, calf's liver, mutton, and a dessert of lemon mousse. *2 rue Planastel, tel. 93/20–68–76. Reservations advised. Dress: casually smart. MC, V. Closed Nov. and Mon. Expensive.*

Peintres has lovely views and reasonable prices. *71 Montee-Bourgade, Haut de Cagnes, tel. 93/20–83–08. Reservations advised. Dress: casual. AE, DC, MC, V. Closed Wed. Moderate.*

Villeneuve-Loubet From Cagnes Ville (the modern city below the old town) take Avenue de la Gate and D2085 (Avenue de Grasse) less than 3.2 km (2 mi) to the Escoffier Museum. If this doesn't interest you, go directly from Cagnes to Saint-Paul-de-Vence.

The **Escoffier Museum** is the birthplace of the king of chefs, Auguste Escoffier (1846–1935). It includes a Provençal kitchen with every sort of cooking utensil imaginable; mementos of his career as head chef of the Carlton in London and as creator of

Peach Melba; and his collection of some 15,000 menus dating back to 1820. *3 rue Escoffier, tel. 93/20–80–51. Admission: 12 frs. adults, 6 frs. students. Open Dec.–Oct., Tues.–Sun. 2:15–6.*

Saint-Paul-de-Vence Take D2 north about 11.2 km (7 mi) to **Saint-Paul-de-Vence.** The atmosphere in this perfect gem of a town is Medieval Chic. None of the hill towns is better preserved. Not even the hordes of tourists—for which the village now exists—can destroy its ancient charm. You can walk the narrow, cobbled streets in perhaps 15 minutes, but you'll need another hour to explore the shops—mostly galleries selling second-rate landscape paintings, but also a few serious studios and giftshops selling everything from candles to dolls, dresses, and hand-dipped chocolate strawberries. Visit in the late afternoon, when the tour buses are gone, and enjoy a drink among the Klees and Picassos in the Colombe D'Or (*see* Dining and Lodging, below). You'll want to light a candle in the 12th-century Gothic church to relieve its wonderful gloom. The treasury is rich in 12th- to 15th-century pieces, including processional crosses, reliquaries, and an enamel Virgin and Child.

The **Maeght Foundation** is one of the world's most famous small museums of modern art. Founded in 1964 by Aimé Maeght, a Paris art dealer, and his wife, it sits on a grassy hill a 10-minute walk above Saint-Paul-de-Vence. In addition to regular exhibits, the museum has a permanent collection of ceramics by Joan Miró, mobiles by Alexander Calder, bronze figures by Alberto Giacometti, and stained-glass windows by Georges Braque. Check for concerts in summer. *Tel. 93/32–81–63. Admission: 35 frs. adults, 25 frs. children. Open Apr.–Oct., daily 10–12:30 and 3–7; Nov.–Mar., daily 10–12:30 and 2:30–6.*

Dining and Lodging **Le Chateau du Domaine St. Martin.** The castle sits on a 14-ha (35-acre) property overlooking Vence. Rooms are exquisitely decorated with antiques, needlepoint, and brocade. Visitors are not credit card numbers but guests in a private castle. Rooms in the tower are smaller and less expensive, but decorated with the same loving attention to detail. The formal dining room is one of the best along the coast. *Rte. de Coursegoules, 06140, tel. 93/58–02–02. 25 rooms with bath. Facilities: restaurant, garden, pool, tennis, helicopter landing pad. AE, DC, MC, V. Very Expensive.*

Mas d'Artigny. There's tranquility and peaceful wooded trails; but unfortunately the public areas, though lavish, are more suited for a convention of professionals than for young lovers. It's not that anything is in bad taste but that the ambience is chain-hotelish. The main reasons to stay are the private swimming pools—one per room—and the bathtubs built for two. *Chemin des Salettes, tel. 93/32–84–54. 59 rooms and 29 suites with bath. Facilities: restaurant, pool, tennis. DC, MC, V. Very Expensive.*

Colombe D'Or. Here Pablo Picasso, Paul Klee, Raoul Dufy, Maurice Utrillo, and others—all friends of the former owner—paid with paintings, which hang today on the walls above the tables. What a vast difference there is between seeing a Calder in a museum and lunching on a terrace with a Calder mobile swaying among the lemon trees. So this is what it means to live with art! Unless you like being an Ugly American, don't visit without having a drink or stopping for lunch or dinner. The restaurant has a reputation for simple, adequate meals in an unforgettable setting. The building has great warmth and character, even though it was constructed only after World War II. The rooms are booked far in advance. Staying here, you can explore Saint-Paul-de-Vence in the early morning, or under a full moon, when the only footfalls are your own. *06570 Saint-Paul-de-Vence, tel. 93/32–80–02. 15 rooms with bath. Facilities: restaurant, pool. AE, DC, MC, V. Closed mid-Nov.–late Dec., part of Jan. Expensive.*

Le Hameau consists of four buildings on the grounds of an old farm set among fruit trees. Try Room 11. *Rte. de La Colle, tel. 93/32–80–24. 14 rooms, some with bath. AE, MC, V. Closed mid-Nov.–mid-Feb. Moderate.*

Hotel Marc-Hely is a family hotel in a private house set back from the road that runs between the coast and Saint-Paul-de-Vence. *535 Rte. de Cagnes, tel. 93/22–64–10. 14 rooms, some with bath. AE, MC, V. Moderate.*

Vence   From Saint-Paul-de-Vence continue north on D2, which runs directly into the old section (*Vieille Ville*) of **Vence** at Avenue M. Maurel. If you haven't seen enough medieval towns, park and walk around. In the center is the Romanesque cathedral, which has a nave (central corridor), four aisles, and no transepts (projecting arms). Of special note is a mosaic by Marc Chagall of Moses in the bullrushes and the ornate 15th-century carved wood choir stalls.

From D2, turn left on Avenue M. Maurel. Cross Avenue Foch and turn right on Avenue H. Matisse to the main attraction of Vence, the **Rosaire (Matisse) Chapel** (open Tues. and Thurs., 10–11:30 and 2:30–5:30). "Despite its imperfections I think it is my masterpiece . . . the result of a lifetime devoted to the search for truth," wrote Matisse, who designed and dedicated the chapel in the late 1940s when he was in his eighties and nearly blind.

Tourrette-sur-Loup   From Vence, drive west about 4.8 km (3 mi) on D2210. There's a limit to how many medieval hill towns you're going to want to see. The three I'd recommend are Peillon, because it's the most uncommercial and the most dramatically situated; Saint-Paul-de-Vence, because it's easy to reach, is surrounded by first-class hotels and restaurants, and is visually a gem; and **Tourrette-sur-Loup,** because it's less commercial than other towns and its shops are filled not with postcards and scented soaps but with the work of dedicated artisans. The village of Moustiers-Sainte-Marie is also recommended, should you make the full-day trip to the Grand Canyon of the Verdon (*see* below.)

The outer houses of Tourrette-sur-Loup form a rampart on a rocky plateau, 389.9 m (1,300 ft) above a valley full of violets. A rough stone path takes you on a circular route around the rim of the town, past the shops of engravers, weavers, potters, and painters. Ask any artisan for a map of the town that locates each of the shops. Also worth visiting is a single-nave 14th-century church, which has a notable wood altarpiece.

Dining   **Le Petit Manoir.** It would be difficult to find a sweeter, friendlier place to eat than this tiny restaurant. *21 Grande-Rue, tel. 93/24–19–19. Reservations advised. Dress: casually smart. MC, V. Moderate–Expensive.*

Gorges du Loup   From Tourrette-sur-Loup, continue west about 8 km (5 mi) on D2210 to Pont-du-Loup. Take D6 north for 6.4 km (4 mi) along the east side of the gorge, then head south on D3, past Gourdon, to D2085, the main road between Grasse and Cagnes.

This is a very scenic drive up one side of a dramatic gorge and down the other. It's less impressive than the Grand Canyon of the Verdon, but a great deal closer to the coast.

Time Out If you're afflicted with a sweet tooth, stop in Pont-du-Loup at **La Confiserie des Gorges du Loup** and watch the good people making sugared tangerines, chocolate-covered orange peels, and rose-petal jam. Pretty unsubtle stuff from the land of the *tarte aux pommes*, but good to munch on as you drive around the gorge.

As you head north on D6, park after the third tunnel and walk back for spectacular views into the depths of the gorge.

The road (D3) that takes you south along the west edge of the gorge reaches dizzying heights. Gourdon is touted as one of the must stops on the tourist route, which should be enough to dissuade you from stopping there unless you're desperate for scented soaps or lavender toilet water.

Grasse From Gourdon, continue south on D3 to D2085. From here, turn left (east), back to Cagnes and Nice; or turn right and make a short detour to Grasse. If you're headed back to Cannes, you have to pass through Grasse en route to N85.

Grasse is bottled and sold on every escorted tour along the coast. The reason is its accessibility from both Cannes and Nice, and its perfumeries, where tourists spend money. The town is also famous for its preserves and for its crystallized fruits and flowers.

If touring a perfume factory in an attractive modern town is your idea of pleasure, visit Grasse. If you had visited 4 centuries ago, when the town specialized in leather work, you would have come for gloves. In the 16th century, when scented gloves became the rage, the town began cultivating flowers and distilling essences. That was the beginning of the perfume industry. Today some three-fourths of the world's essences are made here from wild lavender, jasmine, violets, daffodils, and other sweet-smelling flowers. Five thousand producers supply some 20 factories and six cooperatives. If you've ever wondered why perfume is so expensive, consider that it takes 10,000 flowers to produce 1 kg (2.2 lb) of jasmine petals, and that nearly one ton of jasmine is needed—nearly 7 million flowers—to distill a quart and a half of essence. Sophisticated Paris perfumers mix Grasse essences into their own secret formulas; perfumes made and sold in Grasse are considerably less subtle. You can of course buy Parisian perfumes in Grasse—at Parisian prices.

Visitors can buy local perfumes and get some sense of how they're made at any of the three perfumeries: **Fragonard** (20 Boulevard Fragonard); **Galimard** (Les 4 Chemins, Route de Cannes), and **Molinard** (60 Boulevard Victor-Hugo). All three are open weekdays during working hours.

A new perfume museum, the **Musée International de la Parfumerie**, was opened early in February 1989, and explains the history and manufacturing process of perfume. Old machinery, pots, and flasks can be admired; toiletry, cosmetics, and make-up accessories are on display; and there is a section devoted to perfume's sophisticated marketing aids, with examples of packaging and advertising posters. *8 pl. du Cours. Admission: 10 frs. adults, 5 frs. children and senior citizens. Open Wed.–Mon. 10–6; closed Tues.*

From Grasse return to Cannes on N85, or to Nice on N85, D35, and A8.

Biot and Vallauris are just a mile or two inland from the coastal road between Cannes and Nice. If you're staying in the Nice area, visit these two towns as you head south along the coast to Cannes. If you're staying in the Cannes area, visit them as you drive north along the coast to Nice.

Biot On the road to Biot is the **Musée National Fernand Léger** (Léger Museum). Donated to France by Léger's widow in 1959, it offers visitors a good opportunity to trace the artist's development from 1904 until his death in 1955. The building has a 1,200-sq-m (4,000-sq-ft) mosaic on the outside wall that is strikingly out of keeping with the surroundings. *Chemin du Val de Pome, tel. 93/33–42–20. Admission: 15 frs. adults, 8 frs. senior citizens, children free. Open Apr.–Oct., Tues.–Sun. 10–noon and 2–7; Nov.–May, 10–noon and 2–6.*

The houses of **Biot** cling to a hillside above the Braque Valley. The town is a handicraft center, specializing in gold and silver jewelry decorated with precious and semiprecious stones, and glassblowing. Suspended in the heavy, tinted glass are tiny bubbles that sparkle in the sun: You can buy the glass or simply watch the ancient process by which it's blown.

When you return to the coastal road (Route 7), you'll pass a **Marineland** with trained-dolphin shows. *Rue Mozart. Admission: 75 frs. adults, 50 frs. children. Open Apr.–Oct., daily 10–9; Nov.–Mar., daily 11–6; first performance at 2:30.*

Vallauris The wares of more than 100 local potters overflow Avenue Georges-Clemenceau and the neighboring streets, such as Rue Sicard and Rue du Plan—some of it high quality, most of it turned out for the high-volume tourist trade. With luck you'll find some tasteful cups and plates. Also for sale are handmade marionettes and olive-wood sculpture.

Bricks and pottery have been made here since the time of Tiberius from a local seam of clay. Picasso revived the declining industry when he lived here from 1952 to 1959; his ceramics are on display in the 16th-century Renaissance castle, and reproductions are for sale in the Madoura studio. Also housed in the castle is an enormous allegorical fresco by Picasso called *War and Peace. Pl. de la Mairie. Admission: 8 frs. Open Wed.–Mon. 10–noon and 2–6; closed Tues.*

The Grand Canyon of the Verdon Drive from the Nice area or the Cannes area to Grasse. Take N85 northwest toward Castellane. Pass Seranon on your right. Just beyond the small village of Villaute, turn left on D21 to Comps-sur-Artuby. Turn right on D71. As you approach the gorge, you'll see the hill town of Trigance on your right.

This trip will take the better part of a day—a full day or overnight if you plan to walk through the canyon. It is an unforgettable trip—the most spectacular you could make on a one-day excursion from the coast. If you like wild gorges and dizzying heights, the Grand Canyon of the Verdon will be an outstanding experience. For thousands of years the Verdon

River has dug a rift in the earth, making a winding corridor up to 689.9 m (2,300 ft) deep and in places only 7.4 m (25 ft) wide!

The route follows the southern rim of this 20.8-km (13-mi) gorge to Moustiers-Sainte-Marie, one of the loveliest and most unspoiled of the medieval hill towns, where you can buy pottery and dine in a charming country restaurant. Then it returns along the northern rim, with frequent vantage points where you can leave your car and peer down into the swirling depths. Highly recommended are two dramatic walks, neither particularly demanding—one a two-hour trip down into the gorge and back; the other a six- to eight-hour trek along the bottom. Should you decide to spend the night, there's a romantic castle-hotel overlooking the gorge at **Trigance.**

The route around the southern rim is the most dramatic. As you approach the gorge, you'll see the medieval town of Trigance crowning a hill on your right.

The views along the gorge are awesome, from a height that will make you feel as though you're piloting a plane. Stop when the spirit moves you, and don't leave your camera in the car. As you leave the gorge behind, the road turns into D19. At the town of **Aiguines,** which has a noble 17th-century château, you can buy a descriptive guide to the gorge that indicates the trails. At the lake (Lac de Ste. Croix), turn right on D957. In about 7.2 km (4.5 mi), D957 intersects with D952. You can turn right and head back along the northern rim of the canyon, but it's worth a 2.4-km (1.5-mi) detour (a left turn on D957) to visit the unspoiled medieval village of **Moustiers-Sainte-Marie,** where serious craftspeople work and sell their wares. There's an attractive Romanesque church with a three-tier bell tower, and a **Pottery Museum** (open summers, Wed.–Mon. 9–noon and 2–7; earlier closings off-season; closed Tues.) displaying the clear, blue-glazed pottery that made the town famous in the 17th and 18th centuries, when there were 12 active potteries here. For good photographs, take the path that winds up above the village to the **Notre-Dame-de-Beauvoir Chapel.**

Time Out   The terrace of **Les Santons** on Place de l'Eglise (tel. 92/74–66–48), a delightful Provençal restaurant, overlooks a mountain torrent flowing through the town. It's a tiny, family-run restaurant, so make reservations.

After resting up in Moustiers-Sainte-Marie, return east on D952, along the northern rim of the gorge. Unless you're in a rush to get back, leave D952 at La Palud-sur-Verdon and take the circular Crest Road (D23) that hugs the edge of the canyon. The Crest Road will return you to D952 near where you left it. Turn right on D952 to Point Sublime and continue east to Castellane. From here, take N85 back to Grasse.

Two Spectacular   The shorter, two-hour walk (round-trip) begins at the parking
Walks   lot at **Samson Corridor.** Follow the marked route to the right just beyond the first tunnel (Tusset Tunnel) after **Point Sublime.** Walk down to the footbridge over the Baou, cross over, and continue through two tunnels to a promontory with a view of the Trescaïre Chaos. Bring a flashlight.

The longer, six- to eight-hour walk begins at the **Chalet de la Maline** (on the Crest Road), and continues for 14.7 km (9.15 mi) to Point Sublime. Follow the red and white arrows along the footpath. Wear sturdy shoes and carry a flashlight, water, and food. Before setting off, phone 92/74–68–20 to make sure that a taxi is available; then call again when you reach Point Sublime and arrange to be picked up. (There may not be a phone at the Chalet de la Maline, which is why it's important to end your hike at the phone booth at Point Sublime.)

Dining and Lodging The **Château de Trigance** commands a splendid view of the valley and the surrounding mountains. There are a few small rooms with a medieval feeling to them—an ideal place to spend the night should you spend a full day at the gorge and not want to drive back after dark. *Trigance, tel. 92/76–91–18. 8 rooms with bath. Facilities: restaurant. AE, DC, MC, V. Closed mid-Nov.–Easter. Expensive.*

The Esterel From Nice, take Autoroute A8 south past Cannes to the La Napoule (N98) exit. Continue south along the coast to Saint-Raphaël. If you're starting in Cannes, take N98 to La Napoule and continue south along the coast to Saint-Raphaël.

This is a half-day trip from Cannes that takes you away from the crowds, into a silent world of tortured, rust-colored rocks thrusting their jagged claws into the sea. The contrast between the fiery red rocks, the deep green pines, and the blue sea inspired the Belgian writer Maurice Maeterlinck to call this region "closer to fairyland than any place on earth."

The Esterel is made up of volcanic rocks (porphyry) carved by the sea into dreamlike shapes. The harshness of the landscape is softened by patches of lavender, cane apple, and gorse. The deep gorges with sculpted parasol pines could have inspired Tang and Sung Dynasty landscape painters. The drive south from La Napoule to Saint-Raphäel takes you along the coast, past tiny rust-colored beaches and sheer rock faces plunging into the sea. The route back to Cannes takes you through the mountains of the Esterel, which have many trails and dramatic views.

You may want to stop in **La Napoule** at the **Château de la Napoule Art Foundation** to see the eccentric and eclectic work of the American sculptor Henry Clews. Clews, who saw himself as Don Quixote and his wife as the Virgin of La Mancha, came from a New York banking family. A cynic and sadist, he had, as one critic remarked, a knowledge of anatomy worthy of Michelangelo and the bizarre imagination of Edgar Allan Poe. His work—as tortured as the rocks of the Esterel—shows an infatuation with big bellies and distorted bodies; his nude of a man with a skull between his thighs is not easily forgotten. *Av. Henry-Clews. Admission: 15 frs. Guided visits Mar.–Nov., Wed.–Mon. at 3, 4, and 5.*

Time Out On your right, just past **Théoule**, is **Villa Anna Guerguy** (tel. 93/75–44–54), a small hotel laced with vines, built into the red rocks high above the sea. The public areas are full of character: attractive if you are looking for seclusion in an unusual, dramatic setting. Stop at least for drinks on the red-tiled patio encircled by pines.

From **Le Trayas** to **Anthéor** is the most scenic part of the drive, beneath the tormented mountains, with deep ravines and razor-sharp ridges. **Agay** has the best protected anchorage along the coast. It was here that Antoine de Saint-Exupéry was shot down in July 1944. He had just flown over his family castle on his last mission.

Saint-Raphaël is a family resort with holiday camps, best known to tourists as the railway stop for Saint-Tropez. It was here the Allied forces landed in their offensive against the Germans in August 1944.

Before returning through the Esterel, you can make a short side trip from Saint-Raphaël to **Fréjus** (the two towns border each other), but I don't recommend it unless you have a special interest in antiquity. The town has not altogether lost the pedestrian character it had as a Roman naval base. It was at Fréjus that Napoleon landed in 1799 on his way back from Egypt, and it was from here that he embarked for Elba.

Caesar made Fréjus a way station on the road between Italy and Gaul. When Emperor Augustus took over, he wanted a powerful fleet and turned the town into a huge naval base—the second largest in the Empire, where galleys were built and men trained for the victory over Mark Antony at Actium. Today there's little sense of the town's former glory. Remains of the 48-km (30-mi) aqueduct can best be seen at the east end of the town. The forum is gone and the Temple of Jupiter is a hospital. The amphitheater (arena), where bullfights are sometimes held, is the most imposing site still to be seen. The **Episcopal Town,** built in the late 10th century, which includes a cathedral, baptistery, cloister, and bishop's palace may be of greater interest. The austere 4th-century baptistery, built with black granite columns from the Roman forum, is one of the oldest in France. The present cathedral dates back to the 10th century, with 12th-century vaulting and handsome 15th-century carved wood choir stalls. Ring the bell on the iron gate to see the lovely, graceful cloister and the amusing 14th-century carvings of creatures from the Apocalypse on the ceiling of the upper arcade.

From Saint-Raphaël return to Cannes on N7—the mountain route through the Esterel. There's a fine desolation here, with different views around every curve. At the sign **Forêt Domaniale de Esterel,** turn right and drive to the top of **Mount Vinaigre** (609 m/2,030 ft). It's all of 31m (100 ft) from the parking lot to the summit. Try to come in the late afternoon when the coastal views are most striking.

Return to N7 and continue east to Cannes.

What to See and Do with Children

The Riviera is an ideal vacation spot for children. Every coastal resort has swimming, water sports, and bike rentals. For teenagers, there's a vigorous nightlife, particularly in Juan-les-Pins, Saint-Tropez, Cannes, and Nice.

Visit the walled medieval towns—the next best thing to sand castles, particularly Peillon. Hike through the Gorge of the Verdon—France's answer to the Grand Canyon. In Monte Carlo, don't miss the Aquarium (on the Rock)—which is under the supervision of Jacques-Yves Cousteau—the Anthropological Museum, and the Doll Museum. Cap Ferrat has a zoo with a trained-monkey show. There's a Marineland at the turnoff to Biot on the coastal road between Nice and Cannes.

Nightlife

Cannes If you want to find out what Cannes is all about, splurge with a drink at the **Carlton Hotel Bar** (58 La Croisette) after 9 PM. The center ring is at the **Studio Circus** (48 boulevard de la République). Popular discos include the **Jackpot** (at the Palm Beach Casino), **Jane's** (in the Gray d'Albion), and the **Galaxy** (in the Palais des Festivals).

There's gambling at the **Casino of the Palais des Festivals** from November through May, starting at 4 PM; and at the **Palm Beach Casino** from June through October, starting at 5 PM. Bring a jacket and your passport.

Nice **La Camargue** (5 place Charles-Félix) is the hottest disco. **Au Pizzaiolo** (4 bis rue du Pont Vieux), in the old city, is cheaper and less forbidding. **Superstar** (3 place de l'Armée-du-Rhin) is another disco on the nightly circuit.

Saint-Tropez The back bar at **L'Escale,** along the harbor, gets the pick of the pack. The mating cries at **Ponche** (rue Remparts) are a few decibels lower. **Les Caves du Roy,** in the Hotel Byblos, is Saint-Tropez's answer to New York's dance clubs. The golden youth gather at **L'Aphrodisiaque** (rue Allard)—at least those who are admitted.

8 Spain

Seville, Córdoba, Granada, and the Costa del Sol

Introduction

The Mosque of Córdoba, the Alcázar of Seville, the Alhambra of Granada—these are the three great monuments of Islamic Spain that you'll be visiting on your trip through Andalusia. Let's take a brief look at the history behind them.

When the Visigoths gained control over Spain in the 5th century, they persecuted the Jews and overtaxed everyone else. When the Muslims took over in 711, they were greeted as liberators. There they remained until 1492.

These Muslims are often called Moors, but there really is no such person: The Spaniards used the term merely to designate those people—Arabs, Syrians, Egyptians, Berbers, and others—who settled in their country. To call them Arabs is equally misleading. The first wave of settlers were Berbers— there was not an Arab among them. The Arabs eventually rose to power in Spain, but they were never more than a small minority of the Muslim population, and their power and influence always exceeded their numbers. As it was the Muslim religion that united these settlers, let's refer to them collectively as Muslims and speak of their kingdom as Islamic Spain.

There were three great centers of Muslim culture: Córdoba, 756–1010; Seville, 1010–1248; and Granada, 1248–1492. Each rose to power, enjoyed a period of glory, and then faded.

The greatest flowering of Moorish culture was during the first 250 years under the Córdoba caliphate. (A caliph is a successor of Mohammed who enjoys both spiritual and temporal power; a caliphate is his office or kingdom.) Undermined by incompetent rulers, the caliphate disintegrated and Islamic Spain broke into 23 separate kingdoms *(taifas)*, of which Seville became the most important.

In the meantime, the Christians, weakened by squabbles of their own—there was no unified Spain then, only a number of warring kingdoms—banded together in the north, where the Muslims had less control, and began what is called the Reconquest. This struggle to restore Christianity continued for over 400 years more.

The first major Christian victory was in Toledo in 1085. When Seville fell in 1248, Muslim culture moved to Granada, where it survived precariously for 244 years. The marriage of Isabella of Castile and Ferdinand of Aragon brought the two strongest Spanish kingdoms together and unified Catholic Spain against the Muslims. Granada finally fell in 1492, about ten months before Columbus sailed for the New World.

Ferdinand and Isabella persecuted the Jews and Moors and hounded them out of Spain. The Spanish Inquisition, which lasted until 1834, was an effort to reestablish a Spanish identity after more than 700 years of Muslim rule. Its first victims were not Jews but pure-blood Spaniards who had converted to Islam. By eliminating the Muslims and the Jews, the Inquisition virtually eliminated the Spanish middle class and plunged the country into a decline from which it has only recently recovered.

It's fashionable but unfair to build up Islamic Spain at the expense of the Catholics—to say that whatever is beautiful is the

Seville, Córdoba, Granada, and the Costa del Sol

inheritance of Muslim culture. Only after many years on Spanish soil did Islamic culture flourish. On the other hand, it's fair to say with Federico García Lorca that "an admirable civilization, a poetry, an architecture, and a delicacy unique in the world—all were lost."

Highlights

Bullfights and flamenco in Seville.

The palace and gardens of the Alhambra—the greatest monument of Islamic Spain.

The fabulous mosque of Córdoba, with a full-size cathedral inside.

Tennis, golf, and sun along the fashionable Costa del Sol.

A back-road adventure to the perched white villages of Andalusia.

Accommodations in ancient palaces and abbeys converted into first-class hotels.

Before You Go

Government Tourist Offices

In the U.S. 665 Fifth Ave., New York, NY 10022, tel. 212/759–8822; 845 N. Michigan Ave., Chicago, IL 60611, tel. 312/644–1992; San

Vicente Plaza Bldg., 8383 Wilshire Blvd., Suite 960, Beverly Hills, CA 90211, tel. 213/658–7188; 121 Bricknell Ave., Suite 1850, Miami, FL 33131, tel. 305/358–1992.

In Canada: 102 Bloor St. W., Suite 1400, Toronto, Ontario M5S 1M8, tel. 416/961–3131.

In the U.K. 57–58 St. James's St., London SW1A 1LD, tel. 071/499–4593.

When to Go

The tourist season runs from Easter to mid-October. The best months for sightseeing are May, June, September, and early October, when the weather is usually pleasant and sunny without being unbearably hot. During July and August try to avoid the inland cities of Andalusia, where the heat can be stifling and many places close down at 1 PM.

As for crowds, Easter is always a busy time, especially in the main Andalusian cities of Seville, Córdoba, Granada, Málaga, and the Costa del Sol resorts. July and August, when most Spaniards and other Europeans take their annual vacation, see the heaviest crowds, particularly in coastal resorts. Holiday weekends are naturally busy, and major fiestas, such as Seville's April Fair, make advance booking essential and cause prices to soar. Off-season travel offers fewer crowds and lower rates in many hotels.

Special Events

Palm Sunday through Good Friday: Holy Week festivities in Seville.
Late April: The Seville Fair, with dancing, processions, and bullfights.
May 1–12: Córdoba festival of decorated patios.
Late June: Seville folk-dance competitions.
Late June–early July: Granada Festival of Music and Dance, with concerts and ballet in the gardens of the Alhambra.

Currency

The unit of currency in Spain is the peseta. There are bills of 500, 1,000, 2,000, 5,000, and 10,000 ptas. Coins are 1 pta., 5, 25, 50, 100, 200, and 500 ptas. The 2- and 10-ptas. coins and the old 100-ptas. bills are rare but still legal tender. At press time (spring 1990), the exchange rate was about 107 ptas. to the U.S. dollar and 175 ptas. to the pound sterling.

Customs

Visitors age 15 and over are not permitted to bring into Spain more than 200 cigarettes or 50 cigars. Alcohol is limited to one liter of liquor over 22 proof and two liters of wine. All foods are prohibited from entering the country.

Dogs and cats are admitted, providing they have up-to-date vaccination records from the home country.

Language

In major cities and coastal resorts you should have no trouble finding people who speak English. In such places, reception staff in hotels of three stars and up are required to speak En-

glish. Don't expect the man in the street or the bus driver to
speak English, although you may be pleasantly surprised.

Reading

John A. Crow, *Spain: The Root and the Flower*, the most read-
able introduction to Moorish Spain.

Jan Morris, *Spain*, a classic, impressionistic guide.

James Michener, *Iberia*, a wordy and somewhat dated tribute.

Ernest Hemingway, *Death in the Afternoon*, the best book
ever written about bullfighting; *The Sun Also Rises*, Spain between the wars; and *For Whom the Bell Tolls*, the Spanish Civil
War.

V. S. Pritchett, *The Spanish Temper*, a perceptive, if at times
dated, portrait of the Spanish people, with insights into the art
of bullfighting.

H. V. Morton, *A Stranger in Spain*, a mid-20th-century English traveler's literate, absorbing reflections on visiting
Spain.

Arriving and Departing

By Plane

If you don't plan to visit Madrid, either fly direct to and from
Málaga, on the Costa del Sol, only 49.91 km (31 mi) east of
Marbella, or fly to Seville, changing planes in Madrid. **Iberia** is
the only airline with direct flights between Málaga and the
United States (from New York, Chicago, and Los Angeles).

If you do plan to visit Madrid, fly direct to Madrid and return
from Málaga or Seville; or conversely, fly direct to Málaga or
Seville and return from Madrid.

Iberia also has direct flights in summer between Madrid and
New York, Miami, and Los Angeles. **TWA** has direct flights between Madrid and New York. In Seville Iberia Airlines is at
Almirante Lobo 3 (tel. 95/422–89–01 for information, 95/421–
88–00 for reservations).

By Train

If your trip begins in Madrid and you're using public transportation, take the Madrid airport bus downtown to the airport
bus terminal at the Plaza Colón (30 minutes) and a cab (20 minutes) to the South Station (Atocha). Express trains take about
6 hours to Córdoba or 7 to Granada, about 7½ hours to Seville,
and about 9½ hours to Málaga. In Spring 1992 a new high-speed
train, the TAV, is scheduled to operate between Madrid and Seville, cutting traveling time to 3 hours between the two cities.

By Car

Rules of the Road Driving is on the right, and horns and high-beam headlights
may not be used in cities. The wearing of seat belts is compulsory on the highway but not in cities (except the M30 Madrid ring
road). Children may not ride in front seats. At traffic circles

give way to traffic coming from the right unless your road has priority. Your home driving license is essential and must be carried with you at all times, along with your car insurance and vehicle registration document. You will also need an International Driving License and a Green Card if you are bringing your own car into Spain. Speed limits are 120 kph (74 mph) on autopistas, 100 kph (62 mph) on N roads, 90 kph (56 mph) on C roads and 60 kph (37 mph) in cities unless otherwise signed.

If your trip begins in Madrid and you're traveling by car, stop in Toledo on your way south, taking routes N401 and N400 to N IV. It's a 5-hour drive from Madrid to Bailen, and another 1½ hours to Córdoba.

Getting Around

By Train or Bus

If you're taking public transportation, get a Chequetren—a book of coupons good for 15% discounts on trains. They're sold at main stations. When you're buying the actual tickets, get them from travel agents displaying blue and yellow RENFE signs, and avoid ticket lines at stations.

If you plan to begin and end your trip in Madrid, there's good, fast train service between Madrid, Córdoba, and Seville; between Seville and Málaga; and between Granada and Madrid. The express from Madrid to Córdoba takes 6 hours, and from Córdoba to Seville, 1 hour. From Seville to Marbella, it's a 3½-hour train ride to Málaga and a 1-hour bus ride from Málaga to Marbella. The train takes 2 hours from Málaga to Granada, and about 6 hours from Granada back to Madrid.

If you plan to begin your trip in Madrid and end it in Málaga, follow the same route as above, but instead of taking the train from Granada to Madrid, take the train from Granada back to Málaga.

In Córdoba, for train information contact the RENFE Travel Office (Ronda de los Tejares 10, tel. 95/747–58–84) or the station (Glorieta Conde de Guadaloupe, tel. 95/747–93–02).

In Marbella, train information is at tel. 95/231–2500, and ticketing from Viajes Melia (Av. Ricardo Soriano 14, tel. 95/277–1895).

Bus information in Seville: tel. 95/441–7111.

If you plan to begin and end your trip in Málaga, buses leave almost every half hour from Málaga to Marbella. The express trip takes about 1 hour. From Málaga take the train to Seville (3½ hours). From Seville take the train to Córdoba (1 hour). The bus trip from Córdoba to Granada takes 3 hours. The train from Granada back to Málaga takes about 2 hours.

By Car

If you're driving, you need a Green Insurance Card. A rented car should have one in the glove compartment. If you're bringing your own car, get the Green Card from your insurance company before you leave home.

Roads marked *A* are turnpikes *(autopista)*. *N* is for national roads, *C* for country roads. You'll be driving mostly on single-lane roads, so expect delays, and leave plenty of time to get where you're going.

Almost all monuments and buildings close from 1:30 to 3 or 4 PM, and remain open until 7 or 8 PM. Many close on Mondays. Plan your itinerary accordingly! If you plan to begin and end your trip in Madrid, take N IV from Madrid to Bailén (about 6 hours). If you arrive in Madrid after an all-night flight, you may want to stop in Bailén before heading to Córdoba, which is another 105.6 km (66 mi) west on N IV. Bailén has a useful government-run hotel, Parador de Bailén. (Carretera N IV, tel. 95/367–01–00).

From Córdoba you have a choice of two roads to Seville. The faster is 142.4 km (89 mi) on N IV. The slower but more scenic route is on C431 for 78.89 km (49 mi) along the Guadalquivir River; south on C432 for 27 km (17 mi) to Carmona (there's another parador hotel here); and then west for 38.4 km (24 mi) on N IV to Seville.

From Seville, you have a choice of routes to Ronda and Marbella, both described on the itinerary below.

When you're ready to leave Marbella, take the coastal road N340 east to Málaga (54.4 km/34 mi) and Motril (another 67.2 km/57 mi); then take N323 north to Granada (67.2 km/42 mi).

The fastest route from Granada back to Madrid is on N323 through Jaén and Bailén. The more interesting route is through Baeza and Ubeda.

If you plan to begin your trip in Madrid and end it in Málaga, follow the same route as above, except from Granada return to Málaga by the inland route—west on N342 and south on N321 (78 miles).

If you plan to begin and end your trip in Málaga, what you have to decide is whether to (1) do your sightseeing and then reward yourself with a few final days of indolence on the Costa del Sol; to (2) recover from your overnight flight to Spain on the Costa del Sol, and then begin your sightseeing; or to (3) begin and end on the Costa del Sol. The following route lets you do all three. It is essentially the same route described above, but in reverse.

Head west along the coast from Málaga to Marbella. The drive takes less than an hour. You can either save Marbella for the end of your trip or stop here now. From Marbella continue west on N340 to San Pedro de Alcántara, and turn north on C339 to Ronda. There are two routes from Ronda to Seville, both discussed on the itinerary below. From Seville there are two roads to Córdoba. The faster is 142.4 km (89 mi) on N IV. The slower but more scenic route is east for 38.4 km (24 mi) on N IV to Carmona; north on C432 for 27.2 km (17 mi); and east on C431 for 78.4 km (49 mi) along the Guadalquivir River to Córdoba. From Córdoba, the shortest route to Granada is on N432. The more interesting route is on N IV to Bailén; N22 to Ubeda; N321 to Baeza and Jaén; and N323 to Granada. From Granada, take N323 south to Motril, and then head west along the coast back to Málaga. You can either fly directly home or spend more time in Marbella.

Essential Information

Important Addresses and Numbers

Tourist Information The major provincial tourist offices of Moorish Spain are in **Córdoba** (Plaza de Colon 15, tel. 95/747–48–63), **Granada** (Plaza de Mariana Pineda, about 6 blocks east of the cathedral, tel. 95/822–66–88; open Mon.–Sat. 9:30–2 and 5–7:30, closed Sun.), and **Seville** (Provincial Tourist Office of Andalusia, Av. de la Constitución 21, 41004 Seville, a short walk from the cathedral, tel. 95/422–14–04; open Sept.–Apr., weekdays 8:30–3, Sat. 9–1:30, closed Sun.; Oct.–Mar., weekdays 9–1:30 and 3:30–8, Sat. 9–1:30, closed Sun.).

The principal municipal tourist offices of the region are in **Córdoba** (Plaza de Judas Levi, in the Judería, halfway between the mosque and the synagogue, tel. 95/729–07–40), **Marbella** (Av. Miguel Cano 1, 29600 Marbella, tel. 952/77–46–93; open weekdays 9–5, Sat. 9–noon), and **Seville** (Paseo de Las Delicias, 41012 Sevilla, tel. 95/423–44–65).

Emergencies For **police,** dial 091.

For medical emergencies, contact: In **Marbella,** Clinica Marbella (Av. Severo Ochoa, tel. day 95/277–42–00, night 95/277–42–82); **Seville,** contact the Emergency Clinic (Jesus del Gran Poder 23, tel. 95/436–24–61).

Consulates **U.S.: Fuengirola** (Av. Saenz de Tejada 1., 27 km/17 mi east of Marbella, tel. 95/247–48–91); **Seville** (Paseo de las Delicias 7, tel. 95/423–18–85).

U.K.: Málaga (Duquesa de Parcent 8, tel. 95/221–75–71).

Opening and Closing Times

Banks Banks are generally open weekdays 8:30–2 and Saturday 8:30–1, but in the summer many banks close at 1 PM weekdays and do not open on Saturday. Money exchanges at airports and train stations stay open later.

Museums Most museums are open from 9:30 AM to 2 PM, and from 4 PM to 7 PM, and are closed one day a week, usually Mondays. Opening hours vary widely, so make sure to check before you set off.

Shops One of the most inconvenient things about Spain is that almost all shops close at midday for at least three hours. Generally store hours are from 10AM to 1:30 PM and 5 PM to 8 PM. Shops are closed all day Sunday, and in many places they are also closed Saturday afternoons.

Shopping

Córdoba Look for filigree silver and embossed leather in the shops of the old Jewish quarter, a short walk from the mosque.

Granada In the narrow streets such as Zacatín and Angel Ganivet, between the cathedral and Reyes Católicos, is the old Moorish silk market (the **Alcaicería**), which has been turned into a tourist district with some interesting pottery and craft shops. Look for marquetry (chess sets, boxes, music boxes, etc.), ceramics, shoulder bags, rugs, and wall hangings.

Reyes Católicos is the main shopping street leading toward the Alhambra. Other shops are on Cuesta de Gomérez, which goes from Reyes Católicos up to the Alhambra. Pottery is sold on Routes N323 and N342, north and east of town.

Marbella You can find designer clothes (particularly beachwear) in the old Moorish quarter, and in boutiques of individual hotels.

Seville The main pedestrian shopping street, **Calle de las Sierpes,** will be a disappointment unless you're into Korean castanets, wood bulls stuck with swords, and imitation Moorish tiles. A few shops sell quality jewelry, pottery, and fans, however, so take a look. You may also find folk costumes and flamenco dresses.

At the Plaza del Duque is a department store, **Corte Inglés,** and a daily craft and jewelry market. Best bet for antiques and ceramics are the stores in the Barrio Santa Cruz. For ceramics in particular, try **Cerámicas Seville.** Note how the pottery is more intricate and sophisticated—less rustic and spontaneous—than the pottery made in Granada.

For lace tablecloths and hand-embroidered clothes, try **Feliciano Foronda,** Alvarez Quintero 52. For folk costumes try **Establecimento Lina** at Plaza Santa Cruz 12, in the Barrio.

Sports

Fishing Dozens of fishing boats are docked at Puerto Banús, 8 km (5 mi) west of Marbella (toward Cadiz), waiting to take you angling for shark.

Golf The Costa del Sol has five championship golf courses, all near **Estepona** (27.2 km/17 mi west of Marbella) and **San Pedro de Alcántara** (11.2 km/7 mi west of Marbella): *Aloha,* tel. 95/278–2–88; *Atalaya Park,* tel. 95/278–18–94; *Las Brisas,* tel. 95/278–03–00; *Guadalmina,* tel. 95/278–13–17; and *Nueva Andalucía,* tel. 95/287–82–00.

Tennis Most hotels have their own courts. There's also **Bjorn Borg's Tennis Club,** and **Lew Hoad's Tennis Club** in Fuengirola (25.6 km/16 mi east of Marbella).

Dining

There is a value added tax (IVA) of 6% or 12% on all meals, depending on the category of the restaurant. At the less expensive cafés and restaurants, this tax will be included in the cost of the dishes. At the more expensive establishments, it is added to the bill. Restaurants do not add a service charge. Ten percent of the total before tax is standard. At bars and cafés, it is customary to leave a tip when the waiter brings your change on a saucer (tip tray).

Ask for water and you'll get bottled mineral water, either *sin gas* (without bubbles) or *con gas* (with). For tap water, which is perfectly safe, ask for *aqua natural.*

The main meal is lunch, which usually doesn't begin until 2 PM. Dinner often starts at 10 PM, sometimes as late as midnight. Restaurants open at 1 PM, so go early if you want quick service for lunch. For dinner, restaurants open around 9 PM and dining rooms in paradors open at about 8:30 PM.

The three-course *menú del día* (menu of the day) is the best bargain, though not usually the best meal. Restaurants are required to have a "menu of the day," but you may have to ask for it.

Spanish food is, as a rule, a food of the people; don't expect gourmet cuisine. The Spaniards usually don't serve their meals steaming hot (extreme heat, they argue, hides the taste), so if you like hot food ask to have it served *muy caliente*. Contrary to what many people think, the Spanish don't like their food highly seasoned; chili is almost never used and pepper is seldom on the table. Nearly everything is cooked with olive oil, which is not necessarily heavy, and *al ajillo* (with lots of garlic). Desserts are usually a let down; best bet is fresh fruit.

The national dish is *paella*, a base of saffron-flavored rice with anything from mussels to chicken, pimientos, peas, and lobster. If it's properly prepared, you'll taste the separate flavor of each ingredient. It's heavy and takes some 20 minutes to prepare, so it's usually served at lunch. Best bet near the coast is paella with fresh seafood.

Another universal dish is gazpacho, a cold blend of puréed tomatoes, cucumbers, green peppers, garlic, oil, salt, pepper, onions, and a touch of vinegar. Taste differs according to the region, but often garlic will be dominant. Try "white gazpacho" with ground almonds and grapes.

On the Costa del Sol, and to a lesser degree in Seville and Granada, you're usually better off with fish than with meat. Specialties include *lubina al sal* (sea bass baked in a shell of salt) and *fritura mixta*—a delicate mix of lightly fried fish.

Don't leave Spain without trying some *tapas*. These tasty tidbits—potatoes, marinated beef, squid, ham, clams, mussels, fish roe, and so on—are served on counters of bars and cafés, and also as appetizers or main dishes in the paradors (government-run hotels). Like the Spaniards, you can go from bar to bar sharing tapas—a happy alternative to a formal dinner. *Raciónes* are larger portions.

Tortilla sacromonte, a potato omelet with diced ham and mixed vegetables, is popular in Granada. ("Tortillas" in Spain are omelets.)

For dessert or for afternoon snacks, try *almendra* (almond-flavored ice cream) or rum raisin (Málaga-style) ice cream. *Granizado de café* is iced coffee.

Southern Spain produces sweet apertif and dessert wines, not table wines. Sherry, produced near Jerez de la Frontera (which is not included on the itinerary but is only an hour out of your way), is the most famous Spanish wine. There are three basic types: (1) the light, dry apertifs *(fino)* such as Tío Pepe or La Ina that should be drunk as fresh as possible (don't get the last glass in an open bottle); (2) the fuller-bodied, nutty-tasting *amontillados*—the cheap ones made from blended wines, the better ones from *finos* that have been left to mature; and (3) the darker, fuller-bodied *olorosos*, which have a higher alcohol content. Sherry has a slightly higher alcohol content than other wines because brandy is added while it's being made. You'll find a lower alcohol content in Spanish sherries than in those you drink at home because extra brandy is added in exported sherries to protect them in transit. There's no such thing as a vintage sherry.

Most restaurants have a cheap, adequate house wine. **Sangria** (a fruit punch with wine, fruit juice, soda, brandy, and slices of oranges and lemons) originated in southern Spain. *Sol y sombra* (brandy and anis) is another popular drink. *Sorbeta de limón* (champagne and sorbet) is a great antidote for hot weather.

Category	Cost*
Very Expensive	over $7,500 ptas
Expensive	5,000 ptas–7,500 ptas
Moderate	2,500 ptas–5,000 ptas
Inexpensive	Under 2,500 ptas

*Price per person, excluding drinks, service and IVA tax.

Lodging

You'll see three signs on Spanish hotels. *H* means "hotel." *HR* is a "residential hotel" with no formal restaurant but often a Spanish-style cafeteria. *HA* designates an "apartment hotel," often with cooking facilities.

Breakfast may or may not be included in the price; ask in advance. Rooms with bathtubs usually cost more than rooms with showers. On the Costa del Sol, rooms with sea views often cost more; specify what you want. Many hotels are undergoing restorations; specify whether you want a newer or older room. When possible, ask to see your room before checking in.

The five main hotel chains are Hotasa (look for the symbol of two animal heads), Husa, Meliá, Sol, and Entursa. All tend to be clean and comfortable, but only the Entursa hotels have any special character.

Paradors. You would think that government-run hotels would be institutionally bland; but the paradors—some 80 of them— are, as a rule, the most tasteful and interesting hostelries in Spain. Many are restored castles, convents, palaces, and royal hunting lodges that have been modernized but allowed to keep their Old World charm. Most are spacious, with large bathrooms, and decorated with antiques, armor, tapestries, and ceramic tiles. Many are also on high ground with magnificent views or in the old, historic sections of ancient cities. Dining rooms serve regional meals and local wines. The only minus—a plus for some—is the absence of nighttime entertainment and recreation, and a certain lack of warmth in the newer ones. Paradors have only a few rooms, so make reservations in advance. The National Tourist Office of Spain has a brochure that describes "parador vacations," which let you stay in one parador or in a different one every night as you travel. Following the itinerary below, you can stay in paradors in Bailén (on the road from Madrid to Córdoba), Córdoba (outside the city), Carmona (outside of Seville), Granada, Pico de Veleta (outside of Granada), Málaga, and Úbeda.

Category	Cost*
Very Expensive	over 10,000 ptas
Expensive	7,500 ptas–10,000 ptas
Moderate	5,000 ptas–7,500 ptas
Inexpensive	2,500 ptas–5,000 ptas

Prices based on a standard double room; IVA tax and service are not included.

Bullfighting

The bullfighting season runs from late March to mid-October. If you don't know anything about it, you're likely to be confused, repelled, or bored.

It's usual to divide the bullfight into a prelude and three acts:

The Prelude. There's a roar of applause as the president enters. He signals and the gates swing open. In come the participants, even the man who will drag the dead bulls offstage. The first to enter are the matadors. Each has his own swagger. They're supposed to look grave and unconcerned. The main actor, on the right, will fight the first and fourth bulls. The youngest, in the center, gets to kill the third and sixth. Everyone now leaves the ring. The president signals again.

Act One, scene one. Enter the bull. No one knows how he will perform. Only the young heifers at the bull ranches are tested; if they charge bravely, they are bred; if not they become meat. The bulls are never tested because they would remember. It is assumed that they will inherit bravery from their mothers.

If the bull comes out charging, he is a single-minded bull who is easy to handle. This one stops. He thought he was being set free to join the herd, but something is wrong. He sniffs. He has seen the flick of a cape. He has never seen one before; his owners have made sure of that. He charges. Of the three *peones* (assistants) now in the ring, he chooses one victim, who scurries over the stockade. The matador watches. He is not a coward: He wants to see how the bull responds—if his vision is good, if he pulls to the left or to the right.

The matador approaches with his cape, red on one side, yellow on the other. The color really doesn't matter, the bull is colorblind. The bull charges, and the matador shows off his skill. The first pass of the cape, the *verónica*, is the most basic, deriving from the way in which St. Verónica is said to have held the cloth she used to wipe Christ's face. With each pass the matador gets closer to the bull, as he learns what he can and cannot do. If the bull stakes a territory, it's more dangerous to fight him there, protecting his ground, than when he's headed for it and has nothing on his mind but getting back. Olé! shout the crowds—a word some say comes from the Moorish cry to Allah.

Act One, scene two. Enter the men on horseback, the *picadores*, holdovers from the days when matadors were royal sportsmen who fought bulls from horses. The horses are terrified, but you can't hear them complain because their vocal cords are cut. Their right eyes are bandaged so they won't see the bulls coming to rip them apart. The bull is goaded to attack the right side of the heavily padded horses while the picadores, in turn, thrust their six-foot lances into his shoulders. The idea is to paralyze the neck muscles so that the head drops and the matador can slay the bull with a sword. The motive is not sadistic; if the picadores pump their pikes or take too long, the audience boos. The bull is encouraged to toss the horses so that he will tire himself out. Much worse than the sight of a dying bull is the sight of a gored horse, writhing in pain, its insides spilling into the ring; pray you don't see this happen. What does happen frequently is that the horse, when tossed, goes down, and with him, the picador, who scurries away while the matadors divert the bull.

Act Two. Enter the *banderilleros*, on foot, who dance away from the bull as he charges, thrusting three pairs of 45.7-cm (18-in) darts, barbed like fishhooks, into the beast's shoulders. This is the least dangerous part of the show, done not to cause pain but to lower the bull's head so the matador can slay him. The bull stands in pain, trying to lick the pools of blood pouring like paint down his back. "As the wounded bull stands there waiting for the kill," wrote English traveler H. V. Morton, "I am reminded of all the tortured Christs in Spain. They wear the same air of spent and hopeless exhaustion. The blood streaks their bodies in the same way."

"No one brought up on Beatrix Potter can understand this," said Morton.

Act Three, scene one. The matador sometimes dedicates the bull to one person; but if he takes off his hat and salutes the whole audience it means he's dedicating the bull to everyone, and we can expect a great performance. With the *muleta*, a small red cape that hides a sword, he now performs his most dangerous and exciting moves. The matador is judged by his artistry and by his willingness to put himself in danger. He shouldn't move his feet as the bull passes. The bull should avoid him, not he the bull. Arching his body shows less skill than standing straight. Kneeling is dangerous; so is passing the cape over his head (losing sight of the bull), and holding the cape behind his body. What he must do is destroy the bull's will—making the bull do what he wants, rendering him harmless. Getting the bull to perform in slow motion increases the danger.

Act Three, scene two. This is called "The Moment of Truth." The matador returns to the stockade for his sword and then advances toward the bull. He looks along the edge of his blade to the narrow space between the bull's shoulders that leads straight to his heart. This is the most dangerous moment. The matador sweeps the cape in front of the bull to draw his head down; if the head doesn't drop, the horns will rip into the matador. The matador lunges forward. Rarely does he strike true. He thrusts again. The bull totters and begins to cough up blood. If the matador can't make a clean kill, the audience boos loudly to disassociate itself from the butchery. Once the bull is down, he's killed with a final thrust into the brain.

The Itinerary

Orientation

Your trip takes you through Andalusia, on a voyage through almost 800 years of Islamic Spain. It also includes a few happy days of self-indulgence on the beaches of the Costa del Sol.

In Córdoba you'll visit an 8th-century mosque that is so vast, it contains a 16th-century Baroque cathedral within its walls. Nearby are the ancient white streets of the Jewish quarter, unchanged from a time when Jews and Arabs lived together in peace.

When people think of romantic Spain—of Carmens and Don Juans—they think of Seville. Here you can discover for yourself whether bullfighting is a butchery or art. After visiting the Alcázar—a Moorish palace of gleaming tiles and arabesques—you'll dine in an old Andalusian house and watch flamenco in the Barrio Santa Cruz—a maze of whitewashed streets overflowing with flowers.

Back roads take you south from Seville to the shining white villages of Andalusia, rising like castles above the fields of wheat and corn. From the past you move into the present in Marbella, the most tasteful and sophisticated resort along the Costa del Sol. You can lead an active life playing golf and tennis, and enjoying a different restaurant every night—or spend your days lounging at your hotel pool at the edge of the sea.

The trip ends in Granada, where you'll check into a palace hotel and explore the Alhambra—a fabled palace worthy of the Arabian Nights.

The Main Route

3–5 Days Day excursion to Córdoba
Two nights: Seville
One night: Marbella
One night: Granada

5–7 Days Day excursion to Córdoba
Two nights: Seville
Two nights: Marbella
Two nights: Granada

7–14 Days Day excursion to Córdoba
Three nights: Seville
One night: Parador of Carmona
Four nights: Marbella
Day excursions to Ronda and the perched white villages of Andalusia
Three nights: Granada
Day excursion to Úbeda and Baeza

Exploring

Córdoba

Except for its great mosque and ancient Jewish quarter, the modern city of Córdoba gives little evidence of its former glory.

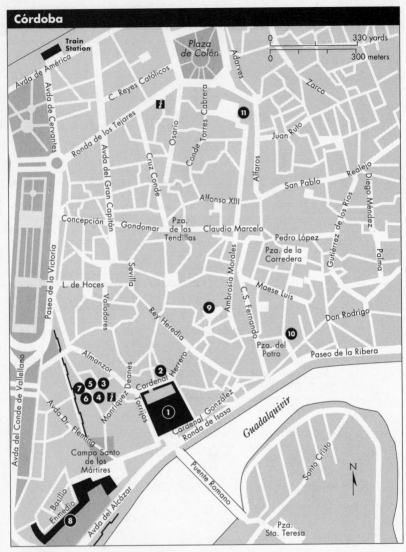

Córdoba

Train Station

Plaza de Colón

0 — 330 yards
0 — 300 meters

Avda de América
Avda de Cervantes
C. Reyes Católicos
Ronda de los Tejares
Avda del Gran Capitán
Cruz Conde
Osario
Conde Torres Cabrera
Adarves
Zarco
Juan Ruto
Alfaros
San Pablo
Realejo
Diego Méndez
Alfonso XIII
Concepción
Gondomar
Pza. de las Tendillas
Claudio Marcelo
Pedro López
Pza. de la Corredera
Gutiérrez de los Ríos
Palma
Paseo de la Victoria
L. de Hoces
Sevilla
Valladares
Rey Heredia
Ambrosia Morales
C.S. Fernando
Maese Luis
Don Rodrigo
Almanzor
Manríquez Deanes
Cardenal Herrero
Torrijos
Pza. del Potro
Paseo de la Ribera
Avda del Conde de Vallellano
Avda Dr. Fleming
Campo Santo de los Mártires
Cardenal González
Ronda de Isasa
Guadalquivir
Santo Cristo
N
Basilio Enmedio
Avda del Alcázar
Puente Romano
Pza. Sta. Teresa

Alcázar, **8**
Cristo de los Faroles, **11**
Judería, **3**
Maimónides Statue, **6**
Mosque, **1**
Museo Arqueológico, **9**
Museo de Bellas Artes, **10**
Museum of Bullfighting, **5**
Plaza Judás Levi, **4**
Synagogue, **7**
Virgin of Lanterns, **2**

The two sights are a must on any tour of southern Spain, but once you've seen them, you'll probably be content to move on. While the mosque is closed (1:30 to 3:30 PM), tour the Jewish quarter and stop for lunch. There are at least two good restaurants nearby.

As you wander through the mosque and the old Jewish quarter, imagine yourself back in the 8th century, when Córdoba was the first and greatest capital of Islamic Spain.

Your ruler is one-eyed Abd-er-Rahman I. His family belonged to a long line of Umayyads, who were slaughtered by another branch of Mohammed's family, the Abbassides. Abd-er-Rahman escaped and fled to Spain, where he began a dynasty that ruled for 300 years. It was in 785, under his rule, that the mosque was begun. In 929, his descendant Abd-er-Rahman III unmasked the fiction that the Arab world was united and declared himself Caliph. The Arab world was now formally split in two—as the Roman world was split between East and West—one capital in Baghdad, the other in Córdoba.

Americans tend to label Muslims as intolerant, but under the Córdoba caliphate nothing could have been more untrue. For almost 50 years the Muslims shared the Visigoth church with the Christians and made no effort to interfere with their services. When the Muslims decided to build a mosque, they gave the Christians money to build themselves another cathedral. How unlike the intolerance the Christians showed the Muslims after the Reconquest!

For 300 years the caliphs of Córdoba ruled the most advanced state in Europe. Arabic, the official tongue, was spoken by both Jew and Christian. Córdoba was said to have a population of 500,000—almost twice what it has today. While the rest of Europe was groping through the Dark Ages, Córdoba had illuminated streets. While education in Northern Europe was limited to a few monastic centers, nearly everyone in Córdoba could read and write. Universities flourished. The Renaissance began here with translations of classical learning.

The Spanish Muslims introduced Europe to waterwheel irrigation, peach trees, and dates. They introduced paper and glass, jasmine and the lute. The world's most accomplished mathematicians, they showed the West how to use Arabic numerals. Without them we'd still be trying to multiply CCXII times MCLXI.

The caliphate eventually crumbled because of incompetent rulers, and Islamic Spain split into warring states, the most powerful of which was Seville. In 1236, Córdoba fell to the Christians. About 100,000 Muslims fled to Granada, where they remained until the last caliph was ousted from power in 1492.

The first place to visit is the **mosque** (Mezquita) near the Guadalquivir River (the entrance is on Cardenal Herrero). Your initial feeling may well be of disorientation—of losing your way in a mysterious forest. Try to remember that in a mosque all paths are supposed to be good, because God is everywhere; that in God's house one can no longer lose the way. How different the feeling from a Christian church, where columns propel the worshiper's gaze forward to the altar, and upward to God.

It's important to realize also that the mosque does not serve the same function as a church. The side facing Mecca has a sanctuary indicating the direction worshipers should face while praying, but the rest of the mosque is a community gathering place—a huge rectangular desert tent where people come to stroll or study. In Islamic times, officials read proclamations here, scholars debated, students attended classes.

The original mosque was not a place of self-abnegation where a worshiper escaped this life in order to find the next: It was a cool oasis (the columns are often compared to palm trees) where people could escape the heat of the sun. Arcaded porticos (rows of columns) kept the mosque open to the outside world. The lines of columns were continued outside in the rows of orange trees in the perfumed courtyard, as if man and nature were working together in the service of God. When the Christians took power, they filled in the arcades in order to build shrines against the outer walls. The natural world was locked out and a living mosque became spiritually dead.

Notice how the columns are of different shapes and made from different materials: granite, marble, jasper, and other stones. This is because they were taken by the Muslims from various places they conquered. There are Roman pillars from Gaul, Visigoth pillars with fleur-de-lis designs, Byzantine pillars from Constantinople. The shorter ones are raised on bases; the longer ones are buried beneath the floor.

As the Muslim population increased, the mosque was enlarged three times. Completed, it measured 176.9 m (590 ft) by 127.4 m (425 ft), one-third of which was the open courtyard.

The horseshoe-shape arches, a trademark of Early Moorish architecture, were used in the original Visigoth church that the mosque replaced. The double arches—one on top of the other—were added to raise the ceiling and create a sense of airiness and space; the idea may have come from the Roman aqueduct at Segovia. Many of the bronze and copper lamps were made from church bells.

It is mind-boggling that you can wander through this forest of pillars for perhaps 30 minutes without even knowing that within its midst is a full-size cathedral! At first, the Christians merely ripped out some of the pillars to create a space that resembled the nave (central aisle) of a church. This satisfied them for nearly 300 years, from 1236 to 1520. The local clergy then petitioned Charles V to build a transept, cover it, and close it in from the rest of the mosque. Charles, unaware of the desecration that was to be performed, gave his consent. When, six years later, he saw the results, he exclaimed, "If I had known what you were to do, you would not have done it. For what you have made here may be found in many other places, but what you have destroyed is to be found nowhere else in the world."

Enter through the **El Patio de los Naranjos** (Courtyard of the Oranges). Try to imagine what it was like before it was walled in, when the ornamental fountains were used for ablutions by the faithful as they entered the mosque.

You will enter into the oldest part of the mosque. Head to the right wall, turn left, and walk till you come to a break in the columns. This is where the original cathedral was. Continue to the far wall, turn left, and walk to the **Mihrab**, the sanctuary facing Mecca. This was the holiest part of the mosque. The gold dome is a synthesis of Byzantine and Islamic art—a reminder that the mosque was built by Christian workers lent by the

Christian emperor in Constantinople. Note the paving stones worn smooth by centuries of worshipers kneeling in prayer.

Suddenly, in the midst of this forest, you step into a gilded Baroque cathedral. What, you wonder, is it doing here? From a world of shadows you have stepped suddenly into a radiant clearing. James Michener calls it a monument of "colossal ugliness." Others have called it a worm in a bright red apple and a Jonah in the whale. Still others are content to find it emblematic of southern Spain: the ruins of a Roman basilica incorporated into a Visigoth church, turned into a Muslim mosque with a Christian cathedral inside. Whatever you think of the cathedral, be grateful it was built, for without it the mosque would surely have been torn down. *Admission free. Open daily 10:30–1:30 and 3:30–5:30.*

Exit through the Courtyard of the Oranges and turn right to the famous Street of the Flowers (Calleja de las Flores). You can't miss it because it's filled with tourists. On this and adjoining streets are numerous tourist shops selling leather goods, filigree jewelry, marquetry, fans, and pins. Other, less famous streets are just as beautiful, so walk around.

Directly behind the mosque is the **Jewish Quarter** (Judería). Like the Barrio in Seville, it is an ancient world of narrow, twisted streets, cool courtyards, beautifully wrought window grilles, and whitewashed walls covered with flowers. The 14th-century **synagogue** (La Sinagoga) is no more than a plain, small room with some Mudejar stucco on the upper walls, but it has rich historical associations and is one of three synagogues left in Spain. *Admission free. Open daily 9:30–1:30 and 3:30–6:30.*

For three centuries, under Muslim tolerance, the Jews of Córdoba enjoyed a golden age. They were doctors, philosophers, diplomats, even generals. In the Judería is a statue of Moses Maimónides (1135–1204), a Jewish physician and one of the most brilliant men that Spain has ever produced.

Walk from the synagogue to the **Zoco,** a large courtyard where craftsmen work around a patio, and where you can stop for a light lunch.

Dining **El Caballo Rojo** is near the mosque. The old converted mansion has a terrace, and dining rooms on three levels. Decor is regional. National specialties include *cordero a la miel* (lamb with honey). *Cardenal Herrero 28, Córdoba, tel. 95/747–53–75. Reservations unnecessary. Jacket suggested. AE, DC, V. Moderate.*

Almudaina is the other top restaurant. It is located in an old converted school at the entrance to the Judería. Fish is a specialty, but the menu varies according to seasonal produce. *Campo Santo de los Martires, tel. 95/747–43–42. No reservations. Dress: casual. AE, DC, V. Moderate.*

Castillo de la Albaida is an old Andalusian home with an open terrace and lovely, peaceful views. *Ctra de Trassierra, Km 4.5, tel. 95/727–34–93. No reservations. Dress: casual. AE, DC, V. Moderate.*

Lodging **The Adarve** is the newest hotel in town and faces the Mezquita on the side opposite its sister hotel, the Maimónides. Built into an old house, it is furnished in smartly contemporary style, though the rooms are relatively small. *Magistral Gónzalez,*

Francés 15, 14003 Córdoba, tel. 95/748–11–12. 103 rooms. Facilities: garage. AE, DC, MC, V. Expensive–Very Expensive.

Parador Nacional de la Arruzafa is a modern parador located 4 km (2½ mi) north of Córdoba, with lovely gardens, a restaurant serving Andalusian specialties, a children's dining area, and private terraces overlooking the city. *Av. de la Arruzafa, 14012 Córdoba, tel. 95/727–59–00. 83 rooms. Facilities: restaurant, separate dining area for children, outdoor pool. AE, DC, MC, V. Expensive.*

The Maimónides is smaller, friendlier, and less expensive than the Meliá. Rooms are a bit worn but clean. The location, in the heart of the historic area next to the mosque, is ideal. The hotel does not have its own restaurant, but next door is the Bandolero with indoor and outdoor dining. *Torrijos 4, 14003 Córdoba, tel. 95/747–15–00. 61 rooms. AE, DC, MC, V. Moderate–Expensive.*

Seville

When foreigners imagine romantic Spain, they think of Seville, the largest city in Andalusia. It was here that Velásquez and Murillo were born; here that Don Juan, the model for *Don Giovanni*, lived; here that Don José first met Carmen. It was Seville that inspired *The Marriage of Figaro* and *The Barber of Seville*. Here Cervantes was imprisoned, and here Don Quixote was born.

The important sights—the cathedral, the Giralda, the Alcázar, and the Barrio Santa Cruz—are all within walking distance of each other. Not far away are the bullring and the María Luisa Gardens—among the loveliest in Spain.

Seville Cathedral. Only St. Peter's in Rome and St. Paul's in London are bigger than the Seville Cathedral. When the Christians overran Córdoba, they decided to build their cathedral inside the mosque; here in Seville they demolished the mosque and built over it. The Christians were overwhelmed by the beauty of Seville and must have felt a need to prove that Christianity could do as well. The size of the cathedral will overwhelm you; walking beneath those massive pillars—the vaults rising 55 m (184 ft) above the transept crossing—is like strolling through a forest of giant sequoias. The gloom is immense, too, the pillars disappearing upward into darkness. How unlike the Alhambra, where life is seen as something to enjoy, not escape.

To the left of the modern doors is the Chapel Royal (Capilla Real), a Renaissance building with an ornamented dome. The sanctuary contains some 15th- and 16th-century choir stalls, as rich as the Spanish imagination, and the tomb of Christopher Columbus. There's a school of thought that says Columbus's remains are still in Santo Domingo, but we're in Seville now, so let's assume he's here. Besides, Seville has been chosen as the site of the 1992 fair to celebrate the 500th anniversary of Columbus's "discovery" of the New World.

The **library** behind the cathedral contains 10 books owned by Columbus, including *Marco Polo*, Plutarch's *Lives*, Seneca's *Tragedies*, and Pliny's *History*. Can you imagine Columbus reading Seneca? His marginal notes all have to do with gold, pearls, ivory, pepper—in other words, making money.

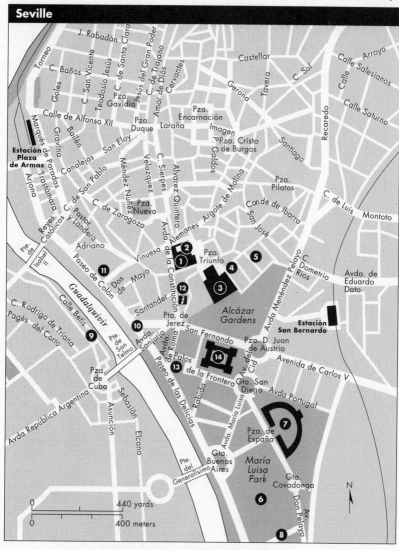

Seville

Alcázar, **3**
Barrio Santa Cruz, **5**
Calle Betis, **9**
Cathedral, **1**
Giralda, **2**
Golden Tower, **10**

Maestranza
Bullring, **11**
María Luisa Park, **6**
Museo Arte
Contemporaneo, **12**
Patio de las
Banderas, **4**
Plaza de America, **8**
Plaza de España, **7**

San Telmo Palace, **13**
Tobacco Factory
(University), **14**

The 96.5-m (322-foot) **Giralda** (minaret) was the only part of the original mosque (other than the Orange Tree Court) that the Christians did not destroy. A 16th-century Renaissance belfry has been added to the original 12th-century structure: How typically Andalusian to have a church bell rung from the top of a Muslim minaret!

You'll notice that the Giralda has a solidity, a monumentality not usually associated with Muslim architecture. This is because it was built by the Almohades, a fundamentalist dynasty that eschewed all ostentation in an effort to restore the strict religious beliefs and simple lifestyle of the Prophet. Gone are the horseshoe-shape arches (inspired by the Visigoths) that you saw in the Córdoba mosque; the arches here are more pointed, in the spirit of the Middle East.

Giraldas were built for the muezzin to call the faithful to service. In small mosques he stood at the door; in large ones he climbed the minaret, faced Mecca, put his forefingers in his ears, and cried, "God is most great" (four times) and "Come to salvation" (twice). In the morning he added, "Prayer is better than sleep." The muezzin could not be drunk, insane, or a woman. Climb the gentle ramp—two horses wide—to a platform at 68.9 m (230 ft) for a breathtaking view of Seville. *Admission: 200 ptas., which includes admission to the Giralda. Open weekdays 11–5, Sat. 11–4, Sun. 2–4.*

Outside the cathedral are horse-drawn carriages *(coche caballos)* waiting to take you for a ride. Be sure to bargain and to agree on a price beforehand. One lovely trip is through María Luisa Park.

On your way from the cathedral and the Alcázar, consider a visit to the **Archives of the Indies** (Archivo General de Indias). Among the documents are signatures of Columbus and Magellan, and a letter Cervantes wrote in 1590, at the age of 43, asking for a job in the New World. If accepted, Cervantes would probably have lived out his life as a public accountant and never written *Don Quixote;* but scrawled across his application are the words, "Let him look for something closer to home." *Open for guided tours Mon.–Sat. 10–1.*

The **Alcázar** is an intricate maze of gleaming tiles, arabesques, carved wood ceilings, and lacelike stucco—a perfect setting, it would seem, for the Arabian Nights. Its stunning profusion of shapes and forms—H. V. Morton calls it "the multiplication table set to music"—will enchant you. Equally fascinating is the fact that this Moorish palace was built for a Catholic king named Pedro the Cruel (1333–1369).

When Pedro came to power in 1350, more than 70 years had passed since the Moors had relinquished power, and the palace that the Almohades had built was nearly in ruins. A man as sensuous as he was cruel, Pedro loved the idea of living with his harem in an exotic Moorish palace, and so he hired the finest Muslim craftsmen to emulate the Alhambra in Granada. These craftsmen were called Mudéjars, and their art was executed according to Muslim designs and techniques, but under a Christian yoke. Pedro's palace was a hybrid structure, half Visigoth, half Moorish; but the fact that it was built at all shows how completely Arabic ideas had infiltrated Spanish thought.

Restorations went on through the 19th century, destroying much of the palace's integrity; nonetheless, it remains one of the greatest and purest examples of Mudéjar architecture in the world. As you tour the rooms, have fun trying to distinguish Christian from Muslim elements and comparing the sometimes glaring harshness of the new tiles to the soft, subtle lyricism of the originals.

If you don't see any paintings, it's because the early Muslims, like the Jews, saw the use of idols as a threat to their concept of the One God, and therefore frowned on representational art. Their need for artistic self-expression found its outlet in geometric forms and calligraphy. The greatest mathematicians of the ancient world, they loved logical, coherent lines. Of all the arts, they respected calligraphy the most. In the West we think of the written word as nothing but an abstract symbol; but to the Arabs, language has a visual dimension as well. Words, to them, not only celebrate beauty, they *are* beauty.

A grand 16th-century staircase takes you to the Royal Apartments—the most touched-up part of the palace, some rooms altered as late as the 19th century. The lacelike delicacy of some of the work is Isabeline—a style named for Isabella, Ferdinand's wife, after they had ousted the Moors from Granada. The need to cover every inch of space with fine designs, as a woman's veil does, was inspired by the Moorish love for detail; yet note how the Spanish work is voluptuous for its own sake, while the Moorish work is only the outward expression of a mathematical love of form.

The Moorish Court of the Maidens (Patio de las Doncellas) was, sadly, given an upper story in the 16th century. Surrounding the court are rooms of finely carved stucco and glazed tiles. The room of Emperor Charles V—he was the one who allowed a Renaissance palace to be in the Alhambra—has a notable collection of tapestries. Also worth seeing is the domed ceiling (cupola) of the Hall of the Ambassadors (Salón de Embajadores). Did Pedro know that the verses on the wall were in praise of Allah?

Also off the Court of the Maidens are the apartments of María de Padilla, Pedro's mistress. It was she alone who gave beauty to Pedro's life. She was simple and pious and very beautiful. At the advice of the court, he married a French princess, Blanche of Bourbon, but after three days he imprisoned her and fled back to María. He married again, but after one day he was back in María's arms.

Don't miss the terraced gardens of the Alcázar, filled with exotic trees, shrubs, and ornamental fountains. You can sit here beneath the magnolia trees and imagine yourself back in the court of Pedro the Cruel. *Admission: 250 ptas. Open Mon–Sat 9–12:45 and 3–5:45, Sun 9–12:45.*

From the gardens, walk to the Flag Court (Patio de las Banderas) and follow a covered passage to the Barrio Santa Cruz, the former Jewish quarter, where the Spanish nobility lived in the 17th century.

The **Barrio Santa Cruz** is one of the most picturesque sights in Spain. Narrow white streets open out into tiny squares that could be in North Africa. The sun-bleached walls give no indication of what's within; be sure to peer through the beautiful wrought-iron doors at the tiled courtyards with their gurgling fountains and orange trees. What a contrast between the simplicity of these homes and the Rococo indulgences of the cathedral!

Among the houses are curiosity shops that sell everything from old jewelry to mirrors, antique ceramics, and daggers.

Time Out | On several squares are restaurants where you can pause for drinks or lunch. Be sure to return at night when the cafés blast their light and music into the dark streets. At Plaza de los Venerables is **Casa Román,** an atmospheric bar with hams hanging from the ceiling. At Plaza de Santa Cruz is **Los Gallos,** where you can watch flamenco.

The Plaza de Doña Elvira has a fountain, and benches for guitarists.

North of the Barrio is **Pilate's House** (Casa de Pilatos). This is a smaller, less crowded version of the Alcázar, with carved wood doors from Lebanon, beautiful old tiles, and a fountain in a central courtyard. A 16th-century ancestor of the present owner returned from the Holy Land and built his palace in what he thought was the style of Pontius Pilate's home; yet it's much more Mudéjar than Roman. Upstairs are some lesser-known paintings by Goya, Murillo, and Velásquez. *Admission: 100 ptas. Open daily 9–6.*

Charity Hospital (Hospital de la Caridad) is a Baroque almshouse with a single-nave church containing paintings by Murillo and Valdés Leal. The best-known work is Leal's morbid *Finis gloriae mundi,* in which a bishop in his coffin is being devoured by cockroaches or worms. Murillo said the painting made him want to hold his nose.

In the crypt below the altar lie the remains of Miguel de Mañara. Inscribed on his tomb are the words, "Here lie the ashes of the worst man the world has ever known." Mañara, who commissioned Leal's paintings, is often mistaken for the original Don Juan. Actually, he saw a play about Don Juan and was inspired to follow in his footsteps. One story tells of how, after a drunken orgy, he saw a funeral procession with a partially decomposed corpse that was himself. According to another legend he made advances to a beautiful nun, but when she turned her head aside he saw that her face was eaten away by a foul disease more horrible than death. Whatever happened, he was so overwhelmed by a sense of his own mortality that he gave away all his possessions, joined the brotherhood, and spent the rest of his life burying the bodies of executed prisoners. Somerset Maugham describes the chapel he built as "a bed-chamber transformed into a chapel for the administration of the last sacrament." *Calle Temprado. Admission: 100 ptas. Open: Mon.–Sat. 10–1 and 3:30–6, Sun. 10:30–12:30.*

After a day of sightseeing, nothing could be lovelier than an early evening stroll along the Guadalquivir River between the **San Telmo** and **Isabel II bridges.** The walk takes you past the early 13th-century **Golden Tower** (Torre de Oro), one of the few remaining monuments of Almohade Spain. Sixty-minute **river cruises** depart from near the tower, usually at 5:45 PM. (**Cruceros Sevilla,** tel. 95/412–19–34).

To escape the summer heat, stroll through the peaceful **María Luisa Garden,** one of the prettiest in Spain, with pools and fountains and quiet, shaded nooks beneath towering beech trees. On one side of the entrance is the **Tobacco Factory,** where some 10,000 girls worked in the 19th century, including Carmen. The building is now part of the University of Seville.

Dining Dinners usually don't begin till 9 or 10, so consider a drink first at the elegant Alfonso XIII on San Fernando, close to the Alcázar (*see* Lodging, below).

La Dorada specializes in fresh seafood, such as *dorada* (tuna) and *lubina* (flatfish), baked in a shell of salt. *Virgen de Aguas Santas 6, tel. 95/445-51-00. Reservations suggested. Jacket suggested. AE, DC, MC, V. Closed Sun. dinner and Aug. Expensive.*

Mesón Don Raimundo serves sophisticated regional meals in an old convent near the cathedral. Decor includes a stuffed deer and a suit of armor—just in case you forget you're in Andalusia. A good bet for lunch, particularly for tapas at the bar. *Argote de Molina 26, tel. 95/422-33-55. Reservations suggested. Jacket suggested. AE, DC, MC, V. Closed Sun. dinner. Expensive.*

El Rincón de Curro is a five-minute walk from Alfonso XIII. Regional specialties are formally and graciously presented in what some consider the best restaurant in the city. *Virgen de Lujan 45, tel. 95/445-02-38. Reservations suggested. Jacket required. AE, DC, V. Closed Aug. and Sun. Expensive.*

Rio Grande is another top restaurant, serving summer meals alfresco on a scenic terrace above the Guadalquivir River near the west end of San Telmo Bridge. The elegant (as opposed to regional) dining room has globe lamps, oil portraits, and potted plants. If you have only one night in Seville, you may prefer a place with more of a barrio atmosphere. *Betis 70, tel. 95/427-39-56. Reservations suggested. Jacket suggested. AE, DC, MC, V. Expensive.*

La Albahaca is a small restaurant in an old patrician house in the heart of the barrio. There's a limited menu, but lots of atmosphere. *Plaza Santa Cruz 12, tel. 95/422-07-14. Reservations suggested. Jacket suggested. AE, DC, V. Closed Sun. Moderate.*

Los Alcázares is a bit travel-posterish but offers good value. It's also conveniently located near the cathedral. Meals are served in a quaint, white-plaster building faced with tiles. *Miguel de Mañara 10, tel. 95/421-31-03. Reservations unnecessary. Dress: casual. Closed Sun. MC, V. Moderate.*

El Burladero, with its bullfighting motif, seems to have been gored by success. It's still popular, though, particularly among *el toro* fans. The bullring is only an ear's throw away. Try the clams in a sauce of onions, tomatoes, and white wine. *Canalejas 1, tel. 95/422-29-00. Reservations suggested. Dress: casual. AE, DC, V. Closed Aug. Moderate.*

Hostería del Laurel is in the barrio, with hanging hams, herbs, and a good reputation for fresh fish dishes, such as *fritura mixta. Plaza de los Venerables 5, tel. 95/422-02-95. No reservations. Dress: casual. No credit cards. Moderate.*

Hostería del Prado, with a "this is the real Spain" ambience, offers tapas and regional cooking. *Prado de San Sebastian, tel. 95/441-67-11. No reservations. Dress: casual. No credit cards. Moderate.*

Modesto is a popular tavern with lots of Spanish snacks on a marble-top bar, and a restaurant upstairs. *Cano y Cueto 5, tel.*

95/441–18–16. No reservations. Dress: casual. No credit cards. Inexpensive.

Lodging **Alfonso XIII** is in a class by itself. It was built to house wealthy guests for an Exhibition in 1929 and has retained the elegance of a stately palace. The rooms are not as grand as you might expect from the price you pay to stay in them (the Alfonso is the third or fourth most expensive hotel in Spain), and certain of the furnishings are worn. However, the courtyard atrium is a museum of Spanish and Moorish tapestries and art. Come here for predinner cocktails even if you don't book a room. *San Fernando 2, 41004 Seville, tel. 95/422–28–50. 149 rooms. Facilities: Formal dining room, outdoor pool, shops, hairdresser, parking. AE, DC, MC, V. Very Expensive.*

The Colón gets an olé! as one of the better large, modern hotels, popular with bullfight aficionados. The bullring is nearby. Seventh-floor rooms have private balconies. *Canalejas 1, 41001 Seville, tel. 95/422–29–00. 211 rooms. Facilities: formal restaurant, 24-hr room service, gym, fax service. AE, DC, MC, V. Very Expensive.*

Doña María is tucked into a side street only minutes from the barrio and the cathedral. No two rooms are alike—some charming with brass, canopied beds, others cramped and plain. There's a top-floor pool and a comfortable Moorish-style lounge with antiques and couches for guests to curl up in. The price is right, too: about half the cost of Alfonso XIII. *Don Remondo 19, 41004 Seville, tel. 95/422–49–90. 61 rooms. Facilities: Breakfast only, rooftop pool, bar. AE, DC, MC, V. Expensive–Very Expensive.*

Nuevo Lar is a slick, modern hotel a short walk from the barrio. *Plaza de Carmen Benitez 3, 41003 Seville, tel. 95/441–03–61. 137 rooms. Facilities: gym, sauna, fax service. AE, DC, V. Expensive–Very Expensive.*

Pasarela is relatively new with modern facilities. *Av. de la Borbolla 11, 41004 Seville, tel. 95/441–55–11. 82 rooms. Facilities: Restaurant serving breakfast only, gym, sauna, parking. AE, DC, V. Expensive–Very Expensive.*

The **Parador Nacional Alcázar del Rey Don Pedro** is in Carmona, west of Seville. It's a 40-minute drive, but how often do you get to sleep in the ruins of a Moorish fort? You won't want to commute more than once, so stay either the night before you arrive in Seville or the night you leave. *Carmona, 41410 Seville, tel. 95/414–10–10. 59 rooms. Facilities: outdoor pool. AE, DC, MC, V. Expensive.*

Murillo is a picturesque hotel on a pedestrian-only street. Front rooms have balconies, and the hotel has many long-term tenants, even though it has no restaurants. *Lope de Rueda 7, 41004 Seville, tel. 95/421–60–95. 61 rooms, 14 suites. Facilities: bar. AE, DC, V. Moderate–Expensive.*

La Rábida is a real find for the budget-minded tourist: an old-fashioned hotel on a quietish street near the center of town. Marble hallways lead to basic rooms surrounding an open courtyard. Rooms are unmemorable but clean, with high ceilings. Breakfast is included in the tariff. *Castelar 24, 41001 Seville, tel. 95/422–09–60. 100 rooms. No credit cards. Moderate.*

Reyes Católicos is a small, modern annex to the nearby Montecarlo Hotel. *Gravina 57, 41001 Seville, tel. 95/421–12–00. 26 rooms. AE, DC, V. Moderate.*

Ducal, less expensive, is an adequate, old-fashioned hotel. *Pla-*

za de la Encarnación 19, 41003 Seville, tel. 95/421–51–07. AE, DC, V. Inexpensive.

Hostal Toledo—one of several very basic family-run hotels in the Barrio Santa Cruz—is in lovely, old, Moorish-style buildings dripping with flowers. Rooms, some of them with bath, but few with air conditioning, cost as little as $15 a night. *Santa Theresa 15, 41004 Seville, tel. 95/421–53–35. 13 rooms. No credit cards. Inexpensive.*

On to Marbella You have a choice of driving directly from Seville to Marbella or following back roads through the **perched white villages** of Andalusia.

If you're anxious to see these villages but have limited time, drive through them en route to Marbella. You'll see only a few of them—but some are better than none. Here's the route to follow: From Seville, take N342 to Morón. Continue south to Pruna and Olvera; then go 3.2 km (2 mi) west on N342, and south to Setenial, Arriate, and Ronda. From Ronda, drive south on N339 to San Pedro de Alcántara, and east on N340 to Marbella. Pick up a large-scale Costa del Sol map at tourist shops in Seville.

A better idea, if time permits, is to drive direct from Seville to Marbella, settle into your hotel, and then break the routine one day with a side trip through Ronda and the other perched villages.

Marbella

Marbella is the most fashionable and sedate resort area along the coast. There is a town with both a charming old Moorish quarter and a modern, T-shirt-and-fudge section along the main drag; but when people speak of Marbella they refer both to the town and to the resorts—some more exclusive than others—stretching 16 km (10 mi) or so on either side of town, between the highway and the beach. If you're vacationing in southern Spain, this is the place to stay. There's championship golf and tennis, fashionable waterfront cafés, and trendy boutiques in the charming, medieval quarter of town.

The "golden bachelor"—the richest catch in Spain—hangs out at the Marbella Club. Petrodollars fill the Arab banks along N340 and underwrite Bjorn Borg's tennis clinic and Regine's nightclub at Puerto Romano. The Arabs, of course, stick to their own *wadi* (domain); what you'll see are people like yourself, shopping in Marbella and relaxing in one of the resorts surrounded by subtropical foliage at the edge of the sea. Marbella does have a certain Florida-land-boom feel to it, but development has been controlled, and Marbella, let's hope, will never turn into another Torremolinos.

Most of your time should be devoted to indolence—swimming in the ocean, sunbathing on sandy beaches or by the hotel pool. When you need something to do, visit the old Moorish section of Marbella and wander along the narrow white-washed lanes radiating from **Plaza de los Naranjos**. Among the trashy souvenir emporia you'll find some tasteful crafts shops like El Rey de la Ceramica, selling pottery from Granada; stores such as **Casa Bonet,** selling place mats and tablecloths; boutiques specializing in beachwear; and a choice of charming cafés for lunch or drinks.

Another trip you won't want to miss is to **Puerto Banús,** 8 km (5 mi) west of Marbella. Less than 20 years ago Puerto Banús was a quiet port with a few bars. Today it has perhaps 100 restaurants and shops; by the time you get there, it may have another 50. Blinked into existence by a group of developers with a sense of style and taste, Puerto Banús is an adult fantasyland, a Yuppyland of Benettons and Picasso Pizzerias, quality restaurants and designer boutiques—all stretching along two streets behind the harbor, with a small, sandy beach at one end. Everything is fun and for sale—just as it is in the restored harborfronts of Boston, Newport, and New York. The uniformly white-washed buildings lend a semblance of order and peacefulness to the profusion of shops—and create an atmosphere more Spanish than Spain. Come for lunch or dinner—restaurants are listed below. Many shops are open till 2 AM. The young take over the piano bars and discos from elevenish, and straggle home at dawn.

Dining   **Don Leone** is another local favorite, with such specialties as artichoke soup, fresh homemade pastas, and Merluza fish with mint leaves. *Muelle Ribera 45, Puerto Banús, tel. 95/281–17–16. Reservations advised. Dress: smart casual. AE, V. Closed Feb. Expensive.*

La Fonda is a small restaurant with tables both inside and on the terrace of an old Andalusian house. Run by one of Madrid's leading restaurateurs, it offers regional specialties such as *pastel de trucha salsa romos* (trout baked in pastry with sauce) and *Pintada en hojaldre* (guinea-hen in puff pastry). *Plaza Santo Cristo 9, Marbella, tel. 95/277–25–12. Reservations essential. Jacket required. AE, DC, MC, V. Expensive.*

La Hacienda Las Chapas, 12.8 km (8 mi) east of town, toward Málaga, is a white adobe building with rustic decorations (beamed ceiling, fireplace, tiled floor, wood tables). Specialties include veal cooked in foil, roast partridge in vine leaves, quail flambé, guinea hen, and maize pancakes. *Ctra. Cadiz, Km 193, Marbella, tel. 95/283–12–67. Reservations essential. Jacket required. AE, DC, MC, V. Closed Mon. and Nov. 15–Dec. 15. Expensive.*

Marbella Club, on N340, 3.2 km (2 mi) west of town, toward Cadiz, is where the private villa owners come to socialize, creating an intimate, community feeling you won't experience in other Marbella resorts. *Ctra. Cadiz, Km 177, Marbella, tel. 95/277–13–00. Reservations essential. Jacket required. AE, DC, MC, V. Expensive.*

La Meridiana, 4.8 km (3 mi) west of town, toward Cadiz, serves meals on the garden terrace of a Bauhaus-type building. *Camino de la Cruz, Las Lomas, tel. 95/277–61–90. Reservations advised. Jacket suggested. AE, DC, V. Closed Mon., Tues. lunch. Expensive.*

The Royale is best known for its fresh fish. *Muelle Ribera-local, Puerto Banús, tel. 95/281–18–98. Reservations advised. Dress: smart casual. AE, DC, V. Closed Feb. Expensive.*

Taberna del Alabardero serves seafood specialties in a setting overlooking the harbour. *Muelle Benabola, Puerto Banús, tel. 95/281–27–94. Reservations advised. Dress: smart casual. AE, DC, V. Closed Sun. and Feb. Expensive.*

Cipriano also enjoys a good reputation for fresh fish. Prices are slightly lower than at Royale, and the atmosphere is more casual. *Muelle de Levante, Puerto Banús, tel. 95/281–10–77. Res-*

ervations advised. Dress: smart casual. AE, DC, V. Closed Feb. Moderate.

Gran Marisquería Santiago is well known for its fresh seafood: sole meunière, halibut with mushroom sauce, fresh salmon with herbs, lobster from the tank. The atmosphere is informal —the restaurant is on the busy waterfront, in back of the main town beach. *Paseo Maritimo, Marbella, tel. 95/277–00–78. Reservations unnecessary. Dress: casual. AE, DC, V. Moderate.*

Shaban is the place for good Indian/Pakistani food. *Muelle Benabola, Puerto Banús, tel. 95/281–50–44. Reservations unnecessary. Dress: casual. AE, V. Closed Feb. Moderate.*

El Balcón de la Vírgen is a friendly, low-priced restaurant in a 16th-century building in the old quarter of Marbella. *Remedios 2, Marbella, tel. 95/277–60–92. Reservations unnecessary. Dress: casual. AE, DC, V. No credit cards. Closed Tues. Inexpensive.*

Lodging The only reason to stay in town is if you're on a tight budget and have no car. Students can stay in small, family-run hotels in the old quarter of Marbella for as little as $10 a night. There are a few reasonably priced, package-tour-type high-rise hotels only a block from the busy town beach. For most visitors, air-conditioning in summer is a must. The ocean is uninviting at times, thanks to improper pollution controls, so a hotel pool is a plus. You may prefer to stay at one of the sparkling white resorts strung along the beach on either side of town. Finding the right one is critical.

Don Carlos, 12.8 km (8 mi), or 15 minutes east of Marbella, on the road toward Málaga, is a large, 17-story white concrete slab at the edge of the sea. The former Hilton attracts an American crowd. Ask for an upper room facing the ocean. The isolated 5.2-ha (13-acre) estate has lovely gardens, and you can walk along a natural beach away from the commercial areas. Otherwise, you need a car. *Ctra. N340, Km 191, 29600 Marbella, tel. 95/283–11–40. 232 rooms. Facilities: restaurants, bars, large gardens, heated outdoor pool, boutiques, tennis. AE, DC, MC, V. Very Expensive.*

The Marbella Club is 3.2 km (2 mi) west of town on the road to Cadiz. The grande dame of Marbella, it is old and aristocratic. It tends to attract an older, established clientele, who request the same room year after year. The fact that the local patricians all belong to the club and come down from their villas for drinks and dinner gives it a certain color and class. The bungalow-style rooms run from cramped to spacious, and the decor varies from Beach Modern to regional; specify what you want, but ask for a room that's been recently renovated. The grounds are exquisite. Breakfast is served on a patio where songbirds flit through the lush, subtropical vegetation. *Ctra. N340, Km 178, 29600 Marbella, tel. 95/277–13–00. 100 rooms. Facilities: restaurant, piano bar, outdoor heated pool, private beach, boutiques, tennis. AE, DC, MC, V. Very Expensive.*

Los Monteros, 6.4 km (4 mi) east of Marbella, on the road to Malaga, prides itself on being one of the most expensive hotels in Spain. The hotel is minutes from the famous Rio Real golf course (free bus service to the greens). A large pool and lovely lawns separate a modern two-story section from a more old-fashioned, seven-story building. Rooms and views vary; specify what you want. Eighty percent of the guests are English, which may explain the somewhat starched formality of many rooms, and the beach chairs perfectly aligned on manicured lawns, like so many pieces of sculpture. *Crtr. N340, Km 187, 29600 Marbella, tel. 95/277–17–00. 170 rooms. Facilities: restaurants, bars, subtropical gardens, outdoor pools, private beach, horseback riding, boutiques, 7 tennis courts. AE, DC, MC, V. Very Expensive.*

Puente Romano, 3.2 km (2 mi) west of town on the road to Cadiz, is just past the Marbella Club. Though under the same management, it has a different atmosphere. More international, Puente Romano offers hosts greater anonymity and a greater number of American guests. It is a very modern hotel/apartment complex of low white stucco buildings on beautifully manicured grounds. Rooms are more luxurious than at the Marbella Club—and more predictable. *Ctra. N340, Km 176, 29600 Marbella, tel. 95/277–01–00. 184 rooms. Facilities: restaurant, piano bar, Regine's nightclub, 2 outdoor pools, private beach, boutiques, tennis. AE, DC, MC, V. Very Expensive.*

Andalucía Plaza. Stay here only if you like being surrounded by Americans or don't mind 600 conventioneers at dinner. *Ctra. N340, Km 185, 29660 Nueva Andalucia, tel. 95/281–47–92. 415 rooms. Facilities: restaurants, bars, subtropical gardens, indoor and outdoor pools, boutiques, tennis. AE, DC, MC, V. Expensive.*

El Fuerte has simple, adequate rooms, in town. There's also a garden with palm trees and a certain faded elegance in the public areas. *Av. del Fuerte 1, 29600 Marbella, tel. 95/277–15–00. 262 rooms. Facilities: restaurants, bars, outdoor pool, tennis courts. AE, DC, MC, V. Expensive.*

Baviera is a budget hotel on the main street opposite the bus station. *Camino del Calvaro, 29600 Marbella, tel. 95/277–29–50. 41 rooms. No credit cards. Inexpensive.*

Students on a budget can stay in small family-run hotels in the old quarter of Marbella for $15–$20 a night. You'll be lucky to find air-conditioning or anyone who speaks English, but rooms will be clean and some will have private showers. Best bet is the friendly **Enriqueta,** (J. Chinchilla 20, 29600 Marbella, tel. 95/277–00–58), which has a TV room. Next best is **Hostal el Mero** (Castillo 14, 29600 Marbella, tel. 95/277–00–60).

On to Ronda Perhaps it was the light after a late-afternoon storm, but the drive through the **perched white villages of Andalusia** was the highlight of my last trip to Spain. There are many such villages, blazing white, clutching the rocky mountainsides above the fields of sunflower and wheat, grape, and maize.

The houses are painted white to ward off the summer heat. Up close, one sees that the streets are dusty and the walls crumbling. But from a distance, the towns seem to rise from the plains like medieval castles. The uniform whiteness gives them an architectural integrity as soothing to the heart as to the eye: Here at last is a world where, visually at least, the individual is subsumed; where everything says "us," not "I." What you'll see is the seasonless, monochromatic world; the family is still the wellspring of life in these Moorish towns, and the true colors come from the perfumed courtyards within.

You owe it to yourself at least once to leave the main highways and wander along the back roads, through fields and pastureland, beneath the perched white villages. The roads are as safe as any in Spain, and marked well enough that with a detailed map, you won't get lost—at least not for long. Drive west on N340 to San Pedro de Alcántara (10.7 km/6.7 mi). Head north on C339 to Ronda (43.2 km/27 mi).

Ronda

Both the modern district and the old Moorish quarter are split in two by a great gorge. The bridge across it, which has a restaurant in the former prison cell above its central arch, is one of the most spectacular sights in Spain. The only problem with Ronda is its popularity; you have no sense of discovery here as you do in the white villages. The old town lies behind walls built during the Moorish occupation, which lasted until 1485. Because of the high elevation, the houses are low and small, with steep roofs, as they are in the colder regions of the north. Park at the **Collegiate Church** (Colegiata de Santa María la Mayor, Plaza de la Ciudad) on your left as you drive through the old town. Of particular note in this former mosque are the Renaissance chancel (where the altar is) and the ornate choir stalls, as well as the minaret bell tower. Walk behind the church (the side away from the road), and turn right to the **Mondragón Palace,** with its twin towers. The terrace overlooks the gorge and the plains below.

The view from the **bridge,** looking down 149.9 m (500 ft), is spectacular. Cross the bridge and enter the new town. On your left is the **bullring.** Built in 1785, it is one of the oldest in Spain. Francisco Romero, the father of modern bullfighting—he introduced the cape, the *muleta,* and most of the rituals—was born in Ronda in 1698. His son Juan Romero introduced the "supporting team," and his grandson Pedro Romero (1754–1839) became one of Spain's greatest bullfighters.

Also on your left, beyond the bullring, are the **Paseo de la Merced Gardens** (Alameda del Tajo). Stroll through the gardens and enjoy a dramatic walk along the cliffs.

For a short excursion from Ronda you should consider a visit to **Cueva de la Pileta** (Pileta Cave), just outside Benaojan. Not only are the caves fascinating for their multiple caverns filled with stalactites and stalagmites, but they contain black and red drawings that predate those at Altimira and indicate that the caves were inhabited more than 25,000 years ago.

Continue north through the modern section of Ronda on C339 to Puerto de Montejaque (16 km/10 mi). Turn left on C344 to **Grazalema** (12.9 km/8 mi), 814.7 m (2,716 ft) up, where you can visit the Church of the Encarnación and wander through the white streets, beneath balconies and patios bursting with flowers.

Now you have a decision to make. To reach **Zahara,** one of the most beautiful of the white villages, the most direct route, over a rough mountain road, is to take C344 another mile west, and then to turn north (right) on Route 521 (12.8 km/8 mi), past Puerto de las Palas. The longer, less dramatic route is to drive northeast 9.6 km (6 mi) from Grazalema to Puerto de Asperilla on C339; then, at the *T,* turn left (north), go about 11.2 km (7 mi), and turn left again on Route 521 to Zahara.

If you're addicted to back roads, follow signs from Zahara to the pretty town of **El Gastor** and then head north to the major road, N342. If you've seen enough, skip El Gastor, and from Zahara continue north on Route 521, and turn left (north) on C339, going 6.4 km (4 mi) to **Algodonales.** This town seems even whiter than the other white towns, perhaps because of the striking contrast with the silvery-green olive groves that surround it.

Whether you go to Algodonales or El Gastor, you'll end up on N342. Turn right (east) to **Olvera** (20.8 km/13 mi from Algodonales). The beauty of this village is compromised only by the presence of the main road. From Olvera, you can make a side trip northeast to **Pruna** (14.4 km/9 mi round-trip).

Drive 3.2 km (2 mi) east on N342, and head south 11.2 km (7 mi) to the perched village of **Setenil**, where the rock forms a natural roof over the streets. This is the most dramatic part of the drive, and should be made in the late afternoon, when the sun is less harsh. From Setenil continue south to **Arriate** and Ronda, and then take C339 back south to the coast. The trip will take the better part of a day.

If this tour hasn't satisfied your wanderlust, try the following itinerary to other white villages and a dramatic mountain peak. Drive east along the coast on Route N340 from Marbella to **Fuengirola** (27.2 km/17 mi). Take the beautiful drive north to **Mijas** (8 km/5 mi). Continue north, past **Alhaurín** to the white village of **Cartama** (19.2 km/12 mi). Cross the Guadalhorca River (3.2 km/2 mi) and turn left (north) on C337 to the white village of **Alora** (20.8 km/13 mi). Continue north on another beautiful road to the **Ruinas de Bobastro** (17.6 km/11 mi). Drive to **Las Atalayas,** turn left at the edge of the lake to **Ardales** (6.4 km/4 mi), return to Alora via **Carratraca** (22.4 km/14 mi), and retrace your steps back to Cartama (24 km/15 mi). Take C337 to **Coin** (12.8 km/8 mi), **Monda,** and **Marbella** (12.8 km/17 mi).

On to Granada As you approach overdeveloped **Torremolinos,** the traffic increases and so do the real estate and video club signs. What Torremolinos has to offer are high-rise hotels with pools and shops along a highway, and a strip of beach. Life here is geared for the package-tour trade.

Lodging **Málaga** is not a destination, but a point of transit. The only place I'd recommend staying in Málaga is the **Parador de Gibralfaro,** which sits on a mountaintop with breathtaking views, about 3.2 km (2 mi) from the center of town. The rustic rooms are reasonably priced, and there is a pleasant dining room with the option of eating on a terrace that offers a spectacular view over Málaga's harbor. *Málaga 29016, tel. 95/222–19–02. 12 rooms. Facilities: restaurant, parking. AE, DC, MC, V. Moderate–Expensive.*

Between Málaga and Salobreña is the **Nerja Cave** (Cueva de Nerja) (open May–mid-Sept. daily 9–9; off-season, 10–1:30, 4–7). If you're partial to caves or are traveling with children, the Nerja Cave is worth an hour of your time. It's not the usual long, dark passageway, but a huge network of limestone caverns with lots of corners to explore. There's classical music, and, best of all, no guide comparing stalactites to Joe DiMaggio's bat or George Washington's nose. Most thrilling are the Cascade Chamber, which hosts an annual festival of music and dance; and a cathedrallike room with a pillar 59.9 m (200 ft) long—the longest-known stalactite in the world.

At **Almuñecar,** turn north on N323 for 65.6 km (41 mi) to Granada. This is a beautiful trip along the western rim of the Sierra Nevadas—a world of wild, red rock, orange and lemon groves, and silver olive trees.

Granada

The main attraction of Granada—perhaps of all Spain—is a Moorish fort and palace known as the Alhambra. You'll want to spend at least a half day here and at the palatial villa called the Generalife. The other musts are the cathedral and the adjoining Royal Chapel (Capilla Real), where Ferdinand and Isabella are buried. You'll also want to wander through the old Moorish quarter to see the Alhambra at dusk, and journey 46.4 km (29 mi) to Pico de Veleta to enjoy the wild mountain views of the Sierra Nevadas.

When Córdoba was at the height of its power, Granada was a mere provincial capital. It was then, in the 9th century, that construction of the Alhambra began—not the palace, but the original fortress that occupies part of the present site.

Granada came to its full glory under the Nasrid dynasty (1232–1492), when the rest of Spain had fallen to the Catholics. As many as 100,000 Muslim refugees fled here before the advancing Christian armies. The city was under constant siege, and its existence depended on the payment of tributes, skillful diplomacy, and the whims of the enemy. The situation was worse than precarious; it was just a matter of time before Granada fell into Christian hands.

When Mohammed V began the Alhambra Palace in 1377, he must have known that he was building the last and perhaps most splendid monument of 700 years of Moorish culture in Spain. It was the work of an old, dying civilization; the product of a reduced and threatened state. As you tour the palace, try to see it as an oasis of peace and beauty where Mohammed V and other sultans sought to escape impending doom—each room an Arabian tale told to stave off death.

Modern Granada is a busy, sprawling town, visually unmemorable. As you climb Alhambra hill, you leave the noise and confusion of modern life behind and enter a green world, where the air is clear and cool. The Alhambra is not one but a series of buildings on a 14-ha (35-acre) plateau, a natural acropolis looming over the modern town of Granada. Think of it as a fortified medieval city with five sections: (1) the Alcazaba, the oldest part of the Alhambra (and also the most touched up), dating back to the days when it served as a military fortress; (2) the 14th-century Alhambra Palace, or Alcázar, where the sultan lived with his harem and entertained important guests; (3) the Royal City, which included a college, houses, workshops, and a great mosque—virtually none of which remain; (4) a Christian palace built after the Reconquest by Charles V (grandson of Ferdinand and Isabella); and (5) the Generalife (technically outside the walls of the Alhambra), the summer villa of the Sultan and his family.

Ask yourself as you walk around: Is the Alhambra the high point of Muslim architecture in Spain, or is it the dying gasp of a

Granada

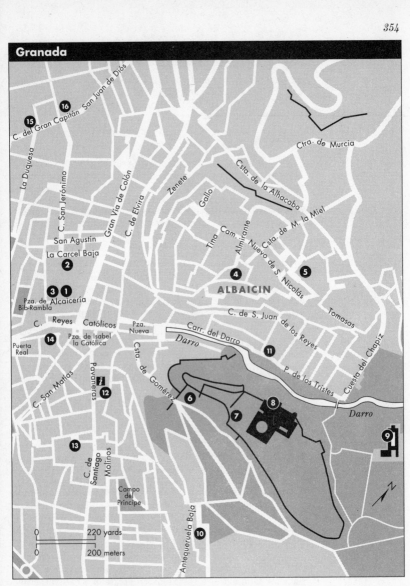

Alabaicín, **4**

Alcaicería, **3**

Alhambra, **8**

Alhambra Precincts, **6**

Casa de los Tiros, **12**

Casa Museo de
Falla, **10**

Cathedral, **2**

Corral del Carbón, **14**

Generalife, **9**

Museo
Arqueológico, **11**

Puerta de la Justicía, **7**

Royal Chapel, **1**

San Jerónimo, **15**

San Juan de Diós, **16**

San Nicolás Church, **5**

Santo Domingo, **13**

decadent culture? One critic calls it "foppish." Another says it looks more like a boudoir than a king's palace. Still another equates the Córdoba mosque with the robustness of early Christian architecture and the Alhambra to the flaccid self-indulgence of Rococo. "No medieval Christian king lived in such feminine exotic surroundings," wrote H. V. Morton in *A Stranger in Spain*. "These pretty vistas, fountains, and arcades, designed it seems for eating of rose-petal jam, for tears, for sighs, provoke the thought that the Alhambra is not unlike a woman who has no other quality than beauty."

You will probably be surprised by the smallness of the rooms. No effort has been made to overwhelm you, as at, say, Versailles. Even the Court of Lions is built on an intimate, human scale. The sultans seemed to be seeking an inner peace, not a way of proving their worth in the eyes of the world.

The material of which the Alhambra is made is wonderfully flimsy. Beneath the ornate stuccowork is nothing but bricks, plaster, and rubble. The wood frame is crudely constructed. The ceilings are nothing but carved plaster, which you could break with a hand. The caliphs built schools and mosques to last, but not palaces, which were merely the headquarters of one man who would someday be replaced. That the decorations have survived 500 years is a miracle.

What you see is not the creation of one man but an accretion of styles over many generations. This explains the seemingly haphazard arrangement of some buildings and the absence of a defined axis. Notice how the builders concealed all solid functional components—walls, arches, ceilings—behind a decorative web of plaster and tile. Lightness was the aim of Moorish architecture as massiveness was for the Egyptians. The goal was worthy of a genie: Not only to fill space with beauty, but to make the walls disappear, to free them of weight; in short, to transcend matter.

As you walk through the Alhambra, try to think of it as a Moorish heaven: an oasis in a dry desert, with fountains, greenery, and shelter from the sun. Picture the slender columns as tent poles or date palms; the flowery capitals (the heads of columns) as vegetation; the designs on the walls as oriental carpets in a nomad's tent. The desert is empty as a whitewashed wall: Is it any wonder that the Moors would want to fill it with color and life?

Our own houses shelter us from nature; in the Alhambra, nature is integrated in the design. We admit sunshine from without; the Alhambra admits it from courtyards within. It's only in recent times that Western architects have begun to catch up with the Arabs—using skylights and atriums, and, following the lead of Frank Lloyd Wright, integrating architecture with the natural environment. For this to happen we had to learn what the Moors apparently knew: that man and nature are one, and that happiness comes from experiencing this oneness.

The road to the entrance is lined, inappropriately, with elms: The Spanish King gave Wellington an estate in return for his struggle against Napoleon, and Wellington returned the favor with a decidedly un-Moorish gift of elms.

Enter through the Gate of Justice (Puerta de la Justicia), so called because it was here that the sultans held court. In the keystone of the horseshoe-shape entry arch is a large open hand of Fatima, daughter of Muhammad by his first wife, each finger symbolizing one of the five requirements of the Islamic faith: belief in the oneness of God, prayer, fasting in the month of Ramadan, pilgrimage to Mecca, and the giving of alms.

Turn into the **Place of the Cisterns** (Plaza de los Aljibes), an open area where water was stored in case enemies destroyed the aqueduct. On your right is the 14th-century sultan's **palace** (Alcázar), which is where you'll want to spend most of your time. On your left, behind a wall, is the oldest part of the Alhambra, which contained military headquarters, government offices, a mint, guards' barracks, and apartments for members of court and official guests.

Turn left into the **Alcazaba** and climb the watchtower (Torre de la Vela) for a great view of Granada. It was on this terrace that the Catholics placed their first cross in 1492, proclaiming the end of 700 years of Muslim rule.

Return to the Place of the Cisterns. Ahead of you is **Emperor Charles V's Palace.** It's fashionable to denigrate this Renaissance structure, to dismiss it as a visual obscenity; but not all critics agree. The important thing is to make up your own mind and to see what your verdict says about your own sensibilities. Charles V, the grandson of Ferdinand and Isabella, tore down many Moorish buildings to construct this palace, which was never completed. It's a perfect square with a circular inner court where bullfights were once held. Michener calls its facade "grotesquely ugly, as if someone had set out to burlesque the worst taste of the time." Washington Irving dismissed it as an "arrogant intruder." Whatever its architectural virtues, Charles's palace is as inappropriately situated as the cathedral in the Córdoba mosque.

From Charles V's palace, turn into the **Court of the Myrtle Trees** (Patio de Comares), which has a long pool down the center, bordered by myrtles. This was the reception area for visitors to the Hall of the Ambassadors (Salón de Embajadores), so try to imagine yourself waiting here for a meeting with the sultan. Notice how nature is included in this Moorish version of paradise: in the dark green hedges standing out against the gleaming white marble; in the sky sailing across the water. Notice, too, how everything converges on the center: a very Eastern notion, where one looks inward (as opposed to outward, toward the world) to find peace, and where beauty is enclosed within walls as the spirit or soul is encased in the body. The reflections create a playful ambiguity about the nature of reality (which is real, which reflection?). There's a sense of unreality, too, in the narrow columns, which seem too slight to support anything.

At the north end of this court is the **Hall of the Blessing** (Sala de la Barca), which leads into the **Hall of the Ambassadors.** The sultan met official visitors and held state receptions here. The lavish decoration—the most splendid in the Alhambra—reflects the importance of this hall in a kingdom that depended on diplomacy, not warfare, for its survival.

Turn right down a gallery to the **Queen's Dressing Room** (Tocador de la Reina) located at the top of a small tower (**Abul Hachach's Tower**). The room has been modernized and painted with arabesques. Washington Irving lived here while writing *The Alhambra.*

Return to the Court of the Myrtle Trees and turn left into the famous **Court of Lions** (Patio de los Leones). This 14th-century court was the drawing room of the harem, at the heart of the palace. The lions offering their rumps to the fountain are probably Phoenician. The fountain was originally a sundial—at each hour water flowed from the mouth of a different lion.

To your right, off the Court of Lions, is the **Hall of the Abencerrajes** (Sala de los Abencerrajes). The honeycomb dome is carved from simple plaster: a beehive (one critic writes) whose honey is light. The hall is named after the noble family whose male members were lured here and executed by the last sultan of Granada; guides will insist you can still see their blood.

From the Hall of the Abencerrajes return to the Court of Lions. Turn right. At the end of the hall is the **Hall of the Kings** (Sala de los Reyes), which houses the portraits of the first 10 Nasrid rulers.

Return to the Court of Lions and take the passageway to the right. This leads into the **Hall of the Two Sisters** (Sala de las Dos Hermanas), which many consider the loveliest room in the palace. It would be fun to dream up an Arabian tale about the two sisters, but they are in fact nothing more than the two slabs of flawless white marble. The honeycomb ceiling seems the work of bees. Many compare it to stalactites or icicles—an appropriate sort of wish fulfillment for a people of the desert.

Exit through the Gate of Justice and walk left around the walls to the **Generalife,** the summer villa of the sultans. All here is cool and restful, sensual and intimate. The two lines of water jets make visual poetry and remind us again that the Arab heaven is a cool place with water. *Admission: 300 ptas. Open Mon.–Sat. 9–8, Sun. 9–6 (Oct.–Mar. 9:30–6); floodlit visits Wed.–Sat. 10–midnight (Oct.–Mar. 8–10 Sat. only).*

Chapel Royal (Capilla Real) is the tomb of the Catholic Monarchs *(Los Reyes Católicos)*, Ferdinand and Isabella. Built in the Isabeline style—a Catholic response to the Moorish love of decoration, but with none of the restraint—it is one of the most lavish sepulchres in the world. Isabella's art collection of great Flemish, Spanish, and Italian paintings is in the sacristy. *Admission: 200 ptas. Open Apr.–Sept., daily 10:30–1 and 4–7; Oct.–Mar., daily 10:30–1 and 3:30–6.*

The Catholic Monarchs wanted to be buried in the city where they won their final victory over the Moors in 1492. Isabella was a year older than Ferdinand. She was a beautiful child, who was pursued at age 14 by Edward IV of England; had she accepted his advances, she might have become Queen of England! Her modesty went to such extremes that when she was dying, she refused to show her bare foot for extreme unction, and her silk stocking was anointed instead. She was devoted to Christ's kingdom and thought God approved of the Inquisition and the expulsion of the Jews. It was she, not her husband, who believed in Columbus.

Isabella is looking away from her husband, just as, on another sepulchre, her daughter Juana the Mad is looking away from her husband, Philip the Handsome.

At age 17 Juana set sail for Flanders to marry 18-year-old Philip of Burgundy. She was insanely jealous of him, and responded to his infidelities with hunger strikes and tantrums. The couple returned to Spain, but Philip hated the stuffiness of the court and fled, leaving Juana alone with her depressions. She tried to flee to him one cold November night, dressed in nothing but her nightgown; and from that time she was known as *Juana la Loca*—Joan the Mad or Crazy Jane. When she was permitted to return to Flanders in 1504, she embarrassed the Spanish court by attacking Philip's lover and cutting off her rival's long hair in public.

When Isabella died, Juana returned to Spain with Philip to claim her inheritance as heir to Castile. Ferdinand acted as her regent, because she was considered unfit to rule. Within a year Philip died. Inconsolable, Juana refused to have him buried and set his corpse on a throne dressed in furs. After the body was embalmed, she never left the coffin and had it opened every night so that she could kiss the dead man's face. For several years she wandered about the country, traveling by night with a hearse that carried her husband's body. Her father, Ferdinand, who outlived Isabella by a dozen years, finally convinced Juana to settle in a mansion, still accompanied by Philip's corpse; and there they remained for 47 years, until her death at the age of 76. It was the child of Juana and Philip, Charles V, who built his palace in the Alhambra and who approved the construction of the cathedral in the Córdoba Mosque.

A short flight of steps leads down to a vault where the simple coffins of Ferdinand, Isabella, Juana, and Philip lie on a stone slab. On the wall is a crucifix. The reality of death is poignantly brought home in the contrast between the splendid tomb and these four lead boxes.

Next to the Chapel Royal is the **cathedral,** built in the 16th and 17th centuries. Sit in its dim interior, preferably during one of the daily organ concerts, and contemplate the different values that went into the creation of this church and the Alhambra. What is unusual is the way in which you're made to enter through a rotunda rather than through a nave (the long central aisle).

One of the highlights of your stay in Granada is the sweeping view of the Alhambra from the terrace of **St. Nicholas Church** (San Nicolás) in the **Albaicín,** the old Moorish quarter. Come at sunset for a sight you won't forget.

If you're interested in architecture, visit the **Carthusian Monastery** (Monasterio de la Cartuja), east of the university on Calle Real de Cartuja, which has a lavishly decorated Baroque church, a magnificent late-Baroque sacristy, and a splendid view. *Admission: 100 ptas. Open Apr.–Sept., daily 10–1 and 4–7; Oct.–Mar., daily 10–1 and 4–6.*

To escape the heat and enjoy some spectacular mountain scenery, either on foot or from your car, drive 46.4 km (29 mi) to **Pico de Veleta**—more than 3,000 m (10,000 ft) up in the Sierra Nevadas. You can ski here from mid-December through early May; one of the lifts may be open now in summer. The road to the top is passable only from July to October, but you don't have to reach the summit to appreciate the view.

Dining There are several good to excellent restaurants in Granada, but none that is consistently first-rate. Several have a great deal of warmth and character.

Parador Nacional San Francisco on Alhambra hill has a restaurant worth visiting—perhaps more for its atmosphere than for its cuisine—if you are staying in the neighborhood. *Recinto de la Alhambra, tel. 95/822–14–93. Reservations required. Dress: smart casual. AE, DC, MC, V. Moderate–Expensive.*

Columbia, in the same neighborhood, has live guitar music on a terrace overlooking the city. *Antequeruela Baja 1, tel. 95/822–74–33. Reservations advised weekends. Dress: smart casual. AE, DC, V. Closed Sun. Moderate.*

Cunini, located behind the flower market near the cathedral, takes top billing. Downstairs is a tapa bar; the upstairs restaurant is best known for its Basque-style soup-stews and its fresh fish. *Pescaderia 9, tel. 95/826–37–01. Reservations advised weekends. Dress: smart casual. AE, DC, MC, V. Closed Sun. eve. Moderate.*

Ruta del Veleta is 4.8 km (3 mi) from Granada on the road to the mountains, so you may want to stop there for lunch or dinner en route to the Pico de Veleta. *44 Cenes de la Vega, tel. 95/848–61–34. Dress: casual. No reservations. AE, DC, V. Closed Sun. eve. Moderate.*

Sevilla, a well-established restaurant near the cathedral, serves traditional Andalusian cuisine, including a local fish soup recipe. The tapas bar is especially good. *Oficios 14, tel. 95/822–12–23. Reservations not necessary. Dress: casual. AE, DC, V. Closed Sun. eve. Moderate.*

Casa Salvador, a distance from the cathedral and the Alhambra, is simple, friendly and a good value. *Duende 16, tel. 95/822–50–09. No reservations. Dress: casual. AE, DC, V. Closed Sun. eve. and Mon. Inexpensive.*

Los Leones, slightly less expensive than Casa Salvador, is similarly friendly but distant from the cathedral and the Alhambra. *Acera del Darro 10, tel. 95/825–50–07. No reservations. Dress: casual. AE, DC, V. Closed Mon. eve. and Tues. Inexpensive.*

Los Manueles is basic, busy, and friendly, with ceramic tiles, and smoked hams hanging from the ceiling. *Zaragoza 2, tel. 95/822–34–15. No reservations. Dress: casual. No credit cards. Inexpensive.*

Lodging Hotels that claim to be in the Alhambra are not in fact within the walls, but only on Alhambra hill, in walking distance of the palace. Try to stay here: It's quiet and cool, and away from the congestion of the town below. Stay in town only if you need a budget hotel or want to be in walking distance of the night spots.

The Alhambra Palace is a lavish, Moorish-style palace halfway up the hill to the Alhambra. Its location on the main road, with cars and buses constantly pulling into and out of insufficient parking spaces, gives it a more harried mood than that of the more isolated Parador. Despite its busyness, however, the Palace is still a conversation piece, with rich carpets, tapestries, and colorful Moorish tiles. Front rooms are preferable. *Peña Partida 2, Granada 18009, tel. 95/822–14–40. 140 rooms. Fa-*

cilities: restaurant, lounge for afternoon tea and cocktails, limited parking. AE, DC, MC, V. Expensive.

Carmén is essentially a high rise on a busy street not far from the cathedral. Rooms are clean but somewhat basic. Inside rooms are quieter—the higher up the better. *Acera del Darro 62, Granada 18005, tel. 95/825–83–00. 205 rooms. Facilities: restaurant. AE, DC, MC, V. Expensive.*

Luz de Granada is the best of the modern hotels in town. Rooms, though small, are clean, comfortable, and reasonably priced. The hotel, however, has an impersonal, group-tour ambience and is inconveniently located northwest of town on the road to Córdoba. *Av. de la Constitución 18, Granada 18012, tel. 95/820–40–61. 173 rooms. Facilities: restaurant, conference facilities, shops, parking. AE, DC, MC, V. Expensive.*

Parador Nacional San Francisco is one of two hotels that are actually on the grounds of the Alhambra (though not within the walls). The former Arab palace was transformed into a Franciscan cconvent when Granada was reconquered in 1492. Rooms are simple and restrained; public areas are full of rare icons, rugs, mosaics, and embroideries. The only noises is from the fountains in the gardens, beneath the vine-covered walls. If you want a tastefully subdued environment where you can experience the tranquility of the Alhambra itself, this is the place to stay. (If you can't get a room in the Parador, make reservations for lunch.) *Recinto de la Alhambra, Granada 18009, tel. 95/822–14–40. 39 rooms. Facilities: restaurant, terrace for afternoon tea and cocktails, garage. AE, DC, MC, V. Expensive.*

América, an alternative hotel much in demand, is clser to the Alhambra than the government parador. Its popularity stems from the warm hospitality expressed by its owners, who have filled the public rooms with an assortment of antiques. Guest rooms are on the small side, but they are comfortable and well maintained. *Real de la Alhambra, Granada, 18009, tel. 95/ 822–74–71. 14 rooms. Facilities: restaurant. Closed Nov.– Apr. AE, DC, V. Moderate–Expensive.*

The **Brasilia** is aging but fine if you just need a place to put your head—particularly the seventh-floor rooms with balconies. *Rocogidas 7, Granada 18005, tel. 95/825–84–50. 68 rooms. Facilities: breakfast only. AE, DC, V. Moderate.*

The **Los Angeles** caters to tour groups and is away from the center of town. But the surroundings are pleasant and peaceful, the staff is friendly, the price is right, and the hotel is one of the very few with a pool. stay in the larger rooms added since 1983. *Cuesta Escoriaza 17, Granada 18008, tel. 95/822–14–24. 100 rooms. Facilities: restaurant, outdoor pool, parking. AE, DC, V. Moderate.*

Parador Nacional de Sierra Nevada is a chalet-style parador near the summit of the Pico de Veleta where you can also stop for meals (reserve ahead). Upper rooms are best. You're above the timberline, so to take a walk, just set off in any direction. Be sure to bring a sweater, even in summer. *monachil, Sierra Nevada 18196, tel. 95/848–02–04. 32 rooms. Facilities: restaurant, skiing. AE, DC, MC, V. Moderate.*

The **Washington Irving,** where the author of *The Alhambra* once stayed, is farther up Alhambra hill. The hotel is one of a kind, but many rooms are very small and plain. If you stay, ask for a large one. *Paseo del Generalife 2, Granada 18009, tel. 95/ 822–75–50. 68 rooms. Facilities: Restaurant, banquet room, shops. AE, DC, MC, V. Moderate.*

Carlos V is a quiet, English-style hotel on the fourth floor of a government building in a residential area. Rooms are furnished with twin beds only. *Plaza de los Campos 4, Granada 18009, tel. 95/822–15–87. 28 rooms. Facilities: restaurant. AE, DC, V. Inexpensive.*

Kenia is a quiet, unassuming hotel in a residential area. *Molinos 65, Granada 18009, tel. 95/822–75–06. 19 rooms. Facilities: terrace for breakfast. AE, DC, V. Closed Oct.–Dec. Inexpensive.*

Baeza

If you're driving from Granada back to Madrid (or from Granada to Córdoba), consider a short side trip to Baeza and Úbeda. Take N323 north to Jaén, then turn right on N321 for 46.4 km (29 mi) to Baeza and another 9.6 km (6 mi) to Úbeda.

Baeza was a former *taifa* capital—one of the feudal kingdoms that developed in Moorish Spain when the Córdoba caliphate collapsed. The Albaicín, the old Moorish quarter of Granada, is named for the Baezan Moors who fled to Granada when the Christians reconquered the town in 1227. This was the first reconquered town in Andalusia; the first mass of the Reconquest was held here on a balcony overlooking the Plaza of the Lions. What you'll see in Baeza are some fine examples of early Spanish Renaissance architecture. The casual visitor can expect to spend less than an hour exploring the important sights, which are all within a few minutes' walk of each other.

Park at the lovely **Plaza of the Lions** (Plaza de los Leones), the square on your right as you drive through town on N321. Above the lions is a draped figure said to be Hannibal's wife. The head is new; the old one was removed during the Spanish Civil War by Republicans who mistook her for the Virgin.

To the right of the square is the tourist office (Casa del Pópulo, tel. 95/374–04–44), where you can pick up a walking guide. To the left is the most elegant 16th-century slaughterhouse *(abattoir)* you ever did see. Stairs lined with 16th-century Renaissance-Plateresque buildings lead from the square to the cathedral. (The Plateresque style combines Gothic, Renaissance, and Arabic elements. "Plateresque" comes from *platero*, meaning "silversmith"; the design is so fine, it seems more the work of a silversmith than of a mason. Though this delicate ornamentation is Arab-inspired, the decorative themes and the symmetry and balance of the buildings themselves are inspired by the Italian Renaissance.)

Follow the steps to the Plaza Santa María. Turn right to reach the **cathedral,** which was remodeled in the late 16th century and has some outstanding chapels (one of them has a 25-peseta treat; deposit a coin and find out for yourself).

Instead of returning to the lions, cross Plaza Santa María and follow a narrow street to the Romanesque church of **Santa Cruz.** Next door is the old 16th-century university, which had a prison for unruly students. Across from the university is the **Jabalquinto Palace** (Palacio de Jabalquinto). The free-flowing, lacelike facade is a great example of the Moorish-inspired Isabeline style, in which every inch of space is covered with intricate designs.

Úbeda

After the Christians took over in 1234, Úbeda became a strong-hold for knights, who continued the fight against the Moors—and among themselves.

The focus of your trip has been Moorish Spain; an hour in Úbeda will introduce you to the art and architecture of Catholic Spain during the Renaissance. If you have more than a passing interest in the arts, you will find many notable Renaissance palaces to explore; or you may be content visiting the buildings on Plaza Vázquez de Molina, and the streets and pottery shops in the gypsy quarter.

Stop at the tourist office (Plaza del Ayuntamiento 2, tel. 95/375–08–97) for a map and descriptive booklet. Leave your car here and walk to the Plaza Vázquez de Molina. Around the corner from the tourist office, on your way to the square, is a crafts shop selling the green glazed pottery for which the town is known. You'll also pass some antiques shops selling old ceramics.

Plaza Vázquez de Molina, the aristocratic center of the old town, is bordered by several historic buildings. **El Salvador Church,** designed in 1536, has an ornamented sacristy of breathtaking exuberance. The Virgin averts her eyes from the pair of topless Italian Renaissance caryatids (female figures) guarding the door. For the key to the church, walk around the left side—to your left as you're facing the entrance—and down a street of whitewashed buildings. Ring the bell on the first door on the right.

Across the street from the church is a 16th-century palace that has been converted into the **Parador Nacional Condestable Dávalos** (Plaza Vázquez de Molina 1, tel. 95/375–03–45).

Another church worth visiting is the Gothic **St. Paul's** (San Pablo)—particularly for its chapels.

If you liked the pottery near the tourist office, visit the studios where it's made, along Calle Valençia in the **gypsy quarter,** a 10-minute walk from St. Paul's. You step through a Moorish stone archway and enter a world of immaculate white walls and angular shadows where time seems to have stopped. Men crouch in doorways as if waiting for time to begin, and old women huddle in doorways like petals of a black flower. The area is quite safe, and, unlike the ancient quarters of Seville and Córdoba, completely unspoiled by the tourist trade.

From Úbeda, take N322 west for 40 km (25 mi) to **Bailén** and then take N IV north (about 6 hours) to Madrid.

What to See and Do with Children

Córdoba: the mosque, which looks like a forest of zebras.

The Costa del Sol: the pools, beaches, and tennis courts; the Nerja caves; the discos at Puerto Banús.

Granada: the gypsy caves on Sacromonte; a hike from Pico de Veleta.

Seville: a walk through the old quarter to a flamenco show at the Plaza de Santa Cruz; a climb to the top of the Giralda; a horse-drawn carriage ride from the cathedral; a bullfight; the discos across the river near Avenida Republica Argentina.

Nightlife

Granada   In **Granada** nightlife centers on the gypsy caves on Sacromonte, the hillside opposite the Generalife. Tourists submit to and sometimes participate in 30-minute flamenco shows, which have been described as "a cosmic low in tourist-racketeering." Two exceptions are **Zincale** (Sacromonte 19) and private shows in the studio of **Mario Maya** (Mon.–Sat. 7 PM–3 AM). If you're seriously interested in flamenco, see it in Seville.

The origin of the gypsies is not known, but it's generally believed that they came from northern India and migrated to Persia about AD 1000. From there they split into two branches—one heading southwest to Egypt and North Africa, the other moving northwest to Europe and the Balkans. "Gypsy" means "Egyptian." Gypsies from Egypt migrated to Spain in the mid-15th century. They preserved the songs and dances of old Andalusia, but did not create them—being better imitators than creators.

In Granada the gypsies perform in caves carved from the hillsides. It's not as primitive as it sounds, for their whitewashed rooms are lit with electricity and heated with tiled stoves. The caves themselves are naturally warm in winter and dry and cool in summer. You may find a passionate or talented dancer here, but most just walk through the steps, clicking their imported castanets, squeezing the myth of Gypsy Spain for every tourist dollar they can get. Go for the experience, expect to be taken, and insist on having a good time.

Marbella   **Marbella** has two casinos, **Casino Nueva Andalucía** (Puerto Banús, tel. 95/281–13–44) and **Casino de Juego de Torrequebrada** (Benalmádena, tel. 95/244–25–45). The latter also has a nightclub.

Other bright spots, both in the town of Marbella and in Puerto Banús, include **Regine's** (Hotel Puente Romano, tel. 95/277–01–00), the disco **Kiss** (Av. Ricardo Sorlano y Ansai, tel. 95/277–40–94), and **Olivia Valere** in Puerto Banús (Gray D'Albion, tel. 95/281–42–83).

Seville   People who know flamenco are less than enthusiastic about the tourist shows in **Seville**—but they're the best you're going to find in southern Spain. For under $10 you get a seat at a table for a 60-minute performance. Hostesses serve drinks. Shows begin at 9:30 and 11:30 PM. The most authentic is at **El Arenal** (Rodo 7, tel. 95/421–64–92).

Consider eating dinner in the barrio and then taking in the flamenco show at **Los Gallos** (Plaza de Santa Cruz 11, tel. 95/421–69–81). Shows are at 9 and 11 PM. After the show, you can visit some of the quarter's colorful bars, such as **Casa Román** on the Plaza de los Venerables.

Discos include **Turin** (Asunción 21, tel. 95/427–50–55), **La Reja** (Santa de Gracia 33, tel. 95/421–41–42), and **Sal de Sevilla** (Castilla 175, tel. 95/433–16–89), which has a gigantic video screen competing with the music for attention. Most discos are in the newer part of the city, across the San Telmo Bridge, on streets such as Calle Fortaleza and Calle del Salado.

Conversion Tables

Distance

Kilometers/Miles To change kilometers to miles, multiply kilometers by .621.
To change miles to kilometers, multiply miles by 1.61.

Km to Mi	Mi to Km
1 = .62	1 = 1.6
2 = 1.2	2 = 3.2
3 = 1.9	3 = 4.8
4 = 2.5	4 = 6.4
5 = 3.1	5 = 8.1
6 = 3.7	6 = 9.7
7 = 4.3	7 = 11.3
8 = 5.0	8 = 12.9
9 = 5.6	9 = 14.5

Meters/Feet To change meters to feet, multiply meters by 3.28.
To change feet to meters, multiply feet by .305.

Meters to Feet	Feet to Meters
1 = 3.3	1 = .31
2 = 6.6	2 = .61
3 = 9.8	3 = .92
4 = 13.1	4 = 1.2
5 = 16.4	5 = 1.5
6 = 19.7	6 = 1.8
7 = 23.0	7 = 2.1
8 = 26.2	8 = 2.4
9 = 29.5	9 = 2.7

Weight

Kilograms/Pounds To change kilograms to pounds, multiply by 2.20.
To change pounds to kilograms, multiply by .453.

Kilos to Pounds	Pounds to Kilos
1 = 2.2	1 = .45
2 = 4.4	2 = .91
3 = 6.6	3 = 1.4
4 = 8.8	4 = 1.8
5 = 11.0	5 = 2.3
6 = 13.2	6 = 2.7
7 = 15.4	7 = 3.2

8 = 17.6	8 = 3.6
9 = 19.8	9 = 4.1

Grams/Ounces To change grams to ounces, multiply grams by .035.
To change ounces to grams, multiply ounces by 28.4.

Grams to Ounces	Ounces to Grams
1 = .04	1 = 28
2 = .07	2 = 57
3 = .11	3 = 85
4 = .14	4 = 114
5 = .18	5 = 142
6 = .21	6 = 170
7 = .25	7 = 199
8 = .28	8 = 227
9 = .32	9 = 256

Liquid Volume

Liters/U.S. Gallons To change liters to U.S. gallons, multiply liters by .264.
To change U.S. gallons to liters, multiply gallons by 3.79.

Liters to U.S. Gallons	U.S. Gallons to Liters
1 = .26	1 = 3.8
2 = .53	2 = 7.6
3 = .79	3 = 11.4
4 = 1.1	4 = 15.2
5 = 1.3	5 = 19.0
6 = 1.6	6 = 22.7
7 = 1.8	7 = 26.5
8 = 2.1	8 = 30.3
9 = 2.4	9 = 34.1

French Vocabulary

Words and Phrases

	English	French	Pronunciation
Basics	Yes/no	Oui/non	wee/no
	Please	S'il vous plaît	seel voo play
	Thank you	Merci	mare-**see**
	You're welcome	De rien	deh ree-**en**
	Excuse me, sorry	Pardon	pahr-**doan**
	Sorry!	Désolé(e)	day-zoh-**lay**
	Good morning/ afternoon	Bonjour	bone-**joor**
	Good evening	Bonsoir	bone-**swar**
	Good-bye	Au revoir	o ruh-**vwar**
	Mr. (Sir)	Monsieur	mih-see-**oor**
	Mrs. (Ma'am)	Madame	ma-dam
	Miss	Mademoiselle	mad-mwa-**zel**
	Pleased to meet you	Enchanté(e)	on-shahn-**tay**
	How are you?	Comment allez-vous?	ko-men-tahl-ay-**voo**
Numbers	one	un	un
	two	deux	dew
	three	trois	twa
	four	quatre	**cat**-ruh
	five	cinq	sank
	six	six	seess
	seven	sept	set
	eight	huit	wheat
	nine	neuf	nuf
	ten	dix	deess
	eleven	onze	owns
	twelve	douze	dues
	thirteen	treize	trays
	fourteen	quatorze	ka-torz
	fifteen	quinze	cans
	sixteen	seize	sez
	seventeen	dix-sept	deess-**set**
	twenty	vingt	vant
	twenty-one	vingt-et-un	vant-an-**un**
	thirty	trente	trahnt
	forty	quarante	ka-**rahnt**
	fifty	cinquante	sang-**kahnt**
	sixty	soixante	swa-**sahnt**
	seventy	soixante-dix	swa-sahnt-**deess**
	eighty	quatre-vingts	cat-ruh-**vant**
	ninety	quatre-vingt-dix	cat-ruh-vant-**deess**
	one hundred	cent	sahnt
	one thousand	mille	meel
Colors	black	noir	nwar
	blue	bleu	blu
	green	vert	vair
	red	rouge	rouge

white	blanc	blahnk
yellow	jaune	jone

Days of the Week

Sunday	dimanche	dee-**mahnsh**
Monday	lundi	lewn-**dee**
Tuesday	mardi	mar-**dee**
Wednesday	mercredi	mare-kruh-**dee**
Thursday	jeudi	juh-**dee**
Friday	vendredi	van-dra-**dee**
Saturday	samedi	sam-**dee**

Useful Phrases

Do you speak English?	Parlez-vous anglais?	par-lay vooz ahng-**glay**
I don't speak French	Je ne parle pas français	jeh nuh parl pah fraun-**say**
I don't understand	Je ne comprends pas	jeh nuh kohm-prahn **pah**
I understand	Je comprends	jeh kohm-**prahn**
I don't know	Je ne sais pas	jeh nuh say **pah**
I'm American/ British	Je suis américain/ anglais	jeh sweez a-may-ree-**can**/ahng-**glay**
My name is . . .	Je m'appelle . . .	jeh muh-**pel** . . .
What time is it?	Quelle heure est-il?	kel ur et-**il**
When?	Quand?	kahnd
Yesterday	Hier	yair
Today	Aujourd'hui	o-zhoor-**dwee**
Tomorrow	Demain	deh-**man**
What?	Quoi?	kwah
What is it?	Qu'est-ce que c'est?	kess-kuh-**say**
Who?	Qui?	kee
Where is . . .	Où est . . .	oo ay
the train station?	la gare?	la gar
the subway station?	la station de métro?	la sta-syon deh may-**tro**
the bus stop?	l'arrêt de bus?	la-ray deh **booss**
the terminal (airport)?	l'aérogare?	lay-ro-**gar**
the post office?	la poste?	la post
the bank?	la banque?	la bahnk
the . . . museum?	le musée . . . ?	leh mew-**zay**
the hospital?	l'hôpital?	low-pee-**tahl**
the telephone?	le téléphone?	leh te-le-**phone**
Where are the rest rooms?	Où sont les toilettes?	oo son lay twah-**let**
Here/there	Ici/là	ee-**see**/la
Left/right	A gauche/à droite	a goash/a drwat
Is it near/far?	C'est près/loin?	say pray/lwan
I'd like . . .	Je voudrais . . .	jeh voo-**dray**

a room	une chambre	ewn **shahm**-bra
the key	la clé	la clay
a newspaper	un journal	un joor-**nahl**
a stamp	un timbre	un **tam**-bruh
I'd like to buy . . .	Je voudrais acheter . . .	jeh voo-**dray** ahsh-**tay**
city plan	un plan de ville	un plahn de**veel**
road map	une carte routière	ewn cart roo-tee-**air**
envelopes	des enveloppes	dayz ahn-veh-**lope**
postcard	une carte postale	ewn cart post-**al**
How much is it?	C'est combien?	say comb-bee-**en**
A little/a lot	Un peu/beaucoup	un puh/bo-**koo**
More/less	Plus/moins	ploo/mwa
I am ill/sick	Je suis malade	jeh swee ma-**lahd**
Call a doctor	Appelez un docteur	a-pe-lay un dohk-**tore**
Help!	Au secours!	o say-**koor**
Stop!	Arrêtez!	a-ruh-**tay**

Dining Out

A bottle of . . .	une bouteille de . . .	ewn boo-**tay** deh
A cup of . . .	une tasse de . . .	ewn tass deh
A glass of . . .	un verre de . . .	un vair deh
Bill/check	l'addition	la-dee-see-**own**
Bread	du pain	due pan
Breakfast	le petit déjeuner	leh pet-**ee** day-zhu-**nay**
Dinner	le dîner	leh dee-**nay**
Fork	une fourchette	ewn four-**shet**
I am on a diet	Je suis au régime	jeh sweez o ray-**jeem**
I am vegetarian	Je suis végétarien(ne)	jeh swee vay-jay-ta-ree-**en**
I cannot eat . . .	Je ne peux pas manger de . . .	jeh nuh puh pah mahn-**jay** deh
I'd like . . .	Je voudrais . . .	jeh voo-**dray**
I'm hungry/thirsty	J'ai faim/soif	jay fam/swahf
Is service/the tip included?	Est-ce que le service est compris?	ess keh leh sair-veess ay comb-**pree**
It's good/bad	C'est bon/mauvais	say bon/mo-**vay**
It's hot/cold	C'est chaud/froid	say sho/frwah
Knife	un couteau	un koo-**toe**
Lunch	le déjeuner	leh day-juh-**nay**
Menu	la carte	la cart

Napkin	une serviette	ewn sair-vee-**et**
Plate	une assiette	ewn a-see-**et**
Please give me . . .	Donnez-moi . . .	doe-nay-**mwah**
Spoon	une cuillère	ewn kwee-**air**
Wine list	la carte des vins	la cart day **van**

German Vocabulary

Words and Phrases

	English	German	Pronunciation
Basics	Yes/no	Ja/nein	yah/nine
	Please	Bitte	**bit**-uh
	Thank you (very much)	Danke (vielen Dank)	**dahn**-kuh (**fee**-lun dahnk)
	Excuse me	Entschuldigen Sie	ent-**shool**-de-gen zee
	I'm sorry	Es tut mir leid	es toot meer lite
	Good day	Guten Tag	**goo**-ten tahk
	Good-bye	Auf Wiedersehen	auf **vee**-der-zane
	Mr./Mrs.	Herr/Frau	hair/frau
	Miss	Fräulein	**froy**-line
	Pleased to meet you	Sehr erfreut	zair air-**froit**
	How are you?	Wie geht es Ihnen?	vee **gate** es **ee**-nen?
	Very well, thanks	Sehr gut, danke	zair goot **dahn**-kuh
	And you?	Und Ihnen?	oont **ee**-nen
Numbers	one	eins	eints
	two	zwei	tsvai
	three	drei	dry
	four	vier	fear
	five	fünf	fumph
	six	sechs	zex
	seven	sieben	**zee**-ben
	eight	acht	ahkt
	nine	neun	noyn
	ten	zehn	tsane
Days of the Week	Sunday	Sonntag	**zone**-tahk
	Monday	Montag	**moan**-tahk
	Tuesday	Dienstag	**deens**-tahk
	Wednesday	Mittwoch	**mit**-voah
	Thursday	Donnerstag	**doe**-ners-tahk
	Friday	Freitag	**fry**-tahk
	Saturday	Samstag	**zahm**-stahk
Useful Phrases	Do you speak English?	Sprechen Sie Englisch?	**shprek**-hun zee **eng**-glish?
	I don't speak German.	Ich spreche kein Deutsch.	ich **shprek**-uh kine doych
	Please speak slowly.	Bitte sprechen Sie langsam.	**bit**-uh **shprek**-en zee **lahng**-zahm
	I am American/British	Ich bin Amerikaner(in)/ Engländer(in)	ich bin a-mer-i-**kahn**-er(in) **eng**-glan-der(in)
	My name is . . .	Ich heiße . . .	ich **hi**-suh
	Where are the rest rooms?	Wo ist die Toilette?	vo ist dee twah-**let**-uh
	Left/right	Links/rechts	links/rechts

Open/closed	Offen/geschlossen	O-fen/geh-**shloss**-en
Where is . . .	Wo ist . . .	**vo** ist
the train station?	der Bahnhof?	dare **bahn**-hof
the bus stop?	die Bushaltestelle?	dee **booss**-hahlt-uh-**shtel**-uh
the subway station?	die U-Bahn-Station?	dee OO-bahn-**staht**-sion
the airport?	der Flugplatz?	dare **floog**-plats
the post office?	die Post?	dee **post**
the bank?	die Bank?	dee **banhk**
the police station?	die Polizeistation?	dee po-lee-**tsai**-staht-sion
the American/ British consulate?	das amerikanische/ britische Konsulat?	dahs a-mare-i-**kahn**-ishuh/ **brit**-ish-uh cone-tso-**laht**
the Hospital?	das Krankenhaus?	dahs **krahnk**-en-house
the telephone?	das Telefon	dahs te-le-**fone**
I'd like to have . . .	Ich hätte gerne . . .	ich **het**-uh gairn
a room	ein Zimmer	I-nuh **tsim**-er
the key	den Schlüssel	den **shluh**-sul
a map	eine Karte	I-nuh **cart**-uh
How much is it?	Wieviel kostet das?	**veel**-feel **cost**-et **dahs?**
I am ill/sick	Ich bin krank	ich bin **krahnk**
I need . . .	Ich brauche . . .	ich **brow**-khuh
a doctor	einen Arzt	I-nen artst
the police	die Polizei	dee po-li-**tsai**
help	Hilfe	**hilf**-uh
Stop!	Halt!	hahlt
Fire!	Feuer!	**foy**-er
Caution/Look out!	Achtung!/Vorsicht!	**ahk**-tung/**for**-zicht
Dining Out A bottle of . . .	eine Flasche . . .	I-nuh **flash**-uh
A cup of . . .	eine Tasse . . .	I-nuh **tahs**-uh
A glass of . . .	ein Glas . . .	ein glahss
Bill/check	die Rechnung	dee **rekh**-nung
Do you have . . . ?	Haben Sie . . . ?	**hah**-ben zee
Food	Essen	**es**-en
I am on a diet.	Ich halte Diät.	ich **hahl**-tuh dee-**et**
I am a vegetarian.	Ich bin Vegetarier.	ich bin ve-guh-**tah**-re-er
I cannot eat . . .	Ich kann . . . nicht essen	ich kan . . . nicht **es**-en
I'd like to order	Ich möchte bestellen . . .	ich **mohr**-shtuh buh-shtel-en

Is the service included?	Ist die Bedienung inbegriffen?	ist dee beh-**dee**-nung **in**-beh-grig-en
Menu	die Speisekarte	dee **shpie**-zeh-car-tuh
Napkin	die Serviette	dee zair-vee-**eh**-tuh
Separate/all together	Getrennt/alles zusammen	ge-**trent**/**ah**-les tsu-**zah**-men

Italian Vocabulary

Words and Phrases

	English	Italian	Pronunciation
Basics	Yes/no	Sí/no	see/no
	Please	Per favore	pear fa-**vo**-ray
	Thank you	Grazie	**grah**-tsee-ay
	You're welcome	Prego	**pray**-go
	Excuse me, sorry	Scusi	**skoo**-zee
	Sorry!	Mi spiace!	mee spee-**ah**-chay
	Good morning/ afternoon	Buona giorno	bwoh-n **jor**-no
	Good evening!	Buona sera	**bwoh**-na say-ra
	Good-bye	Arrivederci	a-ree-vah-**dare**-chee
	Mr.(Sir)	Signore	see-**nyo**-ray
	Mrs.(Ma'am)	Signora	see-**nyo**-ra
	Miss	Signorina	see-nyo-**ree**-na
	Pleased to meet you	Piacere	pee-ah-**chair**-ray
	How are you?	Come sta?	**ko**-may **sta**
	Very well, thanks	Bene, grazie	**ben**-ay **grah**-tsee-ay
	And you?	E lei?	ay **lay**-ee
	Hello (over the phone)	Pronto?	**proan**-to
Numbers	one	uno	**oo**-no
	two	due	**doo**-ay
	three	tre	tray
	four	quattro	**kwah**-tro
	five	cinque	**cheen**-kway
	six	sei	say
	seven	sette	**set**-ay
	eight	otto	**oh**-to
	nine	nove	**no**-vay
	ten	dieci	dee-**eh**-chee
	eleven	undici	**oon**-dee-chee
	twelve	dodici	**doe**-dee-chee
	thirteen	tredici	**tray**-dee-chee
	fourteen	quattordici	kwa-**tore**-dee-chee
	fifteen	quindici	**kwin**-dee-chee
	sixteen	sedici	**say**-dee-chee
	seventeen	diciassette	dee-cha-**set**-ay
	eighteen	diciotto	dee-**cho**-to
	nineteen	diciannove	dee-cha-**no**-vay
	twenty	venti	**vain**-tee
	twenty-one	ventuno	vain-**too**-no
	thirty	trenta	**train**-ta
	forty	quaranta	kwah-**rahn**-ta
	fifty	cinquanta	cheen-**kwahn**-ta
	sixty	sessanta	seh-**sahn**-ta
	seventy	settanta	seh-**tahn**-ta
	eighty	ottanta	o-**tahn**-ta
	ninety	novanta	no-**vahn**-ta
	one hundred	cento	**chen**-to
	one thousand	mila	**mee**la

Colors	black	nero	**neh**-ro
	blue	azzurro	a-**tsu**-ro
	green	verde	**vehr**-day
	red	rosso	**ros**-so
	white	bianco	bee-**ang**-ko
	yellow	giallo	**ja**-lo
Days of the Week	Monday	lunedì	**loo**-neh-dee
	Tuesday	martedì	**mahr**-teh-dee
	Wednesday	mercoledì	**mare**-co-leh-dee
	Thursday	giovedì	**jo**-veh-dee
	Friday	venerdì	**ven**-air-dee
	Saturday	sabato	**sah**-ba-toe
	Sunday	domenica	doe-**men**-ee-ca
Useful Phrases	Do you speak English?	Parla inglese?	**par**-la een-**glay**-zay
	I don't speak Italian	Non parlo italiano	non **par**-lo ee-tal-**yah**-no
	I don't understand	Non capisco	non ka-**peess**-ko
	Slowly!	Lentamente!	**len**-ta-men-tay
	I don't know	Non lo so	noan lo **so**
	I'm American/ British	Sono americano/a Sono inglese	**so**-no a-mey-ree-**ka**-no/a; **so**-no een-**glay**-zay
	My name is . . .	Mi chiamo . . .	mee kee-**ah**-mo
	What time is it?	Che ore sono?	kay **o**-ray **so**-no
	When?	Quando?	**kwahn**-doe?
	Yesterday/today/ tomorrow	Ieri/oggi/ domani	**yer**-ee/**o**-jee/ do-**mah**-nee
	Tonight	Stasera	sta-**ser**-a
	What?	Che cosa?	kay **ko**-za
	What is it?	Che cos'è	kay ko-**zay**
	Who?	Chi?	kee
	Where is . . .	Dov'é?	doe-**veh**
	the bus stop?	la fermata dell'autobus?	la fer-**ma**-ta del ow-toe-**booss**
	the train station?	la stazione?	la sta-tsee-**oh**-nay
	the subway station?	la metropolitana?	la may-tro-po-lee-**ta**-na
	the terminal	il terminal?	eel ter-mee-**nahl**
	the post office?	l'ufficio postale?	loo-**fee**-cho po-**sta**-lay
	the bank?	la banca?	la **bahn**-ka
	the store?	il negozio?	ell nay-**go**-tsee-o
	the cashier?	la cassa?	la **ka**-sa
	the . . . museum?	il museo . . .?	eel moo-**zay**-o
	the hospital?	l'ospedale?	lo-spay-**day**-lay
	the elevator?	l'ascensore?	la-shen-**so**-ray
	a telephone?	un telefono?	oon tay-**lay**-fo-no
	Where are the rest rooms?	Dov'é il bagno?	doe-**vay** eel **bahn**-yo

Here/there	Qui/lá	kwee/la
Left/right	A sinistra/a destra	a see-**neess**-tra/ a **des**-tra
Straight ahead	Avanti dritto	avahn-tee **dree**-to
Is it near/far?	È vicino?/lontano?	ay vee-**chee**-no/ lon-**tah**-no
I'd like . . . a room the key a newspaper a stamp	Vorrei . . . una camera la chiave un giornale un francobollo	vo-**ray** **oo**-na **ka**-may-ra la kee-**ah**-vay oon jor-**na**-lay oon frahnn-ko-**bo**-lo
I'd like to buy . . . some soap a city plan a road map of . . . a country map envelopes a postcard	Vorrei comprare . . . una saponetta una planta della cittá una carte stradale di . . . una carta geografica delle buste una cartolina	vo-**ray** kom-**pra**-ray **oo**-na sa-po-**net**-a **oo**-na **plahn**-ta day-la chee-**ta** **oo**-na **cart**-a stra-**dah**-lay dee **oo**-na **cart**-a jay-o-**grah**-fee-ka day-lay **booss**-tay **oo**-na car-toe-lee-na
How much is it?	Quanto costa?	**kwahn**-toe **coast**-a
A little/a lot	Poco/tanto	**po**-ko/**tahn**-to
More/less	Più/meno	pee-**oo/may**-no
I am ill/sick	Sto male	sto **ma**-lay
Please call a doctor	Chiami un dottore	kee-**ah**-mee oon doe-**toe**-uray
Help!	Aiuto!	a-**yoo**-toe
Stop!	Alt!	ahlt
Fire!	Al fuoco!	ahl **fwo**-ko

Dining Out

A bottle of . . .	una bottiglia di . . .	**oo**-na bo-**tee**-lee-ah dee
A cup of . . .	Una tazza di . . .	**oo**-na **tah**-tsa dee
A glass of . . .	Un bicchiere di . . .	oon bee-key-**air**-ay dee
Bill/check	Il conto	eel **cone**-toe
Bread	Il pane	eel **pa**-nay
Breakfast	La prima colazione	la **pree**-ma ko-la-**tsee**-oh-nay
Dinner	La cena	lah **chen**-a
Fixed-price menu	Menù a prezzo fisso	may-**noo** a **pret**-so **fee**-so
Fork	La forchetta	la for-**ket**-a
I am on a diet	Sono a dieta	**so**-no a dee-**et**-a

I am vegetarian	Sono vegetariano/a	**so**-no vay-jay-ta-ree-**ah**-no/a
I cannot eat . . .	Non posso mangiare . . .	non **po**-so man-**ja**-ray
I'd like . . .	Vorrei . . .	vo-**ray**
I'm hungry/thirsty	Ho fame/sete	o **fa**-may/**set**-ay
Is service included?	Il servizio è incluso?	eel ser-**vee**-tzee-o ay een-**kloo**-zo
It's good/bad	È buono/cattivo	ay **bwo**-no/ka-tee-vo
It's hot/cold	È cald/freddo	ay **kahl**-doe/**fred**-o
Knife	Il coltello	eel kol-**tel**-o
Lunch	Il pranzo	eel **prahnt**-so
Menu	Il menù	eel may-**noo**
Napkin	Il tovagliolo	eel toe-va-lee-**oh**-lo
Please give me . . .	Mi dia . . .	mee **dee**-a
Spoon	Il cucchiaio	eel koo-kee-**ah**-yo
Waiter/Waitress	Cameriere/cameriera	ka-mare-**yer**-ay/ka-mare-**yer**-a
Wine list	La lista dei vini	la **lee**-sta **day**-ee **vee**-nee

Spanish Vocabulary

Words and Phrases

	English	Spanish	Pronunciation
Basics	Yes/no	Sí/no	see/no
	Please	Por favor	pore fah-**vohr**
	Thank you (very much)	(Muchas) gracias	(**moo**-chas) **grah**-see-as
	You're welcome	De nada	day **nah**-dah
	Excuse me	Con permiso	con pair-**mee**-so
	Pardon me/what did you say?	¿Perdón?/Mande?	pair-dohn/mahn-deh
	Could you tell me?	¿Podría decirme?	po-**dree**-ah deh-**seer**-meh
	I'm sorry	Lo siento	lo see-**en**-toh
	Good morning!	¡Buenos días!	**bway**-nohs **dee**-ahs
	Good afternoon!	¡Buenas tardes!	**bway**-nahs **tar**-dess
	Good evening!	¡Buenas noches!	**bway**-nahs **no**-chess
	Goodbye!	¡Adiós!/¡Hasta luego!	ah-dee-**ohss**/ah-stah-**lwe**-go
	Mr./Mrs.	Señor/Señora	sen-**yor**/sen-**yore**-ah
	Miss	Señorita	sen-yo-**ree**-tah
	Pleased to meet you	Mucho gusto	**moo**-cho **goose**-to
	How are you?	¿Cómo está usted?	**ko**-mo es-**tah** oo-**sted**
	Very well, thank you.	Muy bien, gracias.	**moo**-ee bee-**en**, **grah**-see-as
	And you?	¿Y usted?	ee oos-**ted**?
	Hello (on the telephone)	Diga	**dee**-gah
Numbers	one	un, uno	oon, **oo**-no
	two	dos	dohs
	three	tres	**tress**
	four	cuatro	**kwah**-tro
	five	cinco	**sink**-oh
	six	seis	sace
	seven	siete	see-**et**-eh
	eight	ocho	**o**-cho
	nine	nueve	new-**ev**-ay
	ten	diez	dee-**es**
	eleven	once	**ohn**-seh
	twelve	doce	**doh**-seh
	thirteen	trece	**treh**-seh
	fourteen	catorce	kah-**tohr**-seh
	fifteen	quince	**keen**-sey
	sixteen	dieciséis	dee-es-ee-**sace**
	seventeen	diecisiete	dee-**es**-ee-see-**et**-ay
	eighteen	diechiocho	dee-**es**-ee-**o**-cho
	nineteen	diecinueve	dee-**es**-ee-new-**ev**-ay
	twenty	veinte	**vain**-teh
	twenty-one	veinte y uno/veintiuno	**vain**-te-oo-no
	thirty	treinta	**train**-tah

forty	cuarenta	kwah-**ren**-tah
fifty	cincuenta	seen-**kwen**-tah
sixty	sesenta	sess-**en**-tah
seventy	setenta	set-**en**-tah
eighty	ochenta	oh-**chen**-tah
ninety	noventa	no-**ven**-tah
one hundred	cien	see-**en**
one hundred one	ciento uno	see-en-toh **oo**-no
one thousand	mil	meel

Colors	black	negro	**neh**-grow
	blue	azul	ah-**sool**
	green	verde	**ver**-day
	red	rojo	**roh**-hoh
	white	blanco	**blahn**-koh
	yellow	amarillo	ah-mah-**ree**-yoh

Days of the Week	Sunday	domingo	doe-**meen**-goh
	Monday	lunes	**loo**-ness
	Tuesday	martes	**mahr**-tess
	Wednesday	miércoles	me-**air**-koh-less
	Thursday	jueves	who-**ev**-ess
	Friday	viernes	vee-**air**-ness
	Saturday	sábado	**sah**-bah-doh

Useful Phrases	Do you speak English?	¿Habla usted inglés?	ah-blah oos-**ted** in-**glehs**?
	I don't speak Spanish	No hablo español	no **ah**-bloh es-pahn-**yol**
	I don't understand (you)	No entiendo	no en-tee-**en**-doe
	I don't know	No sé	no **seh**
	I am American/ British	Soy americano(a)/ inglés(a)	soy ah-meh-ree-**kah**-no(ah)/ in-**glehs**(ah)
	My name is . . .	Me llamo . . .	may **yah**-moh
	What time is it?	¿Qué hora es?	keh **o**-rah es?
	It is one, two, three . . . o'clock.	Es la una; son las dos, tres	es la **oo**-nah/sohn lahs dohs, tress
	Yes, please/No, thank you	Sí, por favor/No, gracias	**see** pohr fah-**vor**/no **grah**-see-ahs
	When?	¿Cuándo?	**kwahn**-doh?
	This/Next week	Esta semana/ la semana que entra	es-tah seh-**mah**-nah/lah seh-**mah**-nah keh en-trah
	Yesterday/today/ tomorrow	Ayer/hoy/mañana	ah-**yehr**/oy/mahn-**yah**-nah
	Tonight	Esta noche	es-tah **no**-cheh
	What?	¿Qué?	keh?
	What is it?	¿Qué es esto?	keh es **es**-toh
	Who?	¿Quién?	kee-**yen**

Where is . . .?	¿Dónde está . . .?	**dohn**-day es-**tah**
the train station?	la estación del tren?	la es-tah-see-**on** del **train**
the subway station?	la estación del Metro?	la es-ta-see-**on** del **meh**-tro
the bus stop?	la parada del autobus?	la pah-**rah**-dah del oh-toe-**boos**
the post office?	la oficina de correos?	la oh-fee-**see**-nah deh koh-**reh**-os
the bank?	el banco?	el **bahn**-koh
the store?	la tienda . . .?	la tee-**en**-dah
the cashier?	la caja?	la **kah**-hah
the . . . museum?	el museo . . .?	el moo-**seh**-oh
the hospital?	el hospital?	el ohss-pea-**tal**
the elevator?	el ascensor?	el ah-**sen**-sohr
the bathroom?	el baño?	el **bahn**-yoh

Here/there	Aquí/allá	ah-**key**/ah-**yah**

Open/closed	Abierto/cerrado	ah-be-**er**-toh/ ser-**ah**-doh

Left/right	Izquierda/derecha	iss-key-**er**-dah/ dare-**eh**-chah

Straight ahead	Derecho	der-**eh**-choh

Is it near/far?	¿Está cerca/lejos?	es-**tah** sehr-kah/ **leh**-hoss

I'd like . . .	Quisiera . . .	kee-see-**ehr**-ah
a room	un cuarto/una habitación	oon **kwahr**-toh/ **oo**-nah ah-bee-tah-see-**on**
the key	la llave	lah **yah**-veh
a newspaper	un periódico	oon pear-ee-**oh**-dee-koh
a stamp	un timbre de correo	oon **teem**-breh koh-**reh**-oh

I'd like to buy . . .	Quisiera comprar . . .	kee-see-**ehr**-ah kohm-**prahr**
a dictionary	un diccionario	oon deek-see-oh-**nah**-ree-oh
soap	jabón	hah-**bohn**
a map	un mapa	oon **mah**-pah
a magazine	una revista	**oon**-ah reh-**veess**-tah
paper	papel	pah-**pel**
envelopes	sobres	so-brehs
a postcard	una tarjeta postal	**oon**-ah tar-**het**-ah post-**ahl**

How much is it?	¿Cuánto cuesta?	**kwahn**-toh **kwes**-tah

A little/a lot	Un poquito/ mucho . . .	oon poh-**kee**-toh/ **moo**-choh

More/less	Más/menos	mahss/**men**-ohss

Telephone	Teléfono	tel-**ef**-oh-no

Telegram	Telegrama	teh-leh-**grah**-mah

	I am ill/sick	Estoy enfermo(a)	es-**toy** en-**fehr**-moh(ah)
	Please call a doctor	Por favor llame un medico	pohr fah-**vor** ya-meh oon **med**-ee-koh
	Help!	¡Auxilio! ¡Ayuda! ¡Socorro!	owk-**see**-lee-oh/ ah-**yoo**-dah soh-**kohr**-roh
	Fire!	¡Encendio!	en-**sen**-dee-oo
	Caution!/Look out!	¡Cuidado!	kwee-**dah**-doh
Dining Out	A bottle of . . .	Una botella de . . .	**oo**-nah bo-**teh**-yah deh
	A cup of . . .	Una taza de . . .	**oo**-nah **tah**-thah deh
	A glass of . . .	Un vaso de . . .	oon **vah**-so deh
	Bill/check	La cuenta	lah **kwen**-tah
	Bread	El pan	el pahn
	Breakfast	El desayuno	el deh-sah-**yoon**-oh
	Dinner	La cena	lah **seh**-nah
	Dish	Un plato	oon **plah**-toh
	Menu of the day	Menu del día	meh-**noo**del **dee**-ah
	Fixed-price menu	Menu fijo o turistico	meh-**noo** **fee**-hoh oh too-**ree**-stee-coh
	Fork	El tenedor	el ten-eh-**dor**
	Is the tip included?	¿Está incluida la propina?	es-**tah** in-clue-**ee**-dah lah pro-**pea**-nah
	Knife	El cuchillo	el koo-**chee**-yo
	Large portion of savory snacks	Raciónes	rah-see-**oh**-nehs
	Lunch	La comida	lah koh-**mee**-dah
	Menu	La carta, el menu	lah **cart**-ah, el meh-**noo**
	Napkin	La servilleta	lah sehr-vee-**yet**-ah
	Please give me	Por favor déme	pore fah-**vor** **deh**-meh
	Spoon	Una cuchara	**oo**-nah koo-**chah**-rah
	Waiter!/Waitress!	¡Por favor Señor/Señorita!	pohr fah-**vor** sen-**yor**/sen-yor-**ee**-tah

Index

Personal Itinerary

Departure *Date*

Time

Transportation

Arrival *Date* *Time*

Departure *Date* *Time*

Transportation

Accommodations

Arrival *Date* *Time*

Departure *Date* *Time*

Transportation

Accommodations

Arrival *Date* *Time*

Departure *Date* *Time*

Transportation

Accommodations

Personal Itinerary

Arrival *Date*   *Time*

Departure *Date*   *Time*

Transportation

Accommodations

Arrival *Date*   *Time*

Departure *Date*   *Time*

Transportation

Accommodations

Arrival *Date*   *Time*

Departure *Date*   *Time*

Transportation

Accommodations

Arrival *Date*   *Time*

Departure *Date*   *Time*

Transportation

Accommodations

Personal Itinerary

Arrival *Date*   *Time*

Departure *Date*   *Time*

Transportation

Accommodations

Arrival *Date*   *Time*

Departure *Date*   *Time*

Transportation

Accommodations

Arrival *Date*   *Time*

Departure *Date*   *Time*

Transportation

Accommodations

Arrival *Date*   *Time*

Departure *Date*   *Time*

Transportation

Accommodations

Personal Itinerary

Arrival *Date*   *Time*

Departure *Date*   *Time*

Transportation

Accommodations

Arrival *Date*   *Time*

Departure *Date*   *Time*

Transportation

Accommodations

Arrival *Date*   *Time*

Departure *Date*   *Time*

Transportation

Accommodations

Arrival *Date*   *Time*

Departure *Date*   *Time*

Transportation

Accommodations

Personal Itinerary

Arrival *Date*   *Time*

Departure *Date*   *Time*

Transportation

Accommodations

Arrival *Date*   *Time*

Departure *Date*   *Time*

Transportation

Accommodations

Arrival *Date*   *Time*

Departure *Date*   *Time*

Transportation

Accommodations

Arrival *Date*   *Time*

Departure *Date*   *Time*

Transportation

Accommodations

Addresses

Name	*Name*
Address	*Address*
Telephone	*Telephone*
Name	*Name*
Address	*Address*
Telephone	*Telephone*
Name	*Name*
Address	*Address*
Telephone	*Telephone*
Name	*Name*
Address	*Address*
Telephone	*Telephone*
Name	*Name*
Address	*Address*
Telephone	*Telephone*
Name	*Name*
Address	*Address*
Telephone	*Telephone*
Name	*Name*
Address	*Address*
Telephone	*Telephone*
Name	*Name*
Address	*Address*
Telephone	*Telephone*

Addresses

Name

Address

Telephone

Name

Address

Telephone

Name

Address

Telephone

Name

Address

Telephone

Name

Address

Telephone

Name

Address

Telephone

Name

Address

Telephone

Name

Address

Telephone

Name

Address

Telephone

Name

Address

Telephone

Name

Address

Telephone

Name

Address

Telephone

Name

Address

Telephone

Name

Address

Telephone

Name

Address

Telephone

Name

Address

Telephone

Notes

Fodor's Travel Guides

U.S. Guides

Alaska
Arizona
Boston
California
Cape Cod
The Carolinas & the
  Georgia Coast
The Chesapeake
  Region
Chicago
Colorado
Disney World & the
  Orlando Area

Florida
Hawaii
The Jersey Shore
Las Vegas
Los Angeles
Maui
Miami & the Keys
New England
New Mexico
New Orleans
New York City
New York City
  (Pocket Guide)

New York State
Pacific North Coast
Philadelphia
The Rockies
San Diego
San Francisco
San Francisco
  (Pocket Guide)
The South
Texas
USA
The Upper Great
  Lakes Region

Virgin Islands
Virginia & Maryland
Waikiki
Washington, D.C.

Foreign Guides

Acapulco
Amsterdam
Australia
Austria
The Bahamas
The Bahamas
  (Pocket Guide)
Baja & the Pacific
  Coast Resorts
Barbados
Belgium &
  Luxembourg
Bermuda
Brazil
Budget Europe
Canada
Canada's Atlantic
  Provinces
Cancun, Cozumel,
  Yucatan Peninsula
Caribbean
Central America
China

Eastern Europe
Egypt
Europe
Europe's Great
  Cities
France
Germany
Great Britain
Greece
The Himalayan
  Countries
Holland
Hong Kong
India
Ireland
Israel
Italy
Italy's Great Cities
Jamaica
Japan
Kenya, Tanzania,
  Seychelles
Korea

Lisbon
London
London Companion
London
  (Pocket Guide)
Madrid & Barcelona
Mexico
Mexico City
Montreal &
  Quebec City
Morocco
Munich
New Zealand
Paris
Paris (Pocket Guide)
Portugal
Puerto Rico
  (Pocket Guide)
Rio de Janeiro
Rome
Saint Martin/
  Sint Maarten
Scandinavia

Scandinavian Cities
Scotland
Singapore
South America
South Pacific
Southeast Asia
Soviet Union
Spain
Sweden
Switzerland
Sydney
Thailand
Tokyo
Toronto
Turkey
Vienna
Yugoslavia

Special-Interest Guides

Bed & Breakfast
  Guide to the Mid-
  Atlantic States

Bed & Breakfast
  Guide to New
  England
Cruises & Ports
  of Call

A Shopper's Guide
  to London
Health & Fitness
  Vacations
Shopping in Europe

Skiing in North
  America
Sunday in New York
Touring Europe